ICT-Based Assessment, Methods, and Programs in Tertiary Education

Serpil Meri Yilan
Agri Ibrahim Cecen University, Turkey

Kasim Koruyan
King Saud University, Saudi Arabia

IGI Global
PUBLISHER of TIMELY KNOWLEDGE

A volume in the Advances in Educational Technologies and Instructional Design (AETID) Book Series

Published in the United States of America by
IGI Global
Information Science Reference (an imprint of IGI Global)
701 E. Chocolate Avenue
Hershey PA, USA 17033
Tel: 717-533-8845
Fax: 717-533-8661
E-mail: cust@igi-global.com
Web site: http://www.igi-global.com

Library of Congress Cataloging-in-Publication Data

Names: Meri Yilan, Serpil, 1987- editor. | Koruyan, Kasim, 1974- editor.
Title: ICT-based assessment, methods, and programs in tertiary education / Serpil Meri Yilan and Kasim Koruyan, editors.
Description: Hershey, PA : Information Science Reference, [2020] | Includes bibliographical references and index.
Identifiers: LCCN 2019047054 (print) | LCCN 2019047055 (ebook) | ISBN 9781799830627 (hardcover) | ISBN 9781799830634 (paperback) | ISBN 9781799830641 (ebook)
Subjects: LCSH: Education, Higher--Computer-assisted instruction. | Postsecondary education--Computer-assisted instruction. | Education, Higher--Effect of technological innovations on. | Postsecondary education--Effect of technological innovations on. | Education, Higher--Information technology. | Postsecondary education--Information technology. | Educational technology.
Classification: LCC LB2395.7 .I33 2020 (print) | LCC LB2395.7 (ebook) | DDC 378.1/7344678--dc23
LC record available at https://lccn.loc.gov/2019047054
LC ebook record available at https://lccn.loc.gov/2019047055

This book is published in the IGI Global book series Advances in Educational Technologies and Instructional Design (AE-TID) (ISSN: 2326-8905; eISSN: 2326-8913)

British Cataloguing in Publication Data
A Cataloguing in Publication record for this book is available from the British Library.

For electronic access to this publication, please contact: eresources@igi-global.com.

Advances in Educational Technologies and Instructional Design (AETID) Book Series

Lawrence A. Tomei
Robert Morris University, USA

ISSN:2326-8905
EISSN:2326-8913

Mission

Education has undergone, and continues to undergo, immense changes in the way it is enacted and distributed to both child and adult learners. In modern education, the traditional classroom learning experience has evolved to include technological resources and to provide online classroom opportunities to students of all ages regardless of their geographical locations. From distance education, Massive-Open-Online-Courses (MOOCs), and electronic tablets in the classroom, technology is now an integral part of learning and is also affecting the way educators communicate information to students.

The **Advances in Educational Technologies & Instructional Design (AETID) Book Series** explores new research and theories for facilitating learning and improving educational performance utilizing technological processes and resources. The series examines technologies that can be integrated into K-12 classrooms to improve skills and learning abilities in all subjects including STEM education and language learning. Additionally, it studies the emergence of fully online classrooms for young and adult learners alike, and the communication and accountability challenges that can arise. Trending topics that are covered include adaptive learning, game-based learning, virtual school environments, and social media effects. School administrators, educators, academicians, researchers, and students will find this series to be an excellent resource for the effective design and implementation of learning technologies in their classes.

Coverage

- Online Media in Classrooms
- Collaboration Tools
- Digital Divide in Education
- Social Media Effects on Education
- Higher Education Technologies
- Web 2.0 and Education
- Bring-Your-Own-Device
- Classroom Response Systems
- Hybrid Learning
- Game-Based Learning

IGI Global is currently accepting manuscripts for publication within this series. To submit a proposal for a volume in this series, please contact our Acquisition Editors at Acquisitions@igi-global.com or visit: http://www.igi-global.com/publish/.

The Advances in Educational Technologies and Instructional Design (AETID) Book Series (ISSN 2326-8905) is published by IGI Global, 701 E. Chocolate Avenue, Hershey, PA 17033-1240, USA, www.igi-global.com. This series is composed of titles available for purchase individually; each title is edited to be contextually exclusive from any other title within the series. For pricing and ordering information please visit http://www.igi-global.com/book-series/advances-educational-technologies-instructional-design/73678. Postmaster: Send all address changes to above address.

Titles in this Series

For a list of additional titles in this series, please visit:
http://www.igi-global.com/book-series/advances-educational-technologies-instructional-design/73678

Handbook of Research on Online Discussion-Based Teaching Methods
Lesley Wilton (University of Toronto, Canada) and Clare Brett (University of Toronto, Canada)
Information Science Reference • © 2020 • 400pp • H/C (ISBN: 9781799832928) • US $265.00

Building STEM Skills Through Environmental Education
Stephen T. Schroth (Towson University, USA) and Janese Daniels (Towson University, USA)
Information Science Reference • © 2020 • 345pp • H/C (ISBN: 9781799827115) • US $180.00

Paradigm Shifts in 21st Century Teaching and Learning
Şenol Orakcı (Aksaray University, Turkey)
Information Science Reference • © 2020 • 400pp • H/C (ISBN: 9781799831464) • US $200.00

Gamification Strategies for Retention, Motivation, and Engagement in Higher Education Emerging Research and Opportunities
Robert Costello (Newcastle College University Centre, UK)
Information Science Reference • © 2020 • 205pp • H/C (ISBN: 9781799820796) • US $155.00

Innovations and Technologies for Soft Skill Development and Learning
Suresh Kumar Nagarajan (VIT University, India) and Mohanasundaram R. (VIT University, India)
Information Science Reference • © 2020 • 330pp • H/C (ISBN: 9781799834649) • US $195.00

Computer Corpora and Open Source Software for Language Learning Emerging Research and Opportunities
Kristina Posavec (University of Zagreb, Croatia)
Information Science Reference • © 2020 • 200pp • H/C (ISBN: 9781799836803) • US $175.00

Virtual and Mobile Learning Activities in Higher Education
Lisbeth Amhag (Malmö University, Sweden)
Information Science Reference • © 2020 • 200pp • H/C (ISBN: 9781799841838) • US $175.00

Handbook of Research on Bilingual and Intercultural Education
María Elena Gómez-Parra (University of Córdoba, Spain) and Cristina Aránzazu Huertas Abril (Universidad de Córdoba, Spain)
Information Science Reference • © 2020 • 550pp • H/C (ISBN: 9781799825883) • US $265.00

IGI Global
PUBLISHER of TIMELY KNOWLEDGE

701 East Chocolate Avenue, Hershey, PA 17033, USA
Tel: 717-533-8845 x100 • Fax: 717-533-8661
E-Mail: cust@igi-global.com • www.igi-global.com

Table of Contents

Detailed Table of Contents

to gender. The study provided some suggestions for EFL learners to benefit from technology in their English language learning.

Automated writing evaluation (AWE) has become increasingly popular in the assessment of writing. The study in this chapter examines the extent to which EFL learners' overall narrative writing performance improves through the AWE feedback system (i.e., Pigai). Eighteen university participants were required to write one paragraph narratives on the web-based Pigai system every week over the course of a month. Findings show a significant improvement in overall scores between the first and last writing task. The analysis of lexical profile further shows a significant improvement in lexical richness, clause density, and paragraph length between the first and last narrative task. The study also reported that the primary error types that occurred in learner narrative writing were lexical, mechanical, and syntactic errors. Results of post-writing interviews also showed a positive attitude towards Pigai. Finally, a positive correlation was observed between automated Pigai scores and human rating scores, supporting the reliability of the AWE system.

This chapter addresses the research gap in providing an extended framework for facilitating learner autonomy and enhancing intrinsic motivation through specifically-designed online tasks to enhance the development of reading skills in higher education. The approach to designing the reading tasks was informed by the comprehensive expansion of Chapelle's model explicitly to provide a theoretical framework for task design to assess the impact of the iPad-enhanced task design on the development of learner autonomy and motivation. Data collection and processing followed an exploratory case study approach applying mixed-method design. The differences in median scores for pre- and post-data were statistically tested using a Mann-Whitney U test. Thematic analysis was used to identify, analyze, and report themes in qualitative data collected for this study. Analysis of the results suggests that changing the culture of instruction and preparing university students for the realities of the digital age seem to be both positive and necessary.

This chapter focuses on distraction at mobile learning environments from different perspectives. It is hoped that this chapter will contribute to the academic discussion on this topic by exploring whether the term 'distraction' accurately describes learners' tendencies to leave the formal, standard, or prescribed content and access the non-standard applications and websites during the academic attempts. This chapter will also introduce a more in-depth discussion on the root causes that drive learners' deviation to the non-standard applications and websites. Furthermore, it will propose and discuss some emerging arguments such as converting 'learning distractions' into 'learning attractions' in a way that might enhance the academic discussion on theory and practice of mobile learning research. Finally, it will introduce three effective techniques and strategies that have the potential to control distractions in mobile learning environments.

Mobile learning has the potential to increase the opportunities to make teaching and learning available beyond the traditional classroom. The main aim of this study was to develop a mobile technologies course delivered online and explore the effects of this online course designed on mobile technologies on the use of ICT skills, attitudes, and views of EFL instructors. While employing mixed methodology, explanatory sequential research design was applied. In this study, participants were selected through convenient sampling and the data were collated through a questionnaire used as pre- and post-tests, followed by semi-structured interviews and class observations. The results of this study indicated that the online training course on mobile technologies had a positive impact on the use of ICT skills and EFL teachers' views in general. Further, attending the mobile technologies course delivered online was very beneficial and effective for the instructors in that it helped them to develop their skills on the use of mobile technologies in English language teaching.

The aim of the research is to analyse pre-service teachers' perceptions about the effectiveness of the digital ecosystem implemented in the area of English morphosyntax in b-learning modality. Based on this goal, a qualitative research approach was adopted. One hundred forty-three learners were enrolled in the subject, and a total of 43 participated in the study. The instrument used to collect data was unstructured individual interviews. The findings suggested students' positive attitudes towards the implemented digital ecosystem. It highlighted that the students were active participants and knew how to manage their learning and how to collaborate with their classmates. The flexibility and accessibility provided by the technological tools available in the model allowed students to combine their personal and professional obligations with lifelong learning. It overcame all the spatial and temporal barriers and developed a kind of learning just-in-time, just-for-students, anytime and anywhere.

Section 3
ICT-Based Programs

The roles of information technology in the contemporary world cannot be over-emphasized considering its enormous usage in the educational sector. This chapter investigates the effectiveness of computer-managed instruction (CMI) on students' performance in tertiary institutions in the North-Central Geopolitical Zone of Nigeria. The control group was taught Computer Science using traditional lecture method (TLM) approach, and the experimental group was taught using CMI approach. A total of 360 students in colleges of education (COE), polytechnic, and university participated in the study by using multi-stage sampling procedures. The null hypotheses were tested using ANCOVA and ANOVA statistical analyses at 0.05 level of significance. Findings revealed that there was a statistical difference in the performance scores of students using CMI and TLM approaches. There was also a statistical difference between private and public tertiary institution students' performance. Additionally, the students from the university had the highest mean when compared with students from COE and polytechnics.

Virtual learning systems (VLSs), commonly referred to as learning or course management systems, have been formally adopted at many higher education institutions. However, knowledge of the actual usage of VLSs is limited in terms of what specific functional and non-functional characteristics are deemed useful and how this influences system usage. Furthermore, little is known about the role of other non-system-related factors related to VLS usage, such as pedagogic, organisational, and individual difference factors. This chapter proposes and describes the virtual learning system usage model (VLSUM), which represents the factors influencing VLS usage in higher education institutions. The VLSUM is based on a conceptual framework integrating multiple dimensions and is confirmed by the results of an empirical study. A mixed-methods research design was adopted in the development of the VSLUM. This model is valuable to educational technologists, instructional designers, and software designers for VLS implementation in higher education.

Technology integration into higher education is considered essential in terms of achieving accountability performance measures that qualify institutions to receive federal grants. The policy presented in this chapter focuses on technology integration into curricula and instruction as a means to enhance student

Foreword

I have great pleasure in writing the foreword to this timely collection of chapters that reflects many of my own interests in language teaching and learning and I'm sure many of yours. The book offers a set of articles from a wide range of contexts, mostly from what is termed the global south, and is focused on higher education. It also shows a good understanding of needs of both learners and teachers in higher education laying emphasis on making sure both learners and teachers enhance and build on what are now referred to as 21st century skills. This skill includes learner autonomy, which has always been a part of the language teaching, but it is still as vital as ever, and is being transformed by the application of technology. The book also recognizes that teachers in higher education are still not often given the support and training that they need to best support learners.

Throughout the book there is an emphasis on the appropriate use of technology and that context matters. There are no one-size fits all answers. The three sections include chapters on assessment, a topic not often covered in books in our field, with chapters providing an overview of the topic, looking at themes like blended assessment and automatic writing assessment. The second section looks at the impact of teaching through a variety of ICT tools and emphasizes the developments we are seeing in the mobile space. The third part reviews technology use at the program level and includes timely literature reviews and evaluations of general and specific e-learning platforms. The whole book is driven from an interest in localized pedagogy, recognizing where we are in the field and effectively taking this forward. You will learn a good deal from taking the time to work through these chapters.

Gary Motteram
University of Manchester, UK

Preface

INTRODUCTION

The use of Information and Communication Technology (ICT) in education has revolutionized learning and teaching for decades. ICT is regarded as a means to promote learners' and teachers' creativity and skills, so it should be paid more attention in learning contexts, especially in developing contexts (Zhou & Purushothaman, 2018). In this regard, numerous articles, journals and books have been published on ICT use in teaching and learning over the last 50 years. However, little is known how ICT impacts learning (Rosén & Billore, 2019).

With the advance of ICTs in learning environments, the roles of learners and teachers have changed. Students have spent their lives using a number of digital devices. These technologies have become part of their daily life (Bax, 2011). In this sense, they are regarded as digital natives, who are naturally skilled at using new and emerging technologies (Prensky, 2001). Still, this does not mean that students are able to apply them freely in their formal learning. Therefore, students of today at the tertiary level, at the very least, need to be aware of the potential effectiveness of these new technologies and their use in learning. Shifting beyond the traditional mode of education, the integration of ICTs has become an advantage for students at tertiary education when used for the right purpose to enhance language learning. Chapelle (2001) emphasizes that the notion of 'communicative competence' has been transformed since the use of computers in language learning and describes communicative competence as 'electronic literacies, i.e. communication in registers associated with electronic communication' (p. 2). Furthermore, Shetzer and Warschauer (2000) argue over learners' autonomous learning and redefine autonomous learners as the ones who 'are able to take charge of their own learning by working on individual and collaborative projects that result in communication opportunities in the form of presentations, Web sites, and traditional publications accessible to local and global audiences' (p. 176), as also reflected in this book. Likewise, teachers' role has changed. Teachers 'who have access to an Internet computer classroom are in a position to teach students valuable lifelong learning skills and strategies for becoming autonomous learners' (Shetzer & Warschauer, 2000, p. 176).

There is a general consensus that computers support the development of learner autonomy and motivation through ICT tools in a technology-enhanced learning environment (Koruyan, 2016; Meri-Yilan, 2019) and the computers make learning more accessible as suggested by Warschauer (2000) claiming that "learning to read, write, and communicate in the electronic medium as valuable in its own right" (p. 46). Therefore, it is important that the use of ICT in learning environments should be reinforced in a sustainable way with a range of pedagogical approaches taking students' needs and interests into the consideration to promote lifelong learning.

Policy makers and other stakeholders including parents very often take it for granted that environments with high-tech tools or facilities would enhance learning. Accordingly, the focus needs to be more on how to train our students and teachers to access consistent, reliable and authentic materials afforded by the use of technology informed by pedagogy as some chapters in this collection attempt to do. Students and teachers should be provided with appropriate support and guidance so that the integrating of technology-supported language learning can be successful and help learners to gradually become autonomous. Technology courses should be part of the integrating programs which are currently non-exist, as nicely put by Thornbury (2011), it seems to be "fashion parade of gadgets and special effects with no real discussion as to what principles might motivate their best use".

Research on ICTs has indicated technology should not be seen as a core solution in a learning environment (Zhang, 2019), but as a tool that should be used appropriately. The focus needs to be on learning process, practice and products. Furthermore, there are many examples of good practice around the world (e.g. Debski & Levy, 1999; Felix, 2001). However, there are still problems with the delivery and design. That might be because teachers simply transfer materials, tasks and activities used in face-to-face settings to online environments without adapting them to the new technological environment and they expect success in language learning (Hampel, 2006). Or the problem is a genuine lack of "conceptualization of how language learning could be enhanced in new, innovative ways with the assistance of mobile devices" (Godwin-Jones, 2011, p. 7). Thus, methods, new pedagogical approaches and practices aligned with the use of technology are necessary for success stories about teaching and learning, because technologies and their applications have potential in contributing to learning, and teachers need guidance and training in implementing and using digital tools with their students. Therefore, ICT-based assessment, methods, and programs should be on the "intersections between content, pedagogy and technology" (Hockly, 2011, p. 212) and context. In this regard, *ICT-Based Assessment, Methods, and Programs in Tertiary Education* contributes to the field with its valuable chapters from different parts of the world to provide solutions to common problems in learning and teaching.

ORGANIZATION OF THE BOOK

The book is organized into three sections based on its title. A brief description of each section follows:

Section 1: ICT-Based Assessment

This section covers six chapters which investigate assessment through ICT tools.

Chapter 1 proposes a research model for the assessment of language learner autonomy (LLA) and aims to establish a scale for its measurement of LLA in a self-access learning environment pointing out the gap in the literature of LLA assessment. The author's model produces a reliable and robust method both to assess LLA and to improve the pedagogical outcomes. This chapter concludes that the intervention increases the levels of students' LLA who are at the bottom of the treatment groups, but those at the top stay the same throughout the course of the intervention, and recommends further exploration of the components of the measurement scale.

Chapter 2 assesses the impact of a blended learning digital ecosystem implemented in an English Phonetics and Phonology subject. The chapter focuses on the development of a digital ecosystem, using Moodle, to create an adequate virtual environment in which learners are able to improve their phonological competence in all its dimensions. The results demonstrate that pre-service teachers have a positive perspective on the digital ecosystem, and they improve their English pronunciation level producing English more accurately. The findings also show that the digital ecosystem provides a more natural environment for pronunciation practice.

Chapter 3 reviews language assessment through ICT by giving a non-systematic analysis of the related literature. The author claims that there is a need to modify traditional language assessment in technology-enhanced language classrooms so that it can be more effective. The chapter draws attention to the research gap which occurs in the role of computers in language assessments posing its research questions (e.g., How can technology be implemented in language assessment?), and then answers those questions giving examples from the related research. This chapter presents innovative digital language assessment tools and discusses how to implement and use these tools.

Chapter 4 sets out a conceptual framework for the design and use of 'blended assessments' that seek to create formative activities that can be characterized by shifting modalities of presentation, variations in time and action. The authors identify three core characteristics of formative blended assessment, which represents a conceptual point of departure for the ongoing development in blended approaches that highlight the integration of technology and assessment in Saudi language programs.

Chapter 5 investigates Yemeni and Saudi EFL learners' use of language learning strategies (LLSs). The authors adopt a correlative design to see if the nation and gender play a role in using LLS on electronic platforms. Their study contributes not only to the definite contexts (i.e. Yemeni and Saudi) but also to the field of LLS in terms of assessment and correlation. It suggests the need to adopt various technology-based strategies for better language input and output.

Chapter 6 investigates a popular automated writing evaluation (AWE) tool Pigai, examining the influence of the writing tool on EFL learner writing development. The authors test the hypothesis that real-time writing feedback from Pigai is beneficial to EFL learner writing development and helpful to identify learner errors in their writing production. They also look at learners' attitude and the correlation of scores provided by Pigai and human raters which is compared and discussed. Findings show a significant improvement in students' overall scores between two writing tasks, and their vocabulary, clause density, and paragraph length between two narrative tasks develop. A positive correlation is also observed between automated Pigai scores and human rating scores, supporting the reliability of the AWE system. Finally, students show a positive attitude towards Pigai. This chapter suggests that the AWE tool can be effective in identifying learner errors and guiding EFL learners to revise their writing by providing qualitative diagnostic sentence-by-sentence feedback. This tool is also faster and more responsive than teacher's feedback.

Section 2: ICT-Based Methods

This section covers seven chapters that explore methods based on ICT tools.

Chapter 7 addresses the research gap in providing an extended framework for facilitating learner autonomy and enhancing intrinsic motivation through specifically designed online tasks to enhance the development of reading skills in higher education. The author expands Chapelle's model explicitly to provide a framework for task design to assess the impact of the iPad-enhanced task design on the development of learner autonomy and motivation. It is suggested that changing the culture of instruction and preparing university students for the realities of the digital age seem to be both positive and necessary moves and a first step that may encourage an active language learning process and enhance students' motivation to read, because reading is the most powerful tool we have in language education. With well-designed iPad tasks as in this chapter, language teachers can support this process by helping students to become well-motivated, autonomous, lifelong learners in a sustainable way with a range of pedagogical approaches taking students' needs and interests into the consideration to promote lifelong learning.

Chapter 8 explores a Quiz tool available on Moodle executing listening comprehension tasks on second language learners registered for the Basic isiZulu module at the University of KwaZulu-Natal, South Africa. The authors examine the process used in the design of listening comprehension activities. This experiment research is conducted over four weeks with a cohort of non-mother-tongue learners of isiZulu. The findings suggest that students benefit from the formative e-assessments of listening comprehension tasks. The chapter concludes that language teachers should engage in a careful and thoughtful planning process in the design of authentic listening comprehension tasks.

Chapter 9 examines collaborative discussion amongst students using Padlet to enhance the teaching and learning of essay writing in Mandarin Language. In this chapter, the focal point is how certain technology, Padlet, is being utilized to transform didactic teaching and learning into innovative pedagogy to create new learning experiences for tertiary undergraduates helping them to improve their writing skills. The authors conclude that students are able to develop their writing skills through active collaboration using Padlet, which provides many opportunities for constructive learning through a resource-based approach where undergraduates support, and learn from one another even though the topics given are considered challenging for the participants and they struggle to produce appropriate content in the early stages. They further suggest that to use this Padlet successfully, instructors need training on how to use the tool and design appropriate activities that can promote students' learning.

Chapter 10 researches the impact of using digital storytelling on motivation and learning strategies in foreign language teaching and discusses how storytelling has been an essential component of human life to transfer culture and knowledge from one generation to another throughout the history. The authors conclude that use of digital storytelling in foreign language teaching has statistically no effect on the students' use of learning strategies and their motivation, and argue that the results contradict with the existing literature.

Chapter 11 provides a critical review about negative aspects of one of the technological tools, iPad, in technology-enhanced learning environments. It contributes to the academic discussion on the different types and sources of distraction and multi-tasking at M-Learning environments and provides solutions to the distraction. The author discusses some emerging arguments such as converting 'learning distractions' into 'learning attractions' in a way that might enhance the academic discussion on theory and practice of mobile learning research. Finally, this chapter introduces three effective techniques and strategies that have the potential to control distractions.

Chapter 12 develops a mobile technologies course delivered online and explores the effects of this online course designed on Mobile Technologies on the use of ICT skills, attitudes and views of EFL Instructors. The chapter suggests that English language instructors, researchers and material designers should try to incorporate different technological tools into the courses or the materials. The author observes that the student involvement increases and they become active learners when their learning environment is arranged through mobile learning. This chapter concludes that attending the Mobile Technologies Course delivered online is very beneficial and effective for the instructors in that it helps them develop their skills on the use of mobile technologies in English language teaching.

Chapter 13 is concerned with blended learning (b-learning) exploring the effectiveness of the technological tools offered through the digital ecosystem implemented in b-learning modality. The author investigates this modality in terms of effectiveness, benefits and flexibility. The results show that the design of the digital ecosystem is effective, flexible to study and practice a second language; enables the participants to have access to resources and tools and in turn, helps them to develop learner autonomy. It also promotes a collaborative learning environment and creates a learning community. This chapter concludes that a number of students demand this kind of education. Finally, it suggests that further research on b-learning and digital ecosystems is necessary on learners' formation, teachers' training and their technological skills.

Section 3: ICT-Based Programs

This section covers five chapters that develop or review programs developed through ICT devices.

Chapter 14 aims to explore the effectiveness of Computer-Managed Instruction (CMI) on students' performance in tertiary institutions in Nigeria, where students' poor academic performance in the tertiary institutions is a major concern for educators. The authors use Computer Managed Instruction Approach (CMIA) for their excremental group and Traditional Learning Approach (TLA) for their control group. The findings reveal that CMIA group performs better than TLA and the results are statistically significantly.

Chapter 15 describes the Virtual Learning System Usage Model (VLSUM), which represents the factors influencing VLS usage in higher education institutions. The chapter addresses the gap and indicates the lack of research on the factors that influence usage of VLSs from a multi-dimensional perspective encompassing, for example, system features, pedagogic aspects, organizational support for online teaching and learning. The author proposes a conceptual framework to assess the role of VLSs from a multi-dimensional perspective and this conceptual framework is empirically tested.

Chapter 16 conducts a systematic review of the literature related to technology integration into higher education in the United States, which is considered essential in terms of achieving accountability performance measures that qualify institutions to receive federal grants. The author presents the policy that focuses on technology integration into curricula and instruction to enhance student achievement. This chapter describes the problems that prevent higher education institutions from integrating technology effectively into their educational systems and proposes key solutions to better integrate technology into higher education classrooms. It suggests that to attain the benefits of described policy and facilitate the use of technology for teaching and learning purposes, policymakers and educational leaders are required to generate context specific policies, recommendations, and practices that establish the fundamental link between technology, learning, and student success.

Chapter 17 does a systematic review of developed Intelligent Tutoring Systems (ITS) based on guidelines proposed by Silva and Neiva (2016). The author consults research papers from a variety of journals in the field. The author considers that with the growth of Information Communication Technology, emerging technologies (e.g., Artificial Intelligence, Voice Searches, Augmented Reality, Virtual Reality and Mixed Reality) learning has been revolutionized. His review in the field of emerging technologies reflects that they are able to engage learners and grab learner attention. The chapter focus, Algorithm, "Silent Observation", has sound footings in micro-research findings on formative assessment and emerging technologies and has a strong pedagogical framework interweaving emerging technologies.

Chapter 18 is concerned with evaluation of e-learning platforms such as Canvas, Blackboard, Moodle and Open Edx. Based on the document analysis method, this chapter presents an evaluative report on globally popular e-learning platforms including Canvas, Blackboard, Moodle and Open edX in terms of their market share, user interface, and features, and reaches a conclusion by comparing and contrasting their differences and similarities.

CONCLUSION

The literature on ICTs warns curriculum planners, designers and practitioners that the use of technology needs informing through a well-designed pedagogy rather than simply being technology driven. This means that ICTs should be part of a comprehensive pedagogical framework. Otherwise, the money spent on the rapid development of digital tools and resources by the educational institutions could be wasted and may result in creating obstacles and challenges rather than sorting the current problems out. To minimize the negatives and maximize the potential use of ICT in language education, it is very important that it is accompanied and used with pedagogy. The chapters in this volume comprehensively cover and discuss the pedagogical aspect of technology accompanied with a theoretically informed framework in technology-enhanced learning environments. The use of technology brings forth a flexible and accessible mode of education and bridges the gap of learning across borders. This enables students at tertiary level to have the access to other universities and academic resource materials globally, thereby expanding their knowledge. Thus, it is crucial to consider the development of technology in education. This is because times have changed, teachers have evolved, and we now have a new breed of ICTs and this would suggest, therefore, that the methods, assessment and programs need updating to take account of developments in ICTs, which requires support and designed taking students' interests and choices into consideration to encourage them to take more control of their learning. The benefits for learning are increasingly being demonstrated and teachers' roles in the information age ought to be both expanding and changing to embrace these changes. This leads to a need for an edited collection of original studies in this area and some of these studies are collected in this book.

This book provides relevant theoretical frameworks along with the latest empirical research findings in the area with a systematic review of the related literature. It is written for professionals, teachers and researchers who would like to improve their understanding of ICT-based assessments, methods, and programs in tertiary education.

The target audience of this book is composed of professionals and researchers who incorporate ICT into various disciplines in tertiary education. Moreover, the book provides insights and support executives and stakeholders concerned with ICT innovation, computer or technology assisted learning, instructional design, educational policy, course management, educational theory and practice, and curriculum design in different fields of tertiary education.

Serpil Meri Yilan
Agri Ibrahim Cecen University, Turkey

Kasım Koruyan
King Saud University, Saudi Arabia

REFERENCES

Bax, S. (2011). Normalisation revisited: The effective use of technology in language Education. *International Journal of Computer-Assisted Language Learning and Teaching*, *1*(2), 1–15. doi:10.4018/ijcallt.2011040101

Chapelle, C. (2001). *Computer applications in Second Language Acquisition*. Cambridge: Cambridge University Press. doi:10.1017/CBO9781139524681

Debski, R., & Levy, M. (Eds.). WORLDCALL: Global Perspectives on Computer-Assisted Language Learning. Amsterdam: Swets & Zeit linger.

Felix, U. (2001). *Beyond Babel: language learning online*. Melbourne: Language Australia Ltd.

Godwin-Jones, R. (2011). Mobile Apps for Language Learning. *Language Learning & Technology*, *15*, 2–11.

Hampel, R. (2006). Rethinking task design for the digital age. *ReCALL*, *18*(1), 105–121. doi:10.1017/S0958344006000711

Hockly, N. (2011). ELT Journal Debate 'Tweeting is for the birds, not for language learning. In T. Pattison (Ed.), IATEFL Brighton Conference Selection (pp. 211–212). Academic Press.

Koruyan, K. (2016). *The influence of technology-enhanced task design on the development of language learner autonomy and motivation in an Anatolian high school; A case study* (Unpublished Doctoral dissertation). Open university, Milton Keynes, UK.

Meri-Yilan, S. (2019). Learning in scaffolded autonomous e-learning environments amongst EAP students in a UK university. *Focus on ELT*, *1*(1), 70–85. doi:10.14744/felt.2019.00002

Prensky, M. (2001). Digital natives, digital immigrants. *On the Horizon*, *9*(5), 1–6. doi:10.1108/10748120110424816

Rosén, C., & Billore, S. (2019). A Cross-Cultural Study of Students' Attitudes towards Digital Language Learning Tools. In *12th Innovation in Language Learning International Conference, Florence, Italy, November 14-15, 2019* (Vol. 12, pp. 100-105). Filodiritto Publisher.

Shetzer, H., & Warschauer, M. (2000). An electronic literacy approach to network-based language teaching. In M. Warschauer & R. Kern (Eds.), *Network-based Language Teaching: Concepts and Practice* (pp. 171–185). Cambridge: Cambridge University Press. doi:10.1017/CBO9781139524735.010

Silva, R. L. S., & Neiva, F. W. (2016). Systematic Literature Review in Computer Science - A Practical Guide. doi:10.13140/RG.2.2.35453.87524

Thornbury, S. (2011). *E is for Education Technology*. Retrieved on January 10 2020 from http://scottthornbury.wordpress.com/2011/05/01/t-is-for-technology/#comments

Warschauer, M. (2000). On-line learning in second language classrooms: An ethnographic study. In M. Warschauer & R. Kern (Eds.), *Network-based Language Teaching: Concepts and Practice* (pp. 41–58). Cambridge: Cambridge University Press. doi:10.1017/CBO9781139524735.005

Zhang, J. (2019). *Technology is not the solution: Visitor experience of the Chengdu Museum in the digital age* (Unpublished Master's Thesis). Uppsala University, Sweden.

Zhou, C., & Purushothaman, A. (2018). Developing creativity and learning design by Information and Communication Technology (ICT) in developing contexts. In M. Khosrow-Pour (Ed.), *Encyclopedia of Information Science and Technology* (4th ed., pp. 4178–4188). IGI Global.

Acknowledgment

We would first like to thank the IGI Global for giving us this opportunity to work on and publish this edited book. We are also grateful to Dr. Gary Motteram, who supported us with his insightful comments and foreword for this book. We are indebted to the authors of this book whose research we believe contributes to the field of ICT. For providing invaluable feedback and editing support, we are thankful to the members of the Editorial Advisory Board of this book including reviewers. Last but not least, personal special thanks should go to my co-editor, Dr. Serpil, who advised me on my chapter along with the editing.

Section 1
ICT-Based Assessment

Chapter 1
A Framework for the Assessment of Learner Autonomy in Language Learning:
Establishment of a Measuring Scale and Bands

Sahar Matar Alzahrani
https://orcid.org/0000-0001-8468-0768
Umm Al Qura University, Saudi Arabia

ABSTRACT

This research reports on the assessment of the improvement in the language learner autonomy (LLA) of a group of Saudi medicine students at tertiary level following an intervention that aims to examine and enhance their LLA in a blended course. Thus, this study proposes a research model for the assessment of LLA in the 21st century and establishes a scale for its measurement. Because LLA is a combination of observable and non-observable behaviors, quantitative and qualitative methods were triangulated in a mixed method research to look at it through the learner voice and metacognition (process perspective) and through the learner gained test scores (product perspective). To overcome the problem that LLA is an unsteady state, the assessment model integrates summative and formative assessment methods. Findings show that the assessment of LLA helps to better understand the process of LLA enhancement and the potential factors that might influence learners' LLA.

DOI: 10.4018/978-1-7998-3062-7.ch001

INTRODUCTION

The current chapter focuses on the assessment of language learner autonomy (LLA) in a blended Self-Access Language Learning (SALL) environment. It is argued that one of the main changes that teachers need to undertake when they aim to empower their learners is to change assessment practices within their classroom (Everhard, 2015a). This requires exerting time and effort. Assessment of LLA is one of the most difficult tasks for the teacher and the researcher in SALL because other variables are in play including the use of technology (Reinders and Lázaro, 2007). Assessment is often undertaken using 'underdeveloped methodologies and assessment tools' (ibid: p. 1). Therefore, this research was carried out to propose a model for the assessment of LLA in the twenty-first century based on the assumption that there are several components underpinning the concept of LLA and that the lack of any one of these components may influence the level of students' LLA. It also aims to establish a scale for the measurement of LLA in a self-access learning environment. The word 'measurement' is used to refer to the quantitative work which provides numerical evidence on the level of learners' LLA; and 'assessment' is used for the broader process of assessment of LLA including the use of quantitative and qualitative data collection methods.

The study in this chapter is based on an experimental mixed-method research which investigates the measurement and the development of LLA of a group of Saudi students at tertiary level in a blended course and proposes a comprehensive framework for LLA assessment in the twenty-first century. This paper aims to answer one research question based on its design of a LLA scale: How can the development of LLA be measured within a blended learning environment?

First, the chapter gives the definition and constituents of learner autonomy, and its relation to assessment. Next, it draws attention to the gap in the literature of LLA assessment and establishes a LLA measurement scale. Ultimately, based on the research on this scale, it shows findings, solutions and recommendations along with further considerations.

BACKGROUND

Defining Learner Autonomy

Learner autonomy has been discussed and defined in the literature of second and foreign language learning. Because of the multidimensionality of learner autonomy, there have been attempts to define it from several perspectives (Smith, 2008). The definitions given by different theorists tend to differ slightly. It is only in the 1990s that learner autonomy was linked to language learning and the development of second language proficiency (Little, 2007; Smith, 2008).

Little (1991, p. 4) significantly contributes to the notion of autonomy with his definition of autonomy as "a capacity for detachment, critical reflection, decision making, and independent action". Since LLA is often considered to be multidimensional, Benson (2001, 2011) suggests that Little adds another (psychological) dimension to the Vygotskyan view of learner autonomy. In this view, autonomy is looked at as a phenomenon that includes both 'individual-cognitive' and 'social interactive' notions, involves 'interdependence', and adopts freedom and choice (ibid). By 'detachment', Oxford (1999) explains that Little does not mean detachment of learners from their communities, institutions, or materials. He rather means that the development of learners' cognition requires them to be socially engaged for assistance purposes and at the same time to be detached for individual-reflection purposes.

Prominent scholars (e.g. Dam, Eriksson, Little, Miliander, and Trebbi) put forward the Bergen definition which combines the promotion of LLA and the importance of interdependence as a form of sociocultural theory which refers to LLA as "a capacity and willingness to act independently and in cooperation with others, as a social, responsible person" (Dam et al. 1990, p. 102). By the twenty-first century, autonomy has formed chapters or sections of the textbooks used for language teacher education (Smith, 2008). However, there has been little or no consensus on what LLA actually is (Little, 2007). The concept integrates ideas from different fields of knowledge including Philosophy, Politics, Pedagogy, and Psychology (Schwienhorst, 2008).

Little's (2007, p. 14) view of LLA argues that "the development of learner autonomy and the growth of target language proficiency are mutually supporting and fully integrated with each other". Benson (2010) defines autonomous language learners as "learners who are in some sense 'in control' of important dimensions of their learning, which might otherwise be controlled by others or by nobody at all". Everhard (2015a, p. 11) quotes Benson's suggestion that "autonomy is best defined as 'a composite of abilities, attitudes or dispositions'". Tassinari (2012, 2016) has a higher-order view of LLA as "the metacapacity, i.e. the second order capacity, of the learner to take control of their learning process to different extents and in different ways according to the learning situation".

Esch (1997) illustrates that learner autonomy involves the sense of independence which is the opposite of learners' dependence on the teacher, rather than as a reference to the individualistic view which emphasizes learning in isolation. In fact, recent views of learner autonomy highlight the interdependence (Dam, 1995; Esch, 1997; Little, 1991; 1999, Tassinari, 2015; Ushioda, 2011) which the advocates of the Vygotskyan sociocultural theory (e.g. Benson, 1996; Little, 1996; Little, 2001; Sinclair, 2000) believe can take place through the communication and support shared among learners or between learners and teachers. This meaning of independence which relies on interdependence as a means to move to independence (Tassinari, 2015) has an implication for the meaning intended for independent learning of autonomous learners as illustrated in the present paper.

The definition of LLA adopted in the current study is a combination of elements drawn from the definitions of Benson (2010), Dickinson (1987), and Little (1999), Littlewood (1996), Tassinari (2016): Learners' "metacapacity, i.e. the second order capacity" ... "to take control of their learning process to different extents and in different ways according to the learning situation" (Tassinari, 2016, p. 120). This metacapacity entails learners' "independent capacity to make and carry out the choices which govern his or her actions" (Littlewood, 1996, p. 428), "to use the acquired knowledge and skills confidently, flexibly, appropriately and independently of the teacher" (Benson. 2010, p. 81), and to judge 'the degree of success' of their learning (self-assessment) (Dickinson, 1987, p. 16; Little, 1999).

The definition adopted in the current paper has the purpose of identifying the components vital to LLA in different learning contexts whether in a classroom or in a more open learning environment (i.e. self-access learning). The autonomy-related components underpinning this definition of LLA draw on the definitions of well-known scholars in the literature of LLA (e.g. Benson, 2010; Dam et al., 1990; Holec, 1981; Little, 1991; Littlewood, 1996; Oxford, 1999; Tassinari, 2016), to mention a few of the most influential ones. These components are:

1) Learners' willingness (i.e. attitude and belief) (Chan, 2001; Everhard, 2015a; Kohonen, 1999, 2012 cited in Everhard, 2015a; Le, 2013; Littlewood, 1997; Sinclair, 2000, 2009; Tassinari, 2012);
2) Learners' confidence (Cotterall, 1995a; Dam and Legenhausen, 2010);
3) Learners' capacities
   (3a) Language competencies (Benson, 2010; Little, 1999, 2003a; Morrison, 2005; Oxford, 1999; Peek, 2015; Schwienhorst, 2008; Sinclair, 1999);
   (3b) Metacognitive knowledge (of self, language, learning process, and strategies or skills) (Le, 2013; Littlewood, 1996);
   (3c) Metacognitive strategies (i.e. planning, reflection, learning management, and self-assessment) (Tassinari, 2012; 2016).

This definition is evidently lengthy, and this was expected by Le (2013) when a comprehensible definition to LLA is to be considered, but it is intended to have an 'explicit' definition (Benson, 2001, p. 94) which combines an explanation of the 'WHAT' and the 'HOW' in relation to capacities of autonomous learners as suggested by Benson (2007a, p. 23) in his criticism to Holec's definition.

Constituents of Learner Autonomy

Measuring students' LLA level requires knowing what capacities or behaviors are being measured. Benson (2007a) asserts that it is tricky to identify disconnected components of autonomy in language and that this question remains debatable. Benson's (2011) view of the concept of autonomy is that it is complex and it comprises many constructs which are all different from the construct of autonomy itself. Benson (2011) lists examples of components of autonomy as were found in educational research such as language awareness, motivation, strategy use, learner beliefs, and metacognition. None of these constructs, not even the construct of autonomy itself, is a 'discrete observable construct' (Benson, 2010, p. 66). Due to the fact that it consists of many constructs, we can tell if a learner is to some degree autonomous when we observe those constructs and treat them as manifestations or 'indexical' behaviors of autonomy (ibid., p. 65). The result is that learners can be autonomous in totally different ways and the construct of autonomy itself can be seen in different forms (ibid). A debate in the literature of learner autonomy about what might constitute the construct of autonomy is undeniable.

In this paper, LLA is believed to encompasses the five main components included in the adopted definition of learner autonomy: willingness (i.e. attitude and belief), confidence, metacognitive knowledge (of self, language, learning process, and strategies or skills), metacognitive strategies (planning, learning management, and self-assessment), and language competences. These five constituents are the components of the model proposed for the assessment of students' LLA (see Figure 1). Figure 1 illustrates the link between these five theoretical constituents and the proposed model for the assessment of LLA.

Figure 1. The final version of the LLA assessment model

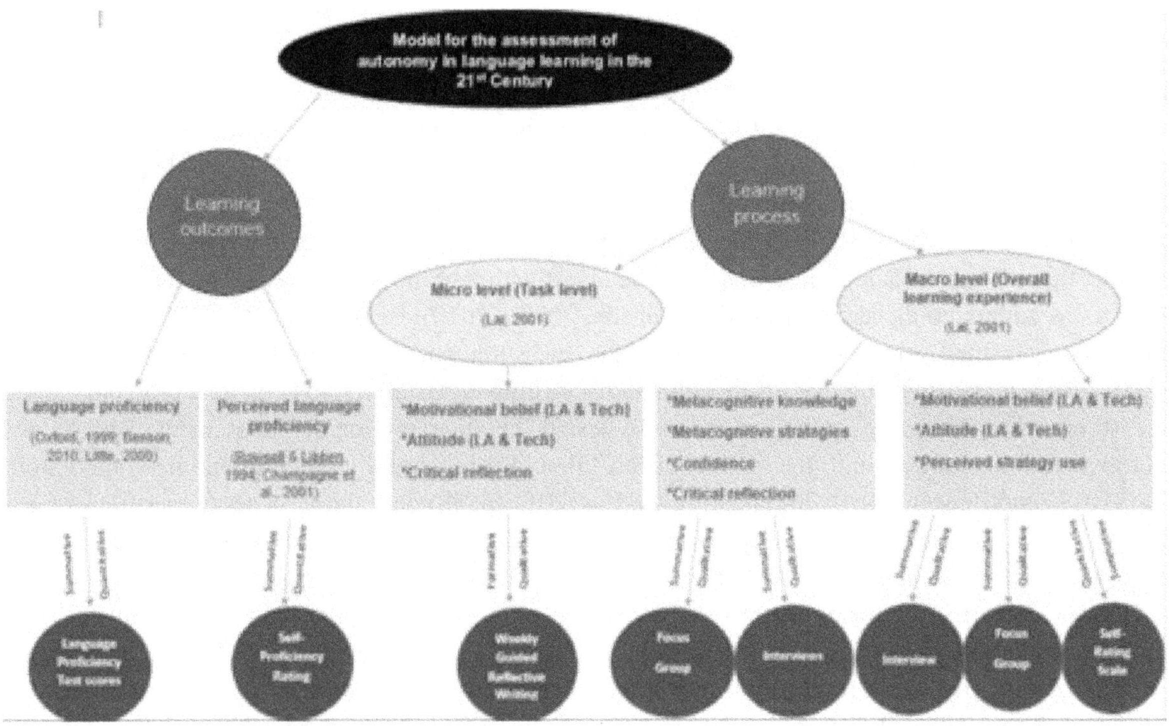

Complexity of Autonomy Assessment

English language teachers doing initiatives to promote language learner autonomy (LLA) are in most cases interested in testing the effectiveness of their efforts in fostering LLA. Moreover, educational institutions policies need to consider the credibility of the conclusions made about students' learning outcomes and LLA when the aim is to integrate LLA enhancement and this shows the importance of its measurement. However, there is disagreement in the literature about LLA definition, manifesting skills, and the appropriateness of the use of quantitative versus qualitative assessment methods.

The term 'secret garden' was used to describe the complexity of assessment (Weeden, et al., 2002, p. 150) and autonomy (Everhrad, 2015b). Everhard (2015a) stresses that autonomy, assessment, and language learning are very interrelated. The assessment of LLA is 'a challenging topic' from which we come up with fundamental research questions such as, how individuals' LLA in different contexts can be described using observable behaviours or descriptive criteria; whether levels of LLA development can be defined; whether LLA growth can help to generate new methods for developing LLA; and whether the development in language proficiency and in LLA are connected (Tassinari, 2015, p. 64).

Even when teachers find evidence for the development of their students' LLA, it is difficult to 'justify its promotion through tangible scales of measurement' (Everhard, 2006, p. 11). This question was under investigation by the authors in Everhard and Murphy's (2015) edited book along with the identification of how assessment in language learning can be used to practice and improve autonomy (Cotterall and Malcolm, 2015). The measurement of autonomy became more problematic because researchers fail to address its problems (Benson, 2010).

Research Gap in the Literature of LLA Assessment

As compared to the increasing number of discussions on the enhancement of LLA, the assessment of LLA and the link between the concepts of learner autonomy and assessment are both neglected (Everhard, 2015a). "This neglect [of LLA assessment] is surprising" and "It is therefore striking that the relationship between assessment and autonomy in language learning, which so clearly warrants rigorous investigation regarding the influences of the one on the other and the resultant implications and ramifications, remains relatively neglected" (Everhard, 2015a, p. 8). A great volume of research in the literature of learner autonomy focused on the investigation of the aspects related to the concept, but only a few addressed the assessment of it (Benson, 2007b; 2010). Benson (2010, p. 77) observes that there is only a small volume of the literature on the 'measurement' of autonomy including his writings (2001, 2010, and 2011); and that his thoughts in his writing (2001, pp. 51-54) on how problematic the measurement of autonomy is are not empirically-tested. The literature on the assessment of LLA does not give sufficient attention to the main question 'Should we measure learner autonomy?' apart from Lai (2011) and Benson (2010, 2011). However, Lai (2011, p. 48) only throws a set of questions on assessment, for example, 'Why should we assess learner autonomy?' and 'Is this a necessary step to take? If so, for whom?', but she does not answer the main question.

However, there is a growing interest in the assessment of LLA (Murase, 2015) but this interest was only able to produce ways of indirectly assessing LLA using its relationship with "observable and measurable factors" (Le, 2013, p. 76). With this increasing interest in the notion of assessment of LLA, it "seems that any actual attempt to measure learner autonomy tends to be perceived in a rather negative way, such as 'problematic' (Benson, 2001, p. 54) or even a combination of 'problematic' and 'difficult' (Lai, 2011, p. 43-5; Mynard, 2006, p. 3)." (Murase, 2015, p. 38). At this point, we can ask questions about what makes it difficult and how we can overcome this difficulty.

Benson (2011) explains that the slow progress in dealing with these problems is because the institutions did not translate autonomy into their credibility requirements although it is practiced as an education goal. Additionally, researchers refuse to address the issue of autonomy assessment because they believe that assessment itself goes against the concept of autonomy (Benson, 2011; Champagne et al., 2001). In fact, it is possible to find ways to address these problems (Benson, 2011). Benson (2001) maintains that 'the measurement of autonomy is problematic' but it 'does not necessarily mean that we should not attempt to measure it' (p. 54).

Benson (2010) describes the need for research to develop tools for LLA measurement and he comments that these tools are needed to provide empirical evidence for our understanding of how LLA develops in different contexts. Murase (2015) asserts that "some form of measurement of autonomy is needed for research purposes at least" and she uses Benson's (2011) acknowledgement of the need for such measurement when the aim is to investigate the effectiveness of an initiative to promote LLA. The quantitative instruments to measure autonomy are 'more convincing to some researchers' (Murase, 2015, p. 36), but there is a lack of effective quantitative instruments or measurement of autonomy (Murase, 2006 cited in Murase, 2015).

Cooker (2012, p. 164) states "I am aware of three studies which have developed statistically-based measures of learner autonomy (i.e. Dixon, 2011; Confessore and Park, 2004; Murase, 2010) but feel they all lacked the important aspect of tapping into subjective learner perceptions of learner autonomy". Reinders and Lázaro's (2007) review has put together the quantitative instruments that were developed in previous studies to measure LLA, e.g. Dixon (2011); Lai (2001); Reinders and Cotterall (2001);

Murase (2015); Mynard (2004, 2006). Even when measurement of LLA is attempted to prove that learners improved in LLA (e.g. Murase, 2015), a scale which can show learners' profile of LLA was not achieved (Cotterall and Malcolm, 2015; Murase, 2015) and this is because the researcher had to come to an understanding of how LLA develops to be able to build the instrument before she continues with the work on the measurement.

In this paper, the measurement of LLA is believed to be technically possible and conceptually appropriate because if LLA is composed of several dimensions of control over learning (Benson, 2010) and is a matter of degrees (Everhard, 2015a), we should be able to measure the extent to which learners can control these dimensions and the degree of their LLA. Also, it was thought to be possible if the construct of LLA was conceptualized and operationalized (Murase, 2015) and if we reduced it into observable concepts that can be measured (Benson, 2010). It is realized that this is not enough to have a reliable measurement of LLA, but the authenticity of learners' behaviors should be checked (Benson, 2001) by including their own self-evaluation using qualitative methods to validate these self-assessment (Dam and Legenhausen, 2010) and by avoiding enforcing any influence on learners' behaviors during the measurement (Murase, 2015).

Based on the belief that measurement of LLA is possible and appropriate, a model is developed and proposed in this paper for the assessment of LLA with a measuring scale in this study. First, the construct of LLA is re-conceptualized to get a theoretical framework for the measurement of LLA, then a learner training program for the enhancement of students' LLA is designed, after that the proposed assessment model is developed, and the assessment model is operationalized to establish a measuring scale. The established scale and bands for the measurement of the change in students' LLA over the course are applied on students' data.

MAIN FOCUS OF THE CHAPTER

The focus of the chapter is to discuss the problems posed in the literature, establish a LLA measurement scale and contribute to the field thanks to findings gathered based on this scale.

Problems of the Measurement of Learner Autonomy

Just as LLA was treated in the literature as a multidimensional concept and was defined from several perspectives (Smith, 2008), it was also measured from different perspectives by different researchers. Some researchers measured it from the process perspective such as metacognitive awareness (Sinclaire, 1999); self-directed learning skills (Ravindram, 2001); learning process at task level (Lai, 2001); metacognitive knowledge about oneself, learning process, and language (Lamb, 2010), while others measured the learning products to assess LLA such as learner proficiency self-rating (Champagne et al., 2001; Rowsell & Libben, 1994); language proficiency test (Benson, 2010; Champagne et al., 2001; Little, 1999; Oxford 1999); language achievement (Oxford, 1999).

Some researchers believe that it can only be measured quantitatively (Chamagne et al., 2001; Lai, 2001) whilst others believe that qualitative methods are suitable for the measurement (Chamagne et al., 2001; Dam & Legenhausen, 2010; Lamb, 2010; Morrison, 2005; Rowsell & Libben, 1994; Simmons & Wheeler, 1995). The time in which the measurement is carried out is also different in the literature. Some researchers preferred the summative measurement at the end of a course or a certain period of time (Lai, 2001); whereas others feel that the formative measurement during the learning experience is better (Lai, 2001; Lamb, 2010; Rivers, 2001). Just as there is no agreement about the definition of LLA, there is also no agreement yet about what skills can manifest this concept.

Figure 2. The scale for the measurement of Language Learner Autonomy

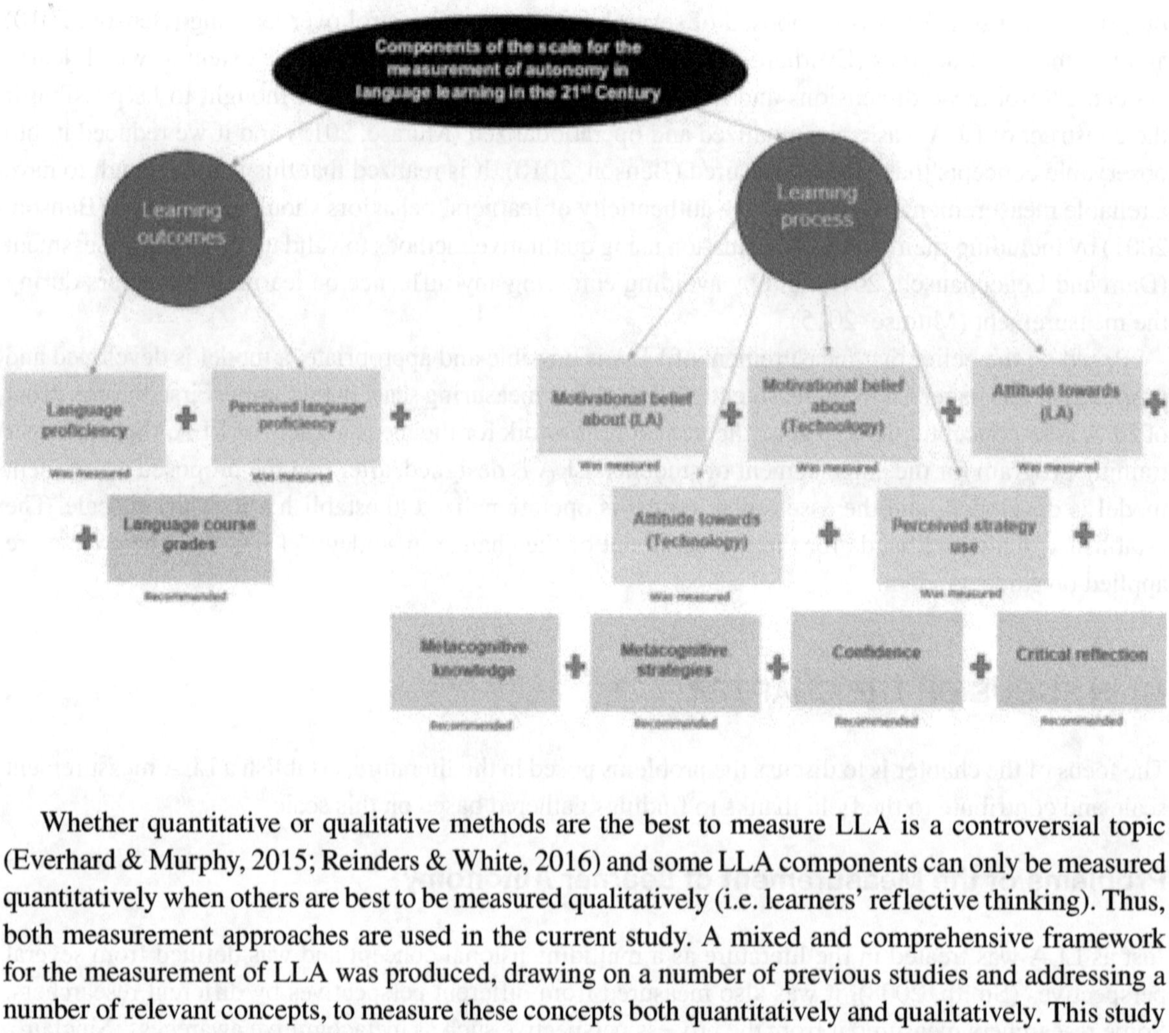

Whether quantitative or qualitative methods are the best to measure LLA is a controversial topic (Everhard & Murphy, 2015; Reinders & White, 2016) and some LLA components can only be measured quantitatively when others are best to be measured qualitatively (i.e. learners' reflective thinking). Thus, both measurement approaches are used in the current study. A mixed and comprehensive framework for the measurement of LLA was produced, drawing on a number of previous studies and addressing a number of relevant concepts, to measure these concepts both quantitatively and qualitatively. This study builds on previous studies which looked at the indirect measurement of LLA through the measurement of one or two related concepts, however, this study is measuring LLA directly by the application of a measuring scale to give a score for students' LLA.

The proposed framework uses summative and formative measures. Summative measurement methods were used to look at the enhancement made by the students in the end of the learning experience, e.g. self-rating scale (SRS form), proficiency self-rating, language proficiency test, focus group and individual interviews. Students' guided weekly reflective writing was used to formatively measure students' metacognitive knowledge. This framework also combines looking at the micro and the macro level of learning. It looks at learner autonomy through the gained tests scores (product perspective) and through the learner voice and metacognition (process perspective).

Focusing on the product perspective, the improvement in students' language proficiency was examined. This was measured pre and post the study using two instruments: One of these instruments was a language proficiency test and the other was a proficiency self-rating form. However, in the process perspective, two levels were looked at: the micro level of learning focusing on the tasks per week. What was measured here is students' critical reflection ability and their metacognitive knowledge. A guided reflective writing form was given to students per week. The other level of learning process was the macro which looks at the overall learning experience. In this level of learning, students' perceived strategy use and metacognitive knowledge were measured. These were measured using a self-rating scale (pre- and post), interviews, and a focus group post the study. Therefore, a mixed and comprehensive model was produced for LLA direct measurement, drawing on previous studies and addressing relevant concepts.

The Establishment of LLA Measurement Scale

Using the proposed framework for LLA assessment (see Figure 1), the scale for the measurement of LLA, as demonstrated in Figure 2, is created and it is an additive scale of the indicators of these constructs with the assumption that all the included indicators are of equal importance.

A 100-point scale is created out of the relevant components and thus is divided into 10 measuring bands as listed in Table 1. Each of these bands has the threshold of 10 scores and the naming method of the Common European Framework of Reference (CEFR) bands in levelling students' language proficiency was used to name the proposed bands. For example, when the student scores from 0-10, then she is at level A1.

Table 1. The bands established for the LLA measurement scale

LLA band name (at a point of time)	Range of scores
E2	91-100
E1	81-90
D2	71-80
D1	61-70
C2	51-60
C1	41-50
B2	31-40
B1	21-30
A2	11-20
A1	0-10

Using this scale with the bands, LLA of the participating students is measured before and after the training along with the change in their LLA. For instance, a student who scores 63 out of a 100 before the study is at the D1 level; and when she scores 85 out of a 100 after the study, then she is at level E1. Multiple data analysis methods were exploited as it is a mixed-method research. The quantitative data are treated statistically to obtain the ultimate LLA variable. The qualitative data from the reflective writing forms were imported to NVivo software to process the queries on the themes needed to answer the research question.

Research Sample

The target population of this research consisted of the Medical and Medical Sciences students studying in their preparatory year at a local university. The sample of the study was composed of three groups of the Medical and Medical Sciences learners, with similar total number of students (25). The participants' sampling in qualitative studies was done differently from the way it is approached in quantitative studies (Dörnyei, 2007).

Three groups were purposely selected out of 28 groups in total of the Medical and Medical Sciences university students (foundation year) as the sample for the experiment to represent the population of the study. However, the selection of this purposive sample was random within the groups of students which were placed on the pre-intermediate level of language proficiency according to the placement test. Each group of the three encompassed 25 students. The reason for selecting three groups was to investigate the effect of learners' technology use on the enhancement of their autonomy-related capacities in order to be able to draw as robust and reliable conclusions as possible about the relationship between students' technology use and LLA enhancement.

The students in the groups were given numbers to use them as their research codes for anonymity purposes. The division of the sample into three groups is meant to add to the validity of the study through the comparison of the results of the three groups who have been exposed to the same experience of learning except for the investigated variable, the supplementary learning material being delivered via the online or the offline mode. One group was intended to be exposed to a Blended Learning (BL) experience by adding an Online Strategy Course with Medical English content to the already existing Face-to-Face Medical English Course which is a pre-requisite course for the students to pass the foundation year; and it is called 'the online treatment group' (ONTG) consisting of 24 students. The second group was planned to be taught using the same content of the Medical English Strategy Course but in an offline mode in addition to the existing Face-to-Face Medical English Course. This group consisted of 26 students and it is called 'the offline treatment group' (OFTG). The third group of participants was determined not to be exposed to any treatment besides the core Face-to-Face Medical English Course; and it is called 'the control group (CG)' encompassing 25 students.

Data Collection Instruments and Procedures

Quantitative data were used to test the proposed model for the assessment of language learner autonomy and, therefore, to establish a measuring scale for language learner autonomy in the twenty-first century. Pre- and post-questionnaires (self-rating scale and proficiency self-rating) along with a pre- and post-proficiency test were used as the quantitative methods. To implement the proposed framework, quantitative and qualitative methods were triangulated in a mixed-method research approach. The findings from the quantitative data were used afterwards for a validation study which is beyond the scope of the current research paper. Qualitative data were collected during (e.g. guided weekly students' reflective writing) or after providing training to the students (e.g. classroom and online observation, one to-one interview, and a focus group interview).

Data Analysis Procedures

Conversely, the model proposed for the assessment of LLA has been set out quantitatively and the quantitative LLA variable has been created to be used to measure students' LLA prior to the experiment (at T1) and after the experiment (at T3). The change that they made in LLA from T1 to T3 has been calculated and the results of the frequency of the LLA variable that was run for T1, T3, and the change made in LLA are reported. Similarly, the results of the significance testing of the differences in the change in LLA across the three groups (ANOVA TEST), between the two treatment groups (Independent T-test), and within each group (Paired T-test) are worked on.

A frequency test was run on the OFTG's LLA change to show an improvement of (M=5.10). Likewise, the ONTG's mean of LLA change revealed an increase of (M=10.03) from the start of the course which was double the OFTG's improvement. However, the CG showed a declined LLA (M= 4.06). The greater enhancement in the LLA of the ONTG compared to the OFTG's may indicate that the use of technology led to this difference between the two groups as it was the only variable that was not given to the OFTG. The decline in the CG's LLA can show that they were getting more dependent on their teacher as a result of learning in a traditional classroom and not being exposed to the treatment.

To look at the significance of the changes made in LLA from the start of the course within each group, a paired sample T-test was carried out. Table 2 shows that the OFTG significantly improved LLA with five points on a -100 to +100 scale. Likewise, the ONTG made a significant 10-point improvement on a -100 to +100 scale. A four-point reduction on a -100 to +100 scale in LLA was significantly made by the CG which can be a result for the lack of training and technology. The significant improvement made by the OFTG and ONTG over the course revealed the positive impact of technology on helping ONTG to make double the increase of OFTG.

A One Way ANOVA test was carried out on the change in LLA score to test the significance of the difference among the three groups and it was found highly significant (see table 2). The post hoc test (S-N-K) showed each one of the groups on a different column which revealed that the three groups are different from each other. The CG showed significantly less LLA after the course than the two groups; and the treatment groups made significantly different amount of increase in their LLA. This result goes in line with the results of the paired sample T-test above that the learner training led to a difference between OFTG and CG and that technology led to a difference between ONTG and OFTG.

Table 2. Significance of students' change in LLA

Groups	Change significance within groups	Change significance between 3 groups	Change significance between 2 treatment grs
Offline	t (25) =3.877, p <0.05	F (2, 72) = 16.712, p < 0.05	p < 0.05
Online	t (23) =4.987, p <0.05		
Control	t (24) = - 2.188, p < 0.05		

An independent sample T-test was run on the change in LLA to test the significance of the difference between the treatment groups and there was a significant difference which supports the above results that technology made a difference in the improvement of LLA. LLA level for everyone has quantitatively been assumed and differences in the levels of LLA in the three groups of the experiment were looked at to be identified. The conclusions made from the quantitative work are tested using students' qualitative responses in the focus group interview, one-to-one interviews, and guided reflective writings along with the researcher's online and offline observations. However, the testing of the quantitative findings is beyond the scope of this research paper.

Findings

Results of LLA Measurement (scale)

In this study, there are many substantive findings about the assessment of LLA. This chapter provides the answer to the research question which seeks to identify how we can measure LLA within a blended learning environment by presenting the findings of the scale components and the suggested modifications. One of the findings of this study is the creation of the measuring scale and the creation of the measuring bands building on the bands of the Common European Framework of Reference (CEFR) for the measurement of language proficiency. It also shows that the assessment of LLA helps to better understand the process of LLA enhancement and the potential factors that might influence learners' LLA.

A reliable, appropriate, and robust way to measure LLA was proposed and validated. It was found that the most reliable and robust way to get tangible evidence and an accurate assessment of LLA is to combine quantitative and qualitative assessment methods in a formative and a summative view and to look at the assessment of LLA at the macro and micro levels. It is appropriate because it avoids assessing it through the use of tests and it incorporates students' voices to do self-assessment to go in line with the essence of this concept and to ensure the authenticity of the findings. This is a reliable and robust method for the assessment because it does not only assess LLA in a certain task, but it goes beyond that to the overall learning experience; it includes formative besides the summative assessment to help with the triangulation and to improve the pedagogical outcomes; and it uses two approaches (i.e. quantitative and qualitative) and multiple methods for data collection to help with the triangulation and the validation of the findings from either approaches or methods. It was also found in this study that learners need training on self-assessment.

Conclusion About Quantitative LLA Measurement

From the results of the quantitative LLA measurement in the three groups, there is not a huge difference between the ceiling of LLA scores (the level of the highest scoring) in the ONTG at T1 (82) and T3 (85), but also not a big difference between the ceiling of the OFTG at T1 (88) and T3 (93). However, the ONTG's base increased whilst the OFTG's base remained the same. That means that the variability within the ONTG decreased over the time which indicates that they were all moving in the same direction of change and that more students were making change in the ONTG than in the OFTG. The ONTG became more homogenous when the LLA scores of the bottom increased more than those of the top. Those students who were at the bottom in the ONTG made greater change than with those at the bottom of the OFTG where everyone was generally just slightly increasing. Regardless of the reliability of students' self-assessment to obtain their LLA scores, this difference in the change between the treatment groups suggests that technology was more effective than the training to cause change in greater number of students in the ONTG than in the OFTG.

It is concluded that the intervention was increasing the levels of students' LLA who are sitting at the bottom of the treatment groups, but those sitting at the top remained similar throughout the course of the intervention. This is explained by the progress made by the low autonomy students in both groups which was much greater (two bands) than in the high autonomy students in both groups (one band). The agreement between what the overall picture of the three groups and the selected case studies say about LLA change leads to posing questions about the accuracy of self-assessment skill in both low and high autonomy students.

Overall, almost everybody (in the ONTG) had a positive score and increased their levels of LLA except three students who decreased in the ONTG and, interestingly, a few more students (6 students) were decreasing in the OFTG. The average LLA change suggests that the ONTG (10) became more autonomous over the time twice as much as the OFTG (5). The negative number in the control group (-4) may indicate that students are getting more dependent on the teacher or are unaware of what they are rating themselves at. They were not excited to help the research or to engage with the research work after the intervention. However, we need to explore whether anyone of the components of the measurement scale is not working in the qualitative approach. This can be done by looking at how each of the components of the scale is working in the qualitative data and whether they work in a similar way.

Relationship Between Quantitative and Qualitative Assessments

An interesting contribution to the area is the exploration of this relationship with a critical assessment perspective when something is studied quantitatively versus qualitatively. To some extent, there is a disconnection between what the quantitative data and what the qualitative data are saying about LLA of the four case studies examined in the case study e.g. Nora's progress in LLA.

Students' quantitative self-rating in the individual components of LLA in the SRS form highlighted the phenomenon found in LLA quantitative measurement (overall LLA scores) in that people who had high levels of LLA at the beginning do not increase very strongly over time whilst we see a greater increase at the lower end. However, looking at what each of the case studies said in the qualitative data about these components, it was found that Nora's LLA was high and perhaps she should have shown a greater increase in her LLA score. It was also found that LLA of Lama and the two low autonomy students (Samia and Nora) was not as high as their LLA scores were showing; and that they should have shown a lower increase in their LLA scores based on the qualitative triangulated data of these four case studies. This is linked to the issue highlighted by (Brantmeier and Vanderplank, 2008; Hung et al., 2016; Oscarson, 1984) in that high achievers tend to under-rate their performance while a tendency for self-overrating is common among low achievers.

SOLUTIONS AND RECOMMENDATIONS

Need for Deconditioning Process Before Training

Learner empowerment and responsibility for learning should be given to learners from the very beginning of the course but teachers must not suppose that learners can control all aspects of learning or that all learners can do that from the outset (Little, 1999). However, not all learners have the same capability for autonomous learning and not all aspects of learning can be managed at the same time (ibid). This study finds that the difference in the extent to which students engage with the training depends on students' capacity to take control of their learning and on their attitudes and beliefs about learner-centered pedagogies (Benson and Cooker, 2013, p. 7; Le, 2013), technology, and metacognitive strategies. Therefore, it is recommended that researchers improve students' attitudes and beliefs about learner-centered pedagogies as well as technology use along with their capacities before they give them training or technology (Le, 2013). This will prepare them for the training and make them accept technology use.

Engagement with technology use and with training (i.e. pedagogy) leads to greater capacities and better attitude and belief about independent learning, technology use, and metacognitive strategies. Consequently, greater engagement with technology use and with the training (i.e. pedagogy) leads to more increase in LLA. Hence, it is recommended that researchers ensure students' engagement with the given training and with technology to help improve their capacities, attitudes, and beliefs about independent learning and eventually improve in LLA.

Suggested Modifications on the Assessment Model

The results of statistics on LLA score and its individual components were satisfying and were showing what was expected to happen in the participating groups, i.e. the ONTG outperforms the OFTG and the CG in the change they make in LLA over time. The qualitative data of the four case studies showed a similar thing but with some issues in self-assessment which resulted in moderate distortion in students' LLA measurement.

One of the findings that came from the qualitative investigation of LLA assessment is the impact of students' confidence and metacognitive strategies on their LLA enhancement. These two components were qualitatively assessed as the data-driven analysis approach was conducted, but they were not included in the measuring scale. Similarly, metacognitive knowledge was considered in the assessment carried out for LLA when it was elicited from students' qualitative reports on their attitudes, beliefs, and perceived strategy use in the interview and FG, but it was not treated statically because it was not originally measured in the SRS. These three concepts were not included in the quantitative measurement of LLA (and accordingly in the LLA score) but they were assessed qualitatively. Therefore, it is recommended that other researchers use this assessment model and consider the inclusion of three concepts (i.e. confidence, metacognitive strategies, and metacognitive knowledge) as separate components for the assessment model, with equal importance, both in the quantitative and qualitative parts of the assessment.

FUTURE RESEARCH DIRECTIONS

The disconnection between the findings of the quantitative and the qualitative data of the four case studies is not about the reliability of the quantitative measurement because a variety of procedures have been undertaken to ensure that the quantitative measurements are as reliable as possible. For example, all the items included in the questionnaire were tested, each individual item was tested to ensure that they map onto what they are meant to be measuring, and the actual data at the ground level for every individual question was looked at. After ensuring that the quantitative side of the assessment is as reliable as possible, the focus was to do the same for the qualitative side. Yet, it is about two different ways of exploring something. It is completely natural that some elements of the quantitative and the qualitative assessments are not the same. The criterion for the self-assessment done in the qualitative data are not the same as the criterion used in their quantitative data. In the quantitative measurement of LLA, it was clear to the students that there was some sort of rating in which they might have given themselves higher scores, but in the qualitative data they were asked to talk about their experience in language learning, how they felt, what they did. They were not aware that they were declaring things about themselves which would be used to rate them. The quantitative measurement used learners' self-assessment to measure observable and no observable constructs. The qualitative assessment revealed the importance of combining both types of assessment methods to be able to capture the authenticity of the observable and no observable autonomy-related constructs. Therefore, this chapter suggests further studies to consider the pros and cons of each data collection instrument and other aspects of the literature.

Also, it was not possible to include students' language course grades (LCG) in the LLA measurement conducted in this study for contextual reasons though it was proposed as part of the initial proposed assessment model. However, further research may look at its inclusion after ensuring that it is systematically measured at T1 and T3 where the same test will be applied at the beginning and at the end.

Additionally, Structural Equation Modelling (SEM) was not done to test the proposed measuring scale and to test the fit of its components because it requires a large sample which is not the case with this study. Further research can run structural equation model on the proposed measurement scale and examine whether its components fit together which would help to test the causal relationship between technology and LLA more accurately than a regression would do.

CONCLUSION

The model proposed for the assessment of LLA in this study encompasses several components to be measured quantitatively and assessed qualitatively. These components are related to the theoretical concepts which are discussed as the fundamental concepts associated to the construct of LLA. It is meant to be used as a research model for researchers who aim to go beyond the assessment for autonomy to work on the measurement and assessment of autotomy in language learning in the 21st century. Reflection was used in this study to integrate quantitative (summative) self-assessment with qualitative (formative and summative) self-assessment with the learning advisor rather than using only one of these approaches to self-assessment. Moreover, the proposed assessment model can be a research model used by action researchers (i.e. teacher-researchers) or researchers with other focuses to either investigate different aspects of LLA, understand LLA, conceptualize evaluation (assessment) of LLA, conduct assessment of LLA, and promote LLA in light of the assessment model components.

ACKNOWLEDGMENT

I would like to thank the administration of the English Language Centre at Umm AlQura University and the students for taking part in this study.

REFERENCES

Benson, P. (1996). Concepts of autonomy in language learning. In R. Pemberton, E. S. L. Li, W. W. F. Or, & H. Pierson (Eds.), *Taking Control: Autonomy in Language Learning* (pp. 27–34). Hong Kong: Hong Kong University Press.

Benson, P. (2001). *Teaching and Researching Autonomy in Language Learning*. London: Longman.

Benson, P. (2007a). Autonomy in language teaching and learning. *Language Teaching*, *40*(1), 21–40. doi:10.1017/S0261444806003958

Benson, P. (Ed.). (2007b). *Learner autonomy 8: Teacher and learner perspectives*. Dublin: Authentik.

Benson, P. (2010). Measuring autonomy: Should we put our ability to the test? In A. Paran & L. Sercu (Eds.), *Testing the Untestable in Language Education* (pp. 77–97). Bristol: Multilingual Matters. doi:10.21832/9781847692672-007

Benson, P. (2011). *Teaching and Researching Autonomy*. Harlow: Pearson.

Benson, P., & Cooker, L. (2013). The social and the individual in applied linguistics research. In P. Benson & L. Cooker (Eds.), *The Applied Linguistic Individual- Sociocultural Approaches to Identity, Agency and Autonomy* (pp. 1–16). Sheffield: Equinox Publishing Ltd.

Brantmeier, C., & Vanderplank, R. (2008). Descriptive and criterion-referenced self-assessment with L2 readers. *System*, *36*(3), 456–477. doi:10.1016/j.system.2008.03.001

Champagne, M. F., Clayton, T., Dimmitt, N., Laszewski, M., Savage, W., Shaw, J., ... Walter, P. (2001). The assessment of learner autonomy and language learning. *AILA Review*, *15*, 45–55.

Chan, V. (2001). Readiness for Learner Autonomy: What do our learners tell us? *Teaching in Higher Education*, *6*(4), 505–518. doi:10.1080/13562510120078045

Confessor, G. J., & Park, E. M. (2004). Factor validation of the learner autonomy profile (Version 3.0) and extraction of the short form. *International Journal of Self-Directed Learning*, *1*(1), 39–58.

Cooker, L. (2012). *Formative (self-) assessment as autonomous language learning* (Unpublished PhD dissertation). University of Nottingham, Nottingham, UK.

Cotterall, S. (1995a). Readiness for Autonomy: Investigating Learner Beliefs. *System*, *23*(2), 195–205. doi:10.1016/0346-251X(95)00008-8

Cotterall, S., & Malcolm, D. (2015). Epilogue. In C. J. Everhard & L. Murphy (Eds.), *Assessment and autonomy in language learning* (pp. 167–175). Basingstoke, UK: Palgrave Macmillan. doi:10.1057/9781137414380_8

Dam, L. (1995). *Learner Autonomy 3: From Theory to Classroom Practice*. Dublin: Authentic.

Dam, L., Eriksson, R., Little, D., Miliander, J., & Trebbi, T. (1990). Towards a definition of Autonomy. In T. Trebbi (Ed.), *Third Nordic Workshop on Developing Autonomous Learning in the FL Classroom*. Bergen, Norway: Institute for praktisk pedagogikk, University of Bergen. http://www.warwick.ac.uk/go/dahla/archive/trebbi_1990

Dam, L., & Legenhausen, L. (2010). Learners reflecting on learning: Evaluation versus testing in autonomous language learning. In A. Paran & L. Sercu (Eds.), *Testing the Untestable in Language Education* (pp. 120–138). Bristol, UK: Multilingual Matters. doi:10.21832/9781847692672-009

Denzin, N. K. (1978). *The Research Act: A Theoretical Introduction to Sociological Methods*. Englewood Cliffs, NJ: Prentice Hall.

Dickinson, L. (1987). *Self-instruction in Language Learning*. Cambridge: Cambridge University Press.

Dixon, D. (2011). *Measuring language learner autonomy in tertiary-level learners of English* (Unpublished PhD dissertation). University of Warwick, UK.

Dörnyei, Z. (2007). *Research Methods in Applied Linguistics: Quantitative, Qualitative, and Mixed Methodologies*. Oxford: Oxford University Press.

Erzberger, C., & Kelle, U. (2003). Making inferences in mixed methods: the rules of integration. In A. Tashakkori & C. Teddlie (Eds.), *Handbook of Mixed Methods in Social and Behavioral Research*. Thousand Oaks, CA: Sage.

Esch, E. (1997). Learner training for autonomous language learning. In P. Benson & P. Voller (Eds.), *Autonomy and Independence in Language Learning* (pp. 164–176). London: Longman.

Everhard, C. J. (2006). The elusiveness of autonomy. *Independence. Newsletter of the IATEFL Learner Autonomy Special Interest Group*, *38*, 9–13.

Everhard, C. J. (2015a). The assessment-autonomy relationship. In C. J. Everhard & L. Murphy (Eds.), *Assessment and Autonomy in Language Learning* (pp. 8–34). Basingstoke, UK: Palgrave Macmillan. doi:10.1057/9781137414380_2

Everhard, C. J. (2015b). Investigating peer- and self-assessment of oral skills as steppingstones to autonomy in EFL higher education. In C. J. Everhard & L. Murphy (Eds.), *Assessment and Autonomy in Language Learning* (pp. 114–142). Basingstoke, UK: Palgrave Macmillan. doi:10.1057/9781137414380_6

Everhard, C. J., & Murphy, L. (Eds.). (2015). *Assessment and autonomy in language learning*. Basingstoke, UK: Palgrave Macmillan. doi:10.1057/9781137414380

Holec, H. (1981). Autonomy and Foreign Language Learning. Oxford, UK: Pergamon.

Hung, Y.-J., Samuelson, B. L., & Chen, S. (2016). The relationships between peer- and self-assessment and teacher assessment of young EFL learners' oral presentations. In M. Nikolov (Ed.), *Assessing young learners of English: Global and local perspectives* (pp. 317–338). Cham, Switzerland: Springer International Publishing. doi:10.1007/978-3-319-22422-0_13

Lai, J. (2001). Towards an analytic approach to assessing learner autonomy. *AILA Review*, *15*, 34–44.

Lai, J. (2011). The challenge of assessing learner autonomy analytically. In C. J. Everhard, J. Mynar, & R. Smith (Eds.), Autonomy in language learning: opening a can of worms (pp. 43-49). Canterbury, UK: IATEFL.

Lamb, T. (2010). Assessment of autonomy or assessment for autonomy? Evaluating learner autonomy for formative purposes. In A. Paran & L. Sercu (Eds.), *Testing the Untestable in Language Education* (pp. 77–97). Bristol, UK: Multilingual Matters. doi:10.21832/9781847692672-008

Le, Q. X. (2013). *Fostering learner autonomy in language learning in tertiary education: an intervention study of university students in Hochiminh City, Vietnam* (Doctoral dissertation). University of Nottingham.

Little, D. (1991). *Learner Autonomy 1: Definitions, Issues and Problems*. Dublin: Authentik.

Little, D. (1996). Freedom to learn and compulsion to interact: Promoting learner autonomy through the use of information systems and information technologies. In R. Pemberton, E. S. L. Li, W. W. F. Or, & H. Pierson (Eds.), *Taking control: Autonomy in language learning* (pp. 203–218). Hong Kong: Hong Kong University Press.

Little, D. (1999). Developing learner autonomy in the foreign language classroom: A social-interactive view of learning and three fundamental pedagogical principles. *Revista Canaria de Estudios Ingleses*, (38), 77-88.

Little, D. (2000). We're all in it together: exploring the interdependence of teacher and learner autonomy. In *The 7th Nordic Conference and Workshops on Autonomous Language Learning*. University of Helsinki.

Little, D. (2001). We're all in it together: exploring the interdependence of teacher and learner autonomy. In *The 7th Nordic Conference and Workshops on Autonomous Language Learning*. University of Helsinki.

Little, D. (2007). Language learner autonomy: Some fundamental consideration revisited. *Innovation in Language Learning and Teaching*, *1*(1), 14–29. doi:10.2167/illt040.0

Littlewood, W. (1996). Autonomy: An anatomy and a framework. *System*, *24*(4), 427–435. doi:10.1016/S0346-251X(96)00039-5

Mellow, J. D., Reeder, K., & Forster, E. (1996). Using time-series research designs to investigate the effects of instruction on SLA. *Studies in Second Language Acquisition*, *18*(3), 325–350. doi:10.1017/S0272263100015059

Mertens, D. M. (2005). *Research and Evaluation in Education and Psychology: Integrating Diversity with Quantitative, Qualitative, and Mixed Methods* (2nd ed.). Thousand Oaks, CA: Sage.

Morrison, B. (2005). Evaluating learning gain in a self-access language learning centre. *Language Teaching Research*, *9*(3), 267–293. doi:10.1191/1362168805lr167oa

Murase, F. (2010). *Developing a new instrument for measuring learner autonomy* (Unpublished doctoral dissertation). Macquarie University, Sydney, Australia.

Murase, F. (2015). Measuring language learner autonomy: problems and possibilities. In C. J. Everhard & L. Murphy (Eds.), *Assessment and Autonomy in Language Learning* (pp. 35–63). Basingstoke, UK: Palgrave Macmillan. doi:10.1057/9781137414380_3

Mynard, J. (2004). Investigating evidence of learner autonomy in a virtual EFL classroom: a grounded theory approach. In J. Hull, J. Harris, & P. Darasawang (Eds.), Research In ELT: proceedings of the international conference (pp. 117-127). School of Liberal Arts and the Continuing Education Center, King Mongkut's University of Technology.

Mynard, J. (2006). Measuring learner autonomy: Can it be done? *Independence. Newsletter of the IATEFL Learner Autonomy Special Interest Group*, *37*, 3–6.

Oscarson, M. (1984). *Self-assessment of foreign language skills: a survey of research and development work Council of Europe*. Strasbourg: Council for Cultural Cooperation.

Oxford, R. L. (1999). Relationships between second language learning strategies and language proficiency in the context of learner autonomy and self-regulation. *Revista Canaria de Estudios Ingleses*, *38*, 109-126. Retrieved from: https://goo.gl/9AxkZo

Peek, R. (2015). Exploring learner autonomy: Language learning locus of control in multilinguals. *International Journal of Multilingualism*, *13*(2), 230–248. doi:10.1080/14790718.2015.1090991

Ravindram. (2001). Towards learner autonomy: evolution in practice: The certificate in independent language learning. In B. Sinclair, T. Lamb, & I. McGrath (Eds.), *Learner Autonomy, Teacher Autonomy: Future Directions* (pp. 60-72). London: Longman.

Reinders, H., & Cotterall, S. (2001). Language learners learning independently: How autonomous are they? *Toegepaste Taalwetenschap in Artikelen*, *65*(1), 85–97. doi:10.1075/ttwia.65.09rei

Reinders, H., & Lázaro, N. (2007). The assessment of self-access language learning: Practical challenges. *Language Learning Journal*, *36*(1), 55–64. doi:10.1080/09571730801988439

Reinders, H., & White, C. (2016). 20 years of autonomy and technology: How far have we come and where to next? *Language Learning & Technology*, *20*(2), 143–154.

Rivers, W. P. (2001). Autonomy at all costs: An ethnography of metacognitive self-assessment and self-management among experienced language learners. *Modern Language Journal*, *85*(2), 279–290. doi:10.1111/0026-7902.00109

Schwienhorst, K. (2008). *Learner Autonomy and CALL Environments*. London: Routledge.

Seeman, T., & Tavares, C. (2000). Involving learners in their own learning: How to get started. In D. Little, L. Dam, & J. Timmer (Eds.), *Focus on learning rather than teaching: Why and how? Papers from the IATEFL conference on learner independence, Krakow, 14-16 May 1998* (pp. 59-70). Dublin: Trinity College.

Sinclair, B. (1999). More than an Act of Faith? Evaluating Learner Autonomy. In C. Kennedy (Ed.), *Innovation and Best Practice* (pp. 96–107). Harlow: Longman.

Sinclair, B. (2000) *Learner Autonomy and its Development in the Teaching of English to Speakers of Other Language (TESOL)* (Unpublished doctoral dissertation). University of Nottingham.

Sinclair, B. (2009). The Teacher as Learner: Developing Autonomy in an Interactive Learning Environment. In R. Pemberton, S. Toogood, & A. Barfield (Eds.), *Maintaining Control: Autonomy and Language Learning* (pp. 175–198). Hong Kong: Hong Kong University Press. doi:10.5790/hongkong/9789622099234.003.0010

Smith, R. (2008). Learner autonomy. *ELT Journal*, *62*(4), 395–397. doi:10.1093/elt/ccn038

Tassinari, M. G. (2012). Evaluating learner autonomy: A dynamic model with descriptors. *Studies in Self-Access Learning Journal*, *3*(1), 24–40.

Tassinari, M. G. (2015). Assessing learner autonomy: a dynamic model. In C. J. Everhard & L. Murphy (Eds.), *Assessment and Autonomy in Language Learning* (pp. 64–88). Basingstoke, UK: Palgrave Macmillan. doi:10.1057/9781137414380_4

Tassinari, M. G. (2016). Assessment for learning; assessment for autonomy. In C. Gitsaki & C. Coombe (Eds.), *Current Issues in Language Evaluation, Assessment and Testing, Research and Practice* (pp. 118–136). Cambridge: Cambridge Scholars Publishing.

Thomsen, H. (2000). Learners' favoured activities in the autonomous classroom. In D. Little, L. Dam, & J. Timmer (Eds.), *Focus On Learning Rather Than Teaching: Why and How?* (pp. 71–86). Dublin: CLCS.

Ushioda, E. (2011). Why Autonomy? Insights from Motivation Theory and Research. *Innovation in Language Learning and Teaching*, *5*(2), 221–232. doi:10.1080/17501229.2011.577536

Vygotsky, L. S. (1978). *Mind in Society*. Cambridge: Harvard University Press.

Weeden, P., Winter, J., & Broadfoot, P. (2002). *Assessment: What's in it for schools?* London, UK: Routledge Falmer.

ADDITIONAL READING

Al-Seghayer, K. (2015). Salient key features of actual English instructional practices in Saudi Arabia. *English Language Teaching*, *8*(6), 89–99. doi:10.5539/elt.v8n6p89

Allwright, R. L. (1988). Autonomy and individualization in whole-class instruction. In A. Brookes & P. Grundy. (Eds.) Individualization and Autonomy in Language Learning (pp. 35-44). ELT Documents, 131. London: Modern English Publications and the British Council.

Alrabai, F. (2016). Factors underlying low achievement of Saudi EFL learners. *International Journal of English Linguistics*, *6*(3), 1–17. doi:10.5539/ijel.v6n3p21

Alzahrani, S., & Watson, J. (2016). The impact of online training on Saudi medical students' attitudes, awareness, and use of language learning strategies in relation to their developing autonomy. *Studies in Self-Access Learning Journal*, *7*(1), 4–15.

Alzahrani, S., & Wright, V. (2016). Design and management of a self-access language learning space integrated into a taught course. *Studies in Self-Access Learning Journal*, *7*(2), 136–151.

Barfield, A., & Brown, S. H. (2007). *Reconstructing Autonomy in Language Education: Inquiry and Innovation*. Basingstoke: Palgrave. doi:10.1057/9780230596443

Boud, D. (1995). *Enhancing learning through self-assessment*. London: Kogan Page.

Brantmeier, C., & Vanderplank, R. (2008). Descriptive and criterion-referenced self-assessment with L2 readers. *System, 36*(3), 456–477. doi:10.1016/j.system.2008.03.001

Cooker, L. (2015). Assessment as learner autonomy. In C. J. Everhard & L. Murphy (Eds.), *Assessment and Autonomy in Language Learning* (pp. 89–113). Basingstoke, New York: Palgrave Macmillan. doi:10.1057/9781137414380_5

KEY TERMS AND DEFINITIONS

Blended Learning: Web-based online approaches both synchronous and asynchronous integrated with a traditional face-to-face taught course- the online part can take place either blended with classroom teaching, complementing face-to-face teaching as homework to do online after a class, or complementing face-to-face teaching in self-access sessions on campus, at home, or on the go (mobile learning).

Control Group: The group of participants who are not exposed to any treatment besides the core Face-to-Face Medical English Course.

Focus Group Interview: A group form of an interview and an economical approach of gathering qualitative data which is used to examine the agreement and disagreement happening among the different participants.

Language Learner Autonomy: Learners' metacapacity to take control of their learning process to different extents and in different ways according to the learning situation. This metacapacity entails learners' independent capacity to make and carry out the choices which govern their actions to use the acquired knowledge and skills confidently, flexibly, appropriately and independently of the teacher and to judge the degree of success of their learning (self-assessment).

Language Learning Strategies: The core of the tasks in the supplementary material that was designed for the learner training which the learners in the two treatment groups were exposed to.

Offline Treatment Group: The group of participants which is taught using the same content of the Medical English Strategy Course given to the online treatment group but in an offline mode in addition to the existing Face-to-Face Medical English Course.

Online Treatment Group: The group of participants which is intended to be exposed to a blended learning experience by adding an Online Strategy Course with Medical English content to the already existing Face-to-Face Medical English Course in the foundation year.

Perceived Strategy Use: The learners' understanding of a preferred and used effective collection of strategies.

Reflective Writing Forms: A qualitative research method designed to collect data about learners' reflective ability to explore their LLA.

Self-Rating Scale: A six-point Likert scale which presents a large number of items about the LLA component parts considered in this study and it is presented to all the students in the three participating groups.

Time 1 (Before the Experiment): The time in which all the measurements are carried out before the treatment.

Time 3 (After the Experiment): The time in which all the measurements are carried out after the treatment.

Chapter 2
Assessing the Impact of a Digital Ecosystem to Learn English Pronunciation

Ana María Pinto-Llorente
https://orcid.org/0000-0002-8538-9902
University of Salamanca, Spain

ABSTRACT

The present research is an innovative study that intends to analyse the effectiveness of a b-learning digital ecosystem implemented in the area of English phonetics and phonology. It also aims to highlight the benefits of some transmissive, interactive, and collaborative resources in learning of the subject. It is a quantitative research with an ex-post-facto design, collecting data through a questionnaire. The results demonstrated that pre-service teachers had positive views towards the digital ecosystem to improve their English pronunciation level and their ability to perceive and produce English more accurately. The findings also emphasized the potential of the digital ecosystem to provide a more natural environment for pronunciation practice and a more individualized instruction focused on learners who become active learners generating knowledge.

INTRODUCTION

Research in second language learning has used different methods in teaching pronunciation. However, it has revealed that there is a need to develop new methods and further investigate, especially teaching English pronunciation in higher education. Therefore, the study in this chapter aims to contribute to the research in the field of phonology, English as a second language and e-learning in higher education by analyzing the effectiveness of a blended learning (b-learning) digital ecosystem implemented in English Phonetics and Phonology subject, which has been traditionally taught face-to-face. The current chapter presents a project which develops a digital ecosystem, using Moodle, the open-source learning platform, to create an adequate virtual environment in which pre-service teachers will be able to improve their phonological competence in all its dimensions. The digital ecosystem was made up of 4 modules: the

DOI: 10.4018/978-1-7998-3062-7.ch002

organs of speech, vowel sounds, consonant sounds, and homophones, homographs, stress, unstressed syllables, weak and strong forms of the words, and intonation. All four modules included different transmissive (podcast and videocast), interactive (online glossary and online questionnaires) and collaborative (forum) technological tools to develop the e-activities and promote interaction between the participants.

The goals of the present quantitative research were to analyse pre-service teachers' perceptions about the effectiveness of the blended learning digital ecosystem implemented in the area of English Phonetics and Phonology, and to highlight the benefits of some transmissive, interactive and collaborative tools such as podcast, videocast, online questionnaires, online glossary and forum in learning English Phonetics and Phonology. The study focused on three research questions:

1. How do pre-service teachers perceive the digital ecosystem in terms of effectiveness?
2. Do pre-service teachers believe that the digital ecosystem implemented provide a natural environment for authentic pronunciation practice?
3. Do pre-service teachers perceive that the digital ecosystem supports individual and collaborative learning throughout technological tools?

The study also tried to test three hypotheses (H):

H1. English pronunciation learning level and the satisfaction of pre-service teachers will be higher with the implementation of the blended learning digital ecosystem.
H2. The digital ecosystem implemented will help pre-service teachers to develop their ability to perceive and produce English more accurately.
H3. The digital ecosystem will supply pre-service teachers with a natural environment for pronunciation practice.

BACKGROUND

Teaching Second Language

Throughout the history of teaching English as second language (L2), reseracher adopted varied methods for teaching pronunciation. As Levis (2005) points out, "the history of pronunciation in English language teaching is a study in extremes. Some approaches to teaching, such as the reformed method and audiolingualism, elevated pronunciation to a pinnacle of importance, while other approaches, such as the cognitive movement and early communicative language teaching, mostly ignored pronunciation" (p.369).

As Larsen-Freeman, 2003, Larsen-Freeman and Long, 1994, and Sánchez, (1997) stated, in the beginning, teaching second language was basically through the memorization of grammar rules and vocabulary lists. That intended to enable learners to read texts, make translations and use the L2 to communicate in written form. Besides, teachers used students' mother tongue in their lesson predominantly, so there was no oral exposure to the L2 and, of course, no interest in pronunciation (Santos, 1999).

The direct method emerged to reject all the principles on which the previous method was based and became the first approach focusing mainly on oral skills. That directly implied the improvement of oral skills and the emphasis on the correct pronunciation (Pastor, 2005). It emerged from a project carried out by the German linguist and the founder of the Berlitz Language Schools, Maximilian Berlitz (1852-

1921) in Rhode Island in 1978. The method rapidly spread throughout Europe and America. The principles and procedures followed in the method were aimed at the exclusive use of the L2, the learning of vocabulary and sentences used in real context. The grammar was taught inductively, and teachers put a great emphasis on correct pronunciation. These principles were reflected in the guidelines followed at Berlitz schools (Richards and Rodgers, 2001).

In the mid of the twentieth century, the audio-oral method emerged, which was based on structuralist linguistics that highlighted Bloomfield and his school, and on behavioural theory with a clear influence of the psychologist Skinner. The conclusions, which were drawn from the formation of certain habits through the repetitions of behaviours in animals, were transferred to people and to second language acquisition (Pastor, 2005; Sánchez, 1997). Lado (1915-1995) presented a clear description of the approach in his work. It was suggested that, when teaching a L2, oral skills must be enhanced and must be acquired through the creation of habits and the learning of certain patterns that must be used automatically in response to a stimulus. There was a specific emphasis on pronunciation and on the immediate correction of mistakes to avoid the acquisition of an incorrect habit.

As Usó (2008) pointed out, the pronunciation had been in the background and it was not until the 1990s when it recovered its importance in the communicative method that was based on cognitive psychology with focus on communication in the L2. Specifically, the acquisition of an adequate communicative competence conformed by a set of competences (grammatical competence, sociolinguistic competence, discourse competence and strategic competence) and an adequate pronunciation. The term communicative competence was coined by Hymes (1972), who considered that it did not only refer to produce grammatically correct sentences, but it must also consider the socio-cultural context in which the interaction takes place. Therefore, it is essential to know the receiver, the moment and place in which communication takes place. A few years later, other linguists such as Canale (1983), and Canale and Swain (1980) defined communicative competence as a competence in which other four competences (linguistic competence also known as grammatical competence, sociolinguistic competence, discourse competence and strategic competence) were interrelated.

In 2001, the European Council published the Common European Framework of Reference for Languages: Learning, teaching and assessment (CEFR). It was part of the general project of linguistic policy that was exemplified in the Rüschlikon (Switzerland) symposium entitled Transparency and Coherence in Language Learning in Europe: Objectives, Evaluation and Certification. That document included a definition of communicative competence, which was composed of a set of competences: linguistic, sociolinguistic and pragmatic competences. In the communicative method, pronunciation played a fundamental role in relation to the oral skills, becoming an essential aspect when determining the communicative competence of a L2 speaker (Iruela, 2007). It is basic for interaction since if the speaker's pronunciation is adequate, there will not be obstacles in communication and there will be greater acceptance by native speakers (Cortés, 2002). As Bartolí (2005) stated, learners who had an adequate pronunciation contributed to their greater self-esteem and confidence. It is necessary that pronunciation receives appropriate treatment (Iruela, 2004). This aspect has not usually devoted the same attention to other aspects of the L2 because teachers do not normally know how to integrate it into the communicative approach.

Derwing and Munro (2005) pointed out that "the study of pronunciation has been marginalized within the field of applied linguistics. As a result, teachers are often left to rely on their own intuitions with little direction. Although some instructors can successfully assist their students under these conditions, many are reluctant to teach pronunciation" (p.379). This statement led us to carry out this research on analyzing pre-service teachers' perceptions about the effectiveness of the b-learning digital ecosystem of English phonetics and phonology subject. Phonetics is a branch of linguistics that deals with the manner in which sounds are perceived, produced and transmitted, so it is the science that deals with speech sounds and the way in which they are produced, transmitted, received, analysed, classified and transcribed. It is concerned with articulatory phonetics, acoustic phonetics and auditory phonetics (Hardcastle, Laver & Gibbon, 2010; Richard & Schmidt, 2013; Yule, 2014). On the other hand, Phonology is also a branch of linguistics, which concerned with the way in which sounds are organized and used in first languages (Hardcastle, Laver & Gibbon, 2010; Richard & Schmidt, 2013; Yule, 2014). There are different definitions of phonological competence. In our study, we will use the definition of the Common European Framework of Reference for Languages (CEFR) (Council of Europe, 2001) in which "Phonological competence involves a knowledge of, and skill in the perception and production of: sound-units (phonemes) of the language and their realization in particular contexts (allophones); phonetic features which distinguish phonemes (distinctive features, e.g. voicing, rounding, nasality, plosion); phonetic composition of words (syllable structure, the sequence of phonemes, word stress, word tones); sentence phonetics (prosody); sentence stress and rhythm; intonation; phonetic reduction; vowel reduction; strong and weak forms; assimilation; elision." (p.116)

Relevant Studies on Teaching Pronunciation Through Technology

According to Derwing and Munro (2005), there has been a growing literature on L2 speech production and perception. However, it has not usually been published in teacher-oriented publications. They also state that a part of the research "may not be perceived as practical because it has been carried out under strict laboratory conditions, so it is not immediately clear how the findings apply to the classroom" (ibid, p.382). This section presents a brief overview of the most relevant studies around teaching pronunciation, technology and blended learning approach.

Wilson (2005) carried out one of the first studies on the use of Moodle in teaching pronunciation. That research combined the use of the platform and an open-source acoustic analysis software called Praat. According to the results, learners became more autonomous in their learning, something that traditionally depended on teacher's evaluation. Moreover, the use of Praat allowed them to analyse their pronunciation level by their own. On the other hand, the combination of Moodle and Praat permitted teacher to find out the weaknesses of each student to help with the areas they needed to improve.

Ashby (2008) published a paper that presented different grant-funded initiatives carried out at the University College London for four years to develop innovations in the teaching, learning and assessment of phonetics at the university. One of those initiative referred to the project Phonline that was a comprehensive attempt to develop an online course in which most of the elements of phonetic training, tutorial materials, exercises, practical training and assessment were embedded and available. Specifically, the project aimed to achieve three main goals. The study was conducted to research and find out solutions within a virtual learning environment to the specific multimedia problems of distance learning in phonetics, to design and implement a distance-learning course in English phonetics and to pilot the course and obtain feedback. An eight-week introductory course in English Phonetics was designed for the pilot study and 25 students across five continents were participated in the study. The overall results obtained showed a high degree of satisfaction towards different aspects of the design, organisation and delivery of the course. A majority of the participants also stated that they would recommend the course to other learners and would undertake further online courses based on the experience with the project.

Ali (2016) presented a research developed at Renner 2 University. The university aimed to develop a comprehensive pedagogical framework for English pronunciation training consisting of a blended learning framework that combined face-to-face teaching of pronunciation with online instruction using technology, called Automatic Speech Recognition. The participants who were French university students majoring in Literature, Arts and Communication showed an advanced level of grammar and syntax. However, their spoken English remained the same with a heavy accent of their mother tongue which could hinder effective communication. The paper analysed how computer assisted pronunciation training software had been used to identify potential improvements to deal with bad pronunciation habits.

Liu and Hung (2016) carried out a study to assess the effectiveness of computer assisted pronunciation instruction and practice in English pronunciation. The participants who were undergraduate students studying general English at a technological university in Taiwan took an eight-week English pronunciation course. The results obtained through a questionnaire at the end of the course revealed a significant improvement in the quality of participants' pronunciation, and their positive opinions towards instruction were enhanced.

A qualitative research was carried out by Pourhosein Gilakjani (2018) to find out Iranian teachers' views toward computer technology in teaching English pronunciation. The researcher used a semi-structured interview to collect data which were analysed according to the Miles and Huberman's process of reducing data, constructing theme and drawing conclusions. The results emphasized that participants' positive attitude towards the use of computer technology increased, since it provided a useful, pleasing and interactive environment that helped participants to have an accurate pronunciation and improve the quality and deliver of pronunciation instruction. The results also revealed that the participants' confidence and motivation towards technology increased because it played a key role that changed their instruction and helped them to teach pronunciation effectively.

The Digital Ecosystem

The digital ecosystem implemented in English Phonetics and Phonology course was designed through the open-source Learning Management System, Moodle. This stands out for having a support and development community, and for being based on a solid educational philosophy (Cole & Foster, 2008). It is a platform for the creation and management of Internet-based courses that provide educators with the necessary tools to create an effective course in a website and allow the participants to enroll in this course. It is a project inspired by social constructionist pedagogy (Rice, 2011) a feature that distinguishes it from other Content Management System (CMS) developed only for a series of tools without an educational theory.

The design was based on the selection of a pedagogical model according to the principles of a constructivist web-based learning environment (Duffy & Cunningham, 1996; Honebein, 1996; Knuth & Cunnigham, 1993) where students are placed at the centre of the teaching-learning process. Considering this premise, the digital ecosystem was designed to:

- provide learners with an experience in the construction of knowledge and in different points of view (Baker & Gossman, 2013; Walsh & Kahn, 2010)
- develop learning in real and relevant contexts for students so that they can transfer what they learn in an academic context to everyday life (Payne, 2009; Willis, 2009)
- allow students to have a relevant role, being place in the centre of the process (Altanopoulou, Tselios, Katsanos, & Georgoutsou, 2015; Blumberg, 2009; Gisbert, 2002)

- set learning in social experience in which takes place (Bell, 2009)
- use multiple modes of representation to meet participants' different learning styles (Pinto-Llorente, Sánchez-Gómez & García-Peñalvo, 2018a) and
- encourage self-awareness of the knowledge construction process (Gan, Menkhoff & Smith, 2015; Pinto-Llorente, Sánchez-Gómez & García-Peñalvo, 2018b).

Regarding the design of the digital ecosystem, the visual organization of the virtual environment was topic format, dividing the environment into an introductory block and other four parts around the contents of the course: (1) the organs of speech; (2) vowel sounds; (3) consonant sounds, and (4) homophones, homographs, stress, unstressed syllables, weak and strong forms of the words, and intonation.

Each block included different materials and e-activities (digital activities) available through the transmissive, interactive, and collaborative resources offered by Moodle. As Gómez (2006) and Pérez et al., (2009) point out, this division of the resources is due to two factors. On one hand, the degree of difficulty of the process of communication; on the other hand, the pedagogical model on which they are based.

Transmissive resources referred to PDF and Word files, podcasts, videocast and links to external websites where participants had access to dictionaries or pages where they could use specific software to create their own podcasts and videocasts. Transmissive resources could be downloaded so that students could access to the contents and the practices developed through podcast and videocast to work with them on different media tools such as smartphones, tablets or computers. As Man-Man (2006) states, this facilitated access to the content of the subject and their practice in a multitude of situations and contexts.

Regarding interactive resources, one of the blocks contained an online glossary a digital tool used to create an online dictionary of key concepts of phonetics and phonology. Each block also included assessment and self-assessment tests. On one hand, the assessment tests were available to carry out the continuous assessment of the learning process and provide students with feedback about their progress. They were enabled with a limited time, allowing a single attempt and applying penalties for the incorrect answers. On the other hand, the self-assessment tests were available during the whole course. The learners could complete them whenever they wanted and the times they needed. The purpose of those tests was to help them practice the contents of the subject and be ready to do the assessment ones. Moreover, the learners could know their level in the course and their needs since they also included feedback.

Concerning collaborative resources, the blocks of the digital ecosystem contained forums divided into two types. Some of the forums were designed to encourage interaction between the participants and create a space in which they could ask the doubts about the content of the course. Other forums were designed to facilitate the development of the group e-activities that were assessed by the teacher as part of the continuous assessment.

MAIN FOCUS OF THE CHAPTER

Research Design

This is a quantitative study with an ex-post-facto design that is defined as "a systematic empirical inquiry in which the scientist does not have direct control of independent variables because their manifestations have already occurred or because they are inherently not manipulable." (Kerlinger, 1973, p.379). The study addressed a descriptive study, using techniques of descriptive and inferential analysis for different strata sample of the study (Arnal, Rincón & Latorre, 1994). To develop the study, the researcher followed the phases established by Buendía, Colás and Hernández (1997). During the first phase, the theoretical and conceptual phase, the researcher set the objectives and hypotheses of the study. During the second phase, the methodological phase, the researcher selected the sample and the variables of the study and prepared the definitive design of the instrument to collect data. In the last phase, the statistical and conceptual phase, the researcher coded and analysed the data to obtain the results that could be generalized and stated the main conclusions.

Participants

87 Spanish pre-service teachers in Primary Education were enrolled in the semestral and compulsory course of English phonetics and phonology. The majority of the participants were women, specifically 78.1% (n=68) of the sample, and 21.9% (n= 19) were men. The age range of the sample components was very wide, ranging from 20 to 58 years old. The 87 participants were divided into four age groups, 20-24 years old (Group 1), 25-29 (Group 2), 30-34 (Group 3) and 35 or more (Group 4). All of them had already completed a university degree, since one of the requirements of the university to study a degree in blended learning modalities was to have completed a degree before. It is also relevant to highlight that the previous degree of most participants was related to education. In addition, most of them (71,5%, n=62) were working full-time or part-time and had a job related to education.

Instrument

The researcher used a test to collect data. It was designed using the option form provided by Google Drive and stored in the digital ecosystem implemented for English Phonetics and Phonology subject. That instrument was designed to collect information about the followings:

1. Sociodemographic pre-service teachers' details.
2. Pre-service teachers' perspectives about the teaching contents provided in the digital ecosystem.
3. Pre-service teachers' perceptions about the e-activities developed.
4. Pre-service teachers' perceptions about some technological tools.
5. Pre-service teachers' self-assessment of their oral skills and pronunciation level.

Alternative responses ranged from open, closed, yes/no to Likert scale depending on the nature of the item. Likert scale questions were coded from 'totally effective' to 'totally ineffective'. For this study 'Totally ineffective' was coded as 1; 'Ineffective' as 2; 'Neither effective nor ineffective' as 3; 'Effective' as 4 and 'Totally effective' as 5.

The external validity of the instrument was guaranteed through the experts in educational research, English as a L2 and educational technology in the design of the questionnaire. On the other hand, the internal consistency of the test was assessed using Cronbach's alpha, high internal consistency α=0.894 was obtained, so their measures were stable and consistent.

Data Collection and Analyses

Data were collected at the end of the first semester using a questionnaire. As stated earlier, the questionnaire was stored in the digital ecosystem of English Phonetics and Phonology subject and it was available to be completed within a week. The researcher collected data and downloaded them to the personal computer for coding. After creating the data matrix, using the software Statistical Package for the Social Sciences (SPSS) 24, the researcher started introducing and debugging data followed by descriptive (frequency and percentages) and inferential analyses (ANOVA).

RESULTS, SOLUTIONS AND RECOMMENDATION

The results of the descriptive analysis revealed that most pre-service teachers (66.8%, n=58) had a positive perception towards their improvement of English pronunciation level through the digital ecosystem designed and implemented in English Phonetics and Phonology subject as found by Ashby (2008). The results, as the inferential analysis determined, differed according to age groups. Specifically, the results of analysis of variance according to the different age groups (p=.000) showed that there were statistically significant differences (CI 95%). It was calculated the Tukey HSD post-hoc test (Figure 1) in order to determine the differences between the groups. The test indicated that the mean scores for Group 1 ($\bar{x}$=4.41, SD=.561) and Group 2 ($\bar{x}$=4.22, SD=.551) were significantly different from Group 3 ($\bar{x}$=3.71, .952) and Group 4 ($\bar{x}$=3.42, SD=.956). The test revealed that Group 1 and Group 2 had considered that they improved their English pronunciation level more than Group 3 and Group 4.

The results of the descriptive analysis (Table 1) of the dependent variable that referred to pre-serviced teachers' perception about the effectiveness of the transmissive (podcasts and videocasts), interactive (online tests and online glossary) and collaborative (forums) technological tools were in general quite positive. Regarding participants' perspective about podcasts, most of them considered that they were effective (38.3%, n=33) and totally effective (45%, n=39). Similar results were obtained in the variable that refers to videocasts. In that case, 37.7% (n=32) stated that they were effective and 48.9% (n=43) totally effective. In both variables, just few of participants considered that they were absolutely ineffective. In relation to the results of the effectiveness of online test, online glossary and forums, most of them considered that they were effective (36,6% n=31, 38,5% n=33 & 44,4% n=38) and totally effective (32,7% n=28, 33,8% n=29 & 38,3% n=33).

It was analysed if there were statistically significant differences (CI 95%) between the different groups on those variables. The results of analysis of variance according to those groups (p=.000) showed that there were statistically significant differences in the dependent variables that referred to the effectiveness of podcasts (p=.000), videocasts (p=.000), online tests (p=.000), online glossary (p=.000) and forums (p=.000). The Tukey HSD post-hoc test was conducted (Figures 2, 3, 4, 5, 6) to find out which the difference between the groups. The results illustrated that the mean scores for Group 1 (Podcasts: $\bar{x}$=4.67 Videocasts: $\bar{x}$=4.69, Online tests: $\bar{x}$=4.75, Online glossary: $\bar{x}$=4.69 & Forums: $\bar{x}$=4.63) and Group 2 (Podcasts: $\bar{x}$=4.58, Videocasts: $\bar{x}$=4.57, Online tests $\bar{x}$=4.51, Online glossary $\bar{x}$=4.65 & Forums: $\bar{x}$=4.50) were significantly different from Group 3 (Podcasts: $\bar{x}$=3.95, Videocasts: $\bar{x}$=4.04, Online tests: $\bar{x}$=3.10, Online glossary: $\bar{x}$=3.40 & Forums: $\bar{x}$=3.77) and Group 4 (Podcasts: $\bar{x}$=3.78, Videocasts: $\bar{x}$=3.78, Online tests: $\bar{x}$=3.35, Online glossary: $\bar{x}$=3.38 & Forums: $\bar{x}$=3.96). The test revealed that groups 1 and 2 gave higher ratings to the effectiveness of all tools than groups 3 and 4.

Figure 1. Results of the Tukey HSD Test of the Dependent Variable English pronunciation level

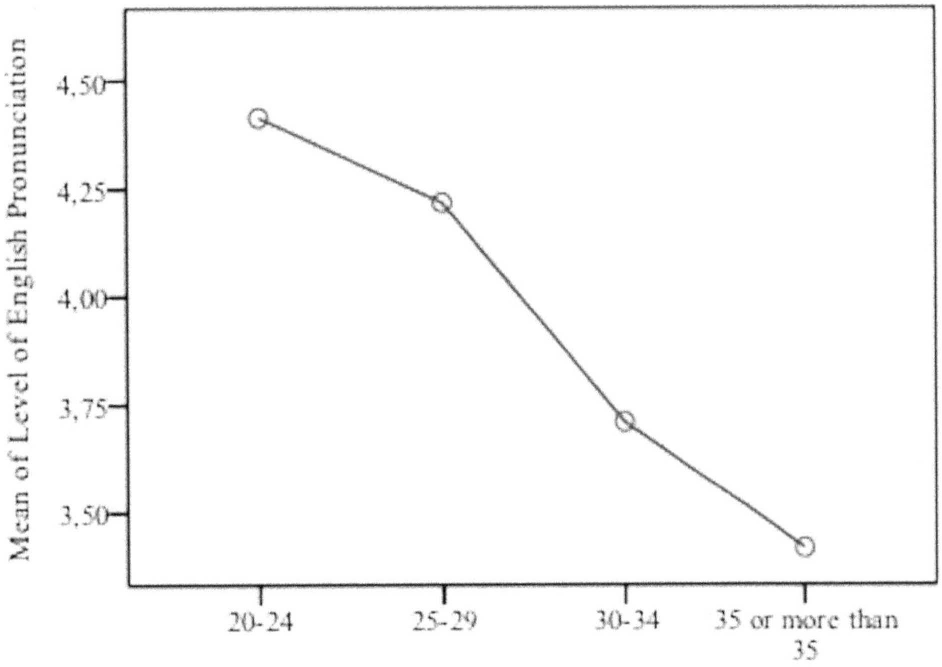

The results of the descriptive analysis (Table 2) regarding the perceptions of the pre-service teachers were also favourable in relation to the dependent variables that refer to the effectiveness of the e-activities available in the digital ecosystem to develop their phonological competence, pronunciation and oral skills. 47.8% (n=42) assessed those e-activities as effective and 27.9% (n=24) as totally effective. Regarding the results of the other two variables, they were quite similar, since 67.9% (n=59) and 71.2% (n=62) considered that they were effective to improve pronunciation and oral skills.

Table 1. Statistics of the Dependent Variables of the Effectiveness of Podcasts, Videocasts, Online test, Online Glossary & Forums

Items	Ineffective	Neither effective nor ineffective	Effective	Totally Effective	$\bar{x}$	Sx
Podcasts	2.2%	14.5%	38.3%	45%	4.26	.787
Videocasts	0.8%	12.6%	37.7%	48.9%	4.35	.728
Online Tests	12%	18.7%	36.6%	32.7%	3.90	.994
Online Glossary	2.8%	24.9%	38.5%	33.8%	4.03	.836
Forums	1.1%	16.2%	44.4%	38.3%	4.20	.743

Figure 2. Results of the Tukey HSD Test of the Dependent Variable level of the Effectiveness of Podcast

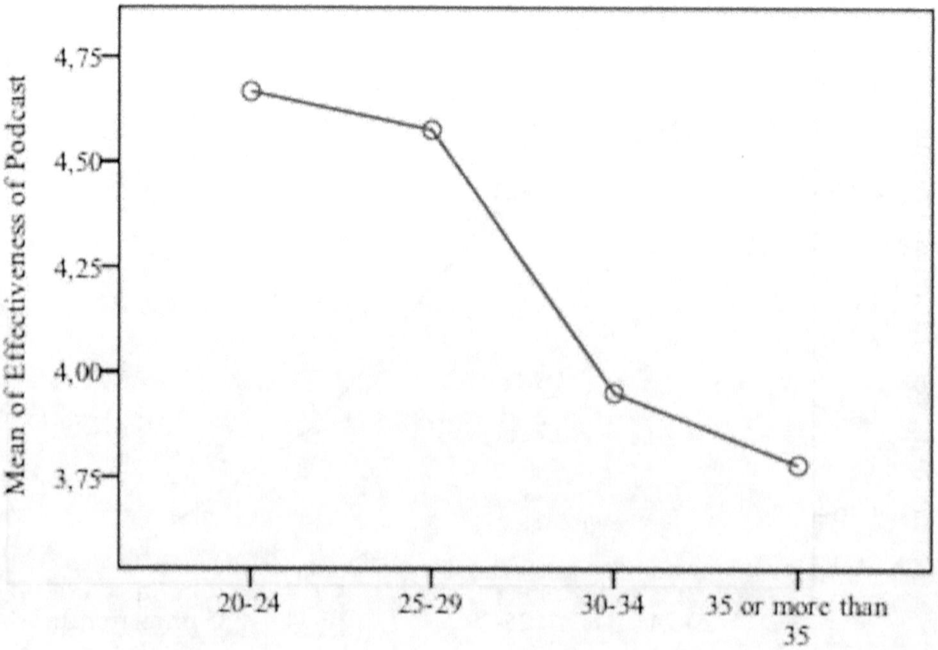

Figure 3. Results of the Tukey HSD Test of the Dependent Variable level of the Effectiveness of Videocast

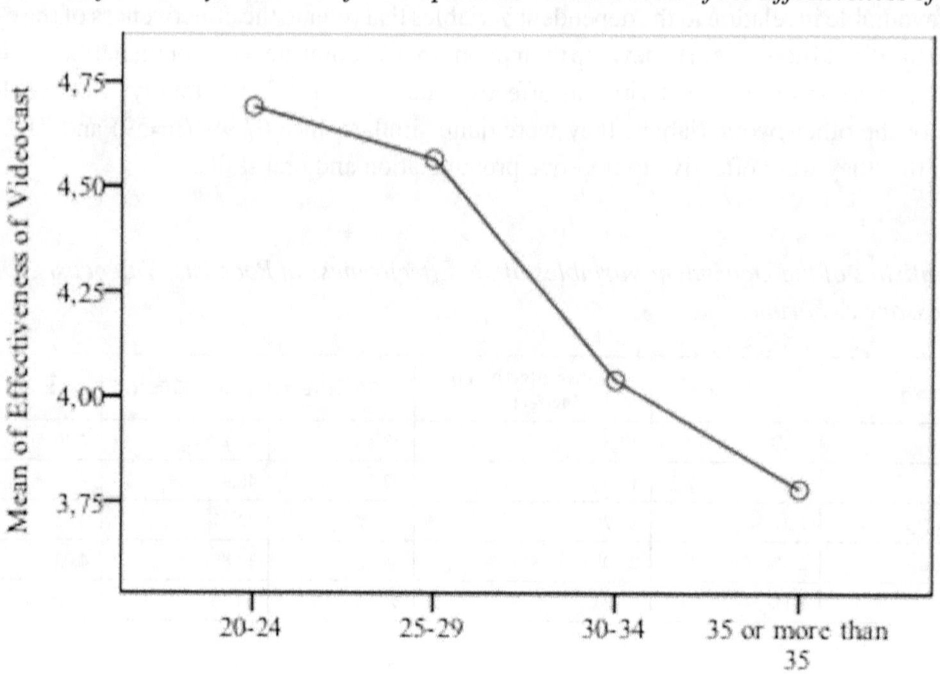

Figure 4. Results of the Tukey HSD Test of the Dependent Variable level of the Effectiveness of Online Tests

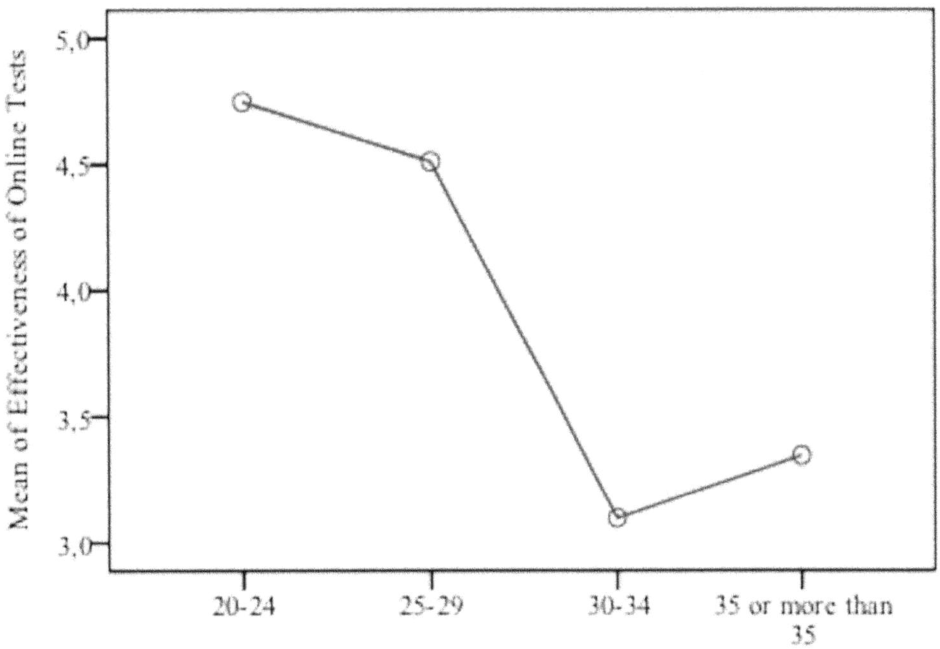

Figure 5. Results of the Tukey HSD Test of the Dependent Variable level of the Effectiveness of Online Glossary

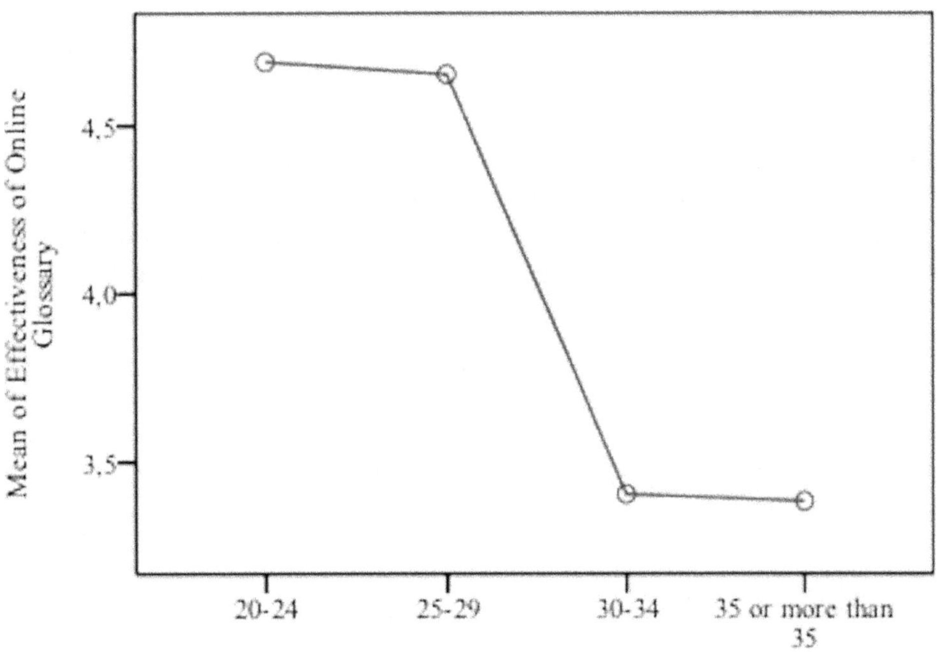

Figure 6. Results of the Tukey HSD Test of the Dependent Variable level of the Effectiveness of Forums

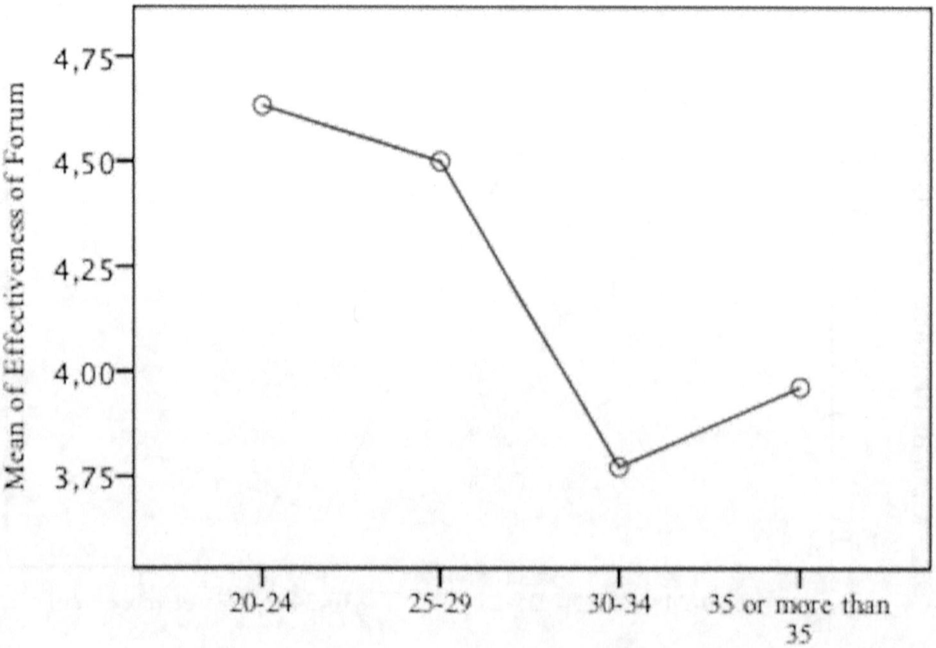

The results of those dependent variables, as the inferential analysis determined, differed according to age groups. Specifically, the results of analysis of variance according to the different age groups (p=.000, p=.000, p=.000) showed that there were statistically significant differences (CI 95%). The Tukey HSD post-hoc test was conducted (Figures 7, 8, 9) to ascertain which groups significantly differed from the others. The test indicated that the mean scores for Group 1 (phonological competence: $\bar{x}$=4.54, SD=.501; pronunciation: $\bar{x}$=4.41, SD=.561; oral skills: $\bar{x}$=4.69, SD=.465) and Group 2 (phonological competence: $\bar{x}$=4.32, SD=.553, pronunciation: $\bar{x}$=3.71, SD=.952; oral skills: $\bar{x}$=4.61, SD=.554) were significantly different from Group 3 (phonological competence: $\bar{x}$=3.44, SD=1.142; pronunciation: $\bar{x}$=3.42, SD=.956; oral skills: $\bar{x}$=4.13, SD=.674 and Group 4 (phonological competence: $\bar{x}$=3.38, SD=1.097; pronunciation: $\bar{x}$=3.36, SD=; oral skills: $\bar{x}$=4.18, SD=.819). The test revealed that Groups 1 and 2 considered that they had improved their English pronunciation level more than Groups 3 and 4.

Table 2. Statistics of the Dependent Variables of the Effectiveness of E-activities to Develop Phonological Competence, Pronunciation & Oral Skills

Items	Totally effective	Ineffective	Neither effective nor ineffective	Effective	Totally Effective	$\bar{x}$	Sx
Phonological Competence	2.8%	5.3%	16.2%	47.8%	27.9%	3.93	.950
Pronunciation	0.3%	3.1%	12.8%	67.9%	15.9%	3.96	.660
Oral Skills	0.3%	2.2%	8.1%	71.2%	18.2%	4.05	.613

Figure 7. Results of the Tukey HSD Test of the Dependent Variable level of the Effectiveness of the E-activities to Develop Phonological Competence

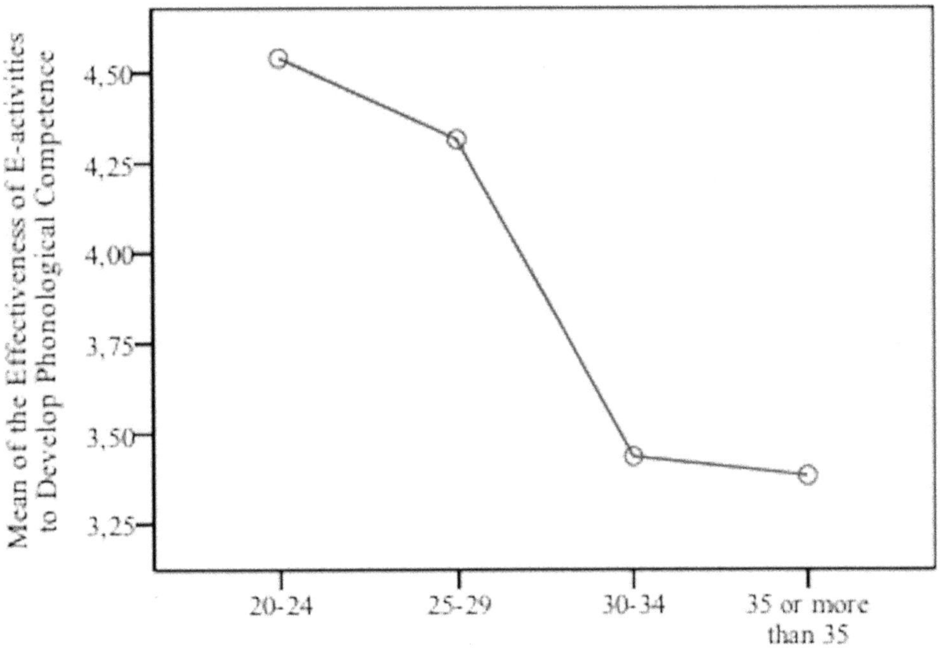

Figure 8. Results of the Tukey HSD Test of the Dependent Variable level of the Effectiveness of the E-activities to Develop Pronunciation

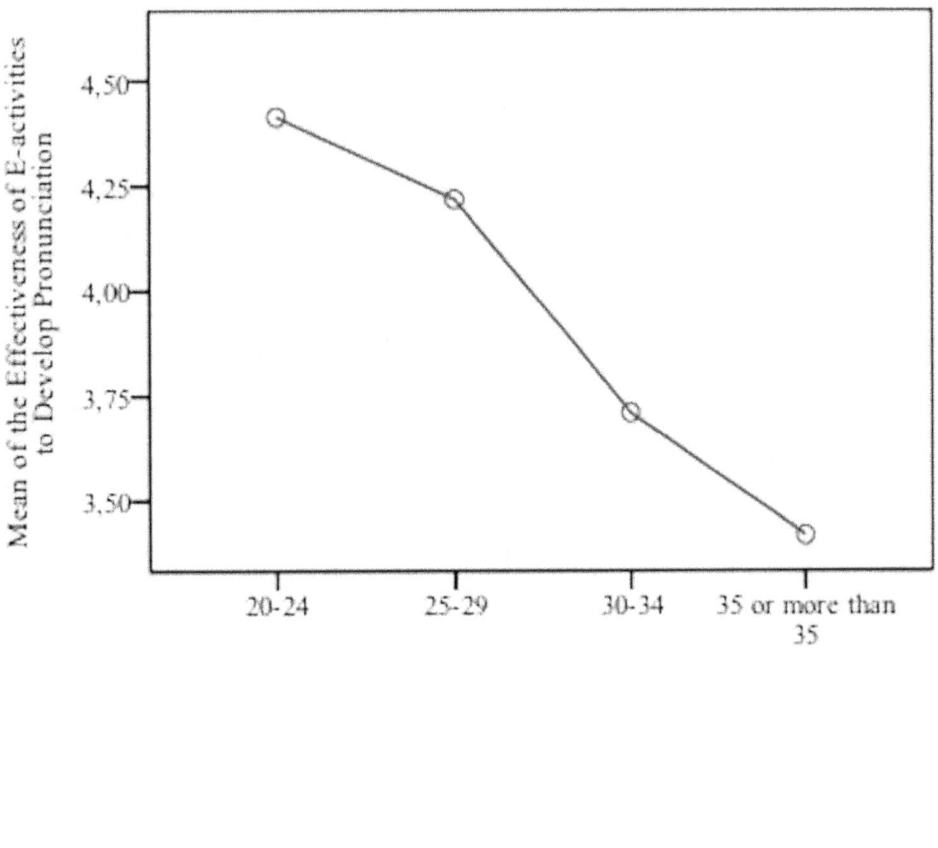

Figure 9. Results of the Tukey HSD Test of the Dependent Variable level of the Effectiveness of the E-activities to Develop Oral Skills

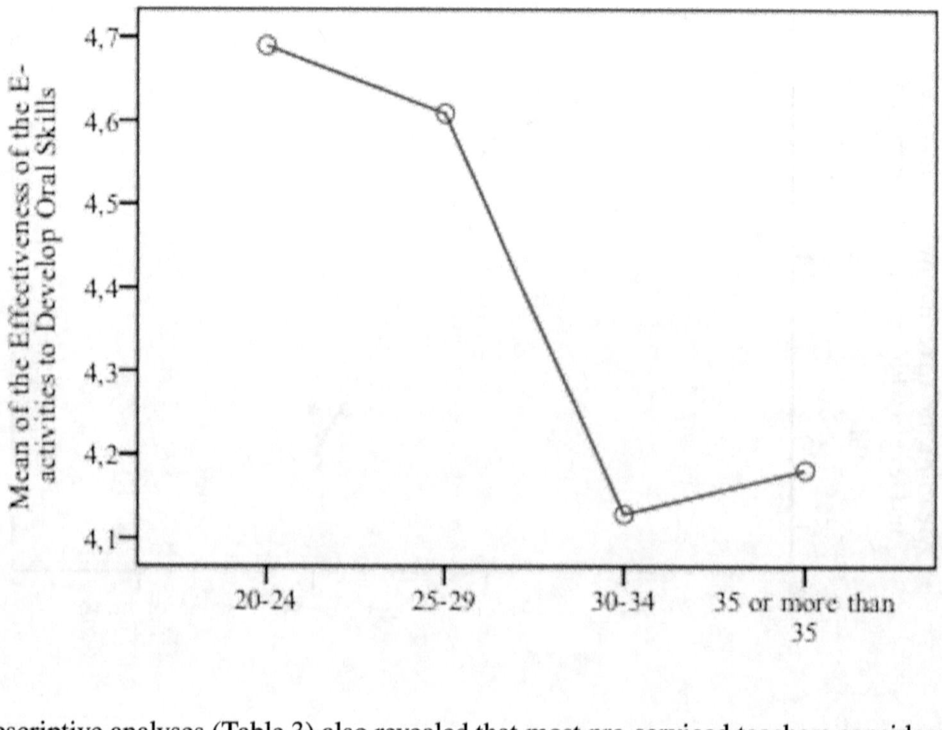

The descriptive analyses (Table 3) also revealed that most pre-serviced teachers considered that the digital ecosystem designed and implemented was effective (42.2%, n=37) and totally effective (41.3%, n=36) to help them to develop their ability to perceive and produce English more accurately. Moreover, more than half of the participants (69,6%, n=61) also assessed the digital ecosystem as effective to help them to be aware of the different English accents. Regarding the results about the effectiveness of the digital ecosystem to provide a natural environment to practice English pronunciation, 45.5% (n=40) assessed it as effective and 45% (n=39) as totally effective.

Table 3. Statistics of the Dependent Variables of the Effectiveness of the Digital Ecosystem to perceive and produce English more accurately, to be aware of the different English Accents & to provide a Natural Environment to practice English Pronunciation

Items	Totally effective	Ineffective	Neither effective nor ineffective	Effective	Totally Effective	$\bar{x}$	Sx
To perceive and produce English more accurately	1.7%	2.8%	8.4%	69.6%	17.6%	3.93	.950
Different English Accents	0.5%	4.1%	12.6%	67.9%	14.9%	3.96	.660
Natural environment to practice English Pronunciation	0.6%	2.2%	6.7%	45.5%	45%	4.05	.613

Figure 10. Results of the Tukey HSD Test of the Dependent Variable level of the Effectiveness of the Digital Ecosystem to help Pre-service Teachers to perceive and produce English more accurately

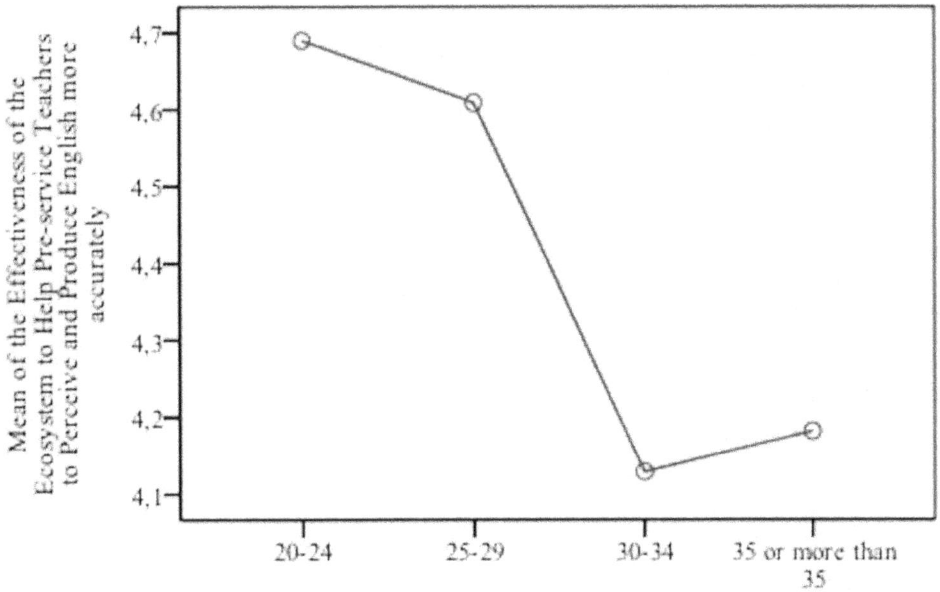

The results of the inferential analysis (Figure 10) emphasized that there were differences between the different age groups in the dependent variable that refer to the possibilities provided by the digital ecosystem to help pre-service teachers to develop their ability to perceive and produce English more accurately. Specifically, the results of analysis of variance according to the different age groups (p=.000) showed that there were statistically significant differences (CI 95%). The Tukey HSD post-hoc test was conducted in order to ascertain which groups significantly differed from the others. The test indicated that the mean scores for Group 1 ($\overline{X}$=4.38, SD=.595), Group 2 ($\overline{X}$=4.24, SD=.843), and Group 3 ($\overline{X}$=4.19, SD=1.031) were significantly different from Group 4 ($\overline{X}$=3.64, SD=1.060). The test revealed that Group 1, Group 2 and Group 3 assessed better the digital ecosystem for that purpose than Group 4.

Finally, the pre-serviced teachers were also asked about the effectiveness of the digital ecosystem to support autonomous and collaborative learning of English pronunciation through technological tools. In line with Wilson's (2005) findings, the results of the descriptive analysis (Table 4) were also quite positive about those dependent variables. Specifically, 48% (n=42) and 27.9% (n=24) of the participants pointed out that the digital ecosystem was effective and totally effective to support autonomous learning. Similar results were obtained in the other variable, since 54.7% (n=46) stated that it was effective and 30.2% (n=26) totally effective.

Table 4. Statistics of the Dependent Variables of the Effectiveness of the Digital Ecosystem to support Autonomous & Collaborative Learning of English Pronunciation

Items	Totally effective	Ineffective	Neither effective nor ineffective	Effective	Totally Effective	$\overline{X}$	Sx
Autonomous Learning	2.5%	8.4%	13.1%	48%	27.9%	3.91	.983
Collaborative Learning	2.0%	3.4%	9.8%	54.7%	30.2%	4.08	.840

Overall, the current research provides specific evidences of the potential of podcasts and videocasts to provide access to the necessary practice with a wide range of accents and contexts to improve English pronunciation level and oral skills (Mbah, Mbah & Iloene, 2014). The direct consequence of that was the possibility to communicate more effectively in different communicative situations and get a significant learning of English pronunciation.

The study proved how the use of different technological tools made possible, as Llisterri (2007) points out, the systematic integration of English pronunciation activities in self-learning, online learning and blended learning environments.

There were evidences of the pedagogical sense of the transmissive, interactive and collaborative tools used in the digital ecosystem. In line with other studies, those tools were suitable for learning in the blended learning modality, since they facilitated the necessary practice for the participants of blended learning modality in which the number of sessions was smaller than in the face-to-face modality (Ruiz, 2008). In those studies, there were evidences on how technology provided an improvement in the quality of education, and on the teaching-learning process and therefore on the learning outcomes (Chacón & Pérez, 2011; Talero & Elizabeth, 2012).

FUTURE RESEARCH DIRECTIONS AMD LIMITATIONS OF THE STUDY

The study suggests that the great potential of the digital ecosystem implemented, and the technological tools used to provide a virtual environment where students can improve their English pronunciation level. These digital ecosystems can represent a great opportunity to allow people to carry out their training throughtout their lives independently. The new virtual learning environments and the technological resources are essential to respond to knowledge society people's needs.

However, this chapter recommends that future research should focus on the use of other technological tools that help to eliminate the weak aspects of the digital ecosystem analysed. Studies should also focus on the potential of these digital ecosystems to train students on other skills and aspects of the second language.

Furthermore, the current study presents two main limitations. On one hand, the researcher focuses on a specific degree, English language teaching in Primary Education. On the other hand, it is the number of participants, only 87 learners enrolled in English phonetics and phonology course.

Regarding these limitations, the quantitative results would probably be different if the study were carried out with students who study at different departments. It is recommended to repeat the research in different context to analyse and compare the results obtained in this research with new studies.

CONCLUSION

The study aimed to analyse the pre-service teachers' perceptions about the effectiveness of a digital ecosystem implemented in English Phonetics and Phonology subject, and to highlight the benefits of some transmissive, interactive and collaborative tools in learning that subject. Regarding the results, the pre-service teachers considered that they improved their English pronunciation level. However, there were differences, younger participanta showed a more positive perception towards the potential of the digital ecosystem and the technological resources used for the development of the e-activities (Abdous, Camarena & Facer, 2009).

There was a more individualized instruction, focused on learners to a large extend that it was due to the e-activities developed in the digital ecosystem in which the participants became active learners, generating knowledge (Evangelidou, 2017; Pinto-Llorente, Sánchez-Gómez & García-Peñalvo, 2018a). An evidence of that active role was the creation of podcast uploaded in the digital ecosystem on their part (Tallei & Coura, 2011). The fact of being active participants and providing them with opportunities to take their own decisions increased their motivation to improve their oral skills and their English pronunciation level (Man-Man, 2006).

It was highlighted how the online tests enabled in the digital ecosystem allowed the participants to self-assess their English pronunciation level and oral skills systematically (Pinto-Llorente, Sánchez-Gómez & García-Peñalvo, 2016) in order to know their strengths, weaknesses and needs. It is necessary not to neglect the teaching of pronunciation when learning a L2, but also try another component of the curriculum design, since it has the same importance as other aspects such as grammar, vocabulary, culture, etc.

REFERENCES

Abdous, M., Camarena, M. M., & Facer, B. R. (2009). MALL Technology: Use of Academic Podcasting in the Foreign Language Classroom. *ReCALL, 21*(1), 76–95. doi:10.1017/S0958344009000020

Ali, S. (2016). Towards the development of a comprehensive pedagogical framework for pronunciation training based on adapted automatic speech recognition systems. In S. Papadima-Sophocleous, L. Bradley & S. Thouësny (Eds.), CALL communities and culture – short papers from EUROCALL 2016 (pp. 7-13). Research-publishing.net. doi:10.14705/rpnet.2016.eurocall2016.530

Altanopoulou, P., Tselios, N., Katsanos, C., & Georgoutsou, M. (2015). Wiki-Mediated Activities in Higher Education: Evidence-Based Analysis of Learning Effectiveness Across Three Studies. *Journal of Educational Technology & Society, 18*(4), 511–522.

Arnal, J., Rincón, D., & Latorre, A. (1994). *Investigación educativa. Fundamentos y metodología.* Barcelona: Labor.

Asbhy, M. (2008). New directions in learning teaching and assessment for phonetics. *Estudios de Fonética Experimental, 17*, 17-44.

Baker, J., & Gossman, P. (2013). The learning impact of a virtual learning environment: Students' views. *Teacher Education Advancement Network Journal, 5*(2), 19–38.

Bartolí, M. (2005). La pronunciación en la clase de lenguas extranjeras. *Phonica, 1*, 1–27.

Bell, G. (2009). *Building Social Web Applications*. Sebastopol, CA: O'Reilly Media.

Blumberg, P. (2009). *Developing Learner-Centered Teaching. A Practical Guide for Faculty*. San Francisco: John Wiley & Sons.

Buendía, L., Colás, P., & Hernández, F. (1997). *Métodos de investigación en psicopedagogía*. Madrid: McGraw-Hill.

Canale, M. (1983). De la competencia comunicativa a la pedagogía comunicativa del lenguaje. In *Competencia comunicativa. Documentos básicos en la enseñanza de lenguas extranjeras* (pp. 63–83). Madrid: Edelsa.

Canale, M., & Swain, M. (1980). Theoretical Bases of Communicative Approaches to Second Language Teaching and Testing. *Applied Linguistics, 1*(1), 1–47. doi:10.1093/applin/1.1.1

Chacón, C., & Pérez, C. (2011). El podcast como innovación en la enseñanza del inglés como lengua extranjera. *Pixel-Bit. Revista de Medios y Educación, 39*, 41–54.

Cole, J., & Foster, H. (2008). *Using Moodle. Teaching with the Popular Open Source Course Management System*. Sebastopol, California: O'Reilly Media.

Cortés, M. (2002). *Didáctica de la prosodia del español: la acentuación y la entonación*. Barcelona: Edinumen.

Council of Europe. (2001). *Common European Framework of Reference for Languages: Learning, teaching, assessment*. Cambridge: Cambridge University Press.

Derwing, T. M., & Munro, M. (2005). Second Language Accent and Pronunciation Teaching: A Research-Based Approach. *TESOL Quarterly, 39*(3), 379–397. doi:10.2307/3588486

Duffy, T. M., & Cunningham, D. J. (1996). Constructivism: Implications for the Design and Delivery of Instruction. In D. H. Jonassen (Ed.), *Handbook of Research for Educational Communications and Technology* (pp. 170–198). New York: Macmillan Library Reference.

Evangelidou, F. (2017). Kavala's 6th Graders towards Mastering Mathematics: A Blended Learning Proposal at Disabled Students' Side. In A. Palalas & P. Pawluk (Eds.), *Blended Learning Theory and Practice Proceedings of the 2nd World Conference on Blended Learning (IABL2017)* (pp. 79-84). Toronto: International Association for Blended Learning and George Brown College.

Gan, B., Menkhoff, T., & Smith, R. (2015). Enhancing students' learning process through interactive digital media: new opportunities for collaborative learning. *Computers in Human Behavior, 51*(B), 652-663.

Gisbert, M. (2002). El Nuevo rol del profesor en entornos tecnológicos. *Acción pedagógica, 11*(1), 48-59.

Gómez, J. (2006). *Moodle 1.5 Manual de Consulta. Propuesta Pedagógica*. Valladolid: GNU Press.

Hardcastle, W. J., Laver, J., & Gibbon, F. E. (2013). *The Handbook of Phonetics Sciences*. Oxford: Blackwell Publishing.

Honebein, P. C. (1996). Seven Goals for the Design of Constuctivist Learning Environment. In B. G. Wilson (Ed.), *Constructivist learning environments: Case studies in instructional design* (pp. 11–24). Englewood Cliffs, NJ: Educational Technology Publications.

Hymes, D. (1972). On Communicative Competence. In J. Pride & J. Holmes (Eds.), *Sociolinguistics* (pp. 269–293). Harmondsworth, UK: Penguin.

Iruela, A. (2007). Principios didácticos para enseñanza de la pronunciación en lenguas extranjeras. *MarcoELE Revista de Didáctica, 4*. Retrieved from https://marcoele.com/principios-didacticos-para-la-ensenanza-de-la-pronunciacion-en-lenguas-extranjeras

Kerlinger, F. N. (1985). *Investigación del comportamiento. Técnicas y metodología*. Nueva Editorial Interamericana.

Knuth, R. A., & Cunnigham, D. J. (1993). Tools for constrcutivism. In T. Duffy, J. Lowyck, & D. Jonassen (Eds.), *Designing environments for constructivist learning* (pp. 163–187). Berlín: Springer-Verlag. doi:10.1007/978-3-642-78069-1_9

Larsen-Freeman, D. (2003). *Techniques and Principles in Language Teaching*. Oxford: Oxford University Press.

Larsen-Freeman, D., & Long, M. (1994). *Introducción al estudio de la adquisición de segundas lenguas*. Madrid: Gredos.

Levis, J. M. (2005). Changing Contexts and Shifting Paradigms in Pronunciation Teaching. *TESOL Quarterly*, *39*(3), 369–377. doi:10.2307/3588485

Liu, S. C., & Hung, P. Y. (2016). Teaching Pronunciation with Computer Assisted Pronunciation Instruction in a Technological University. *Universal Journal of Educational Research*, *4*(9), 1939–1943. doi:10.13189/ujer.2016.040902

Llisterri, J. (2007). La enseñanza de la pronunciación asistida por ordenador. In *XXIV congreso internacional de AESLA. Aprendizaje de lenguas, uso del lenguaje y modelación cognitiva: Perspectivas aplicadas entre disciplinas* (91-120). España, Madrid: UNED.

Man-Man, P. (2006). Developing Students' listening and speaking Skills Through ELT Podcasts. *Education Journal*, *34*(2), 115–134.

Mbah, E. E., Mbah, B. M., Iloene, M. I., & Iloene, G. (2014). Podcasts for Learning English Pronunciation in Igboland: Students' Experiences and Expectations. *The EUROCALL Review*, *22*(2), 57–68. doi:10.4995/eurocall.2014.3635

Pastor, S. (2005). La enseñanza de segundas lenguas. In A. López & B. Gallardo (Eds.), *Conocimiento y lenguaje* (pp. 361–399). Valencia: PUV.

Payne, C. R. (2009). *Information Technology and Constructivism in Higher Education Progressive Learning Frameworks*. Hershey, PA: IGI Global Snippet. doi:10.4018/978-1-60566-654-9

Pérez, M. T., Arratia, O., Martín, M. A., & Galisteo, D. (2009). *Innovación en docencia universitaria con Moodle. Casos prácticos*. Alicante: Editorial Club Universitario.

Pinto-Llorente, A. M., Sánchez-Gómez, M. C., & García-Peñalvo, F. J. (2016). Assessing the Effectiveness of Interactive and Collaborative Resources to Improve Reading and Writing in English. *International Journal of Human Capital and Information Technology Professionals*, *7*(1), 66–85. doi:10.4018/IJHCITP.2016010105

Pinto-Llorente, A. M., Sánchez-Gómez, M. C., & García-Peñalvo, F. J. (2018a). A Research on Students' Perceptions on a B-Learning English Environment to Improve Written Skills. In V. Ahuja & S. Rathore (Eds.), *Multidisciplinary Perspectives on Human Capital and Information Technology Professionals* (pp. 179–201). Hershey, PA: IGI Global. doi:10.4018/978-1-5225-5297-0.ch010

Pinto-Llorente, A. M., Sánchez-Gómez, M. C., & García-Peñalvo, F. J. (2018b). Students Skills in a Blended Learning Environment: A Qualitative Research. In A. Borchers (Ed.), *Technology Management in Organizational and Societal Contexts* (pp. 249–280). Hershey, PA: IGI Global. doi:10.4018/978-1-5225-5279-6.ch011

Pourhosein Gilakjani, A. (2018). Teaching Pronunciation of English with Computer Technology: A Qualitative Study. *International Journal of Research in English Education*, *3*(2), 94–114. doi:10.29252/ijree.3.2.94

Rice, W. (2011). *Moodle 2.0 E-Learning Course Development*. Birmingham: Packt publishing.

Richards, J. C., & Rodgers, T. S. (2001). *Approaches and Methods in Language Teaching*. Cambridge: Cambridge University Press; doi:10.1017/CBO9780511667305

Richard, J. C., & Schmidt, R. (2013). *Longman Dictionary of Language, Teaching and Applied Linguistics*. New York: Routledge; doi:10.4324/9781315833835

Ruiz, C. (2008). El Blended-learning: Evaluación de una experiencia de aprendizaje en el nivel de postgrado. *Investigación y Posgrado*, *23*(1), 11–36.

Sánchez, A. (1997). *Los métodos en la enseñanza de idiomas: evolución histórica y análisis didáctico*. Madrid: SGEL.

Santos, I. (1999). *Lingüística Aplicada a la enseñanza-aprendizaje del español como lengua extranjera*. Madrid: Arco Libros.

Talero, A., & Elizabeth, S. (2012). El podcast en la enseñanza de la lectoescritura. *Revista Virtual Universidad Católica del Norte*, *37*, 9–26.

Tallei, J. I., & Coura, J. (2011). El uso del podcasts en la enseñanza secundaria. *Revista de humanidades, tecnología e cultura*, *1*(1), 234-242.

Usó, L. (2008). La enseñanza de la pronunciación en LE: Algunas consideraciones. *Phonica*, *4*, 104–130.

Walsh, L., & Kahn, P. (2010). *Collaborative Working in Higher Education. The Social Academy*. New York: Routledge.

Willis, J. (2009). *Constructivist Instructional Design (C-ID). Foundations, Models, and Examples*. Charlotte, NC: Information Age Publishing.

Wilson, I. (2005). Using Praat and Moodle for teaching segmental and supra segmental pronunciation. *TESOL Quarterly*, *3*, 33–43.

Yule, G. (2014). *The Study of Language*. Cambridge: Cambridge University Press.

ADDITIONAL READING

Baker, A., & Murphy, J. (2011). Knowledge base of pronunciation teaching: Staking out the territory. *TESL Canada Journal*, *28*(2), 29–50. doi:10.18806/tesl.v28i2.1071

Dell'Aria, C., & Incalcaterra McLoughlin, L. (2013). Developing Phonological Awareness in Blended-learning Language Courses. In L. Bradley & S. Thouësny (Eds.), *20 Years of EUROCALL: Learning from the Past, Looking to the Future. Proceedings of the 2013 EUROCALL Conference*, Évora, Portugal (pp.78-85). 10.14705/rpnet.2013.000142

Derwin, T. M., & Munro, M. J. (2009). Putting accent in its place: Rethinking obstacles to communication. *Language Teaching*, *42*(4), 476–490. doi:10.1017/S026144480800551X

Foote, J. A., Trofimovich, P., Collins, L., & Urzúa, F. (2013). Pronunciation teaching practices in communicative second language classes. *Language Learning Journal*, 1–16.

Gilakjani, A. P. (2012). A study of factors affecting EFL learners' English pronunciation learning and the strategies for instruction. *International Journal of Humanities and Social Science*, *2*(3), 119–128.

Kochaksaraie, M. N., & Makiabadi, H. (2018). Second Language Learners' Phonological Awareness and Perception of Foreign Accentedness and Comprehensibility by Native and Non-native English Speaking EFL Teachers. *Journal of Teaching Language Skills*, *36*(4), 103–140.

Kwary, D. A., & Fauzie, S. (2018). Students' achievement and opinions on the implementation of e-learning for phonetics and phonology lectures at Airlangga University. *Educação e Pesquisa*, *44*. Retrieved from http://www.scielo.br/scielo.php?script=sci_arttext&pid=S1517-97022018000100432

Mohammed, F. O. (2014). The Use of Phonological Awareness Skills in Teaching Phonetics and Phonology for University Students. *Journal of the Humanities and Social Sciences*, *19*(1), 101–116. doi:10.9790/0837-1919101106

Nadiera, N., & Hamidah Yamat, H. (2019). Phonics Teaching Techniques: A Mixed Method Study with Lower Primary English Teachers in Malaysia. *International Journal of Scientific and Research Publications*, *9*(4), 618–624. doi:10.29322/IJSRP.9.04.2019.p8875

Pinto-Llorente, A. M., Sánchez-Gómez, M. C., & García-Peñalvo, F. J. (2015). To Be or Not to Be Successful? That Does Not Only Depend on Technology, But Also on Human Factors. *Journal of Cases on Information Technology*, *17*(1), 51–69. doi:10.4018/JCIT.2015010104

KEY TERMS AND DEFINITIONS

Active Learning: It is a type of learning in which teaching tries to involve learners in the learning process. Students are actively engaged in the development of the lessons, activities, etc., and improve skills such as reflection, problem solving, and critical thinking, etc.

Autonomous Learning: It refers to a situation in which learners are responsible for their learning. They take charge of their own learning and are actively involved, taking individual decisions according to their necessities or preferences focused on the goals they need to achieve.

Blended Learning: A kind of education modality that combines both face-to-face and online lessons.

Collaborative Learning: It refers to a situation in which a group of students learn together and have an active role in creating and sharing knowledge.

Higher Education: It is the third level of education. It is beyond secondary education and is normally provided by universities or colleges.

Learner-Centered Pedagogy: It refers to a pedagogy that places students at the centre of the teaching-learning process. Students are more active and participative, and the process turns knowledge into a negotiation between teachers and students. Furthermore, this pedagogy starts from students' interests and objectives, and it carries out a learning process based on real situations and materials, using the current technologies to favour this process.

Learning Community: It refers to a group of students who work collaboratively, share knowledge and have common learning objectives.

Quantitative Research: It is a structured and rigour methodological approach focused on quantifying the problem and finding out how frequent the results are in order to project these results to a larger population. The techniques used to collect quantitative data are mainly questionnaires.

Chapter 3
Assessing Language Learning in Technology-Enhanced Environments

Zeynep Çetin Köroğlu
https://orcid.org/0000-0002-9456-8910
Bayburt University, Turkey

ABSTRACT

Modern language classrooms need to be modified to adapt to the rapidly-enhanced technological innovations in terms of designing, planning, teaching, and assessing. In line with the growing trend and interest in exploring the internet, technology-based tools, and environments for assessment purposes of foreign language learning, this chapter takes a critical look at language assessment through ICT by addressing the research gap in the field and discussing through a non-systematic review of related research. In addition, innovative digital language assessment tools are presented, and related research questions are answered in relation to, especially a language skill, speaking. The current chapter aims to shed light on how ICT, technology-enhanced environments, and innovative digital tools can be used for language assessment.

INTRODUCTION

Technology in language assessment was introduced in the 1960s with the aim of making the testing process more effective (Chapelle & Voss, 2017). Some developments in language testing have been made since then, and these developments can be categorized under three themes chronologically. The fist remarkable development is computer-adaptive testing that enables administering an interactive testing to each test takers during the assessment process (Chapelle & Voss, 2017). This type of testing refers to both research and practice that use of technology to monitor and reflect students' or test takers' performance and skills based on an algorithm set up by the test developer (see Chalhoub-Deville, 1999). The second theme is effective technology use in testing which is provided by automated writing evaluation (AWE) that decreases the intensive work of evaluation such as assessing students' essays. The third theme is

DOI: 10.4018/978-1-7998-3062-7.ch003

efficiency- oriented research that focuses on comparison of score meaning for computer enhanced tests and others' scoring (Chapelle & Voss, 2017). It is clear that various terms are used to refer computer-based language assessment such as computer-adaptive, computer-aided, computer-assisted, computer-enhanced, computer-mediated, computer-supported, and technology-enhanced. However, all these terms suggest that computer has a supporter, mediator or peripheral role in language assessment (Yu & Zhang, 2017). The main problem is that computers shouldn't be perceived as a delivery program by assessors and educators. On the contrary, it is quite necessary that they must consider computer as an integral part of language assessment (Yu & Zhang, 2017). The current chapter aims to shed light on how ICT, technology-enhanced environments, and innovative digital tools can be used for language assessment.

Considering this, the current chapter draws attention to the research gap which occurs in the role of computers in language assessments. Some studies (Mullamaa, 2010; Salehi & Salehi, 2012; Teo, 2012; Wang, 2005) have focused on ICT and its integration in both language learning, teaching and assessment but there is lack of discussing ICT based assessment approaches and these approaches' administration with necessary digital tools. Therefore, this chapter aims to conduct a non-systematic review of the related literature and explore the studies which have been carried out related with ICT and assessment in recent years, current digital tools, websites and applications and future research suggestions of the issue. It also intends to answer the following research questions based on the review:

1. What are the positive and negative sides of technology integration in language assessment?
2. What does related literature suggest on technology integration in language assessment and what are the future research directions for types of language assessment?
3. What ICT tools can be implemented for language assessment?

BACKGROUND

Salmon (2002) indicates that we need to focus on technology's contributions to pedagogy and pedagogy's needs in general instead of focusing on what it can do for us. As one of the most significant areas of pedagogy, assessment has evolved with the technology. Thus, technology can make possible the representation of models, systems or domains and its manipulation and modifications. This is only thanks to having developed these tools in the past (Pellegrino & Quellmalz, 2010). Although early technological implementations in large-scale testing were comparatively simple, efficient and low-cost (Bennett, 2008; Quellmalz, & Pellegrino, 2009), the boundaries of evaluating complicated learning types are being pushed by a new generation of formative assessments.

The computer's capacity to capture student input enables users to gather proof of procedures like problem-solving sequences and strategy use. If learning and related materials become digital, the evaluation will also have to follow this path so that the learning mode and the evaluation mode match (Russell & Haney, 2000). However, if all multiple-choice tests are put on a computer, sufficient progress will not be made on how technology is used for training in schools. Sadly, there has been little progress in using the evaluation machine. Educators shifted the first major educational tests to the computer almost ten years ago and intended to utilize the technology to introduce new methods of measurement. These efforts went no further due to the adaptability, cost, technical unpredictability, need to preserve the scope of the decision-making, and adequacy of multiple choices (Schmidt, 2002a). Good assessment and evaluation should engage students with the assessment criteria. Assessment should support and enhance personalized and meaningful learning. It should also feedback which leads to development and improvement. Furthermore, good and well-designed assessment should focus on students' improvement, development and effort. It stimulates dialogue among students and teachers. From this perspective, language assessment in technology-enhanced environments requires well designed and essential components for both students and teachers. According to Chapelle (2010), three domains are important for using computer technology in language assessment and evaluation:

- **Efficiency:** Computer technology use can enhance and improve efficiency in test development, test delivery, and scoring. Students' speaking and writing performances are scored through computer-adaptive testing and automated scoring.
- **Equivalence:** This means that students' computer-based and paper-based test performances should be comparable.
- **Innovation:** Innovation suggests that with the help of the integration of technology, language ability can be re-conceptualized (Chapelle & Douglas, 2006, p. 107). They define language ability as "the ability to select and deploy appropriate language through the technologies that are appropriate for a situation".

Besides this, several studies have looked at language assessment through ICT. According to Chapelle and Voss (2016), people may feel less comfortable talking to a computer screen even though they get used to reading something on it. The modification and implementation of computer technologies in language assessment is a more complex and controversial issue in language teaching and learning. Various variables may have effects on the reliability and validity of the test. Even students' familiarity with testing software affects its effectiveness in language assessments and test results.

On the other hand, developing technologies create and provide lots of opportunities for language assessment in different formats, such as scenario-based language assessment, virtual environment-based language assessment, digital formative assessment, and others. Even with the use of multimedia in language testing, teachers or assessors check different language skills than they would with tests involving audio alone (Chapelle & Voss, 2016). From this perspective, recent related research is presented in this section.

Recent research has studied and analyzed ICT and language teaching in detail (Mullamaa, 2010; Salehi & Salehi, 2012; Wang, 2005). Teo (2012) looked at whether computer-assisted dynamic assessment promotes metacognitive reading strategies. Participants of the study were freshmen English students in Taiwan. Teo states that mediation is a difficult task to complete in a larger classroom, which is an essential element of dynamic assessment. Thus, in this study, the computer played a mediator role which interacted and responded to students in a web-based computerized dynamic assessment (C-DA). The study was carried out as action research which aimed to improve participants' metacognitive reading strategies. The students' performances were captured by computer for review by the human instructor. The study revealed that computers can be used as a mediator in C-DA (Teo, 2012) and be a part of reading skills assessment.

Another study was carried out by Nakatsuhara, Inoue, Berry and Galaczi (2017) investigating the effects of internet-based video conferencing technology on speaking skills assessment. The research aimed to find out similarities and differences between standard and computer-mediated face-to-face tests. This research examined the results of test and participants' language performance, test management, and classification behavior for both methods. Results of this study showed that the two different test formats generated similar results, but both the participants' functional output and the examiners' behavior changed (Nakatsuhara et al, 2017). They emphasized that using a video conferencing mode for speaking assessment has required traditional format of testing looking at construct validity, reliability, the interaction between interlocutors. However, it is stated by Kim and Craig (2010, 2012) that video conferencing in L2 speaking assessment is quite rare.

Kim and Craig researched the validation of video conferencing for speaking skills assessment with 40 test-takers. The participants were tested using both face-to-face and video conferenced oral interviews. The quantitative findings of their study indicated that there was no statistical significance between the two testing modes. Additionally, they compared two test modes in terms of computer familiarity, non-verbal linguistic cues, comfort, and interest. The authors proposed that video conferenced interviews were similar to face-to-face interviews in terms of reliability, construct validity, authenticity, interactivity, effect, and practicality (Kim & Craig, 2012).

Another study carried out by Early and Swanson (2008) researched the functionality, challenges, and advantages of digital tools and how these tools were used by undergraduate foreign language students. In the study, instructors and students completed surveys and were interviewed. The data from tools were then collected and analyzed. Results of the study showed that oral proficiency improved with the support of both traditional and technology-enhanced methods of assessment (Early & Swanson, 2008).

In traditional speaking assessment, students felt pressure due to peer presence and their answers were less authentic and creative. However, in digital voice recording, students felt more comfortable and relaxed. In addition to this, they had time to think and identify their errors in their speaking performance. They experimented with more vocabulary and felt a sense of success in their language proficiency (Early & Swanson, 2008). Like the students, instructors had a positive perception on the use of voice recording in speaking skills assessment. They thought that traditional assessment of oral performance was time-consuming and did not engage students. Moreover, it did not provide a second chance to students and caused classroom management problems. On the other hand, digital voice recording increased time for instruction and more options for evaluation in terms of place (Early & Swanson, 2008). Additionally, with the help of digital voice recording, language instructors could easily evaluate students' progress and have more reliable data.

Another hybrid and distance learning study carried out by Blake et al, (2008) investigated a phone delivered the automated speaking assessment to assess participants' speaking performances at the end of the course as the proof of learning in an online learning environment. The results showed that students' oral proficiency development in an online context was similar to those who learned content in the language classroom. One of the main features of the study was that researchers utilized both the online course and assessment tool to investigate their effectiveness for speaking skills. Additionally, in this study, the course content was delivered through CD/DVD programs, web pages, and synchronous chat programs (Blake et al, 2008). It showed that digital tools used for assessing foreign language speaking skills were useful, effective, and had the required features of language testing.

However, digital tools for writing assessment are not as effective as speaking assessment tools. According to Godwin Jones (2008), one of the challenges in digital writing assessment tools is developing a highly sophisticated tool to provide useful feedback at various levels of English language learners. Thus, most of the digital assessment tools evaluate surface features such as spelling and grammar, but other important features of writing, such as cohesion and general issues of global composition, are missing (Godwin Jones, 2008).

Language testing with digital tools offers the above-mentioned positive impacts on language pedagogy both for instructors and students. However, it has negative points as well. Firstly, computer adaptive testing has difficulty in designing necessary and appropriate techniques to assign the required number of items of appropriate difficulty levels to test takers. Secondly, automated scoring systems to assess language skills such as speaking, writing, reading, or vocabulary, are still problematic in terms of reliability, validity, construct validity issues (Yu & Zhang, 2017).

Considering all these studies, some research questions have arisen and will be answered in the following section.

MAIN FOCUS OF THE CHAPTER

Research Methodology

The current chapter was designed and written in the form of non-systematic narrative review of language assessment in technology- enhanced learning environment. The reasons for selecting this type of method were the abundance of publications and information related to the topic, different perspectives and lack of consensus on it (Ferrari, 2015). Additionally, non-systematic reviews aim to identify and summarize what has been previously published, avoid duplications and address new research directions (Ferrari, 2015), which helps to answer the research questions posed in this chapter.

A Non-Systematic Review of Language Assessment through ICT

The aim of this section is to answer the questions and present information about language assessment through ICT tools.

What are The Positive and Negative Sides of Technology Integration in Language Assessment?

Various positive sides of technology integration in language assessment have been discussed through the previous section. For example, digital learning environment helps language learners to set their own pace of study and teachers can track their students' development more effectively with more engaging digital textbooks, interactive presentations, and videos to enhance learners' motivation to learn and to become more successful in their learning. Although there have been numerous advantages of technology use in language assessment, there are disadvantages to technology when it is implemented or embedded in language learning environments. Bennett (2002) classifies these drawbacks under five headings:

- Hardware and software reliability: High-stake testing interruptions can have substantial impact on the results of students
- Safety: Controlling access to the students' information and questions (although these are problems with paper-based examinations, too, well-understood systems can handle them)
- Measurement problems: For example, a knowledge of screen-based work and differences in internet speed will influence the achievement of students
- Question type limitations which are ready to use question types
- Students' familiarity with computers and access to them

However, according to García Laborda, (2007, p.8) "the benefits of online testing should overcome any of its drawbacks, as it can be faster, more efficient, and less costly than traditional paper-and-pencil testing. Additionally, multimedia prompts can help make the test feel more 'real'. Adaptive tests can facilitate the difficulty of rapid diagnosis, and self-correcting tests can accelerate the process of correction, feedback, and reporting". There are emerging approaches and terms in language assessment. This is a result of developing technologies, such as digitally enhanced language assessment, technology-based language assessment, ICT-based language assessment (internet communication technologies), AI-based language assessment (artificial intelligence), VLE-based language assessment (virtual learning environments), and digital formative assessment. According to Pellegrino and Quellmalz (2010), these new generations of language assessment makes possible to determine where, how, what, when, and why assessment takes place and its relationship with learning and teaching.

As one of the common characteristics, these content-rich language assessment types include high-quality interactive web-based materials which are used for source material in language testing. According to Chalhoub-Deville (2001, p. 97), "advances in technology should encourage test developers to move beyond the thinking that has long dominated paper-and-pencil testing and inspire the use of 'disruptive' applications, by which assessments are conceptualized and implemented in innovatively different ways". This is because language learning and teaching have been continuously reshaped the development of technologies and, as an outcome of this development, language assessment should also be improved in this direction. Getting significant results through test delivery on computers is inevitable, but efficiency should not be the ultimate goal (Bennett, 2002b). Implementing technology in language assessment needs to help language teachers to give better instruction and motivate students to achieve better learning. In other words, language testing leads to experience of learning (Bennett, 2002b). Similar to Bennett's point of view, Gipps (2005) indicates that the aim of test design in the new assessment type is not to build costly computer systems that offer data for summative assessment, but provide useful, meaningful information and constructive feedback to help language learners to become more successful in their learning.

What Does Related Literature Suggest on Technology Integration in Language Assessment and What are the Future Research Directions for Types of Language Assessment?

Developments in technology-based language assessments at school level are generally moving forward in two directions. The first one is by using ICT to support exams and tests. The second one is by administering pilot tests for assessments. At university level, if a university uses a learning management systems (LMS) such as Edmodo (2019) or Second Life, it may include or apply online tests and quizzes for assessment (Gipps, 2005). Studies generally consider computer technologies as a teaching or assessment tool rather than an integral part of teaching foreign languages. However, digital technologies have been extensively used for language teaching and assessment, especially in higher education. The reconceptualization of computer-enhanced language assessment will be a guiding principle of innovation in assessment practices (Yu & Zhang, 2017). From this perspective, more recent studies have integrated technological tools as an integral part of this process and it is possible to see the integration of these technologies in the assessment phase (See Chapelle & Voss, 2016; Kim & Craig, 2012; Nakatsuhara et al, 2017).

A significant point in integrating technologies in language pedagogy is students' and language instructors' familiarity with these technologies. A student who takes a test on iPad or mobile phone is similar to having a test on the computer for skillful users of these electronic devices (Ling, 2016). Additionally, the development of artificial intelligence computer technologies has led them to become more interactive and smarter. Resources and effort-intensive face-to-face traditional language tests have given rise to practical alternatives formed by developing technologies to improve the learning experience of students. Three of these new alternatives will be discussed and presented under this heading. They are virtual learning environment-based language assessment (VLE), scenario-based language assessment (SBA) and digital formative assessment.

VLE-Based Assessment

VLEs are virtual places that educators and learners can use to display and exchange ideas and communicate with each other. Another definition made by Green, Brown, and Robinson (2008) is that learning management systems or course management systems (LMS/ CMS) are software packages that permit teachers and students to receive course content through a web-based environment. Moreover, teachers may use this environment to teach a part of the course content or a whole course. Another important feature of VLEs is its interactive nature. Teachers can easily combine various resources, such as notes, quizzes, and questionnaires with VLEs, or a chat feature if it exists (Dudenay & Hockly, 2007). If it doesn't exist in a software package, language teachers can arrange a meeting through a videoconferencing using Skype as external tool (Herrera Mosquera, 2017). Research asserts that VLEs have a positive effect across various contexts (Barker & Gossman, 2013, Yıldırım et. al., 2018). Additionally, they are preferred by language teachers in terms of pedagogical usefulness, technological advantages and ease of use (Mosquera, 2017).

There are two types of VLEs: institution-led and teacher-led. The former is prepared and created for commercial purposes and sold to schools by a company. Teachers can then use uploaded activities and course content (Walker & White, 2013). In the latter, the teacher can create and upload their teaching materials to VLE, but it might be more time-consuming and exhausting for them. VLEs can be used as a virtual assessment environment if the software is designed suitably for language assessment purposes. In other words, if the quizzes, questionnaires or exams on a course are uploaded and used as digital tools, it would be virtual environment-based language assessment. Tomlinson (1999) states that VLEs provide differentiated instruction that can modify resources, content, activities and address students' needs. Students need personalized language assessment as well to improve their learning experience with this assessment. Thus, more reflective, self-regulated individuals need useful assessment instruments capable of monitoring their learning progress. As discussed in previous sections, most of the digital tools offer personalized assessment for language learners. For instance, the use of voice recording with the purpose of speaking skills assessment or video conferencing use.

It is possible to see that there are various forms of virtual environments (VE). The first one is a web-based virtual environment that permits communication among individuals via a live voice. With this technology, individuals are represented by computer-animated characters, namely avatars, and can communicate in real-time (Ockey, Gu & Keehner, 2017). Another type of virtual environment is a voice-enabled one. With the help of this type, language teachers, instructors or examiners can collect data samples in real-time that can be assessed through human raters or machines. This type is useful for speaking skills assessment (Ockey et al, 2017). Moreover, test takers and examiners can have access to VEs from anywhere via internet-connected devices.

The development of three-dimensional graphics (3D motion-speech synchronization), video communication platforms and designing virtual environments with the purpose of testing, is a creative and effective way to engage students in the testing process. Moreover, VEs should present an authentic environment which addresses students' sensory experience, their knowledge and beliefs from the real-world and should trigger students to take action (Dede, Salzman, Loftin, and Ash, 2000).

Edmodo can be classified as a VSO and an LMS (learning management system) that is an educational social networking website with various features. Students, teachers and even students' parents can easily communicate and interact in an online space. Teachers can set tasks and give assignments using Edmodo. Additionally, the teacher can provide website links and additional resources to aid students. An important feature is that teachers can collaborate and share information with other teachers all around the world. The tool can be accessed.

Another virtual learning environment is Schoology (2019), which has similar features to Edmodo. Assignments for students, course information and teaching material can be presented with this digital tool. It acts not only as a website that provides course information, but also as a useful tool for discussions, assessment, and interaction outside of the class. Additionally, the tool works in collaboration with Dropbox, Powerschool or GoogleDrive allowing students to upload files. Moodle and Blackboard can also be given as other examples of VLEs.

Scenario-Based Language Assessment (SBA)

SBA is a technology-based approach which assesses learners in a meaningful and purposeful context (O'Reilly & Sabatini, 2013). The assessment can take place in a setting, such as simulated cafeteria, with simulated characters, such as close friends or a teacher and have a purpose, such as the completion of a task as an assignment. SBA aims to develop autonomous and embedded language abilities for learners in a simulated real-life language context. Furthermore, due to SBA's design capabilities, it is possible to examine learner background understanding, metacognitive, self-regulatory and linguistic strategies, and motivation or involvement that operates within an SBA as performance moderator (O'Reilly & Sabatini, 2013; Sabatini et al, 2014).

Scenarios are useful to discuss and identify because they represent patterns of everyday life (Haynes, Spence and Lenze, 2009). Moreover, it is a useful way of testing learners' understanding of a given topic and their reaction towards an exact situation. SBA is perceived as both summative and formative assessment which informs language learners on how effective activities are in fulfilling the course's aim and improving the learning experience of students and motivate them at the same time (Haynes, Spence and Lenze, 2009).

SBA can be carried out with the 'questionmark' website which offers lots of options to create tests such as surveys, quizzes, tests and exams on any topic, for any course or curriculum. The website enables students to be assessed on their laptops, tablets or smartphones. Additionally, it uses an intuitive browser-based app for the author, and tag questions are organized in hierarchical and searchable item banks. It delivers high-stake tests and exams securely. The website uses Online Proctoring to ensure the integrity of distance learning tests and exam results. Teachers, school administrators and stakeholders have access to analyze and report on student results. It provides instant results and constructive feedback. Moreover, it can be integrated with Blackboard, D2L, Canvas, Moodle, Sakai and similar tools.

Digital Formative Assessment

Formative assessment can be defined as "all those activities undertaken by teachers, and/or by their students, which provide information to be used as feedback to modify the teaching and learning activities in which they are engaged" (Black & Wiliam, 1998, p.82). Formative assessment, namely assessment for learning, has become more effective and meaningful for learning rather than summative assessment. In other words, assessment of learning. The main focus of assessment has changed dramatically in the 21st century thanks to blended learning (Baleni, 2015). Formative assessment, when it is digitally embedded, provides immediate feedback in quality online courses. It is clear that the use of digital formative assessment tools (DFATs) in education is increasing rapidly (Fabera, & Visscherb, 2018).

According to Nicol (2007, p.3) good assessment and feedback should:

- Help clarify what good performance is (goals, criteria, and standards)
- Encourage 'time and effort' on challenging learning tasks
- Deliver high-quality feedback that helps learners self-correct
- Encourage positive motivational beliefs and self-esteem
- Encourage interaction and dialogue around learning (peer and teacher-student)
- Facilitate the development of self-assessment and reflection in learning
- Give learners a choice in assessment: content and processes
- Involve students in decision-making about assessment policy and practice
- Support the development of learning communities
- Help teachers adapt to teaching to student needs.

As can be understood from the items presented above, effective assessment and feedback should have various features to support and evaluate the students' learning. These features should exist in technology-enhanced language assessment as well. Digital assessment tools should encourage students' motivational beliefs and self-esteem, unlike face-to-face speaking tests which increase anxiety and peer pressure (Paker & Höl, 2012). In addition, students do not have a second chance for their performances. However, with a digital speaking assessment tools, students may feel more comfortable, be able to relax and have more chances. Therefore, their anxiety levels decrease, and they can perform better. Assessment should also support learning communities where collaborative learning is highly effective.

Teachers can create digital learning communities with the help digital tools which allow groups to be assessed on digital platforms. For instance, an oral speaking test can be carried out with a video conferencing session and students can take the test as a group after a competed group learning activity. Digital language assessment should also ensure an opportunity for interaction and dialogue between students and teachers. Most of the current digital language assessment tools have chat features which enable interaction and communication such as Webpa, Edmodo synchronously or asynchronously.

Another important feature of a good assessment is feedback and students' self-correction. In traditional assessment, immediate and corrective feedback is provided in the testing process. Providing feedback is not difficult in digital assessment tools or websites either. Thus, the ability of digital tools or software programs enable language teachers to provide feedback. Vincent (2016) states that "when teachers know their students well, they can build strong connections that lead to better learning. Knowing students' interests, strengths, and weaknesses help teachers tailor learning experiences for their students. Formative assessment involves the teacher collecting information about what students know, don't know, and want to learn." In this respect digital formative assessment should include (Kigandi, 2010 cited in Baleni, 2015):

- Assessment tasks which represent real-life situations and which are meaningful for the learning process
- Assessment activities in digital formative assessment which help learners to understand meaning and link their previous knowledge to the new information
- The ability to add learner information in an online environment for peer learning through discussion forums
- Digital formative assessment activities accompanied by feedback
- Rubrics which can be presented to students to make them see their achievement level and expected level of achievements
- Assessment tasks which support self-assessment, and reflection of students

What ICT tools can be implemented for language assessment?

As previously discussed in this chapter, computer technologies are increasingly being used in "designing, developing and delivering test content as well as scoring and reporting examinee test performance" (Sawaki, 2012, p. 426). It is clear that technology use is common in every aspect of language assessment. The use of technology for designing, developing and delivering is possible via various technological, digital, synchronous or asynchronous tools which are constantly being developed. It is not possible to present all these positive digital tools, but many of them are discussed and presented in this part of the chapter.

First of all, presentations are an indispensable part of various lessons in language teaching. Presentations can be turned into interactive slideshows with Pear Deck (2019). Students can follow the teacher's presentation on their computer, tablet or mobile phone or a device which has an internet connection. Additionally, students can respond or answer a question. Moreover, the website can make flashcards that can be exported into a quiz preparation website such as Quizlet (2019). By using Pear Deck, teachers can pose interactive questions to students and gather students' answers and responses individually through the website. Furthermore, students' answers can be evaluated. The website can be used both for interactive teaching and evaluation.

Another multimedia assessment tool is Spiral (2019). It is an interactive learning and assessment tool which provides instant feedback, interactive videos, collaborative learning tasks, flipped classroom activities and so on. Teachers can create groups through Spiral and students can discuss topics and complete assigned tasks. When the teacher shows exemplary responses, each student can see what they did. For assessment, teachers can grade assignments individually or automatically. The statistics for each question can also check to what extent the class has understood.

An additional interactive and flexible presentation tool is Lesson Up. It can be used for flipped learning and in-class activities. This website offers various features for designing a good lesson: using online videos, adding key terms, questions for assessing students' understanding, and curated websites. The tool also supports autonomous learning so that students can set their own learning pace. Students can go forward or backwards through lessons and they can even change their responses to questions. The tool provides visual reports about students' progress as well.

Flipgrid (2019) encourages students to respond in video format which can be used for both teaching and assessment. Thus, students can talk about their video responses to in-class activities. The tool can be useful for speaking skills assessment, especially in flipped classrooms, Students can therefore learn theoretical knowledge at home by using learning materials which have been pre-taught by the teacher. Class time is generally spent practicing and learning from peers (Çetin Köroğlu & Çakır, 2017). Students can be more engaged through Flipgrid in speaking skills assessment because it provides a modifiable video response opportunity.

GoClass (2019) is another website which delivers interactive lessons to students' mobile devices. Similar to Flipgrid, Goclass is suitable for using in flipped or blended classrooms. Language teachers can prepare self-paced lessons or assign a task before the lessons. Students have more time to practice and deepen their understanding. However, the website has a fixed structure for lesson preparation. It could be more restrictive for certain lessons.

These useful websites can be used for both teaching and assessing language learners' language skills. Additionally, language teachers can combine and use them in projects, sources of essays, creating an online discussion, group work or peer assessment.

Webpa (2019) is an additional online tool for assessment. It is very useful for reflection and peer and self-assessment. One important feature of Webpa is its flexibility. Teachers can determine assessment criteria, size of groups and aims of tasks due to pedagogical requirements (JISC, 2010).

PebblePad (2019) can be used to create blogs, pages, records, and reflections. These portfolios can be reused with multiple audiences. The sketchbook tool makes students more engaged in their learning and provides a conceptual understanding with peer and self-review (JISC, 2010).

There is an additional tool, developed by AJE (2019), which evaluates the quality of English manuscripts. The designers of this tool aim to save time, money and effort for publishers and journal editors. The tool works due to a dataset of over 100,000 papers. Speaking skills assessment is challenging, logistically complex and resource-intensive (Çetin Köroğlu & Çakır, 2017, Nakatsuhara et al, 2017). It is impossible to carry out a speaking skill assessment in geographically remote areas (Nakatsuhara et al, 2017). Even though face-to-face tests for speaking skills assessment offer benefits for reciprocal communication, it is not always possible from an administrative point of view. As an online conference and webinar tool, ZoomUs (2019) is a good option for video conferencing for L2 speaking assessment. Other voice recording tools can also be used for L2 speaking assessment such as audacity, odeo and yackpack. Students can record their responses or prompts through these online tools and language teachers can evaluate individually or implement these threads to classroom discussion. Gipps (2005) says one of the main issues in technology-enhanced assessment is marking or scoring students' tests which are carried out by human action. Implementation of artificial intelligence and its effective use may diminish scoring and the burden of marking in language assessment.

Video-conferencing technology has removed the physical barrier to help human being to communication with people from all over the world. Interaction with electronic devices can be made and supported by artificial intelligence (AI) technology to carry out various daily tasks such as creating reminders. AI has become a part of our lives. For example, self-parking cars have been launched. Another example is the robot Sofia. She can answer people's questions, talk to them and even joke. In this respect, artificial intelligence implementation in language testing can decrease human effort and workload in scoring and marking. An increasing amount of supplier companies (Speexx, Busuu, Duolingo) provide AI-enabled language-learning applications for hundreds of languages to businesses and the public. However, MIT researchers figured out that AI in language assessment is biased and unfair (Hao, 2019). This result stems from the fact that it cannot detect differences in accents, pauses, and cultural context in the tested language. The implementation of AI in language assessment is a controversial and complicated issue because of various reasons.

SOLUTIONS AND RECOMMENDATIONS

It is believed that digital assessment will improve language learning and support meaningful experiences for learners. This chapter has presented a non-systematic review of the related literature on language assessment through ICT and the following recommendations are made to help a smooth integration of digital tools in relation to language assessment.

There are possible ways to integrate technological tools into language assessment that are stated by the scholars. These are as follow:

- The foundation of evaluation tasks may be multimedia or interactive components of the internet
- Internet evaluation and cooperative or group evaluation can be performed via chat rooms and panels. Peer assessment can be carried out with these digital tools and environments
- A transcript can be utilized to evaluate students' participation in online discussions
- Questions and problems can be posed to students through discussion boards. Assignments and feedback can be sent through e-mail that is a helpful, convenient, and easy way to deliver (Gipps, 2005)
- The students' answers can be registered via computers, tablets or podlets, and employees can submit feedback online regardless of whether the labeling is automated or not

As has been discussed above, technology-enhanced assessment has pros and cons. It provides the following benefits:

- Greater diversity and authenticity in evaluation layout
- Improved student involvement by interactive formative evaluations with adaptive reviews
- Adjustability in timing and location of assessments
- The capture of broader abilities and characteristics. For instance, by simulating, e-portfolios, and interactive matches, not evaluated merely by other means
- Efficient submission, marking, moderation, and data storage processes
- Accurate, exact outcomes with the likelihood of combining human and computer marking
- Immediate feedback
- Increased possibilities for students to respond to feedback through tools. For example, e-portfolios
- Innovative strategies centered on creative media use, online self-assessment, and peer review
- Accurate curriculum design and implementation (JISC, 2010)

In addition to these benefits of using technology for language assessments, it is evident that innovation takes place when teachers, students, and test developers realize technology as a tool to develop new methods and approaches for testing (Chapelle & Douglas, 2006).

Fist, innovation occurs in dialogue and communication via online interaction. Time constraints and distance can be overcome through online interaction which is possible using blogs, forums, voice boards, and e-mail. In addition, teachers can provide feedback to students for better learning with these tools. This can be provided quickly through interactive tools such as interconnected mobile phones when students make a mistake in formative assessment. Another innovative side of using technology in language assessment is its authenticity that language skills can be practiced through online simulations, video technologies or virtual reality environments. Speed and ease of processing is a further innovation. This allows testing systems to provide feedback to language learners, students and curriculum developers. Consequently, data transfer between institutional systems occurs without delay (JISC, 2010).

To sum up, technology offers a vast amount of opportunities in terms of language teaching and learning and assessment. However, the main concern of language teachers and test developers should be to select appropriate digital materials and components suitable for their students. Additionally, the aim is not to design costly digital systems which only work for numerical data in language assessment. Rather to shift digital language assessment into a learning experience which is long-lasting and effective. In line with the growing trend and interest in exploring the internet, technology-based tools and environments for assessment purposes of foreign language learning, in the present chapter language's assessment through ICT is discussed within the framework of related research. Besides, innovative digital language assessment tools are presented. How to implement and use these tools are discussed in terms of language skills. In addition, related questions were asked throughout the chapter to make readers more concerned with the issue. It is expected that the readers will search for further information to answer the questions.

FUTURE RESEARCH DIRECTIONS

This study highlighted the integration of computer technologies such as visual, audio, animation, simulation, virtual reality or eye tracking, etc. content into test content (Yu & Zhang, 2017). A further study can explore the impacts of research innovative multimodal and interactive tasks, the inter-operability of such tasks on different platforms and their effects on the performance of testers (Yu & Zhang, 2017). This chapter just did a non-systematic analysis rather an empirical study. A further study can be carried out with innovative eye-tracking devices to interpret and observe students' eye movements during language testing. These devices can be used in various test atmospheres and provide opportunities to deter and detect students' irrelevant behaviors or cognitive process (Dolgunsöz, 2016; Yu, He, & Isaacs, 2017). Another research area of the language assessment field is comparability studies which should focus on comparability between different digital platforms and multimodal tasks and these interactive tasks' effects on test takers' performances (Yu & Zhang, 2017). Another point is unfortunately, speech recognition programs and devices don't recognize advanced level of language use and research should be carried out for speech recognition (Chapelle & Voss, 2017). In this sense, future studies can investigate conversational features, such as length of turn, turn interruptions/overlaps, and gaps between turns (Nakatsuhara et al. 2017). In addition, another research can be carried out on computer literacy such as test takers' response to time, keyboarding speed etc. (Setzer, Wise, van den Heuvel, & Ling, 2013).

CONCLUSION

This chapter has presented language assessment through ICT by giving a non-systematic analysis of the related research. It indicated that computer-adaptive language testing or computer-mediated language testing may give language learners a more positive test experience by diminishing their anxiety levels, especially regarding speaking skill performance. Another positive side of these tests is that it increases efficiency and flexibility in test administration and scoring. AI indirectly led to a decrease in human workload. Despite AI having been received negatively in language testing, it has become a part of it.

The chapter also showed that one another positive side of the new testing trends is that providing feedback automatically or more easily is not a difficult issue anymore. This is because learners can receive instant, detailed and automated feedback due to their performances. Therefore, future language assessment will go beyond one-time testing and a model, to more personalized, motivated and engaged learning and testing experience (Chan, Bax, & Weir. 2017).

The chapter indicated that recent studies have focused on the effectiveness of technological tools, software programs or interactive websites on language assessment. Additionally, there are research gaps in investigation of software related, language learner related and comparability related issues which were discussed in previous heading. Other contributions of this non-systematic review of related literature are presenting innovative and recent assessment types in language pedagogy, presenting effective and well-designed digital tools and digital platforms which support technology-enhanced language testing, and providing solutions to possible problems of technology-enhanced language assessment.

The chapter concluded that developed technological tools, software programs or interactive websites can be used to promote student engagement, motivation, and ultimately enhance the quality of the testing experience for language learners. This is because language testing should support language learning during the testing process as well. Additionally, the chapter suggested what the previous scholars indicated that formative assessment, dynamic assessment, interactionist dynamic assessment, interventionist dynamic assessment, virtual environments for language testing, computer-based dynamic assessment should be implemented in language classrooms as testing methods (Fabera & Visscherb, 2018; Ockey et. al, 2017; Teo, 2012).

REFERENCES

AJE. (2019). Available online: https://www.aje.com/

Balçıkanlı, C. (2010). Learner Autonomy in Language Learning: Student Teachers' Beliefs. *The Australian Journal of Teacher Education, 35*(1). doi:10.14221/ajte.2010v35n1.8

Baleni, Z. (2015). Online formative assessment in higher education: Its pros and cons. *The Electronic Journal of e-Learning, 13*(4), 228-236.

Barker, J., & Gossman, P. (2013). The learning impact of a virtual learning environment: Students' views. *Teacher Education Advancement Network Journal, 5*(2), 19–38.

Bennett, R. E. (2002a). *Inexorable and inevitable: the continuing story of technology and assessment.* Paper presented at 28th Conference of the International Association for Educational Assessment, Hong Kong.

Bennett, R. E. (2002b). Using electronic assessment to measure student performance (Issue Brief); partly based on: How the Internet will help large-scale assessment reinvent itself. *Education Policy Analysis Archives, 9*(5).

Bennett, R. E. (2008). *Technology for large-scale assessment.* ETS Report No. RM-08-10. Princeton, NJ: Educational Testing Service.

Bennett, R. E. (2015). The changing nature of educational assessment. *Review of Research in Education, 39*(1), 370–407. doi:10.3102/0091732X14554179

Benson, P. (2001). *Teaching and researching autonomy in language learning*. London: Longman.

Benson, P. (2011). *Teaching and researching autonomy* (2nd ed.). London: Pearson Education.

Black, P., & Wiliam, D. (1998). Assessment and classroom learning. *Assessment in Education: Principles, Policy & Practice*, *5*(1), 7–74. doi:10.1080/0969595980050102

Blake, R., Wilson, N. L., Cetto, M., & Pardo-Ballester, C. (2008). Measuring oral proficiency in distance, face-to-face, and blended classrooms. *Language Learning & Technology*, *12*(3), 114–127.

Capper, C. A., & Frattura, E. M. (2009). *Meeting the needs of students of all abilities: How leaders go beyond inclusion*. Thousand Oaks, CA: Corwin Press.

Chalhoub-Deville, M. (2001). Language testing and technology: Past and future. *Language Learning & Technology*, *5*(2), 95–98.

Chan, S., Bax, S., & Weir, C. (2017). *Researching participants taking IELTS Academic Writing Task 2 (AWT2) in paper mode and in computer mode in terms of score equivalence, cognitive validity and other factors.* IELTS Research Reports Online Series 2017/14. British Council/Cambridge English Language Assessment/IDP: IELTS Australia. Retrieved from https://www.ielts.org/-/media/research-reports/ielts_online_rr_2017-4.ashx

Chapelle, C. A., & Douglas, D. (2006). *Assessing language through computer technology*. Cambridge, UK: Cambridge University Press. doi:10.1017/CBO9780511733116

Chapelle, C. A., & Voss, E. (2016). 20 years of technology and language assessment in Language Learning &Technology. *Language Learning & Technology*, *20*(2), 116–128.

Chen, C.-F. E., & Cheng, W.-Y. E. (2008). Beyond the design of automated writing evaluation: Pedagogical practices and perceived learning effectiveness in EFL writing classes. *Language Learning & Technology*, *12*(2), 94–112.

Craig, D. A., & Kim, J. (2010). Anxiety and performance in video-conferenced and face-to-face oral interviews. *Multimedia-Assisted Language Learning*, *13*(3), 9–32. doi:10.15702/mall.2010.13.3.9

Dede, C., Salzman, M., Loftin, R. B., & Ash, K. (2000). The design of immersive virtual learning environments: Fostering deep understandings of complex scientific knowledge. In J. M. Jacobson & R. B. Kozma (Eds.), *Innovations in science and mathematics education: Advanced designs for technologies of learning* (pp. 361–413). Mahwah, NJ: Lawrence Erlbaum Associates.

Dolgunsöz, E. (2016). Using eye-tracking to measure lexical inferences and its effects on reading rate during EFL reading. *Dil ve Dilbilimi Çalışmaları Dergisi*, *12*(1), 63–78.

Dudeney, G., & Hockly, N. (2007). *How to Teach English with Technology*. Pearson Education Limited.

Early, P., & Swanson, P. B. (2008). Technology for oral assessment. In C. M. Cherry & C. Wilkerson (Eds.), *Dimension* (pp. 39–48). Valdosta, GA: SCOLT Publications.

Edmodo. (2019). Available online: https://www.edmodo.com

Fabera, J.M., & Visscherb, A.J. (2018). The effects of a digital formative assessment tool on spelling achievement: Results of a randomized experiment. *Computers & Education.*

Flipgrid. (2019). Available online: https://info.flipgrid.com/

García Laborda, J. (2007). On the net: Introducing standardized EFL/ESL exams. *Language Learning & Technology, 11*(2), 3–9.

Gipps, C. V. (2005). What is the role for ICT-based assessment in universities? *Studies in Higher Education, 30*(2), 171–180. doi:10.1080/03075070500043176

GoClass. (2019). Available online: https://www.goclass.com/

Godwin-Jones, R. (2008). Web-writing 2.0: Enabling, documenting, and assessing writing online. *Language Learning & Technology, 12*(2), 7–13.

Green, T. D., Brown, A., & Robinson, L. (2008). *Making the Most of the Web in your Classroom: A Teacher's Guide to Blogs, Podcasts, Wikis, Pages and Sites*. Thousand Oaks: Corwin.

Hao, K. (2019). This is how AI bias really happens—and why it's so hard to fix. *MIT Technology*. Review retrieved from https://www.technologyreview.com/s/612876/this-is-how-ai-bias-really-happensand-why-its-so-hard-to-fix/

Haynes, S. R., Spence, L., & Lenze, L. (2009). Scenario-based assessment of learning experiences. *Proceedings of the 39th ASEE/IEEE Frontiers in Education Conference.*

JISC. (2010). *Effective Assessment in a Digital Age*. Retrieved from www.jisc.ac.uk/digiassess

Kiddle, T., & Kormos, J. (2011). The effect of mode of response on a semi-direct test of oral proficiency. *Language Assessment Quarterly*, *8*(4), 342–360. doi:10.1080/15434303.2011.613503

Kim, J., & Craig, D. A. (2012). Validation of a video conferenced speaking test. *Computer Assisted Language Learning, 25*(3), 257–275. doi:10.1080/09588221.2011.649482

LessonUp. (2019). Available online: https://www.lessonup.com/en/

Litman, D., Strik, H., & Lim, S. G. (2018). Speech Technologies and the Assessment of Second Language Speaking: Approaches, Challenges, and Opportunities. *Language Assessment Quarterly, 15*(3), 294–309. doi:10.1080/15434303.2018.1472265

McFarlane, A. (2001). Perspectives on the relationships between ICT and assessment. *Journal of Computer Assisted Learning, 17*(3), 227–235. doi:10.1046/j.0266-4909.2001.00177.x

McFarlane, A. (2002). *Educating the inheritors of the information age. Inaugural Lecture, 18 November 2002*. Bristol: University of Bristol.

Mitul, M. (2018). *Artificial Intelligence in Testing: Tools and Advantages.* Retrieved from https://maruti-tech.com/artificial-intelligence-in-testing/

Mosquera, L. H. (2017). Impact of implementing a virtual learning environment (VLE) in the EFL classroom. *Íkala, revista de lenguaje y cultura, 22*(3), 479-498.

Mullamaa, K. (2010). ICT in language learning – benefits and methodological implications. *International Education Studies, 3*(1), 38–44. doi:10.5539/ies.v3n1p38

Nakatsuhara, F., Inoue, C., Berry, V., & Galaczi, E. (2017). Exploring the Use of Video-Conferencing Technology in the Assessment of Spoken Language: A Mixed-Methods Study. *Language Assessment Quarterly, 14*(1), 1–18. doi:10.1080/15434303.2016.1263637

Nicol, D. (2007). *Principles of good assessment and feedback: Theory and practice.* Paper presented at the REAP International Online Conference on Assessment Design for Learner Responsibility.

Ockey, G. J., Gu, L., & Keehner, M. (2017). Web-based virtual environments for facilitating assessment of L2 oral communication ability. *Language Assessment Quarterly, 14*(4), 346–359. doi:10.1080/15434303.2017.1400036

Paker, T., & Höl, D. (2012). Attitudes and perceptions of the students and instructors towards testing speaking communicatively. *Pamukkale Universitesi Egitim Fakultesi Dergisi, 32*(2), 13–24. doi:10.9779/PUJE544

Pear Deck. (2019). Available online: https://www.peardeck.com

PebblePad. (2019). Available online: https://www.pebblepad.co.uk/

Pellegrino, J., & Quellmalz, E. (2010). Perspectives on the Integration of Technology and Assessment. *Journal of Research on Technology in Education, 43*(2), 119–134. doi:10.1080/15391523.2010.10782565

Quellmalz, E. S., Timms, M. J., & Buckley, B. (2010). The promise of simulation-based science assessment: The calipers project. *International Journal of Learning Technology, 5*(3), 243–263. doi:10.1504/IJLT.2010.037306

Quizlet. (2019). Available online: https://quizlet.com

Russell, M., & Haney, W. (2000). Bridging the gap between testing and technology in schools. *Education Policy Analysis Archives, 8*(19), 19. doi:10.14507/epaa.v8n19.2000

Salehi, H., & Salehi, Z. (2012). Integration of ICT in language teaching: Challenges and barriers. *In Proceedings of the 3rd International Conference on e-Education, e-Business, e- Management Learning, 27*, 215–219.

Santiago, D., King, T., & Clarke, P. (2018). *AI-Driven Test Generation: Machines Learning from Human Testers.* Retrieved from https://www.pnsqc.org

Sawaki, Y. (2012). Technology in language testing. In G. Fulcher & F. Davidson (Eds.), *The Routledge handbook of language testing* (pp. 426–437). Abingdon, UK: Routledge.

Schoology. (2019). Available online: https://www.schoology.com/

Setzer, J. C., Wise, S. L., van den Heuvel, J. R., & Ling, G. (2013). An Investigation of examinee test-taking effort on a large-scale assessment. *Applied Measurement in Education*, *26*(1), 34–49. doi:10.1080/08957347.2013.739453

Spiral. (2019). Available online: https://spiral.ac/

Teo, A. (2012). Promoting EFL students' inferential reading skills through computerized dynamic assessment. *Language Learning & Technology*, *16*(3), 10–20.

Tomlinson, C. (1999). *The Differentiated Classroom: Responding to the Needs of All Learners*. Alexandria, VA: Association for Supervision and Curriculum Development.

Vincent, T. (2016). *Know Students Better: A Visual Guide to Formative Assessment Tools.* Retrieved from https://learninginhand.com/blog/know

Walker, A., & White, G. (2013). *Technology Enhanced Language Learning. Connecting Theory and Practice*. Oxford, UK: Oxford University Press.

Wang, L. (2005). The advantages of using technology in second language education: Technology integration in foreign language teaching demonstrates the shift from a behavioral to a constructivist learning approach. *T.H.E. Journal*, *32*(10), 39–42.

Webpa. (2019). Available online: https://webpa.lboro.ac.uk/login.php

Weller, M. (2002). Assessment issues on a web-based course. *Assessment & Evaluation in Higher Education*, *27*(2), 109–116. doi:10.1080/02602930220128698

Yildirim, G., Elban, M., & Yildirim, S. (2018). Analysis of use of virtual reality technologies in history education: A case study. *Asian J. Educ. Train.*, *4*(2), 62–69. doi:10.20448/journal.522.2018.42.62.69

Yu, G., He, L., & Isaacs, T. (2017). *The Cognitive Processes of taking IELTS Academic Writing Task 1: An Eye-tracking Study*. IELTS Research Reports Online Series, British Council, IDP: IELTS Australia and Cambridge English Language Assessment. Available online: www.ielts.org/ /media/researchreports/ielts_online_rr_2017-2.ashx

Yu, G., & Zhang, J. (2017). Computer-Based English Language Testing in China: Present and Future. *Language Assessment Quarterly*, *14*(2), 177–188. doi:10.1080/15434303.2017.1303704

ZoomUs. (2019). Available online: https://zoom.us/hc/en-us

ADDITIONAL READING

Aygun, S., & Aydin, S. (2016). The use of e-portfolios in EFL writing: A review of literature. International Association of Research in Foreign Language Education and Applied Linguistics. *ELT Research Journal*, *5*(3), 205–217.

Burston, J., & Monville-Burston, M. (1995). Practical design and implementation considerations of a computer-adaptive foreign language test: The Monash/Melbourne French CAT. *CALICO Journal*, *13*(1), 26–46.

Chapelle, C. A., Cotos, E., & Lee, J. (2015). Diagnostic assessment with automated writing evaluation: A look at validity arguments for new classroom assessments. *Language Testing*, *32*(3), 385–405. doi:10.1177/0265532214565386

Chapelle, C. A., & Voss, E. (2017). Utilizing Technology in Language Assessment. In E. Shohamy, I. Or, & S. May (Eds.), *Language Testing and Assessment. Encyclopedia of Language and Education* (3rd ed.). Cham: Springer. doi:10.1007/978-3-319-02261-1_10

Davies, P. (2000). Computerised Peer-Assessment, Innovations in Education and Training International. *IETI*, *37*(4), 346–355.

Eckes, T. (2014). Examining testlet effects in the Test DaF listening section: A testlet response theory modeling approach. *Language Testing*, *31*(1), 39–61. doi:10.1177/0265532213492969

Ferrari, R. (2015). Writing narrative style literature reviews. *Medical Writing*, *24*(4), 230–235. doi:10.1179/2047480615Z.000000000329

Heinz, P. J. (2004). Towards Enhanced Second Language Reading Comprehension Assessment: Computerized versus Manual Scoring of Written Recall Protocols. *Reading in a Foreign Language*, *16*(2), 97–124.

Hoque, M. E. (2013). *Computers to help with conversations: Affective framework to enhance human nonverbal skills* (Doctoral dissertation). Available from ProQuest Dissertations and Theses database.

Jacobs, E. L. (2001). The effects of adding dynamic assessment components to a computerized pre-school language screening test. *Communication Disorders Quarterly*, *22*(4), 217–226. doi:10.1177/152574010102200407

Palomo-Duarte, M., Berns, A., Dodero, J. M., & Cejas, A. (2014). Foreign language learning using a gamificated APP to support peer-assessment. In Proceedings of *TEEM' 14: Second international conference on technological ecosystem for enhancing multiculturality, Salamanca, Volume 1*. 10.1145/2669711.2669927

Papp, S., & Walczak, A. (2016). The development and validation of a computer-based test of English for young learners: Cambridge English young learners. In M. Nikolov (Ed.), Assessing young learners of English: Global and local perspectives (Educational linguistics, Vol. 25, pp. 139–190). New York: Springer.

Park, K. (2014). Corpora and language assessment: The state of the art. *Language Assessment Quarterly*, *11*(1), 27–44. doi:10.1080/15434303.2013.872647

Race, P., Brown, S., & Smith, B. (2005). *500 Tips on Assessment*. Abingdon: Routledge Falmer.

Salmon, G. (2002). E-tivities: The Key to Active Online Learning. London; Sterling, VA: Kogan Page Limited.

KEY TERMS AND DEFINITIONS

Artificial Intelligence (AI): The technology which has the ability of a computer program or a machine to think and learn.

Computer Adaptive Testing: The application of computers to assessment processes, including the delivery of tests, the capture of responses and marking by either computer or human marker.

Digital Formative Assessment: A type of assessment made through providing immediate feedback in online environments.

ICT: Technologies that provide access to information through telecommunications.

Learning Management Systems or Course Management Systems (LMS/CMS): A software application or Web-based technology used to plan, implement, and assess a specific learning process.

Scenario-Based Assessment (SBA): A technology-based approach which assesses learners in a meaningful and purposeful context. It can be used to assess various language skills such as speaking and writing.

Virtual Learning Environments (VLE): An online system comprising a range of tools to support learning and the management of learning.

Chapter 4
Conceptualizing Formative Blended Assessment (FBA) in Saudi EFL

Mansoor S. Almalki
https://orcid.org/0000-0002-3214-9876
Taif University, Saudi Arabia

Paul Gruba
University of Melbourne, Australia

ABSTRACT

This chapter sets out a conceptual framework for the design and use of 'blended assessments' that seek to create formative activities that can be characterized by shifting modalities of presentation, variations in time and action, and moves from individual to group work. The study's framing is built upon longitudinal participatory action research based on the research questions. In addition to auto-ethnographic observations, 13 Saudi participants—three course coordinators, seven instructors, and three students—were asked to participate in focus groups and individual interviews. Using qualitative data analysis software, three core characteristics of formative blended assessment were identified: (1) multi-modal activities, flexibility, and peer encouragement, for example, were seen to be an 'advantage'; (2) alignment of pedagogies and assessment tasks were perceived in a 'compatibility' theme; and (3) the possibility of dishonest behaviors and administrative challenges were classed under 'complexity'.

INTRODUCTION

In line with global trends, adopting blended approaches to English as a Foreign Language (EFL) programs in the Saudi higher education system have been met with a series of challenges that include, for example, lack of teacher training, a hesitancy to shift away from traditional pedagogies, and poor support for infrastructure (Al-Qahtani & Higgins, 2013). The integration of digital tools in face-to-face settings, nonetheless "has clearly emerged as the most promising use of technology for second language learn-

DOI: 10.4018/978-1-7998-3062-7.ch004

ing" (Chapelle, 2016, p. xi). One key area of promise, the integrated use of technology in assessment practices to create 'blended assessments', has received little attention to date. Because of their alignment with current approaches in blended language learning; however, such assessments have the potential to be a powerful agent of innovation in the Saudi context: assessment practices, as has been argued, can truly drive the 21st century curriculum (Wyatt-Smith & Cumming, 2009).

Blended learning offers greater choice compared to other methods (Littlejohn and Pegler, 2007). Blended learning method can be an answer to the growing issues related to curriculum delivery, access and academic program quality (Picciano, 2009). Blending different approaches in the current teaching and learning programs in higher education can have positive outcomes and support university students with greater flexibility without any limitation of time and place (Vaughan, 2007). Blended courses are observed increasing student engagement in their learning, enhance teacher-student interaction and add flexibility in the curriculum through improvement opportunities. Students have a problem with taking greater responsibility for their learning, partly through gaining competency in the new technologies. Faculty members also find it hard to develop blended courses due to a lack of time, support and resources, and they also have to gain competency in ICT applications (Vaughan, 2007). For the institution, blended learning is an opportunity to expand educational boundary and reduce the problems currently arising.

The rationale for conducting this study is to investigate the characteristics of blended learning and to analyse the data and make recommendations to allow the advantages of ICT in blended learning in Saudi context. Currently, the traditional system is unable to respond, and there is insufficient time and commitment by the universities to plan and build for the future. Therefore, an initiative leading towards blended learning is promising. The chapter's aim is look at the usefulness and influence of blended learning on teaching and learning. Therefore, in this chapter, the design and use of blended assessments are investigated in a study grounded in a key question: Situated in the Saudi context, what are the language course coordinators', instructors' and students' understandings and preferences in the design of formative blended assessment tasks and activities for language learning programs?

BACKGROUND

This section reviews the literature on blended learning starting with the definition of blended learning. It highlights the area of innovation needed, and impetus for the innovation.

Definition of Blended learning

According to Mandl and Kopp (2006), blended learning is the felicitous combination of the benefits e-learning offers with the advantages of traditional face-to-face-learning settings. In other words, it is the combination of learning in class and learning online in formal education. In the literature, term blended learning is defined as hybrid, blended and mixed modes (Swan, 2009). Blended learning in this chapter refers to the notion that students generally attend face-to-face classes and have online access to the course content and activities.

Area of Innovation

It is important to discuss the nature of the curriculum and assessment of EFL in terms of the challenges that the instructors and course coordinators face. Some of the challenges in EFL education are the lack of student motivation, underachievement, poor pedagogical strategies, high stakes testing, and a lack of qualified or capable instructors.

In Saudi Arabia, English instructors can be classified into three groups: (a) native speakers, (b) bilinguals, and (c) instructors from Pakistan and India (Khan, 2011). The native speakers are generally considered less qualified because their credentials mainly involve passing CELTA or TESOL. Bilingual instructors usually originate from Egypt and other Arab countries. Despite the insights of Arab culture, bilingual instructors are often not effective because of their lack of motivation. Instructors from regions such as India and Pakistan are certified and are considered to be the most effective; however, they lack an understanding of the Arab culture, which affects their usefulness.

University-level English is poor in Saudi Arabia, particularly in terms of writing (McMullen, 2009). Learning English is difficult for students because of anxiety over the complexities of the language, which sometimes lead to a lack of motivation to improve their English language skills (Mohammed, 2011). EFL in primary, middle, and secondary schooling is important in Saudi Arabia. Students of EFL in Saudi Arabia at the college level have moved through an EFL curriculum that starts during the first years of primary school. Only 45 minutes a week is dedicated to English at primary school level. However, as the student progresses into intermediate and secondary levels, their EFL time allowance is increased to approximately four hours every week (Elyas & Picard, 2010).

Blended designs for assessment are significant in Saudi Arabia because the Saudi government is currently working on improving the education system, specifically in regard to the English proficiency of students. The attempt to improve the English proficiency of college students in Saudi Arabia is prioritized in Saudi because of the acknowledgment that proficiency in English is needed in order to be competitive in the increasingly globalized world (Elyas & Picard, 2010).

Despite the support of the government towards English education in the curriculum at the tertiary level, success has still not completely achieved (Khan, 2011). Some of the problems encountered by Saudi Arabian leaders include the lack of incorporation of IT in language education, lack of opportunities for language exposure in the target language of English, and a lack of experience of instructors and students in incorporating technology in the classroom (Khan, 2011; Mohammed, 2011). These barriers suggest a need for further policies and practices to address the improvement of English proficiency in college students.

Our search of the literature suggests that blended designs for assessment have never been examined within the context of Saudi Arabia, and there is a seeming lack of empirical research on how blended assessment operates in the EFL system. It is intended that the results of this study will provide new information on how the design principles of blended assessment may be applicable in EFL in college education in Saudi Arabia. An initial step, however, is to explore the language learning metaphors currently being used.

Blended assessments differ from traditional measures of language proficiency in number of ways. Unlike measures created in static 'paper and pencil' formats designed for a single use at a set point in time (e.g., Hill, 2012; Jamieson, 2011), blended assessments consist of variations in modality, time and action, as well as differences across individual and group work (Gruba & Hinkelman, 2012). For example, whereas a traditional assessment would be presented on paper to test writing in class for an individual student, a blended design would allow the student to write collaboratively with others through a networked online tool for the length of term project. Given that project-based language learning prepares students for complex future work (Dooly & Sadler, 2016), it is now clear that a focus on blended assessment designs are required to spur innovation.

Based on experience in Saudi higher education, we argue that there is strong demand for not only for technology integration but also for assessment practices that offer reliable, tamper-free evaluations of the language proficiency. Indeed, from our perspective, there appears to be an increasing need in Saudi Arabia for assessments of language proficiency that can be productively used for the purposes of institutional enrolment, employment, and other certification purposes.

Impetus for the Innovation

Work on the principled design, use and revision of blended assessment is needed for three reasons: (1) improved recognition of new literacies abilities amongst contemporary students to prepare them for 21st century work (Kress, 2009; Motteram, 2016); (2) constructive alignment with prevailing global trends in technology integration (Horizon Report, 2017); (3) clearer focus and development of language teacher capabilities (Haines, 2016).

According to this chapter, reflecting on various theories of innovation implementation can help provide explanations for shortcomings of pre-existing practices in Saudi Arabia. For example, this chapter believes there are significant barriers to ensuring uniformity and standardisation of assessment practices, and one of these barriers is the absence of enforced regional, state, and national guidelines for language assessment. Without these guidelines and the enforcement of any overarching protocol for assessment of language, the classroom instructor is left with almost no framework. In some circumstances, heads of department may offer leadership in this area. However, not very often than in our experience, the classroom instructor is left unchecked (and unaided) in the instruction and assessment of language.

While innovations such as blended assessment offer new ways to evaluate students' competence in language, these interventions also provide evaluation of the competence of instructors of language. Some instructors may consider this threatening. However, this chapter can only see such reform as positive, and through this chapter, this chapter aims to indicate this.

MAIN FOCUS OF THE CHAPTER

The framing of this chapter is built upon longitudinal participatory action research based primarily on qualitative accounts investigating core characteristics of formative blended assessment in technology-enhanced language learning within its real-life context from the participants' perspective. In purely quantitative studies, participants have more opportunity to reveal their thoughts and feelings through qualitative methods, such as interviews, than by simply ticking boxes in a questionnaire, especially since participants' thoughts are "unobservable construct" which is difficult to measure quantitatively (Dörnyei and Ushioda, 2011, p. 193). Thus, in order to look at the nature of students to address the research questions, qualitative data were gathered through auto-ethnographic observations, focus group and interviews to provide potentially rich data. One of the main aims of applying a qualitative approach in the study is to explore and understand the blended learning assessment process. It also helps to interpret the outcomes to build, as Creswell (2013) puts it, a holistic picture based on the researchers' interpretations and the participants' views about the phenomenon to find answers to the research questions. Another aim for using qualitative methods in the study is to obtain an 'inside view of the phenomenon, getting as close as possible to the subject of the research to collect resonant, fertile data" (Walliman, 2005, p. 247).

In addition to auto-ethnographic observations, the study presented in this chapter asked thirteen Saudi participants – three course coordinators, seven instructors and three students – to participate in focus groups and individual interviews. Using qualitative data analysis software, the study identified three core characteristics of formative blended assessment: (1) multi-modal activities, flexibility, and peer encouragement, for example, were seen to be an 'advantage'; (2) alignment of pedagogies and assessment tasks were perceived in a 'compatibility' theme; and (3) the possibility of dishonest behaviors and administrative challenges were classed under 'complexity'. Taken together, these themes represent a conceptual point of departure for the ongoing development in blended approaches that highlights the integration of technology and assessment in Saudi language programs.

Participants Selection

The first step in recruiting participants was to determine their suitability and readiness to proceed through all the study. The study deemed this as important and necessary so that they could get a deeper understanding of the phenomenon being investigated, and from all possible relevant perspectives. Moreover, the study tried to make sure that potential participants had experience with technology in language teaching (for the course coordinators and instructors) and experience with language assessment (for the students). For the ease of data collection, it was also imperative for the authors as researchers to consider the students' language proficiency. Therefore, those who seemed to be advanced in language proficiency (to the extent that they would be able to be interviewed in English) were invited to participate.

A total number of ten staff members and three students showed personal and professional interest in participating in this study. The participants were divided into three distinct groups of course coordinators, instructors, and students because, as this study was initiating innovation, it was imperative to consider the viewpoints of all stakeholders, as these viewpoints might differ in some ways. The course coordinators are the managers, the instructors are the facilitators, and the students are the end users of the learning system.

Procedure

This study started the data collection by inviting potential participants to join the study. The study asked a selected number of potential participants to fill out entry surveys and provide demographic and other related information. The aim of this procedure was to identify the suitability and appropriateness of the potential participants to join to the study. Having handed out the surveys, the study discussed the questions and made sure they were understood, especially by the BA students.

Thirteen participants (7 instructors, 3 course coordinators, 3 students) completed the entry surveys and showed readiness to participate in the study. The entry surveys were collected from the participants over three days.

The semi-structured interviews took place at a Saudi university at different times. These interviews took more time to complete than the previous stage because all participants were engaged in their teaching/studying responsibilities and their schedules had to be accommodated to avoid possible disruptions to their activities. All instructors and students were invited to come to the office allocated for this study, which was convenient for all of them. The course coordinators asked the authors to come to their workplace for interviewing them as they found this easier with their schedules.

Each participant was asked questions relating to blended learning and blended assessment conceptualizations and perceptions; in particular, about the language skills that they thought should be assessed in EFL using blended assessment. Participants noticeably preferred the productive skills of English (speaking and writing). This is connected to the fact that most of the study participants raised the cheating issue as an ongoing factor that may hinder the effectiveness of BA in their institution. They believed that in speaking and extended writing it would be easier for instructors to determine the validity of the assessment. Also, after initial assessment in these areas, instructors would have some idea of their students' performance levels and their level of English, and so cheating opportunities in assessing speaking and writing online would be limited.

Data Analysis

The set of three "innovation initiation" characteristics that are set out in Rogers and Shoemaker (1971, p. 15) were adopted as our central framework for analysis:

1. Relative advantage: the degree to which blended designs for assessments are perceived as better than the designs they are replacing.
2. Compatibility: the degree to which blended designs for assessments are perceived as consistent with existing values and past experiences, and able to meet the needs of potential adopters.
3. Complexity: the degree to which blended designs for assessments seen to be difficult to understand and use.

Using this core framework, a thematic analysis of the qualitative data with the goal of identifying patterns and trends (Miles, Huberman, & Saldana, 2012) were conducted. After a series of analytical iterations, four main themes emerged: (a) multi-approach, (b) encouragement, (c) formative assessment, and (d) challenges.

FINDINGS, SOLUTIONS AND RECOMMENDATIONS

This section both presents findings and discusses them based on the related literature. As shown in this section, the Multi-approach theme contains the most clusters, as well as the second greatest number of coded examples (18). The greatest number of coded examples falls under the Encouragement theme (19), followed by Multi-approach (18), Formative assessment (16) and Challenges (8). In the table, Relative Advantage, Compatibility and Complexity are listed as types of innovations likely to enhance or reduce the possibility of adoption.

Relative Advantage of Blended Assessments

According to Rogers and Shoemaker (1971), the 'relative advantage' of an innovation occurs when stakeholders see that the proposed change, if implemented, will be preferable to what it will be replacing. In Saudi context, study participants indicated that blended assessments could be better than current

Table 1. Multi-faceted nature of blended assessment

Factor	*Definition*	*Sample data*
Integration	Traditional and online approaches are merged.	*"Blended [learning and assessment] means when we blend two types of approaches to teach and where we provide such a nice atmosphere where we blend and we present a very cosy and harmonious atmosphere of learning to the students"* (Soliman, interview 7).
Learner focus	Assessment design is grounded in perceived student needs.	*"Things are moving from [a] traditional or teacher-centred classroom to [a] student or learner-centred classroom, giving autonomy to the students or the learners to take initiative"* (William, interview 2).
Novelty	New ideas and approaches are implemented in EFL assessment tasks.	*"This is a new concept and most of the teachers, especially who are teaching in the EFL situation, now they are fully obsessed with the idea of blended approaches"* (Jack, interview 1).

approaches if designs were multifaceted and included considerations of technological integration, learner focus, and conceptual novelty (Table 1).

A majority of the participants defined blended designs for learning and assessment as the mixing or integration of two approaches, face-to-face instruction and online instruction. Soliman, an EFL instructor, defined blended learning assessment in terms of the mixing of traditional and modern approaches to meet the learning needs of students. He said, "as the name is really suggestive, so blended approaches mean when we blend two types of approaches to teach and where we provide such a nice atmosphere where we blend and present in a very cosy and harmonious atmosphere of learning to the students" (Soliman, interview 7). As indicated by their perceptive and deductive extrapolations of the meaning of blended approaches, a lack of formal exposure to the core concepts and foundations of blended assessment points to the fact that it is seen as new and innovative concept to ESL instructors in this context.

The second theme, encouragement, pertains to ways in which blended assessments may help motivate students to be more involved in their studies of English. Factors which encourage students to be better motivated include interactivity, the possibility of feedback, and the availability of resources to students (Table 2).

Table 2. Encouragement as a relative advantage

Factor	*Definition*	*Sample data*
Interactive	Refers to the interactive nature of blended assessment.	*"Outside of class it's even better; it also gives them opportunities to practice English with other people"* (Ali, interview 8).
Feedback	Refers to the feedback that students receive from blended assessment.	*"I send what is called the feedback along with the result to the students"* (Sami, interview 4).
Resources	Refers to the availability of resources useful to students.	*"I think the technology is providing a lot of resources"* (William, interview 2).

Blended assessment was perceived to be interactive. It was seen as providing students with the opportunity to relate with ease and facility to their own and other instructors. Interactivity can also be achieved even when students are alone because students can utilize technological programs that allow them to practice language though them as if they are interacting with another person. Ali, an EFL instructor, believes that a blended approach, being interactive, is attractive to students: "Outside of class it's even better; it also gives them opportunities to practice English with other people" (Ali, interview 8). The potential alluded to here is congruent with what Egbert (2005) and Egbert and Hanson-Smith (2007) wrote as three essential components of successful computer-assisted learning initiatives, which are: learners need opportunity to interact and negotiate meaning, they need to be able to interact with authentic audiences, and they need to be involved with authentic tasks.

Feedback was also singled out as a possible motivating factor for students to participate in blended assessment. The blended assessment approach allows for a more convenient way for instructors to provide feedback as a result of the available technology. In face-to-face instruction feedback can frequently occur as a natural consequence of interaction between instructors and students. Despite the perceived ease of providing feedback as a result of online components of blended assessment, some concerns were raised. Adam expressed concerns about the informality of some technological platforms in providing feedback stating, "I consider it a little too informal if it would be through blogs and all that. But if it is acceptable with the institution, then, yeah, it's fine" (Interview 9).

Blended assessment also offers extensive resources wherein independent learning can be developed and encouraged. Isaac, an EFL instructor, explained that the internet provides a global platform for students in which the available information seems limitless; with that students are provided with the opportunity to be exposed to more variety and increased knowledge. Overall, the results of this theme suggest that blended assessment can not only be useful in improving the language assessment of students, but it can also be effective in assisting students to become more engaged in assessment tasks in class.

Multi-Approach

The participants stated that they understood and preferred designs of formative blended assessment tasks as a multi-approach view of language learning, encompassing the elements of integration and innovation. This is consistent with recent findings on blended and classroom-based assessment (Gruba & Hinkelman, 2012).

In the review of the themes emerging from the analysis of the transcripts, evidence indicates that apart from their views on defining blended assessment, both instructors and students have similar preferences and understanding concerning formative blended assessment. The elements associated with formative blended assessment tended to be articulated in a manner consistent with the available literature on classroom-based assessment and blended language assessment (Gruba & Hinkelman, 2012; Harris et al., 2009; Hill & McNamara, 2012).

Integration

Blended learning assessment can be described as being about integration in that it involves the delivery of the language assessment tasks through both traditional and online means. This is the subject of a large number of studies on improving blended learning environments (Al-Qahtani & Higgins, 2013; Jia, Chen, Ding, & Ruan, 2012) and becoming mainstream in language assessment in blended delivery (Garrett, 2009, Levy, 2009; Oxford & Jung, 2007).

It would have been easy for the participants to have said that they didn't like the traditional forms of assessment and instead they wanted new ways of assessing, based on technology and the use of computers – but this is not what they said. They want both. They could see the value in past, older forms of assessment, and they could also see the potential benefits of what technology has now made possible.

Innovation

As well as integration, the findings indicated that innovation is a significant preference in multi-approach blended designs. Innovation typically goes hand in hand with multimodality, and Garrett (2009) uses the word *innovation* to describe creative communication strategies that use technology. A similar notation can be found in a study conducted by Gruba and Hinkelman (2012), who refer to *multimodal* being part of blended assessment. These authors signify the rising trend of using new technologies, and the innovative developments in how these are used.

Innovation in assessment, which refers to innovative responses in the face of continuous change, is a necessary aspect of blended assessment. Chen and Kessler (2013) highlighted the value of innovation in noting the increasing use of media to be prominent in accessing the course modules and the various preferences students' exhibited in knowledge access. Deng and Carless (2010) questioned practices of incorporating innovation into assessment, noting that the examination remains the predominant pedagogy in non-English speaking societies. This tallies with the findings in this research, where the participants supported the use of traditional forms of assessment, but also embraced the innovative changes enabled by technological developments.

The participants stated that they understood and preferred designs of formative blended assessment tasks that offered relative advantages over conventional strategies. In understanding the context of the beliefs and ideologies of the course coordinators, instructors, and students on formative blended assessment in language learning, it was apparent that the participants were generally very optimistic about the potential of utilizing formative blended assessment in language learning. They saw benefits in this means of assessment and they appreciated the encouragement and collaboration that they perceived as going hand in hand with formative blended assessment in language learning. It was possible to presume from the participant responses that the perceived *benefits* of blended assessment for EFL instruction could serve as motivational factors driving the design of the blended assessment curriculum in the institution.

Benefits

The benefits of blended learning and assessment attracted much attention among educators as well as students who were exposed to these learning modalities. These perceived benefits include improvement of communication between instructors and students, more effective methods of teaching technical skills to students, and the provision of assistance to instructors. These findings are consistent with the commentary on the themes of benefits, found in previous studies (Jamieson, 2011), and encouragement (Harris et al., 2009).

Encouragement and Collaboration

The participants stated that there were greater opportunities to exploit the relative advantage of increased potential for collaboration – where course coordinators, instructors and students all contribute to the assessment design. These comments tended to be consistent with what has been previously known concerning the role of communication in blended assessment. Thus, the responses gathered tend to support the proposition that the development of collaboration among participants in blended assessment needs greater emphasis (Graham, 2009).

Some of the participants inferred that as communication competency improves so does the collaborative learning experiences of the EFL students. They added that in blended assessment systems the students are motivated to participate in online interactions, which provide the students more opportunity to articulate their thoughts in written form.

In terms of encouragement, the responses from the participants stressed the motivational influence of formative blended assessment. The majority of the comments inferred that it was the interactive possibilities of online software for assessment that led to increased desire and satisfaction with the assessment and learning experience. It was for these reasons that the concepts of encouragement and collaboration have been grouped together as a sub-category of the purported relative advantages of formative blended assessment (FBA).

The responses of the participants are not surprising and reflect the tenets of both contemporary EFL theory and motivational theory. For example, concerning the latter, the defining feature of formative assessment is that task and feedback occur at a time when the student (and instructor) still has ample opportunity to rectify unsatisfactory language learning performance. Motivation and encouragement are noticeably higher when the individuals perceive that their effort actually affect a particular outcome (Harris et al., 2009). Thus, the synergy between greater opportunity for socialisation and feedback appears to increase positive perceptions of FBA.

Compatibility of Blended Assessments

In line with Rogers and Shoemaker (1971), the compatibility of an innovation occurs when a proposed change is perceived as being consistent with existing values and past experiences. If a characteristic of an innovation is that it is considered to be compatible, then it is more likely to reach the implementation phase of an innovation; here, participants expressed ways that they could imagine new assessment regimes merging into their existing views of classroom proficiency measurements.

Table 3. Defining formative assessment practices

Factor	*Definition*	*Sample data*
Progress	Refers to the progress in student learning as a result of formative assessment.	*"Students also must be knowing that, okay this is how much I have done and this is what I'm supposed to work on now"* (Jack, interview 1).
Tests	Refers to the use of tests during assessment.	*"Having exams"* (Omar, interview 13).
Measure	Refers to the achievement measured in formative assessment.	*"Teachers and students must be knowing what's going on there and how much they have learned so far in my classroom"* (Jack, interview 1).

Many of the participants perceived blended assessment as a way to examine the learning progress of students. Adam explained the rationale for determining the progress of students by saying, "If your students are making progress [then you learn] how best you can help" (Interview 9). According to Kader, assessment should assist in checking the students' rate of progress or learning.

As in the previous comments, the facilitation of enhanced means of collecting data concerning student progress is a central theme in the reports by Russell and Airasian (2012). Another way in which blended assessment was understood by the participants was as a means of measuring the achievement of students. The focus of measuring a student's achievement was on examining if students learn what they are supposed to learn according to the curriculum. Isaac explained that, "It's done according to a standard evaluation tool. For example, here the standard for evaluation, the expectations for evaluating the students have been made clear to us by the university" (Interview 10). Blended assessment gives instructors a more dynamic approach to measure the achievement of students because of the available tools in online approaches.

Some participants like Turki and Omar view blended assessment as merely tests or exams, failing to recognize the reason behind such tests. There seems to be a difference between how instructors and students perceive blended assessment. Instructors tend to have a more rounded view of blended assessment and tend to see blended assessment as an opportunity to not only track the progress of students in a meaningful and accurate way, but also to measure their achievement. Among students, however, formative assessment was typically perceived as simply tests.

As well as viewing formative blended assessment as being a multi-approach system and offering relative advantages, the participants stated that they understood and preferred designs of formative blended assessment tasks that were compatible with the goal of encouraging learning. Moreover, the participants' responses suggested that regardless of modality, formative assessment is designed to check students' performance. The concept of compatibility refers to the role of formative assessment in checking the performance of students for the greater purpose of ensuring that learning can be maximised. This is the main principle of formative assessment.

The participants associated their conceptions of the design of formative blended assessment tasks with several forms of context specific challenges and issues involving government and educational institution feedback. These themes were found to be consistent with studies of Saudi educator training (Al-Hazmi, 2003). Curriculum delivery issues mentioned by the participants that were consistent with the literature included ethics in learning standards (Liang & Bonk, 2009), authenticity, and reliability (Chapelle, 2008).

Complexity of Blended Assessments

Complexity characteristics, according to Rogers and Shoemaker (1971), are of concern when stakeholders see a possible innovation as user-friendly, and it is perceived as easy to understand and use. The fourth theme, challenges, refers then to the different challenges that instructors or students may experience in blended assessment. This theme was relevant because it provided insights into what affects instructors when they plan blended learning and assessment. Some of the perceived challenges include gaining facility in using technology, distraction from the availability of information and resources, and a lack of administrative support. Table 4 contains all the main clusters that emerged from the theme challenges.

Table 4. Challenges

Factor	*Definition*	*Sample data*
Facility	Refers to the necessary training needed to implement blended assessment.	*"I personally believe, if you use these machines in the classroom you should be well trained and you have to be very, very judicious"* (Jack, interview 1).
Distraction	Refers to blended assessment as a possible source of distraction.	*"Some of the students are playing with the gadgets"* (Jack, interview 1).
Administrative support	Refers to the lack of administrative support in implementing blended assessment.	*"Sometimes in the classroom and certain language labs the computers are available but we just [use them] when it comes to reading and writing, just to test their reading and writing ability and progress"* (Kader, interview 6).
Monitor	Refers to the need for monitoring to prevent cheating.	*"Nobody is monitoring them. But if there should be some ground rules that this is a test in a way, so you don't do this, you don't do that"* (Adam, interview 9).

Not having the appropriate skills to implement and use the 'machines' involved in blended language assessment can be a challenge both for instructors and students. Soliman explained the significance of having training and facilities in using technology within the context of blended assessment. Soliman noted the need for a basic knowledge in using computers given that technology plays a major role in many aspects of the way of living of people today:

Soliman: "*They must have some sort of knowledge about the bandwidth in the fast internet connection if they are slow so[or] they well get disconnected after two or three or four minutes, so it will not be good for them*" (Interview 7).

Without the proper knowledge or facility in using computers, students may lose their motivation, which can have a negative impact on their learning:

R: "*Just that they won't use it?*"
Soliman: "*Yes, de-motivation. So they must be able to use it, they must be able to know how the system works and if they don't have this much, they may go for short training in computer technology*" (Interview 7).

A difference can be gleaned from the responses of the participants on the whole compared to earlier studies into blended approaches. While the participants of this study appeared to be primarily concerned with operating information technology systems, the participants of previous studies appear to have been more concerned with attaining/accessing state of the art technology (Levy & Stockwell, 2006).

The lack of administrative support in the use of technological equipment can also be a challenge in a successful implementation of blended assessment system. Instructors need support and proper training in using the technology, especially in the early stages of developing programmes which use computers. The educational institution also needs to be able to provide the tools and the equipment needed to implement the curriculum within a blended learning system. Students may also need administrative support to gain facility in using technology.

Distraction as a result of the availability of different programs and technological systems can be a challenge in blended approaches. Without proper monitoring, both instructors and students can deviate from the goals of blended assessment, resulting in educational goals not being achieved. Sultan noted that blended approaches can be useful in getting the attention of students, but instructors need to be careful in ensuring that the attention of students is on the right topic:

"My opinion [is] that it is good to get attention, good to make the studies more interesting and to get them involved and there are chances that students may detract or distract sometimes, but if the teacher is attentive and he himself knows these techniques, he can better teach – instead of teaching in a traditional way" (Interview 3).

The previous comments of Sultan highlight a problem, but also infer a potential solution for the issue. While the use of online media presents a problem of potential online distraction to students, one means for the teacher to address this issue could be to navigate the online assessment components prior to their session with the students in order to detect distractions. For example, there may be situations where students need to type in a new URL or search for a particular word using a search engine. This the time when students are most likely to be distracted. Thus, through teacher preparation, distractions can be decreased. Also, as highlighted by Sultan, there is a need for diligent monitoring of student use of online components in any assessment program. Authors such as Levy and Stockwell (2006) and Egbert et al. (2011) state that it is the teacher that makes the difference in the context of language learning, and not the technology. This highlights the important role a teacher can play to implement the technology successfully.

Some instructors prefer a more proactive approach in addressing cheating by monitoring the activities of students. Instructors believed that they and the course coordinators should be given a means of monitoring possible cases of dishonesty, in the face of the freedom that students have to access technology. The lack of structured monitoring to detect the cheating in blended assessment indicates the need for instructors to have the initiative to monitor cheating in their own ways. Formative blended assessment leads to changes in how instructors practice the teaching profession. Primarily these changes come about because of the use of technology in assessment, and because such use requires the provision of feedback, administrative support, competency of instructors both in teaching and management of technology, and the overall sustainability of the practice of using this new assessment modality.

FUTURE RESEARCH DIRECTIONS AND IMPLICATIONS

Following are details of some of the significant implications for practice confronting instructors engaged in formative blended assessment:

Instructors will be under increasing surveillance to ensure that their assessment plans match the prescribed curriculums of their institutions. This will be an important quality standard measure as increasingly automated systems of assessment lead to more scrutiny of teaching and learning. With the increase in uniformity of assessment practices using a range of media there will also be a need for teachers to provide feedback that is more uniform from class to class. Differences in instructor to student feedback, and feedback from class to class, will be more noticeable. One stark implication of an increase in the application of formative blended assessment regimes is that education providers intending on implementing these programs will need to be equipped with the appropriate hardware and software to conduct these assessments. One of the challenges for both formative blended assessment scheme designers and the instructors themselves who are required to implement these programs will be ensuring that the outcome programs are able to achieve an optimal level of integration between different means of information exchange. More importantly, an implication of blended systems is that designers and teachers must be able to apply innovative means to encourage assessment and learning.

A further implication of formative blended assessment regimes is that a supporting environment is required. Such a climate of endorsement will require support from the most senior executives directing the education institution for unit coordinators, lecturers, and tutors. One specific example of change may involve how, in the past, students were required to keep paper-based learning diaries. Such diaries may be replaced by digitalised learning diaries, and these diaries could be made part of the formative blended assessment regime. Thus, there will be greater pressure on teachers and administrators to encourage the use of information technology in language assessment.

CONCLUSION

Three main characteristics of formative blended assessment were identified in this study, namely advantages, compatibility and complexity. Blended learning assessment has advantages enhancing multi-modal activities, flexibility and peer encouragement, as well as being aligned with 21st century pedagogies and assessment tasks. However, it is a complex structure with challenges, but overall it has the potential to play a part in language teaching and learning in tertiary education in Saudi Arabia.

The participants' views are indicators of their acceptance of formative blended assessment into new learning and teaching environment, and their reflections on aspects of blended learning assessment are a useful indicator for curriculum designers using technology multimedia in language teaching and learning. Furthermore, the participants indicated that blended assessments could be better than current approaches if designs were multifaceted and included considerations of technological integration, learner focus, and conceptual novelty

This chapter presented that blended assessments can help motivate students to be more involved in their learning process and get more constructive feedback through the available technology along with participating in online interactions, which provide the students more opportunity to articulate their thoughts. It also showed that multi-approach blended assessment design has benefits such as integration, innovation, encouragement and collaboration, and compatibility.

Overall, the results suggest that blended assessment can not only be useful in improving the language assessment of students, but it can also be effective in assisting students to become more engaged in assessment tasks in class. It is also apparent that the participants in the study were generally very optimistic about the potential of utilizing formative blended assessment in language teaching and learning.

REFERENCES

Al-Hazmi, S. (2003). EFL teacher preparation programs in Saudi Arabia: Trends and challenges. *TESOL Quarterly*, *37*(2), 341–344. doi:10.2307/3588509

Al-Qahtani, A., & Higgins, S. (2013). Effects of traditional, blended and e-learning on students' achievement in higher education. *Journal of Computer Assisted Learning*, *29*(3), 220–234. doi:10.1111/j.1365-2729.2012.00490.x

Chapelle, C. A. (2008). Utilizing technology in language assessment. In *Encyclopedia of Language and Education: Language Testing and Assessment*. Heidelberg: Springer Verlag.

Coffey, J., Hammer, D., Levin, D., & Grant, T. (2011). The missing disciplinary substance of formative assessment. *Journal of Research in Science Teaching*, *48*(10), 1109–1136. doi:10.1002/tea.20440

Creswell, J. W. (2013). *Qualitative inquiry & research design: Choosing among five approaches*. Los Angeles, CA: Sage.

Deng, C., & Carless, D. (2010). Examination preparation or effective teaching: Conflicting priorities in the implementation of a pedagogic innovation. *Language Assessment Quarterly*, *7*(4), 285–302. doi:10.1080/15434303.2010.510899

Dooly, M., & Sadler, R. (2016). Becoming little scientists: Technologically-enhanced project-based language learning. *Language Learning & Technology*, *20*(1), 54–78.

Dörnyei, Z., & Ushioda, E. (2011). *Teaching and researching: Motivation*. Harlow, England: Pearson Education.

Egbert, J. (2005). *CALL essentials: Principles and practice in CALL classrooms*. Alexandria, VA: TESOL.

Egbert, J., Akasha, O., Huff, L., & Lee, H. (2011). Moving forward: Anecdotes and evidence guiding the next generation of CALL. *International Journal of Computer-Assisted Language Learning and Teaching*, *1*(1), 1–15. doi:10.4018/ijcallt.2011010101

Egbert, J., & Hanson-Smith, E. (Eds.). (2007). *CALL environments: Research, practice, and critical issues* (2nd ed.). Alexandria, VA: TESOL.

Elyas, T., & Picard, M. (2010). Saudi Arabian educational history: Impacts on language teaching. *Education, Business and Society*, *3*(2), 136–145. doi:10.1108/17537981011047961

Flick. (2009). *An introduction to qualitative research.* London: Sage.

Garrett, N. (2009). Computer-assisted language learning trends and issues revisited: Integrating innovation. *Modern Language Journal*, *93*(S1), 719–740. doi:10.1111/j.1540-4781.2009.00969.x

Gruba, P., & Hinkelman, D. (2012). *Blending technologies in second language classrooms*. Basingstoke, UK: Palgrave McMillan. doi:10.1057/9780230356825

Haines, K. (2016). Expanding the knowledge base of teachers' use of communication tools for language learning. *System*, *62*, 102–112. doi:10.1016/j.system.2016.07.008

Hill, K. (2012). *Classroom-based assessment in the school foreign language classroom.* Frankfurt am Main: Peter Lang. doi:10.3726/978-3-653-01984-1

Hill, K., & McNamara, T. (2012). Developing a comprehensive, empirically based research framework for classroom-based assessment. *Language Testing*, *29*(3), 395–420. doi:10.1177/0265532211428317

Jamieson, J. (2011). Assessment of classroom language learning. In C. Chapelle (Ed.), *Handbook of research in second language teaching and learning*. New York, NY: Routledge.

Jia, J., Chen, Y., Ding, Z., & Ruan, M. (2012). Effects of a vocabulary acquisition and assessment system on students' performance in a blended learning class for English subject. *Computers & Education*, *58*(1), 63–76. doi:10.1016/j.compedu.2011.08.002

Khan, I. A. (2011). The teacher of English: Pedagogic relevance in Saudi Arabia. *English Language Teaching*, *4*(2), 112–120. doi:10.5539/elt.v4n2p112

Leakey, J., & Ranchoux, A. (2006). BLINGUA. A blended language learning approach for CALL. *Computer Assisted Language Learning*, *19*(4/5), 357–372. doi:10.1080/09588220601043016

Levy, M. (2009). Technologies in use for second language learning. *Modern Language Journal*, *93*(S1), 769–782. doi:10.1111/j.1540-4781.2009.00972.x

Levy, M., & Stockwell, G. (2006). *CALL Dimensions: Options and Issues in Computer-Assisted Language Learning*. Mahwah, NJ: Routledge.

Littlejohn, A., & Pegler, C. (2007). *Preparing for Blended e-Learning*. London: Routledge. doi:10.4324/9780203961322

Mandl, H., & Kopp, B. (2006). *Blended Learning*. Forschungsfragen und Perspektiven.

McMullen, M. G. (2009). Using language learning strategies to improve the writing skills of Saudi EFL students: Will it really work? *System: An International Journal of Educational Technology and Applied Linguistics, 37*, 418-433.

Miles, M., & Huberman, A. (1994). *Qualitative data analysis: An expanded sourcebook*. Beverly Hills: Sage.

Mohammed, A. (2011). EFL effective factors: Anxiety and motivation and their effect on Saudi college student's achievement. *Proceedings of the 4th International Conference of Education, Research and Innovations*.

Motteram, G. (2016). Membership, belonging, and identity in the twenty-first century. *ELT Journal*, *70*(2), 150–159. doi:10.1093/elt/ccw001

Picciano, A. G. (2009). Blending with purpose: The multimodal model. *Journal of Asynchronous Learning Networks*, *13*(1), 7–18.

Rogers, E. M., & Shoemaker, F. F. (1971). *Communication of innovations: A cross-cultural approach* (2nd ed.). New York: Free Press.

Saldana, J. (2012). The coding manual for qualitative researchers (No. 14). Sage.

Swan, K. (2009). Introduction to the Special Issue on Blended Learning. *Journal of the Research Center for Educational Technology*, *5*(1), 1–3. http://www.rcetj.org/index.php/rcetj/article/view/20/25

Vaughan, N. (2007). Perspectives on blended learning in higher education. *International Journal on E-Learning*, *6*(1), 81–94.

Walliman, N. (2005). *Your research project: a step-by-step guide for the first-time researcher*. Los Angeles: Sage.

Walters, F. S. (2010). Cultivating assessment literacy: Standards evaluation through language-test specification reverse engineering. *Language Assessment Quarterly*, *7*(4), 317–342. doi:10.1080/15434303.2010.516042

Wyatt-Smith, C., & Cumming, J. (Eds.). (2009). *Educational assessment in the 21st Century*. Dordrecht: Springer. doi:10.1007/978-1-4020-9964-9

ADDITIONAL READING

Alebaikan, R. (2010). *Perceptions of blended learning in Saudi universities*. Unpublished PhD thesis, University of Exeter, Exeter, England.

Alshumaimri, A., Aldridge, T., & Audretsch, D. (2010). The university technology transfer revolution in Saudi Arabia. *The Journal of Technology Transfer*, *35*(6), 585–596. doi:10.100710961-010-9176-5

Baleni, Z. G. (2015). Online formative assessment in higher education: Its pros and cons. *Electronic Journal of e-Learning*, 13(4), 228–236.

Boelens, R., De Wever, B., & Voet, M. (2017). Four key challenges to the design of blended learning: A systematic literature review. *Educational Research Review*, *22*, 1–18. doi:10.1016/j.edurev.2017.06.001

Dlab, M., Katic, M. A., & Candrlic, S. (2015). Ensuring formative assessment in e-course with online tests. In *Proceedings of the 10th Int. Conf. Comput. Sci. Educ.*, pp. 322–327. 10.1109/ICCSE.2015.7250264

Krasnova, T., & Demeshko, M. (2015). Tutor-mediated support in blended learning. *Procedia: Social and Behavioral Sciences*, *166*, 404–408. doi:10.1016/j.sbspro.2014.12.544

Moraño, J., Roselló, M., & Ruiz, L. (2015). Blended learning at maths with aerospace engineering freshmen. In *Proceedings of the IEEE Frontiers in Education Conference*, pp. 1-4.

Timmers, F., Walraven, A., & Veldkamp, P. (2015). The effect of regulation feedback in a computer-based formative assessment on information problem solving. *Computers & Education*, *87*, 1–9. doi:10.1016/j.compedu.2015.03.012

Wanner, T., & Palmer, E. (2015). Personalising learning: Exploring student and teacher perceptions about flexible learning and assessment in a flipped university course. *Computers & Education*, *88*, 354–369. doi:10.1016/j.compedu.2015.07.008

Willey, K. (2016). Combining a collaborative learning framework with an e-learning tool to improve learning and professional development in blended learning environments. In *Proceedings of the IEEE Future Technologies Conference*, pp. 1303–1304. 10.1109/FTC.2016.7821769

Zhang, Z., Cao, T., Shu, J., Zhi, M., Liu, H., & Li, Z. (2017). Exploration of blended teaching pattern based on hstar and smart classroom. In *Proceedings of the Int. Symp. Educ. Technol.*, pp. 3–7. 10.1109/ISET.2017.10

KEY TERMS AND DEFINITIONS

Blended Assessment: It is a type of assessment differing from traditional assessment and unlike paper and pencil formats as well as including collaborative and individual work.

Blended Learning: The notion that students generally attend face-to-face classes and have online access to the course content and activities.

Collaboration: A kind of work where course coordinators, instructors and students all contribute to the assessment design.

Formative Assessment: The task and feedback occur at a time when the student (and instructor) still has ample opportunity to rectify unsatisfactory language learning performance.

Innovation: Using technology for creativity, for example, implementing blended assessment when measuring students' writings or tasks.

Integration: It involves the delivery of the language assessment tasks through both traditional and online means.

Multi-Approach: Encompassing the elements of integration and innovation.

Chapter 5
Assessment of Language Learning Strategies in Technology-Enhanced Learning Environment

Wagdi Rashad Ali Bin-Hady
https://orcid.org/0000-0002-4116-113X
Hadhrmout University, Yemen

Abdu Al-Kadi
https://orcid.org/0000-0003-3805-7507
Ibb University, Yemen

Ali Abbas Falah Alzubi
https://orcid.org/0000-0001-6252-9522
Najran University, Saudi Arabia

Hassan Saleh Mahdi
University of Bisha, Saudi Arabia

ABSTRACT

This chapter reports on the Yemeni and Saudi EFL learners' use of language learning strategies (LLSs) in technology-mediated language learning contexts. The study examines whether nationality and gender play a significant role in using LLSs on electronic platforms. The study adopted a correlative design in which 100 Yemeni and Saudi university students were recruited to respond to an online close-ended questionnaire. Drawing on Oxford's classification of learning strategies, the findings of this study showed that metacognitive and cognitive strategies were used more frequently compared to the other LLSs. Moreover, the findings of t-test showed a significant difference in the use of LLSs attributed to nationality in favor of the Saudi learners and no significant difference in the choice of LLSs attributed to gender. The study provided some suggestions for EFL learners to benefit from technology in their English language learning.

DOI: 10.4018/978-1-7998-3062-7.ch005

INTRODUCTION

Language learning can be affected by a number of factors such as age, gender, personality, motivation, self-concept, life-experience, learning style, excitement, anxiety, and technology (Wenden & Rubin, 1987; Williams & Robert, 1997; Zhou & Wei 2018). Language learners naturally follow effective ways to learn the target language. In the classroom, they are consistently exposed to new input and challenging tasks given by their instructors. When processing new information and performing language tasks, language learners use learning strategies, either consciously or unconsciously (Al-Maktary, 2018; Lee, 2010; O'Malley & Chamot, 1990; Yanju & Yanmei, 2016). Prior research findings have revealed that successful language learners employ language learning strategies (LLSs) better than their counterparts (Al-Maktary, 2018; Maldonado, 2016; Metcalfe & Noom-Ura, 2013; Yanju & Yanmei, 2016). This belief inspired educators and researchers to explore the LLSs that successful learners tend to use. Such strategies are suggestively useful for less successful learners to develop certain language skills (Al-Maktary, 2018; Maldonado, 2016; Lee, 2010).

The advent of technology has created several opportunities for students to learn easily and quickly. It has given learners more responsibility and autonomous learning roles to tackle their language learning in almost instructor-free learning settings regardless of time and place (Ahmed, Al-kadi & Hagar, 2020; Alzubi, 2019). Since the amount of information to be processed by language learners is high in language classrooms, learners use different language learning strategies in performing language tasks and processing the new input they face on their own in virtual spaces. They tend to employ cognitive, metacognitive, and socio-affective strategies to process, understand, remember, and assess language learning input they obtain on their own. Nevertheless, not all learners have the same ICT facilities. For instance, in some contexts inadequate access to the Internet is still a salient barrier that prevents implementing ICT for effective language learning. Thereby, it is important to consider accessibility to educational technology in different contexts. The previous studies which examined the impact of ICT on language instruction were conducted in contexts with either high or low internet connection. There is a need to fill this gap by assessing the use of LLSs in two different technology-enhanced language learning contexts. This chapter is a report of a descriptive study that explored differences in utilizing LLSs in a technology-enhanced language environment. The context of language (Khamkhien, 2010; Oxford, 1990) and genders of learners are very important players that could affect language learning strategies (Božinović, & Sindik, 2011; Zare, 2010). More pointedly, the study intended to elucidate whether there were differences in the use of learning strategies between Yemeni and Saudi EFL learners, and ascertained differences in use of LLSs between the two samples due to differences in access to the ICTs tools. It also sought to examine if there was any difference regarding the gender of learners.

The following questions guided the investigation:

1. Which language learning strategies are highly used in ICT-enabled learning environments?
2. Are there any significant differences in the use of LLSs in ICT-enhanced learning environments attributed to the learning settings?
3. Are there any significant differences in the use of LLSs in ICT-enhanced learning environments attributed to gender?

BACKGROUND

This section provides background information about language learning strategies (LLSs). It also explores such strategies in connection with another concept such as gender. Mainly, it discusses whether males and females use LLSs in the same way or differently. Assessment of the use of such strategies within the digital environment is also reviewed.

Language Learning Strategy (LLS)

A plethora of LLS definitions and classifications exists in the literature. For instance, Wenden and Rubin (1987) defined learning strategies as "any sets of operations, steps, plans, routines used by the learner to facilitate the obtaining, storage, retrieval, and use of information" (p. 19). Another definition suggested by Richards and Platt (1992) portrayed strategies as "intentional behavior and thoughts used by learners during learning so as to better help them understand, learn, or remember new information" (p.209). According to Stern (1975), "the concept of learning strategy is dependent on the assumption that learners consciously engage in activities to achieve certain goals and learning strategies can be regarded as broadly conceived intentional directions and learning techniques" (p. 261). LLSs in these definitions are conceptualized as a broad concept. For the purpose of the present study, LLSs refer to all strategies that learners of English use to achieve better results. This paper adopts the definition of Lee (2010), who viewed LLSs as "learning skills, learning-to-learn skills, thinking skills, problem skills or, in other words the methods which learners use to intake, store and retrieve during the learning process" (p.134). The study was inspired by Oxford's (1990) quote that language learning strategies "are especially important for language learning because they are tools for active, self-directed movement, which is essential for developing communicative competence" (p.1). Griffiths (2013) introduced a very simple and comprehensible definition of language learning strategies, viewing them as activities that learners choose consciously for regulating their own language learning. A more updated definition of LLSs by Oxford emerged in 2011 describing L2 learning strategies as "the learner's goal-directed actions for improving language proficiency or achievement, completing a task, or making learning more efficient, more effective, and easier" (p. 167).

LLSs have been classified and undertaken by many scholars. To mention a few, Rubin (1987), O'Malley and Chamot (1990), Oxford (1990), and Stern (1975) are among other authors who have contributed vigorously to LLSs, and their works have been widely quoted and referenced. Rubin (1987) made the distinction between strategies contributing directly to learning and those contributing indirectly to learning. According to Rubin, there are three types of strategies used by learners: communication strategies, learning strategies, and social strategies. Cognitive learning strategies and meta-cognitive learning strategies composing the learning strategies are those direct strategies that contribute to the development of language learning process constructed by the learners. Communication strategies are less directly related to language learning since their focus is on the process of participating in a conversation and getting meaning across or clarifying the speaker's intention. Speakers use communication strategies when facing difficulty since their communication ends outrun their communication means or when confronted with misunderstanding by a co-speaker (Hismanoglu, 2001). Social strategies refer to those activities engaged by language learners. Such activities afford them opportunities to practice their knowledge. Although these strategies provide exposure to the target language, they contribute indirectly to learning since they do not lead directly to obtaining, storing, retrieving, and using language (Rubin & Wenden, 1987).

One of the most comprehensive and widely used classifications of LLSs is the taxonomy of Oxford (1990). In fact, Oxford elaborated Rubin's (1987) classification and divided language learning strategies into two main categories (i.e. direct and indirect), which were further subdivided into six groups. Direct strategies include memory strategies, cognitive strategies, and compensation strategies. Indirect strategies, on the other hand, encompass metacognitive strategies, affective strategies, and social strategies. Similarly, O'Malley and Chamot (1990) pointed out that learning strategies are involved in the procedural knowledge where LLS are employed consciously in early stages of learning and later performed without the person's awareness. O'Malley and Chamot (1990) claimed the benefits of applying cognitive theory to strategies and identified three primary categories: cognitive strategies, metacognitive strategies, and socio-affective strategies. Nevertheless, Lessard-Clouston (1997) argued that LLSs and strategy training should move beyond descriptive categorizations of LLSs. It should seek answers to a number of language learning related issues such as (a) language learning strategies that appear to work best in different contexts, (b) language proficiency in language learning strategies use and training, (c) assessment and measurement of language learning strategies, and (d) learning settings.

Addressing these issues in a variety of settings assists in building the theory that seems necessary for more language learning strategies work related to current L2/FL teaching practice. However, the difficulty in researching LLSs is that they are not observed directly, but inferred from language learners' behavior. Over the years, different researchers have employed a variety of approaches to explore LLSs. The approach used by good language learners through researching into the good language learning strategies revealed a number of positive strategies so that positive strategies which could also be used by low-level language learners trying to become more successful in language learning (Al-Maktary, 2018). However, there is always the possibility that low-level language learners also use the same strategies of good language learners to become successful in language learning; however, this may not be guaranteed due to the interference of other factors.

LLSs and Gender

Different beliefs emerged regarding the correlation between LLSs choice and gender. A few studies reported that male learners use LLSs differently from female learners (e.g. Božinović & Sindik, 2011; Ho & Ng, 2016). However, the majority of studies showed no difference between male and female learners in the use of LLSs (e.g. Alhaisoni, 2017; Viriya & Sapsirin, 2014). Still, few others found little difference (Alhaysony, 2017). Aljuaid (2010) used Oxford's (1990) Strategy Inventory for Language Learning (SILL) to explore which LLSs Saudi EFL female learners used. The study found that metacognitive strategies were the most frequently used while memory strategies were the least. Generally, the learners used LLSs with high and medium averages. Alhaisoni (2017) examined the use of LLSs at Ha'il University with EFL learners, Saudi Arabia. The study reported no significant difference in the use of LLSs attributed to gender. Furthermore, Alhaysony (2017) studied the use of LLSs among 134 EFL Saudi learners at Aljouf University in terms of gender and duration. The study revealed that female learners used LLSs more frequent than male learners did at the overall use of strategies. However, such difference was not significant. In different contexts, the case may differ. Ho and Ng (2016) investigated the use of LLSs in relation to gender among 535 male and 1173 female students at Malaysian public universities. The study reported that males and females used LLSs differently. Furthermore, in Thailand,

Viriya and Sapsirin (2014) studied the use of learning style and language learning strategies among 150 learners. The study found that genders of learners had no effect on the use of language learning strategies. Moreover, Dubrovnik, Božinović and Sindik (2011) used SILL questionnaire to check LLSs among learners of German, Spanish, French and Italian. The finding revealed that female learners significantly outperformed male learners in the choice of LLSs other than social strategies. The present study also focused on whether gender has an impact on the use of LLSs.

Assessment of LLSs in ICT-based Environments

LLSs have been conventionally highlighted through the works of a myriad of researchers (O'Malley & Chamot, 1990; Oxford, 1990; Oxford & Burry-Stock, 1995; Richards & Platt, 1992; Wenden & Rubin, 1987). The revolution of technology such as computers, smartphones, and internet applications has facilitated the process of language learning in terms of knowledge access, independent learning, more learner-centered learning and the practice of language (Alzubi & Singh, 2017). Hence, research interests have been shifted to explore the use of learning strategies within a digital learning environment. The advancement in technology has permeated every part of modern life as everything has become digitalized (Ali & Bin-Hady, 2019). Zhou and Wei (2018) accentuated the need for language learners to develop strategies to learn a new language with the help of information and communication technology (ICT). Teachers need to teach their students such strategies. Bekleyen and Hayta (2015) investigated Turkish EFL students' use of LLSs with mobile technology. The findings showed that students employed different LLSs to develop their English. The study showed that students' use of LLSs with the help of mobile technology did not exceed the use of computer technology for the same purpose. In a similar vein, Nurhaeni and Purnawarman (2018) studied the correlation between learners' autonomy and using smartphones in developing their English. The study pointed out that using smartphones affect learners' use of LLSs. Cognitive and social/affective strategies were developed highly while metacognitive strategies were the lowest.

Yemen and Saudi Arabia have quite similar cultural heritage and - at the top of this heritage is that they share the same language (Arabic). However, the two countries are economically heterogeneous. In terms of English education, it is believed that students' proficiency levels are the same because of the cultural and language background. Some previous studies showed that Saudi learners of English have low English proficiency specifically new college students (Ahmad, 2016); the same is true for Yemeni learners (Al-Sohbani, 2016; Bin-Hady, 2016). With reference to the implementation of technology in the education system, in the Saudi Arabian context, the Ministry of Education has paid a lot of attention to the adoption of technology in the education systems (Al-Ahdal, 2013; Alqasham, 2018). In Yemen, as the country is being plagued by corruption and the ongoing war, implementing technology in education is critical.

This literature review provides a background to address the issue of LLSs in teaching and learning English as a foreign language with a specific reference to the Saudi and Yemeni contexts. The strategies discussed above can inspire researchers to investigate the learning strategies used by the Yemeni and Saudi language learners when they are present in the virtual world, using web applications. Through the assessment of LLSs, the current study demonstrates how frequently LLSs were used by EFL learners in order to acquire English within ICT environment. It also examines differences in the use of LLSs attributable to learning context and gender.

MAIN FOCUS OF THE CHAPTER

The current study follows the correlative research design. Correlative design is defined as "procedures in quantitative research in which investigators measure the degree of association (or relation) between two or more variables using the statistical procedure of correlational analysis" (Creswell, 2012, p. 21). Thus, the study expounds the relationship between LLSs and ICT tools, and the relationship between the Yemeni and Saudi use of LLSs in ICT environment. The study was conducted in two EFL contexts: the Yemeni context and Saudi context. This study was built on Oxford's (1990) taxonomy of learning strategies. As Oxford's SILL was released before the emergence of most of the current technological innovations, which have penetrated L2 education, the taxonomy was adopted with some modifications to make it more relevant to the themes of the current investigation.

The population of the study is undergraduates enrolled in the English programs at four universities in the cities of Taiz and Hadramout in Yemen, and Najran and Bisha in Saudi Arabia. The study assigned convenience sampling which is defined by Dörnyei (2007) as "a type of nonprobability or nonrandom sampling where members of the target population that meet certain practical criteria such as easy accessibility, geographical proximity, availability at a given time" (pp.98-99). The study targeted 200 male and female learners: one hundred in each country, as they were accessible to the researchers in their affiliated universities. They were aged between 19 and 23. However, the responses were only one hundred, 70 Yemeni and 30 Saudi, 59 males and 41 females. While these participants were assumed as linguistically homogeneous, they are heterogamous in terms of technology ownership and usage.

A five-Likert scale closed-ended questionnaire was administered online to collect the data (see Appendix 1). It was adapted from Oxford's (1990) SILL in connection with ICT-based environments. In creating their questionnaire, the researchers also took positive aspects of Bekleyen and Hayta (2015) with some modifications to the items which suit the research settings. The questionnaire consisted of 33 items: memory strategies (five items), cognitive strategies (ten items), compensation strategies (four items), metacognitive strategies (four items), affective strategies (six items), and social strategies (four items). The initial version of the survey was piloted, and its validity and reliability were checked. The questionnaire was sent to four professors of Applied Linguistics specialized in Computer-Assisted Language Learning and Mobile-Assisted Language Learning. Some issues related to item rewording, categorizing LLSs, and suitability of the local context were adjusted. Overall, the internal consistency of the instrument was calculated (0.91) and this value is generally high.

Data Analysis

The collected data was analyzed using the Statistical package for Social Sciences (SPSS). Two kinds of analysis were used: descriptive analysis to extract the means, standard deviations, and percentages of the participants' responses on the questionnaires and independent samples t-test to correlate the data collected based on the variables of gender and country of the participants (Appendix 2). In addition, Leven's test was computed to check the equality of variances between the number of participants in relation to gender and country.

Results

This study discusses three issues relevant to the assessment of LLSs use in the ICT environment. The results are displayed in this section according to the order of the research questions. To begin with, data relevant to the first research question, "which language learning strategies are highly used in ICT-enabled learning environments?" are outlined in Table 1. As the table shows, the metacognitive and cognitive strategies are the most commonly used language learning strategies by the learners. The results showed that the mean scores of metacognitive strategies were 3.80 and 3.75 for cognitive strategies which are considered according to Oxford and Burry-Stock (1995) as high average. The remaining LLSs of memory, compensation, affective and social strategies are used in medium average (above 2.5 and below 3.5). To sum up, learners used LLSs in the ICT environment rated from high (meta-cognitive and cognitive) to medium average (compensation, memory, affective and social strategies).

Table 1. LLSs Use in the ICT Environment

Category	Items	M	SD	Percentage	Order
Memory Strategies	5	3.386	0.770	67.72	3
Cognitive Strategies	10	3.753	0.630	75.06	2
Compensation Strategies	4	3.288	0.841	65.75	5
Metacognitive Strategies	4	3.803	0.792	76.05	1
Affective Strategies	6	3.280	0.821	65.60	6
Social Strategies	4	3.290	0.917	65.80	4
Total	33	3.505	0.602	70.10	

The second research question of this study revolved around differences in the use of LLSs assigned to different learning settings. The aim was to ascertain if there was any significant difference in the use of LLSs in ICT-enhanced learning environments attributed to the learning settings. It required calculating the total mean scores for all the LLSs used by the Yemeni learners to be compared with the Saudi learners for the use of the same LLSs. Table 2 shows that Yemeni learners used LLSs with overall mean scores of 3.42 with a standard deviation of 0.6 which is considered as medium use of LLSs. On the other hand, the Saudi learners used LLSs within overall mean scores of 3.69, and a standard deviation of 0.5, which is considered as high level use. Moreover, the degree of significance between the use of LLSs is calculated using t-test and Sig. value (Sig= .035) which is statistically considered as a significant difference in favor of the higher mean score, i.e. Saudi learners. To present the difference within each category of LLSs, it can be seen- as Table 2 shows that there is a significant difference between the Yemeni and Saudi learners in using LLSs specifically in memory, cognitive and compensation language learning strategies.

Table 2. Correlation between Yemeni and Saudi Learners of the Use of LLSs in ICT Environment

Category	Nationality	N	Mean	Std. Devi.	DF	T	Sig (2 tailed)
Memory	Yemeni	70	3.2886	.77545	98	1.960	.053
	Saudi	30	3.6133	.72003	58.882		
Cognitive	Yemeni	70	3.6529	.64059	98	2.491	.014
	Saudi	30	3.9867	.54566	63.992		
Compensation	Yemeni	70	3.1750	.85799	98	2.077	.040
	Saudi	30	3.5500	.74971	62.426		
Metacognitive	Yemeni	70	3.7036	.80453	98	1.933	.056
	Saudi	30	4.0333	.72437	60.645		
Affective	Yemeni	70	3.2476	.82178	98	-.600	.550
	Saudi	30	3.3556	.82899	54.507		
Social	Yemeni	70	3.2393	.89830	98	-.844	.401
	Saudi	30	3.4083	.96375	51.609		
Total	Yemeni	70	3.4221	.60060	98	-2.139	.035
	Saudi	30	3.6980	.56784	57.882		

The third research question is about the use of LLSs in the ICT-based environment for male and female learners. To answer this question, the total mean scores for all the LLSs used by the male learners were compared with the female learners for the use of the same LLSs in the ICT environment. Table 3 shows that both male and female learners used LLSs with a mean score of 3.50, which is considered as high average and with a standard deviation of 0.66 for females and 0.55 for males. Furthermore, to check the significance, a t-test for independent-sample was used. The total Sig value is .968, which means there is no statistically significant difference in mean scores of LLSs between male and female learners.

Table 3. Comparison between Male and Female Learners' Use of LLSs

Strategy	Gender	N	Mean	Std. Deviation	Df	T	Sig. (2-tailed)
Memory	Male	59	3.3119	.78808	98	-1.157-	.250
	Female	41	3.4927	.74040	89.513		
Cognitive	Male	59	3.8000	.57084	98	.894	.373
	Female	41	3.6854	.70836	73.873		
Compensation	Male	59	3.2119	.88183	98	-1.080-	.283
	Female	41	3.3963	.77656	92.552		
Metacognitive	Male	59	3.8644	.71517	98	.937	.351
	Female	41	3.7134	.89366	73.488		
Affective	Male	59	3.2175	.86118	98	-.912-	.364
	Female	41	3.3699	.76150	92.375		
Social	Male	59	3.3559	.91114	98	.862	.391
	Female	41	3.1951	.92789	85.187		
Total	Male	59	3.5028	.55681	98	-.040-	.968
	Female	41	3.5078	.66814	75.757		

SOLUTIONS AND RECOMMENDATIONS

As data in Table 1 exhibits, meta-cognitive and cognitive language learning strategies were the highest type of strategies that both Yemeni and Saudi learners commonly employed (Mean values: 3.803 and3.753 respectively). The other types of LLSs were used at a medium rate. To put this result in the context of previous studies in other EFL contexts, it is useful to refer to the results of similar studies here. For instance, Ho and Ng (2016) pointed out that the use of metacognitive strategies lead learners to a more independent and self-directed language learning process as they try to explore, plan, manage and evaluate their own learning. Similarly, Ping and Luan (2017) found that learners with high language proficiency employed more strategies ranging from high to medium levels compared to moderate and low language proficiency learners who employed all the strategies within the medium strategy range. This finding is in line with Al-Buainain (2010) who found that Qatari EFL learners used LLSs from a high to medium range, and the highest strategy according to the author was the metacognitive strategies that the Qatari learners used at the percentage of 75.3%. Similarly, this finding is also in agreement with Alhaisoni (2017) who conducted a study on 701 male and female Saudi EFL learners at Ha'il University. The finding revealed that learners preferred to use cognitive and metacognitive strategies frequently while affective and memory strategies were the least preferred. Ho and Ng (2016) also support this by finding that metacognitive strategies were the highest among Malaysian students. This study finding shows that EFL learners used LLSs from high to medium average while Alhaysony (2017) and Alhaisoni's (2017) findings reported that Saudi learners' use of LLSs ranged from medium to low. This can be justified by the integration of ICT in this study for assessing the use of LLSs in EFL. Bekleyen and Hayta (2015) found that Turkish learners utilized different LLSs to enhance their English competence owing to the use of mobile and computer technologies. Zhou and Wei (2018) stated that integrating LLSs within technology provides learners with practical solutions to become more effective learners. The study confirms

Zhou and Wei's (2018) argument that the availability of new technologies and language learning tools has grown much faster than the preparation of language teachers. Hence, EFL teachers need training in how to invest technology and in teaching English to maximize the exposure to this target language.

This study was conducted in two different ICT contexts, namely Yemen and Saudi Arabia. As the findings indicate, the Saudi participants outperformed Yemeni participants in terms of the frequency of LLS use. This difference could be attributed to the heavy usage of the Internet, which is more applicable to the Saudi learners than their Yemeni counterparts. This is supported by the pervasiveness of mobile technologies and convenience of online resources that require appropriate strategies for language learning effectiveness (Zhou & Wei, 2018). Previous studies (e.g. Cevdet, 2010; Ping & Luan, 2017; Salahshour & Sharifi, 2013) revealed significant differences between the use of LLSs and learners' proficiency levels – proficient learners employ LLSs more frequently than their less proficient counterparts.

As the data in Table 3 indicates, there is no significant difference between the use of LLSs between male and female learners. In a similar vein, Viriya and Sapsirin (2014) found that both male and female learners' use of LLSs falls within the same averages. This finding contradicts the notion that male and female learners applied LLSs differently (Liyanage & Bartlett, 2012). Ho and Ng's (2016) study revealed that female and male learners used LLSs differently. Similarly, Alhaysony (2017) found that Saudi female learners used LLSs more frequently than male learners did, yet the difference is insignificant.

Implications

The study contributes to the field of language learning strategies in terms of assessment and correlation. It has implications for EFL tertiary learners, teachers, and decision-makers. It urges EFL learners in general and Yemeni and Saudi learners in particular to utilize available technological tools to build on their English communicative competence by using different LLSs that suit their learning contexts. In this way, teachers can motivate their students in using such technology in their learning and encourage their students to use language-learning strategies properly. The study also urges the decision-makers, especially in Yemen, to develop the infrastructures of classrooms with technologies and internet connection, thus, both teachers and learners can benefit from technology in the learning and teaching process of English language.

LIMITATIONS AND FUTURE RESEARCH DIRECTIONS OF THE STUDY

While the chapter puts forward significant findings, it is worthwhile to mention unavoidable limitations in terms of instrumentation and sampling of the current study. The authors believe that the results would have been more reliable by triangulating methods of data collection. It would have been better if the sample were selected randomly and each university got a specific representativeness from the total sample. For triangulating data collection sources, further research may adopt a mixed-method approach, employing a variety of data collection tools. These limitations serve as 'food for thought' that may inspire other researchers to continue research in the field of technology-based learning strategies and to explore new uncharted areas.

CONCLUSION

This chapter has demonstrated that the average use of LLSs within the ICT-based learning environment surpasses the use of LLSs within Yemeni and Saudi contexts. Learning with ICTs provides various opportunities for learners to use LLSs differently to traditional learning strategies. This suggests the need to adopt various technology-based strategies for better language input and output. Although technology has become the lifeline for many, it is not common in some learning contexts such as Yemeni context. Also, handing out devices to learners may be seen as the means and the end rather than the means to an end. The availability of technology does not ensure better learning outcomes. Thus, the technology needs to be informed by pedagogy. Classroom teachers should join efforts to reorient English learning by adopting strategies for technology-enhanced learning paradigms, especially in contexts where exposure to the target language mostly happens in virtual spaces rather than the conventional classroom.

REFERENCES

Ahmad, J. (2016). Technology assisted Language learning is a silver bullet for enhancing language competence and performance : A case study. *International Journal of Applied Linguistics and English Literature*, *5*(7), 118–113. doi:10.7575/aiac.ijalel.v.5n.7p.118

Ahmed, R., Al-kadi, A., & Hagar, T. (2020). Preface. In A. Rashad, A. Al-kadi, & T. Hagar (Eds.), *Enhancements and limitations to ICT-based informal language learning: Emerging research and opportunities* (pp. xii–xx). Hershey, PA: IGI Global. doi:10.4018/978-1-7998-2116-8

Al-Ahdal, A. A. M. H. (2013). Integration of information and communication technology (ICT) into the education system of Yemen: The need of the hour. *International Journal of Social Sciences & Education*, *3*(1), 40–47.

Al-Buainain, H. (2010). Language learning strategies employed by English majors at Qatar University: Questions and queries. *ASIATIC*, *4*(2), 92–120.

Al-Kadi, A. (2018). Towards humanizing ELT: Revisiting the need for English in the medical context in Yemen. *Eric database* (ERIC Number: ED591138).

Al-Maktary, H. (2018). A cross-sectional study of oral communication strategies by successful EFL learners. *International Journal of Foreign Language Teaching & Research*, *6*(24), 23–37. http://jfl.iaun.ac.ir/article_611572.html

Al-Sohbani, Y. A. Y. (2016). An investigation of the reasons behind the weaknesses in English among public secondary school leavers. *Journal of Teaching and Teacher Education, 4*(2), 41-51.

Alhaisoni, E. (2017). Language learning strategy use of Saudi EFL students in an intensive English learning context. *Asian Social Science*, *8*(13), 115–127. doi:10.5539/ass.v8n13p115

Alhaysony, M. (2017). Language learning strategies use by Saudi EFL students: The effect of duration of English language study and gender. *Theory and Practice in Language Studies*, *7*(1), 18–28. doi:10.17507/tpls.0701.03

Ali, J.K.M., & Bin-Hady, W. R. A. (2019). A study of EFL students' attitudes, motivation and anxiety towards WhatsApp as a language learning tool. *Arab World English Journal,* (5), 289-298. Doi:10.24093/awej/call5.19

Aljuaid, H. (2010). Language learning strategies: Perceptions of female Saudi EFL learners. In *Papers from the Lancaster University Postgraduate Conference in Linguistics & Language Teaching, 2010*, 2–24.

Alqasham, F. H. (2018). Exploring Saudi EFL learners' agency toward the use of WhatsApp for English learning at Qassim University. *International Journal of Linguistics*, *10*(6), 10–43. doi:10.5296/ijl.v10i6.13857

Alzubi, A. A. F. (2019). *The effects of smartphones mediated language learning strategies on the learner autonomy of Saudi Arabian undergraduates* (Unpublished Ph.D. thesis). Universiti Sains Malaysia.

Alzubi, A. A. F., & Singh, M. K. M. (2017). The use of language learning strategies through smartphones in improving learner autonomy in EFL reading among undergraduates in Saudi Arabia. *International Journal of English Linguistics*, *7*(6), 59–72. doi:10.5539/ijel.v7n6p59

Bekleyen, N., & Hayta, F. (2015). Language learning in new era: Do mobile phones help? In A. Akbarov (Ed.), *The practice of foreign language teaching: Theories and applications* (pp. 434–445). New Castle, UK: Cambridge Scholars Publishing.

Bin-Hady, W. R. A. (2016). *Communicative competence in teaching English at secondary schools: A critical investigation in Yaff'ae district of Yemen*. GRIN Verlag. doi:10.13140/RG.2.2.17234.40645

Božinović, N., & Sindik, J. (2011). Gender differences in the use of learning strategies in adult foreign language learners. *Metodički obzori: časopis za odgojno-obrazovnu teoriju i praksu, 6*(11), 5-20.

Cevdet, Y. Õ. (2010). The relationship between language learning strategies, gender, proficiency and self-efficacy beliefs: A study of ELT learners in. *Procedia: Social and Behavioral Sciences*, *2*(2), 682–687. doi:10.1016/j.sbspro.2010.03.084

Creswell, J. W. (2012). *Educational research: planning, conducting, and evaluating quantitative and qualitative research* (4th ed.). Boston: Pearson Education.

Dörnyei, Z. (2005). The psychology of the language learners: Individual differences in second language acquisition. In Annual Review of Psychology. London: Lawrence Erlbaum.

Dörnyei, Z. (2007). *Research methods in applied linguistics*. New York: Oxford University Press.

Griffiths, C. (2013). *The strategy factor in successful language learning*. Bristol, UK: Multilingual Matters. doi:10.21832/9781847699428

Hismanoglu, M. (2001). Language learning strategies in foreign language learning and teaching. *The Internet and TESL Journal, 8*. Retrieved December 3, 2019, from http://iteslj.org/Articles/Hismanoglu-Strategies.html

Ho, A. P., & Ng, L. (2016). Gender-based differences in language learning strategies among undergraduates in a Malaysian public university. *Issues in Language Studies*, *5*(2), 1–17. doi:10.33736/ils.1631.2016

Khamkhien, A. (2010). Factors Affecting Language Learning Strategy Reported Usage by Thai and Vietnamese EFL Learners. *Electronic Journal of Foreign Language Teaching*, *7*(1), 66–85.

Lee, C. K. (2010). An overview of language learning strategies. *ARECLS*, *7*, 132–152.

Lessard-Clouston, M. (1996). ESL vocabulary learning in a TOEFL preparation class: A case study. *Canadian Modern Language Review*, *53*(1), 97–119. doi:10.3138/cmlr.53.1.97

Liyanage, I., & Bartlett, B. J. (2012). Gender and language learning strategies: Looking beyond the categories. *Language Learning Journal*, *40*(2), 237–253. doi:10.1080/09571736.2011.574818

Maldonado, M. (2016). Communication strategies used by different level L2 English learners in oral interaction. *Revista signos*, *49*(90), 71-93. doi: 09342016000100004 doi:10.4067/S0718

Metcalfe, J., & Noom-Ura, S. (2013). Communication strategy use of high and low proficiency learners of English at a Thai University. *LEARN Journal*, *6*(1), 66–87.

Nurhaeni, & Purnawarman, P. (2018). The use of smartphone and learning strategies. *Indonesian EFL Journal*, *4*(1), 43–48. . doi:10.25134/ieflj.v4i1.797

O'Malley, J. M., & Chamot, A. (1990). *Learning strategies in second language acquisition*. Cambridge: Cambridge University Press. doi:10.1017/CBO9781139524490

Oxford, R. L. (1990). *Language learning strategies: What every teacher should know*. Boston: Heinle Publishers.

Oxford, R. L. (2011). Strategies for learning a second or foreign language. *Language Teaching*, *44*(2), 167–180. doi:10.1017/S0261444810000492

Oxford, R. L., & Burry-Stock, J. A. (1995). Assessing the use of language learning strategies worldwide with the ESL/EFL version of the strategy inventory for language learning (SILL). *System*, *23*(I), 1–23. doi:10.1016/0346-251X(94)00047-A

Ping, H. A., & Luan, N. L. (2017). Effects of learners' language proficiency on their language learning strategies. *Malaysian Journal of Languages and Linguistics*, *6*(1), 10–25. doi:10.24200/mjll.vol6iss1pp10-25

Richards, J., & Platt, C. (1994). *Reflective teaching in second language classrooms*. Cambridge: Cambridge University Press. doi:10.1017/CBO9780511667169

Rubin, J. (1987). Learner strategies: theoretical assumptions, research history and typology. *Learner strategies in language learning*, 15-30.

Salahshour, F., Sharifi, M., & Salahshour, N. (2013). The relationship between language learning strategy use, language proficiency level and learner gender. *Procedia - Social and Behavioral Sciences*, *70*(1957), 634-643. doi:10.1016/j.sbspro.2013.01.103

Stern, H. H. (1975). What can we learn from the good language learner? *Canadian Modern Language Review*, *31*(4), 304–319. doi:10.3138/cmlr.31.4.304

Viriya, C., & Sapsirin, S. (2014). Gender differences in language learning style and language learning strategies. *Indonesian Journal of Applied Linguistics, 3*(2), 77–88. doi:10.17509/ijal.v3i2.270

Wenden, A., & Rubin, J. (1987). *Learner strategies in language learning*. Englewood Cliffs, NJ: Prentice Hall.

Williams, M., & Robert, L. (1997). *Psychology for language teachers: A social constructivist approach*. Cambridge: Cambridge University Press.

Yanju, S., & Yanmei, S. (2016). Communication strategies used by Middle Eastern postgraduate students at service encounters in University of Malaya. *European Journal of Language and Literature Studies, 5*(1), 40–45. doi:10.26417/ejls.v5i1.p40-45

Zare, P. (2010). An investigation into language learning strategy use and gender among Iranian undergraduate language learners. *World Applied Sciences Journal, 11*(10), 1238–1247.

Zhou, Y., & Wei, M. (2018). Strategies in technology-enhanced language learning. *Studies in Second Language Learning and Teaching, 8*(2), 471–495. doi:10.14746sllt.2018.8.2.13

ADDITIONAL READING

Cohen, A. D. (2014). *Strategies in learning and using a second language*. Routledge. doi:10.4324/9781315833200

Griffiths, C. (2004). Language learning strategies: Theory and Research. *Research Paper Series, 1*(1), 1–25. Retrieved from http://www.crie.org.nz/research-papers/c_griffiths_op1.pdf

Griffiths, S., & Cansiz, G. (2015). Language learning strategies: A holistic view. [SSLLT]. *Studies in Second Language Learning and Teaching, 5*(3), 473–493. doi:10.14746sllt.2015.5.3.7

Mart, I. M. P. (1996). The importance of language learning strategies in foreign language teaching. *Cuadernos de Filología Inglesa, 5*(1), 103–120.

Mitits, L. (2015). *Language learning strategies and multilingualism*. Kavala, Greece: Saita publications.

Nacera, A. (2010). Languages learning strategies and the vocabulary size. *Procedia: Social and Behavioral Sciences, 2*(2), 4021–4025. doi:10.1016/j.sbspro.2010.03.634

Oxford, R. (1999). Relationships between second language learning strategies and language proficiency in the context of learner autonomy and self-regulation. *Revista Canaria de Estudios Ingleses, 38*, 108–126.

Su, Y. (2018). A Review of language learning strategy research. *Theory and Practice in Language Studies, 8*(5), 522–527. doi:10.17507/tpls.0805.10

Sumarni, & Rachmawaty, N. (2019). Gender differences in language learning strategies. *Ethical Lingua, 6*(1), 13–22. doi:10.17509/ijal.v3i2.270

Tan, K. C., & Kaur, S. (2015). Types of language learning strategies used by tertiary English majors. *TEFLIN Journal, 26*(1), 17–35. doi:10.15639/teflinjournal.v26i1/17-35

Timirbaeva, G. R. (2013). Language learning strategies and their impact on learner autonomy. Paper presented at the *2013 International Conference on Interactive Collaborative Learning (ICL) Kazan National Research Technological University*, Kazan, Russia. 10.1109/ICL.2013.6644666

KEY TERMS AND DEFINITIONS

Assessment: The ability of measuring or judging the using/ applying of something in certain activity or task. It refers to how frequent each one of the six LLSs is used more by EFL learners to learn/acquire English within the information and communication technology (ICT) environment.

Correlation Research: A type of procedures in quantitative research used to measure the relationship between two or more variables.

EFL Yemeni/Saudi Learners: Refers to undergraduates enrolled in the English programs at four universities in the cities of Taiz and Hadramout in Yemen, and Najran and Bisha in Saudi Arabia.

Language Learning Strategies: The behavioral, mental, or physical procedures that learners use to quicken the acquisition of certain skill or system within the overall language learning process.

Technology-Enhanced Language Learning (TELL): A type of learning using technological means and devices.

APPENDIX 1

This questionnaire is designed to assess language learning strategies in technology-enhanced learning environments. In order to compete our study, the researchers appreciate your help in responding to following items as precisely as possible. We assure you that the date will be only used in this research and will remain confidential. Your name is not compulsory. Please read each statement and indicate your choice of responses with (✓) that tells the frequency you do the statement through technology.

Table 4. Survey: assessment of language learning strategies in technology-enhanced learning environments

	The statement	Always	often	sometimes	rarely	never
1	I write down the new words and meanings using electronics notes to repeat them.					
2	I examine how English words are used on the internet to learn them easily.					
3	I search the Internet for pictures to remember new words easily.					
4	I search the Internet for words that rhyme with new words to remember them.					
5	I search the Internet for places associated with new words.					
6	I watch English movies/ short stories on the Internet.					
7	I use online dictionaries to check the meaning of new words.					
8	I listen to and repeat audio files in English.					
9	I study and practice grammar using websites.					
10	I read short stories, novels, newspapers, magazines, etc. on the Internet.					
11	I search the Internet for information about topics, homework, etc.					
12	I search the Internet to learn the correct use of vocabulary and sentence structures.					
13	I make use of translation facilities on the Internet.					
14	I use note applications to write important information in English.					
15	I check the meaning of new words using dictionaries based on their parts.					
16	I search the Internet for unfamiliar words.					
17	I search the Internet for gestures I can use when I cannot think of a word.					
18	I search the Internet looking for similar words that I can use when I forget the exact word.					
19	When I cannot think of a word in English, I call/text a friend.					
20	I search for how other people learn English on the Internet.					
21	I record my voice and listen to it again.					
22	I search the Internet for ways to improve my English.					
23	I pay attention when someone is speaking English on the Internet.					
24	Using technology makes me feel more relaxed when I feel afraid of using English.					
25	I search the Internet for ways to encourage myself when being afraid of making mistakes.					
26	I use recorders and camera to check if I am tense when using English.					
27	I chat with friends through social networks about my feelings when learning English.					
28	I write my feelings using memos or diaries.					
29	I reward myself when I do well English by playing games.					
30	I look for people on the internet to correct me when I talk.					
31	I practice English with other students through social networks.					
32	I ask for help from English speakers on the Internet.					
33	I read about the culture of English speakers on the Internet.					

APPENDIX 2

Table 5. Statistical data including mean scores and standard deviations of LLSs in ICT-based environment as answered by the respondents to the questionnaire items

Questionnaire item	N	M	SD
I write down the new words and meanings using electronics notes to repeat them.	100	3.5400	.99919
I examine how English words are used on the internet to learn them easily.	100	3.7500	1.10440
I search the Internet for pictures to remember new words easily.	100	3.3000	1.22680
I search the Internet for words that rhyme with new words to remember them.	100	3.2600	1.25223
I search the Internet for places associated with new words.	100	3.0800	1.07007
I watch English movies/ short stories on the Internet.	100	3.7000	1.34465
I use online dictionaries to check the meaning of new words.	100	3.9300	1.17426
I listen to and repeat audio files in English.	100	3.7000	1.04929
I study and practice grammar using websites.	100	3.2900	1.10367
I read short stories, novels, newspapers, magazines, etc. on the Internet.	100	3.6300	1.06035
I search the Internet for information about topics, homework, etc.	100	3.9900	.98980
I search the Internet to learn the correct use of vocabulary and sentence structures.	100	3.9700	1.05844
I make use of translation facilities on the Internet.	100	3.9000	1.04929
I use note applications to write important information in English.	100	3.4200	1.24056
I check the meaning of new words using dictionaries based on their parts.	100	4.0000	1.00504
I search the Internet for unfamiliar words.	100	3.5700	1.18283
I search the Internet for gestures I can use when I cannot think of a word.	100	3.0500	1.27426
I search the Internet looking for similar words that I can use when I forget the exact word.	100	3.5400	1.25867
When I cannot think of a word in English, I call/text a friend.	100	2.9900	1.27521
I search for how other people learn English on the Internet.	100	3.7300	1.10878
I record my voice and listen to it again.	99	3.0000	1.37766
I search the Internet for ways to improve my English.	99	4.2727	.94565
I pay attention when someone is speaking English on the Internet.	99	4.3232	.97759
Using technology makes me feel more relaxed when I feel afraid of using English.	99	4.2222	.95357
I search the Internet for ways to encourage myself when being afraid of making mistakes.	99	3.9091	1.15256
I use recorders and camera to check if I am tense when using English.	99	2.6364	1.33596
I chat with friends through social networks about my feelings when learning English.	99	3.3131	1.20074
I write my feelings using memos or diaries.	99	2.9596	1.26103
I reward myself when I do well English by playing games.	99	2.8384	1.40485
I look for people on the internet to correct me when I talk.	99	3.1616	1.48260
I practice English with other students through social networks.	99	3.4848	1.10991
I ask for help from English speakers on the Internet.	100	3.1500	1.36608
I read about the culture of English speakers on the Internet.	100	3.4300	1.15693

Chapter 6
Assessing Foreign Language Narrative Writing Through Automated Writing Evaluation: A Case for the Web-Based Pigai System

Chia-An Lin
National Taipei University of Technology, Taiwan

Yen-Liang Lin
National Taipei University of Technology, Taiwan

Pei-Shan Tsai
National Taipei University of Technology, Taiwan

ABSTRACT

Automated writing evaluation (AWE) has become increasingly popular in the assessment of writing. The study in this chapter examines the extent to which EFL learners' overall narrative writing performance improves through the AWE feedback system (i.e., Pigai). Eighteen university participants were required to write one paragraph narratives on the web-based Pigai system every week over the course of a month. Findings show a significant improvement in overall scores between the first and last writing task. The analysis of lexical profile further shows a significant improvement in lexical richness, clause density, and paragraph length between the first and last narrative task. The study also reported that the primary error types that occurred in learner narrative writing were lexical, mechanical, and syntactic errors. Results of post-writing interviews also showed a positive attitude towards Pigai. Finally, a positive correlation was observed between automated Pigai scores and human rating scores, supporting the reliability of the AWE system.

DOI: 10.4018/978-1-7998-3062-7.ch006

INTRODUCTION

The rapid development of the internet and intelligent technology over the past twenty years has revolutionized the learning and teaching of English as a foreign language (EFL). During this time, computer-assisted language learning tools for automated writing evaluation (AWE) have become increasingly popular in EFL writing instruction across different educational levels (Huang & Renandya, 2018; Link & Hegelheimer, 2015; Zhang & Hyland, 2017). To improve English language writing, established commercialized programs such as *Criterion* (e.g., Attali & Burstein, 2006), *MY Access* (e.g., Vantage Learning, 2007), *Project Essay Grade* (e.g., Page, 2003) and *WriteToLearn* (e.g., Liu & Kunnan, 2016) have been used by large numbers of students and teachers internationally to improve writing skills for both native English speakers and EFL learners. These programs have proven useful, allowing English language learners to independently and immediately revise and improve their written work (Chen & Cheng, 2008). AWE tools were also designed to benefit teachers by reducing heavy grading loads by providing immediate, automatically-generated quantitative assessments and qualitative diagnostic feedback on large numbers of written works (Aryadoust & Riazi, 2017; Bai & Hu, 2017; Chen & Cheng, 2008). Recent AWE tools such as *LightSide* (Mayfield & Rosé, 2013), *Writing Pal* (Roscoe et al., 2017), *CorrectEnglish* (Wang et al., 2013) and *Pigai* (Li, Lu, & Li, 2015; Lu & Li, 2016) have been developed to be innovative learning platforms that provide individualized feedback, particularly for EFL contexts.

This chapter investigates one popular AWE tool, *Pigai*, examining the influence of the writing tool on EFL learner writing development. *Pigai* is beneficial to learners because it provides real-time feedback on learner's writing in a bilingual interface which is particularly suitable for Chinese-speaking leaners (Li et al., 2015). After users submit a written piece, *Pigai* immediately gives an overall score and comments based on vocabulary, sentence, discourse and content. Sentence-by-sentence feedback for the writing task is also provided. Although some studies examining *Pigai* have found it to be effective in diagnosing (Chao & Liu, 2017) and in improving overall English language writing (Huang & Renandya, 2018; Li et al., 2015; Zhang, 2016), specific errors and linguistic features of learner writing that improve over time have not yet been reported. In addition to its effect on learner writing development, how the AWE tool compares to human raters still remains unknown. This study assesses the performance of four aspects of student writing (i.e., vocabulary, sentence, discourse, and content), and examines primary error types of writing, learner attitudes towards AWE system, and the correlation between *Pigai* and human scoring. The study is designed to answer the following research questions:

1. To what extent does the AWE feedback system (i.e. *Pigai*) improve English narrative writing? Which aspects of writing benefit most from the *Pigai*?
2. What are the primary error types in narrative writing tasks identified through *Pigai*?
3. What are learners' attitudes towards using the *Pigai* feedback system?
4. How consistent are the scores provided by *Pigai* relative to human raters?

Based on the above research questions, this study tests the hypothesis that real-time writing feedback from an AWE system, i.e. *Pigai*, is beneficial to EFL learner writing development and helpful to identify learner errors in their writing production. Furthermore, learner's attitude and the correlation of scores provided by *Pigai* and human raters is also compared and discussed.

BACKGROUND

This chapter reviews the theoretical foundations and existing literature on assessment of writing by different AWE tools and how the tools facilitated the learning process. Emphasis is given to the development of different linguistic knowledge and writing skills through the use of AWE tools.

Assessment of Writing in AWE Tools

Writing can be assessed by multiple criteria and rubrics, including vocabulary, grammar, content, organization, and discourse. AWE tools basically follow similar evaluation criteria. Currently, there are several AWE tools helping writers to improve the quality of English writing, each with different strengths (Table 1). The focal tool of this study, *Pigai*, evaluates and reports on the appropriate length of organization, transitions of discourse, spelling and punctuation of mechanics, syntax and vocabulary of written work. It provides an overall score and comments, as well as sentence-by-sentence feedback, so users can revise and acquire knowledge by the extension of each sentence they have written in the system (e.g., Chao & Liu, 2017; El Ebyary & Windeatt, 2019; Li et al., 2015).

The most commonly used AWE tool is *Criterion*, developed by Educational Testing Service. Most research to date examining the development of English writing has used *Criterion* (e.g., Liao, 2015; Li et al., 2015; Li et al., 2014). The scoring system of *Criterion* consists of two complementary applications, critique and e-rater, making it suitable for the classroom setting (Li et al., 2014). The critique application can detect the errors and then categorizes them into grammar, usage, mechanics, and discourse elements of organization and development, while the e-rater application can provide an overall score by considering the writing quality. A second commonly used AWE tool, *MY Access*, developed by *IntelliMetric*, provides not only diagnostic feedback and holistic scores, but also "a variety of writing assistance features including *My Editor*, *Thesaurus*, *Word Bank*, *My Portfolio*, *Writer's Checklist*, *Writer's Guide*, *Graphic Organizers*, and *Scoring Rubrics*" (Chen & Cheng, 2008, p. 99). Other AWE tools such as *CorrectEnglish*, developed by Vantage Learning and *Intelligent Academic Discourse Evaluator*, developed by Iowa State University, are also widely used. *CorrectEnglish* features for the interactive platform, presented in seven languages, include English grammar learning, and different formatting styles, including APA, MLA, CBE, and Chicago style (Wang et al., 2013). *Intelligent Academic Discourse Evaluator* analyzes research articles at the level of discourse elements in 50 academic disciplines, helping the development of academic writing (Cotos, 2011). Although different AWE tools have different features, all provide immediate, individualized, and corrective feedback, pointing to drawbacks in learner writing and further assisting learners to improve the quality of writing.

Table 1. Comparison with Automated Writing Evaluation

Name of AWE Tools	Developer (Publish Year)	Areas of Scores and Feedback
MY Access	IntelliMetric (2007)	1. Focus & Meaning 2. Content & Development 3. Organization 4. Language, Use & Style 5. Mechanics & Convention
Criterion	Educational Testing Service (2009)	1. Grammar 2. Usage 3. Mechanics 4. Style 5. Organization & Development
Intelligent Academic Discourse Evaluator	Iowa State University (2009)	1. Text analysis of moves 2. Texts, emphasis on functional meaning
Pigai	Jukuu (2013)	1. Vocabulary 2. Sentence 3. Discourse 4. Content
CorrectEnglish	Vantage Learning (2013)	1. Grammar 2. Mechanics 3. Word choice 4. Organization 5. Argument structure

AWE tools operate on the premise of providing quality, real-time feedback to learners. This interactive feedback between AWE tools and learners has overall been shown to benefit learner outcomes. Through the AWE tools, users submit their written work, and the system can then provide immediate and helpful feedback, which allows users to focus on discourse, then actively revise their own work and enhance understanding (Bai & Hu, 2017; Cotos, 2011; Huang & Renandya, 2018). Not only did AWE tools provide effective feedback and improve writing, but most participants responded that the feedback let them concentrate on improving their writing and reported having positive impressions of the tools. This is important as it signals that AWE tools can be self-sustaining and used independently by learners. Similarly, as learners gain familiarity with the power of these tools, learners report that they use them less for simple revision, but instead for enhancing the quality and impact of a written work (Huang & Renandya, 2018; Tuzi, 2004). This means that not only do AWE tools provide basic language assistance, but that they also unlock self-learning potential in learners and provide opportunities to maximize the power of writing. However, for lower-proficiency learners there is evidence that the automated features of AWE tools may actually decrease learning – information on organization, logic, or that requiring individualized feedback is not provided by AWE tools (Li et al., 2015). Depending on the tool itself, long term writing skill development may be limited by the limitations of the tool itself; *Criterion*, for example, does not catch all grammatical errors and is prone to providing incorrect feedback (Li et al., 2015).

Learning Outcomes Using AWE Tools

Studies have shown that AWE tools help learners improve their grammar (e.g., Liao, 2015; Zhang, 2016), vocabulary (e.g., Wang et al., 2013), and organization (e.g., Tuzi, 2004) in writing production. Liao (2015), for example, traced the learning of 66 sophomore students through an essay-writing process using *Criterion*, and found significant improvement between first and final drafts, with a decrease in grammatical errors such as fragments, subject-verb agreement, and run-on sentences. A further study followed a single English major student using *Pigai* in a similar writing process, showing that with the help of an AWE tool the student was able to strengthen syntactic complexity and diversity (e.g., subordinating clauses and inverted sentence) by responding to AWE feedback (Zhang, 2016). AWE tools have also been shown to improve writing accuracy, allowing learners to be aware of and correct grammatical errors (Wang et al., 2013). Beyond grammar and vocabulary, AWE tools improve learners' understanding of how to organize their writing; AWE tools do not just benefit the technical aspects of writing, but also lead the user to develop better writing skills in general. In this regard, users are guided to re-think and organize the ideas during the writing process, thereby increasing overall writing quality (Tuzi, 2004). Not only did the AWE tool improve quality of output, but also increased length (word count) and connective incidence. Lu and Li (2016) reported an increase in length and overall use of more difficult, academic language, and that students applied more connective words and phrases in their final revision (Lu & Li, 2016). It was evident that the use of AWE enhanced both writing skills and students' lexicon.

In addition to improving the quality of English writing, participants in the majority of previous studies report holding positive attitudes towards the technology because the feedback provided by AWE helped improve their writing proficiency and enhance linguistic skills, language accuracy and encouraged them in their writing (e.g., Li et al., 2015). Nevertheless, the benefits reported in previous studies were not consistent. Huang and Renandya (2018), for example, examined whether lower-proficiency EFL learners (i.e. students scoring below 50 in TOFEL iBT) can improve their writing with the implementation of *Pigai*. Their results showed no significant difference between the control group and the experimental group, indicating that the revision quality may not always be improved with the use of an AWE tool (Huang & Renandya, 2018). Furthermore, some users reported confusion with and limited efficacy of feedback because they were not able to follow up with questions or clarifications (Wang et al., 2013). Some teachers and instructors also held negative views, reporting that AWE tools only allowed for basic language development and not meaningful linguistic growth, and further suggested that human feedback and assessment were important aspects that are not available in AWE tools (Chen & Cheng, 2008). Despite these differences in attitudes towards AWE tools, there is evidence to support the use as a language learning tool. This study examines the effect of one AWE tool, *Pigai*, on a group of Taiwanese EFL learners to explore how it can facilitate the development of learner writing and learner attitude toward the AWE tool.

MAIN FOCUS OF THE CHAPTER

Introduction to *Pigai*

Pigai is an AWE tool that provides automatic assessment of written works, giving the user an overall score of writing, general comments, and web-based feedback. *Pigai* works by analyzing written works that a user submits, and providing real-time sentence-by-sentence feedback for each written work. First, students write and submit their work directly on the *Pigai* interface. Upon submission, the feedback is immediately generated. The users are then invited to modify and resubmit their work on the interface. The analysis engine of *Pigai* includes 192 dimensions, categorized into four aspects: vocabulary, sentence, discourse and content. Scores for vocabulary are based on lexical richness (type-token ratio, i.e., the number of unique words divided by the number of total words) and lexical sophistication (i.e., academic words). Scores for sentence evaluated average sentence length, grammar accuracy and density of subordinate clauses. The evaluation of discourse included paragraph structure, paragraph length, number of paragraphs and use of connectives. Scores for content examined the relevance among sentences and paragraphs. Additionally, the feedback provided by the AWE tool contains the errors and extended learning, including learning tips, tips to correct, phrases for high marks, tips for collocations, and syntax checking (Guan & Liu, 2015). As seen in Figure 1, the system gives an overall score and general feedback on student writing.

Figure 1. An example of the feedback provided by Pigai

Context and Sampling

This study employed a mixed-methods approach to analyze the influence of *Pigai* on the development of L2 English writing skills of students in a university in Taiwan. The participants recruited for this study were twenty-two first-year English majors (8 male, 14 female), aged approximately 19 years old, who took the course "English grammar" taught by the researcher before the experiment started. During the course, all participants acquired some fundamental knowledge about English grammar and elements of narrative writing. They were intermediate proficiency level (B1 or B2) of English in overall language skills according to the CEFR (Common European Framework of Reference for Languages) scale. All of the students participating in this study were all volunteers and were given a small gift voucher for the participation.

Data Collection Process

Before the start of the experiment, the participants received training to familiarize themselves with the *Pigai* AWE feedback system as unfamiliarity with a system may result in negative effects of writing performance and learner attitudes (e.g., Huang & Renandya, 2018). After that, all participants were required to write one narrative paragraph on *Pigai* every week for one month on the following four narrative writing tasks: *A Memorable Trip*, *An Embarrassing Experience*, *My Unforgettable Summer Vacation*, and *A Memorable Experience in My Childhood*. Thirty minutes were allotted for writing, and 20 minutes allotted for revision for each submission. The control of the writing time makes the results more comparable. During the process of writing, the participants were not given any specific guidelines about how to structure their writing or what to write. To assess user attitude toward the AWE tool, all the participants who took part in this study were required to be interviewed. In the interview, they were asked to answer questions based on their experiences of using *Pigai*. The interview questions (see Appendix) included their perceptions of the AWE tool, the helpful features of *Pigai*, and strengths and weaknesses of AWE feedback. All the interviews were audio-recorded and then transcribed in Chinese and translated into English. Finally, to compare results of *Pigai* to that of a human rater, the writings of each participant were evaluated by experienced teachers who have taught EFL for over 10 years (including one native and one non-native English speakers) using similar rubrics as *Pigai*.

Data Analysis

In order to assess the influence of *Pigai* on writing improvement and the impact of the feedback system, various aspects of feedback are examined: relationship between revision frequency and final scores, lexical profile of the final revision in the first and the last narrative containing lexical sophistication, lexical richness, average sentence length, clause density and paragraph length (Agustin-Llach & Jiménez-Catalán, 2018; Laufer, 1994). Lexical richness is calculated by type-token ratio, i.e., the number of unique words divided by the number of total words. Lexical sophistication refers to the number of words used from the academic word list (AWL) (Coxhead, 2000). Clause density was measured by dividing the number of clauses by the number of sentences. To calculate the average lexical profile, the computer first individually calculates the writing at the level of word, sentence or paragraph, and finally the written piece. Then, it computes the average score and shows the percentage in a line graph. Each item in the lexical profile of the final revision of the first and the last narrative was analyzed by paired sample *t*-test to examine whether each item improved significantly from the first to the final writing production. The data also included revision frequency by each participant and their final scores, and the Pearson correlation analysis between the frequencies and final scores is tested. The correlation analysis was also applied to the analysis of scores from *Pigai* and experienced teachers in order to understand whether the scores between AWE and human raters are consistent.

Table 2. Average Score of the First Draft and Final Revision in Four Narratives

Narrative Tasks	Average (with SD)		Significance (*P* value)
	First Draft	Final Revision	
The First Narrative	77.06	79.90	.010*
The Second Narrative	76.41	80.47	.008*
The Third Narrative	77.35	80.36	.010*
The Final Narrative	77.98	81.31	.007*
* $p < .05$			

First drafts from each narrative were used to evaluate primary error types. Four error categories were included: mechanical errors (e.g., spelling, capitalization), semantic errors (e.g., collocation, sentence structure), syntactic errors (e.g., subject-verb disagreement, verb tense), lexical errors (e.g., noun, verb, conjunction). Each error identified through *Pigai* was manually checked and assigned to its error types by the researchers, and the numbers of each type were calculated. With regard to the evaluation of learners' attitudes towards *Pigai*, all the participants were individually interviewed by a trained researcher with the purpose of obtaining user experiences after using *Pigai* for the experiment. Participant interviews (see Appendix) constituted qualitative data, and participants were asked about the strengths and limitations of *Pigai*, reflections and attitudes towards AWE feedback systems, and comments or suggestions for the use of the system. To understand students' responses to the interview questions, content analysis was utilized in this study.

Table 3. Lexical Profile of the Final Revision in the First and the Final Narrative

Lexical Profile	Average (with SD)		Significance (*P* value)
	The First Narrative	The Last Narrative	
Lexical Sophistication	5.87 (0.66)	5.78 (0.67)	.005*
Lexical Richness	5.28 (0.34)	5.31 (0.35)	.001*
Average Sentence Length	18.42 (5.35)	17.07 (4.02)	.024*
Clause Density	1.01 (0.42)	1.07 (0.43)	.018*
Paragraph Length	186.47 (42.09)	187.33 (41.80)	.001*
* $p < .05$			

Findings

This study examines the effects of one AWE tool, *Pigai,* on EFL student narrative writing, primary error types in writing, learner attitudes towards *Pigai*, and the correlation between *Pigai* and human scoring. This section presents the findings of the empirical analysis based on the four research questions.

Effects of Pigai Feedback on Narrative Writing

This study first investigated the effect of *Pigai* on EFL narrative writing. Table 2 presents the differences in average scores between first and last drafts, showing a significant improvement across all four narratives. With the input and feedback provided by *Pigai*, learners can make interactional adjustments to what they write, proving to benefit their written production. Through feedback, learners better understand the errors they make, interaction which then facilitates language acquisition (Brown & Lee, 2015; Ellis, 2015).

Lexical profile includes lexical sophistication, lexical richness, average sentence length, clause density, and paragraph length. Table 3 shows the mean score of lexical profile and significance of differences between the final revision in the first narrative and in the final narrative. Lexical richness, clause density and paragraph length all show a significant improvement, suggesting the three linguistic aspects of the final narratives were markedly improved compared to those of the first narrative. For example, lexical richness increased from 5.28 to 5.31, meaning that students used more and various academic words in the last narrative than in the first narrative. However, there is a significant decrease in lexical sophistication and average sentence length between first and final drafts. This means that they did not use more difficult words in the final narrative.

However, by comparing the two narratives, the reason why the average sentence length in the final narrative is shorter is because of an uneven distribution of sentence lengths: 38% of sentences are 13.328-15.85 words long, while 27% are 18.375-20.9 words long. For the average sentence length in the first narrative, 26% of sentences were 15.85-18.375 words long. In addition, by examining the average scores of the two narratives, the average score in the final narrative is not higher due to the lower average sentence length. Therefore, in this case, learners who wrote shorter sentences did not necessarily have a better grasp of a language.

Figure 2. Relationship between Revision Frequency and Final Scores

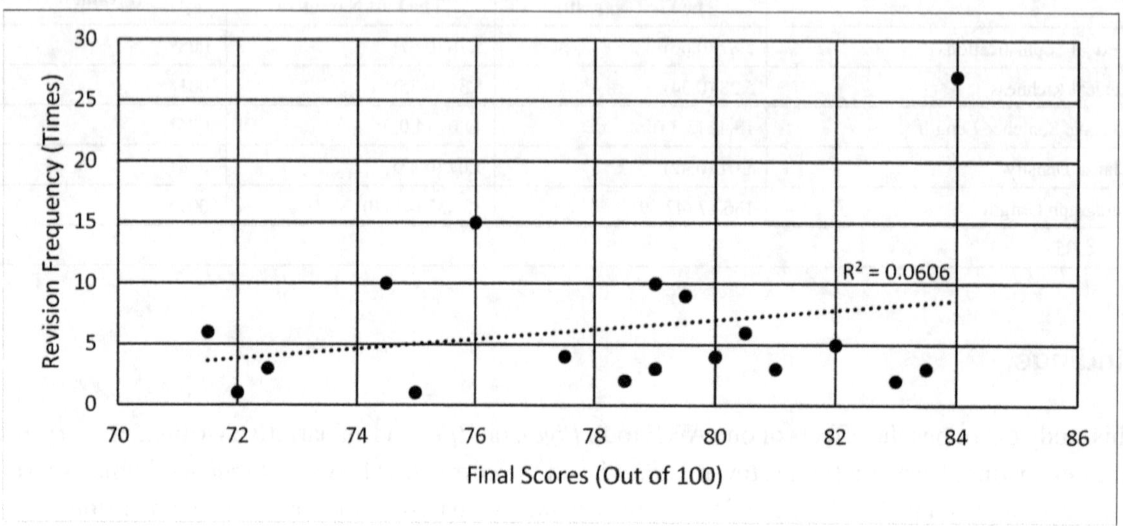

Furthermore, the relationship between revision frequency and final scores can help explain whether students improved their writing by interacting with the provided feedback. Figure 2 presents participants' final scores and revision frequency of the second narrative, showing a positive correlation between score and revision frequency. This indicates that the more times participants revised their writing, the higher score they got; in other words, by interacting with the feedback provided by *Pigai*, participants can get higher scores after revising their writing. Similar to second narrative, the other three narratives also showed positive correlation between scores and revision frequency.

Errors of English Narrative Writing

This study also examined error frequencies in first drafts in an effort to better understand the most common error types that learners made. To do this, error frequencies for first drafts of the four narrative paragraphs were calculated. In total, four main error-types were observed, as shown in Table 4. The primary error types identified through *Pigai* were lexical errors, mechanical errors and syntactic errors, which often stemmed from negative transfer from learners' L1, under generalization (e.g., ignorance of L2 syntactic rules) and approximation (e.g., misuse of near-synonyms and lexemes with similar sound/form). For lexical errors with nouns, students often did not make it clear whether the noun is countable or uncountable, such as 'informations', and the feedback provided by *Pigai* suggested that 'information' should be an uncountable noun. Other noun errors like 'a number of picture' and 'a pair of sneaker' were detected by *Pigai*, and the feedback suggested that the noun should be in the plural form of 'a number of pictures' and 'a pair of sneakers', respectively. Furthermore, there were two observed causes of mechanical errors. First, students used cellphones or computers to type their paragraphs, so they sometimes forgot to capitalize the first word of a sentence. For example, they often typed 'i' or 'we' in the beginning of a sentence instead of 'I' or 'We'. They also spelled words incorrectly which may reflect an input error rather than a true spelling error. For example, a student typed 'jewlry' and 'temparature' rather than 'jewelry' and 'temperature' in the first draft. As for syntactic errors, the most common subject-verb disagreement error was that the verb did not correspond to the subject in the sentence, such as 'I still remembers that I fell down on the street because of the heavy wind,' (the verb 'remember' should follow the subject 'I') and 'The memories is so unforgettable that I recall it from time to time during summer' (the subject 'the memories' is plural form, so the verb 'is' should become 'are'). Participants reported in the interview that their most common errors in writing English were mechanical and lexical errors. For example, a student answered that she sometimes did not know whether the noun was countable or not, and another student said that she was afraid of vocabulary because she usually spelled words incorrectly. In contrast to a similar study by Liao (2015) which concluded that "fragments, subject-verb disagreement, run-on sentence, and ill-formed verbs were identified as the primary grammatical error types" (p. 314), this study found that lexical errors, mechanical errors, and syntactic errors were the most common error types. However, according to Ferris (1999), the most common error types in both studies are 'treatable errors', making their results similar in terms that "errors occur in a patterned, rule-governed way (e.g., subject-verb agreement, run-ons and comma splices, missing articles, verb form errors)" (p. 6), and "can be fixed when learners review the rules governing these errors" (Liao, 2015, p. 309).

Table 4. The Percentage of Error Types in First Drafts of Four Narrative Paragraphs

Rank	Error Type	Percentage
1	Lexical Errors	32.48%
2	Mechanical Errors	23.50%
3	Syntactic Errors	22.22%
4	Semantic Errors	21.79%

On the other hand, by looking at total errors in the first draft, there is a decrease of total errors from the first narrative to the last narrative, and the error numbers declined from 77 to 44 (Table 2). As a consequence, the feedback from *Pigai* successfully makes participants notice their mistakes, resulting in a gradual decrease of grammatical errors. In addition, most participants responded that the feedback on first drafts made them notice errors, and in further drafts they were able to self-monitor, noticing when they made similar mistakes.

Figure 3. Total Errors of the First Draft in Four Narratives

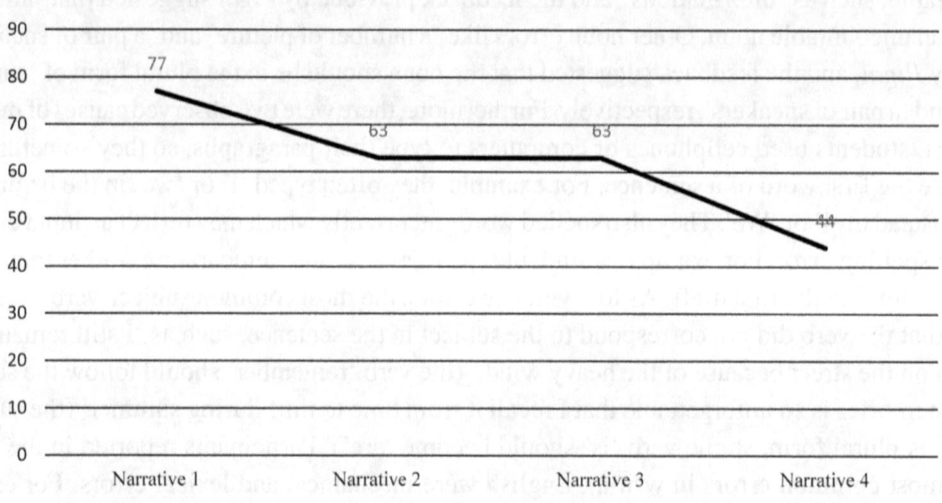

Attitudes towards Pigai

Participant interviews are considered a useful way to evaluate user impression of *Pigai*. All participants reported the merits of the feedback provided by *Pigai* and the quality of their writing was improved accordingly. Some of the responses are presented below.

"Yes, it can provide formal or advanced vocabulary. Most people may use basic vocabulary to make sure they don't make mistakes, but if you use some formal or advanced vocabulary, it may be better to your writing; therefore, I think providing recommended vocabulary is helpful" (Student 3, personal communication, June 18, 2018).

"Yes, the feedback system can identify grammatical errors you made, so you can directly revise your writing." (Student 4, personal communication, June 19, 2018)

"I think it is helpful to your writing for short-term training. However, for long-term training, you may need more complicated or advanced writing skills; then, I don't think *Pigai* will help you a lot at that time. Of course it can help you improve writing from basic level to intermediate level, but if you want to write in advanced level, you may need to find another way" (Student 2, personal communication, June 20, 2018).

"I think it is useful and convenient for those who want to enhance their writing skills by themselves" (Student 3, personal communication, June 18, 2018).

When the participants were asked about the most helpful aspect of the AWE feedback. The extended learning in the system (i.e. recommended expressions, learning hints, and extended differentiation) was considered the most beneficial function. On the usefulness of the generated suggestions for expressions, 77% of participants agreed that *Pigai* helped select a more appropriate use of words or phrases for replacement. Consequently, participants could acquire more knowledge about the appropriate lexical choices in narrative writing. For example:

"I think recommended expression is the most helpful because it focuses on phrases and sentence structures so that I can write better. Moreover, the score increased obviously if you use the feedback in recommended expression; basically, you can get more than 0.5 point" (Student 2, personal communication, June 20, 2018).

Although the extended differentiation (with frequency of use in target corpora) was found to be beneficial, 33% of participants reported that they did not fully understand the information of extended differentiation. This may be because it is not easy for them to interpret the frequency information of a word in a corpus. For example:

"Compared to extended differentiation, recommended expression is helpful to me. Because I still don't understand whether how many times a word occurred in the corpus is good for me or not, it didn't help me a lot" (Student 2, personal communication, June 20, 2018).

The system was also reported to be convenient, to give relevant, sentence-by-sentence feedback and efficient scores, to record the data within each individual's learning portfolio and suggested appropriate expressions and synonyms. The feedback provided by *Pigai* can offer formal vocabulary options which the user can choose in order to improve writing. *Pigai* also checks for grammatical errors, and users can immediately respond to suggestions to revise their writing. Finally, the way *Pigai* provides feedback is convenient and immediate, as opposed to human feedback which takes time. However, there was one negative comment about the feedback system, with one participant reporting that the function of *Pigai* is only able to help in the process of advancing from basic to intermediate writing levels; to advance beyond intermediate levels, *Pigai* would be insufficient and writers would need to find alternate learning tools or feedback options.

"The weakness is that the feedback system still made some mechanical errors; in other words, the writing errors identified by the system may not correspond to my expressions" (Student 2, personal communication, June 20, 2018).

"The weakness is that the system identified some errors which you write correctly, but you didn't know why they were wrong" (Student 5, personal communication, June 20, 2018).

Interview responses also identified some weaknesses of *Pigai* including correct usages marked as incorrect, vague feedback and a lack of face-to-face consultation. Five participants thought that the feedback did not correspond to the writer's intended meanings. In other words, the system detected an error and provided a better expression; however, it may not be the same as the original meaning. On the other hand, sometimes the system provided incorrect feedback (the original sentence was correct, but the system detected it as incorrect and offered incorrect suggestions).

Table 5. The Correlation of Scores from Pigai and Human Raters

		Pigai	Human Raters
Pigai	Pearson correlation	1	.744**
	Sig. (2-tailed)		.000
	N	18	18
Human Raters	Pearson correlation	.744**	1
	Sig. (2-tailed)	.000	
	N	18	18
** Correlation is significant at the 0.01 level (2-tailed).			

"I suggest that teacher should cooperate with *Pigai*. For example, first, I can get the feedback from *Pigai*; then, the teacher can check for the second time, so I can receive the feedback again. Hence, this way may be beneficial to my writing" (Student 2, personal communication, June 20, 2018).

As for any other comments and suggestions, two participants suggested that the writing should be corrected by both teachers and by *Pigai*. First, students can type their writing in *Pigai*, and then they can revise the more fundamental grammatical errors before being submitted to a teacher. This way, when teachers subsequently check their work, their workload can be reduced and allow them to focus on the content and the relevance of their writing (this is not reliable to be checked by the computer alone). This double-check method is suggested by participants to be an effective and more accurate way to check writing and enhance writing skills of students. The issue of human feedback incorporating with AWE feedback has also been discussed in other AWE studies (e.g., Chen & Cheng, 2008).

The Correlation of Scores from Pigai and Experienced Teachers

This section reports the correlation of scores from *Pigai* and those of experienced EFL teachers in an effort to better understand whether the way that the system gives scores is similar to human raters. To do this, scores provided by *Pigai* and by experienced teachers were collected, and then the data were analyzed through correlation analysis. A positive correlation was observed between *Pigai* scores and human rating scores, suggesting consistency between human and machine raters, though *Pigai* appeared to be stricter. Table 5 presents the correlation of scores from *Pigai* and two experienced teachers (Taiwanese and Canadian) as human raters (first narrative tasks). The scores are highly correlated in the first narrative; as for the rest of three narratives, the data also show the scores of *Pigai* and human raters are moderately positively correlated with the Pearson correlation coefficient r ranging from .05 to .07 (p <.05). That is, the scores given by *Pigai* is consistent with human raters.

SOLUTIONS AND RECOMMENDATIONS

Based on the findings presented in the previous section, the AWE feedback proved to be effective. There was an overall decrease in errors and a significant increase of overall scores, lexical richness, clause density, and paragraph length. The AWE tool used, *Pigai*, provided individualized feedback according to specific learner input, focused learners' attention on problematic aspects of their language use and led to self-correction, provoking adjustments to linguistic form or content until an acceptable level of understanding was achieved. The process of revision may also lead to intrapersonal interaction (Cotos, 2011; Ellis, 2015); learners appear to construct a better understanding of discourse phenomena and eventually produce better output. Participant interviews also supported these finding, indicating that participants generally showed a favorable attitude towards the feedback provided by *Pigai*. They reported that the automated evaluation system could help them identify the previously unattended language problems and correct the lexical, mechanical, syntactic, and semantic errors in writing. The strengths of the AWE identified in this study are also consistent with previous studies (e.g., Dikli & Bleyle, 2014; Li et al., 2015).

Although a number of previous studies (e.g., Huang & Renandya, 2018) found no clear improvement in revision quality with the use of *Pigai*, this study has shown a positive effect of using an AWE tool supporting the Interaction Hypothesis, that "interaction facilitates SLA because conversational and linguistic modifications that occur in discourse provide learners with necessary comprehensible linguistic input" (Muho & Kurani, 2014, p. 47). In particular, lexical richness, clause density and paragraph length all show a significant improvement, suggesting the three linguistic aspects of the final narratives were markedly improved compared to those of the first narrative. It appears that the feedback system of *Pigai* may help students acquire knowledge of vocabulary, which could then be used in following narratives. On the other hand, there was a significant decrease in lexical sophistication and average sentence length. This means that there was not an increased use of more difficult words or longer sentences from the first to final narrative tasks. However, this is not necessarily a reflection of decreased writing performance. They may use concise language and decrease use of unnecessary vocabulary. From the available data it is unclear if shorter sentences are a reflection of improved language skill, and as a result more investigation on this question is needed.

This study found a positive correlation between AWE and human scoring, showing consistency and equal efficacy of the automated reporting system; however, some users in this study reported a preference for correction by teachers. Previous studies have reported discrepancies (Roscoe, Crossley, Snow, Varner & McNamara, 2014; Wang & Brown, 2007) when analyzing the differences between AWE tools and human scoring. Wang and Brown (2007), for example, found that the AWE tool (*Intellimetric*) consistently gave higher scores and therefore higher rates of passing than human raters. A further study found that human raters produce a higher quality of scoring than that of an AWE tool, *Writing Pal* (Roscoe et al., 2014). Scores given by human raters were more highly correlated to scoring rubric subscales than scores given by the AWE system; in other words, human raters appeared to realize how students organized their ideas and arguments, and how they applied their general knowledge, reading comprehension and vocabulary skill in essays (Roscoe et al., 2014).

FUTURE RESEARCH DIRECTIONS

Although this study has demonstrated the pedagogical merits of AWE, some possible limitations to the use of AWE were recognized. First, some of the lexical profile used in the study, such as lexical difficulty and average sentence length, were not improved over the one-month experiment through the AWE system alone. As the development of lexicon may require a long period of time or additional assistance from an instructor, future studies may consider a longer term (e.g., a semester) with intense use of *Pigai* and teacher guidance would probably result in the improvement of these elements of lexical profile. Replicating this intervention on more groups/participants may also be required to validate the findings of this study. Second, the data discrepancies between the AWE and the human scoring are statistically equal, but accuracy of these data could still be improved. It is, for example, unknown if a larger cohort of professional teacher feedback tested against the same *Pigai* feedback would maintain a positive correlation. More teachers as human raters can be invited in future studies to increase sample size and thereby include a greater diversity of human perspectives and scoring styles, and then compare these to those of *Pigai*. The pedagogical implications of the present study relate to the implementation of *Pigai* in EFL writing classes. Due to some weaknesses of *Pigai*, such as correct usages labeled as errors and actual error that was missed, EFL teachers are suggested to incorporate *Pigai* to help students improve EFL writing by scaffolding learners' interpretations of the machine-generated feedback. For example, students can submit their writing through *Pigai* in order to revise lexical, syntactic and semantic errors first, and then teachers guide learners to revise their own writing particularly in organization, logic, or more sophisticated aspect of composition; therefore, this incorporation would be expected to more effectively facilitate the development of writing.

CONCLUSION

The present study was designed to assess EFL narrative writing development with the support of *Pigai*, a well-known AWE tool. It was found that the AWE tool can be effective in identifying learner errors and guide EFL learners to revise their writing by providing qualitative diagnostic sentence-by-sentence feedback. One of the significant findings to emerge from this study is that by looking through the lexical profile of final revisions in the first and last narratives, lexical richness, clause density, and paragraph length were significantly improved. A significant improvement can also be seen between the first draft and final revision of each narrative, showing the beneficial effect of the AWE system on revising written production. *Pigai* also successfully helped students notice errors, leading to the decrease of total number of errors in subsequent revisions, a sign that they were becoming aware of their mistakes and self-correcting. The study has also shown that the AWE system could efficiently help identify leaner errors, showing that the primary error types that occurred in narrative writing were lexical errors, mechanical errors, and syntactic errors. Most of the students also held positive attitudes towards the use of *Pigai* because the feedback helped them notice the errors they made and provided recommended expressions. With regard to the consistency, a positive correlation was shown between *Pigai* and human raters, suggesting that the way that the system assesses is similar to that of experienced teachers. This result can be used to help students who are originally hesitant to use an automated feedback system; not only is the feedback similar to that of teachers but it is faster and more responsive.

REFERENCES

Agustin-Llach, M. P., & Jiménez-Catalán, R. M. (2018). Teasing out the role of age and exposure in EFL learners' lexical profiles: A comparison of children and adults. *International Review of Applied Linguistics in Language Teaching*, *56*(1), 25–43. doi:10.1515/iral-2015-0075

Aryadoust, V., & Riazi, M. (2017). Role of assessment in second language writing research and pedagogy. *Educational Psychology*, *37*(1), 1–7. doi:10.1080/01443410.2016.1227089

Attali, Y., & Burstein, J. (2006). Automated essay scoring with e-rater V. 2. *The Journal of Technology, Learning, and Assessment*, *4*. Retrieved from http://www.jtla.org

Bai, L., & Hu, G. (2017). In the face of fallible AWE feedback: How do students respond? *Educational Psychology*, *37*(1), 67–81. doi:10.1080/01443410.2016.1223275

Brown, H. D., & Lee, H. (2015). *Teaching by principles: An interactive approach to language pedagogy*. White Plains, NY: Pearson Education.

Burstein, J., Chodorow, M., & Leacock, C. (2004). Automated essay evaluation: The Criterion online writing system. *AI Magazine*, *25*, 27–36.

Chao, I., & Liu, E. (2017). Developing an automated essay scoring and feedback system for learners of English in Taiwan. In *4th Annual International Conference of the Asian Association for Language Assessment*. Taipei, Taiwan: The Language Training and Testing Center.

Chen, C. F. E., & Cheng, W. Y. E. (2008). Beyond the design of automated writing evaluation: Pedagogical practices and perceived learning effectiveness in EFL writing classes. *Language Learning & Technology*, *12*(2), 94–112. Retrieved from http://llt.msu.edu/vol12num2/chencheng/

Cotos, E. (2011). Potential of automated writing evaluation feedback. *CALICO Journal*, *28*(2), 420–459. doi:10.11139/cj.28.2.420-459

Dikli, S., & Bleyle, S. (2014). Automated essay scoring feedback for second language writers: How does it compare to instructor feedback? *Assessing Writing*, *22*, 1–17. doi:10.1016/j.asw.2014.03.006

El Ebyary, K., & Windeatt, S. (2019). Eye tracking analysis of EAP students' regions of interest in omputer-based feedback on grammar, usage, mechanics, style and organization and development. *System*, *83*, 36–49. doi:10.1016/j.system.2019.03.007

Ellis, R. (2015). *Understanding second language acquisition* (2nd ed.). Oxford, UK: Oxford University Press.

Ferris, D. (1999). The case for grammar correction in L2 writing classes: A response to Truscott (1996). *Journal of Second Language Writing*, *8*(1), 1–11. doi:10.1016/S1060-3743(99)80110-6

Gass, S., & Mackey, A. (2007). Input, interaction, and output in second language acquisition. In J. Williams & B. VanPatten (Eds.), *Theories in second language acquisition: An introduction* (pp. 175–199). Mahwah, NJ: Lawrence Erlbaum.

Guan, X. F., & Liu, Q. X. (2015). The introduction of a great help in college English composition teaching. In *Proceedings of the 2015 Joint International Social Science, Education, Language, Management and Business Conference* (pp. 133-136). Atlantis Press.

Huang, S., & Renandya, W. A. (2018). Exploring the integration of automated feedback among lower-proficiency EFL learners. *Innovation in Language Learning and Teaching*, 1–12. doi:10.1080/17501229.2018.1471083

Laufer, B. (1994). The lexical profile of second language writing: Does it change over time? *RELC Journal*, *25*(2), 21–33. doi:10.1177/003368829402500202

Learning, V. (2007). *MY Access! Efficacy Report*. Newtown, PA: Author. Retrieved from http://www.vantagelearning.com/school/research/myaccess.html

Lee, I. (2017). *Classroom writing assessment and feedback in L2 school contexts*. Singapore: Springer Singapore. doi:10.1007/978-981-10-3924-9

Li, J., Link, S., & Hegelheimer, V. (2015). Rethinking the role of automated writing evaluation feedback in ESL writing instruction. *Journal of Second Language Writing*, *27*, 1–18. doi:10.1016/j.jslw.2014.10.004

Li, Z., Link, S., Ma, H., Yang, H., & Hegelheimer, V. (2014). The role of automated writing evaluation holistic scores in the ESL classroom. *System*, *44*, 66–78. doi:10.1016/j.system.2014.02.007

Li, Z. X., Lu, Z. H., & Li, X. W. (2015). AWE-based corrective feedback on developing EFL learners' writing skill. In *Critical CALL – Proceedings of the 2015 EUROCALL Conference* (pp. 375-380). Padova, Italy: Research-publishing.net.

Liao, H. C. (2015). Using automated writing evaluation to reduce grammar errors in writing. *ELT Journal*, *70*(3), 308–319. doi:10.1093/elt/ccv058

Liu, S., & Kunnan, A. J. (2016). Investigating the application of automated writing evaluation to Chinese undergraduate English majors: A case study of "WriteToLearn". *CALICO Journal*, *33*(1), 71–91.

Lu, Z. H., & Li, Z. X. (2016). Exploring EFL learners' lexical application in AWE-based writing. In S. Papadima-Sophocleous, L. Bradley, & S. Thouësny (Eds.), CALL communities and culture – short papers from EUROCALL 2016 (pp. 295-301). Dublin, Ireland: Research-publishing.net.

Muho, A., & Kurani, A. (2014). The role of interaction in second language acquisition. *European Scientific Journal*, *16*, 44–54. Retrieved from https://eujournal.org/index.php/esj/article/view/4696/4488

Page, E. B. (2003). Project essay grade: PEG. In M. D. Shermis & J. C. Burstein (Eds.), *Automated essay scoring: a cross-disciplinary perspective* (pp. 43–54). Lawrence Erlbaum.

Ranalli, J., Link, S., & Chukharev-Hudilainen, E. (2017). Automated writing evaluation for formative assessment of second language writing: Investigating the accuracy and usefulness of feedback as part of argument-based validation. *Educational Psychology*, *37*(1), 8–25. doi:10.1080/01443410.2015.1136407

Roscoe, R. D., Crossley, S. A., Snow, E. L., Varner, L. K., & McNamara, D. S. (2014). Writing quality, knowledge, and comprehension correlates of human and automated essay scoring. In *The Twenty-Seventh International Flairs Conference* (pp. 393-398). AAAI Press.

Roscoe, R. D., Wilson, J., Johnson, A. C., & Mayra, C. R. (2017). Presentation, expectations, and experience: Sources of student perceptions of automated writing evaluation. *Computers in Human Behavior*, *70*, 207–221. doi:10.1016/j.chb.2016.12.076

Tuzi, F. (2004). The impact of e-feedback on the revisions of L2 writers in an academic writing course. *Computers and Composition*, *21*(2), 217–235. doi:10.1016/j.compcom.2004.02.003

Wang, J., & Brown, M. S. (2007). Automated essay scoring versus human scoring: A comparative study. *The Journal of Technology, Learning, and Assessment*, *6*(2), 4–28. Retrieved from https://eric.ed.gov/?id=EJ838612

Wang, Y. J., Shang, H. F., & Briody, P. (2013). Exploring the impact of using automated writing evaluation in English as a foreign language university students' writing. *Computer Assisted Language Learning*, *26*(3), 234–257. doi:10.1080/09588221.2012.655300

Warschauer, M., & Ware, P. (2006). Automated writing evaluation: Defining the classroom research agenda. *Language Teaching Research*, *10*(2), 157–180. doi:10.1191/1362168806lr190oa

Zhang, Z. (2016). Student engagement with computer-generated feedback: A case study. *ELT Journal*, *71*(3), 317–328. doi:10.1093/elt/ccw089

Zhang, Z. V., & Hyland, K. (2017). Student engagement with teacher and automated feedback on L2 writing. *Assessing Writing*, *36*, 90–102. doi:10.1016/j.asw.2018.02.004

ADDITIONAL READING

Cotos, E. (2011). Potential of automated writing evaluation feedback. *CALICO Journal*, *28*(2), 420–459. doi:10.11139/cj.28.2.420-459

Huang, S., & Renandya, W. A. (2018). Exploring the integration of automated feedback among lower-proficiency EFL learners. *Innovation in Language Learning and Teaching*, 1–12. doi:10.1080/17501229.2018.1471083

Li, J., Link, S., & Hegelheimer, V. (2015). Rethinking the role of automated writing evaluation feedback in ESL writing instruction. *Journal of Second Language Writing*, *27*, 1–18. doi:10.1016/j.jslw.2014.10.004

Liao, H. C. (2015). Using automated writing evaluation to reduce grammar errors in writing. *ELT Journal*, *70*(3), 308–319. doi:10.1093/elt/ccv058

Liu, S., & Kunnan, A. J. (2016). Investigating the application of automated writing evaluation to Chinese undergraduate English majors: A case study of "WriteToLearn". *CALICO Journal*, *33*(1), 71–91.

Wang, Y. J., Shang, H. F., & Briody, P. (2013). Exploring the impact of using automated writing evaluation in English as a foreign language university students' writing. *Computer Assisted Language Learning*, *26*(3), 234–257. doi:10.1080/09588221.2012.655300

Warschauer, M., & Ware, P. (2006). Automated writing evaluation: Defining the classroom research agenda. *Language Teaching Research*, *10*(2), 157–180. doi:10.1191/1362168806lr190oa

Zhang, Z. V., & Hyland, K. (2017). Student engagement with teacher and automated feedback on L2 writing. *Assessing Writing*, *36*, 90–102. doi:10.1016/j.asw.2018.02.004

KEY TERMS AND DEFINITIONS

Automated Writing Evaluation: The technology to evaluate essays and provide scores and feedback for users.

Extended Differentiation: The reference of extended learning which tells users how many times the word they use occurs in the corpus or which helps users make the differentiation between similar words.

Extended Learning: Different kinds of references for users to learn and revise their essays (e.g., recommended expression, synonyms learning, learning hints, and extended differentiation).

Lexical Profile: The analytical statistics of writings based on corpora and cloud computing in *Pigai* and categorized into various aspects (e.g. average word length, lexical richness, lexical sophistication, average sentence length, clause density, and paragraph length).

Lexical Richness: Type-token ratio, that is, the number of unique words divided by the number of total words.

Lexical Sophistication: Words are categorized by *Pigai* for different levels of (e.g., frequently used word, academic word, and informal word). Lexical sophistication refers to the number of words used are from the academic word list.

Pigai: A web-based system which users can submit their writings in and receive an overall score and sentence-by-sentence comments and feedback.

Recommended Expression: The reference of extended learning which provides some better or more formal words similar to the word that users use in writing.

APPENDIX

The Interview Questions

1. How do you think about the AWE system?
2. Are you satisfied with the overall scores and comments?
3. What kind of aspect, vocabulary, sentence, discourse, or content, is the most helpful to you? Why?
4. Do you think that AWE feedback helps you improve your writing? Why?
5. What kind of errors do you usually make in your writing?
6. Do you think that the AWE feedback helps you notice the errors you make?
7. How do you revise your writing by looking through AWE feedback? For example, do you revise all the errors provided by the AWE feedback, or you just choose some parts of it? Why?
8. What kind of AWE feedback is the most helpful to you? Why?
9. Do you think that extended learning under the AWE feedback like recommended expression, synonyms learning, learning hints, or extended differentiation, are helpful to you? Why?
10. Can you identify the strengths and weaknesses of AWE feedback?
11. Which way do you prefer, corrected by teachers or corrected by AWE system?
12. Do you have any comments or suggestions for the use of AWE system?

Section 2
ICT-Based Methods

Chapter 7
An Expanded Framework for Facilitating Learner Autonomy and Enhancing Intrinsic Motivation Through Specifically-Designed Online Tasks:
Technology-Enhanced Language Learning

Kasim Koruyan
King Saudi University, Saudi Arabia

ABSTRACT

This chapter addresses the research gap in providing an extended framework for facilitating learner autonomy and enhancing intrinsic motivation through specifically-designed online tasks to enhance the development of reading skills in higher education. The approach to designing the reading tasks was informed by the comprehensive expansion of Chapelle's model explicitly to provide a theoretical framework for task design to assess the impact of the iPad-enhanced task design on the development of learner autonomy and motivation. Data collection and processing followed an exploratory case study approach applying mixed-method design. The differences in median scores for pre- and post-data were statistically tested using a Mann-Whitney U test. Thematic analysis was used to identify, analyze, and report themes in qualitative data collected for this study. Analysis of the results suggests that changing the culture of instruction and preparing university students for the realities of the digital age seem to be both positive and necessary.

DOI: 10.4018/978-1-7998-3062-7.ch007

INTRODUCTION

Technology-enhanced language learning refers to language learning that takes place in a technology-rich environment and the range of technologies used in language learning (Motteram, 2013). As Skehan (2003) argues, technology-enhanced classrooms are playing an important role in relation to motivation and autonomy in language learning. Sotiriou and Primalis (2013) also suggest that technology and its applications can be very powerful aids when delivering reading lessons, and that they can stimulate students' interest in reading. However, merely by providing technological tools, learning does not mean take place unless they are informed by pedagogy.

As far as learning English is concerned, despite English being generally accepted as an internationally important language for academic and professional success, Turkish students are reluctant to read in general and in English in particular. Indeed, a recent survey has reported that Turkish students had the poorest results in English exams in European countries (Education First, 2013). Commenting on the results of the survey, Bülbül, Mısırlıoğlu, Ceyhun, Araz and Altuğ (2014) suggested that by and large Turkish people and students in particular lack interest in reading, particularly in English. Some of the reasons for this may include:

- students' attitudes towards the learning situation (crowded classrooms),
- the way the English language is taught (teacher-centered classes),
- that the teaching and learning materials are based on the audio-lingual method, and
- difficulties in reading and writing in English due to learning differences.

As a result, many students have become dissatisfied with learning English. This type of dissatisfaction has been highlighted by their lack of interest in reading and their passivity towards English being taught in the classroom (Boyno, 2011). Thus, changing the culture of instruction and preparing university students for the realities of the digital age seem to be both positive and necessary moves and a first step that may encourage an active language learning process and enhance students' motivation to read. As Krashen (2004) suggests, reading is the most powerful tool we have in language education.

An exploration of the use of iPad-supported tasks for English language learning and reading in particular will contribute to the understanding of the nature and role of students' motivation with regard to learning English in the Turkish context. Another core problem, according to Boyno (2011), is that Turkish students are not given the chance to develop a sense of taking responsibility for their learning, because the concept of learner autonomy is absent in Turkish education. Consequently, students are not motivated to make their own choices and to take the initiative in terms of their learning; instead, they are told what they need to do. Saraç's observations (2013, p. 21) confirm that learners remain exposed to traditional educational methods where the teacher is the "sage on the stage" rather than the "guide on the side". Indeed, learners may not want to become autonomous learners, because they are accustomed to being "spoon-fed" and controlled (Deci & Flaste, 1995, p. 85), which may also explain a lack of motivation to learn English.

As a result, a teacher-centered, textbook-reliant, audio-lingual teaching method is commonly found to prevail in language classrooms in Turkey (Büyükkantarcıoğlu, 2004). This may be because the English language curriculum has not considered the needs and characteristics of students. Thus, this study conducted a needs analysis about students' interests and learning preferences before designing the online reading tasks and using 'FluencyWorlds', an interaction application. To encourage change, iPads were used to help students to take at least some responsibility for their learning while doing group presentations, and increase their motivation along with pedagogical interventions. Yet, teachers also need to facilitate this process and adopt a learner-centered approach. The iPads-enhanced task design is embedded in the researcher's pedagogical approach to teaching, which aims at increasing learner autonomy. Hence, online reading tasks were designed to allow students to use their iPads to enhance their language learning and reading skills. Thus, through technology-enhanced task design, students were encouraged to exercise control over their learning of English and given the opportunity to become active participants in and outside the classroom. An examination of how students in the English Preparatory Program (EPP) use iPads in a task-based approach to develop their reading skills in English will contribute to the understanding of the role of learner autonomy and intrinsic motivation in the Turkish education context.

Therefore, this chapter addresses the research gap in providing an extended framework for facilitating learner autonomy and enhancing intrinsic motivation through specifically designed online tasks to develop reading skills in higher education. It sets out to answer two research questions:

1. How does the introduction of technology-enhanced task design affect the motivation of students to read in English in EPP?
2. To what extent does the introduction of technology-enhanced task design enable students to exercise control over their English language learning in EPP?

Next section describes learner autonomy and motivation in language learning, and their relationship with information and communication technology (ICT) followed by related studies in the field. After this, the chapter shows the methodology, outlining an exploratory case study approach with mixed methods. Then, it analyses the findings and discusses those findings in relation to the research questions. Finally, this chapter draws conclusions from the study and future research directions and limitations of the study.

BACKGROUND

Definitions of Autonomy in Language Learning

In recent years, interest in learner autonomy has grown considerably in the field of language learning (e.g. Benson, 2011; Dam, 1995; Kohonen, 1992; Little, 2007). Despite the proliferation of research on autonomy over the last 30, its definition remains unclear, particularly in relation to language learning, as Benson and Voller (1997) indicate that "monolithic definitions of autonomy and independence have proved elusive" (p. 13).

Even though the exact definition of autonomy is still in debate, there appears to be some consensus about certain aspects of the concept in language learning. "The ability to take charge of one's own learning" (Holec, 1981, p. 3) appears to be the most cited definition and it may take many shapes, such as the ability to take the initiative, to be aware of learning progress and to evaluate learning outcomes, which require the ability and capacity for "critical reflection" (Little, 1991, p. 4). Kohonen (1992) approaches the concept from the sociocultural perspective by stating that "autonomy thus includes the notion of interdependence that is being responsible for one's own conduct in the social context" (p. 19). In other words, autonomous language learners are able to work collaboratively with others and solve conflicts or problems in constructive ways.

Following the same line of argument as Kohonen (1992), Little (2007) proposes that learner autonomy is "the product of an interactive process" (p. 18). Students learn collaboratively through interaction with each other (Vygotsky, 1978) and interdependent autonomy is possibly more applicable to the classroom environment. Thus, learner autonomy is understood in two different ways: the first highlights the individual dimension (Holec, 1981), while the second foregrounds the social dimension (Kohonen, 1992). As a result, the conceptualization of autonomy has shifted from seeing it as an independent phenomenon (the independence of the individual) to accepting its interdependence (the interdependence of a group) aspect. In this sense, autonomy can be related to the psychological need within self-determination theory (SDT) for an important intrinsic motivational component, 'relatedness'. For the purpose of this study, Holec's and Kohonen's definitions, along with Dam's conceptualization (1995), which brings both approaches together, that is "a readiness to take charge of ones' learning … independently or in co-operation with others" (p. 1) are used.

According to Littlewood (1996, p. 428), taking responsibility for one's own learning depends on two major components of autonomy, namely 'ability' and 'willingness'. Ability depends on both "knowledge" about choices offered to the learner and the 'skills' for implementing those choices, whereas willingness entails 'motivation' and 'confidence'. Dam (2011) also stresses students' willingness and capacity to learn as key elements in promoting learner autonomy. Thus, developing learners' autonomy means developing their 'ability' and 'willingness', together with their knowledge, skills, intrinsic motivation and confidence. Little (1990, p. 12) warns, however, that students may initially not accept or be reluctant to take responsibility for their own learning due to their previous learning experience, as observed, for example, by Borg and Al-Busaidi (2012) with Omani students. The key to developing language learner autonomy, therefore, seems to be gradually supporting students to become autonomous users of the second language (L2) as reflected in their conscious use of strategies, self-evaluation of their progress and reflection of their learning (Dam, 1995). Therefore, language teachers should empower their students to self-evaluate their learning through their support and guidance, which is the approach the researcher has chosen for this study

Thus, autonomy, specific to the current study's context in the chapter, is taken to mean exercising control over certain aspects (e.g., collaborating, self-evaluating and reflecting) of the learning of English independently or interdependently. Accordingly, online reading tasks in this study were designed in a way that the participants would have opportunities to work both independently and with their group, in and outside the classroom.

Motivation in Language Learning

Much has been written to establish that motivated students learn a L2 better than those who are not (e.g. Deci & Ryan, 1985; Dörnyei & Ushioda, 2011; Gardner, 1985). The importance of motivation in second and foreign language learning has been increasingly recognized ever since Gardner and Lambert (1959) introduced the social-psychological approach.

The pioneering study by Gardner (1985) and his socio-educational model led the field of motivational research until the 1990s. However, a number of researchers (e.g. Crookes & Schmidt, 1991; Dörnyei & Ushioda, 2011; Oxford & Shearin, 1994) have criticized Gardner's model for focusing too narrowly on integrative and instrumental dimensions of motivation and paying little attention to the role of motivation in L2 classrooms.

As a result, to gain an in-depth understanding of motivation to learn a language in an institutional context, other approaches and concepts, such as intrinsic/extrinsic motivation and SDT, have been introduced expanding Gardner's socio-educational construct. Due to lack of space, these concepts are not examined comprehensively, but intrinsic motivation will be briefly discussed below.

Corder's phrase "[g]iven motivation, anyone can learn a language" (cited in Skehan, 1989, p. 49) highlights the importance of motivation in language learning. Despite its generally unchallenged position and the amount of research undertaken in this field, there is no shared understanding of the exact nature of motivation and it is still an "elusive concept" (Dörnyei, 1998, p. 128).

However, several researchers have explored motivation extensively, and there seems to be an agreement over particular aspects, such as the force, desire or reason that initiates the persistence to achieve a goal. For this study, the common points of the definitions expounded by Williams and Burden (1997), Dörnyei and Ottó (1998) and Gardner (1985) (i.e. reasons to do an action, initiate and sustain it) are used. This is because the introduction of the iPad-enhanced task design and interactive application may arouse initial interest, due to the attraction of the electronic gadget and novel tasks, and enable students to internalize, at least to some extent, what they are doing. However, it may not lead to students investing time and effort to sustain their interest in learning a language.

Intrinsic/Extrinsic Motivation and Self-Determination Theory in Language Learning

According to Deci and Ryan (1985), self-determined individuals have common innate psychological needs for competence, relatedness and autonomy. Individuals have a feeling of competence when they face and overcome "optimal challenges" successfully, and they experience relatedness when they care for and are cared for by others. Thus, innate psychological needs are closely related to intrinsic motivation. Deci and Ryan (2000) argue that intrinsically motivated students are those who, by feeling competent and self-determined, simply enjoy doing the activity itself, have fun and expand their own feeling of achievement while working on a language task. The online reading tasks in this study are designed in a way to intrinsically motivate students and help them to exercise control over their learning through the use of the iPad. Therefore, this research will explore the impact of technology-supported learning for fostering reading skills, on learners' intrinsic motivation and self-determination. It aims to examine whether the integration of technology-enhanced task design into classrooms helps to enhance students' intrinsic motivation and their ability and willingness to read in English within and beyond the classroom.

Extrinsic motivation, on the other hand, refers to learning the L2 as a means to an end, often stemming from external factors, such as receiving external rewards or avoiding punishments (Deci and Ryan, 2000). Extrinsic motivation may be sufficient at the initial stage of L2 learning but, when the initial excitement begins to wear off, it may be impossible to sustain throughout what Dörnyei (1998, p. 117) calls "the long and often tedious learning process". The iPad itself represents an element of extrinsic motivation, and it is an external push into the classroom to help students take on some responsibilities for their learning and become motivated providing its use is based on a pedagogically informed approach to task design in learning contexts.

The guiding principle for the tasks is to support students in making active and sustained contributions to their language learning, in gaining satisfaction from the learning process before the initial excitement (of iPads) wears off. Thus, by transforming external regulation into their own internal control processes, EPP students may develop intrinsic motivation that, to some extent, may help overcome the problems outlined earlier.

According to Selçuk (2015), the success rate of students learning English in Turkey was 50% in 2011, and the proportion of students who did not show interest in lessons was very high. Exploring possible sources that triggered this in EFL classes, Selçuk (2015) observed that class material, reading topics, and perceiving reading in English as boring were demotivating factors. Rahman, Jumani and Basit (2010) researched Pakistani students learning English and found that textbooks and lack of use of modern technological aids demotivated the participants.

As far as reading habits are concerned, investigating those of high school students in three provinces in Turkey, Bülbül et al. (2014) found that Turkish people did not have a positive attitude towards reading books and 70% of young people in Turkey did not read books at all.

Technology-Enhanced Language Learning

Selinger (2001) states that:

ICT is found in all sectors of the workplace in developed countries, and it is becoming increasingly used in the developing world. Children of today, at the very least, need to become aware of the potential of new technologies in all aspects of their lives (no page number).

In Turkey, there have been some attempts to introduce ICT into the education system as well as to other parts of social life over the last three decades, and more recently FATIH project (Movement for Enhancing Opportunities and Improving Technology) in high schools (Koruyan, 2016). Those attempts have been made to integrate ICT into schools and universities so that students can gain the knowledge and skills required for the information age in general. Another point made by Selinger (2001) is that even though we are in a digital age and some, or maybe the majority of students have access to gadgets such as mobile phones, PCs and/or laptops and use social media, this should not mean that they are able to use those tools for educational purposes. This is because merely by providing technological tools, learning will not occur on its own (Healey, 1999, p. 136), but rather, as Motteram (2013, p. 182) suggests, how to deploy those technologies in classroom practice and "how they mediate that practice" are more important. Therefore, students still need training in the use of the technology for learning (Gönen & Akbarov, 2015).

Therefore, careful guiding of students, training of both teachers and students and designing of online learning tasks are needed so that learners can benefit from the use of ICT in this digital age. Without proper guidance, accessing unrestricted information can in fact prevent learners from taking more responsibility (Murray, 1999), and may demotivate them. The literature (e.g. Hampel, 2006; Kurek & Hauck, 2014) on ICT and language learning and teaching also warns us that the use of technology needs to be informed by pedagogy rather than simply being technology-driven as mentioned earlier. This means that ICT should be part of a comprehensive pedagogical framework. The Ministry of National Education (MoNE) has also failed to provide pedagogical training for teachers and students while implementing the FATIH project which would have enabled them to design tasks and/or discover more about what the e-pad has to offer (Koruyan, 2016). For example, Gönen and Akbarov's survey results with university students in Turkey (2015) showed that students "need assistance to use mobile technologies for language learning purposes" (p. 120), and as Kurek and Hauck (2014) suggest, we should create engaging and exciting learning opportunities and environments not only to give our students more chances to exercise control over the learning of English but also to motivate them by using technology. Accordingly, the focus should be more on how to train students to access consistent, reliable and authentic materials afforded by the use of technology informed by pedagogy as this study attempted to do.

The Role of ICT in Relation to Autonomy and Motivation in Language Learning

The role of ICT in developing autonomy and motivation has been vaunted over the years, with a number of assertions (e.g. Benson, 2011; Murray, 2005; Yaprak, 2014) made in favor of computer-enhanced language learning, for example, motivating aspects of technology-enhanced language learning (e.g. Murray, 2005), and autonomy and motivating aspects of technology (e.g., Hampel & Hauck, 2006; Meri, 2012; Samur et. al., 2015; Ushioda, 2000). The present study aims to build on these studies in a specific Turkish context.

Research mostly indicates that there is a correlation between positive affective states and additional incentives to learn a language (Ellis, 2003). In other words, technology-enhanced task design can act as an additional incentive to link autonomy and motivation as affective states. Through the use of the iPad and appropriately designed tasks, students can participate individually and collaboratively in activities, such as carrying out online research and presenting the results as a group in the class. This can help learners to enhance their intrinsic motivation to learn the language and improve their reading skills (Chapelle & Jamieson, 2008, p. 65), along with developing strategies for reading online.

Hence, the aims of the reading tasks designed for this study are to provide learners with "meaning-based activities closely related to learners' actual communicative needs and with some real-world relationship" (Levy & Stockwell, 2006, p. 249) in which learners have to "achieve a genuine outcome", such as solving a problem. This, in turn, will lead them to seek out opportunities for exposure to and using English outside the classroom. Therefore, from the sociocultural perspective, the guiding principle for the tasks is to support students in making active contributions to their language learning and to intrinsically motivate them.

Furthermore, the advent of technologies has clearly influenced language learning materials and task design. However, according to Chapelle (2000) the development of materials is not often clearly informed by theories of L2 learning, and she proposes a set of criteria for task design in CALL: language learning potential, learner fit, meaning focus, authenticity, positive impact and practicality. The tasks designed for this study follow these criteria. Some researchers (e.g. Hampel, 2006; Hauck & Youngs, 2008) have expanded her framework and applied it in synchronous computer-mediated communication environments for distance education. Although Chapelle provides us with a basic theoretical framework, learner autonomy and motivation do not explicitly appear in this framework. Some CALL researchers (e.g. Blin, 1999) also indicate that they do not always find comprehensive frameworks used to explore the development of learner autonomy. Therefore, it is crucial that attention be given to the way in which tools such as iPads are used and indeed to the very purpose of using these tools in formal educational settings within a comprehensive pedagogical framework. This requires a clear vision of language learning objectives and task design, which is the starting point of this study. This study, therefore, further expands Chapelle's model explicitly to provide a framework for task design to assess the impact of the iPad-enhanced task design on the development of learner autonomy and motivation. As a result, the tasks were designed to encourage a learner-centered approach providing opportunities for student interaction, collaboration and communication inside and outside the classroom to enhance students' intrinsic motivation as found in the Chinese context whereby intrinsic motivation was increasingly enhanced by a task-based EFL program (Lau, 2009).

Exploring Malaysian undergraduate students' motivational aspects in CALL classrooms, Abdul-Razak (2000) found that students in classes that used computers enjoyed English more than those who did not use computers, and it helped increase their interest, motivation and autonomy for language learning. Al-Shammari (2007) investigated undergraduate students' attitudes towards CALL in Turkish Arabia and the post-treatment questionnaire data revealed that students' positive attitudes increased and they were motivated by using computers and took responsibility for their language learning. Finally, in the US context, Ducate and Lomicka (2013) investigated the use of a mobile device, the iPod touch and they found that students felt that the iPod enabled them to have more exposure to language outside the classroom and that their learning increased more than if they did not have the device. They said that using the iPod was motivating, fun and interesting. Thirty-seven studies from 1970 to 2006 summarized by Grgurovic, Chapelle and Shelley (2013) indicated that overall results favored a technology-supported pedagogy in language learning.

Concerning the Turkish context, Samur et al. (2015) conducted a study investigating Grade 9 Anatolian High School students' perceptions about using e-pads in their language studies. Their data revealed that students appreciated having access to more authentic materials and that using tablet in their language studies intrinsically motivated them and that they exercised control over their learning. Mutlu and Eroz-Tuga (2013) investigated first-year university students who were trained through ICT for 5 weeks in language learning strategies to promote learner autonomy and enhance motivation at a university in Turkey. They found that the participants' strategy uses improved, they were more willing to take responsibility for their language learning, and their motivation was enhanced. They concluded that computer-assisted language learning (CALL) played a positive role in promoting university students' autonomy. Yaprak (2014) presented a framework informed by Chapelle (2000) for the design of collaborative tasks in a CALL environment at a university in Turkey to find out about university undergraduate students' initial attitudes towards CALL tasks, and she used group discussions to determine their final attitudes. She found that a computer-assisted interactive and collaborative learning environment offered opportunities for interaction and collaboration via a discussion forum which supported language tasks that empowered the learners to be more autonomous. As a natural outcome of Task-based Language Learning (TBLL) and CALL, she concluded that studying in a multimedia environment intrinsically motivated language students to activate and improve their reading skills. Finally, investigating Anatolian High school students' motivation and autonomy in a technology-enhanced environment by expanding on Chapelle's (2000) framework, Koruyan (2016) found that the overall results indicated that students who participated in his study were willing and able to exercise control over the learning of English and their intrinsic motivation to engage in reading tasks was increased through participation in technology-enhanced language learning tasks.

This study expanded on the existing research and focused on higher education, because research regarding the impact of ICT on autonomy and motivation in language learning is still lack in the Turkish context and more studies are needed to establish this relevance in practice.

MAIN FOCUS OF THE CHAPTER

Exploratory Case Study Approach

The approach taken in this study was that of a case study which used both qualitative and quantitative methods. The case study looked at two classes in the English Preparatory Program, exploring technology-enhanced task-based language learning. Yin, one of the most well-known advocates of case study research, describes it as consisting of "an empirical enquiry that investigates a contemporary phenomenon in depth and within its real-life context, … in which multiple sources of evidence are used" (2009, p. 14). This study can be described as an exploratory case study analyzing and interpreting the language learning process resulting from the introduction of technology-supported task-based learning from the perspective of participants.

Participants

This study was conducted with a total of 32 participants aged between 19 and 23 (23 females and 9 males) in the EPP at a Turkish university. Their English level was pre-intermediate according to the placement test. The researcher informed them about the research, the research tool, and methodology. They declared their consent and he assured them their anonymity. The students were chosen on volunteering basis and the institution was chosen because they use iPad for their project-based learning and the researcher had an easy access to conduct the study.

Design and Administration of the Online Reading Tasks

The pedagogical focus of this study is to facilitate learner autonomy by encouraging learners to take some control of their learning and enhance motivation through online tasks specifically designed to enhance the development of reading skills. Table 1 presents the criteria proposed by Chappelle (2000, p. 8).

Table 1. Criteria for CALL tasks (Chappelle, 2000, p. 8)

Language learning potential: The degree of opportunity presents for beneficial focus on form.
Learner fit: The amount of opportunity for engagement with language under appropriate conditions given learner characteristics.
Meaning focus: The extent to which learners" attention is directed toward the meaning of the language.
Authenticity: The degree of correspondence between the learning activity and target language activities of interest to learners out of the classroom.
Positive impact: The positive effects of the CALL activity on those who participate in it.
Practicality: The adequacy of resources to support the use of the CALL activity.

In addition to the criteria in Table 1, the tasks and activities in those tasks in the study were designed to encourage learners to collaborate with each other, and to provide opportunities for active participation and discussion. Hampel (2006, p. 113) suggests that task design should take account of the affordances of technology for specific purposes. For the purpose of this study, online dictionaries and YouTube videos were provided via hyperlinks. Further, because online reading is different from reading hard copy text, different reading strategies could be developed through online reading activities, which would enhance learner autonomy. There were three tasks, and each task involved reading text and was divided into a number of steps involving learners in activities. Each task was completed over a number of lessons each lasting 50 minutes. One of the tasks, which is 'Fun Festivals' was carried out through the 'bugclub' interactive website followed by general comprehension, vocabulary and grammar questions. In addition to those tasks, the 'FluencyWorlds' interactive app. was used to simulate daily conversations, such as getting to know each other in an authentic environment, doing online shopping, seeing a doctor or going to the cinema in the target language (TL). The participants felt like they were having a conversation with a native speaker. On this app., they can practice the language as much as they can and check their mistakes and corrections by getting immediate feedback. The criteria used for the design of the tasks are explained below:

- **Language learning potential**: The main focus of the reading activities of these communicative tasks was on meaning. However, students worked on linguistic aspects (i.e. vocabulary) of the reading. Focus on form was planned to take place either at the beginning or at the end of the lessons, which this chapter explained where and when necessary depending on the objective of the lesson.
- **Learner fit**: The reading topics were chosen from the needs analysis conducted before conducting this study, paying careful attention to students' interests, age and language capacity (Chappelle, 2000) to enable them to participate actively and willingly in the learning process, both independently and interdependently.
- **Meaning focus**: The learner's attention was predominantly on the meaning of the language while carrying out the reading tasks. The negotiation of meaning took place during students' discussion and interaction with each other to exchange information gathered from what they had read and researched on the internet, both inside and outside the class (Ellis, 2003).
- **Authenticity**: The brainstorming activities and YouTube videos along with activities on 'FluencyWorlds' application drew on learners' prior experience and use authentic material that the learner is likely to encounter outside the classroom. Nunan (2004) also stresses the importance of introducing authentic texts into the learning situation.
- **Positive impact:** CALL activities were intended to have a positive impact on students by allowing them to engage and interact with each other during pair or group work to share and exchange information. The tasks also allowed students to build on their cultural knowledge (Hauck & Youngs, 2008).
- **Practicality:** It is very useful and effective for students to go online, search and find information to complete their tasks in seconds with/without their teacher's guidance where and when necessary, and in this sense an iPad was very practical for online searching.
- **Collaboration**: Pair and group work, whole class feedback, group presentations, class blog discussions and focus group enabled collaboration within and between the groups. The collaboration provided an opportunity for negotiation of meaning and communication in the target language.
- **Interaction**: The tasks allowed students to meet and interact with each other in and outside the class to work collaboratively, which was intended to enhance students' language development (Ellis, 2003) and reading skills. In the final steps of the tasks, students were provided with the op-

portunity to reflect on their thoughts in the form of discussion, which encourages more collaborative autonomous learning among students (Hampel, 2006).

- **Developing strategy**: Instructions guided students to help them with the development of strategies (e.g. students supported their presentation with YouTube clips and visual images to give a clearer message of their presentations to the other groups) and helped them to work with the iPad in and outside the class by searching online and conducting interviews. Students looked at visual materials that allowed for open interpretation, used online dictionaries provided via hyperlinks, highlighted words when they needed it, and they searched for information from the links provided (non-linearity).
- **Creativity**: Students supported their presentations with creating YouTube videos and pictures. They also showed creativity by suggesting how the use of iPads in language classrooms could be improved.
- **Affordances of modes**: The tasks take the affordances of different modes, such as visual images, YouTube video clips and online dictionaries, into consideration, which helps to convey the meaning of the reading text.
- **Reflection**: Students were becoming aware of their learning (Murphy et al., 2005) by reflecting on the learning process at the end of each group presentation and on the class blogs about the activities, lessons, atmosphere of the class and their presentations.
- **Self-evaluation**: Furthermore, students had the opportunity to evaluate their own reading levels at the pre- and post- tasks stages. Evaluating learning is very important for the development of learner autonomy (Dam, 1995).

The online reading tasks were administered in the class. The students were divided into 4 groups in both classes. Task instructions were displayed on the Smart Board for the students to follow. The researcher presented the pre-reading activities (e.g. warm-up and lead in) through the Smart Board to set the context of the reading task, then left the students to do the rest of the activities on their own and at their own pace, allowing him to observe and note down in my journal the students' reactions to online reading tasks during the remainder of the lesson.

Data Collection Methods and Analysis

To enhance reliability, clarify potential doubts and reduce the scope for bias within the case study, the results gathered from different methods of data collection were compared to achieve triangulation. Lincoln and Guba (1985) point out that triangulation is a check on data and constructions of data.

This study draws on diverse sources of data, such as interviews, closed and open-ended questions from the questionnaires, reflections through class blog and focus group and a researcher journal. Pre- and post-task questionnaires were distributed to all students in both classes. Pre-and-post-task interviews were conducted with a number of students, who indicated their willingness to participate through the pre-task questionnaire for the pre-task interview and at the completion of reading tasks for the post-task interview.

The researcher was an instrumental in obtaining the research findings and then interpreting them. Therefore, to minimize potential bias, two professional researchers were recruited to review the data, such as interview transcripts and interpretations. In addition, the participants were consulted to check that interpretation concurred with their experiences. In this way, findings were verified to ensure that the results produced were reliable and supported conclusions drawn.

In line with Burton (2000), both quantitative and qualitative research techniques can be legitimately used in case studies together with an appropriate statistical program. A frequently-used test of the of pre- and post- test differences in a case like this study is a Mann-Whitney U test because the data in this study were not normally distributed (Hatch & Lazaraton, 1991). This test also enables comparison of two non-paired groups that do not need to be of equal size as in the case of this study (Creswell, 2012).

The qualitative data which consisted of interviews, open-ended questions in the questionnaires, class blog discussions, focus group and researcher journal entries were analyzed through thematic analysis using NVivo software. Thematic analysis is a widely used qualitative analytical method (Roulston, 2001).

Table 2. Data extract from qualitative tools for initial analysis of the main themes

Data extract from post-task interviews	Coded as
1. The introductions were very nice and I love them (motivation).	1. Motivation
2. The video clips and photos were very effective (the impact of ICT on motivation)	2. Motivation
3. The pictures from the Fun Festival made me think positively about the culture of that country. I wish I could visit that country (ICT may motivate to read more about the festivals and bridge between learning in the classroom and outside world which may encourage students to read more have the desire to visit the place)	3. Motivation
4. We learnt how to be critical and how to discuss what we learn with confidence and learnt how to find information in a short time.	4. Autonomy

The content of the table is coded as follows:

- Red color represents learner autonomy and its aspects/sub-themes.
- Yellow color represents motivation and its aspects/sub-themes.
- Green color represents the positive impact of the affordances of ICT on learner autonomy and motivation.
- The coding is explained in the text in bold (e.g., IM stands for intrinsic motivation)

Table 3. Data extract from qualitative tools for initial analysis of the main themes

Data extract from post-task interviews	Coded as
ST: No, it was enjoyable and everybody worked together very well. **[Intrinsic motivation]- [Collaboration = Learner Autonomy]**	**IM, COLL/LA**

Findings

This chapter sets out the pre-and-post tasks results in relation to the research questions. First, the overall results from the questionnaires will be reported and illustrated with quotes from interviews, class blog discussion and notes from the research journal and focus group followed by an analysis in relation to the research questions.

Motivation

The data presented in this section answer to the first research question: How does the introduction of technology-enhanced task design affect the motivation of students to read in English in EPP?

Table 4. Average responses to items in relation to different aspects of motivation

Aspects of motivation	Average scores (Highest: 5.0)	
	Pre-task	Post-task
Attitudes towards the learning situation	3.1	4.7
Intrinsic motivation	4.1	4.9
Extrinsic motivation	3.9	3.7

The results before introduction of the tasks in Table 4 demonstrate that students' responses to items indicating intrinsic motivation received the highest average score (4.1). Thus, students' initial motivation was driven internally to learn the language. Students responded positively on extrinsic motivation (3.9), while their attitudes towards the learning situation scored the lowest (3.1) among the motivational aspects. However, the overall trend of the subjects' responses after the implementation of the tasks thorough iPad were very positive about the different aspects of motivation I was exploring. Intrinsic motivation and attitudes towards learning English received the highest mean scores, while extrinsic motivation was the lowest. These results were corroborated by the qualitative findings. Indicators for motivation and its variations (e.g. motivation and sub-categories) were recorded many times during the post-tasks interview, class blog discussions and open-ended questions. This chapter does not propose to present and discuss all the data due to word limit. So, it will focus on intrinsic motivation.

Intrinsic Motivation

Pre-task data show that some students seemed to have a high level of intrinsic motivation to read. They positively expressed their intention to read and enjoy more English, put more effort into and spend more time reading English if they used iPads in the classrooms with more interesting activities (average = 4.1). This may be because students thought that the iPad would provide easier access to authentic and conventional resources, be cheap, save time, enhance practice and/or help them learn English. It may also be because they thought that using an iPad was fashionable. Some students responded that the iPad would 'contribute to education' as well.

The following post-task interview comment also illustrates the findings:

"The activities were motivating, and I love them very much... they were really nice and interactive" (S/1).

As a result, the activities appeared to have had a very positive influence on students' motivation to learn English.

The post-task results suggest that all students showed strong tendencies to be intrinsically motivated. There was strong agreement (average = 4.9) with the statements related to this construct (i.e. since they started using the iPad in technology-enhanced task-based learning, students have been having fun, enjoying learning English, spending more time and putting more effort into reading English, and they also very much drew satisfaction from searching and finding information about the reading topics, then presenting the findings in the class).

Students were asked to explain their answers whether they felt very motivated while carrying out the tasks. They found it motivating watching the goals in the Women's World Cup, watching the video clips about the topic; preparing presentations and conducting interviews; reflecting their ideas at the end of the lessons. In addition, they also found the lessons on these topics very unusual and enjoyable.

There were also lots of comments that reflected intrinsic motivation in the post-task questionnaire qualitative data. These comprised the encouragement to read more, spending more time and putting more effort into reading in English – such as using bugclub.com and practice their English on 'FluentWorlds' app. – finding more about other cultures, enjoyable and interesting English lessons, active participation, opportunities to reflect on their ideas, and interaction among the students and with bugclub.com while reading and with 'FluentWorlds' app. Those results were supported by students' interview comments:

"I love the lessons in this class" (S/2).

"I loved watching the best goals in the Women's World Cup and … just wow … " (S/3).

"I quite like the activities about 'the movies and holidays' on the FluencyWorlds app… you can have a normal conversation with people on this app like real and they reply to you and ask questions, like: 'how are you?'' where are you from?' and other stuff … and when I can't pronounce a word or phrase, it gives you option to read and tap on the correct option to reply to their questions … I both improve my reading and speaking … it is really cool" (S/4).

There were some specific comments about how the online aspects of the designed materials motivated students to read and interact with the 'FluencyWorlds'. For example, some students (S/2,3,4,6,7,8).) used the opportunities provided to spend more time on reading stories in English:

"I tried to read online newspapers … I used 'bugclub' website which you suggested to me … I love it, it is really a nice website" (S/6).

"I have nearly finished all the topics at beginner level on the application you gave us … yes, 'Fluency-Worlds' … I really like this application … It gives you a constant feedback while chatting with them in this application" (S/2).

In addition, some others found the lessons designed for this study to be very motivating and enjoyable:

"The lessons were very motivating, fun and enjoyable" (S/7).

Students' intrinsic motivation was increased by being involved in the learning process as a result of tasks which were enabled by the iPad:

Table 5. Mann-Whitney U test results: Questionnaire items related to motivation

Variables	Test	N	Median Scores	Mann-Whitney U value	Level of significance P
Intrinsic motivation	Pre	32	4	761	0.001
	Post	32	5		
	Total	64			
Extrinsic motivation	Pre	32	3	313	0.001
	Post	32	4		
	Total	64			
Attitudes towards learning situation	Pre	32	3	39.5	0.001
	Post	32	5		
	Total	64			

"This way, I am involved in the activities like presentation and when I do it myself, I learn and get more benefits ..." (S/1).).

They also liked reflecting on their ideas at the end of the lessons:

"I loved the ideas when we discussed the presentations and what we learnt from them at the end of our presentations" (S/5).

Interaction and collaboration among learners intrinsically motivated them to achieve the tasks:

"We worked together and helped each other, and we finally managed to complete our presentation ..." (S/3).

Those responses corroborate with explanations in the post-task questionnaire and focus group discussion that participation in the online tasks using their iPad led the learners to spend more time on reading. Their initial expectations in the pre-task questionnaire matched with their post-task reading habits in English. Class blog contributions also echoed the results from the post-task questionnaire and interviews:

[Blog 1] We enjoyed the lessons, because they were quite interactive, especially at the beginning and end of the lesson.
[Blog 2] Yes, we loved the lesson today, we watched perfect goals.

The contributions highlight the positive impact of the lessons on students' intrinsic motivation to read beyond the classroom. I also noted similar observation in my journal.

It is important to note that the increase in students' intrinsic motivation seems to be predominantly a result of the iPad-enhanced tasks and materials designed for this study. However, my teaching style, which was different from that of other teachers, is also likely to account for some of the change in the students' approach to learning along with the atmosphere in the class and topics chosen.

There were numerous comments and postings about reading tasks, activities, themes, affordances of technology, and the influence of the use of the iPad that indicated how they fostered their intrinsic motivation.

Table 5 shows the results of Mann-Whitney U tests performed on the motivation responses.

For this measure, and then for the other four for each student, the median pre- and post-task score was calculated, and then compared these median pre- and post-task scores using the Mann-Whitney U test. For all aspects of motivation, the pre- and post-task median rank is significantly different ($P < 0.001$). Therefore, the probability of the results occurring by chance is very low. In other words, it is highly unlikely that the difference between pre- and post-task questionnaire responses has occurred by chance.

Reading Habits

This study also looked at the students' reading habits after they experienced the iPad reading tasks designed for the study by using the post-task questionnaire data.

Table 6. Responses to reading habits

Frequency of reading	Every day	Three or four times a week	Once a week	Once a month	Never
Pre-task: English for please	2	3	7	7	13
Post-task: English for please	20	10	2	0	0
Pre-task: English for study	9	9	12	2	0
Post-task: English for study	27	5	0	0	0

Table 6 illustrates participants' reading habits, pre-task data show that 5% of the learners expressed a lack of motivation to read books for pleasure because they never read in English at all, while 31% read once a month and only 4% read daily for pleasure. However, students appeared to focus more on their study because 55% read in English once a week, 24% three to four times a week and 21% every day for study purposes.

Table 7. Participants' average responses to items in relation to different aspects of autonomy

Aspects of autonomy	Average scores (Highest: 5.0)	
	Pre Task	Post Task
Collaborative learning	3.7	4.9
Willing/able to exercise control over the learning of English	3.2	4.9
Exercising control over the learning of English	3.1	4.7
Learning strategies	3.5	4.9

The pre-task interview findings supported these responses, as illustrated by the following quote:

"I normally don't like reading and you are expecting me to read English books" (S/4).

Post-task data show that participants read more frequently than before, with 62.5% of students now reading every day and 31.5% reading three or four times a week for pleasure at the outset of this study. Similar results were also obtained for reading English for study purposes; all students (100%) read daily and three or four times a week. Changes in reading habits suggest that the technology-enhanced tasks and interactive app. encouraged students to read more, since 94% of the learners found reading topics (very) interesting.

Autonomy

The data presented in this section answer to the second research question: To what extent does the introduction of technology-enhanced task design enable students to exercise control over their English language learning in EPP??

The results in Table 7 illustrate that collaborative learning was a positively supported variable with an average score of 3.7, which shows that students seemed to prefer collaboration followed by learning strategies (3.5), while exercising control/ willing/able to exercise control obtained a moderate, yet lower score, with an average of 3.1 and 3.2 respectively:

"We are working together as our teachers suggest and I like working with my friends because we ask each other questions when we don't know..." (S/2).

This is corroborated by the needs analysis results, which also shows that most of the students would prefer to work in a group and with partners.

Students also appeared to be moderately willing and able to exercise control over the learning of English (average = 3.2) and they did not seem to want their teachers to direct them all the time, because they negatively responded to a statement in the questionnaire: "The teacher should explain every language point to me in the class." As for reading, whether they read English on their own initiative or only when instructed to do so by their teacher, few of them read on their own. Here, both constructs, learner autonomy and intrinsic motivation, seem to be interrelated; in other words, a close relationship between language learner motivation and autonomy is observed. They also used dictionary and asked meanings of words from each other to overcome the difficulty of short texts.

Post-data, however, show that the overall tendency in the responses about aspects of autonomy. The figures show that all variables received very high average scores. There were several comments which reflected various kinds of autonomous behaviors in the post-task interview, class blog discussion and open-ended questionnaire items. The following comments illustrate these findings:

"I am now able to do research which is important for me because of my study, I will do formal research, and this gave me some kind of initial step ... I actually liked it because I realized that I learned lots of things ... searching for information around the topics as a group ... yes, I feel my language has improved" (S/6).

As for collaborative learning, there were many activities that provided the learners with opportunities to collaborate, such as discussing headings, pictures, YouTube videos, preparing presentations and delivering them as a group. The results illustrate that the learners appeared to enjoy reading together, which influenced their language learning progress positively. Furthermore, collaboration encouraged them to put more effort into their learning, that is improved their reading skills as they had agreed strongly with the statements representing collaborative learning (average = 4.9).

When they explained their answers to questionnaire items, about group discussions and pair work, students stated that working together, exchanging and brainstorming ideas made them think differently. This might be because they worked together and benefited from discussions, and as a result gained confidence.

Some of them explicitly expressed that they like working together on the presentations and that group discussion improved their confidence, as S/2 put it:

"... I liked working with my group because was enjoyable and I learnt very much" (S/2).

Students appeared to prefer to work in groups and participate in group discussions, along with interacting with the 'FluentWorlds' activities by writing down how to pronounce some words they heard in their language and repeat these words with each other.

Furthermore, the results suggest that students were more willing and able to exercise control over the learning of English after using the iPads and carrying out the specially designed tasks. They scored highly positively (average = 4.9) on statements that addressed willingness to conduct interviews, to search on the internet to find information about "fun festivals", "women's football", "Malala's story" and interacting with activities on 'FluencyWorlds' app., and to present their results to the class.

The following reflections from the interviewees provide further evidence that they are willing and able to take responsibility for conducting interviews:

"The interview activity gave me the confidence to go and ask other students questions in the school ... yes, definitely I will do in during my study in the department" (S/8).

The iPads also contributed to the students" willingness and ability to exercise control over the learning of English:

"The iPad makes our learning more accessible and easier because I can search online for information for my lessons, as I did when I searched for information on festivals and doing the activities on the app. [FleuncyWorlds]" (S/5).

Autonomous learners are creative learners who are able to make suggestions for improvements. Students were given choices to suggest how to use the iPad and improve the lessons. There were numerous references indicating students' creativity. Students made linguistic and non-linguistic recommendations. They were able to suggest how they could improve their reading and listening:

"...we can read and record ourselves with 'FleuntWorlds' app, and then listen to our pronunciation and our teachers can correct us" (S/4).

Students also deployed various learning strategies, such as metacognitive, cognitive, social and affective strategies, during execution of the reading tasks (average=4.9). Searching on the internet seemed to enable them to use different learning strategies, such as consulting online dictionaries or looking for information from different web resources. Some of the students used metacognitive strategies, such as organizing an activity and self-monitoring when they were preparing and delivering their presentations and conducting interviews. They also monitored their own progress in English reading. There were a number of comments in the post-task qualitative data which reflected various kinds of learning strategies applied during task execution:

"We prepared our presentation by organizing the information and dividing it to each group member to present one part" (metacognitive) (S/7).

Students used social and cognitive strategies to find the meaning of unknown words:

"I guessed the meaning from the context and used Google Translate" (cognitive) (S/6).

"I asked my classmates when I find it difficult" (social) (S/2).

Some learning strategies hinted at and/or mentioned explicitly in the contributions to the class blog and focus group were:

- Searching websites to find information.
- Helping each other during presentations.
- Using Google Translate to look up unknown vocab.

Table 8. Mann-Whitney U test results: Questionnaire items related to autonomy

Variables	Test	N	Median Scores	Mann-Whitney U value	Level of significance P
Collaborative Learning	Pre	32	4	331	0.001
	Post	32	5		
	Total	64			
Willing/able to exercise control over the learning of English	Pre-	32	3	167	0.001
	Post	32	5		
	Total	64			

Table 8 shows the median scores of the responses to the questions regarding aspects of autonomy. The median scores are significantly different ($P < 0.001$) and the post-task median scores (5) are greater than the pre-test medians (3 and 4); therefore, as in motivation, the probability that the differences arose by chance is very low.

Students were further encouraged to employ the metacognitive strategy of self-evaluation.

Table 9. Responses to self-evaluation of fluency level in reading English

Pre-task	Excellent: 0	Above average: 3	Average: 24	Weak: 5
Post-task	Excellent: 15	Above average: 16	Average: 2	Weak: 0

As seen in Table 9, a clear majority (75%) of students evaluated their reading fluency level in English as average, while none circled excellent and 10% considered themselves above average. In contrast, 15% rated themselves as weak in pre-task data. However, past-task data show that a clear majority of participants perceived their reading level as having improved after execution of the reading tasks designed for this research through iPad. Students evaluated their reading fluency level in English as excellent (44%) and above average (%50). No student selected the 'weak' option. Therefore, the specially designed reading tasks supported by use of the iPad appear to have contributed to an improvement in the students' reading levels. Interviewees (S/1,4,5) monitored their own progress and reading level:

"…because, I am getting better and better with this way … I realized that my reading skill is improving as well … I read the stories you gave us, and I slowly understand them better compared to before …" (S/2).

The above statements confirmed that both students' self-awareness of the improvement of reading skills and their fluency level in reading has improved as well.

As for reflection, the findings provided a good amount of evidence of students' reflections which have already been reported in the previous sections. As noted by some students, the discussions and feedback stages at the end of the lessons created an environment that fostered student autonomy, which allowed them to reflect on their presentations, the overall classroom atmosphere and activities.

To sum up, the findings illustrate that creating a comfortable, healthy and relaxed environment for reflecting on learning is a key to developing learning strategies, autonomy and intrinsic motivation.

SOLUTIONS AND RECOMMENDATIONS

Students' intrinsic motivation in language learning has been examined and differences have been found between the pre- and post-task data, with significant increase shown in the post-task data. Before the intervention, the majority of the students were not interested in reading, as Course (2014) found with her students, and a very few students read in English regularly. Altınyelken (2010) attributed the lack of reading habits to an exam-driven education system in which children are cognitively and intellectually underdeveloped and neglected. Drawing on Ushioda's results (1998), Dörnyei and Ushioda (2011) relate learners' lack of motivation to external factors, such as teaching methods and learning tasks. A further reason may be related to the lack of interactivity in the classroom. Thus, students may simply not want to read and/or may even give up reading altogether. This resonates with Little's (1990, p. 12) warning that initially learners may not want to take control over the learning of English, because of a lack of autonomous learning experience, a tendency also observed by Borg and Al-Busaidi (2012) in Oman and by Course (2014) in Turkey. It is, therefore, important to create a learning environment where students are able to engage and interact with each other and use social strategies to ask for help when it is needed.

It has also been noted that stimulating an L2 environment for reading skills is widely recognized to be a prerequisite for successful language learning (Ellis, 2003; Krashen, 2004).

In addition, as well as Course (2014), other studies (Dam, 1995; Yaprak, 2014) found that the use of new pedagogical practices and such practices supported by iPad use have a positive impact on students' intrinsic motivation in language learning in general and reading in English in particular. Students in this study displayed stronger intrinsic motivation compared to the pre-task data. This study echoed findings by Course (2014) who found that her students' intrinsic motivation increased after her intervention project about reading English stories in English language classrooms. The results of this study provide evidence that the students' intrinsic motivation was increased through a technology-enhanced task-based language learning approach which is further supported by the wider literature (e.g. Abdul-Razak, 2000; Al-Shammari, 2007; Murray, 2005) in the field. This could be a means to an end, providing authentic materials to the students to read more and enjoy the learning process, as found by Samur et al. (2015) with Turkish students. Their participants indicated that they would access more online materials and enjoy their language study with the use of iPads (Samur et al., 2015). Therefore, the iPad along with specially designed tasks and 'FluentWorlds' app. could serve to both stimulate students' interest and help them in their reading. As reported by Krashen (2004), creating a stimulating L2 environment for students to enjoy reading is widely acknowledged to be an important factor for language learning acquisition.

Before the use of the e-pad and application of the online reading tasks, students were not very willing to exercise control over the learning of English, as research by Course (2014) and Boyno (2011) in the Turkish context has also confirmed. This could be linked to the Turkish education system as reflected in students' comments. However, having experienced the task design, interactive app. 'FluentWorlds', the iPad, different teaching approach, the topics chosen, a collaborative and non-threatening learning atmosphere successfully transformed their reluctance into enthusiasm and willingness to try deploying various strategies (Oxford, 2011), taking risks and using the opportunities that provided to exercise control over their learning of English.

Overall, technology-enhanced task-based language learning enabled the participants in this study to develop the different capacities that are key to self-determination theory. These were the ability and willingness together with their knowledge, skills, intrinsic motivation and confidence to exercise control over the learning of English (Dam, 1995). For example, the participants in this study found the reading tasks and the activities in those tasks interesting which had a positive impact on their intrinsic motivation to read more, learn better and further their learning, and they showed initiative by taking control of their learning and improving their English by reading very simple stories in English outside the classroom as indicated by the participants.

They also used learning strategies which helped them read effectively and reflected on, (Little, 1991; Murphy et al., 2005) and evaluated their learning process. Finally, some of them felt more secure by working together and/or with others which improved their sense of relatedness (Deci and Ryan, 1985). In other words, the students demonstrated increased intrinsic motivation, competence, relatedness and autonomy, which are common innate psychological needs for self-determined learners. This result is consistent with results from studies Yaprak (2014) and Mutlu and Eroz-Tuga (2013) regarding the positive influence of ICT on the development of learner autonomy and enhancing intrinsic motivation.

FUTURE RESEARCH DIRECTIONS AND LIMITATIONS OF THE STUDY

The findings of this study confirmed Koruyan (2016)'s research model developed from Chapelle's theoretical framework (2000). Overall, the chapter suggests further studies to design and evaluate a technology-enhanced learning environment paying attention to the following points:

- A follow-up study is needed using the technology-enhanced tasks with more classes, as well as comparing student responses with those from students in classes where technology-enhanced task design has not yet been introduced.
- For this follow-up study, teachers should be given more pedagogical control and recognition so that they can design their own tasks according to their students' needs and interests.
- Whatever is found out in the context of language learning and teaching in this study should be immediately transferable to the learning and teaching of any other subject matter (e.g. Science and Humanities) as I take out one level of mediation from the learning and teaching process that is the foreign language (Kurek and Hauck, 2014).

Finally, this chapter suggest that the following questions should be investigated:

- Is the enhanced motivation in this study sustained?
- How easy do other teachers find it to work with the framework and models in this study? What kind of preparation do they really need?
- To what extent are Turkish teachers willing to exercise control over their teaching and how this can be encouraged?
- How can teachers in Turkish universities and teachers in countries with very traditional views of teaching best be supported to help their learners exercise control over their language learning?

CONCLUSION

This research has addressed the research gap in providing an extended framework for facilitating learner autonomy and enhancing intrinsic motivation through specifically designed online tasks to enhance the development of reading skills in higher education. It has expanded Chapelle's model explicitly to provide a framework for task design to assess the impact of the iPad-enhanced task design on the development of learner autonomy and motivation.

The findings indicate that with an approach and expanded framework to task design that takes account of the affordances of technology, it is possible to enhance the EPP students' intrinsic motivation to read and help them improve their language learning. The post-task data also illustrates that the introduction of technology-enhanced task design had a positive impact on students' attitudes towards reading in English. Before this research, students did not have positive attitudes towards reading in English, possibly due to the dominant pedagogical approach in the Turkish education system, which remains – to this day – behaviorist and teacher-centered. However, the design, the themes of the reading materials, and the atmosphere in the class seemed to have stimulated students' interest in searching on the internet and to have helped them to read more around the topic. They continued reading for pleasure on the 'bugclub' website, as indicated by the participants. The findings further suggest that scaffolding and transparency in task instructions, which were achieved by displaying the latter on the Smart Board, and therefore making them constantly available to the learners also played a crucial role in their motivation, helping them to carry out the tasks step by step in a comparatively independent way. In addition, it can be affirmed that a multimedia environment, offering resources such as the visual and aural input on YouTube that they engaged with, intrinsically motivated students to improve their reading skills. Overall, the introduction of technology-enhanced task-based learning positively affected the motivation of these EPP students to read in English.

While talking about the ways in which they approached their language learning through the reading tasks used in this study, students' comments indicated they were exercising a degree of control over their learning, along with a capacity to reflect critically on their approach to the online reading tasks. The findings provide some insight into the ways in which the technology-enhanced task design with an appropriate framework has helped convert students from being dependent on their teacher to taking greater responsibility for their learning, both independently and interdependently. The iPad and the tasks seemed to contribute to the students' willingness and ability to exercise control over their learning of English, which they did by deploying various learning strategies, such as metacognitive to overcome the difficulty some experienced in understanding the reading texts. The students also gained confidence in self-assessment and were able to evaluate their progress, which is the metacognitive strategy closely associated with autonomous learning, and they also felt confident to make suggestions for improving the use of the iPad and the lessons. This shows their active involvement in the learning process.

The overall results from this study indicate that EPP students who participated in this study were willing and able to exercise control over the learning of English and their intrinsic motivation to engage in reading tasks was increased through participation in technology-enhanced language learning tasks informed by the expanded.

REFERENCES

Abdul-Razak, Z. N. (2000). *Motivational Factors and Learners' Strategies in the English as a Second Language Classroom at Universiti Technology Malaysia with Special Reference to Computer Assisted Language Learning* (Unpublished PhD thesis). University of Stirling.

Al-Shammari, M. H. (2007). *Turkish English as a Foreign Language: Learners' Attitudes toward Computer Assisted Language Learning* (Unpublished PhD thesis). West Virginia University.

Altınyelken, H. K. (2010). Pedagogical renewal in sub-Saharan Africa: The case of Uganda. *Comparative Education, 46*(2), 151–171. doi:10.1080/03050061003775454

Benson, P. (2011). *Teaching and Researching Autonomy in Language Learning*. Harlow: Pearson Education.

Benson, P., & Voller, P. (Eds.). (1997). *Autonomy and Independence in Language Learning*. London: Longman.

Blin, F. (1999). CALL and the development of learner autonomy. In R. Debski & M. Levy (Eds.), *WORLDCALL: Global Perspectives on Computer-assisted Language Learning* (pp. 133–149). Lisse: Swets & Zeitlinger.

Borg, S., & Al-Busaidi, S. (2012). *Learner Autonomy: English Language Teachers" Beliefs and Practices*. London: The British Council.

Boyno, M. (2011). *An Analysis of the Factors Influencing Learner Autonomy in the Turkish EFL Context* (Unpublished PhD thesis). Çukurova University.

Bülbül, S., Mısırlıoğlu, E., Ceyhun, G., Araz, N., & Altuğ, U. (2014). Factors affecting reading habit and media follow-up in Turkey. *Türkiye Atletizim Federasyonu Preventive Medicine Bulletin, 13*(1), 47–56. doi:10.5455/pmb.1-1361624478

Burton, D. (2000). *Research Training for Social Scientists*. London: Sage. doi:10.4135/9780857028051

Büyükkantarcıoğlu, N. (2004). A sociolinguistic analysis of the present dimensions of English as a foreign language in Turkey. *International Journal of the Sociology of Language, 165*(165), 33–58. doi:10.1515/ijsl.2004.006

Chapelle, C. (2000). Innovative language learning: Achieving the vision. *ReCALL, 13*(1), 3–14. doi:10.1017/S0958344001000210

Chapelle, C., & Jamieson, J. (2008). *Tips for Teaching with CALL: Practical Approaches to Computer-assisted Language Learning*. New York: Pearson-Longman.

Course, S. (2014). Critical reading in EFL in a Turkish high school context. *International Journal of Language Academy, 2*(3), 133–156. doi:10.18033/ijla.108

Creswell, J. W. (2012). *Educational research: planning, conducting, and evaluating quantitative and qualitative research* (4th ed.). Boston: Pearson Education.

Crookes, G., & Schmidt, R. (1991). Motivation: Reopening the research agenda. *Language Learning, 41*(4), 469–512. doi:10.1111/j.1467-1770.1991.tb00690.x

Dam, L. (1995). *Learner Autonomy 3: From Theory to Classroom Practice*. Dublin: Authentik.

Dam, L. (2011). Developing learner autonomy with school kids: principles, practices, results. In D. Gardner (Ed.), *Fostering Autonomy in Language Learning* (pp. 40–51). Gaziantep. Available at http://ilac2010.zirve.edu.tr/Fostering_Autonomy.pdf

Deci, E. L., & Flaste, R. (1995). *Why We Do What We Do*. New York: Penguin Books.

Deci, E. L., & Ryan, R. M. (1985). *Intrinsic Motivation and Self-determination in Human Behavior*. New York: Plenum. doi:10.1007/978-1-4899-2271-7

Deci, E. L., & Ryan, R. M. (2000). Intrinsic and extrinsic motivations: Classic definitions and new directions. *Contemporary Educational Psychology, 25*(1), 54–67. doi:10.1006/ceps.1999.1020 PMID:10620381

Dörnyei, Z. (1998). Motivation in second and foreign language learning. *Language Teaching, 31*(3), 117–135. doi:10.1017/S026144480001315X

Dörnyei, Z., & Ottó, I. (1998). *Motivation in action: a process model of L2 motivation*. Working Papers in Applied Linguistics 4. London: Thames Valley University.

Dörnyei, Z., & Ushioda, E. (2011). *Teaching and Researching Motivation* (2nd ed.). Harlow: Longman.

Ducate, L., & Lomicka, L. (2013). Going Mobile: Language Learning with an iPod Touch in Intermediate French and German Classes. *Foreign Language Annals*, *26*(3), 45–468. doi:10.1111/flan.12043

Ellis, R. (2000). Task-based research and language pedagogy. *Language Teaching Research*, *4*(3), 193–220. doi:10.1177/136216880000400302

Ellis, R. (2003). *The Study of Second Language Acquisition*. Oxford: OUP.

Gardner, R. (1985). *Social Psychology and Second Language Learning: The Role of Attitudes and Motivation*. London: Edward Arnold.

Gardner, R., & Lambert, W. E. (1959). Motivational variables in second language acquisition. *Canadian Journal of Psychology*, *13*(4), 266–272. doi:10.1037/h0083787 PMID:13855818

Gönen, K., & Akbarov, A. (2015). Digital Natives in Higher Education Related to Language Learning. *Journal of Foreign Language Teaching and Applied Linguistics*. Available at www.j-fltal.org/storage/j-fltal-12.pdf

Grgurovic, M., Chapelle, C., & Shelley, M. (2013). A meta-analysis of effectiveness studies on computer technology-supported language learning. *ReCALL Journal*, *25*(2), 165–198. doi:10.1017/S0958344013000013

Hampel, R. (2006). Rethinking task design for the digital age. *ReCALL*, *18*(1), 105–121. doi:10.1017/S0958344006000711

Hampel, R., & Hauck, M. (2006). Computer-mediated language learning: Making meaning in multimodal virtual learning space. *The JALT CALL Journal*, *2*(2), 3–18.

Hatch, E., & Lazaraton, A. (1991). *The Research Manual: Design and Statistics for Applied Linguistics*. Rowley, MA: Newbury House.

Hauck, M., & Youngs, B. (2008). Telecollaboration in multimodal environments: The impact on task design and learner interaction. *CALL*, *21*(2), 87–124. doi:10.1080/09588220801943510

Healey, D. (1999). Theory and research: autonomy in language learning. In J. Egbert & E. Hanson-Smith (Eds.), *CALL Environments: Research, Practice and Critical Issues* (pp. 391–402). TESOL.

Holec, H. (1981). *Autonomy and Foreign Language Learning*. Oxford: Pergamon Press.

Kohonen, V. (1992). *Experiential Language Learning: Second Language Learning as Cooperative Learner Education*. Cambridge: CUP.

Koruyan, K. (2016). *The influence of technology-enhanced task design on the development of language learner autonomy and motivation in an Anatolian high school; A case study* (Unpublished Doctoral dissertation). Open university, Milton Keynes, UK.

Krashen, S. (2004). *The power of reading: insights from the research*. Portsmouth, NH: Libraries Unlimited, Heineann.

Kurek, M., & Hauck, M. (2014). Closing the "digital divide" – a framework for multiliteracy training. In G.J. Pettes, & L. Williams (Eds.), Digital Literacies in Foreign and Second Language Education: Research, Perspectives, and Best Practice. CALICO Monograph Series 12. San Marcos, TX: CALICO.

Lau, M. A. I. (2009). *TBL in English Language Learning in Macau: Effects on Chinese Tertiary Learners' Beliefs and Motivations* (Unpublished PhD thesis). The University of Nottingham.

Levy, M., & Stockwell, G. (2006). *CALL Dimensions: Options and Issues in Computer-assisted Language Learning*. Lawrence Erlbaum Associates.

Lincoln, Y. S., & Guba, E. (1985). *Naturalistic Inquiry*. Beverley Hills, CA: Sage. doi:10.1016/0147-1767(85)90062-8

Little, D. (1991). *Learner Autonomy 1: Definitions, Issues, Problems*. Dublin: Authentik.

Little, D. (2007). Language learner autonomy: Some fundamental considerations revisited. *Innovation in Language Learning and Teaching, 1*(1), 14–29. doi:10.2167/illt040.0

Littlewood, W. (1996). Autonomy: An autonomy and a framework. *System, 24*(4), 427–435. doi:10.1016/S0346-251X(96)00039-5

Meri, S. (2012). Autonomous computer-assisted language learning: Turkish primary school students' perceptions of Dyned software. *International Conference „ICT for Language Learning*, 1–4.

Motteram, G. (Ed.). (2013). *Innovations in learning technologies for English language teaching*. London: The British Council.

Murphy, L., Hauck, M., Nicolson, M., & Adams, H. (2005). Reflection and self-evaluation. In S. Hurd, & L. Murphy (Eds.), Success with Languages. Abingdon: Routledge in association with The Open University.

Murray, D. (2005). Technologies for second language literacy. *Annual Review of Applied Linguistics, 25*, 188–201. doi:10.1017/S0267190505000103

Murray, G. (1999). Autonomy and language learning in a simulated environment. *System, 27*(3), 295–308. doi:10.1016/S0346-251X(99)00026-3

Mutlu, A., & Eroz-Tuga, B. (2013). The role of computer-assisted language learning (CALL) in promoting learner autonomy. *Eğitim Arastırmaları-Eurasian Journal of Educational Research, 51*, 107–122.

Nunan, D. (2004). *Task-based Language Teaching*. Cambridge: CUP. doi:10.1017/CBO9780511667336

Oxford, R., & Shearin, J. (1994). Language learning motivation: Expanding the theoretical framework. *Modern Language Journal, 78*(1), 12–28. doi:10.1111/j.1540-4781.1994.tb02011.x

Oxford, R. L. (2011). *Teaching and Researching Language Learning Strategies* (2nd ed.). Harlow: Pearson Education.

Rahman, F., Jumani, N. B., & Basit, A. (2010). Motivating and demotivating factors among learners. *International Journal of Academic Research, 2*(1), 206–212.

Roulston, K. (2001). Data analysis and 'theorizing as ideology. *Qualitative Research, 1*(3), 279–302. doi:10.1177/146879410100100302

Samur, Y., Garipağaoğlu, B. C., & Karadeniz, S. (2015). Student perceptions on tablet computer use. In *First International Congress on 'LE: Digital Life Environments'*. Istanbul University.

Saraç, S. (2013). Learner autonomy in Turkish territory context. *Independence, 56*, 21–2.

Selçuk, M. (2015). *Demotivation in EFL classes*. Available at https://www.academia.edu/864982/Demotivation_in_EFL_Classes

Selinger, M. (2001). *Information and communication technology in schools*. Available at http:\\www.imfundo.org/papers/ict_in_s.doc/

Skehan, P. (1989). *Individual Differences in Second Language Learning*. London: Arnold.

Skehan, P. (2003). Focus on form, tasks, and technology. *Computer Assisted Language Learning, 16*(5), 391–411. doi:10.1076/call.16.5.391.29489

Sotiriou, C., & Primalis, D. (2013). Literature strikes back! Teaching literature with technology. In T. Pattison (Ed.), IATEFL Liverpool Conference Selection (pp. 130–131). Academic Press.

Ushioda, E. (2000). Tandem language learning via e-mail: From motivation to autonomy. *ReCALL, 2*(2), 121–128. doi:10.1017/S0958344000000124

Vygotsky, L. S. (1978). *Mind in Society*. Cambridge, MA: Harvard University Press.

Williams, M., & Burden, R. (1997). *Psychology for Language Teachers: A Social Constructivist Approach*. Cambridge: CUP.

Yaprak, Z. (2014). Computer-assisted collaborative language learning: With special reference to TBLL. *Turkish Studies, 9*(6), 1117–1137. doi:10.7827/TurkishStudies.6783

Yin, R. K. (2009). *Case study research: Design and methods*. Thousand Oaks, CA: Sage.

ADDITIONAL READING

Hauck, M. (2007). Critical success factors in a TRIDEM exchange. *ReCALL, 19*(2), 202–223. doi:10.1017/S0958344007000729

Kress, G. (2003). *Literacy in the New Media Age*. London: Routledge.

Meskill, C. (1999). Computers as tools for sociocollaborative language learning. In K. Cameron (Ed.), *Computer Assisted Language Learning (CALL): Media, Design and Applications* (pp. 141–162). Lisse: Swets & Zeitlinger.

Scharle, A., & Szabo´, A. (2000). *Learner Autonomy: A Guide to Developing Learner Responsibility*. Cambridge: CUP.

KEY TERMS AND DEFINITIONS

Affordances of Modes: Different modes of technology offer different potentials such as YouTube.

Authenticity: The quality of tasks/activities the learner is likely to encounter outside the classroom.

Collaboration: Learners work together.

Creativity: Original ideas to create something.

Learner Fit: Being suitable for learners' needs and interests.

Practicality: Easy access to materials or internet search via iPad.

Reflection: Careful thought about a subject.

Chapter 8
Towards the Implementation of E-Assessment in L2 IsiZulu:
An Examination of Four Listening Comprehension Tests

Shamila Naidoo
https://orcid.org/0000-0002-1013-2221
University of KwaZulu-Natal, South Africa

Roshni Gokool
University of KwaZulu-Natal, South Africa

ABSTRACT

This chapter reports on a quantitative study that investigated the adoption and implementation of e-assessments of listening comprehension tasks on second language learners registered for the Basic isiZulu module at the University of KwaZulu-Natal, South Africa. Specifically, the chapter examines the process used in the design of listening comprehension activities. It focuses on the pedagogical implications of adopting such tasks within the assessment rigour. Drawing on Hemmati and Ghaderi's study, the focus is on the format of questions. The experiment was conducted over four weeks with a cohort of non-mother-tongue learners of isiZulu. Encouragingly, the findings of the experiment suggest that formative e-assessments of listening comprehension tasks are beneficial to students. Language teachers should, however, engage in a careful and thoughtful planning process in the design of relevant and authentic listening comprehension tasks.

INTRODUCTION

Computer-based assessments or electronic assessments (e-assessments) in the learning and teaching of a second language (L2) are rapidly changing the way language teachers assess in tertiary education. The plethora of online assessment tools and software available for language teachers to use has reshaped the

DOI: 10.4018/978-1-7998-3062-7.ch008

way languages are taught, learned and assessed. However, an important consideration is that technology is not about "whether we use technology, but how we use it" (Mercado, 2017, p. 2), which means that technology should be for a purpose to benefit both learners and teachers. Technology offers learners new ways "to learn, practice and strategize", and teachers can "make the instructional process more diverse, effective, efficient, engaging and contextually meaningful" (Mercado, 2017, p. 2). Technology affords multi-modal opportunities, that is, aural, written and with visual prospects for learners and language teachers to execute work within complex tasks (Ellis, 2018, p. 17). For instance, Moodle is the selected open-source learning management system (LMS), available to all academics at the University of KwaZulu-Natal (UKZN), South Africa. In 2016, Moodle was launched as the official LMS at UKZN and as the mandatory phase-in across all disciplines (UKZN, 2015). Academics were provided with rudimentary Moodle training to use software to complement the teaching and learning process. Training consisted of navigating through the platform, uploading lecture material and notes and posting messages. Features such as discussion forums, chats and assessment tools were excluded from the training. Thus, the norm was posting messages related to the discipline, and uploading lecture notes. However, very little Moodle intervention occurred in teaching, learning and assessment.

As with many global tertiary institutions, South African institutions are faced with large student enrolments (Snowball, 2014). Consequently, teaching workloads have escalated, particularly the assessment of large cohorts of students. At UKZN, English is used as the language of instruction. However, the university is located in a province where the majority are L1 speakers of isiZulu. Hence, the implementation of UKZN's compulsory language rule for non-mother-tongue speakers of isiZulu (UKZN, 2014). This has resulted in a significant increase in student enrolment within the Basic IsiZulu module. Traditional pen-and paper-based assessments became challenging and impractical, and it was apparent that an alternative mode of assessment was required. Assessing in an electronic environment was not implemented in the teaching and learning of African languages in South Africa. Academics who teach in the Basic isiZulu module have experimented using the Quiz tool available in Moodle as part of the assessment rigor. The rationale for adopting and implementing the Quiz tool as formative assessments is to integrate technology in the teaching and learning of isiZulu and to create an opportunity for digital generation students to interact with online assessments innovatively. Formative assessments are implemented for developmental purposes, thereby providing students with the opportunity to review and improve their performance.

Additionally, the software tool provides academics with an alternate method of assessing large cohorts of students and reducing time spent on administrative aspects during the assessment. Although there are many benefits to computer-based assessments, the researchers are specifically concerned with the implications of integrating such assessments into the Basic isiZulu module. In particular, the researchers are concerned with synchronizing established L2 acquisition methodological principles with a computer-assisted language learning (CALL) tool such as Moodle. This chapter thus explores an unchartered area of research within the field of teaching and learning L2 isiZulu. Given the lack of empirical research relating to the design and implementation of online assessments for teaching isiZulu as L2, this chapter contributes to the existing literature on e-assessments and focuses particularly on exploring listening comprehension tests in an L2 isiZulu e-assessment. The general objective of this chapter is to highlight the adoption and integration of e-assessments in a Basic isiZulu module. Based on action research methodology and through an iterative process over a semester, the online listening comprehension tests were tailored and included in the assessment format. However, the specific objective of this chapter is to present an analysis of four formative online listening comprehension tests. Being aware that listening is the "Cinderella skill" in L2 teaching (Nunan, 1997), the researchers deliberately focused on this skill from the inception of the course. The listening comprehension tests were designed applying aspects of grammar that were taught before posting the formative assessments. Several questions and statements were varied and recurred across the four tests. Therefore, natural speech was reinforced. Participants were assessed with multiple-choice (MCQs) and True/False type questions. The objectives of this chapter include comparing the results from the True/False and MCQ format assessments and determining the difficulty index of the assessment questions.

In designing the four formative tests, the researchers had the following objectives:

1. To identify and apply principles relevant to the development of online listening comprehension material,
2. To identify and apply principles relevant to constructing online questions for listening comprehension test,
3. To determine the difficulty index of the test,
4. To analyze the results of the four formative tests, focusing specifically on:
   4.1. Comparing the results from the True/False and MCQ format tests
   4.2. Comparing the results between the visual cue and no cue tests
5. To determine if there is a correlation between the results of this study and that of Hemmati and Ghaderi (2014).

BACKGROUND

Defining Listening Comprehension

Rost identified three components of listening (cited in McDonough, Shaw & Masuhara, 2013). These were decoding, comprehension and interpretation. Decoding relates to speech perception and engages word recognition and grammatical parsing. Comprehension entails making inferences and using prior knowledge to make sense of what is heard. Interpretation refers to the listener's ability to make comparisons and evaluate meaning. Does listening necessarily imply comprehension? Vandergrift and Baker (2015, p. 392) explained the listening comprehension construct as:

- an ability to process, in real-time, an extract of authentic spoken language;
- understand the linguistic information in the extract; and
- decipher inferences implied in the extract.

They further explained that comprehension requires "cognitive processing that is flexible and adaptable to the task demands to construct in memory a mental representation of what has been comprehended". Vandergrift and Baker (ibid.) noted the following significant points about listening comprehension:

- As listening takes place in real-time, the listener cannot control the speed of input, and there is no option to review the information;
- Working memory is activated during listening because the listener has to decipher the sound stream and apply phonological knowledge to create words and meaning; and

- Prosodic features like tone and stress can feature prominently in the comprehension process during listening.

Listening comprehension imposes higher cognitive demands, more especially for a L2 learner. Vandergrift and Goh (2012, p. 270) explained that this is because L2 learners have "incomplete knowledge" of the target language, they experience "gaps in understanding" and they have to pay close attention to the speaker.

Online Assessments or A-Assessments in Listening

Online assessments or e-assessments are a well-researched area in the higher education context (Gikandi, Morrow & Davis, 2011; Mukandutiye, Sevilla & Makhanu, 2014; Walker, Topping & Rodrigues, 2008). Studies have reported the successful implementation of the Quiz tool at tertiary education institutions (Mukandutiye et al., 2014; Rarh & Goel, 2011; Singh & Gokool, 2018). Govindasamy (2001) examined the pedagogical implications of using online learning and Snowball (2014) reported on the benefits of using online learning for large classes. The Singh and Gokool (2018) study was conducted at UKZN and focused on IsiZulu. Students' perceptions were used as the research data to explore aspects of the Quiz tool. The Singh and Gokool (2018) study indicated room for improvement, specifically relating to the design of tests. While the e-quiz discussed by Singh and Gokool (2018) consisted of MCQs, short answer formats, fill in the blanks and matching type questions; the aural component was absent, as no listening comprehension tests were included.

To the researchers' knowledge, no other studies related to listening comprehension tests in an online environment have been reported for the African languages. In fact, limited attention has been given to the teaching, learning and assessing of African languages through technology. Hence, it is envisaged that this unexplored area of research will provide further insight into the field of information and communications technology (ICT) assessments and methods.

Global studies based on ICT language assessments are thriving. Research conducted on listening comprehension tests are well documented, providing different perspectives on how best to implement listening comprehension tests using technology (Chang, Warden, Liang & Chou, 2018; Farangi & Kheradmand Saadi, 2017; Hamdan & Al-Hawamdeh, 2018; Li, 2019). Whilst many of these recent studies concur that listening comprehension is one of the fundamental skills in second language acquisition, the methods and design used in testing differ. Farangi and Kheradmand Saadi (2017) tracked the use of two strategies, Dynamic Assessment and Schema Theory, reporting that the use of these two strategies improved learners' listening comprehension skills over time. In their study, Dynamic Assessment was implemented by conducting a pre-test, followed by an enrichment activity. The enrichment activity addressed the specific challenges that learners encountered during the comprehension test. The enrichment activity was followed by a post-test. In implementing Schema Theory, the researchers conducted a pre-test, followed by a treatment. The treatment utilized shadowing and the use of semantic maps. Shadowing requires the learner to engage in oral repetition. Semantic mapping focuses on vocabulary revision. After the treatment phase, a post-test is conducted. Farangi and Kheradmand Saadi (2017) report that both strategies, Dynamic Assessment and Schema Theory, record improved performance in listening comprehension. In the study by Chang et al. (2018), the researchers investigated the use of computer-assisted learning indoors and u-learning or ubiquitous outdoor learning. The latter entails learners being tested in authentic contexts or immersive activities. The findings in the Chang et al. (2018)

study indicate that u-learning has more positive benefits for listening comprehension. Traditionally listening comprehension activities focused on the audio component. However, listening frequently has a visual accompaniment. According to Hamdan and Al-Hawamdeh (2018, p. 1123) audio-only listening tests can obstruct comprehension, inhibiting performance. They propose that the audio-visual dialogue feature provides a 'linguistic experience' for the learner. Therefore, in their experimental study Hamdan and Al-Hawamdeh (2018) report on the effects of 'face' (i.e. audio-visual dialogues) listening comprehension. The results indicate that learners perform better in listening comprehension tests when audio-visuals are included. Li (2019), like Farangi and Kheradmand Saadi (2017), focuses on vocabulary, in particular 'aural receptive vocabulary knowledge in listening comprehension'. The study concludes that vocabulary knowledge is vital in overall listening comprehension performance. The afore-mentioned studies exemplify the various approaches used in enhancing listening comprehension skills. Therefore, this study contributes to the ongoing discussion on the use of ICT and assessments.

However, this study focuses on Basic isiZulu, a L2 module offered to speakers of non-Nguni languages at UKZN. There is constant evaluation of the e-assessment techniques used within the module. This is done for two reasons; namely to enhance e-learning and to consider the pedagogical implications of the e-learning tests.

Two catalysts for the enquiry are presented in this chapter. Firstly, the researchers conducted an evaluation, which focused on the written/visual and aural formats and how these affected student performances in Basic isiZulu. Under test conditions, two groups were given a comprehension text. Both groups had visual access to the comprehension. Whilst the questions were presented in a visual format for one group, the other group had to listen to the statement and select True or False. The learner results from this assessment indicated that for 7/10 questions, learners who had access to the visual option performed better.

These results correspond with the observation that while learners may achieve competence in written aspects of the language, their oral and aural skills lag. Cognizant of the role that the sensory modality plays in L2 learning, the researchers deliberately sought to implement VARK in teaching and assessment. VARK is the acronym for visual, aural, reading and writing and kinesthetic (Ramirez, 2011, p. 270).

The second catalyst for this study was an experiment conducted by Hemmati and Ghaderi (2014), in which a listening activity was administered to four groups of L2 learners. Group 1 was assigned the No Preview (NP) option. They listened to the exercise and thereafter viewed the questions and selected answers from the options provided. Group 2 was given the Full Question Preview (FQP) option. They viewed the questions and the options first and then listened to the exercise and answered the questions. Group 3 was given the Question Option Preview (QOP) option. They only viewed the questions, then listened to the exercise and viewed the questions and answers. Group 4 had the Answer Option Preview (AOP) where they only viewed the answers, then listened to the exercise and viewed the questions and answers. Hemmati and Ghaderi (2014) found that the NP format had the minimum mean and the FQP had the maximum mean. There was thus a correlation between the findings from the Hemmati and Ghaderi (2014) study and the sample isiZulu evaluation. These results triggered a more rigid and scientific study of isiZulu listening comprehension activities which are discussed in this chapter.

Teaching and Assessing Listening Comprehension

Listening comprehension is described, by Nunan (1997, p. 47), as the "Cinderella skill of second language learning". Historically, the emphasis was placed on speaking and writing. However, oracy (listening and speaking) has been recognized as an essential complement to literacy for L2 learners. Listening is used more than the macro skills of speaking, reading and writing (Lieske, 2007, p. 39). It follows that in the teaching and assessment of listening activities, material development and assessment tools must be scientifically valid. Brown (2017) documented various approaches to teaching listening. Initially, the Structural Linguistics approach of teaching phonetics, stress and intonation were used to facilitate the understanding of listening. Thereafter, reading comprehension activities were converted into listening comprehension, and the test remained answering of questions. In other words, "reading comprehension was imported into listening comprehension" (Brown, 2017, p. 146). In current times, task-based listening comprehension is popular. Here the learner has to listen and use the information to complete a task. Lieske (2007) identified five elements of effective listening material:

- Content validity;
- Purposefulness and transferability;
- Retrieval of information from long-term memory;
- Teaching new listening skills; and
- Authenticity

Validity implies that the listening skill has primacy in the test and should not only be unidirectional, but bidirectional and/or multidirectional. All four tests in this study are designed with one speaker reading a monologue, followed by questions. It could be argued that this unidirectionality is a design flaw. However, given that the tests are designed for a beginner L2 group, and the focus is on the listening skill, the element of content validity is assured. All listening comprehension activities should be directly linked to the aspects taught in class and applicable in general listening and conversation. During face-to-face lectures, learners were formally taught the grammatical rules for the use of question words. Written translation exercises and written comprehension tests were completed. Thereby, the element purposefulness is realised. To achieve the element of authenticity, the grammaticality, enunciation and lexicon used must mimic real-world speech. The scenarios for the tests, together with the language used, were designed to present authentic situations using commonly heard vocabulary. An example from a test question, shown in Figure 1, is used to illustrate Lieske's element of retrieval of information. The aural question is *Bangaki abangane bakaZanele* / 'How many friends does Zanele have? '

The traditional isiZulu numbers are provided as an answer option. However, in the comprehension test, the listener hears the anglicized form *abawu-3* and not the traditional *abathathu*. The listener, therefore, has to access information from long-term memory. Transferability, the accompaniment to the element of purposefulness, also influences such a question, as the learner recognises the two options that may be used to express numbers. Furthermore, as per Bloom's Taxonomy (Bloom, 1956, Churches, 2010), higher-order functions are required. In this example, it is a knowledge application.

Figure 1. Statement from test – Purposefulness and Transferability

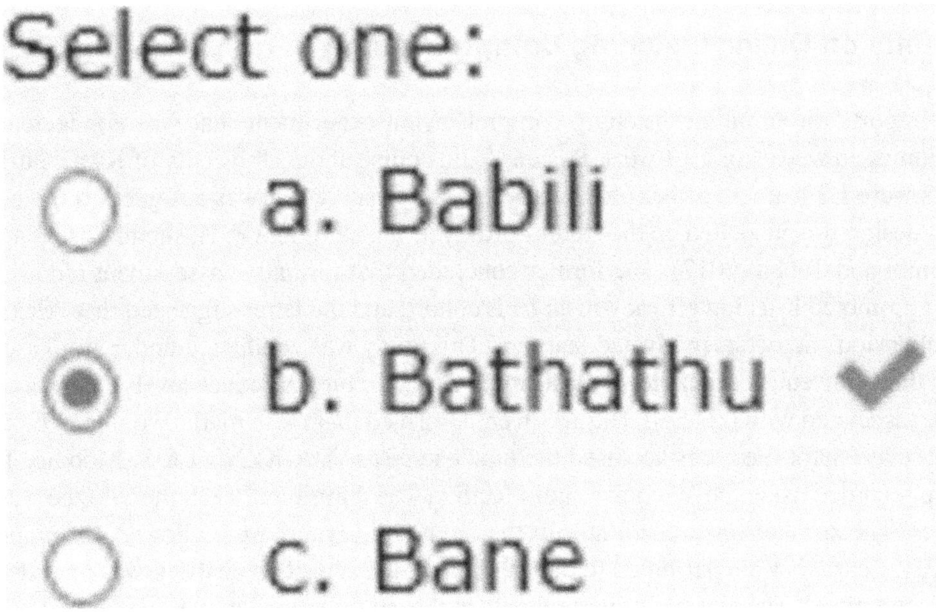

Lieske's fourth element – teaching new listening skills - relates to task-focused instruction. For logistical reasons and given the level of competence of the learners, this element was not incorporated into the tests in this study.

There is a plethora of perspectives on how online assessment should be developed. Harding, Alderson & Brunfaut (2015) recommended a diagnostic process, similar to the process undertaken to determine a medical condition. There is also extensive debate on the format options for listening comprehension tests. The two options pertinent to this study are True/False and MCQ. These options are not without controversy (Bender, 2003). According to Brindley (1998, p. 177) "evaluating whether a proposition is True or False is a legitimate and quite common purpose for listening", but there is a fifty percent chance of guessing the correct answer. Yi'an (1998, p. 40) expressed reservations about the use of MCQ as it allowed the weaker listener to guess an answer.

Nicol (2007, p. 54) noted the disjuncture between MCQs and high-level cognitive thinking. This was reiterated by Mehta and Mokhasi (2014, p. 198), who reported that MCQs are less conducive to assessing the higher-order functions of Bloom's Taxonomy, namely interpretation, synthesis and knowledge application. Brindley (1998, p. 178) also reported that concerning assessing listening, MCQs are flawed as such questions do not resemble normal language usage. Referring to Hansen and Jensen (1994), Brindley (1998, p. 178) also expressed concern about the processing demands imposed by MCQs on the testee. The latter must listen to aural input and match that with the MCQ options. This places stress on the working memory. On the other hand, Hémard and Cushion (2003, p. 137), reporting on a comprehensive study relating to a web-based interactive language learning platform, found that it was appropriate for beginner classes to commence with MCQ type questions.

MAIN FOCUS OF THE CHAPTER

Experiments on Online Listening Comprehension

This study reports on an online listening comprehension experiment that was conducted over four weeks beginning in week 4 of a 13-week Basic isiZulu course at the University of KwaZulu-Natal. The participants were L2 learners of isiZulu. Each week a formative test was assigned to the cohort. The experiment design was modelled on the studies of Bayat, Jamshidipour & Hashemi (2017) and Caruso, Gadd Colombi and Tebbit (2017). The former concluded that formative assessment reduced levels of anxiety and promoted listening efficacy in an EFL cohort, and the latter suggested that "flexible listening comprehension" activities motivated learners. This study was conducted under similar conditions. Learners at their convenience completed the formative test. To further reduce levels of stress and anxiety (commonly associated with L2 tests), learners were informed that these marks would not be considered for the final class mark. Learners accessed the quiz exercises via UKZN's LMS, Moodle. The monologues were recorded using the Windows audio facility. The duration of each monologue was less than four minutes. The speaker was a facilitator in the module. Learners were allowed 15 minutes for the entire activity. Learners were permitted to play and pause the activity. Feedback was provided after the answers are submitted. The number of participants in this study is shown in Table 2.

While the Hemmati and Ghaderi's (2014) study, which was the catalyst for the present study, focused on the performance of learners under four different preview format conditions viz. NP, FQP, QOP and AOP, the focus in this experiment is on the format of questions. The Basic isiZulu cohort listened to a monologue in all four tests. In Test 1, learners listened to a statement and selected from the True/False option. There was a single word cue to remind the listener of the question. Test 4 had the same format, but no cue. Test 2 had an MCQ format with no cue. Test 3 also had an MCQ format but with the answer options visible. An example of the format for Formative 1 and 4 is shown in Figure 2. Figure 3 presents the format for Formative 2 and 3.

Figure 2. Format for Formative 1 and Formative 4

Figure 3. Formats for Formative 2 and Formative 3

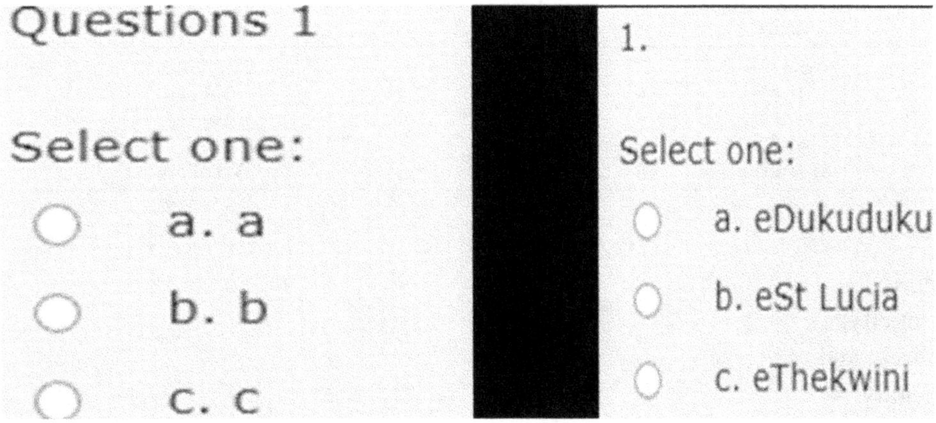

Developing Material to Teach Listening

The Basic isiZulu listening activities were informed by Lieske's (2007) five elements of effective listening material. In a beginner class like Basic isiZulu, it was deemed prudent to take a conservative approach as learners have no prior knowledge of isiZulu. The listening tests were designed to be gradually more complex. The listening discourse is similar to reading comprehension and unidirectional. No dialogues or multiple speaker conversations were introduced. Notwithstanding this, the tests designed were valid, considering the competence of the learners. Lieske's fourth element – teaching new listening skills – was not achieved in the Basic isiZulu tests. This element relates to task-focused instruction, an aspect that the researchers will consider for future exercises. In this study, the formative assessments were based on three tenses. Formative 1 and Formative 2 were based on the Present Tense, Formative 3 on the Past Tense and Formative 4 on the Future Tense. Formative 1 and Formative 4 required the learners to listen to a statement and select from the True/False option, focusing on comprehension. Formative 2 and Formative 3 required learners to listen to a question containing a question word and to select an answer from three options provided. Learners had already encountered the question words in class, during written and oral assessments. Formative 2 and Formative 3 required the application of higher-order functions, for example, making deductions. Thus, Lieske's elements were consciously included in the design of the listening comprehension material.

Assessing Listening Comprehension

Given that this study was conducted with a beginner class with no prior knowledge of isiZulu, the researchers skipped the comprehensive diagnosis and went immediately to identifying a suitable format for the test, opting for the True/False and MCQ formats. The latter was deemed appropriate for the level of the learners, as opposed to other options available in Moodle, for example, matching, short answer, drag and drop etcetera. In formulating the test questions, the researchers adhered to the five main criteria for an assessment tool identified by Vandergrift and Goh (2012, p. 255). These are:

- Validity;

Table 1. Interpreting the Difficulty Index (Tamil, 2015)

Range	Difficulty Level
20 and below	Very difficult
21-40	Difficult
41-60	Average
61-80	Easy
81 & above	Very Easy

- Reliability;
- Authenticity;
- Washback; and
- Practicality

The four tests were deemed valid, as the content is 'familiar'. The listener would have encountered grammatical constructions and vocabulary during face-to-face lectures and the tests focussed on these specific aspects. For example, the tests were designed to measure the listener's ability to understand the use of the question words. Therefore, the question words, which were taught in face-to-face lectures, were gradually introduced and repeated across the four tests. Moreover, the content of the tests is 'predictive', meaning that in a real-life situation, the listener is likely to encounter such a narrative. While the language used is real-life, rendering the assessment tool *authentic*, a weakness was that only one speaker was utilized, thus not creating adequate variation in accent and dialect. Appropriate *washback* or feedback was provided immediately after the test was submitted, i.e. both the mark and a display of the correct answers. The assessment tool was easily accessible to learners via Moodle. Moodle marked the assessment and collated the marks for the teacher, making the administration of the instrument *practicable*. The *reliability* of the instrument, i.e. producing "similar results with a similar population under similar conditions" (Vandergrift and Goh (2012, p. 255), could not be determined for now as the same test would need to be completed with another cohort of learners. This will be done when the next cohort is enrolled. Nonetheless, in the next section, the quantitative results of an item analysis are presented, thereby validating the reliability of the instrument.

The Difficulty Index

Item analysis examined the learner responses to each question, which in this study was a total of forty questions or ten per test. Item analysis was used to determine the Difficulty Index. This was done by arranging the marks of respondents in merit order for each question. One-third of the high scores and one-third of the low scores were then selected. These two groups were considered high achieving (H) and low achieving (L) groups, respectively. An acceptable range of percentages to calculate the Difficulty Index is 25% to 50% (Fourie, Summers & Zweygarth, 2010). The formula to calculate Difficulty Index is:

$$p = \frac{H + Lx100}{N}$$

H = number of respondents in the high achieving group who answered correctly
L = number of respondents in the low achieving group who answered correctly
N =total number of respondents in the two groups H and L

The Difficulty Index was, therefore, the proportion of the total number of learners in the two groups, H and L, who selected the correct response.

Table 1 illustrates the ranges for interpreting the Difficulty Index.

This study was a retrospective quantitative evaluation. Marks were retrieved from the Moodle database, which stores all quiz marks after automatic marking. The total number of respondents for each test is presented in Table 2. The one-third H and L were extracted from these total numbers.

Table 2. Calculation of H and L

	Total Number of Respondents	$\frac{1}{3}$ H	$\frac{1}{3}$ L
Formative 1	122	41	41
Formative 2	88	29	29
Formative 3	71	24	24
Formative 4	60	20	20

The Difficulty Indices are presented in Table 3.

Table 3. The Difficulty Indices

	Q1	Q2	Q3	Q4	Q5	Q6	Q7	Q8	Q9	Q10	Number of questions rated as Difficult
Formative 1 T/F with cue	61	44	49	46	48	39	n/a	57	55	49	1
Formative 2 MCQ	46	32	55	44	36	28	35	36	23	57	6
Formative 3 MCQ with cue	58	51	24	32	43	70	56	38	20	47	4
Formative 4 T/F	11	35	21	53	48	42	38	49	38	44	5

Critical Analysis of Results

In the following discussion, the difficulty indices are analyzed. One question from Formative 1 and five questions from Formative 4 fall into the difficult range. The difficult question in Formative 1 was *Ugogo kaNokuthula unguMaZungu*/Nokuthula's granny is MaZungu. The comprehension did not explicitly state whose granny MaZungu was. However, by inference, respondents should have realized that MaZungu was Nokuthula's granny.

In Formative 4, the statement in Question 1 reads *Isibongo sami singuCele*/My surname is Cele. The statement in Question 9 reads *Ngingumfundi eUKZN*/I am a student at UKZN. These are simple statements which learners use in oral practice and the researchers were baffled about the rating. There is speculation that the respondents were reading in the first person, assuming the role of Xoliswa Cele and therefore answering in the first person. Regarding Questions 2 and 3, *umama kaXoliswa unguSandile*/ Xoliswa's mother is Sandile and *ubaba kaXoliswa unguThembani*/ Xoliswa's father is Thembani, it is assumed that respondents did not identify the correct gender of the name. A challenge with vocabulary may account for the difficulty level with Question 7. The traditional isiZulu word *hlanu*/five is used in the monologue, but the statement question contains the anglicized version *ezingu-5*. There is a similar problem in Formative 3, Question 3 which asks *Bafundani abangane*/what are the friends studying. The monologue states that the friends are studying to become teachers, using the anglicized option *othisha*. But, the correct option is *abafundisi*/teachers, a traditional term for teachers.

In Formative Assessments 2 and 3, the comprehension and understanding of the question words are assessed. The following question words *when*, *what*, *who*, *how many* and *how* were used in the tests. Six questions from Formative 2 and four questions from Formative 3 fell into the difficult range. In Formative 2, the question word *phi*/where is used twice. In question 1, it is used in the sentence *USizwe uvelaphi*/ where does Sizwe originate from? In question 2, it is repeated in the sentence *USizwe uvakashela kuphi*/ where does Sizwe visit. The former is rated average and the latter difficult. Two grammatical variations of the question word were used, and it is apparent that many respondents are not familiar with the second variant *kuphi*. Similarly, when the question word *ubani*/who, is used in Question 4, *uSizwe uvakashela ubani*/who does Sizwe visit, the rating is average. But when the same question word is repeated in Questions 5 and 6, located at the beginning of the sentence with a relative clause, *Ubani osesikoleni*/who attends school and *Ubani onepulazi*/who owns a farm, the rating alters to difficult.

In Formative 3, two new question words were introduced, *ngani*/how and *nini*/when. According to responses, the latter is categorized as difficult. The question is *Abangane baye nini olwandle*/when did the friends go to the beach? The answer options are days of the week. Therefore, respondents would have concluded or even guessed that this question asked 'when'. However, in the actual monologue, it is stated that today is Friday, and the visit to the beach happened yesterday (i.e. Thursday). Respondents were required to determine the correct answer option through the process of deduction. Interestingly, the question word *ubani*/who, is clearly understood in certain contexts. For example, in Formative 3, Question 7 asks *Ubani obone ushaka*/who saw the shark? The difficulty level was average. However, the same question word used in Question 8 asks *Ubani oshaye utshani*/who ran away, and the difficulty level is higher. It is likely that respondents were not familiar with the expression *shaye utshani*, so the difficulty cannot be attributed to the comprehension of the question word. A slightly different postulation is offered for the difficulty encountered with the question word *ni*/what. In Formative 2, Question 9 reads *Unani uBulelani*/what does Bulelani have? Responses fall into the difficult range. Question 10 reads *Wena unani*/what do you have? Responses fall into the average difficulty range. As a beginner group, respondents are probably more familiar with the use of the second person, as opposed to the third person.

Statistically, the MCQs pose more difficulty than the True/False questions. In total, six of the latter were rated as difficult as opposed to ten MCQs (cf. Table 3). The researchers attribute this to the use of the Identificative Copulatives in the True/False format. In total, fourteen of the twenty questions in Formative 1 and Formative 4 contained Identificative Copulatives. For example, in Formative 1, *UNokuthula ungumfundi*/Nokuthula is a student. In Formative 4, *UXoliswa ungumfundi eThusini*/Xoliswa is a student at UKZN. Such examples are considered less complex as the listener is simply required to translate the statement and associate it with a sentence in the monologue. The latter will contain cues or words that occur in the question statement. In Formative 2 and Formative 3 sentences occur with question words. For example, in Formative 2, *USizwe uvelaphi*/where does Sipho originate from? The listener has to first translate a sentence with a question word; then, establish an association between parts of the question sentence with a sentence in the monologue. The question word does not appear in the monologue, thereby reducing possible cues to an answer. The absence of overt cues renders this a more complex process than the choice in the True/False format.

Informed by the analysis, the researchers have identified two challenges that account for the difficulty index scores. Firstly, the respondents have low vocabulary retention. The examples of inability to identify traditional terms and expressions illustrate this. Secondly, the application of Bloom's higher-order functions, for example, knowledge application, poses a challenge. This is evidenced by the respondents' inability to recognize the same question word in different contexts, for example with different verbal agreements and relative constructions. These challenges suggest that the teachers in this module need to review their teaching technique, specifically with relation to vocabulary and selected aspects of grammar.

Correlation of Results With the Hemmati and Ghaderi's (2014) Study

The Hemmati and Ghaderi's (2014) study recorded better performance with the FQP option, where their learners were able to view the questions and answer options before listening. While the experiment reported in this study is not a replication of that study, the results corroborate that of Hemmati and Ghaderi (2014). With the True/False option, the visibility of cues produced only one question falling into the difficult range, but as this was the first test, the level of work was considerably easier as opposed to the fourth test. With the MCQs, when the visual options were available, the number of questions falling into the difficult range was 4, as opposed to 6 when there were no cues.

The decreasing average mark, shown in Table 4, is consistent with the increasing complexity of work. Moodle calculated the average marks.

Table 4. Average Marks

	Average Mark
Formative 1 T/F with cue	6.54
Formative 2 MCQ	5.16
Formative 3 MCQ with cue	5
Formative 4 T/F	4.22

SOLUTIONS AND RECOMMENDATIONS

The perfect timing of the introduction of the compulsory isiZulu module and the phasing in of Moodle at UKZN was coincidental. Unfortunately, in terms of data collection, the researchers were not strategic and did not collect data to effect a credible comparison of written versus online tests, or visual versus aural comprehension tests. Hence, this study is limited in that it focuses exclusively on listening comprehension. Additionally, the researchers did not investigate any challenges that learners may have experienced in transitioning to an online mode of assessment, given that other university modules employ mainly the pen and paper mode for testing. While cognizant that these factors definitely impact on learner performance, the researchers are of the opinion that neither of these shortcomings impacts significantly on the scientific validity of the research undertaken. This research study focuses on the formats of online listening comprehension tests, and the way forward for assessment is undoubtedly online. Furthermore, the researchers did not receive any negative feedback from learners regarding challenges with the use of technology. On the contrary there were positive comments about the use of e-assessment. This research investigation has nevertheless highlighted several issues that require attention.

With the difficulty indices from the formative assessments established, it is necessary to re-conceptualize some aspects of teaching. The use of pronouns must be taught differently; grammatical variation must be highlighted; more innovative teaching methods need to be employed to ensure vocabulary retention and some brain gym activities might be necessary to sharpen the deductive skills of learners.

The critical analysis of the results is instructive. Learner performance was better with the True/False format as opposed to the MCQ. While more challenging at a cognitive level, the inclusion of MCQs is advantageous as it mimics real-world speech. Consider that in normal discourse it is unlikely that a speaker will say *Khetha yebo noma cha*/Select yes or no. *UXoliswa uzohamba ngebhasi ukuya eFlagstaff*/Xoliswa will travel by bus to Flagstaff. It is more likely that a speaker will say *UXoliswa uzohamba ngani ukuya eFlagstaff*/How will Xoliswa travel to Flagstaff. For such reasons the researchers would reconsider the use of the True/False format. Perhaps in the first Formative Assessment, when learners are being familiarized with e-assessment and listening comprehension activities in particular, the True/False format may be convenient. Thereafter, other formats are preferable.

For the evaluation of the understanding and use of question words, the researchers recommend limiting the number of question words per test. Formative 2 and Formative 3 contained four and five question words, respectively. It is preferable to include three question words per test and structure the questions to allow for all grammatical variants. For example, the question word *ni*/what, could be included with vowel verbs as in *Wenzeni uNokuthula*/What did Nokuthula do, and with the Associative Copulative as in *UNokuthula unani*/What does Nokuthula have. This allows for reinforcement of the question word in different grammatical contexts. Reinforcement could also be situated within the Dynamic Assessment strategy used by Farangi and Kheradmand Saadi (2017), where enrichment activities are individualized. Hence, a learner who struggles with differentiating the use of *ni*/what with copulative and associative structures should be referred to further exercises.

The analysis indicated that learners experience difficulty with vocabulary retention. Farangi and Kheradmand Saadi (2017) and Li (2019) identified vocabulary retention as crucial to improving listening comprehension skills, with the former using semantic mapping as a strategy to improve vocabulary retention. The implementation of a similar strategy is recommended for the Basic isiZulu module.

The results of this study corroborate that of Hemmati and Ghaderi (2014) with respect to the visual cues aiding performance. The researchers believe that the initial listening comprehension activities should be user friendly and therefore contain visual cues, where learners can read and listen to the questions and/or monologues. However, if listening is to maintain primacy in the test, listeners should be rapidly weaned off the visual cues. On the other hand, a different type of visual is recommended for inclusion in the Basic isiZulu module, namely audio-visual conversations. This suggestion emanates from the study of Hamdan and Al-Hawamdeh (2018). Moreover, in the age of information and data visualization, it is a shortcoming, not to provide conversation in an audio-visual format.

The Basic isiZulu module is situated on a university campus where the majority of students are L1 speakers of isiZulu. This creates a wonderful opportunity for L2 learners to interact with L1 speakers. But, carpe diem has not prevailed. Logistical challenges should be resolved to facilitate the implementation of u-learning as the study by Chang et al. (2018) indicates that this strategy yields long term positive benefits for developing the listening comprehension skill.

FUTURE RESEARCH DIRECTIONS

The four listening comprehension tests presented in this study were uni-directional or in Nunan's (1997) terms, 'non-reciprocal'. Nunan (1997) suggests a range of interesting and interactive listening activities. For example,

- listening to a news broadcast and then tasking learners with matching the places with events;
- listening to a news broadcast and reading about the same event in a newspaper article and then tasking learners to make comparisons between the two reports;
- following a sequence of instructions; and
- responding to a computerized message

A variety of listening comprehension activities would benefit the Basic isiZulu learners and definitely promote L2 comprehension ability.

McDonough et al. (2013) suggest that listening comprehension activities should be linked to a theme. The Basic isiZulu module utilizes a manual for teaching and learning. Various themes, for example, at the restaurant, at the hospital, at the beach, are available in the manual. Relevant listening comprehension exercises could be developed around these themes.

An investigation into how e-learning can be designed and implemented into L2 teaching of African languages has considerable potential for future research. Research into listening comprehension can be expanded into developing relevant, meaningful and authentic listening tasks. Focus on learner performance in the variety of available question formats, avails itself to substantial research. Hemmati and Ghaderi (2014) report on the various MCQ tests conducted by inter alia Underwood (1989), Brindley and Slater (2002), Chung (2002), Yagawa and Green (2008) and Jafari and Hashim (2012). These studies focus on MCQ testing. If one considers Nunan's suggested interactive activities listed above each of these has the potential for research. Clearly, there is a long road ahead to finding format efficacy for listening comprehension tasks. Kerr, Muller, McKinon & Mc Inerney (2016) determined that there was a correlation between engaging in formative assessment and performance in summative assessment. Similar studies would be relevant for Basic isiZulu, and other African languages. This could lead to further technological integration into summative assessments, thus supporting UKZN's call for Moodle integration within the teaching and learning practice.

In introducing the online listening comprehension activities, it was hoped that learner motivation would be ignited. However, it seems as though learners are most often motivated by marks. The researchers found that gentle reminders to complete the formative assessments were not heeded by many learners, evidenced by the chronologically decreasing number of respondents in the four tests. Replicating the research of Caruso et al. (2017) will be an informative exercise, as it will possibly explain how to motivate learners to use the Moodle platform and take responsibility for their own learning.

Finally, comparative work with other disciplines, particularly in terms of formats used, is possible.

CONCLUSION

The adoption and implementation of e-assessments in African languages in South African higher education are still in their infancy. This chapter explored the use of the Quiz tool available in Moodle to execute a listening comprehension assessment. Incorporating online listening comprehension tests into L2 teaching and learning is a complex process. Listening comprehension activities should be relevant and authentic to the 21st-century learner and should comply with the principles of validity, reliability and practicality. This chapter reports on the Difficulty Index of each item in four formative assessments, and analyzes how different types of questions, such as MCQ and True/False, perform under test conditions. The study provides interesting and valuable insights into the pedagogical implications, which language educators should take into consideration when designing and implementing listening comprehension e-assessments. Listening comprehension is no longer the 'Cinderella' of L2 teaching and learning. It is now the Aladdin's Lamp full of potential, waiting to be explored by innovative and creative ways of assessment.

ACKNOWLEDGMENT

This research received no specific grant from any funding agency in the public, commercial, or not-for-profit sectors.

REFERENCES

Bayat, A., Jamshidipour, A., & Hashemi, M. (2017). The beneficial impacts of applying formative assessment on Iranian university students' anxiety reduction and listening efficacy. *Online Submission*, *5*(2), 1–11. doi:10.18298/ijlet.1740

Bender, D. A. (2003). MCQ, EMSQ or multiple true/false questions? *Bioscience Education*, *2*(1), 1–3. doi:10.3108/beej.2003.02000009

Bloom, B. S., Engelhart, M. D., Furst, E. J., Hill, W. H., & Krathwohl, D. R. (1956). *Taxonomy of Educational Objectives: The Classification of Educational Goals*. New York: David McKay.

Brindley, G. (1998). Assessing listening abilities. *Annual Review of Applied Linguistics*, *18*, 171–191. doi:10.1017/S0267190500003536

Brown, G. (2017). Teaching listening comprehension. In G. Brown (Ed.), *Listening to Spoken English* (pp. 158–186). London, UK: Routledge. doi:10.4324/9781315538518

Caruso, M., Gadd Colombi, A., & Tebbit, S. (2017). Teaching how to Listen. Blended Learning for the Development and Assessment of Listening Skills in a Second Language. *Journal of University Teaching & Learning Practice*, *14*(1), 14.

Chang, C.-C., Warden, C. A., Liang, C., & Chou, P.-N. (2018). Performance, cognitive load, and behaviour of technology-assisted English listening learning: From CALL to MALL. *Journal of Computer Assisted Learning*, *34*(2), 105–114. doi:10.1111/jcal.12218

Churches, A. (2010). *Bloom's digital taxonomy*. Retrieved from http://burtonslifelearning.pbworks.com/f/BloomDigitalTaxonomy2001.pdf

Ellis, R. (2018). *Reflections on task-based language teaching*. Multilingual Matters.

Farangi, M. R., & Kheradmand Saadi, Z. (2017). Dynamic assessment or schema theory: The case of listening comprehension. *Cogent Education*, *4*(1), 1312078. doi:10.1080/2331186X.2017.1312078

Fourie, S., Summers, B., & Zweygarth, M. (2010). Difficulty and discrimination indices as quality assurance tools for assessments in a South African problem-based pharmacy programme. *Pharmacy Education*, 10.

Gikandi, J. W., Morrow, D., & Davis, N. E. (2011). Online formative assessment in higher education: A review of the literature. *Computers & Education*, *57*(4), 2333–2351. doi:10.1016/j.compedu.2011.06.004

Govindasamy, T. (2001). Successful implementation of e-learning: Pedagogical considerations. *The Internet and Higher Education*, *4*(3), 287–299. doi:10.1016/S1096-7516(01)00071-9

Hamdan, J. M., & Al-Hawamdeh, R. F. (2018). The Effects of 'Face' on Listening Comprehension: Evidence from Advanced Jordanian Speakers of English. *Journal of Psycholinguistic Research*, *47*(5), 1121–1131. doi:10.100710936-018-9582-7 PMID:29637485

Harding, L., Alderson, J. C., & Brunfaut, T. (2015). Diagnostic assessment of reading and listening in a second or foreign language: Elaborating on diagnostic principles. *Language Testing*, *32*(3), 317–336. doi:10.1177/0265532214564505

Hémard, D., & Cushion, S. (2003). Design and evaluation of an online test: Assessment conceived as a complementary CALL tool. *Computer Assisted Language Learning*, *16*(2-3), 119–139. doi:10.1076/call.16.2.119.15879

Hemmati, F., & Ghaderi, E. (2014). The effect of four formats of multiple-choice questions on the listening comprehension of EFL learners. *Procedia: Social and Behavioral Sciences*, *98*, 637–644. doi:10.1016/j.sbspro.2014.03.462

Kerr, S., Muller, D., McKinon, W., & Mc Inerney, P. (2016). An online formative assessment tool to prepare students for summative assessment in physiology. *African Journal of Health Professions Education*, *8*(1), 72–76. doi:10.7196/AJHPE.2016.v8i1.581

Li, C.-H. (2019). Using a Listening Vocabulary Levels Test to Explore the Effect of Vocabulary Knowledge on GEPT Listening Comprehension Performance. *Language Assessment Quarterly*, *16*(3), 328–344. doi:10.1080/15434303.2019.1648474

Lieske, C. (2007). Teaching Effective Second Language Listening. 島根大学外国語教育センタージャーナル, *2*, 39-51.

McDonough, J., Shaw, C., & Masuhara, H. (2013). *Materials and Methods in ELT*. Sussex, UK: John Wiley & Sons.

Mehta, G., & Mokhasi, V. (2014). Item analysis of multiple choice questions-an assessment of the assessment tool. *International Journal of Health Sciences and Research, 4*(7), 197–202.

Mercado, L. (2017). *Technology for the Language Classroom: Creating a 21st Century Learning Experience*. London: Macmillan International Higher Education. doi:10.1057/978-1-137-49785-7

Mukandutiye, D., Sevilla, J., & Makhanu, E. (2014). Adoption of e-assessment in Strathmore University. In *Proceedings of IST-Africa Conference* Mauritius. IEEE.

Nicol, D. (2007). E-assessment by design: Using multiple-choice tests to good effect. *Journal of Further and Higher Education, 31*(1), 53–64. doi:10.1080/03098770601167922

Nunan, D. (1997). Listening in language learning. The Language Teacher: The Japan Association of Language Teaching, 21(9), 47-51.

Ramirez, B. U. (2011). The sensory modality used for learning affects grades. *Advances in Physiology Education, 35*(3), 270–274. doi:10.1152/advan.00010.2011 PMID:21908836

Rarh, V., & Goel, A. (2011). A Methodology for E-quiz Content Production for E-learning. In *Proceedings of Second International Conference on Emerging Applications of Information Technology*. IEEE. 10.1109/EAIT.2011.72

Singh, U. G., & Gokool, R. (2018). Students' perceptions of the Moodle Quiz E-assessment tool in an isiZulu language course. *Journal for Language Teaching= Ijenali Yekufundzisa Lulwimi= Tydskrif vir Taalonderrig, 52*(1), 128–150. doi:10.4314/jlt.v52i1.7

Snowball, J. (2014). Using interactive content and online activities to accommodate diversity in a large first year class. *Higher Education, 67*(6), 823–838. doi:10.100710734-013-9708-7

Tamil, A. M. (2015). *Calculating Difficulty, Discrimination and Reliability Index/Standard Error of Measurement*. Retrieved from https://ppukmdotorg.wordpress.com/2015/04/02/calculating-omr-indexes/comment-page-1/

UKZN. (2014). *Language Policy and Plan*. Retrieved from http://ukzn.ac.za

UKZN. (2015). *Phasing in Moodle from 2016 to 2018*. Retrieved from https://www.ukzn.ac.za/wp-content/miscFiles/docs/general-docs/phasing-in-of-moodle-2016---2018.pdf

Vandergrift, L., & Baker, S. (2015). Learner variables in second language listening comprehension: An exploratory path analysis. *Language Learning, 65*(2), 390–416. doi:10.1111/lang.12105

Vandergrift, L., & Goh, C. C. (2012). *Teaching and learning second language listening: Metacognition in action*. New York: Routledge. doi:10.4324/9780203843376

Walker, D. J., Topping, K., & Rodrigues, S. (2008). Student reflections on formative e-assessment: Expectations and perceptions. *Learning, Media and Technology, 33*(3), 221–234. doi:10.1080/17439880802324178

Yi'an, W. (1998). What do tests of listening comprehension test?-A retrospection study of EFL test-takers performing a multiple-choice task. *Language Testing*, *15*(1), 21–44.

ADDITIONAL READING

Bañados, E. (2013). A blended-learning pedagogical model for teaching and learning EFL successfully through an online interactive multimedia environment. *CALICO Journal*, *23*(3), 533–550. doi:10.1558/cj.v23i3.533-550

Chang, C.-C., Warden, C. A., Liang, C., & Chou, P.-N. (2018). Performance, cognitive load, and behaviour of technology-assisted English listening learning: From CALL to MALL. *Journal of Computer Assisted Learning*, *34*(2), 105–114. doi:10.1111/jcal.12218

Gilakjani, A. P., & Sabouri, N. B. (2016). The significance of listening comprehension in English language teaching. *Theory and Practice in Language Studies*, *6*(8), 1670–1677. doi:10.17507/tpls.0608.22

Goh, C. C. (2018). Metacognition in second language listening. The TESOL Encyclopedia of English Language Teaching, 1-7.

Hamada, Y. (2016). Shadowing: Who benefits and how? Uncovering a booming EFL teaching technique for listening comprehension. *Language Teaching Research*, *20*(1), 35–52. doi:10.1177/1362168815597504

Hamdan, J. M., & Al-Hawamdeh, R. F. (2018). The Effects of 'Face' on Listening Comprehension: Evidence from Advanced Jordanian Speakers of English. *Journal of Psycholinguistic Research*, *47*(5), 1121–1131. doi:10.100710936-018-9582-7 PMID:29637485

İnceçay, V., & Koçoğlu, Z. (2017). Investigating the effects of multimedia input modality on L2 listening skills of Turkish EFL learners. Education and Information Technologies. *The Official Journal of the IFIP Technical Committee on Education*, *22*(3), 901–916.

Jones, L. (2013). Supporting listening comprehension and vocabulary acquisition with multimedia annotations: The students' voice. *CALICO Journal*, *21*(1), 41–65. doi:10.1558/cj.v21i1.41-65

Rubin, J. (1994). A review of second language listening comprehension research. *Modern Language Journal*, *78*(2), 199–221. doi:10.1111/j.1540-4781.1994.tb02034.x

Shohamy, E., & Inbar, O. (1991). Validation of listening comprehension tests: The effect of text and question type. *Language Testing*, *8*(1), 23–40. doi:10.1177/026553229100800103

KEY TERMS AND DEFINITIONS

Difficulty Index: It is a statistical function examining one-third of the high scores and one-third of the low scores in a test.

E-Assessment: It is computer-based testing.

Formative Assessment: Assessments used for students' developmental purposes.

Item Analysis: An examination of responses to every question in a test.

Listening Comprehension: A real-time function during which spoken language is processed.

Moodle: A free open-source software platform.

Nguni Languages: Nguni group of languages consists of isiZulu, isiXhosa, SiSwati, and isiNdebele.

Second Language Acquisition: A process involved in the learning of a second language.

Summative Assessment: The final grading of a student.

Chapter 9
Collaborative Discussion Using Padlet to Enhance the Teaching and Learning of Essay Writing in Mandarin Language

Yap Teng Teng
University of Malaya, Malaysia

Azlin Zaiti Zainal
https://orcid.org/0000-0002-0149-9742
University of Malaya, Malaysia

Vinothini Vasodavan
University of Malaya, Malaysia

Emily Lau Kui-Ling
https://orcid.org/0000-0002-9173-6595
University of Malaya, Malaysia

ABSTRACT

Writing skills demand the best pedagogical practices to engage students who struggle with essay writing. In line with the fast-paced, ever-evolving digital advancement, instructors are encouraged to transform their teaching method by integrating technology to help to improve students' writing skills. To do so, one of the ways is to adopt technological tools such as collaborative learning tools in their writing courses to make learning more interactive, interesting, and stimulating. This research, therefore, attempts to examine how Padlet can be utilized to transform didactic teaching and learning into innovative pedagogy to create new learning experiences for tertiary undergraduates. The undergraduates were instructed to use Padlet in their writing task, and this provides many opportunities for constructive learning through a resource-based approach where undergraduates learn from one another and the instructor shows well-written examples or incorrect sentences posted by the undergraduates.

DOI: 10.4018/978-1-7998-3062-7.ch009

INTRODUCTION

In this twenty first century, the rapid growth of technologies has shaped the way humans interact with each other from different parts of the world. These changes have also shaped the way people acquire knowledge, and teach with technologies (Almerich, Orellana, Rodríguez, & García, 2016; Guolifang et al, 2019). Due to that, learning can happen anytime and anywhere beyond boundaries via Internet (Bilici, Guzey, & Yamak, 2016). The development of educational technology creates a golden opportunity for lecturers to apply and integrate various tools such as iPad, Smartboard, laptop, mobile, web-based tool and much more (Bilici et al., 2016). However, higher education institutions are facing great challenges to ensure that faculty members (lecturers) are well-equipped with the skills and knowledge to incorporate technology that often evolve rapidly into teaching and learning process (Almerich et al., 2016; Bower, 2016). There is currently empirical evidence showing that lecturers are incorporating technology in the classroom to a certain level (Angeli & Valanides, 2009; Almerich et al., 2016), and this indicates that research on technology integration in higher education should not be limited to examining lecturers' usage of technology in teaching but should also focus on students' learning processes when using technology in the classroom. Another area of concern when using technology is to transform didactic form of teaching and learning into innovative pedagogy to create new learning experiences for students (Angeli & Valanides, 2009).

The quality of teaching practices indirectly influences the students' learning and outcome considering the fact that lecturers are the powerful agent to propose, implement and experience the use of technology in teaching and learning process (Almerich et al., 2016; Ward & Parr, 2010). As a result, they need to be well equipped themselves not only with the knowledge of technology but also with the ability to design learning tasks that incorporate technology beyond transmission of knowledge and drill-and-practice (Koh, Chai, Benjamin, & Hong, 2015). This is because just having technological knowledge does not guarantee that the instructors can implement technologies into their teaching practice effectively. Lecturers need to restructure learning activities to promote critical thinking, problem-solving, communication, collaboration and knowledge construction through social learning environment (Learning Partnership for 21st Century, 2016). In the local context, this is also aligned with the aspiration of the Ministry of Higher Education (MOHE) for blended learning model to be the main pedagogical approach in the higher educational institution as stated in the Malaysian Higher Education Blueprint 2013-2025. Hence, students will benefit from the use of technologies such as video-conferencing, live streaming, and Massive Open Online Courses (MOOCs) for learning without boundaries (MOHE, 2015). To achieve teaching and learning via technology, MOHE together with the higher education institutions are working towards building the capabilities of the academic community as stated in the National e-learning Policy. According to the policy, by 2020, 75% of higher education instructors will have had knowledge on technological pedagogical content knowledge (TPACK) and basic skills in e-learning to implement blended learning mode in teaching and learning processes (MOHE, 2015).

The policy vision can only be achieved if lecturers have the knowledge and skills that can assist them to employ technological resources in their curricular designs by planning effective teaching and meaningful learning experience for the students. The knowledge and skills are especially important to support students in overcoming the challenges that they experience in learning a particular subject. The focus of this study is writing skill, which is one of the most difficult skills while learning Mandarin. Previous studies show that writing classes tended to focus on traditional methods of memorizing and repetition techniques which lead to poor writing skills among the students (Afrin, 2016; Thomas, 2017).

Although there are many studies on the use of collaborative tools in teaching writing skills in general (Chen, 2019; Chen & Yu, 2019,) there is a scarcity of studies on the use of collaborative learning tools for the teaching and learning of Mandarin writing skills in particular, especially studies focusing on how collaborative tools can help students in the development of content. As suggested by Yilmaz and Keser (2016), different social interaction tools have different functions and that their use in teaching and learning can have different impacts on student interaction which may facilitate the development of writing skills. Thus, it is important to examine how a collaborative tool such as Padlet affects students' learning writing skills. While there is an increasing number of studies investigating the role of Padlet in collaborative learning, there remains a paucity of studies on the use of Padlet for writing skills. This research, therefore, attempts to fill the gap by examining how Padlet can be used to strengthen students' mastery and understanding of topics and how it can help students to enhance their ability to write content.

BACKGROUND

Computer-Supported Collaborative Learning (CSCL)

CSCL is also known as technology that supports collaborative learning by enhancing interaction among group members through joint activity and creation of knowledge (Koschmann, 2002; Lipponen, Rahikainen, Lallimo, & Hakkarainen, 2003; Resta & Laferriere, 2007). In other words, students can engage in meaningful learning within a CSCL environment, discussing and applying knowledge as they work together on learning tasks.

However, the rapid growth of social media and collaborative learning (CL) tools such as wikis, blogs and podcasts require different technical applications that lecturers need to learn in order to integrate CL tools in their teaching and learning. Through CSCL, learners can interact with their peers to promote meaning-making (Koschmann, 2002; Koschmann, Stahl, & Zemel, 2004; Stahl, Koschmann, & Suthers, 2006). Meaning-making happens through the process of social negotiation that promotes learners to formulate different perspectives, ideas and stance to be contributed in a group (Dillenbourg, Baker, Blaye, & O'Malley, 1996; Koschmann, 2002). Besides that, learners construct new knowledge through social negotiation that tends to foster higher phases of collaborative knowledge construction and knowledge building (De Wever, Keer, Schellens, & Valcke, 2010; Johnson & Johnson, 1996; Schrire, 2006; Tang & Tan, 2017). Knowledge construction is achieved when learners create meaning for personal learning rather than receiving it directly from peers. Meanwhile, knowledge building is developed intentionally when a group of learners are collaboratively involved in meaning-making by solving, discussing and comparing ideas or problems (Scardamalia & Bereiter, 2003, 2006; Suthers, 2006).

In CSCL, high quality engagement in joint activity depends on the collaboration among learners that lead to conceptual understanding because engagement mediates the relationship between motivation and learning (Tal, Krajcik, & Blumenfeld, 2006). Collaborative group engagement provides opportunities for students to work on inquiry-based practices to solve authentic problems (Sinha, Rogat, Adams-Wiggins, & Hmelo-Silver, 2015). Thus, CSCL is a component for learners to work collaboratively in joint activities through technology such as CL tools as mediation which is beyond the transmission of knowledge.

Collaborative Learning (CL) Tools in Higher Education

In this 21st century, new opportunities and affordances for learning have arisen due to the advancement of CL tools, mobile learning, and interactive surfaces (Bishop & Elen, 2014). CL tools also can serve as a user-friendly platform that provides immediate learner response and structural levels, and values each participant's opinion (McAfee, 2006). Most of the time, CL tools are known as Web 2.0 application. This internet technology enables and promotes Web content development through social collaboration. Through Web 2.0, various information resources can be accessed promptly and globally (Biasutti, 2017; Fırat & Koksal, 2017; Oliver, 2010).

Hence, from the context of higher education, CL tools could be incorporated in teaching to transform learning process to be less linear and beyond the traditional classroom setting to allow students to acquire social knowledge construction through sharing, discussing and producing various concepts in learning in a dynamic and instantaneous manner (De Wever, Van Keer, Schellens, & Valcke, 2009; Garcia, Elbeltagi, Brown, & Dungay, 2015; Lee & Markey, 2014). Examples of the CL tools include content creation (blogs, wikis, and podcasts); social networking sites (Facebook, Twitter, YouTube); bookmarking (tagging and RSS feeds) and communication tools (instant messaging (IM) and discussion forum. Many CL tools do not need to be installed in any devices or require a high specification hardware (Dewitt, Alias, & Siraj, 2015). This is because almost all LMS have embedded and offer essential CL tools, such as blogs, wikis, podcast, text messaging/chat and discussion forum to organize and control learners' joint activities.

A number of studies have found that CL tools have potential to facilitate learning in online learning environments. Using CL tools, most of the activities related to education, such as reading a text and discussing it online, writing online content, creating audio and video can be carried out. CL tools are proven to be useful for learning since they are known for task-specific collaborations with goals and work-oriented activities (Cheung & Vogel, 2013; Dewitt et al., 2015). Integrating different types of CL tools in learning increases interactions among learners since it allows the students not only to be a passive user of the available tools but also to create, share, contribute and comment on the content through various file formats that can be shared or edited online and develop student-centered personalized learning environments (Cheung & Vogel, 2013; Churchill, 2011; DeWitt, Alias, & Siraj, 2014; Sigala, 2007). In their study, Yilmaz, Karaoglan Yilmaz and Kilic Cakmak (2017, p.963) found that students working in groups using Facebook as a platform, "have tendencies to test, evaluate and regulate themselves by observing the knowledge sharing and interaction behaviours". This implies that collaborative tools have the potential to promote students self-regulation in learning. This implies that lecturers in higher education need to be aware of the educational potential of CL tools and be ready to explore and implement CL tools for the benefit of students' learning through social interactions and cognitive process during collaborative learning.

The Use of ICT to Enhance Writing Skills

Writing is considered as a key principle for language production. It is also regarded as a challenging skill to be learned by students (Fareed, Ashraf, & Bilal, 2016). The language production here can be English as a second language (ESL), English or Mandarin as a foreign language (E/MFL). As far as students' academic life is concerned, writing skill is considered as a vital part of communication because it allows them to express, share and transfer meaning in a well-constructed text (Afrin, 2016). One of the authors in his book expresses that writing is a physical and mental art where human expresses and organizes them into sentences that are comprehensible to a reader (Afrin, 2016). Therefore, this section is divided into two sub sections. First, factors that hinder student writing skills are discussed. Next, the use of CL tools to promote writing skills among students in higher education institution (HEI) is explained. According to the past literature, many students experience difficulty in linguistic skills, especially writing skills due to insufficient idea, high dependency on the first language (L1), anxiety in writing, lack of motivation and inefficient pedagogy (Afrin, 2016; Fareed et al., 2016). Besides, majority of the students who enter HEI are freshmen (Thomas, 2017). Hence, they have trouble in writing skills.

Students Writing Skills Challenges

Previous studies showed that poor writing skills resulted from two main factors: the learner and the lecturer. From the learner perspective, students face anxiety in writing because they struggle with the structural components of the language which lead to poor ideas in text composition. This situation also causes lack of confidence in students, since teaching strategies fail to address students' learning style and prior knowledge (Fareed et al., 2016; Mercer-Mapstone & Matthews, 2017). This situation is also associated with their lack of motivation when students are continuously involved in didactic learning method that focuses on rote learning and exam-oriented language production rather than promoting creative skills (Dar & Khan 2015). HEI should move away from teaching and learning process that focus on memorizing and repetition towards teaching students the essential skills such as problem solving, knowledge building and collaborative skills (Dewitt, Alias, & Siraj, 2015). It is important to create opportunities for students to identify a suitable source of information, and rephrase the selected information to be used appropriately in an academic writing context (Gonye, Mareva, Dudu, Sib, 2012). From the lecturer's perspective, students show negative attitudes towards learning writing skills because of ineffective teaching methods used by the lecturers (Fareed et al., 2016; Wang, 2015). Some examples of ineffective pedagogy include inconsistency in giving feedback to students' work and lack of engaging tasks that could motivate students (Pineteh, 2013). It is very common to see lecturers limit themselves in teaching writing skills by using paper and pencil approach which consequently limits the students from having conversation and debate before making an attempt to write (Alsamadani, 2017). In addition to that, previous studies also suggested that lecturers could transform their teaching method by integrating technology in order to improve and inculcate interest among students to improve their writing skills (Fareed et al., 2016; Graham & Perin, 2007; Wang, 2015). In order to do that, lecturers need to adopt CL tools such as wikis, blogs, Padlet, and forum discussion in their writing courses to make learning more interesting and fun. Hence, to incorporate CL tools to teach writing skills, lecturers should be well-equipped with the knowledge and skills of using CL tool to promote students' writing development.

CL Tools to Promote Writing Skills

In this twenty-first century era, teaching language took a new dimension due to the advancement of technology. In HEI, new way of learning writing skill with educational technology is needed and no longer only through practice and reinforcement (Altınmakas & Bayyurt, 2019; Wang, 2015). There are many CL tools that can be integrated in lessons to help students acquire writing skills. According to previous studies, tools such as wikis offer students the room to communicate with peers by sharing, presenting and collaborate information in one document. Wikis are used for collaborative writing due to the free editing feature available for students to review and restructure content at any point of time (Altanopoulou, Tselios, Katsanos, Georgoutsou, & Panagiotaki, 2015; Biasutti & El-Deghaidy, 2012; Wang, 2015). Through wiki, each student could contribute to the benefit of the group when each of them works together to achieve the learning goals and objectives. Collaborative writing has a great prospective since group members could improve writing skill that focus on grammar and language accuracy from each other (Davidson, 2012; Wang, 2015).

The type of collaboration when students use CL tools should also be considered by lecturers to ensure that they produce writing of high quality. Based on Storch's (2002) study of ESL peer interaction in a face-to-face collaborative writing task environment, it is suggested that interaction patterns can be categorized into four types: 1) collaborative 2) dominant/dominant 3) dominant/passive and 4) expert/novice. The findings indicated that more learning uptake was evident when learners interact in a collaborative manner and that peer interaction patterns affected quality of writing. The patterns found to be conducive for learning and improve the quality of writing were the collaborative, and the expert/novice patterns but not the dominant /dominant or the dominant/passive type of interaction. Li and Zhu's (2017) study, which was conducted in the context of ESL learners' wiki-writing for English for academic purposes (EAP) course appears to support this conclusion. They found that the group that demonstrated collaborative pattern produced a research proposal of a higher quality and performed better in terms of coherence and rhetorical structure compared to groups that did not display a collaborative pattern.

Awareness of the role of different CL tools and how they may be used in different ways are crucial for writing stages. There are various steps involved in collaborative writing. According to Navarre (2019, p. 83), these steps may include "group forming, brainstorming ideas, coordinating meeting schedules, researching, exchanging information gathered from the research, outlining and planning the content, crafting the first draft, reviewing and editing and repeating some steps for a second/final draft". Because of this, it is important to recognize how CL tools can support collaborative writing at different stages. In their study of learners' writing in Spanish as a foreign language using ICT tools such as wikis and chats to compare learners' individual and collaborative writing, Elola and Oskoz (2010) found that different ICT tools seemed to be used in different ways by learners. Learners used chats to discuss the overall organization and sections of the essay such as the introduction, body and conclusion and to search for information to address real time concerns. Learners who used wikis were, however, more focused on linguistics aspects at the paragraph level such as coherence of sentences, grammatical structures and vocabulary use. All learners in their study also felt that collaborative writing helped to improve the overall quality of their work. Their study highlights the importance of understanding the role of specific CL tools in designing writing tasks for students.

Kessler (2009) proposed that collaborative writing using technology can promote learner autonomy. In his study of pre-service EFL teachers, Kessler (2009) found that participants can work autonomously on a long-term collaborative task using wiki. However, they appeared to be more focused on content and formatting rather than form. He found that while they were able to demonstrate the ability to work autonomously on the collaborative task, they did not show willingness to correct grammatical errors that did not appear to affect the meaning. Kessler attributed this to the informal setting of the writing task and the nature of the grammatical errors which the participants felt were not severe.

Besides wiki, blog is also another form of CL tools that facilitate students to improve their writing skills in non-traditional ways. Blogging practice allows students to express themselves through writing and attract many people to comments when their articles have been published (Alsamadani, 2017,). In HEI, learning writing skills through blogging is one of the way students socialize, debate, discuss and express their ideas and thoughts with peers and within large sociocultural system (Alsamadani, 2017; Chen, 2015). Besides that, students who write collaboratively were able to produce higher quality of writing than those who wrote individually because students were able to revise and improve their writing style by taking into consideration of readers' point of view (Wang, 2015). Collaboration among students can be cultivated when they receive feedback from peers and take control over the expression of the writing skills (Alsamadani, 2017; Fareed et al., 2016). Therefore, it is important for the lecturers to design learning tasks that incorporate with shared goal for meaningful learning to take place when using CL tools because wiki and blog are eventually used as medium of information sharing online but not for interaction (Dewitt et al., 2015). In the context of writing, Navarre (2019) suggested that tools such as wikis appear to be more appropriate for asynchronous editing compared to document-sharing tools that are more suitable for synchronous editing.

Lecturers need to be aware of the affordances of particular CL tools and how they can be utilized for students' specific learning needs. In this study, a CL tool, Padlet, was used to organize interactive activity for argumentative writing practices in the context of essay writing in Mandarin among undergraduates to allow them to generate new ideas and benefit from them when using this tool. The use of Padlet is an interesting way to develop writing skills it provides a platform to compile and showcase all the students' written work. As suggested by Bikowski (2015), students should be encouraged to use a variety of technologies for collaboration and that Padlet can support students' learning in a creative way. In this way students are exposed to a different method of learning writing where this would raise their awareness of the many different learning opportunities afforded by ICT. Padlet also engages learners to participate actively in learning process as it allows them to write their ideas and make amendments on their writing rather than merely listen and memorize what is taught in class. Using Padlet this way can make classroom activities more interactive, fun, and motivate students in their learning.

The Needs for Mandarin Writing Competency

Mandarin is the most widely spoken language in the world. About 1.2 billion people or around 16% of the world's population use Mandarin or Chinese language as their first language (Hao, 2020). It is also one of the five official languages of the United Nations. This informs the importance of Mandarin competency worldwide. As a matter of fact, the mainland China is one of the largest economic entities in the world, with its booming business and consumer affluence on the rise. In terms of the Malaysian-China ties, Malaysia has been China's top trading partner within ASEAN since 2008 with bilateral trade volume hitting as high as US$108.6bil (RM443bil) from US$96bil (RM392bil) in 2018. This makes Malaysia the top three trade partner of China in Asia (*The Star*, 19 Feb 2019). By the sheer economic and communicative values of the Mandarin language, the innovation in enhancing Mandarin writing skill could go a long way in future endeavors, especially in relation to education and business.

Generally, in the case of learning Mandarin, one of the most difficult skills is the writing skill. Some of the common problems in writing are deficiency in vocabulary choices, lack of ideas as well as poor command of the structural components of the language. These challenges lead to inability to clearly express opinions and thoughts in text composition. Commonly, every student in the classroom has different level of intellectual or cognitive strength. The good students are better in grammar and expression, therefore their writing is stronger. Weaker students need more clarifications and examples to engage with the topic. The traditional teaching approach is inadequate to address the challenges faced by students. The traditional way mainly involve the lecturer giving the topic to the students and then the students would write individually based on the given topic and this is followed by the lecturer's feedback on individual students' writing. This one-to-one feedback helps students discover and remedy their problems. However, it is limited as students often only see their own shortcomings, and they often feel incompetent, helpless and demotivated. Furthermore, students' may not understand the lecturer's comments, especially on how to develop the content. Also, it can be time consuming for the lecturer to comment on all aspects, from grammar to content, on all individual essays. The lecturer, on the other hand, feels frustrated and being flustered as well.

Specifically, in the case of this group of students, they faced three major problems at the start of the writing process. Firstly, they lacked understanding of the topic given. Students could not understand clearly what is required to write from the given topic. Secondly, they were unable to provide relevant contents related to the topic. The ideas were poorly expressed and their opinions were vague. The proposed opinions of pros and cons mostly could not be strongly substantiated. Thirdly, the overall structure was disorganized. There were incomplete sentences and their arguments were flawed. In view of these problems, there was a need to consider ways to support the development of these learners' argumentative writing skills.

As an alternative to the traditional teaching methods, the researchers tried to integrate Padlet in the teaching of argumentative writing. At present, research involving the use of Padlet in writing is lacking, particularly research that looks at the writing process. This research attempts to address the gap by looking at how the use of Padlet can help learners in developing their understanding of topic. In this research, Padlet was utilized to transform didactic teaching and learning of Mandarin writing skills into innovative pedagogy to create new learning experiences for Year 2 University of Malaya's undergraduates. Through the platform of Padlet, each classmate can get inspiration from other classmates' write-up. Padlet adds fun to the classroom and promotes student confidence allowing students to learn from their peers' strengths and improve on their weaknesses.

The current research was driven by these two questions: 1) How can Padlet be used to strengthen students' understanding of the topic? 2) How can Padlet be used to enhance the students' ability to write good content?

MAIN FOCUS OF THE CHAPTER

Participants

TIC 1004 Competency Chinese Language 2 is a core course for Semester 2 year one undergraduates. In the year 2019, there were 14 undergraduates who took this class. Their first language is Mandarin. They were tasked with essay writing practices. One of them includes argumentative writing.

Data Collection Procedures

The data collected were from three writing assignments at the beginning of the semester in the academic year 2018/2019. The participants were 14 students (in a single class) from first year second semester Bachelor of Chinese Language and Linguistics program at the Faculty of Languages and Linguistics. They were introduced to Padlet at the beginning of the course and in Week 3, students were tasked to use Padlet individually. In Week 8, mid-term of the semester, the students had a writing test. The final writing test was administered in Week 15. Three writing assessments were marked according to the rubrics as shown in Table 1 below:

Table 1. The rubric assessment of three test of writing assignment

分数 **Marks (Grade)**	评分标准 **Assessment Criteria**
25-30 (A)	切题、文笔佳、观点独到、题目有新意、运用指定的表达方式、结构性强 Clearly presents a main idea. Well-planned and well-thought out. Includes title, introduction, and statement of main idea, transitions and conclusion. Exceptionally well-presented and argued; ideas are detailed, well-developed, supported with specific evidence & facts, as well as examples and specific details.
20-24 (B)	切题、文笔中等、有内容、题目切题、运用指定的表达方式、颇有结构 There is A main idea supported throughout most of the paper. Good overall organization, includes the main organizational tools. Well-presented and argued; ideas are detailed, developed and supported with evidence and details, mostly specific.
15-19 (C)	略有切题、文笔平平、内容普通没新意、稍偏离指定的表达方式、结构性弱 Vague sense of a main idea, weakly supported throughout the paper. There is a sense of organization, although some of the organizational tools are used weakly or missing, Content is sound and solid; ideas are present but not particularly developed or supported; some evidence, but usually of a generalized in nature.
0-14 (D)	离题、不完整、错字多、偏离指定的表达方式、没有结构 No main idea, No sense of organization. Content is not relevant.

Remarks: The marks scored will be converted to 100% => 80, 70-79, 60-69, >50.

During the first lecture, students were introduced to Padlet and were asked to bring their laptop during class every Tuesday and Wednesday. Networked computers with Internet connectivity is required to be able to use Padlet in classroom. Padlet was used for two types of teaching and learning activities in the classroom for two hours for each class. For the first activity, students were asked to write individually, and for the second activity, students were divided into seven groups. Using Padlet, the lecturer provided the class with lesson notes, topics and guidelines of writing assignments, supplementary materials, and review selected writing samples and provided extra links that support and enhance learning. Students were asked to post their writing works or assignments periodically, and the lecturer would evaluate and post her comments on the Padlet wall. Any confusions that students felt could be resolved based on the lecturer's comments as they could immediately apply the feedback in their writing.

Students could check their friends' posts once they have shared their posts. They could easily view their classmates' writing in real time and comment on each other's post. Students were allowed to post additional writing exercises on lessons learned in the class, and make regular comments on the peer's writing task. In addition, students were encouraged to work on various activities which involved selected writing topics. Students were also given the freedom to do research on a relevant topic of interest and present the information found related to their chosen topic. Padlet was also used as a common platform of written communication among the class members.

Focus group interviews were conducted with all the 14 students in Week 14, the final week of the semester. The students were divided into three groups. The instructor conducted an interview with each group separately during the final session. The purpose of the focus group interview was to find out students' thoughts regarding Padlet. They were asked questions about their experience of using Padlet and how they perceived the usefulness of Padlet in learning essay writing in Chinese. Each focus group interview was audio-recorded and subsequently transcribed.

Data Description

The shared topics can be of varied interests, for example, a discussion of a film, articles on specific topics and related photos, and so forth as shown by Figure 1.

Figure 1. Individual writing sharing after the discussion on selected topics

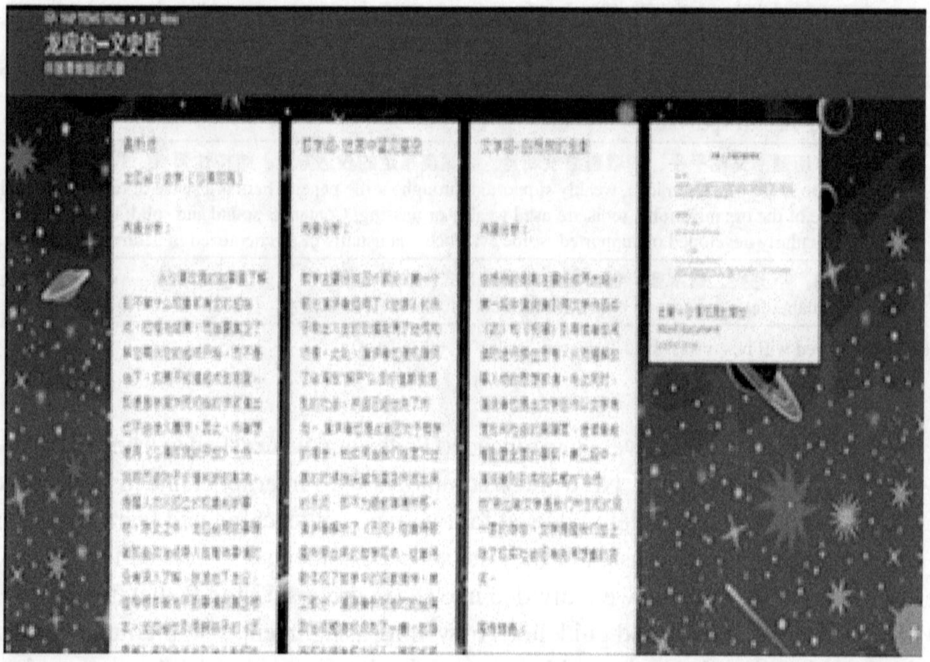

As shown in Figure 1, the Padlet wall displays the writings of three different groups reflecting three different perspectives on the same topic, namely "Literature is essential for a good leadership". The three groups of students interpreted the title and content of the article from three different perspectives. The first group wrote on how philosophical thoughts affect a leader, the second group wrote from the angle of the history of cultivation on how to rebrand a leader, and the third group wrote on the subtle influence of literature on the leader. Everyone collectively shared their ideas on the Padlet wall. After everyone uploaded their writing to this wall, the students would explain their content in their respective groups. This established the atmosphere of collaborative learning. With the use of Padlet, everyone could share their content and this encouraged students' active involvement in their learning. Through observation, it is found that the students know their own content, but they also paid attention to the content of their classmates. This kind of attention also shows that the students were motivated in their learning as Padlet provided them with a platform to learn in a fun and interactive manner compared to the traditional lecture-based method. Padlet also enabled them to be more focused in completing their task as they concentrated on giving feedback on the writings shared by their classmates on the Padlet wall.

Figure 2. One of the activities on individual writing using Padlet during lecture

During class, all the students would post their essays on the Padlet wall. Based on Figure 2, the parts highlighted in yellow refer to the lecturer and student comments based on the essays posted on the Padlet wall. Active discussion on the comments took place in class as students responded each other's work. It is also very important for the lecturer to give constructive feedback on the essays posted to help students with the development of their ideas. Some of the comments highlighted in Figure 2 are based on the topic 'Fake Diplomas'. The comments include: "How does the corruption of the education system affect the creation of fake diplomas?", "How does a fake diploma affect the education system of a country?" After discussion, the students were able to develop their ideas further as seen in the following examples:

“假文凭事件必然会影响到我国的教育发展。所谓“上梁不正下梁歪“我国领袖拥有假文凭事件会使得那些想要抄捷径国民更加有理由效仿之。试想想,如果老师拥有假文凭,没受到专业的训练那么他可能无意间灌输错误的知识给学生,不但会影响学生的未来,还会丢失了国家的人才。 *[The fake diploma event will inevitably affect the development of education in our country. The idiom, "fish rot from the head down" describes this kind of leadership. If our leaders have fake diplomas, it will set the kind of bad example of those who want to cut corners. Just think, if the teacher has a fake diploma and is not trained professionally, he may inadvertently instill the wrong knowledge to the students, which will not only affect the future of the students, but also the talents of the country."*

Students know how to quote idioms to express their thoughts and stand. Another example like:

“[对于假文凭的需求是为了得到更好的就业机会?还是在为自己所铺排的最轻松的成功之道在找借口?这其中买家和卖家都忽略了人品和诚信的重要性。前者以投机取巧为由,后者以盈利为主,才导致了这个市场的不间断循环。假文凭的诱惑之大足以让人们忘了为人根本吗?] *The need for a fake diploma is to get a better job opportunity? Still looking for an excuse for the easiest way to succeed for yourself? Both buyers and sellers ignore the importance of character and integrity. The former* *is based on opportunistic and the latter is based on profit, which leads to the uninterrupted cycle of this market. Is the temptation of a fake diploma enough to make people forget to be human?"*

The examples above demonstrate that the students utilized questioning methods to express their thoughts and ideas. Through this Padlet wall, they could easily learn from each other, where this helps to strengthen their content writing.

Figure 3. Activities 1: Individual Writing by using Padlet during lecture

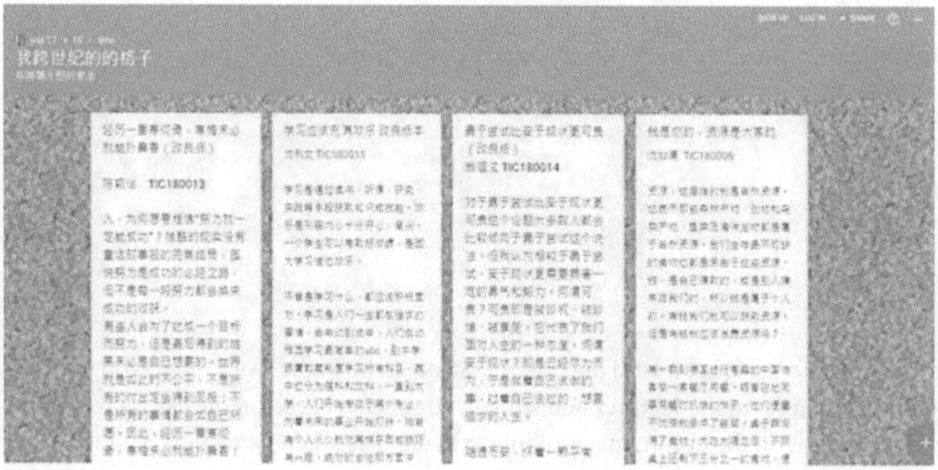

Figure 3 shows the amended version of students writing task based on the comments and discussion which took place during the activities in the classroom. During the semester, the students were assigned writing practice task based on seven essay topics. Each topic would be written on the Padlet wall. In the early stages, the lecturer would randomly choose two students to discuss the topic; one would develop ideas to support the topic and another, the counter argument. The points of both students' views would be shown on the Padlet wall. They were given 15 minutes to write their view of the topic. In these primary stages we found that majority of the students' writing were not clear whether they supported or opposed the motion. After the lecturer gave comments on the wall, pair work was carried out. This session was for everyone to brainstorm ideas related to the topic. The students were given instructions to go home to search for related information, and rewrite a complete essay on their own topic, and then upload it to a new Padlet wall created by the lecturer. An example of one of the topics is "*A good network is king*". Many of the students were not able to support the given topic with relevant ideas. They were able to give the content on agreeing points but not able to expand their ideas on what is involved to build a good network. They responded with short sentences on Padlet. After the discussion based on the Padlet, they went through their peers' work where some of the ideas given were clear but some were not and commented on them. The lecturer then gave comments on the students' posts on the wall of the Padlet. Based on their peers and lecturer's comments, the students developed a better understanding of each individual topic. They also got to know their weakness. Although there were instances of incomplete sentences and lack of confidence to share their idea on the Padlet wall at the beginning, based on the comments given by their peers and lecturer, they were finally able to write a better paragraph as follows:

"[人脉即人际关系、人际网络、体现人的人缘、社会关系,通过各种渠道所达到的领域。根据辞典里的说法,人脉的解释为"经由人际关系而形成的人际脉络",经常用于政治或商业的领域,但其实不论做什么行业,人人都会使用人脉。]…. "People are interpersonal beings through interpersonal networks, human relationships, social relationships, and these are established through various mediums. According to the dictionary, the interpretation of the network is "interpersonal context formed through interpersonal relationships,'' which is often used in political or commercial fields, but in fact, everyone uses the network regardless of the industry…".

Findings

First, the focus group interview data was transcribed. This is followed by applying value coding, focusing on the participants' attitudes and beliefs about the Padlet adopted in the course. The students soon realized that the use of Padlet for teaching and learning differed considerably from the traditional method they were accustomed to either in school or in previous foundation levels. The transcribed data was then sorted and grouped into identical categories under the keywords: (a) concentration; (b) practical; (c) impressive; (d) understand, and (e) interesting. There were different ways that the students explained their thoughts on their experience with the use of Padlet: "interesting" "helps in classroom", "concentration", and "impressive to me" among some of them.

"…Padlet is interesting helped me concentrated in the classroom." (T14)

"I like to read peers' sharing on Padlet." (T09)

"By using Padlet for learning writing is so practical, therefore, I think I can score better marks in final exam". (T07)

"I know Padlet that can assist me in learning Chinese Writing." (T08)

"I think I have to learn new tool to upgrading my writing skills, Padlet is impressive to me."(T02)

"I prefer to integrate Padlet in my presentation writing tasks, it is very practical." (T01)

"all materials shared in Padlet are meaningful, relevant, practical…." (T12)

"lecturer using Padlet during the classroom, can help me more concentrated in learning writing" (T03)

"I like to use Padlet to learn how to share video for related writing topic … it is good for brainstorming during classroom." (T13)

The purposes of this research were to understand how Padlet could be used to strengthen students' understanding of a writing topic and how Padlet could be used to enhance the students' ability to write good content. Based on their responses, it can be summarized that the students were very interested to write essays with Padlet in the classroom and that that they liked this learning atmosphere very much. Based on their peers' contents, they learnt to express their opinion on the different writing topics. They expressed their understanding of the writing structure and also learned more about the essay topic and the related arguments. From the lecturer's comment, they could recognize their mistakes and discover different opinions and ideas. Their feedback on writing through Padlet also enabled them to exercise their ability to think, about the topic from different angles, and exchanging their opinions with other students, "*I am very inspired by myself, discovering my own shortcomings and learning how to write the title*." (T05). Most of the students felt that using Padlet is very interesting, stimulates the motivation to write, and helped them to see that different characteristics of their friends' writing can help them improve their writing skills.

During the whole semester the teaching and learning of both lecturer and students involved several steps including group forming, brainstorming ideas, researching related materials such video, newspapers cutting, in order to exchange information gathered in each Padlet. Most of the time, students would try to outlining and planning the content, crafting the first draft, reviewing and editing and repeating some steps (as stated in Navarre, 2019) for their draft. Because of this, it is important to recognize how CL tools can support collaborative writing at different stages in Chinese essay writing.

Students were tasked with three essay writing assignments throughout the semester. The first assignment was conducted in Week 3, the mid-term assignment was conducted in Week 8 and the final assignment was conducted during the final examination in Week 15. Their writings were assessed to gauge the effectiveness of Padlet integration in the classroom. Each assignment carries a 100% weightage. Results yielded are as follows in Table 2:

Table 2. Results of Students' Writing Assignment

No of Student	Total Marks	First Writing (WEEK 3)	Midterm Writing (WEEK 8)	Final Writing (WEEK 15)
14	100	100	100	100
	>80	(1)7.1%	(7)50%	(10)71%
	70->79	(2) 14.3%	(7)50%	(4)29%
	60->69	(11)78.6%	0	0
	>50	0	0	0

From these three writing assessments such as first assignment (conducted in Week 3), mid-term assignments (conducted in Week 8 and final assignment is during the final examination) all the students passed. Three writing tests were conducted in classroom. In the beginning, the result showed the majority of students (78.5%) were scored the lowest marks in the range marks 60-69. On the Week 8, when mid-term test was conducted, the results showed 50% of students scored in the range marks between 70 and 80. Final test indicated that almost 70% of the students scored grade A at the end of the semester. The Padlet offers a better collaboration between both lecturer and students teaching and learning experiences. It creates an experiential opportunity with which students could experiment with hands-on learning of writing argumentative essay. As suggested by Kessler (2009), a range of collaborative tasks should be provided for learners in order to find optimal conditions for particular groups of language learners and their unique needs. This positive accomplishment affirms that enjoyment and collaborative learning style can improve Mandarin writing skills.

SOLUTIONS AND RECOMMENDATIONS

The use of Padlet as an interactive ICT tool requires students and lecturer to collaborate for it to be effective in the classroom. As highlighted earlier, the use of Padlet encouraged learners to refine their ideas for their essays. Learners were able to view and comment on each other's work posted on the Padlet wall. Through the activity, they learned to scaffold their peers' work and also gained a better understanding of the writing topic where this helped them to improve their writing. This finding is in line with the findings of previous studies (e.g. Alsamadani, 2017; Chen, 2015; Wang; 2015).

Furthermore, the findings of this study highlight not only the importance of collaboration between learners but also the instructor's use of an appropriate ICT tool in facilitating students' writing process. There is a need for the instructor to recognize the affordances of different ICT tools and how they can be utilized to support learners' writing development. As writing is not a linear process, it is essential to understand how technology can support the different stages of writing. In the case of this study, Padlet was used by learners to give feedback on their peers' ideas at the early stages of writing so that learners could refine their ideas for their next draft. Idea generation is an essential stage for learners to be able to write argumentative writing effectively. Padlet affords this learning opportunity through its feature where learners' writing can be displayed and viewed on a Padlet wall by students' enrolled in the class. Previous researchers found that learner collaboration can be fostered when learners received peer feedback and made use of the feedback to improve their writing (Alsamadani, 2017; Fareed et al., 2016). The instructor could use this feature of Padlet to encourage collaboration between learners when they post their ideas and comment on each other's ideas.

Other than promoting collaboration between learners, the use of Padlet in this study appeared to enhance learner motivation in writing. One of the writing challenges faced by the learners in this study was that they found it difficult to express their ideas to write an argumentative essay. However, with the use of Padlet, learners reported that they felt more motivated to write. Previous studies have shown that one of the writing challenges faced by learners include learning anxiety and low motivation (Afrin, 2016; Fareed et al., 2016). Although this study did not aim to examine their learning motivation before and after using Padlet, the findings indicated that the use of Padlet helped with their motivation. This implies that Padlet has the potential to increase learner motivation in classroom and its use for the purposes of idea generation and content development should be considered by writing instructors.

Nevertheless, as shown by the findings, the students tended to focus more on the content of their peers' writing and not so much on the structural aspects of writing such as grammar and vocabulary choice. This finding seems to be in line with the findings of Kessler's (2009) study. In his study, it was found that participants could work independently as they collaborated on a task using wiki. But their focus was predominantly on the content and less on form. Similarly, in the present study, Padlet was mainly used by the students to address writing issues related to content. This implies that although Padlet is useful to support peer collaboration, students would also need to be guided by the instructor to comment on the structural aspects of writing and not just on content alone. It is also acknowledged that even though Padlet also could be used to encourage students to be less dependent on the instructor to provide them with feedback, it is also important for the instructor to raise their awareness of the different aspects of writing that could be improved. The instructor could perhaps first demonstrate the aspects of writing to be commented on based on a writing sample before getting learners to comment on their peers' writing. This demonstration by the instructor could perhaps be done at different stages of writing, from idea generation to the final draft.

To implement the suggestions recommended in this section it is important that good network connectivity is established to enable sustained use. In addition, a limitation of using Padlet is that a monthly fee is needed for using Padlet, which could become a burden for the lecturer. Faculty supports at the macro level in ensuring good network connection and providing appropriate ICT tools and facilities are important to encourage instructors to use ICT tools such as Padlet to promote collaborative learning and enhance teaching in the classroom.

FUTURE RESEARCH DIRECTIONS

For future research directions, it is suggested that more research focusing on the role of collaborative tools on the enhancement of grammar and syntax in writing is needed given their importance in the accuracy of writing and in language learning. Also, since this research involved a small number of participants, a qualitative approach was adopted, where this included interviews with the instructor and students in focus groups. Future research could consider employing quantitative research methods such as questionnaires survey. This could be used to examine the students' learning style, characteristics, and their achievements while comparing feedback methods to promote a more comprehensive understanding of Mandarin writing research. In addition, carefully controlled experiments could also be conducted, investigating variables such as student performance in writing, anxiety in writing, and motivation in writing before and after the use of Padlet.

CONCLUSION

This research is an initial attempt to apply Padlet in the teaching of essay writing, or more specifically, argumentative writing. The lecturer used Padlet for the first time with the students, and it was found that they made improvements in their writing. The Padlet wall is a good sharing platform and plays a very important role in the classroom. It supports the development of various skills needed for students to write an effective argumentative writing and engages them in their learning. The students in this study were able to express their thoughts on the topics based on their readings and receive comments on them. Although the topics given are considered challenging for these students and they struggled to produce appropriate content in the early stages, they were able to develop their writing skills through active collaboration using Padlet. Synchronous interaction was promoted between lecturers and students as they focused on common writing concerns. The feedback received through Padlet helped the students to overcome the problems of generating content and to apply critical thinking skills to support their arguments in a more structured way. Nevertheless, for successful implementation of innovation, the instructor's leadership and guidance are critical. The instructor will need to know how to use the tool and design appropriate activities that can promote students' learning. It is also important for instructors to know the technical requirements needed. As the saying goes, "workers must first sharpen their tools".

REFERENCES

Afrin, S. (2016). Writing Problems of Non-English Major Undergraduate Students in Bangladesh: An Observation. Open Journal of Social Sciences, 4(3), 104–115. doi:10.4236/jss.2016.43016

Almerich, G., Orellana, N., Rodríguez, J., & García, I. (2016). Teachers' information and communication technology competences: A structural approach. *Computers & Education, 100*, 110–125. doi:10.1016/j.compedu.2016.05.002

Alsamadani, H. A. (2017). The Effectiveness of Using Online Blogging for Students' Individual and Group Writing. *International Education Studies, 11*(1), 44. doi:10.5539/ies.v11n1p44

Altanopoulou, P., Tselios, N., Katsanos, C., Georgoutsou, M., & Panagiotaki, M. (2015). Wiki-Mediated Activities in Higher Education. *Evidence-Based Analysis of Learning Effectiveness Across Three Studies, 18*, 511–522.

Angeli, C., & Valanides, N. (2009). Epistemological and methodological issues for the conceptualization, development, and assessment of ICT-TPCK: Advances in technological pedagogical content knowledge (TPCK). *Computers & Education, 52*(1), 154–168. doi:10.1016/j.compedu.2008.07.006

Biasutti, M. (2017). A comparative analysis of forums and wikis as tools for online collaborative learning. *Computers & Education, 111*, 158–171. doi:10.1016/j.compedu.2017.04.006

Biasutti, M., & El-Deghaidy, H. (2012). Using Wiki in teacher education: Impact on knowledge management processes and student satisfaction. *Computers & Education, 59*(3), 861–872. doi:10.1016/j.compedu.2012.04.009

Bikowski, D. (2015). The pedagogy of collaboration: Teaching effectively within an evolving technology landscape. In G. Pickering & P. Gunashekar (Eds.), *Innovation in English Language Teacher Education* (pp. 223–231). New Delhi, India: British Council.

Bilici, S., Guzey, S., & Yamak, H. (2016). Assessing pre-service science teachers' technological pedagogical content knowledge (TPACK) through observations and lesson plans. *Research in Science & Technological Education, 5143*(April), 1–15. doi:10.1080/02635143.2016.1144050

Bishop, J., & Elen, J. (2014). Emerging Technologies. In M. Spector, M. Merrill, M. Bishop, & J. Elen (Eds.), *Handbook of Research on Educational Communications and Technology* (pp. 673–674). New York, NY: Academic Press.

Bower, M. (2016). Deriving a typology of Web 2.0 learning technologies. *British Journal of Educational Technology, 47*(4), 763–777. doi:10.1111/bjet.12344

Chen, R. T.-H. (2015). L2 Blogging: Who Thrives and Who Does Not? *Language Learning & Technology, 19*(192), 177–196. Retrieved from http://llt.msu.edu/issues/june2015/chen.pdf

Chen, W. (2019). An Exploratory Study on the Role of L2 Collaborative Writing on Learners' Subsequent Individually Composed Texts. *The Asia-Pacific Education Researcher, 28*(6), 563–573. doi:10.1007/s40299-019-00455-3

Chen, W., & Yu, S. (2019). Implementing collaborative writing in teacher-centered classroom contexts: Student beliefs and perceptions. *Language Awareness*, *28*(4), 247–267. doi:10.1080/09658416.2019.1675680

Cheung, R., & Vogel, D. (2013). Predicting user acceptance of collaborative technologies: An extension of the technology acceptance model for e-learning. *Computers & Education*, *63*, 160–175. doi:10.1016/j.compedu.2012.12.003

Churchill, D. (2011). Web 2.0 in education: A study of the explorative use of blogs with a postgraduate class. *Innovations in Education and Teaching International*, *48*(2), 149–158. doi:10.1080/14703297.2011.564009

Dar, M. F., & Khan, I. (2015). Writing anxiety among public and private sectors Pakistani undergraduate university students. *Pakistan Journal of Gender Studies*, *10*(1), 121–136.

Davidson, R. (2012). Wiki use that increases communication and collaboration motivation. *Journal of Learning Design*, *5*(2), 38–49. doi:10.5204/jld.v5i2.110

De Wever, B., Van Keer, H., Schellens, T., & Valcke, M. (2010). Roles as a structuring tool in online discussion groups: The differential impact of different roles on social knowledge construction. *Computers in Human Behavior*, *26*(4), 516–523. doi:10.1016/j.chb.2009.08.008

De Wever, V. K., Van Keer, H., Schellens, T., & Valcke, M. (2009). Structuring asynchronous discussion groups: The impact of role assignment and self-assessment on students' levels of knowledge construction through social negotiation. *Journal of Computer Assisted Learning*, *25*(2), 177–188. doi:10.1111/j.1365-2729.2008.00292.x

DeWitt, D., Alias, N., & Siraj, S. (2014). The design and development of a Collaborative mLearning prototype for Malaysian secondary school science. *Educational Technology Research and Development*, *62*(4), 461–480. doi:10.1007/s11423-014-9340-y

Dewitt, D., Alias, N., & Siraj, S. (2015). Collaborative learning: Interactive debates using Padlet in a higher education institution. *The Turkish Online Journal of Educational Technology*, *2015*, 88–95.

Dillenbourg, P., Baker, M., Blaye, A., & O'Malley, C. (1996). The evolution of research on collaborative learning. In H. Spada & P. Reimann (Eds.), *Learning in humans and machines* (pp. 189–211). Oxford: Elsevier Science.

Elola, I., & Oskoz, A. (2010). Collaborative writing: Fostering foreign language and writing conventions development. *Language Learning & Technology*, *14*(3), 51–71.

Fareed, M., Ashraf, A., & Bilal, M. (2016). ESL Learners' Writing Skills: Problems, Factors and Suggestions. *Journal of Education & Social Sciences*, *4*(2), 83–94. doi:10.20547/jess0421604201

Fırat, E. A., & Koksal, M. S. (2017). The relationship between use of Web 2.0 tools by prospective science teachers and their biotechnology literacy. *Computers in Human Behavior*, *70*, 44–50. doi:10.1016/j.chb.2016.12.067

Garcia, E., Elbeltagi, I., Brown, M., & Dungay, K. (2015). The implications of a connectivist learning blog model and the changing role of teaching and learning. *British Journal of Educational Technology, 46*(4), 877–894. doi:10.1111/bjet.12184

Gonye, J., Mareva, R., Dudu, W. T., & Sib, J. (2012). Academic writing challenges at universities in Zimbabwe: A case study of great Zimbabwe university. *International Journal of English and Literature, 3*(3), 71–83.

Graham, S., & Perin, D. (2007). A meta-analysis of writing instruction for adolescent students. *Journal of Educational Psychology, 99*(3), 445–476. doi:10.1037/0022-0663.99.3.445

Hao, S. (2020). Tolerance of diversity: Identity integration among People of all Ethnic groups. In *China's Solution to Its Ethno-national Issues* (p. 179). China Social Sciences Press, Springer; doi:10.1007/978-981-32-9519-3_6.

Johnson, D. W., & Johnson, R. T. (1996). Cooperation and the use of technology. In D. Jonassen (Ed.), *Handbook of research for educational communications and technology* (pp. 1017–1044). London: MacMillan.

Kessler, G. (2009). Student-initiated attention to form in wiki-based collaborative writing. *Language Learning & Technology, 13*(1), 79–95.

Koh, J., Chai, C., Benjamin, W., & Hong, H. (2015). Technological Pedagogical Content Knowledge (TPACK) and Design Thinking: A Framework to Support ICT Lesson Design for 21st Century Learning. *The Asia-Pacific Education Researcher, 24*(3), 535–543. doi:10.1007/s40299-015-0237-2

Koschmann, T. (2002). Dewey's Contribution to the Foundations of CSCL Research. Proceedings of CSCL 2002, 17–22. doi:10.3115/1658616.1658618

Koschmann, T., Stahl, G., & Zemel, A. (2004). The Video Analyst's Manifesto. In *Proceedings of the 6th International Conference on Learning Sciences* (pp. 278–285). International Society of the Learning Sciences.

Lee, & Markey, A. (2014). A study of learners' perceptions of online intercultural exchange through Web 2.0 technologies. ReCALL, 26(3), 281–297. doi:10.1017/S0958344014000111

Li, M., & Zhu, W. (2017). Good or bad collaborative wiki writing: Exploring links between group interactions and writing products. *Journal of Second Language Writing, 35*, 38–53. doi:10.1016/j.jslw.2017.01.003

Lipponen, L., Rahikainen, M., Lallimo, J., & Hakkarainen, K. (2003). Patterns of participation and discourse in elementary students' computer-supported collaborative learning. *Learning and Instruction, 13*(5), 487–509. doi:10.1016/S0959-4752(02)00042-7

McAfee, P. (2006). Enterprise 2.0: The dawn of emergent collaboration. *MIT Sloan Management Review, 47*(1), 21–28. doi:10.1109/EMR.2006.261380

Mercer-Mapstone, L. D., & Matthews, K. E. (2017). Student perceptions of communication skills in undergraduate science at an Australian research-intensive university. *Assessment & Evaluation in Higher Education, 42*(1), 98–114. doi:10.1080/02602938.2015.1084492

Ministry of Higher Education (MOHE). (2015). Malaysia Education Blueprint 2015-2025 (Higher Education) (Vol. 2025). Ministry of Education Malaysia. doi:10.5923/j.ijis.20120206.05

Navarre, A. (2019). *Technology-Enhanced Teaching and Learning of Chinese as a Foreign Language*. Routledge.

Oliver, K. (2010). Integrating Web 2.0 across the curriculum. *TechTrends*, *54*(2), 50–60. doi:10.1007/s11528-010-0382-7

Pineteh, E. A. (2013). The academic writing challenges of undergraduate students: A South African case study. *International Journal of Higher Education*, *3*(1), 12. doi:10.5430/ijhe.v3n1p12

Resta, P., & Laferriere, T. (2007). Technology in Support of Collaborative Learning. *Educational Psychology Review*, *19*(1), 65–83. doi:10.1007/s10648-007-9042-7

Scardamalia, M., & Bereiter, C. (2003). Knowledge building: theory, pedagogy, and technology. In J. W. Guthrie (Ed.), *Encyclopedia of Education* (2nd ed., pp. 1370–1373). New York: MacMillan Reference.

Schrire, S. (2006). Knowledge building in asynchronous discussion groups: Going beyond quantitative analysis. *Computers & Education*, *46*(1), 49–70. doi:10.1016/j.compedu.2005.04.006

Sigala, M. (2007). Integrating web 2.0 in e-learning environ- ments: A socio-technical approach. *International Journal of Knowledge and Learning*, *3*(6), 628–648. doi:10.1504/IJKL.2007.016837

Sinha, S., Rogat, T., Adams-Wiggins, K., & Hmelo-Silver, C. (2015). Collaborative group engagement in a computer-supported inquiry learning environment. *International Journal of Computer-Supported Collaborative Learning*, *10*(3), 273–307. doi:10.1007/s11412-015-9218-y

Stahl, G., Koschmann, T., & Suthers, D. (2006). Computer-supported collaborative learning: An historical perspective. Cambridge Handbook of the Learning Sciences, 2006, 409–426. doi:10.1145/1124772.1124855

Storch, N. (2002). Patterns of interaction in ESL pair work. *Language Learning*, *52*(1), 119–158. doi:10.1111/1467-9922.00179

Suthers, D. (2006). Technology affordances for intersubjective meaning-making. *International Conference for Computers in Education*, 1(2), 1–24.

Tal, T., Krajcik, S., & Blumenfeld, C. (2006). Urban schools' teachers enacting project- based science. *Journal of Research in Science Teaching*, *43*(7), 722–745. doi:10.1002/tea.20102

Tang, K. S., & Tan, S. C. (2017). Intertextuality and Multimodal Meanings in High School Physics: Written and Spoken Language in Computer-supported Collaborative Student Discourse. Classroom Discourse, 8(1), 19–35. doi:10.1080/19463014.2016.1263576

The Star. (2019, February 19). Malaysia-China bilateral trade up 13% in 2018. The Star.

Thomas, S. (2017). Journalogue: Voicing student challenges in writing through a classroom blog. *Journal of Educational Technology & Society*, *20*(1), 112–122.

Wang, Y. C. (2015). Promoting collaborative writing through wikis: A new approach for advancing innovative and active learning in an ESP context. *Computer Assisted Language Learning, 28*(6), 499–512. doi:10.1080/09588221.2014.881386

Ward, L., & Parr, J. M. (2010). Revisiting and reframing use: Implications for the integration of ICT. *Computers & Education, 54*(1), 113–122. doi:10.1016/j.compedu.2009.07.011

Yilmaz, R., Karaoglan Yilmaz, F. G., & Kilic Cakmak, E. (2017). The impact of transactive memory system and interaction platform in collaborative knowledge construction on social presence and self-regulation. *Interactive Learning Environments, 25*(8), 949–969. doi:10.1080/10494820.2016.1224905

Yilmaz, R., & Keser, H. (2016). The impact of interactive environment and metacognitive support on academic achievement and transactional distance in online learning. *Journal of Educational Computing Research*. doi:10.1177/ 0735633116656453

ADDITIONAL READING

Dewitt, D., Alias, N., & Siraj, S. (2015). Collaborative learning: Interactive debates using Padlet in a higher education institution. *The Turkish Online Journal of Educational Technology, 2015*, 88–95.

Fareed, M., Ashraf, A., & Bilal, M. (2016). ESL Learners' Writing Skills: Problems, Factors and Suggestions. *Journal of Education & Social Sciences, 4*(2), 83–94. doi:10.20547/jess0421604201

Li, G., Sun, Z., & Jee, Y. (2019). The more technology the better? A comparison of teacher-student interaction in high and low technology use elementary EFL classrooms in China. *System, 84*, 24–40. doi:10.1016/j.system.2019.05.003

Li, L. (2014). Understanding language teachers' practice with educational technology: A case from China. *System, 46*, 105–119. doi:10.1016/j.system.2014.07.016

Vasodavan, V., DeWitt, D., & Alias, N. (2018). Collaborative Assessment Survey: A Measure of Group Teamwork. In Redesigning Assessment for Holistic Learning: A quick guide for higher education (pp. 50–52). Kuala Lumpur, Malaysia: Academic Enhancement and Leadership Development Centre (ADeC), University of Malaya. Retrieved from https://umcms.um.edu.my/sites/adec/pdf/rahole2017/FY20180503Updated_QG_Higher_Edu_20180730.pdf

Vasodavan, V., Dewitt, D., & Alias, N. (2019). TPACK In Higher Education: Analysis of The Collaborative Tools Used By Lecturers. *The Asia Pacific Journal of Curriculum & Teaching, 7*(1), 9–17.

KEY TERMS AND DEFINITIONS

Collaborative Learning: Learning that occurs when two or more students learn something together towards achieving common learning goals.

Collaborative Teaching: A form of innovative pedagogical approach where Educator/ Lecturer/ Instructor design learning tasks and instructional materials based on collaborative learning tools such as Blog, Padlet, Podcast, Forum Discussion and so forth to support students' learning from one another.

Mandarin Language: Mandarin is spoken in Mainland China, Taiwan, Malaysia, and Singapore. The current trend is that Mandarin has become the standard and common language of the Chinese language and is becoming more and more widely spoken internationally.

Padlet: An online interactive wall used for maintaining interactions and communication for collaborative learning.

Writing Skills: Writing is an essential competency of language. Good writing skills are needed for all the students in order to accomplish their educational and employable requirements. This research referred to argumentative essay writing in Mandarin.

Chapter 10
The Effect of Using Digital Stories in Teaching English as a Second Language:
Digital Stories in Teaching English

Fatma Gizem Karaoglan Yilmaz
Bartin University, Turkey

Busra Koseoglu
Bartin University, Turkey

Cansu Ayvali
Bartin University, Turkey

Tugba Ozturk
Ankara University, Turkey

ABSTRACT

The purpose of this study is to analyze the effect of using digital storytelling on motivation and learning strategies in foreign language teaching. This study was conducted with 20 students enrolled in the preparatory class to learn English as a foreign language for a year in 2018-2019 academic year in a state university in Turkey. Motivation scale and learning strategies scale were used to obtain data. According to the result, there was no significant distinction between digital storytelling and the use of learning strategies in foreign language teaching. This study indicates that the use of digital storytelling in foreign language teaching had no effect on the development of students' use of learning strategies.

DOI: 10.4018/978-1-7998-3062-7.ch010

INTRODUCTION

Advances in information and communication technologies have been transforming educational implications and experiences. Digital learning tools are emerging as a promising means of enhancing learning environments (Ozcinar & Ozturk, 2013). Developments in software, use of internet technology for educational purposes (Çakır & Yıldırım, 2009) and accessing information easily and instantly have made digital literacy gain great importance along with the traditional literacies (Küngerü, 2016). Digital storytelling, in this context, has emerged as a tool used for a variety of reasons in different disciplines such as education, health and communication (Çıralı, 2014) among other digital technologies. Originated from the traditional storytelling, which is a natural way of human communication (Chung, 2006), digital storytelling has made its use in education inevitable. The role of this new storytelling used in both teaching and learning by teachers and students is explained in many studies (Bromberg, 2013; İncikabı, 2013; Kordaki, 2014; Robin, 2006, 2008; Silseth, 2013). Digital storytelling as an educational tool provides guidance and space for students and at the same time teaches communication skills (Gömleksiz & Pullu, 2017). The storytelling has been one of the most frequently used methods in many ways in education, from past to now in almost all levels (Turgut & Kışla, 2015). With today's technology, digital stories, which are mostly computer or web based traditional stories (Ciğerci & Gültekin, 2017), are multimedia forms that promote critical thinking and lead innovative learning (Gömleksiz & Pullu, 2017). The digital storytelling might be a powerful tool for educators to use in their classroom practices (Robin, 2008) as well.

The use of digital storytelling in language education is also an important area to focus on. However, its use is still new, and this raises a need of new scientific investigations. In the present study, two educational aspects of digital storytelling in foreign language teaching will be explored. These aspects are motivation and learning strategies.

Motivation, which is a theoretical structure used to explain the initiation, orientation and quality of behavior, especially of the purpose-oriented behavior (Brophy, 2004), refers to the individual's endeavor to produce behaviors in line with the target in order to meet their needs (Ülgen, 1995). Motivation is generally considered as a basis for almost every learning activity (Tugan, 2015) and an indispensable factor in learning a language (Özçalışan, 2012).

Learning strategies are a set of behaviors or thoughts that are expected to affect the processes of obtaining the information during the process of learning, storing it in their memory and retrieving it when necessary (Çalışkan, 2016). Also, they help the individual process and construct the information while facilitating self-learning (Sökmen, 2006). As in many areas of education, learning strategies are also given importance in foreign language education. From this perspective, language learning strategies can be described as the various processes that foreign language learners use in their learning process to make learning easier and faster (Boylu, 2015).

Although there is a growing body of research concerned with digital storytelling, to our knowledge, this is the first study showing the relationship between motivation and learning strategies, which are very essential for the effective learning process in digital storytelling in foreign language teaching. From this point of view, it is aimed in the present study to examine the effect of digital story on motivation and learning strategies in foreign language teaching.

For that purpose, the remainder of this article will explore the following research questions:

1. Is there a significant difference between the motivation post-test scores of the experimental and control groups?
2. Is there a significant difference between the learning strategies post-test scores of the experimental and control groups?
3. Is there a significant difference between the motivation pretest and post-test scores of the students in the experimental group?
4. Is there a significant difference between the learning strategies pre-test and post-test scores of the students in the experimental group?

BACKGROUND

In this section, theoretical background is presented about digital story telling in foreign language teaching and two important variables as learning strategies and motivation in this context.

Technology and Language Education

Throughout their daily lives, students are constantly imposed to computers, video cameras, mobile phones, digital music players and electronic games (Smeda, Dakich, & Sharda, 2014). In that sense, technology integration in education is important to meet a society's needs that covers the 21st century skills (Bacanak, Karamustafaoğlu, & Köse, 2003; Doğan & Robin, 2008). In education, the use of technology can open doors to students to have prosperous learning practices and attend to learning motions (Karaoglan Yilmaz & Durak, 2018).

In terms of foreign language education, technology and foreign language education are intertwined and not separated (Singhal, 1997). Language is a dynamic process, in that sense, one of the best approaches to learn a language is to offer in interactive and authentic environments to the students. The Internet and computer technologies are powerful means to assist the approaches in language teaching (Nishioka, 2016; Wang, 2005). Now, the effect of technology is considered to be significant in teaching and learning of the target language (Nomass, 2013). In this study, more specifically the contribution of digital storytelling to language learning is examined.

Integration of Traditional Story Into Technology: Digital Story

Throughout the history, storytelling has been an essential component of human life to transfer culture and knowledge from one generation to another, to share values with wisdom, and to preserve heritage (Bromberg, Techatassanasoontorn, & Andrade, 2013; Heo, 2009; Razmi, Pourali, & Nozad, 2014; Smeda et al., 2010; Wang & Zhan, 2010). Storytelling, which has existed long before the emergence of written sources (İnceelli, 2005), has been one of the most commonly used educational teaching methods (Turgut & Kışla, 2015; Uslupehlivan & Kurtoğlu Erden, 2016). In his study, Pedersen (1995) states that telling a story is an original way of teaching. Because storytelling is a pedagogical instrument that has been employed in education to convey knowledge from one generation to another for ages, even in modern times (Smeda et al., 2010), it is used by educators as a way of explaining complex ideas, concepts or information to students (Yılmaz, Üstündağ, & Güneş, 2017). Integrating the visual images with the written text –as happens in digital storytelling- helps the students understand the topic better (Robin,

2008) and allows students to interact with both visual and written texts (Kajder & Swenson, 2004). Due to the fact that storytelling activities are a part of meaning making (Razmi et al., 2014), they take an important place in education (Turgut & Kışla, 2015) and increase participation as well as help students reflect on the daily life; thus, they have been regarded as a key method in language teaching for centuries (Kurudayıoğlu & Honey, 2014).

The stories, which are oral and written cultural products that facilitate cognitive changes by affecting memory (Çıralı Sarıca & Koçak Usluel, 2016) have been digitalized through the advances in information and communication technologies (Kurudayıoğlu & Bal, 2014; Uslupehlivan & Kurtoğlu Erden, 2016). Thus, the tradition of telling and listening stories has gained a new meaning with the existence of technology (Rahimi & Yadollahi, 2017; Turgut & Kışla, 2015). Thanks to the use of computers and emergence of various applications and systems, there have been several important developments in the way the stories are presented (Gils, 2005).

On looking at conceptual framework of digital storytelling, Smeda et al. (2010, p.2) define it as "a modern incarnation of the traditional art of oral storytelling". Heo (2009, p.407) describes as "the field of storytelling using digital media to tell a story". According to Robin (2006), in general, all of the definitions (Chung, 2006; Ciğerci & Gültekin, 2017; Lambert, 2002; Meadows et al., 2003; Price, Strodtman, Brough, Lonn, & Luo, 2015) refer to the storytelling incorporating multimedia tools as images, audio and video. Basically, digital storytelling is the case of creating a short film that combines a scenario or an original story with various multimedia components such as images, music, video and narration which is often the voice of an author (Doğan & Robin, 2008).

The process of transition from consumer to producer position is a critical process in the digital storytelling development (Kocaman Karoğlu, 2015) with Web 2.0 technologies enabling the users to produce content and exchange information (Küngerü, 2016), giving students the opportunity to seek for information, create and understand their own materials, communicate with other individuals and assess the materials they create (Gömleksiz & Pullu, 2017). Thus, the stories produced by the individuals are more accessible and more visible (Kengürü, 2016).

Digital stories contribute to the improvement of students' language and especially speaking skills (Wilson, 1997), improve their past experiences and help them build strong social interactions and provide ways to participate in active and authentic learning (Smeda et al., 2010). Educational use of digital stories often refers to a process consisting of self-discovery, learning and new knowledge (Wang & Zhan, 2010) and in that sense, these tools could be employed in language learning. In the classroom, it is used for a variety of aims such as teaching the content, making students active researchers and storytellers (Doğan & Robin, 2008). It can improve the age-appropriate talents of the students and enable them to focus on the lesson more carefully (Turan & Sezginsoy Şeker, 2018). Moreover, it can go beyond attracting students' attention and inspire less motivated students (Suwardy et al., 2013). Compared to the traditional practical methods, digital storytelling materials can offer more enhanced educational practices because of a variety of the reasons such as it is re-usable and more attractive (Gils, 2005). Also, digital storytelling enables students to use the materials on personal technologies (for example, music on MP3 devices and photos and videos on digital cameras) conveniently (Heo, 2009) which are very helpful in language learning. As the digital stories' basic component is the language, the effect of creating digital stories on language learning is also appealing (Doğan & Robin, 2008). Much has been written on this subject and it has been found that storytelling enables students to learn actively in foreign language teaching (Turgut & Kışla, 2015). Digital storytelling has the potential to develop a wide variety of learning skills, literacy and cognitive/academic skills (Rahimi & Yadollahi, 2017). Students can develop their communication capabilities –which is essential in language learning- express their ideas and create meaningful stories (Robin, 2008).

Like in traditional storytelling, digital stories revolve around a selected theme and commonly have a certain perspective. Different from the traditional storytelling, it is created by combining digital graphics, texts, sound recordings, video and music mixes to provide information on any subject (Robin, 2006). Digital storytelling, as a means of expression, has different types (Küngerü, 2016). However, it is possible to divide the main types into three particular groups: personal narratives, historical narratives/documentaries, informative/instructive narratives (Robin, 2006). Digital storytelling, which can be considered as a bridge that connects the abstract concepts with the process of creation, sharing and discussion (Price et al., 2015), can be used for teaching and learning by both teachers and students (Kordaki, 2014; Robin, 2006; Wang & Zhan, 2010). Teachers can use or create digital stories to teach content of the course which involves presenting an idea, reinforcing understanding of a given topic and reviewing materials (Çıralı Sarıca & Koçak Usluel, 2016; Robin, 2006, 2008; Wang & Zhan, 2010). Digital stories can also be a powerful means for students to create their own stories (Robin, 2006). By enabling students to participate in the process (Gils, 2015), the students learn to do research on a topic, make inquiries, voice their opinions, create meaningful texts and develop their communication skills. Students who participate in this experience may learn to criticize the work of others as well as to criticize their work by performing social work (Robin, 2008).

The digital storytelling creation is a multi-stage process including various learning activities (Karaoglan Yilmaz & Durak, 2018). Center for Digital Storytelling (2005) develops seven essentials of digital storytelling (Robin, 2006: 710) upon which digital storytelling is centered as shown in Figure 1. These elements are;

- Point of View – what is the perspective of the author?
- A Dramatic Question – a question that will be answered by the end of the story.
- Emotional Content – serious issues that speak to us in a personal and powerful way.
- The Gift of your Voice – a way to personalize the story to help the audience understand the context.
- The Power of the Soundtrack – music or other sounds that support the storyline.
- Economy – simply put, using just enough content to tell the story without overloading the viewer with too much information.
- Pacing – related to Economy, but specifically deals with how slowly or quickly the story progresses.

Demirer (2013) remarks that the digital storytelling with these seven components provides the storywriter with an opportunity to convey the key points with his own voice. The story can make them laugh or make them feel sad by leaving an emotional effect on the audience, and thus prevent the readers from getting bored and raise their interest in the story (Demirer, 2013).

The Effect of Digital Story Use on Motivation in Foreign Language Teaching

Motivation is a force, desire or reason that initiates the persistence to achieve a goal. It is a crucial psychological state that students with low motivation cannot improve their foreign language skills (Doğan, 2009). The factors such as internal and external orientations, perception of success or failure (Doğan, 2009) and the positive attitude towards the language and culture learned could be regarded as essential factors necessary for success in foreign language learning (Özçalışan, 2012).

Figure 1. The seven essentials of digital storytelling (Robin, 2006)

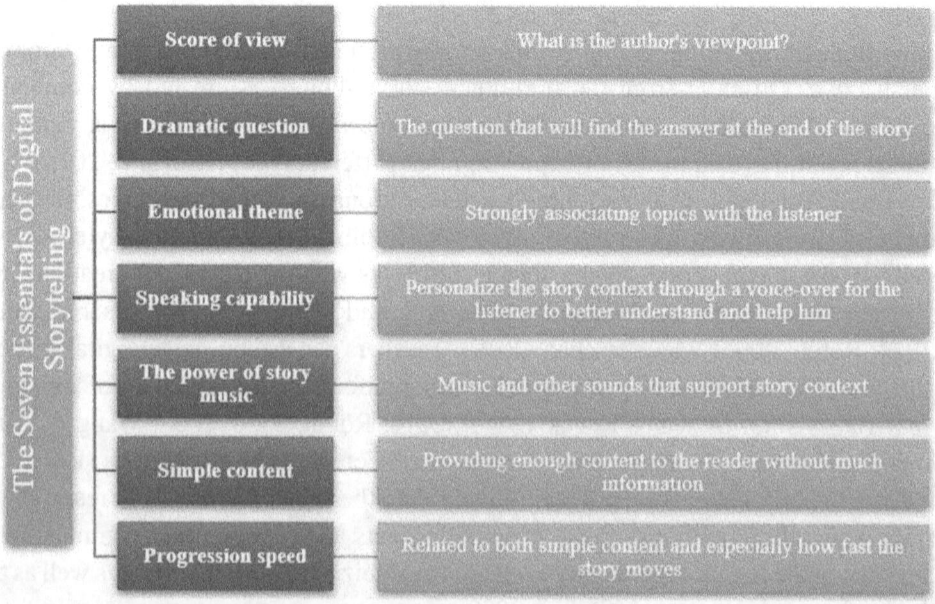

Researchers point out that motivation is a critical factor determining the language learning success (Arslan & Akbarov, 2010; Çelik, 2010). Mehdiyev, Usta and Uğurlu (2016) suggest that motivation can affect positively or negatively the perceptions and behaviors related to language learning. According to Gardner (2007), motivation plays a part in the second language learning process. While Hadžımehmedagıć and Akbarov (2014) assert that motivation is regarded as a very significant factor leading to success in the second language acquisition, Dornyei (1994), in his study, argues that one of the main determinants of the foreign language learning achievement is motivation. Görgen, Kömür and Deniz (2009) point out that motivational factors are one of the variables affecting the language learning process. While researchers such as Atay (2004), and Cheng and Dörnyei (2007) conclude that this variable is an important factor in foreign language acquisition, Kaboody (2013) states that this motivation to develop students in the target language is considered as a complicated process.

According to Dreon et al. (2011), creating content and links related to students' lives helps to motivate them and aim to teaching. In order to achieve this motivation in teaching, appropriateness of these content and connections to the student's desire, the characteristics of the material used and the attractiveness of the environment are seen important (Tatlı & Aksoy, 2017) and here, digital storytelling could play an important and promising role in motivating the students. Moreover, the story can be used as a way of facilitating the discussion on a given topic ad sense making (Robin, 2006). Since narrative stories are effective, memorable and entertaining as educational tools (Neuhauser, 1993), teaching a complicated subject with stories may make students become more oriented towards the course –thus, motivated- and learn meaningfully by stimulating their emotions in their imagination (Turgut & Kışla, 2015). Furthermore, working with digital stories created with multimedia tools could be considered as a way of providing exciting experiences (Hathorn, 2005). Digital storytelling focuses on a chosen theme and accommodates a certain perspective (Turan & Sezginsoy Şeker, 2018). Thus, those students who want to produce their own digital stories may help raise their interest and motivation (Robin, 2006). The participation of students to their own learning practices promotes in-depth learning (Bromberg et al., 2013). In addition, it also helps students develop their multidimensional communicative competencies through a student-centered approach as well as motivate them towards the target language (Razmi et al., 2014 and Tatlı & Aksoy, 2017).

The Relationship of Digital Story Use With Learning Strategies in Foreign Language Teaching

Taşdemir and Tay (2008) explained the learning strategies as the strategies that enable the student to learn in the shortest and the most effective way through teaching and learning methods and techniques. Belet and Yaşar (2007) remark that learning strategies promote learners to become aware of their own learning processes and enhance the effectiveness of the learning process. In their study, they mention that the use of learning strategies improves students' reading comprehension and writing skills and is effective in developing positive attitudes towards language learning.

Here, digital storytelling could help with learning strategies thanks to its components. For instance, in writing up a scenario for the story, the students' writing skills could be improved, the memories of the students actively involved in the process could be also affected (Çıralı Sarıca & Koçak Usluel, 2015). Thus, a strong and efficient way to learn, recall and reflect contributes to the students' learning (Levett-Jones, Bowen & Morris, 2015). Digital storytelling is important for the students to create content and links about their lives, increase and accelerate their level of understanding (Dreon et al., 2011).

MAIN FOCUS OF THE CHAPTER

Research Design

In this study, quantitative research method was employed and quasi-experimental design was used. Data were obtained by using the pretest-posttest control group design, which is a type of the quasi-experimental ones in which the effect on the dependent variable was investigated by interfering with the independent variable (Büyüköztürk, Kılıç-Çakmak, Akgün, Karadeniz, & Demirel, 2018).

Participants

In this study, the study group was chosen based on a convenience sampling method. The participants consist of 20 students. Ten students are in the experimental group and ten students are in the control group, enrolled in the preparatory class to learn English as a foreign language for a year in 2018-2019 academic year in a state university in Turkey. Ages of the students range between 18 and 21 while the average is 19 years-old. There are four female and 16 male students.

Data Collection Tools

In the quantitative dimension of this study, Turkish version of Motivated Strategies for Learning Questionnaire (MSLQ), which is a scale produced by Pintrich, Smith, Garcia and McKeachie (1991), was used. Validity and reliability of the scales, which were administered as two separate scales as "Motivation

Scale" and "Learning Strategies Scale", were ensured by using the data obtained from 852 undergraduate students. As a result, it was found that both of these two scales had construct validity with confirmatory factor analysis results and all of the items and subscales in the scale were distinctive with the reliability results.

Data Collection Process

In the first week of the study, which was a 6-week study, students were informed about the research and then the pretest was administered. As of the second week, based on the course content, approximately 5 minutes long digital stories were created by students with Toondoo which is used for making cartoon and then they animated these cartoons with Movie Maker software. In the last week of the study, posttest was administered to the experimental and control groups. The digital story making stages are shown in Figure 2 which demonstrates how a digital story should be created by following the stages as 1) identifying a digital story, 2) creating a scenario, 3) cartooning stories and 4) organizing the visuals along with images with appropriate sound or music and 5) finally presenting the digital story.

Figure 2. Digital story preparation process

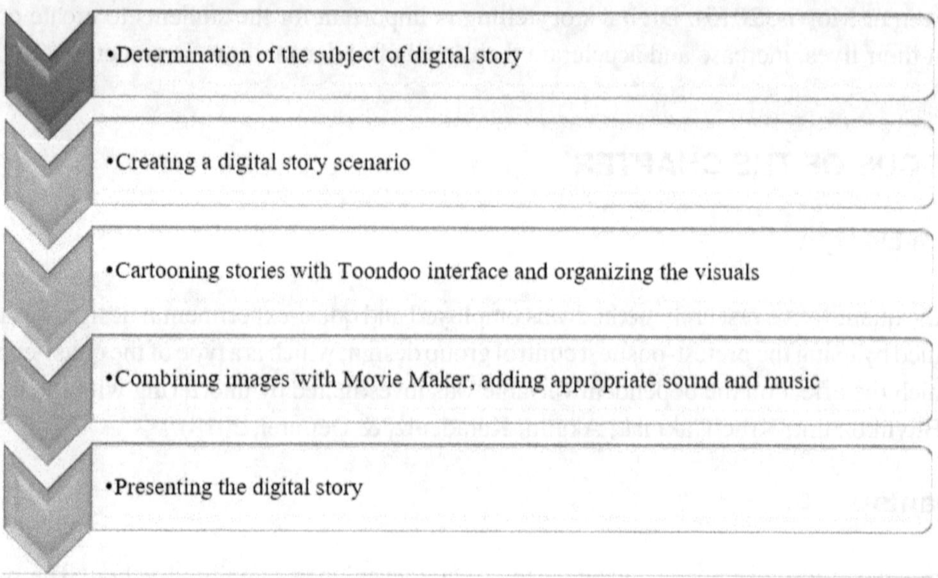

Data Analysis

In order to run data analysis to find out whether there is an effect of digital story use on motivation and learning strategies in foreign language teaching, first of all, normality test was used to determine if data are modeled by a normal distribution. Results showed that the data demonstrated non-normal distribution. Therefore, Mann-Whitney U test was used since the distribution of data did not meet the normality assumption as well as Wilcoxon test was used since variables were nonparametric (Büyüköztürk, 2007).

Findings

Findings About the Motivation Scale Posttest Scores of the Experimental and Control Groups

Mann Whitney U test was used to find out whether there is a significant difference between the motivation scale posttest scores of the study groups. While the mean values from the posttest scores of the students in the experimental group are 149.00, the average of the students in the control group is 154.00. Mann Whitney U test results from the experimental group and the control group are presented in Table 1.

Table 1. Mann Whitney U test results according to experimental and control groups motivation scale posttest scores

Group	N	Mean Rank	Sum of Ranks	U	p
Experimental	10	9.95	99.50	44.500	.677
Control	10	11.05	110.50		

Based on the analyses, it was found that there is no significant difference between the experimental and control groups in terms of digital storytelling and their motivation in foreign language teaching ($U{:}44.5$, $p>.05$). This finding indicates that digital storytelling in foreign language teaching has no effect on the students' motivation who study foreign languages.

Findings About the Learning Strategies Scale Posttest Scores of the Experimental and Control Groups

Mann Whitney U test was used to find out whether there is a significant difference between the learning strategies scale posttest scores of the study groups. While the mean values in the experimental group are 218.80, the average of the students in the control group is 248.30. Mann Whitney U test results from the learning strategies scale administered to experimental group after the implementation and to the control group students are presented in Table 2.

Table 2. Mann Whitney U test results according to experimental and control groups learning strategies posttest scores

Group	N	Mean Rank	Sum of Ranks	U	p
Experimental	10	9.15	91.50	36.500	.307
Control	10	11.85	118.50		

Based on the analyses, it was found that there is no significant difference between the experimental and control groups in terms of learning strategies in foreign language teaching ($U{:}36.5$, $p>.05$). This finding indicates that digital storytelling in foreign language teaching has no effect on the use of learning strategies for foreign language learners.

Findings About the Motivation Scale Pretest and Posttest Scores of the Experimental Group

Wilcoxon test was used to find out whether there is a significant difference between the motivation scale pretest and posttest scores of the study groups. While the mean motivation pretest scores of the students in the group are 144.50, the posttest score average is 149.00. The results of the Wilcoxon test on whether the students' motivation for foreign language teaching with digital storytelling before and after the experiment show a significant difference which is presented in Table 3.

Table 3. Wilcoxon test results according to motivation scale posttest scores of experimental group before and after the experiment

Pretest-Posttest	N	Mean Rank	Sum of Ranks	z	p
Negative ranks	6	4.17	25.00	.255	.799
Positive ranks	4	7.50	30.00		
Ties	0				

Analyses in Table 3 show that there is no significant difference between the pretest and posttest scores of the experimental group (z=.255, p>.05). According to the results, it is observed that digital storytelling in foreign language teaching has no substantial effect on motivation. However, when the average scores are examined, the motivation posttest scores of the students participating in digital storytelling in foreign language teaching are higher than the pretest scores, although the result does not constitute a statistically significant difference.

Findings About the Learning Strategies Scale Pretest and Posttest Scores of the Experimental Group

Wilcoxon test was used to find out whether there is a significant difference between the learning strategies scale pretest and posttest scores of the experimental group. While the mean pretest scores of the students in the group are 212.60, the posttest score average was 218.80. The results of the Wilcoxon test on whether students' use of learning strategies for foreign language teaching with digital storytelling before and after the experiment show a remarkable difference as could be seen in Table 4.

Table 4. Wilcoxon test results according to learning strategies post-test scores of experimental group before and after experiment

Pretest-Posttest	N	Mean Rank	Sum of Ranks	z	p
Negative ranks	5	5.20	26.00	.153	.878
Positive ranks	5	5.80	29.00		
Ties	0				

Analyses in Table 4 show that there is no significant difference between the pretest and posttest learning strategies scale scores ($z=.153$, $p>.05$). According to these results, it is seen that digital storytelling in applied foreign language teaching has no substantial effect on students' use of learning strategies. However, when the average scores are examined, the posttest learning strategies scores of the students participating in digital storytelling are higher than the pretest scores, although the result does not constitute a statistically significant difference.

SOLUTIONS AND RECOMMENDATIONS

The present study has attempted to explore the effect of digital storytelling on learning strategies and motivation of the students in foreign language teaching. It was revealed that use of digital storytelling in foreign language teaching has no effect on the development of students' use of learning strategies and their motivation. However, it was found that the motivation posttest scores of the students participating in digital storytelling in foreign language teaching are higher than the pretest scores and the posttest learning strategies scores of the students participating in digital storytelling are higher than the pretest score. A possible reason could be that of the program of the students in which they are enrolled. Accordingly, they study at a preparatory program aiming to teach English and the students might have been already motivated towards learning a foreign language. As for the learning strategies, teachers might design a learning setting more enhanced with digital storytelling tools as well as integrate into the course taking into account of cognitive, behavioral and metacognitive skills of the students.

This contradicts with existing literature. In terms of learning strategies, Rahimi (2017) remarks that digital stories develop students' diverse learning skills and cognitive abilities. Kordaki (2014) points out that it facilitates theoretical thinking and contributes to creativity. Signes (2008) emphasizes that digital stories are important in education in terms of teaching students how to combine some fundamentals. Wang (2010) argues that teachers can utilize digital stories to provide instructional contents such as the display of an idea and the expression of a subject. Robin (2008) mentions that digital storytelling is a well-placed technology application in order to overcome some obstacles in teaching and to employ the technology efficiently in the classroom of teachers. While Gils (2015) points out that digital storytelling offers more alternatives than traditional teaching approaches, enabling individual learning and improving students' learning, Campbell (2012) suggests that teachers find multimedia-rich digital stories as a powerful learning tool to teach curriculum subjects.

In terms of motivation, it has been reported by many researchers that motivation is an indispensable factor in language education (Özçalışan, 2012; Tugan, 2015) and this tendency of motivation is supported by digital storytelling (Bromberg, 2013; Robin et al., 2005; Smeda, 2010; Yang, 2012). According to

Smeda et al. (2010), digital storytelling increases students' motivation and encourages them to solve problems (Smeda et al., 2010). It provides the student with a rich, original learning experience, provides them with autonomy, and present and discuss their outputs with a related target audience (Kearney, 2009; Kearney & Schuck, 2006), attracts and intensifies the interest of students (Yang & Wu, 2012). For Stockwell (2013), one of the reasons why technology is frequently used in language learning is to motivate the students towards the course and here, digital storytelling could represent an ideal technology use to boost students' motivation.

FUTURE RESEARCH DIRECTIONS

The present study's results could be expanded with further research with following dimensions:

- The dependent variable examined in this study can be examined in different aspects by increasing the diversity of students.
- Motivation and learning strategies as independent variables that constitute the problem statement of this study can be investigated with different variables.
- In teacher training programs in relation to teaching foreign languages, prospective teachers' use of digital story telling could be further explored for them to gain the necessary knowledge and skills to integrate these tools in their lessons.

CONCLUSION

This study examined the use of digital stories in foreign language teaching according to the learning strategies variable. It concludes that when compared with experimental and control group students, and the learning posttest scores of the students who participated in digital storytelling in foreign language teaching were examined according to pretest scores, there is no significant distinction between digital storytelling and the use of learning strategies in foreign language teaching. This study indicates that the use of digital storytelling in foreign language teaching has no effect on the development of students' use of learning strategies.

REFERENCES

Al Kaboody, M. (2013). Second language motivation; the role of teachers in learners' motivation. *Journal of Academic and Applied Studies*, *3*(4), 45–54.

Arslan, M., & Akbarov, A. (2010). Türkiye'de yabancı dil öğretiminde motivasyon - yöntem sorunu ve çözüm önerileri. *Selçuk Üniversitesi Edebiyat Fakültesi Dergisi*, *24*, 179–191.

Atay, D. (2004). İngilizce öğretmenlerinin motivasyon stratejileri. *HAYEF: Journal of Education*, *1*(1), 99–108.

Bacanak, A., Karamustafaoğlu, O., & Köse, S. (2003). Yeni bir bakış: Eğitimde teknoloji okuryazarlığı. *Pamukkale Üniversitesi Eğitim Fakültesi Dergisi, 14*(14), 191–196.

Belet, Ş., & Yaşar, Ş. (2007). Öğrenme stratejilerinin okuduğunu anlama ve yazma becerileri ile Türkçe dersine ilişkin tutumlara etkisi. *Eğitimde Kuram ve Uygulama, 3*(1), 69–86.

Boylu, E. (2015). *Yabancı dil olarak türkçe öğrenenlerin dil öğrenme stratejilerini kullanma düzeyleri*. Ankara: Yayımlanmamış Yüksek Lisans Tezi. Gazi Üniversitesi.

Bromberg, N. R., Techatassanasoontorn, A. A., & Andrade, A. D. (2013). Engaging students: Digital storytelling in information systems learning. *Pacific Asia Journal of the Association for Information Systems, 5*(1), 1–22. doi:10.17705/1pais.05101

Brophy, J. (2004). *Motivating students to learn*. Lawrence Erlbaum Associates. doi:10.4324/9781410610218

Büyüköztürk, Ş. (2007). Sosyal bilimler için veri analizi el kitabi (7. Bs). Ankara: Pegem Akademi.

Büyüköztürk, Ş., Akgün, Ö. E., Özkahveci, Ö., & Demirel, F. (2004). The validity and reliability study of the turkish version of the motivated strategies for learning questionnaire. *Educational Sciences: Theory and Practice, 4*(2), 231–239.

Büyüköztürk, Ş., Kılıç Çakmak, E., Akgün, Ö. E., Karadeniz, Ş., & Demirel, F. (2018). Bilimsel araştırma yöntemleri (24. Bs.). Ankara: Pegem Akademi.

Çakır, R., & Yıldırım, S. (2009). What do computer teachers think about the factors affecting technology integration in schools? *İlköğretim Online, 8*(3), 952-964.

Çalışkan, M. (2016). Öğrenme sürecine etkin katilma: Öğrenme stratejileri ve yürütücü biliş. In M. Yavuz (Ed.), Yeni nesil okul-araştıran okul içinde (pp. 37-76). Konya: Eğitim Yayınevi.

Campbell, T. A. (2012). Digital storytelling in an elementary classroom: Going beyond entertainment. *Procedia: Social and Behavioral Sciences, 69*, 385–393. doi:10.1016/j.sbspro.2012.11.424

Çelik, M. (2013). Interest-based language teaching to increase motivation and output in Turkey. *Sosyal ve Beşeri Bilimler Araştırmaları Dergisi, 24*, 29–44.

Center for Digital Storytelling. (2005). *Seven elements of digital storytelling*. https://www.storycenter.org/history.html

Cheng, H. F., & Dörnyei, Z. (2007). The use of motivational strategies in language instruction: The case of EFL teaching in Taiwan. *International Journal of Innovation in Language Learning and Teaching, 1*(1), 153–174. doi:10.2167/illt048.0

Chung, S. K. (2006). Digital storytelling in integrated arts education. *The International Journal of Arts Education, 4*(1), 33–50.

Ciğerci, F. M., & Gültekin, M. (2017). Use of digital stories to develop listening comprehension skills. *Issues in Educational Research, 27*(2), 252–268.

Çıralı, H. (2014). *Dijital hikâye anlatımının görsel bellek ve yazma becerisi üzerine etkisi*. Ankara: Yüksek Lisans Tezi. Hacettepe Üniversitesi.

Demirer, V. (2013). *İlköğretimde e-öyküleme kullanımı ve etkileri*. Konya: Yayınlanmamış Doktora Tezi. Necmettin Erbakan Üniversitesi.

Dikbaş, Y., & Hasırcı, Ö. K. (2008). Öğrenme stratejileri öğretiminin ve ders işlenişinde kullanımının öğrencilerin akademik başarılarına ve tutumlarına etkisi. *Ahi Evran Üniversitesi Kırşehir Eğitim Fakültesi Dergisi*, *9*(2), 69–76.

Dogan, B., & Robin, B. (2008). Implementation of digital storytelling in the classroom by teachers trained in a digital storytelling workshop. In *Society for Information Technology & Teacher Education International Conference* (pp. 902-907). Association for the Advancement of Computing in Education (AACE).

Doğan, Ö. (2009). *İngilizce hazırlık okuyan öğrencilerin motivasyon düzeyleri*. Eskişehir: Yüksek Lisans Tezi. Osmangazi Üniversitesi.

Dörnyei, Z. (1994). Motivation and motivating in the foreign language classroom. *Modern Language Journal*, *78*(3), 273–284. doi:10.1111/j.1540-4781.1994.tb02042.x

Dreon, O., Kerper, R. M., & Landis, J. (2011). Digital storytelling: A tool for teaching and learning in the youtube generation. *Middle School Journal*, *42*(5), 4–10. doi:10.1080/00940771.2011.11461777

Gardner, R. C., & Lambert, W. E. (1959). Motivational variables in second-language acquisition. *Canadian Journal of Psychology/Revue. Canadian Psychology*, *13*(4), 266–272. doi:10.1037/h0083787

Gils, F. V. (2005). Potential applications of digital storytelling in education. In *3rd Twente Student Conference on IT* (Vol.7). University of Twente, Faculty of Electrical Engineering, Mathematics and Computer Science Enschede.

Gömleksiz, M. N., & Pullu, E. K. (2017). Toondoo ile dijital hikâyeler oluşturmanın öğrenci başarısına ve tutumlarına etkisi. *Electronic Turkish Studies*, *12*(32), 95–110. doi:10.7827/TurkishStudies.12717

Görgen, İ., Kömür, Ş., & Deniz, S. (2013). İngilizce öğretmen adaylarının güdüleme stratejilerini değerlendirmeleri. *Sosyal ve Beşeri Bilimler Araştırmaları Dergisi*, *23*, 147–160.

Gregori-Signes, C. (2008). Integrating the old and the new: Digital storytelling in the EFL language classroom. *Greta*, *16*(1&2), 43–49.

Hadžimehmedagić, M., & Akbarov, A. (2014). The importance of frequent usage of various motivational strategies in second language acquisition. *Linguistics, Culture and Identity in Foreign Language Education*, 1157.

Hakan, K., Aydin, B., & Bulent, A. (2015). An investigation of undergraduates' language learning strategies. *Procedia: Social and Behavioral Sciences*, *197*, 1348–1354. doi:10.1016/j.sbspro.2015.07.388

Hathorn, P. P. (2005). Using digital storytelling as a literacy tool for the inner-city middle school youth. *The Charter Schools Resource Journal*, *1*(1), 32–38.

Heo, M. (2009). Digital storytelling: An empirical study of the impact of digital storytelling on pre-service teachers' self-efficacy and dispositions towards educational technology. *Journal of Educational Multimedia and Hypermedia*, *18*(4), 405–428.

İnceelli, A. (2005). Dijital hikâye anlatımının bileşenleri. *The Turkish Online Journal of Educational Technology, 4*(3), 132–142.

İncikabı, L., & Kıldan, A. O. (2013). An analysis of early childhood teacher candidates' digital stories for mathematics teaching. *International Journal of Academic Research, 5*(2), 77–81. doi:10.7813/2075-4124.2013/5-2/B.10

Kajder, S., & Swenson, J. A. (2004). Digital images in the language arts classroom in the curriculum: Language arts. *Learning and Leading with Technology, 31*(8), 18–21.

Karaoglan Yilmaz, F., & Durak, H. (2018). Examining pre-service teachers' opinions about digital story design. *Education and Information Technologies, 23*(3), 1277–1295. doi:10.100710639-017-9666-2

Kearney, M. (2009). Towards A Learning Design for Student-Generated Digital Storytelling. In *Future of Learning Design Conference*. New South Wales, Australia: University of Wollongong. Retrieved from http://ro.uow.edu.au/cgi/viewcontent.cgi

Kearney, M., & Schuck, S. (2006). Spotlight on authentic learning: Student developed digital video projects. *Australasian Journal of Educational Technology, 22*(2), 189–208. doi:10.14742/ajet.1298

Kocaman-Karoğlu, A. (2015). Öğretim sürecinde hikâye anlatmanın teknolojiyle değişen doğası: Dijital hikâye anlatımı. *Eğitim Teknolojisi Kuram ve Uygulama, 5*(2), 89–106.

Kordaki, M. (2014). On the design of educational digital stories: The Ed-W model. *Procedia: Social and Behavioral Sciences, 116*, 1631–1635. doi:10.1016/j.sbspro.2014.01.447

Küngerü, A. (2016). Bir ifade aracı olarak dijital öykü anlatımı. *Abant Kültürel Araştırmalar Dergisi, 1*(2), 190–202.

Kurudayıoğlu, M., & Bal, M. (2014). Ana dili eğitiminde dijital hikâye anlatımlarının kullanımı. *Sakarya Üniversitesi Eğitim Fakültesi Dergisi*, (28), 74-95.

Lambert, J. (2002). *Digital storytelling: Capturing lives, creating community.* Berkeley, CA: Digital Diner Press.

Levett-Jones, T., Bowen, L., & Morris, A. (2015). Enhancing nursing students' understanding of threshold concepts through the use of digital stories and a virtual community called 'Wiimali'. *Nurse Education in Practice, 15*(2), 91–96. doi:10.1016/j.nepr.2014.11.014 PMID:25487056

Meadows, D. (2003). Digital storytelling: Research-based practice in new media. *Visual Communication, 2*(2), 189–193. doi:10.1177/1470357203002002004

Mehdiyev, E., Gonca, U. S. T. A., & Uğurlu, C. T. (2016). İngilizce dil öğreniminde motivasyon. *Elektronik Sosyal Bilimler Dergisi, 15*(57), 361–371.

Neuhauser, P. C. (1993). *Corporate legends and lore: The power of storytelling as a management tool.* New York: McGraw-Hill.

Nishioka, H. (2016). Analysing language development in a collaborative digital storytelling project: Sociocultural perspectives. *System, 62*, 39–52. doi:10.1016/j.system.2016.07.001

Nomass, B. B. (2013). The impact of using technology in teaching English as a second language. *English Language and Literature Studies*, *3*(1), 111–116.

Özçalışan, H. (2013). *Yükseköğrenim öğrencilerinin ingilizceyi öğrenme motivasyonları*. Yüksek Lisans Tezi. Kocatepe Üniversitesi, Afyon.

Ozcinar, H., & Ozturk, H. T. (2013). Methods for Analyzing Computer-Mediated Communication in Educational Sciences. In N. Sappleton (Ed.), *Advancing Research Methods with New Media Technologies* (pp. 228–249). London: IGI Global. doi:10.4018/978-1-4666-3918-8.ch013

Pedersen, E. (1995). Storytelling and the art of teaching. *Forum*, *33*(1), 2–5.

Price, D. M., Strodtman, L., Brough, E., Lonn, S., & Luo, A. (2015). Digital storytelling: An innovative technological approach to nursing education. *Nurse Educator*, *40*(2), 66–70. doi:10.1097/NNE.0000000000000094 PMID:25290965

Rahimi, M., & Yadollahi, S. (2017). Effects of offline vs. online digital storytelling on the development of EFL learners' literacy skills. *Cogent Education*, *4*(1), 1–13. doi:10.1080/2331186X.2017.1285531

Razmia, M., Pouralib, S., & Nozad, S. (2014). Digital storytelling in EFL classroom (oral presentation of the story): A pathway to improve oral production. *Social and Behavioral Sciences*, *98*, 1541–1544. doi:10.1016/j.sbspro.2014.03.576

Robin, B. (2006, March). The Educational Uses of Digital Storytelling. In *Society for Information Technology & Teacher Education International Conference* (pp. 709-716). Association for the Advancement of Computing in Education (AACE).

Robin, B. R. (2008). Digital storytelling: A powerful technology tool for the 21st century classroom. *Theory into Practice*, *47*(3), 220–228. doi:10.1080/00405840802153916

Sarıca, H. Ç., & Usluel, Y. K. (2016). Eğitsel bağlamda dijital hikâye anlatımı: Bir rubrik geliştirme çalışması. *Eğitim Teknolojisi Kuram ve Uygulama*, *6*(2), 298–309.

Sarıca, H. Ç., & Usluel, Y. K. (2016). The effect of digital storytelling on visual memory and writing skills. *Computers & Education*, *94*, 298–309. doi:10.1016/j.compedu.2015.11.016

Silseth, K. (2013). Surviving the impossible: Studying students' constructions of digital stories on World War II. *Learning, Culture and Social Interaction*, *2*(3), 155–170. doi:10.1016/j.lcsi.2013.04.004

Singhal, M. (1997). The Internet and foreign language education: Benefits and challenges. *The Internet TESL Journal*, *3*(6), 107.

Smeda, N., Dakich, E., & Sharda, N. (2010, July). Developing a framework for advancing e-learning through digital storytelling. In *IADIS International Conference E-Learning* (pp. 169-176). Academic Press.

Smeda, N., Dakich, E., & Sharda, N. (2014). The Effectiveness of digital storytelling in the classrooms: A comprehensive study. *Smart Learning Environments*, *1*(1), 6. doi:10.118640561-014-0006-3

Sökmen, İ. (2006). *İngilizce öğretmenlerinin strateji öğretimi ile ilgili inançları*. Eskişehir: Yüksek Lisans Tezi. Anadolu Üniversitesi.

Stockwell, G. (2013). Technology and motivation in English-language teaching and learning. In *International perspectives on motivation* (pp. 156–175). London: Palgrave Macmillan. doi:10.1057/9781137000873_9

Suwardy, T., Pan, G., & Seow, P. S. (2013). Using digital storytelling to engage student learning. *Accounting Education, 22*(2), 109–124. doi:10.1080/09639284.2012.748505

Taşdemir, A., & Tay, B. (2007). Fen bilgisi öğretiminde öğrencilerin öğrenme stratejilerini kullanmalarının akademik başarıya etkileri. *Uludağ Üniversitesi Eğitim Fakültesi Dergisi, 20*(1), 173–187.

Tatlı, Z., & Aksoy, D. A. (2015). Yabancı dil konuşma eğitiminde dijital öykü kullanımı. *Marmara Üniversitesi Atatürk Eğitim Fakültesi Eğitim Bilimleri Dergisi, 45*, 137–152.

Tendero, A. (2006). Facing yourselves: The effects of digital storytelling on teacher education. *Contemporary Issues in Technology & Teacher Education, 6*(2), 174–194.

Tugan, S. E. (2015). *The relationship among foreign language classroom anxiety, motivation and achievement of Turkish EFL students*. İstanbul: Yayımlanmamış Yüksek Lisans Tezi. Fatih Üniversitesi.

Turan, T., & Şeker, B. S. (2018). The effect of digital stories on fifth-grade students' motivation. *Journal of Education and Future, 13*, 65–78.

Turgut, G., & Kışla, T. (2015). The use of computer-aided story in education: Literature review. *Turkish Online Journal of Qualitative Inquiry, 6*(2), 97–121. doi:10.17569/tojqi.57305

Ülgen, G. (1995). *Eğitim psikolojisi: Birey ve öğrenme*. Ankara: Bilim Yayınları.

Uslupehlivan, E., & Erden, M. K. (2016). *Usage of digital storytelling method in higher education. International Conference on Quality in Higher Education, Sakarya, Turkey.*

Wang, L. (2005). The advantages of using technology in second language education. *The Journal, 32*(10), 38–42.

Wang, S., & Zhan, H. (2010). Enhancing teaching and learning with digital storytelling. *International Journal of Information and Communication Technology Education, 6*(2), 76–87. doi:10.4018/jicte.2010040107

Wilson, J. A. (1997). *A program to develop the listening and speaking skills of children in a first grade classroom* (Master Thesis). University of Virginia.

Yang, Y. T. C., & Wu, W. C. I. (2012). Digital storytelling for enhancing student academic achievement, critical thinking and learning motivation: A year-long experimental study. *Computers & Education, 59*(2), 339–352. doi:10.1016/j.compedu.2011.12.012

Yılmaz, Y., Üstündağ, M. T., & Güneş, E. (2017). Öğretim materyali olarak dijital hikâye geliştirme aşamalarının ve araçlarının incelenmesi. *Abant İzzet Baysal Üniversitesi Eğitim Fakültesi Dergisi, 17*(3), 1621–1640. doi:10.17240/aibuefd.2017.17.31178-338851

ADDITIONAL READING

Behmer, S., Schmidt, D., & Schmidt, J. (2006, March). Everyone has a story to tell: Examining digital storytelling in the classroom. *In Society for Information Technology & Teacher Education International Conference* (pp. 655-662). Association for the Advancement of Computing in Education (AACE).

Karaoglan Yilmaz, F. G., Özdemir, B. G., & Yasar, Z. (2018). Using digital stories to reduce misconceptions and mistakes about fractions: An action study. *International Journal of Mathematical Education in Science and Technology*, *49*(6), 867–898. doi:10.1080/0020739X.2017.1418919

Morgan, H. (2014). Using digital story projects to help students improve in reading and writing. *Reading Improvement*, *51*(1), 20–26.

Ohler, J. (2006). The world of digital storytelling. *Educational Leadership*, *63*(4), 44–47.

Sever, T. (2014). *An investigation into the impact of digital storytelling on the motivation level of students*. Unpublished MA Thesis. Çanakkale Onsekiz Mart University, Institute of Educational Sciences, Çanakkale.

Valkanova, Y., & Watts, M. (2007). Digital story telling in a science classroom: Reflective self-learning (RSL) in action. *Early Child Development and Care*, *177*(6-7), 793–807. doi:10.1080/03004430701437252

Verdugo, D. R., & Belmonte, I. A. (2007). Using digital stories to improve listening comprehension with Spanish young learners of English. *Language Learning & Technology*, *11*(1), 87–101.

Yang, Y.-T. C., & Wu, W.-C. I. (2012). Digital Storytelling for enhancing student academic achievement, critical thinking, and learning motivation. A year-long experimental study. *Computers & Education*, *59*(2), 339–352. doi:10.1016/j.compedu.2011.12.012

KEY TERMS AND DEFINITIONS

Digital Story: Digital story can be defined as video presentations rich in multimedia elements.

Digital Storytelling: Digital storytelling can be defined as the process of creating a short film by combining a text or an original story with multimedia elements such as picture, sound recording, and video.

Digital Teaching: Digital teaching can be defined as any type of teaching that is accompanied by technology or by instructional practice that makes effective use of technology.

Foreign Language Education: Foreign language education can be defined as the teaching of a modern language that is neither an official language nor the mother tongue of a significant part of the population.

Foreign Language Learning: Foreign language learning can be defined as learning of a nonnative language outside of the environment where it is commonly spoken.

Language Learning: Language learning can be defined as developing the ability to communicate in the second/foreign language.

Learning Strategies: Learning strategies are tactics students use to assist them in the learning process.

Motivation: Motivation can be defined as an internal drive that activates behavior and gives it direction.

Chapter 11
Distraction at Mobile Learning Environments:
A Critical Review

Ahmed Mokhtar Abdelaziz
Saudi Aramco, Saudi Arabia

ABSTRACT

This chapter focuses on distraction at mobile learning environments from different perspectives. It is hoped that this chapter will contribute to the academic discussion on this topic by exploring whether the term 'distraction' accurately describes learners' tendencies to leave the formal, standard, or prescribed content and access the non-standard applications and websites during the academic attempts. This chapter will also introduce a more in-depth discussion on the root causes that drive learners' deviation to the non-standard applications and websites. Furthermore, it will propose and discuss some emerging arguments such as converting 'learning distractions' into 'learning attractions' in a way that might enhance the academic discussion on theory and practice of mobile learning research. Finally, it will introduce three effective techniques and strategies that have the potential to control distractions in mobile learning environments.

INTRODUCTION

Since '*Mobile Learning*' became a well-recognized concept in literature in 2005 (Crompton, 2013; Wong, 2015), research on it has been growing at a rapid rate, especially with the introduction of smart handheld devices such as smart phones and tablets (Crompton, Burke, Gregory, & Gräbe, 2016). Since then, researchers have explored, identified, and shared several affordances as well as challenges that have been associated with Mobile Learning (M-Learning) (Burden & Kearney, 2016; Clarke & Svanaes, 2014; Kaalberg, 2014; Kucirkova, Messer, Sheehy & Panadero, 2014; Mingyong, 2015; Mullen, 2014; Ouyang and Stanley, 2014; Rodríguez, Riaza, & Gomez, 2017; Sung, Chang & Yang, 2015). Amongst the most challenging issues that researchers in the field of M-Learning have explored is learners' distraction caused by mobile devices (Fang, 2009).

DOI: 10.4018/978-1-7998-3062-7.ch011

Mingyong (2015) explained that mobile technologies "might distract students' attention from the main focus of the teaching process because students might use those devices for other purposes in and outside classroom" (p. 505). Many other researchers share the same concern (Gallegos & Nakashima, 2018; Gikas and Grant, 2013; Harman & Sato, 2011; Jalil & Sabir, 2019; Junco, 2012; Serah, 2014; Kirschner & Karpinski, 2010; Traxler, 2010).

Despite a wealth of research on the topic, to-date, an in-depth understanding of distraction at M-Learning remains however marginal. Hence, it is useful to investigate whether the term 'distraction' accurately describes learners' tendency to leave the formal content and access non-standard applications and websites during the lessons. It would also be interesting to explore the root causes that lead to learners' deviation to non-standard applications and websites during the academic attempts. Furthermore, it is possible that discussing how to convert *'learning distractions'* into *'learning attractions'* would enhance the academic discussion on theory and practice of mobile learning. Finally, identifying techniques and strategies that can effectively control distractions at M-Learning environments might provide useful insights to program designers, practitioners and administrators.

Reflections on these concepts will be introduced in light of the findings of a PhD study conducted in a M-Learning environment at Saudi Aramco Industrial Training Centres (SAITCs) in Saudi Arabia (Abdelaziz, 2018). In light of this, the following are the research questions for this study:

1. What are the different types and sources of distraction and multi-tasking at M-Learning environments?
2. What are the potential solutions to control distraction at M-Learning environments?

The following section presents a background on the issue followed by the methodology employed, the findings, discussion, and conclusion.

BACKGROUND

This section includes an overview on M-Learning environment with a brief description of its definition, elements, affordances, and challenges. It also provides a focused background on research on the issue of distraction at M-Learning environments.

M-Learning Environment

In a general sense, a learning environment is the medium where learning and teaching take place. It is the sum of the internal and external circumstances and influences surrounding and affecting a person's learning (Jawaid & Aly, 2014), and it is "dependent upon each and everything in an educational organization like curriculum design, teaching methods, teachers' behaviour with students, the atmosphere during teaching sessions, the social and academic environment and support system during stress" (Jawaid & Aly, 2014, p. 319). The Glossary of Education Reform referred to 'learning environment' as "the diverse physical locations, contexts, and cultures in which students learn" (n.p.). Similarly, for Bates (2019), a learning environment includes:

- the characteristics of the learners;
- the goals for teaching and learning;
- the activities that will best support learning;
- the assessment strategies that will best measure and drive learning; and
- the culture that infuses the learning environment. (p. 272)

Recognizing how mobile devices may play a role in maintaining, altering, adding, and/or augmenting the relationship between these components of learning environments, and also exploring the emergent dynamics, aspects, and features of M-Learning environments is evolutionary. For example, a lot of research in the field of M-Learning is progressively exploring the emerging behaviours and roles of instructors and learners, the forms of interaction, the role of the digital learning materials and content, and the types of learning, engagement, and performance as well as many other aspects of M-Learning environments (Crompton, 2013).

In this respect, a plethora of literature found that M-Learning has numerous affordances and challenges that affect the M-Learning environment. What distinguishes M-Learning over conventional learning is its ability to function in formal (e.g., workshops and classrooms) and informal (e.g., museums, zoos) environments (Sung et al., 2015), to meet the urgency of learning needs and knowledge acquisition (Lin, Chen & Chen, 2008), and to place learners in the centre of challenging and active learning environments (Laurillard & Pachler, 2007). Moreover, it enables learning to be independent of time and location constraints, supports learners with different learning needs, and provides learners with immediate feedback (Ouyang and Stanley, 2014).

Furthermore, M-Learning has been argued to empower learners by enabling them "to select and assess relevant information, redefine their goals, and reconsider their understanding of concepts within a shifting and growing frame of reference" (Koole & Ally, 2006, p. 4). Additionally, M-Learning further supports collaboration amongst learners and instructors at multiple levels. Traditionally, collaboration and participative authenticity required learners to be physically present in the learning context. This is not a requirement anymore with mobile technologies and simulated authenticity as they blur or fracture the boundaries and allow learners to be "located in their normal spaces and contexts where the conditions of the real-world contexts are replicated" (Burden & Kearney, 2016, p. 31).

Finally, according to MoLeNet (2007), M-Learning has the potential to:

- help bridge the gap between mobile phone literacy and ICT literacy;
- help to raise the self-confidence and self-esteem of non-traditional learners;
- take place outside, whilst travelling, in the workplace or in the classroom; and
- be used to capture evidence and for assessment (para. 6).

On the other hand, using mobile technologies for learning purposes is still questionable. For example, Ricky and Rechell (2015) argued that "students prefer using mobile devices and flexible technologies for entertainment to acquiring information and communicating with others but they seldom use them for educational purposes" (p. 98). Several other challenges of using mobile technologies for pedagogical purposes have been reported by various researchers; however, it is argued that amongst the identified shortcomings of mobile learning, *distraction* has been reported as the most challenging feature of M-Learning environments (Abdelaziz, 2018).

Research on Distraction at M-Learning Environments

According to Peter and Bijik (2018), distraction refers to "diversion of a person's or a group of peoples' attention from something of utmost importance to other less important or secondary tasks" (p. 10). Hence, in a M-Learning context, distraction may refer to the learner's deviation from learning from the formal or standard content and away from the lesson objectives to non-standard applications and websites which include, but are not limited to social media applications and websites such as YouTube, Twitter, Facebook, Instagram, Snapchat, etc., video-games whether application-based or web-based, news websites, personal emails, podcasts, forums, text messages, etc.

Fang (2009) confirmed that distraction is "a problem that no educator can afford to ignore as ubiquitous computing and M-Learning environments become commonplace" (p. 2). Similarly, Mingyong (2015) reported that one of the main negative effects of mobile technologies is that they "might distract students' attention from the main focus of the teaching process because students might use those devices for other purposes in and outside classroom" (p. 505).

The increased multi-tasking at M-Learning environments impairs learning by the distraction caused by phone ringing, texting, and constant visits to social medial platforms (Gallegos & Nakashima, 2018; Harman & Sato, 2011; Jalil & Sabir, 2019; Junco, 2012; Kirschner & Karpinski, 2010; Serah, 2014). Likewise, Gikas and Grant (2013), Tella (2003) and Traxler (2010) warned that learning across different contexts and at different times may produce fragmented knowledge and incomplete schemata.

However, so far much of the discussion on distraction has been one-sided and has not looked at the issue from all angles. A few studies indicated that the linkage between distraction at M-Learning environments and the mobile devices is not justifiable. Hoffmann (2017), for example, clarified:

It is important to acknowledge that distractions do not come from the devices; rather, distractions are a problem with the pedagogy. Whether a student has a device or not, if he/she is not engaged he/she will find a distraction. Students used to pass notes or talk to their neighbours; now mobile devices offer a different medium for distraction. (p. 40)

Hence, it appears that literature on M-Learning has not provided a comprehensive and in-depth understanding of the issue of distraction and the effective techniques of controlling it; the argument which forms a strong basis for conducting this study.

MAIN FOCUS OF THE CHAPTER

This section provides a brief account on the study context; methods of data collection, sampling, researcher's position in the study, data synthesis and analysis; and findings.

Study Context

The study was conducted at one of Saudi Aramco's Industrial Training Centres (SAITCs) in Saudi Arabia. In 2016, SAITCs started piloting the use of iPads for *Academic* (English, Math, and Science) and *Job Skills* (Electrical, Welding, Mechanical, and other craft specialization) training purposes. A completely new training program with function-based interactive digital content was designed for the iPad training program at SAITCs, and all instructors and trainees were given iPads with the standard digital content installed on them. Further to that, instructors had received on-the-job training on using the iPad for teaching and learning purposes, and the trainees had been given adequate orientation on using the devices for learning before the conduct of the study. It is also worth mentioning that the trainees at SAITCs were generally recent high school and vocational college graduates, ranging in age from 18 to 23 years. Upon completing the training program which spans over one to two years based on the program (high school or vocational), craft, and placement test scores, the SAITCs graduates join the company workforce as regular technicians. These features made SAITCs an ideal context to conduct research on M-Learning environments and to explore its emerging affordances and challenges more in-depth.

Data Collection

Commencing on this study, a case study approach was adopted, where quantitative and qualitative data from questionnaires, semi-structured interviews, unstructured observations, and program documents were collected respectively. Open-ended items in the questionnaire enabled the researcher to identify some emerging and premature themes that needed further exploration and validation. The statistical analysis of the quantitative part of the questionnaires, on the other hand, helped to capture some trainees' and instructors' tendencies towards distraction at mobile learning. As a result, the data gathered from questionnaires guided the researcher's thinking when formulating the questions for the semi-structured interviews.

The researcher conducted interviews with 14 trainees and 20 instructors in order to listen to their unique points of view and to examine how mobile devices impacted their learning from their unique perspective. Each participant was interviewed once for approximately 35 minutes. Data saturation, that is no new themes, perspectives, or perceptions were evident in the data, was achieved at script 29. The researcher realized that saturation was achieved at this stage because participants in the sample were similar in their experiences with respect to the research domain (Guest, Bunce, & Johnson, 2006).

Besides, the unstructured observations were collected during the period of conducting the questionnaires and interviews, as they were not bound by a specific time. The researcher continued to note down all relevant observations, whether new or repeated, while conducting the other methods of data collection. The observations generated complementary data which led to further insights and a better understanding of the phenomenon under study.

Finally, documentary evidence such as email messages and reports on the implementation and evaluation of the iPad program as well as screenshots of some content pages and videos were employed as a method to cross-validate information gathered from the questionnaires, interviews, and observations.

This mixed method approach enabled the researcher to collect systematic data and to develop his findings in a coherent and robust way.

Sampling

The entire population participating in the iPad pilot program at SAITCs (133 trainees and 29 instructors) took part in the questionnaire. For the interviews, non-probability purposive sampling was adopted. Despite the disadvantages that may arise from its non-representativeness, non-probability sampling is employed to deliberately and purposely recruit knowledgeable, interested, uninterested, and unbiased participants (Ary et al., 2010; Cohen et al., 2007). Non-probability sampling is grounded in the principle that researchers can target a specific group that is actually representing itself, rather than the wider population (Cohen et al., 2007).

Researcher's Position in the Study

The researcher was an insider at the context of this study, working as a chairman of an English Language Unit at one of the SAITCs. As an insider, the researcher had sufficient knowledge about the trainees' and instructors' backgrounds, how they may respond to the data collection methods, how much time they would take to respond to the questionnaires, their favourite ways of sharing their insights, and how much data they would share in writing versus orally. These considerations helped him to make decisions about the questions to include in the questionnaires and the interviews, whether they should be translated or not, which specific instruments would collect sufficient data that would help in answering specific research questions and areas of focus, and the order in which the data collection methods would be employed.

Moreover, a detailed account of the actions taken and positions adopted during this study has been declared in order to help in limiting the negative impact of the researcher's potential bias as an insider. This has been achieved by showing the measures taken to ensure rigour and trustworthiness of the research such as triangulation of the data, comparing the findings of this research with previously-published research findings, and integrating the process of member checking, where the researcher's interpretations of the data were shared with 3 study participants who had the opportunity to discuss and clarify the interpretation and contribute new or additional perspectives on the topic under the study. The researcher adopted an epistemological approach whereby the findings and knowledge are constructed through interactions between the researcher and the participants by reflecting on and interpreting data collected through various qualitative and quantitative methods of data collection (Baxter & Jack, 2008; Guba, 1981; Hancock & Algozzine, 2016; Lincoln & Guba, 1985; Russell, Gregory, Ploeg, DiCenso, & Guyatt, 2005).

Data Synthesis and Analysis

Synthesizing data which means combining, integrating, and summarizing findings was carried out on an inductive basis. Broad generalizations, conclusions, and themes were generated from the transcripts, participants' discussions, observations, and the quantitative data (Gale et al., 2013; Fereday & Muir-Cochrane, 2006). Thomas (2006) explained that the "primary purpose of the inductive approach is to allow research findings to emerge from the frequent, dominant, or significant themes inherent in raw data, without the restraints imposed by structured methodologies" (p. 238). This study adopted Hancock and Algozzine's (2016) framework (questions below) to synthesize the large amounts of data generated from different resources. Answering these following questions facilitated the process of data synthesis:

- What information from different sources goes together?
- Within a source, what information can be grouped?
- What arguments contribute to grouping information together?
- What entities bounded by space and time are shared?
- How do various sources of information affect findings?
- What information links various findings together?
- What previous work provides a basis for analysis?
- What questions are being answered?
- What generalizations can be made? (Hancock & Algozzine, 2016, p. 63)

To answer these questions, the researcher followed a process of four steps (Ary et al., 2010, p. 565) which included:

- **Stage 1-Data Reduction:** The researcher printed out all the qualitative data, sorted them by questions, and color-coded them by theme. He gathered similar ideas and comments and used relevant quotations from participants to support the emerging themes.
- **Stage 2-Data Display:** The researcher displayed the quantitative data in percentages to enable readers to immediately recognize, compare and contrast the data. Qualitative data was displayed in a thematic manner where a concept or a theme was introduced, and description followed.
- **Stage 3-Data Consolidation:** The researcher combined both sets of data quantitative and qualitative to create a new set of findings.
- **Stage 4-Data Integration and Reporting**: The researcher integrated the data and interpretations into a coherent whole.

The researcher bracketed his understanding of the phenomenon - as much as he could - throughout the different stages of data analysis by consciously subduing the tendency to integrate the descriptions by research participants into existing theoretical structures, and by giving a clear description of the process of analysis to allow the reader to evaluate the attempt to achieve bracketing (Ashworth & Lucas, 2000).

Findings

Study participants confirmed that some trainees tended to drift to social media and non-standard applications and websites during the lessons for various reasons. According to the questionnaire results, 27% of the instructors thought that the mobile devices distracted their trainees' attention from the main objectives of the teaching and learning experience. Furthermore, of 133 trainee-respondents, those who never or rarely engaged with distractions during the lessons ranged between 44 (33%) and 112 (84%) trainees, yet those who engaged with distractions during the lessons ranged between 21 (16%) and 79 (59%) trainees (Table 1).

Instructor 3 from the Basic Operations Training Unit gave the following simile in his attempt to explain why trainees tended to leave the standard content on their iPads and engage with other applications and websites:

The iPad is like a candy store for the trainees! They love to go there, pick a piece of candy and run! Certainly, there is some distraction going on, but I think we can do something to utilize their love to this store.

This love to *run to non-standard applications* has impacted some of the trainees' social and learning behaviours in several ways and resulted in new features of the M-Learning environment as will be discussed below.

The Rise of Distraction vs. the Fall of Destruction

Findings of the study indicated that a major feature of a M-Learning environment is that there is -in a general sense- a rise in trainees' *distraction,* which refers to using social media, video games, and other non-standard applications, versus a decrease in *destruction,* which refers to horse playing, shouting, and other unwanted behaviours.

Table 1. Trainee Engagement with Distractions and Non-Standard Applications

Which of the following activities do you engage in on your iPad during the lessons? How often?					
Survey Items	**Never**	**Rarely**	**Sometimes**	**Often**	**Always**
Sending and receiving personal emails	46.6% (62)	20.3% (27)	21.8% (29)	5.3% (7)	6.0% (8)
Sending and receiving company emails	49.6% (66)	12.0% (16)	20.3% (27)	7.5% (10)	10.5% (14)
Scheduling appointments or tasks	23.3% (31)	17.3% (23)	26.3% (35)	18.0% (24)	15.0% (20)
Reading online newspapers	27.8% (37)	15.0% (20)	23.3% (31)	21.8% (29)	12.0% (16)
Playing video games	47.4% (63)	19.5% (26)	17.3% (23)	11.3% (15)	4.5% (6)
Watching videos on YouTube for fun	34.6% (46)	24.8% (33)	21.8% (29)	11.3% (15)	7.5% (10)
Using Social networks (such as What's app, Facebook, snapchat, twitter, LinkedIn)	59.4% (79)	12.0% (16)	19.5% (26)	3.0% (4)	6.0% (8)
Reading sports news	51.9% (69)	14.3% (19)	18.8% (25)	6.0% (8)	9.0% (12)
Participating in blogs, forums, and wikis	72.2% (96)	12.0% (16)	9.8% (13)	2.3% (3)	3.8% (5)
Listening to music	51.1% (68)	15.8% (21)	20.3% (27)	6.8% (9)	6.0% (8)

An interesting observation in the context of this study is that trainees are much quieter and more engaged with their devices, but less engaged with each other. This phenomenon is observed in a wide sense, especially during the breaks. There is less physical and social interaction amongst trainees as opposed to increased engagement with the device. This finding is not only based on onsite observations and comparison between trainees enrolled in the iPad pilot program and those in the conventional training programs only, but on comments from the interviews and the questionnaires as well. Instructor 6 from the Math and Science Training Unit shared the following example:

In the past, when I walked around, I could see trainees chatting, talking, and joking with each other. Nowadays, I walk by classrooms or corridors, and I see trainees watching something on their iPads with full attention. They are not interacting with each other as they used to.

Trainees are not interacting with each other as much as they used to. There are often faint smiles on their faces while having their earphones on and probably watching fun videos or engaged with someone else via chatting applications as opposed to the loud giggles and shouts that used to be heard from trainees socializing and challenging each other in the corridors and the rest halls. Also, trainees are no longer seen passing pencils, books, or notebooks in an improper or unsafe way, throwing them across the room. An instructor elaborated on this phenomenon:

In a textbook-based environment, misbehaviours can happen because some trainees complete their tasks or activities earlier than the others, and, thus have free time to do nothing but cause class troubles. Now, they can finish the assigned tasks and go ahead for some more interesting tasks to do on the iPads.

In this regard, it is observed that *discipline* in a M-Learning environment is characterised as less demanding because many behavioural issues that used to require corrective and disciplinary actions from the instructors and management are disappearing. Some study participants attributed this change in trainees' social behaviours to their increased engagement with their devices. Another Job Skills instructor gave the following example: "The iPad is motivating to the trainees, and it has actually changed some bad behaviours. For example, there is no sleeping in class anymore".

Thus, it can be concluded that conventional misbehaviours have been more replaced with distractions, but the question that needs due attention is: if engagement with non-standard applications is seen by practitioners as creating a trouble-free and a more comforting environment, how is this affecting the learning process? Do learners take these distractions into the lessons? The answer to these questions will be reflected on in the next section.

Learning Distractions vs. Learning Attractions

Ostensibly, non-standard applications and websites are taken into the classroom, but it can be argued that they impact the learning process in different ways. Based on the data collected from key personnel, instructors, and trainees during the interviews, non-standard applications and websites turn to be a mixed blessing depending on the distance between them and the topic under study. The more distant and irrelevant to the prescribed learning materials they are, the more negative their impact on the learning process can be as they become *learning distractions*. Conversely, the more proximate and relevant to the prescribed or mandated learning materials and course objectives they are, the more positive their impact on the learning process can be as they may form *learning attractions* for trainees. Hence, it can be concluded that what describes a M-Learning experience as effective is the level of learners' desire to and experience in searching for and integrating enriching learning materials to the topic under study, arguably in a well-moderated context as represented in Figure 1 "Interaction with Non-Standard Applications and Websites, 2018" below.

Figure 1. Interaction with Non-standard Applications and Websites

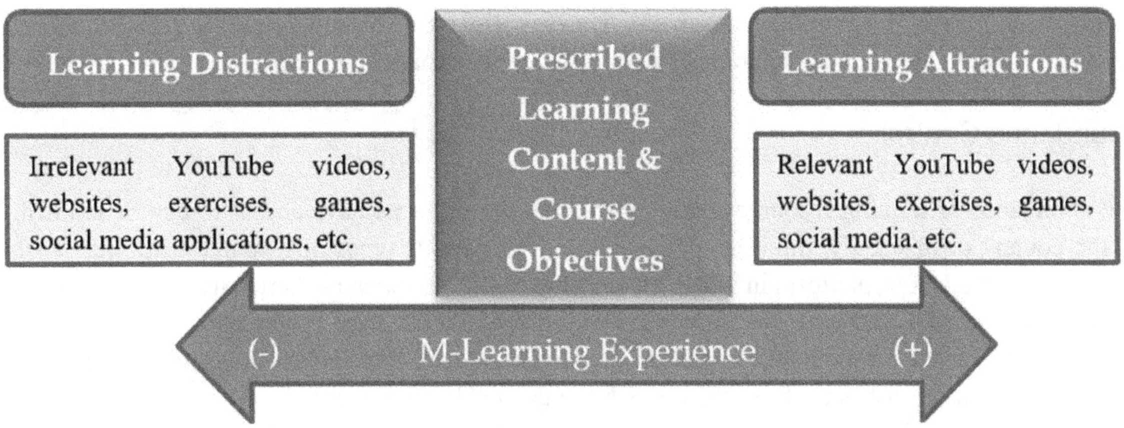

The questionnaire results supported this finding by indicating that engagement with supplementary materials and online resources can enrich lessons inside and outside the classroom. Of 133 trainee-respondents, 92 (69%) used other resources such as YouTube videos to better understand their lessons on their iBooks. Likewise, of 29 instructor-respondents, 28 (96.5%) used various extra resources and materials on the iPads to enhance the content of their lessons.

In addition, various comments from the interviews and questionnaires suggest that mobile technologies provide various types of supplementary resources that can enrich the lessons and make them easier to learn. A Job Skills Instructor shared an experience he had:

I was giving my trainees a short course on troubleshooting today. There is a company called "Synoptic" which creates and develops a lot of troubleshooting scenarios, fully animated, fully interactive, real cases as if you are already in the plant and you have some equipment which is not functioning. Trainees feel very enthusiastic to do such challenging and interactive activities, and with the iPad, they can visit these learning materials inside and outside the classroom and learn more by themselves.

Hoffmann (2017) reported similar conclusions. He reported that "games, although initially thought of as a distraction by many, have academic qualities if connected correctly to the content. For example, Angry Birds can be connected to physics and Clash of the Clans can be used to develop problem solving and team building strategies" (p. 40).

Hence, it can be concluded that the richness, interactivity, and appeal of the learning materials in the official content play an important role in determining the direction and level of trainees' drifting from it. Further to that, instructors' ability to orchestrate the lessons and adopt effective teaching and monitoring techniques in addition to trainees' commitment levels can all control the direction of engaging with the non-standard applications and websites. For example, it was observed in this study that lessons which have been designed with rich, interactive, and appealing materials are more likely to keep trainees focused on the lesson at hand. Trainees tended to leave the prescribed content when they were either bored or felt unaccomplished. It is then when they move to the other applications and websites as either learning *attractions* or *distractions*.

Arguably therefore, leaving the standard or prescribed content, and drifting to other applications and websites may be a call for change to curriculum designers, educators, and practitioners. The trainees can be asked to assess the prescribed content and the training methods and to share their insights and recommendations for potential enhancements. Unless satisfied with the learning materials and/or the instructors' teaching methods, the trainees will look for other sources of learning.

Abundance Control

The abundance of training resources and applications that trainees have access to can be confusing. At the context of this study, trainees appreciated having various types of resources, but they wished they had one toolbox or platform in which all learning resources (such as dictionaries, videos, chatting rooms, bolls, quizzes, and other learning-oriented tools) could be saved. Some participants confirmed that searching through too much information may cause information overload and thus distract rather than guide them. An instructor from the English Language Unit commented:

When searching for information, we do get information overload and much of the material is not moderated, i.e. it could range from elementary information to PhD level. Trainees can be distracted easily, and a lot of time could be wasted just sifting through the vast amount of information.

Besides, other participants highlighted that YouTube videos - which are referred to by trainees as the most valuable source of information to them - may introduce information and ideas that are not matching the corporate standards; especially since selecting these videos is usually left to the discretion of the instructors and trainees. A suggested solution is to develop sufficient company-specific videos that explain the organization's unique processes and share them on one handy platform, thus decreasing confusion and distraction. A questionnaire respondent (trainee) commented: "Shooting videos on Saudi Aramco sites with employees doing real tasks, and having them on the iBooks rather than getting general or irrelevant videos would help a lot".

Hence, there is a good opportunity for program designers, educationalists, and practitioners to guide the learners' drift from the prescribe content and to create learning attractions in more useful way by developing interactive, relevant, appealing materials, sharing them on a user-friendly platform, and utilizing effective pedagogical methods.

Accessing Non-Standard Applications: Impact on High-Performing and Dominating Learners

Participants of this study reported that accessing non-standard applications on mobile devices may have some positives implications. For example, it may help high-performing trainees who tend to finish their tasks and activities quickly to receive immediate rewards by being able to access fun and preferable non-standard applications and websites. The same, at a lower scale, is also applicable to some mediocre trainees; the thing which helps them to increase their efficiency over time.

This aspect of M-Learning environments has the potential to help in different ways. It can abolish the feeling of boredom and demotivation which may result from the prolonged time that slower trainees consume for their task completion while high-performing trainees are waiting for what to do next. Furthermore, it can help in maintaining good control in the classroom as high-performing and dominating learners may find platforms that take them from causing troubles in the classroom when they are done with their tasks and activities. An instructor from the English Language Unit elaborated on this phenomenon:

In a textbook-based environment, some classroom issues or misbehaviours can happen due to the fact that some high-performing trainees complete their tasks or activities earlier than the others, and, thus have free time to do nothing but cause class troubles. Now, they can finish the assigned tasks and go ahead for some more interesting tasks to do. This makes the classroom less disruptive.

Distraction Control Techniques

In light of the discussion above, the concerns and issues about distraction at M-Learning environments need to be re-evaluated and due attention should be directed to turning *distractions* (leaving the standard content) into real, effective learning opportunities or *attractions*. However, distractions -as the name suggests and as they are mostly used in literature now- are correlated with unwanted practices and negative behaviours, and thus, require effective classroom management and novel monitoring techniques to ensure learning is happening and to prevent learners from losing focus. This becomes critical, especially since measuring the usefulness of trainees' engagement with the non-standard applications and websites is not an easy job for instructors and administrators. It will require analysis of too much data collected from individual trainees' devices on their engagement with the different applications. The decision to control trainees' access to the non-standard applications and websites in the classrooms in order to neutralize their impact has so far been a safe, effective, and less demanding option.

In this respect, the study participants identified three effective methods of controlling trainees' access to the non-standard applications and websites inside the classrooms: **instructor as monitor**, **device monitoring,** and **trainee self-monitoring**. These can help guide the practice at similar M-Learning environments.

The Instructor as a Monitor

The Instructor as a Monitor technique requires a change in the instructors' position inside the classroom. Instructors are moved more to the back of the classroom where they have to teach more from behind the trainees or at least from a shoulder-to-shoulder position. This change has been reported as a chief result of the instructors' need to see the screens of his trainees' mobile devices. Instructors' suspicion about trainees' engagement with distractions, passing answers of exercises and quizzes, and turning screens into an idol mode have all been reported as major reasons for instructors to change their positions. An instructor from the Math & Science Unit shared this example:

Some trainees may try to send messages to each other during the lessons and quizzes. Therefore, I currently tend to stand at the back of the classroom more while teaching or proctoring to see the screens of the students' devices. I want to see what they are doing, whether they are watching videos, and whether they are sending messages.

Simultaneously, instructors need to keep their trainees engaged in the learning activities through the implementation of effective group/pair work activities and through empowering trainees to share the lesson with the teacher by teaching parts of it. It has been observed that group work activities in which trainees are assigned specific roles to play such as a group leader, monitor, reporter, and notetaker enable the instructors to orchestrate their classes more effectively and keep trainees more focused on the lessons at hand. Existing research also emphasized instructors' role as a monitor at M-Learning classes (Nedungadi & Raman, 2012; Shih, 2011). Lang (2017) argued that "most of us can shut out distractions when we are pursuing something that really matters to us. So if we want to deal with distractions in teaching, an obvious place to turn would be toward our goals for the classroom: Who creates them? How much do they matter? And how well do students understand them?" (n.p.). Thus, it can be argued that engaging trainees in the learning experience and the process of developing learning goals can be a good method to minimize or avoid the negative impact of distractions in the classroom.

Nonetheless, a question may arise here. What does it require to utilize the extra resources on the mobile devices positively or more effectively? The simple answer goes into two directions:

- First, the emerging role of instructors as selectors.
- Second, the collection of the extra resources.

Regarding the first point, the researcher suggests that utilizing the resources to positively impact learning may require a more complex and emerging role of instructors at M-Learning classes which is the *selector* role. Instructors have to be equipped with the right knowledge and skills of how to guide learners' selection of learning tools and applications, and yet remove distractors in a way that ensures maximum and effective utilization of mobile devices. They also need to know which applications and resources can make their teaching more entertaining to their trainees. Existing research supports this finding. For example, according to Toshalis and Nakkula (2012):

Faced with the noise of myriad digital distractions and their threats to productivity and cognitive complexity, teachers need to understand that classroom engagement is as much about selective disengagement - unplugging, as it were - as it is about the decision to focus attention and apply effort. (p. 22)

As for the second point (collection of the extra resources), comments on the questionnaires and interviews indicated the need for one toolbox or platform in which all learning tools and resources (dictionaries, videos, chatting rooms, bolls, games, quizzes, drawings, and other tools) can be saved. Trainees commented that shooting more videos at the company worksites with employees doing real tasks and having them on the iBooks rather than getting general or irreverent videos from YouTube would be useful. This would make the trainees less confused and less distracted about the content they are studying in relation with the actual tasks and duties that they will perform at the worksites in the future. Finally, involving trainees in shooting such videos has the potential to increase their motivation and focus on the activities.

Device Monitoring Applications

Another technique that helps instructors to control distractions is through *device monitoring applications* which can lock trainees from using social media and other non-standard applications and websites (Figure 2). An instructor from the Academic Section elaborated on this:

In addition to walking around, I am currently using a fantastic App. called 'Classroom' to control my trainees' gadgets. I can see all of my students' iPad screens at all times. If I see something that I do not want to see, I just touch a button and block it.

Figure 2 shows that this application provides many functions which enable the instructors to focus on teaching and trainees to focus on learning. These include but are not limited to:

- Identifying offline trainees;
- Starting, focusing, or pausing trainees' work; and
- Monitoring what trainees see with Screen View features.

Figure 2. Mobile Monitoring Applications

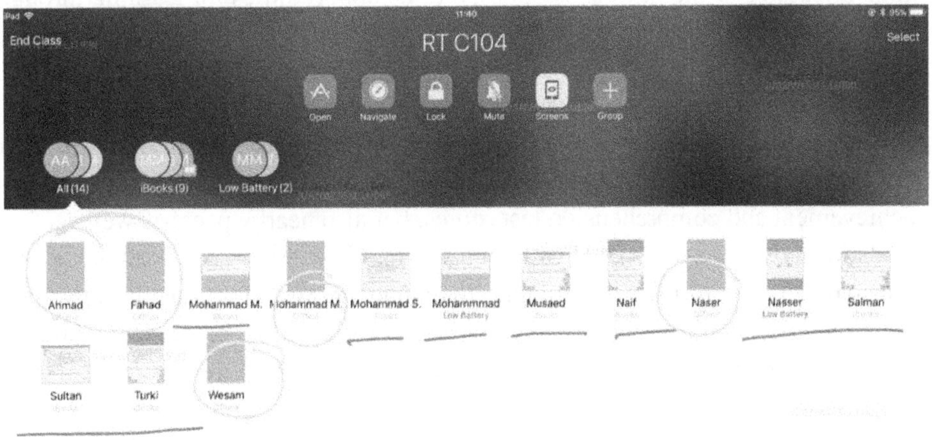

Similarly, Henderson and Yeow (2012) argued that installing monitoring software on learners' mobile devices "allows teachers to have more control over their students to ensure they are staying on task and also not viewing content which they should not be" (p. 81).

However, such applications have been reported by the senior instructors and program coordinators as requiring continuous upgrades which sometimes require upgraded features of the devices and the infrastructure to ensure constant device connectivity. This requires additional administrative work and monitoring from both instructors and senior instructors.

Learners' Self-Monitoring

Finally, *trainees' self-monitoring*, which originates from trainees' sense of commitment and responsibility for managing their learning and completing their training program, as well as understanding that they still can visit all social media and non-standard applications during their free time. A trainee said: "If I watch movies during the class, of course the teacher will know and catch me. Moreover, we know that everything in the company is trackable. It is our responsibility to learn and respect the company's rules".

This approach may bring the idea of *student voice programs* on the table. Toshalis and Nakkula (2012) recommended that *student voice programs* which demonstrate a commitment to the facilitation of student agency and to the creation of policies, practices, and programs that revolve around the students' interests and need be adopted.

These three monitoring techniques have been reported as effective and helpful in minimizing classroom issues and keeping trainees focused on their learning. Arguably therefore, program administrators and staff development experts may need to consider these three methods when training novice instructors on the dynamics and requirements of running M-Learning classes.

SOLUTIONS AND RECOMMENDATIONS

Engagement with non-standard applications and social media as well as multi-tasking at M-Learning classes distracts trainees' attention from the main objectives of the teaching and learning experience. Several studies reported similar findings. Barker, Krull, and Mallinson (2005), for example, found that learners are often surrounded by distractions coming from the portable, smart devices at M-Learning environments. Shannon (2016) concluded that "learners may be motivated by an association with the social and entertainment features of the device, as opposed to its opportunities for learning through portability" (p. 296). Finally, several researchers concluded that multi-tasking and engagement with distractions during academic attempts correlate negatively with student learning, performance, and achievement (Alkahtani et al., 2016; Fox, Rosen, and Crawford, 2009; Fried, 2008; Kirschner and Karpinski, 2010; Lee, Lin, and Robertson, 2012: Mingyong, 2015). Likewise, Pedro, de Oliveira Barbosa, and das Neves Santos (2018) reported that multi-tasking behaviours with media devices have the potential to affect not only users' achievement and comprehension test scores, but also nearby peers as well.

All these detrimental effects associated with multitasking - affecting not only students who willingly multitask but also those nearby - raise a significant challenge for instructors: can the advantages brought about by the inclusion of mobile devices in a classroom setting still be harnessed, while avoiding the potential for distraction they may pose, and how? (Pedro, et al., 2018, p. 10)

However, since mobile devices have become an indispensable tool, facilitating research, communication with instructors and peers, and saving considerable time so enabling greater achievement, they cannot be dismissed as mere toys or distractions. Heinrich (2011) elaborates that while mobile devices "bring with them technical and management issues, these are far outweighed by increased student motivation, progress and collaboration" (p. 50). This perspective supports the findings of this study to turn *learning distractions* into *learning attractions* at M-Learning environments. Fang (2009) argued that these types of *'distractions'* are actually opportunities for change in the classroom:

With many of the world's best professors sharing their video lectures through educational portals..., students have access to the best lectures online in many subject areas. These might be the real "distractors" for professors if they do not reform their teaching. (Fang, 2009, p. 5)

On the other hand, existing research supports the finding that multi-tasking could be for the benefit of the trainees as it may help them to increase their focus in completing the activities and tasks in order to obtain further opportunities on their preferred applications and websites. For example, according to Alkahtani et al. (2016), "multi-tasking is preferred due to the pressures of increased efficiency today. The reason is due to the concept of multi-tasking, which is finishing more within a short period of time" (p. 1006). Similarly, other researchers argued that moving back and forth between applications and activities may provide *'mental breaks'* which have the potential to increase focus. Weslake and Christian (2015) argued that "these brain breaks may or may not involve movement and generally take the form of a learning game, or similar activity" (p. 3). Nevertheless, the counter argument is that people are fatiguing -not refreshing- themselves with the excessive engagement with technologies and multi-tasking. Richtel (2010) argued that "when people keep their brains busy with digital input, they are forfeiting downtime that could allow them to better learn and remember information or come up with new ideas" (p. 1).

However, to reinforce the opportunities in M-Learning environments by controlling learning distractions and turning them into learning attractions, greater efforts need to be invested by curriculum designers, policymakers, instructors, and administrators. The followings are some recommendations that can guide the theory and practice in this respect:

1. The learning content should be digitally designed with rich, interactive, and appealing materials that are more likely to keep the learners motivated and focused on the lesson at hand. Learners tend to leave the prescribed content when they are either bored or feel unaccomplished.
2. Various types of supplementary resources that can enrich the lessons and make them easier to learn should be provided. However, they should be provided in one toolbox or platform in which all learning resources (such as dictionaries, videos, chatting rooms, bolls, quizzes, and other learning-oriented tools) could be saved. This has the potential to facilitate searching through too much information; thus, decreasing or eliminating information overload and learners' distraction.
3. Exercises and activities on the digital content have to be time-based, bound to be completed at a specific frame of time. They should be designed in a way that builds on a scale of difficulty. If an activity is completed in less time than expected, a more challenging task should be given. This may enable learners to pace themselves well on the completing the activities, increase their engagement with the tasks, and decrease or eliminate the feelings of boredom which result in their deviation to the non-standard applications and websites.
4. Sufficient company-specific videos that explain the organization's unique processes should be created and shared on one handy platform. In this respect, program designers and practitioners should also provide room for the learners to develop personalized digital materials and encourage

them to share their products on a user-friendly platform, utilizing effective delivery and assessment methods. This may play a positive role in decreasing trainees' confusion and distraction and, also, increasing their motivation to learning and participation.

5. Professional development and teacher training programs should improve instructors' ability to orchestrate the lessons and adopt effective teaching and monitoring techniques at M-Learning classes. There should be more focus on the emerging roles of instructors at the digital environment such as the instructor as a monitor to learners' devices, as media selector, and a collector of effective digital learning materials. Instructors have to be equipped with the right knowledge and skills of how to guide learners' selection of learning tools and applications, and yet remove distractors in a way that ensures maximum and effective utilization of mobile devices. They also need to know which applications and resources can make their teaching more entertaining to their trainees.
6. Increasing instructors' and learners' awareness about the common technical issues that may arise at M-Learning environments and potential solutions is essential. Learning more about those technical issues and the possible techniques of fixing them has the potential to decrease distraction that may result from them.
7. Effective device control software and techniques which can lock trainees from using social media and other non-standard applications and websites should be availed at M-Learning environments. Installing monitoring software on learners' devices allows for more control over them to ensure that the learners are staying on task and to eliminate their access to distractors.
8. Student Voice Programs which demonstrate a commitment to the facilitation of student agency and to the creation of policies, practices, and programs that revolve around the students' interests need be adopted. Involving learners more through such programs has the potential to increase their awareness about self-monitoring and their personal commitment and responsibility for managing their learning and completing their training programs successfully.

These recommendations are hoped to be effective and helpful in minimizing classroom distractions and keeping trainees focused on their learning at the context of this study.

FUTURE RESEARCH DIRECTIONS

This study is focused on an issue which has been characterized as a major shortcoming of mobile learning; namely distraction, as well as some possible solutions to it. In this respect, the findings of this study have the potential to help the field of technology enhanced learning and the use of information and communication technologies (ICTs) in education. More specifically, this study can offer some guidance to the researchers, professionals, digital content designers, instructors, and program policymakers who want to improve their understanding of the issue of distraction at M-Learning environments.

In light of this, one strength of this study is its context. Being conducted in a rich oil company which avails the most up-to-date technologies for each trainee and instructor, specialized digital content for its specific operations, outstanding infrastructure, and ongoing technical support makes this context ideal for research on the features of M-Learning environments. Hence, it would be interesting to see if the results of this research would be similar at other environments which offer different businesses, other than the oil and petro-chemical business. Moreover, it would be interesting to see if research on learners of other age groups would generate similar results. Finally, other potentially fruitful areas for further research that emerged from the study are:

- Methods of controlling learning distractions and turning them into learning attractions.
- Methods of effective mobile device control techniques and applications.

CONCLUSION

This research contributes to the academic discussion on the different types and sources of distraction and multi-tasking at M-Learning environments and the potential solutions to control them (Fox et al., 2009; Fried, 2008; Kirschner & Karpinski, 2010; Lee et al., 2012; Mingyong, 2015). It showed that distraction in M-Learning environments may appear due to various reasons which include learner's tendency to switch to social media and non-standard applications (Gikas & Grant, 2013), overwhelming learners with too much information and abundant resources (Chen et al., 2008), lack of standardization in learning aids and resources which have conflicting information, and lack of effective engagement with the learning materials. It has also been discussed that distraction may mean something else by learners. They may find more interesting 'learning attractions' (more motivating tutors or learning materials) somewhere online away from the prescribed lessons. Hence, benefiting from the extra resources that mobile technologies provide and turning them to *learning attractions* rather than *distractions* requires integrated actions from M-Learning stakeholders, especially policymakers. Also, while digital content designers and developers need to create and develop relevant appealing resources and collect them accessible on one handy platform, instructors need to use pedagogy and curriculum to integrate the technology effectively into learning and encourage trainees more to participate in the creation of policies, practices, and extra digital resources.

Also, it has been argued that navigating through the device applications and websites may be used as a means of availing mental breaks that can refresh learners' minds or abolish feelings of boredom and demotivation, but this needs careful design in order to avoid the negative implications of multi-tasking and exposure to fragmented knowledge. Finally, three methods of controlling negative aspects of distraction have been identified: the instructor as a monitor, device monitoring applications, and trainee self-monitoring (Fang, 2009; Henderson & Yeow, 2012; Toshalis & Nakkula, 2012).

Hence, the researcher suggests that more intensive research on distraction at M-Learning environments need to be conducted to explore possibilities of controlling *distractions* and turning them to real effective learning *attractions* and to investigate of the potentially effective device control methods and techniques.

REFERENCES

Abdelaziz, A. (2018). *Developing Employability and Job-Related Skills at Mobile Learning Environments: a case study at an industrial training centre*. Lancaster: Lancaster University.

Alkahtani, M., Ahmad, A., Darmoul, S., Samman, S., Al-zabidi, A., & Matraf, K. B. (2016). Multitasking Trends and Impact on Education: A Literature Review. *World Academy of Science. Engineering and Technology International Journal of Educational and Pedagogical Sciences, 10*(3), 1006–1012.

Ary, D., Jacobs, L., & Razavieh, A. (2010). *Introduction to research in education*. New York: Holt, Rinehart and Winston.

Ashworth, P., & Lucas, U. (2000). Achieving Empathy and Engagement: A practical approach to the design, conduct and reporting of phenomenographic research. *Studies in Higher Education*, *25*(3), 295–308. doi:10.1080/713696153

Barker, A., Krull, G., & Mallinson, B. (2005). A proposed theoretical model for m-learning adoption in developing countries. Proceedings of mLearn, 2005(4), 1-10.

Bates, A. W. (2019). *Teaching in a Digital Age – Second Edition*. Vancouver: Tony Bates Associates Ltd. Retrieved 23 January 2019 from https://pressbooks.bccampus.ca/teachinginadigitalagev2/

Baxter, P., & Jack, S. (2008). Qualitative Case Study Methodology: Study Design and Implementation for Novice Researchers. *Qualitative Report*, *13*(4), 544–559. Retrieved from https://nsuworks.nova.edu/tqr/vol13/iss4/2

Bower, M., Sturman, D., & Alvarez, V. (2016). Perceived utility and feasibility of wearable technologies in higher education. *Mobile Learning Futures–Sustaining Quality Research and Practice in Mobile Learning, 15th World Conference on Mobile and Contextual Learning, mLearn 2016 Sydney, Australia, October 24-26, 2016 Proceedings.*

Burden, K., & Kearney, M. (2016). Conceptualising authentic mobile learning. In D. Churchill, J. Lu, T. Chiu, & B. Fox (Eds.), *Mobile learning design: Theories and application* (pp. 27–42). Singapore: Springer. doi:10.1007/978-981-10-0027-0_2

Chen, N., & Hsieh, S., & Kinshuk. (2008). Effects of Short-Term Memory and Content Representation Type on Mobile Language Learning. *Language Learning & Technology*, *12*(3), 93–113.

Clarke, B., & Svanaes, S. (2014). *Tablets for Schools: An Updated Literature Review on the Use of Tablets in Education*. Retrieved 16 Apr. 2015 from: http://www.e-learningfoundation.com/Websites/elearningfoundation/images/PDF%20Documents/T4S-Use-of-Tablets-in-Education.pdf

Cohen, L., Manion, L., & Morrison, K. (2007). *Research Methods in Education* (6th ed.). London: Routledge. doi:10.4324/9780203029053

Crompton, H. (2013). A Historical overview of m-Learning: Toward Learner-Centered Education. In Z. Berge & L. Muilenburg (Eds.), *Handbook of mobile learning*. New York: Routledge.

Crompton, H., Burke, D., Gregory, K. H., & Gräbe, C. (2016). The use of mobile learning in science: A systematic review. *Journal of Science Education and Technology*, *25*(2), 149–160. doi:10.100710956-015-9597-x

Fang, B. (2009). From distraction to engagement: Wireless devices in the classroom. *EDUCAUSE Quarterly*, *32*(4), 4–9.

Fereday, J., & Muir-Cochrane, E. (2006). Demonstrating rigor using thematic analysis: A hybrid approach of inductive and deductive coding and theme development. *International Journal of Qualitative Methods*, *5*(1), 80–92. doi:10.1177/160940690600500107

Fox, A. B., Rosen, J., & Crawford, M. (2009). Distractions, distractions: Does instant messaging affect college students' performance on a concurrent reading comprehension task? *Cyberpsychology & Behavior, 12*(1), 51–53. doi:10.1089/cpb.2008.0107 PMID:19006461

Fried, C. B. (2008). In-class laptop use and its effects on student learning. *Computers & Education, 50*(3), 906–914. doi:10.1016/j.compedu.2006.09.006

Gale, N. K., Heath, G., Cameron, E., Rashid, S., & Redwood, S. (2013). Using the framework method for the analysis of qualitative data in multi-disciplinary health research. *BMC Medical Research Methodology, 13*(1), 117. doi:10.1186/1471-2288-13-117 PMID:24047204

Gallegos, C., & Nakashima, H. (2018). Mobile Devices: A Distraction, or a Useful Tool to Engage Nursing Students? *The Journal of Nursing Education, 57*(3), 170–173. doi:10.3928/01484834-20180221-09 PMID:29505077

Gikas, J., & Grant, M. M. (2013). Mobile computing devices in higher education: Student perspectives on learning with cellphones, smartphones & social media. *Internet and Higher Education, 19*, 18–26. doi:10.1016/j.iheduc.2013.06.002

Guba, E. (1981). Criteria for assessing the trustworthiness of naturalistic inquiries. *Educational Resources Information Center Annual Review Paper, 29*, 75–91.

Guest, G., Bunce, A., & Johnson, L. (2006). How Many Interviews Are Enough? An Experiment with Data Saturation and Variability. *Field Methods, 18*(1), 59–82. doi:10.1177/1525822X05279903

Hancock, D. R., & Algozzine, B. (2016). *Doing case study research: A practical guide for beginning researchers*. New York, NY: Teachers College Press.

Harman, B. A., & Sato, T. (2011). Cell phone use and grade point average among undergraduate university students. *College Student Journal, 45*(3), 544–550.

Heinrich, P. (2011). The iPad as a tool for education: A study of the introduction of iPads at Longfield AcademyNottingham: NAACE: The ICT Association.

Henderson, S., & Yeow, J. (2012). iPad in Education: A Case Study of iPad Adoption and Use in a Primary School. *45th Hawaii International Conference on System Science (HICSS)*, 78–87. 10.1109/HICSS.2012.390

Hoffmann, M. (2017). An exploratory study: Mobile device use for academics. *Research in Social Sciences and Technology, 2*(1).

Jalil, J., & Sabir, S. (2019). Mobile Phone Usage and Distraction in Learning Sessions. *Pakistan Armed Forces Medical Journal, 69*(1), 54–59.

Jawaid, M., & Aly, S. M. (2014). Learning environment in undergraduate institutes in Pakistan: Determining factors and suggestions. *Journal of Postgraduate Medical Institute (Peshawar-Pakistan), 28*(3).

Junco, R. (2012). Too much face and not enough books: The relationship between multiple indices of Facebook use and academic performance. *Computers in Human Behavior, 28*(1), 187–198. doi:10.1016/j.chb.2011.08.026

Kaalberg, K. (2014). *Enhancing Teaching and Learning Through iPad Integration In*. Las Vegas: Department of Teaching and Learning, College of Education, The Graduate College, University of Nevada.

Kirschner, P. A, & Karpinski, A. C. A. (2010). Facebook® and academic performance. *Computers in Human Behavior, 26*(6), 1237-1245. doi:10.1016/j.chb.2010.03.024

Koole, M., & Ally, M. (2006). Framework for the Rational Analysis of Mobile Education (FRAME) Model: Revising the ABCs of Educational Practices. *International Conference on Networking, International Conference on Systems and International Conference on Mobile Communications and Learning Technologies (ICNICONSMCL'06)*, 216. Available in: https://auspace.athabascau.ca/bitstream/2149/612/1/01628461.pdf

Kucirkova, N., Messer, D., Sheehy, K., & Panadero, C. (2014). Children's Engagement with Educational iPad Apps: Insights from a Spanish Classroom. *Computers & Education, 71*, 175–184. doi:10.1016/j.compedu.2013.10.003

Lang, J. (2017). *The Distracted Class*. Retrieved November 10, 2017, From: http://www.chronicle.com/article/The-Distracted-Classroom/239446

Laurillard, D., & Pachler, N. (2007). Pedagogical forms of mobile learning: framing research questions. In N. Pachler (Ed.), *Mobile learning: towards a research agenda* (pp. 33–54). London: WLE Centre, IOE.

Lee, J., Lin, L., & Robertson, T. (2012). The impact of media multitasking on learning. *Learning, Media and Technology, 37*(1), 94–104. doi:10.1080/17439884.2010.537664

Lin, H. Y., Chen, C. Y., & Chen, W. C. (2008). Scaffolding m-Learning approach of automotive practice courses in senior vocational high school. In *Frontiers in Education Conference, 2008. FIE 2008. 38th Annual* (pp. F1H-12). IEEE.

Lincoln, Y. S., & Guba, E. A. (1985). *Naturalistic inquiry*. Beverly Hills, CA: Sage. doi:10.1016/0147-1767(85)90062-8

Mingyong, Z. (2015). Investigation into the use of mobile technology in English teaching and learning in institutes of higher vocational education in Hubei province in China. In *Futuristic Trends on Computational Analysis and Knowledge Management (ABLAZE), 2015 International Conference on* (pp. 505-509). IEEE. 10.1109/ABLAZE.2015.7155037

MoLeNet. (2007). *What is the mobile learning?* Retrieved March 23, 2017, from: http://www.molenet.org.uk/about.html

Mullen, C. (2014). *iPad iPedagogy: A study of teacher perceptions on the impact of the iPad on teaching and assessment practices at a third level college in the United Arab Emirates* (MEd dissertation). The British University in Dubai.

Nedungadi, P., & Raman, R. (2012). A new approach to personalization: Integrating e-learning and m-learning. *Educational Technology Research and Development, 60*(4), 659–678. doi:10.100711423-012-9250-9

Ouyang, J. R., & Stanley, N. (2014). Theories and research in educational technology and distance learning instruction through Blackboard. *Universal Journal of Educational Research, 2*(2), 161–172. doi:10.13189/ujer.2014.020208

Pedro, L. F. M. G., & de Oliveira Barbosa, C. M. M. (2018). A critical review of mobile learning integration in formal educational contexts. *International Journal of Educational Technology in Higher Education, 15*(1), 10. doi:10.118641239-018-0091-4

Peter, J. B., & Bijik, A. H. (2018). Effect of Technology Distraction on Learning among Students in Higher Institutions in Central Nigeria. *Technology, 14*, 16.

Richtel, M. (2010). Digital devices deprive brain of needed downtime. *New York Times, 24*(8), 1-4.

Ricky, Y. K. N., & Rechell, Y. S. L. (2015, December). Using mobile and flexible technologies to enable, engage and enhance learning in Vocational Education and Training (VET). In *Teaching, Assessment, and Learning for Engineering (TALE), 2015 IEEE International Conference on* (pp. 96-101). IEEE.

Rodríguez, A. I., Riaza, B. G., & Gómez, M. C. S. (2017). Collaborative learning and mobile devices: An educational experience in Primary Education. *Computers in Human Behavior, 72*, 664–677. doi:10.1016/j.chb.2016.07.019

Russell, C., Gregory, D., Ploeg, J., DiCenso, A., & Guyatt, G. (2005). Qualitative research. In A. DiCenso, G. Guyatt, & D. Ciliska (Eds.), *Evidence-based nursing: A guide to clinical practice* (pp. 120–135). St. Louis, MO: Elsevier Mosby.

Serah, N. (2014). Challenges Facing Effective Information and Communications Technology (Ict) Implementation In Selected Public Secondary Schools In Nakuru North District Nakuru County. Kenyatta University, The School Of Business.

Shannon, J. (2016). M-learning: Effectiveness, Unknowns and Opportunities. *International Journal of Scientific Development and Research, 1*(9), 292–300.

Shih, R. C. (2011). Can Web 2.0 technology assist college students in learning English writing? Integrating Facebook and peer assessment with blended learning. *Australasian Journal of Educational Technology, 27*(5), 829–845. doi:10.14742/ajet.934

Sung, Y., Chang, K., & Yang, J. (2015). How Effective are Mobile Devices for Language Learning? A Meta-Analysis. *Educational Research Review, 16*, 68–84. doi:10.1016/j.edurev.2015.09.001

Tella, S. (2003). M-learning — Cybertextual travelling or a herald of post-modern, education. In H. Iahti & P. Seppälä (Eds.), *Mobile learning* (pp. 7–21). Helsinki, Finland: IT Press.

The Glossary of Education Reform. (2013). *Learning Environment*. Retrieved From: https://www.edglossary.org/learning-environment/

Thomas, D. R. (2006). A general inductive approach for analyzing qualitative evaluation data. *The American Journal of Evaluation, 27*(2), 237–246. doi:10.1177/1098214005283748

Toshalis, E., & Nakkula, M. J. (2012). Motivation, engagement, and student voice. *Education Digest, 78*(1), 29.

Traxler, J. (2010). Distance education and mobile learning: Catching up, taking stock. *Distance Education, 31*(2), 129–138. doi:10.1080/01587919.2010.503362

Weslake, A., & Christian, B. J. (2015). Brain Breaks: Help or Hindrance? *TEACH COLLECTION of Christian Education, 1*(1), 4.

Wong, L.-H. (2015). A Brief History of Mobile Seamless Learning. In L.-H. Wong, M. Milrad, & M. Specht (Eds.), *Seamless Learning in the Age of Mobile Connectivity* (pp. 3–40). Springer. doi:10.1007/978-981-287-113-8_1

ADDITIONAL READING

Chen, Q., & Yan, Z. (2016). Does multitasking with mobile phones affect learning? A review. *Computers in Human Behavior, 54*, 34–42. doi:10.1016/j.chb.2015.07.047

Gallegos, C., & Nakashima, H. (2018). Mobile Devices: A Distraction, or a Useful Tool to Engage Nursing Students? *The Journal of Nursing Education, 57*(3), 170–173. doi:10.3928/01484834-20180221-09 PMID:29505077

Green, M. (2019). Smartphones, Distraction Narratives, and Flexible Pedagogies: Students' Mobile Technology Practices in Networked Writing Classrooms. *Computers and Composition, 52*, 91–106. doi:10.1016/j.compcom.2019.01.009

Jalil, J., & Sabir, S. (2019). Mobile Phone Usage and Distraction in Learning Sessions. *Pakistan Armed Forces Medical Journal, 69*(1), 54–59.

Laxman, K., & Holt, C. (2017). Bring Your Own Device or Bring Your Own Distraction. *International Journal on E-Learning, 16*(3), 245–263.

Mendoza, J. S., Pody, B. C., Lee, S., Kim, M., & McDonough, I. M. (2018). The effect of cellphones on attention and learning: The influences of time, distraction, and nomophobia. *Computers in Human Behavior, 86*, 52–60. doi:10.1016/j.chb.2018.04.027

Ozer, O., & Kılıç, F. (2018). The effect of mobile-assisted language learning environment on EFL Students' academic achievement, cognitive load and acceptance of mobile learning tools. *Eurasia Journal of Mathematics, Science and Technology Education, 14*(7), 2915–2928. doi:10.29333/ejmste/90992

Shafriri, Y., & Levy, D. (2018). Uniqueness Profile of Mobile Applications for Learning. In *International Conference on Learning and Collaboration Technologies* (pp. 376-390). Springer. 10.1007/978-3-319-91152-6_29

Wilkinson, K., & Barter, P. (2016). Do mobile learning devices enhance learning in higher education anatomy classrooms? *Journal of Pedagogic Development, 6*(1), 14–23.

KEY TERMS AND DEFINITIONS

Device Control Software: A special software or application that can control the learners' devices and can lock the learners from using social media and other non-standard applications and websites.

Digital Content: Formal, standard, or prescribed learning content designed with interactive multimedia.

Learning Attractions: Learners' deviation from learning from the formal or standard content to non-standard applications and websites which support the lesson objectives.

Learning Distractions: Learners' deviation from learning from the formal or standard content and away from the lesson objectives to the non-standard applications and websites.

Learning Environment: The medium where learning and teaching take place. It is the sum of the internal and external circumstances and influences surrounding and affecting a person's learning.

Mobile Learning: A type of learning that allows learners, as individuals or groups, to gain knowledge, ideas, skills, or concepts not already known or recognised from formal or informal contents using mobile technologies at anytime and anywhere.

Multi-Tasking: Dealing with more than one task, application, or program at the same time.

Chapter 12
Mobile Technologies Course Design:
The Use of ICT Skills, Attitudes, and Self-Efficacy in EFL Instructors

Ozlem Zengin
https://orcid.org/0000-0002-7464-6301
Sabancı University, Turkey

ABSTRACT

Mobile learning has the potential to increase the opportunities to make teaching and learning available beyond the traditional classroom. The main aim of this study was to develop a mobile technologies course delivered online and explore the effects of this online course designed on mobile technologies on the use of ICT skills, attitudes, and views of EFL instructors. While employing mixed methodology, explanatory sequential research design was applied. In this study, participants were selected through convenient sampling and the data were collated through a questionnaire used as pre- and post-tests, followed by semi-structured interviews and class observations. The results of this study indicated that the online training course on mobile technologies had a positive impact on the use of ICT skills and EFL teachers' views in general. Further, attending the mobile technologies course delivered online was very beneficial and effective for the instructors in that it helped them to develop their skills on the use of mobile technologies in English language teaching.

INTRODUCTION

Technological advances have affected almost every part of our daily lives, and in education they have tremendously affected teaching and learning. In the last few decades, some teachers have been incorporating technology into teaching to add variety to their teaching approaches and help students increase their motivation. Considering the effects of the use of technological devices in education, Mobile-Assisted Language Learning (MALL) has emerged as a growing trend. MALL encourages the idea that learning

DOI: 10.4018/978-1-7998-3062-7.ch012

may be enhanced by using mobile devices and presents the systematic way of how to utilize mobile learning. Mobile learning suggests the mode of learning by using mobile devices like smart phones, and any other portable devices. Mobile learning may also make teaching and learning available beyond the traditional classroom. Li (2008) stated that "… it focuses on the mobility of the learning practice, and emphasizes the interaction between the learner and the learning content, peers or the instructors which can improve effectiveness, flexibility and convenience of learning" (p.694). Hence, learning enhanced through mobile devices has become a trend in the field of digital learning (Jeng, Wu, Huang, Tan & Yang, 2010).

However, as mobile technologies continue to evolve and monumentally shape the nature of teaching and learning, teachers struggle to incorporate technologies and electronic resources into pedagogically sound activities (Recker et al., 2005; Snyder, Dillow, & Hoffman, 2007; Wells, & Lewis, 2006).

Considering the needs of the learners in the 21st century, the integration of technology has become an indispensable part of teaching and learning process, leading to technology enhanced learning and teaching. However, educators, leaders, and policy makers face challenges improving teacher quality and strengthening the teaching profession to meet the needs of all 21st century learners as teachers are not sufficiently prepared for their students who are digital literate and digital native (Aydin, 2013; Hubbard, 2008; Wiebe & Kabata, 2010).

In-service training of the language teachers and keeping up with recent developments in education are of utmost importance in Turkey; thus, many projects including the use of effective technologies have been implemented in schools. One of the recent projects by the government is the FATIH Project, through which the Ministry of National Education (MoNE) aims to implement the effective integration of technology at schools. Forty-two thousand schools were aimed to be equipped with good technological infrastructure and tablets by the end of 2014. However, the huge investments in the purchase of the technological equipment are not observed in the training of the teachers to use these technologies. Hence, some problems have risen in terms of finding the teachers who are qualified enough to teach with technology as training element from this project was missing and this has negatively affected the successful implementation.

The integration of technology in education has motivated many researchers around the world to investigate its effectiveness and to explore various aspects of Information Communication Technology (ICT) in education. This chapter will be referring to the studies about teacher training in terms of technology considering the scope of this study. According to Moersch (as cited in Ertmer, 2003), teachers who have finished any technology courses are still unable to create small or whole group activities using technology meaningfully. Although the Higher Education Council (HEC) suggests three or more credit hours of technology instruction, many faculties of education feel technology use is not modeled effectively to put this into action. Thus, the present study aimed to provide a solution through offering a technology integration model for English Language Teachers, which could be used as an in-service course package for English as a foreign language (EFL) teachers. An online training course was designed through hands-on practices and experiential learning for practicing instructors to be able to equip them with sufficient knowledge on the use of educational technology and in particular on the use of mobile technologies while teaching English.

The main aim of this study was to develop an online course for mobile technologies and explore the effects of this online course designed on mobile technologies on the use of ICT skills, attitudes and EFL instructors' views. The subsidiary aims of the study were to train EFL instructors on mobile technologies in language teaching and make them feel comfortable while using different mobile applications.

Some studies on technology integration in teacher education programs in other fields were documented. However, the number of studies on the technology integration in English Language Teacher training programs is limited, and most of them are related to the use of some web tools, excluding the mobile applications used in teaching. Furthermore, 21st century skills require teachers to apply technological tools in their teaching to meet students' needs better (ISTE, 2008). This study also aimed to inform English language teachers who are already working in the field of ICT in ELT. Therefore, it intends to ask the following research questions:

1. What are the needs of EFL instructors related to use of Internet, computer and mobile technologies in teaching?
2. Is there a significant difference in acceptance of mobile technologies of EFL instructors before and after taking the online course on mobile technologies?
3. Is there a significant difference in mobile technologies self-efficacy of EFL instructors before and after taking the online course on mobile technologies?
4. Is there a significant difference in the attitudes of EFL instructors towards incorporating mobile learning into teaching before and after taking the online course on mobile technologies?
5. Is there a significant difference in the perceptions related to the usefulness and ease of use of mobile learning of EFL instructors before and after taking the online course on mobile technologies?
6. Is there a significant difference in the perceptions related to the effect of mobile learning on student engagement in learning of EFL instructors before and after taking the online course on mobile technologies?
7. To what extent do EFL instructors use the target mobile applications in teaching after the completion of the online course?
8. What are the EFL instructors' views related to the characteristics of the mobile technologies course they attended?

BACKGROUND

ICT in Foreign Language Education

As ICTs have become indispensable, educators may use them to enrich learning processes. By using videos or any free software, English teachers may aim to cater for learners' needs more through different learning technologies. Some researchers (e.g., Carmen et al., 2003; Hampel, 2006) claim that using ICTs has a positive effect on the foreign language teaching and learning process. ICT tools have eliminated the time and space limitation (Samuel & Bakar, 2006) and classroom interaction has gone beyond the time and space constraints (Frayer, 1997, cited in Samuel & Bakar, 2006). According to Carmen et al. (2003), the use of technological tools in teaching and learning could enhance students' competencies. To this end, Gimbert and Cristol (2004) put forward that instruction enhanced through technology resulted in increased student learning. However, only a limited number of students have a chance to receive education from teachers integrating technology into their teaching processes.

Learning and Teaching in the 21st Century

Today technology plays a leading role affecting students' learning process. For example, learning could take place beyond the classroom. Thanks to the affordances of technology (Hampel, 2006), teachers can implement innovative teaching strategies and designing interesting activities (Duhaney, 2000). The 21st century students are called 'Generation Z' who effortlessly update the information through technology (Oral, 2013). They are able to use the Internet easily and look for information on the Internet by using any mobile devices. With the help of technology, students are provided with more collaborative work as well. OECD (2010) claims that technology enables access to the higher-order skills, which are also referred as the 21st century skills. Such skills are necessary to be acquired by the students now to survive in this digital era.

Considering the global economy continues to develop in today's world, workers are expected to change their jobs at least seven times in their work life (OECD, 2019). Thus, employees in the 21st century are required to have science and mathematics skills, creativity, fluency in information and communication technologies, and the ability to solve complex problems, which are highly important for local, national, and global level citizenship (Dede, 2010). The 21st century education aims to prepare students for a world where many cognitive tasks are performed by computers through expert thinking and complex communications (Dede, 2010). As a result of this, a need has arisen to help students gain 21st century skills which are creativity, critical thinking, communication, collaboration and digital literacy.

The 21st century is rather different than the 20th one in terms of the skills people need to acquire work, citizenship, and self-actualization. Regarding social cohesion, Digital Competency is a necessary component of the educational system to ensure the individual development and participation in 21st century (Martín & Tyner, 2012; OECD, 2011). In this respect, teachers could have the ability to train citizens on the use of ICT in their individual and social development (European Commission, 2012, 2013 and 2014; OECD, 2012; Sánchez-Antolin, Ramos & Sánchez Santamaría, 2014). To this end, all curricula should be updated in terms of their objectives and assessments so that students could attain those skills. In order to prepare students to face the challenges of 21st century, teachers should have the technological knowledge and experience on using technology effectively, which is arguably compulsory in the 21st century. Teaching in the 21st century demands teachers to design interesting and interactive activities for students to address students' needs and abilities better so that students could be active learners (ISTE, 2008). To this end, teachers are expected to use various mobile technologies to maximize student learning and teaching process.

Studies on ICT into Teacher Education

The research on the use of technology in learning and teaching processes has gained a paramount importance in the field of education and teacher-related issues are regarded as key components to use technology successfully in educational context. (Cochran- Smith, 2004; Fullan, 993; Gillingham & Topper, 1999; Sarbib, 2002; Townsend & Bates, 2007).

Veen (1993) conducted a study on teachers' beliefs about the adoption of ICT. The results highlighted that content, pedagogy and teachers' competence in ICT use are key determinants on to what extent they use ICT in their teaching. This result has also been affirmed by other studies as teachers' competence and attitudes are highly important when they are to use technology effectively (Farenga & Joyce, 2001; Means, 1994; Veen, 1993).

In the USA, the Ministry of Education carried out a project called 'Preparing Tomorrow's Teachers to Use Technology', which aimed at improving and enhancing the technology preparation of pre-service teachers. Brush (2003) carried out a study to support this project. For this reason, Arizona State University pre-service teachers were provided with opportunities to develop, implement and evaluate their own instructional activities that utilize technology effectively and appropriately in authentic situations. Pre-service teachers were also given the myriad of tools necessary to integrate technology into teaching and learning activities.

Butler-Pascoe and Wiburg (2003) conducted a study on the need to design a technology-training course to help teachers use technology effectively. The results indicated that they should have the training to integrate technology in their teaching since a professional development program enables teachers to design effective lessons in foreign language teaching through technology.

In his study, Ping (2005) tried to find out pre-service teachers' technology competency and the change of individual attitudes as a result of taking technology- specific courses. He also tried to investigate their perspectives and experiences throughout their teaching preparation experience. He found out that learning to teach with information technology is an idiosyncratic and developmental process situated in multiple individual and social contexts. The use of information technology helped the pre-service and teachers upgrade their content knowledge, and developing the meaning of inclusive education, a sense of identity, collegiality and leadership potential. Technology experiences changed their views of teaching and their own perceptions of themselves as teachers.

Ince (2015) conducted a study on teachers' perceptions on the use of technology. The results showed that most of the teachers think blended learning might affect English language teaching in positive way. Moreover, in Güneş's study (2015), similar results were conveyed. The findings of the study indicated teachers have positive attitudes toward using computer technology in their teaching. The findings of the interview were consistent with the questionnaire data by indicating that teachers use computers for both their personal and educational purposes.

In a study by Baek et al. (2008), the leading factors to encourage teachers to incorporate technology in their teaching were investigated. The results presented such factors as adapting to others' expectations, receiving attention, using technology in terms of basic functions, reducing physical fatigue, class preparation and using technology at advanced level. Açıkalın (2009) did a research to explore the views of pre-service elementary school teachers on the use of Internet. The results indicated a positive tendency on how these teachers regard technology use in class. Aydın (2007) investigated the attitudes of 115 Turkish pre-service EFL teachers towards the Internet. The results provided that most of the participants viewed Internet as a positive tool in educational context as for accessing information. Odabasi (2000) carried out a study on ICT use among faculty members and their perceptions on ICT as regards to its effectiveness. The results highlighted that many faculty members did not know the current applications or web tools to be used in their classes. However, they stated that the use of ICT in class could increase student motivation and help to enhance student learning.

In a study carried out with teachers, Stansberry and Kymes (2007) asked teachers to create e-portfolios for four semesters and then checked the teacher willingness in using e-portfolios for their own teaching. They found that contrary to students' uneasiness at the portfolio, several teachers favored the process stating that technology use could turn the classroom into a dynamic place. In another study, Vallance and Martin (2008) designed a 12-week blended course in Singapore. The discussions of the participants were recorded, and their actions were monitored while they were doing the activities. At the end of the 12-week program, it was seen that the pedagogical beliefs of the participants changed, and they gained better competency to design a course to enhance learning. In another study by Karakaya (2010) who tried to find out teachers' attitudes and perceptions on the use of technology, the results revealed that a great majority of teachers attribute positive remarks for integrating technology in language teaching as they stated the use of technology leads to enhanced learning.

In a study in the USA, Jayachandran (2009) suggested a way to integrate technology into the classroom effectively by examining how two foreign language pre-service teachers use technology while teaching. The findings in this study indicated that the preparation for technology use affects the incorporation of technology into the lessons positively. In another study by Hismanoglu (2012), a technology module was used as a treatment. The results indicated that there was a statistically significant difference between prospective EFL teachers' ICT attitudes before and after ICT- interwoven training, which sheds light on the importance of including more ICT-related courses in the curriculum. On the other hand, Özdemir's study (2013) revealed that the treatment, here it is the online educational technology course on Moodle, did not have a significant impact on the attitudes and self-efficacy of the pre-service teachers about using computer technologies but it had a significant impact on the computer literacy of pre-service teachers towards computers.

MAIN FOCUS OF THE CHAPTER

Research Design

In this study, mixed method research design was used and both qualitative and quantitative data were collected to get in depth information related to designing a Mobile Technologies course. As part of mixed method approach, explanatory sequential research design was applied. To answer the research questions 1, 2, 3, 4, 5 and 6 data were collected through questionnaires. To answer the research questions 7 and 8, data were collected through classroom observations and semi-structured interviews. This study was conducted to a group of instructors that the researcher could access and thus the participants were selected through convenient sampling regarding their teaching experience, age and education background.

Figure 1. Design of the study Adapted from Creswell, 2007

Context

This study was conducted at a private university in the preparatory program in Ankara, Turkey. Students learn English for academic purposes to pursue their academic studies on the condition that they pass the proficiency exam of the university, which is equivalent to CEFR B2 level.

Subjects/Participants of the Study

The participants of the study consisted of the instructors working for the previously mentioned preparatory program. Each instructor held a bachelor's degree in English Language Teaching or related programs, having various levels of experience in language teaching. Most held Certificate in English Language Teaching (ICELT), Certificate in Teaching English to Speakers of Other Languages (CELTA) or Diploma in Teaching English to Speakers of Other Languages (DELTA), which are offered by Cambridge University and indicators of higher level of field-specific qualifications. Moreover, some held Master's and Doctoral degrees while some others were still graduate students at the time of the study (Table 1).

Table 1. Demographic Information about the Participants

Gender	Degree	N
Male	ICELT	1
	DELTA	1
	MA in progress	0
	MA	0
Female	ICELT	3
	DELTA	10
	MA in progress	2
	MA	5

Instruments

To gather the data for this study, a questionnaire entitled *"The Use of Mobile Technologies in Foreign Language Education"* prepared and adapted by the researcher, a classroom observation tool and interview schedule were used.

The Use of Mobile Technologies in Foreign Language Education Questionnaire

First, a questionnaire was mainly adapted from Pollara (2011) and Abu-Al-Aish (2014) developed by the researcher. It aimed to evaluate the acceptance of mobile technologies, self-efficacy regarding mobile technologies, the attitudes of EFL instructors towards incorporating mobile learning into teaching, the perceptions related to the usefulness and ease of use of mobile learning and the perceptions related to the effect of mobile learning on student engagement in learning.

This questionnaire consisted of four parts and 58 items in total. Exploratory Factor Analysis (EFA) was run for part 2 and part 4 of the questionnaire. Each part focused on different aspects. The first part was prepared by the researcher and aimed to conduct a needs analysis for the instructors. The second part was adapted from Mobile Acceptance Questionnaire designed by Abu-Al-Aish (2014). The third part was adapted from the instrument designed by Yasan (2018). The final part was adapted from the questionnaire developed by Pollara (2011). The first part was about teachers' experience on the use of Internet, computer and mobile technologies in teaching. Based on the results of this part of the questionnaire, the online course objectives and the course content were identified and evaluated. The second part was on the acceptance of mobile technologies; third part was about mobile phone self-efficacy and their prior knowledge about the applications used in the study. The fourth part was on the perceptions regarding the usefulness, ease of use of mobile learning and the effect of mobile learning on student engagement in learning. The questionnaire was given to instructors at once without any time interval and they were expected to finish it in 10 minutes as pre or post-tests. The questionnaire was divided into 4 parts: part 1 was used for needs analysis, parts 2, 3 and 4 were used as pre-and-post-test during this study.

This questionnaire was reviewed by two experts in English language teaching and materials design, two experts in the use of mobile technologies in teaching and two English instructors in terms of the face validity and clarity. Although the reliability and validity measurements were obtained beforehand, this instrument was checked in terms of validity and reliability and were found satisfactory, EFA was run by the researcher. A pilot study was conducted to check validity and reliability of the questionnaire. Accordingly, EFA was performed through SPSS 22 to find out the factor structures for part 2 and part 4, which revealed four factor- structure among all the items.

Finally, to the internal consistency for part 2 and part 4 of the questionnaire, Cronbach's alpha coefficients were calculated. The Cronbach's alpha coefficients for part 2 were .91 for Performance Expectancy factor, .94 for Effort Expectancy factor, .92 for Personal Innovativeness factor and .93 for Behavioral Intention factor. The Cronbach's alpha coefficients for part 4 were .93 for Perceptions on student engagement factor, .94 for Perceptions on usefulness factor, .91 for Perceptions on ease of use factor and .92 for Attitudes towards incorporating mobile learning into teaching factor. In addition to that, each item had high correlation with the corresponding factor, indicating the internal consistency of the scale in terms of the criterion suggested by Nunnanly (1978) as of .70.

Classroom Observation Tool

To investigate to the extent which EFL instructors use the target applications in their teaching, a classroom observation tool was developed by the researcher and reviewed by two experts in English Language Teaching and technology use for validation. When the participants completed the online course, they were required to prepare a 50-minute lesson plan and they were observed by the researcher using this tool, which evaluated to the extent which target applications have been used and how teachers used the applications to enhance student-centered learning by ticking boxes to check frequency of use.

Interview Schedule

The interviews aimed to find out about the perceptions and future plans of EFL instructors in terms of mobile technologies integration in their actual teaching. They also aimed to receive some feedback about the online course. The data collected from the interview were used to support the data collected through the questionnaires and the classroom observation tool. The questions in this form were also reviewed by an expert in English language teaching.

Online Course Learning Management System (LMS)

Moodle, which is a free online learning management system (LMS) developed by Martin Dougiamas, was used as an LMS in this study. Based on the competencies of the participating instructors obtained from part 1 of the Mobile Technologies questionnaire, an online course on Moodle was designed to help the instructors develop their competencies in the use of mobile technologies in English Language Teaching. Having analyzed the needs analysis results drawn from part 1, the course objectives were determined through Bloom's Digital Taxonomy. Namely, depending on the instructors' needs, the course objectives and the course content were identified. This online course lasted 6 weeks and included 6 different sections, each of which focused on different mobile technologies grouped under specific categories ranging from vocabulary teaching to mind mapping. For each section, the instructors were expected to spend approximately one or two hours depending on their technology use competency. The main page of the online course on Moodle was displayed in Figures 2 and 3.

Figure 2. Mobile Technologies Course Moodle Page 1

Figure 3. Mobile Technologies Course Moodle Page 2

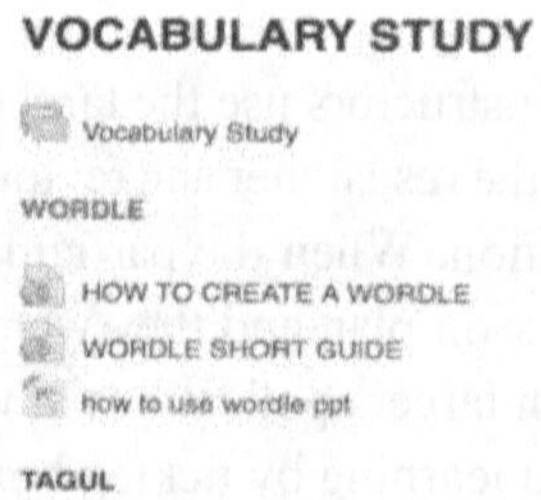

Web 2.0 Applications used for This Study

In this study, various applications like Lnoit, Glogster, Quizlet, Plickers and Aurasma were included.

Data Collection

Data collection procedures are presented in Table 2. The table summarized how the study was conducted within a limited timeframe.

Table 2. Data Collection Procedures

Tasks	Duration
Selection/Adaptation of Instruments	10 weeks
The permissions from institution	4 weeks
Pilot study	6 weeks
EFA Analysis	4 weeks
Participants Selection	2 weeks
Pre-Test	1 week
Development/Redesign of the Course	4 weeks
The implementation of the study	22 instructors + 6 weeks
Post-Test	22 instructors + 1 week
Classroom Observations	3 instructors +1 week
Interviews	3 instructors +1 week

Results

Research Question 1. What are the needs of EFL instructors related to use of Internet, computer and mobile technologies in teaching?

The findings obtained from part 1 were analyzed through descriptive statistics in terms of means and percentages. Based on the results of the needs analysis, they are moderate in terms of using computer and the Internet in learning and teaching (54.55%). Majority of them had been using mobile devices for more than 3 years (86.36% for mobile phone, 63.64% for PDA, 72.73% for Tablet PC). The details of the results are displayed in Table 3.

Table 3. The Results of Needs Analysis about the Experience on Mobile Devices

	Never		Less than 1 year		1-3 years		More than 3 years		Total
	N	%	n	%	n	%	N	%	
Mobile Phone	0	0.00	2	9.09	1	4.55	19	86.36	22
PDA (personal digital assistant, smartphone, IPad, etc.)	1	4.55	1	4.55	6	27.27	14	63.64	22
Tablet PC	2	9.09	2	9.09	2	9.09	16	72.73	22

The instructors used mobile devices mostly for Internet browsing (77.27%) and messaging (61.90%). Regarding their mobile applications, the results indicated that majority of them used mobile applications moderately (45.45%) or poorly (18.18%).

Consequently, the results of the needs analysis indicated that the majority of the participants used mobile devices for basic skills in daily life such as messaging and they did not tend to integrate mobile applications into teaching English.

Research Question 2: Is there a significant difference in acceptance of mobile technologies of EFL instructors before and after taking the online course on mobile technologies?

The acceptance level of EFL instructors on mobile technologies before taking the online course was positive considering the results of the second part of the questionnaire overall. However, as this part consisted of 4 different constructs as part of mobile acceptance level, the responses to relevant items were also investigated. The results in the pre/post tests are presented in Table 4.

Table 4. Results of Acceptance Level of EFL Instructors in pre-post tests

Acceptance Level		Pre-test	Post-test
Performance Expectancy (PE)	Teaching productivity Finding M-learning useful	50% 63.64%	63.63% 68.18%
Effort Expectancy (EE)	M-learning requires effort Becoming skillful is difficult	36.37% 27.28%	22.73% 22.73%
Personal Innovativeness (PInn)	Willingness to use in teaching	68.18%	72.72%
Behavioral Intention (BI)	Planning to use new mobile technologies in teaching Enjoying using M-learning systems in their teaching	59.09% 50.01%	72.72% 68.18%

The results of the Wilcoxon Signed Ranks Test indicated a significant difference between pre-test (Mdn=2.55) and post-test results, Mdn=4.05, $z = -3.796$, $p<.05$.

Research Question 3: Is there a significant difference in mobile technologies self-efficacy of EFL instructors before and after taking the online course on mobile technologies?

The mobile technologies self-efficacy of EFL instructors before taking the online course was positive considering the results of the third part of the questionnaire overall. They mostly stated that if there was no one who showed them how to use mobile applications, they would not feel as comfortable or capable (81.82%). Their second claim was that if they had someone around to help them, they would feel more capable as well (68.18%). Regarding these, it can be claimed that the participants would need someone to guide them or some training throughout the course. Besides, the feeling that they would be helped whenever they needed was important to them as they indicated in the pre-test questionnaire.

The findings of the post-test were also similar to those in the pre-test. The participants indicated positive tendency in terms of mobile technologies self-efficacy. Having taken the online course, it can be assumed that they felt more confident and competent in using mobile technologies as their responses to the item " I would complete a task using mobile phone if there was no one around to tell me what to do as I go" weighted from 'Neutral' to 'Disagree' or from 'Disagree to 'Strongly Disagree'.

The results of the Wilcoxon Signed Ranks Test indicated there was a significant difference between pre-test (Mdn=3.50) and post-test results, Mdn=2.50, $z = -3.601$, $p<.05$.

Research Question 4: Is there a significant difference in the attitudes of EFL instructors towards incorporating mobile learning into teaching before and after taking the online course on mobile technologies?

The attitudes of EFL instructors towards incorporating mobile learning into teaching before taking the online course was positive considering the results of the part 4 of the questionnaire. Item 18 which indicated students could be taught how to use mobile devices in their learning and item 23 which indicated they would want their students to access course content and activities on mobile devices were responded positively by most of the participants (more than 80%). From this point, it can be assumed that the participants believed students could be easily encouraged to use mobile devices in language learning and they would expect their students to use mobile devices for course-related issues. Apart from these, the results also indicated that the participants were eager to learn how to use different mobile applications in their teaching (72.72%). Overall, before taking the online course, the participants were willing to integrate mobile technologies into their classroom teaching.

Considering the results of the post-test, it can be claimed that the participants were still willing to use different mobile technologies into their teaching. They even believed their students would benefit more if they used mobile devices in learning as the percentage to this item increased from 59% to 68%.

The results of the Wilcoxon Signed Rank Test for EFL instructors' attitudes showed there was a significant difference between pre-test (Mdn=2.80) and post-test results, Mdn=3.90, $z = -3.640, p<.05$, which revealed that EFL instructors' attitudes towards ICT use increased positively with the help of the online course.

Research Question 5: Is there a significant difference in the perceptions related to the usefulness and ease of use of mobile learning of EFL instructors before and after taking the online course on mobile technologies?

The perceptions of EFL instructors related to the usefulness and ease of use of mobile learning were positive in general in both pre-and-post-tests. Considering the results of the pre-test, it can be seen that the participants supported the idea that students should use mobile devices in language learning process and could benefit from mobile learning in terms of completing classroom activities, quizzes and communicating with their peers outside class regarding the course content. Further, the instructors have tendency to encourage their students to benefit mobile learning in language learning. As an LMS was used to share classroom documents with the students in the institution where this study was conducted, it was predictable that these instructors expect their students to have access to outside class materials on mobile devices as well. The item that received the lowest responses from the participants was on incorporating mobile learning into classroom instruction (59.09%) and item 11, which was on taking quizzes on mobile device (59.09%).

Regarding the results of the post-test, it can be claimed that the participants supported the idea that mobile learning would be useful for their students in language learning process. They also stated mobile learning should be integrated into classroom instruction more since the percentage to this item increased from 59.09% to 77.27%.

The results of the Wilcoxon Signed Ranks Test indicated there was a significant difference between pre-test (Mdn=2.75) and post-test results, Mdn=4.00, $z = -3.852, p<.05$.

The results on the perceptions related to the ease of use in the pre-test showed that the participants thought students could easily use the mobile applications designed and used in the classroom and language learning. The item indicating students would not require a lot of effort to use mobile applications in the classroom had the highest positive response (77.27%). This shows these instructors believe their students can easily understand how to use the mobile applications in the classroom. The item (Mobile learning opportunities would allow students to learn and study in places they couldn't normally) which received the second highest responses showed with the help of mobile learning, students would have a chance to learn and study in places they normally could not (72.73%). Considering this item, it can be assumed that these participants think mobile learning would enable students to study in different places, encouraging the idea of mobility of learning. The item that received the lowest responses from the participants was that students would complete classwork and assignments if they could use their mobile device (54.55%).

As for the results of the post-test, it can be claimed that the participants still thought their students could easily use mobile applications in language learning process. The results of the post-test indicated a slight increase in all items. Considering the all items, the responses weighted from 'Neutral' to 'Agree' or from 'Agree to 'Strongly Agree'

The results of the Wilcoxon Signed Ranks Test indicated there was a significant difference between pre-test (Mdn=2.60) or post-test results, Mdn=3.80, z = -3.919, p<.05.

Research Question 6: Is there a significant difference in the perceptions related to the effect of mobile learning on student engagement in learning of EFL instructors before and after taking the online course on mobile technologies?

The perceptions of EFL instructors related to the effect of mobile learning on student engagement were negative in general in pre-test. The results in the pre-test indicated that the participants were on the idea that students would not be more likely to engage in activities related to do course outside class. For instance, item 5 indicating the students would be more likely to engage in class discussion outside of class if they could post their thoughts from their mobile device received the lowest responses (18.18%). This item was followed by item 3 which stated that the students would be more likely to participate in class activities outside of class time if they could do so through their mobile device (22.73%). In light of these two items, it can be claimed that these instructors thought integrating mobile learning into English language teaching would not affect their students' engagement outside class studies although they thought it would in classroom activities as indicated in item 1 (63.64%) and 2 (54.54%).

However, the results of the post-test showed a positive attitude in terms of these participants' ideas on student engagement both inside and outside class studies. To give an example, the responses for item 5 increased from 18.18% to 40.91% and the responses for item 3 increased from 22.73% to 54.54%.

Research Question 7: To what extent do EFL instructors use the target mobile applications in teaching after the completion of the online course?

This question was checked through class observations by the researcher. The classroom observations were analyzed according to the questions in the form by doing content analysis through topic coding. The themes arisen from the content analysis were presented in Figure 4.

The mobile applications used in the observed lessons were Plickers, Padlet and Quizlet. The instructors also used whiteboard, projector and their laptops during the lessons. While teaching, the instructors used mobile applications to access, present and process the information included in the lesson. They used Plickers as part of vocabulary teaching before while-reading stage in the lesson and presented unknown words through Plickers.

Throughout the observed lessons, all instructors attempted to teach in a more student-centered fashion. Namely, the classroom activities were designed in a student-centered way. For example, while teaching vocabulary or creating mind maps using technology, students were actively engaged in the lessons, which indicates enhanced student involvement in learning and teaching processes. In this way, the students were active participants rather than being passive.

Figure 4. Themes from classroom observations

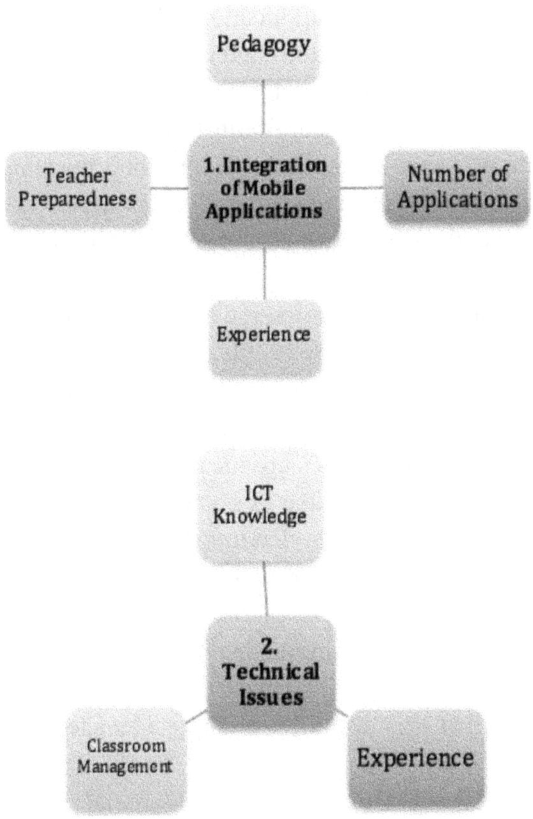

Figure 5. Themes from Interviews

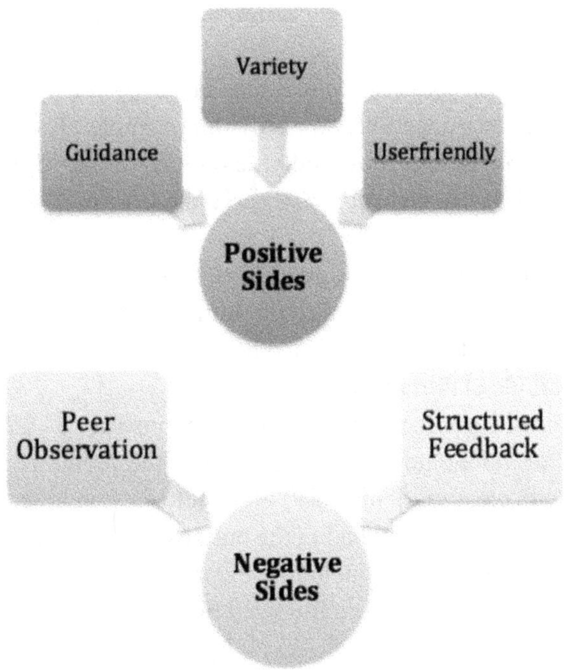

In terms of the frequency of the use of mobile applications, the applications were used at around 30% of the 50-minute lessons. While using the applications, the instructors seemed confident and while setting the task, they all gave very clear instructions and guided students effectively. When students had difficulty, all the instructors helped them confidently.

Regarding the observed lessons, overall all of the instructors were well-prepared, and it was clear that they enjoyed the integration of mobile applications into their teaching. However, they sometimes had difficulty while managing class and teaching through technology.

Research Question 8: What are the EFL instructors' views related to the characteristics of the mobile technologies course they attended?

This question was answered through semi-structured interviews conducted to 3 instructors who took the online course. While analyzing the interview results, topic coding was used and some themes were derived from the qualitative data as can be seen in Figure 5.

The first question in the interview was about what instructors liked the most in the course. In general, all 5 instructors stated that they liked most of the activities provided in the course, especially the variety of the mobile applications presented in the course as stated by 4 instructors. Another activity they really liked in the course was the guidelines and video tutorials provided in the course. They stated that the instructions and explanations were straightforward, which helped them understand how to use the relevant mobile applications effectively.

The second question was about what instructors liked the least in the course. As most of them were very pleased to have taken this course, they couldn't specifically point out any points they did not like. However, two instructors stated that they would have appreciated feedback right after the classroom observations.

The third question focused on what things the instructors found challenging or problematic in the online course. Overall, all of them stated there was not anything specifically problematic for them during the course. They highlighted their appreciation on the clear guidelines and video tutorials. One instructor stated that a sample video recorded in a class where mobile applications were used effectively could have been added to the online course so that they could have a chance to see the actual delivery of the technology-enhanced classrooms.

The fourth question was about how the challenges they faced in the course could have been overcome in the future. As the challenge they faced was on providing sample classroom videos, they all stated that some classroom videos could be integrated into the online course. Moreover, one instructor stated that it would also be useful if they had a chance to observe the lessons of their colleagues who took the online course.

The last question focused on what they would change or keep in this course. They all agreed that the content of the course should not be changed in the future as it was very useful for them. However, some of them stated that one module could be added to the course to observe each other's lessons and the course should include sample classroom videos.

Considering all these points, it can be claimed that all the instructors were pleased with the course content and the variety of the mobile applications offered in the online course. They were especially very happy to be provided with clear guidelines and video tutorials on how to use the target mobile applications. However, the major concern they had in the online course was the fact that they had not been provided with any sample classroom videos including the use of any mobile applications. Next section discussed the results in relation to the literature followed by implications.

SOLUTIONS AND RECOMMENDATIONS

The responses to the first research question, which aimed to find out the needs of EFL instructors so as to develop the mobile technologies course, revealed that despite their experience in the use of mobile technologies, they did not widely use these technologies for teaching. In order to design a training program, analyzing the needs plays a crucial role as documented in the literature. This is because needs analysis is an important means of conducting research prior to designing and evaluating lessons/materials/syllabuses and it helps draw a profile of participants/course in order to determine and prioritize the needs of them (Richards et al, 1992). For instance, The Commonwealth of Australia (2000) states when professional development is determined and implemented to meet the needs of the students and teachers, it becomes more fruitful and effective. Alldhali (2002), conducted a study to design a training program on educational technology for female science teachers considering their needs. The results of the needs analysis indicated these teachers need training on computer, the Internet and virtual reality. Another study by Unal and Ozturk (2012) revealed that the ICT training provided in the context was ineffective as it lacked real needs of the participants like the pedagogical aspects of technology integration. Previous research on approaches to course design involving the use of technology has found a number of challenges, such as a lack of technological skills (Hampel, 2006) or only superficial digital proficiency (Kurek & Hauck, 2014). Thus, Hampel (2006, p. 112) rightly reminds us that "we cannot expect learners and teachers to be competent users of the new media who are unaware of the affordances and how to use them constructively". Misjudgements to this effect are likely to affect teachers' and students' performance negatively. As Veen (1993) suggested a training program should be designed based on the participants' needs rather than being "one size fits all".

The second research question of this study aimed to find out the difference in the mobile acceptance level of the EFL instructors before and after taking the online course. The results suggested that the online course had a positive effect on the instructors' mobile acceptance level. This shows that the training provided to the EFL instructors was effective.

As the literature related to the effect of taking an online course designed on mobile technologies on mobile acceptance level is very limited, it was not possible to make comparisons with similar studies in terms of the increase in mobile acceptance level since mobile acceptance level has mostly been used to develop a new course by examining which construct of mobile acceptance level is more effective. However, the results could be compared with the studies on the integration mobile acceptance level through (TAM) and (UTAUT). As in the study of Venkatesh et al., (2003), the UTAUT could explain about 70% of variance in the intention of taking a course on different technologies. Moreover, this model offers different useful tools for managers and teachers, which would enable them to assess the use of the new technology (Ibrahim & Jaafar, 2011).

In this study, as there was a positive change in the acceptance level of the instructors, it could be claimed that each area in the mobile acceptance level could have positive effect. This result is consistent with other studies on technology acceptance as Performance Expectancy (PE) and Effort Expectancy (EE) have been found to affect behavioral intention while using M-learning positively (Jairak, Praneetpolgrang & Mekhabunchij, 2009; Vankatesh et al., 2003; Wang, Wu & Wang, 2009). However, in some other studies only Effort Expectancy (EE) was found to significantly affect the use of M-learning (Chong et al., 2011; Liu, Li & Carlsson, 2010; Wang, Wu and Wang 2009).

The third research question aimed to find out whether there was a significant difference in the mobile technologies self-efficacy of EFL instructors before and after taking the online course. The results related to the self-efficacy of the instructors showed a positive tendency in both pre and post-tests, which echoes some studies in the literature. As reported by Dexter, Anderson and Becker (1995) teachers need to know how and why to use technology meaningfully. In this current study, the instructors expected guidance from the researcher at the beginning of the course although they were provided with video tutorials and guidelines for each application in the course. Having completed the course, their expectation has changed to some extent and as they were provided with adequate guidance throughout the course, they felt more comfortable with the use of target mobile applications. Correspondingly, Yıldırım (2000) also suggested the best way to encourage teachers to use the new technologies is to enhance their competency level in the use of technology.

The fourth research question in this study aimed to check if there was a significant difference on the attitudes of EFL instructors towards incorporating mobile learning into teaching before taking the online course. The results in both pre-and-post tests indicated the participants were willing to integrate mobile technologies into their classroom teaching. After going through the online course, they were more eager to take incorporate mobile learning into their teaching because they believe that their students would benefit more the lessons designed through mobile applications.

As the instructors in this current study supported the idea of integrating mobile learning into learning and teaching, there are many studies on the use of mobile technologies to enhance learning and teaching in school environment (Hung et al., 2013). The results of such studies showed that mobile learning can integrate real and digital world resources to improve the learning achievement and reduce cognitive load (Hung et al., 2013; Hwang et al., 2013). Jayachandran's study (2009), which investigated two pre-service teachers who aimed to integrate technology into teaching, revealed their willingness as they looked for different technologies for classroom teaching. In terms of teachers' attitudes towards technology use in teaching and learning, Ince (2015) referred to the perception of many teachers on the potential positive effect on blended learning in English language teaching. Güneş's study (2015) conveyed, similar results indicating that teachers had positive attitudes toward using computer technology in their teaching experience. Similarly, Karakaya's study (2010) revealed that a great majority of teachers attribute positive remarks to integrating technology in language teaching. On the other hand, there are also some studies which show going through an online course do not have an effect on teachers' attitudes and self-efficacy levels. Özdemir's study (2013) revealed that the online educational technology courses on Moodle did not have a significant impact on the attitudes and self-efficacy of the pre-service teachers about using computer technologies, but it had a significant impact on the computer literacy of pre-service teachers towards computers.

The fifth research question focused on assessing whether there was a significant difference in the perceptions related to the usefulness and ease of use of mobile learning of EFL instructors before and after taking the online course. The findings for this question were overall positive in both pre-and post-tests as the instructors thought that students could easily understand and use the mobile applications designed for the classroom. Besides, the instructors thought that mobile learning would enable students to study in different places, encouraging the idea of mobility of learning.

Such results are aligned with some studies in the literature in terms of being beneficial for student learning. A study conducted by Song (2008) indicated that mobile learning could improve the participants' vocabulary learning. Pei-Lin and Chiu-Jung (2015) showed that phrase learning by mobile phones developed the performance of the participants significantly. The study by Cavus and Ibrahim (2009) revealed that the target words could be easily learned thanks to an SMS system. However, there are other studies, which contradict with these studies in the literature. To give an example, a study conducted by

Stockwell (2007) indicated vocabulary learning through mobile devices did not have a significant effect on students' achievement.

The sixth research question in this study tried to examine if there was a significant difference in the perceptions related to the effect of mobile learning on student engagement in learning of EFL instructors before and after taking the online course. The results showed a significant difference in the comparison of the results of pre-and-post tests. In contrast to the findings of the previous research questions, the perceptions of EFL instructors related to the effect of mobile learning on student engagement were negative in general in the pre-test. The results of an item on student engagement indicated that integrating mobile applications on outside class studies would not affect student engagement positively or it would not change their attitudes. However, this revealed the use of mobile applications in class would affect student engagement positively.

The study carried out by Vallance and Martin (2008) indicated that designing courses through technology supported and improved learning in classes, suggesting increased classroom engagement in learning. Some teachers appreciated the use of technology in teaching by stating technology use could turn the classroom into a dynamic place, where students are actively involved in learning process (Stansberry & Kymes, 2007). Other studies by Al-Fahad (2009); Wang, et al. (2009); and Rogers, et al. (2010) showed that students were more active in the learning process and more engaged in classroom activities when a lesson was designed through the effective use of technology. In terms of increased classroom engagement, Guenther et al. (2008) and Wyatt et al. (2010) highlighted the enhanced collaboration among students in classes though mobile learning. Finally, Botzer and Yerushalmy (2007) stated that the mobility of learning environment and the ease of use of the application enhanced student engagement in the learning process.

The seventh research question aimed to find out to what extent EFL instructors use the mobile applications they studied in the online course they had attended. While using the applications, the instructors were mostly confident and could guide their students effectively, which indicates the positive effect of taking the online course. In terms of student learning, students were actively involved and there was enhanced student involvement in the lessons through the use of mobile applications.

Such results are consistent with some earlier findings in the literature. The study conducted by Dexter et al. (1995) pointed out that when instructors have positive attitudes towards technology integration in English Language Teaching, more effective results in terms of English teaching will be observed, which is the similar case in the current study. Considering that these instructors had positive attitudes towards incorporating mobile technologies into teaching in the pre-and-post tests, they could teach effectively in the observed lessons. Furthermore, Ibrahim (2010) pointed out that the use of new technologies plays a key role in language teaching and learning as it contributes to the field of education in terms of the way teachers teach the content. The observed lessons in this current study indicated more student-centered teaching and learning, which echoes with the literature that states the effect of the use of emerging technologies in the design of lessons transform them from teacher-centered to more student-centered (Matzen & Edmunds, 2007; Mumtaz, 2000; Snoeyink & Ertmer, 2001; Warschauer & Kern, 2000). Moreover, using emergent technologies enables teachers to individualize the classroom instruction and make the lessons more student-centered (Lee, 2010).

The eighth research question focused on the views of the instructors who took the course on the characteristics of the online course. The results revealed that attending the Mobile Technologies Course that was delivered online was very beneficial and effective for them in that it helped them to develop their skills on the use of mobile Technologies in English Language teaching.

Regarding all the questions in the interview, the instructors stated that they liked the variety of the mobile applications presented in the course and the guidelines and video tutorials provided on Moodle. They all also agreed that the content of the course should not be changed in the future as it was very useful for them. However, they stated that it would be nice to receive feedback right after the classroom observation and they could have been given a chance to see the actual delivery of the technology-enhanced classrooms by adding a sample video lesson on Moodle and they could have observed each other's lessons as well.

Aligned with this study, there are some studies which suggested the similar results. A study investigating the experiences of high school language art teachers on technology integration after taking a technology course was carried out by Byous (2007) suggested that receiving such a course was effective for technology implementation and respectively affected in-class integration positively. To this end, Brennan (1991) put forward that teacher attitudes towards technology use could be enhanced by providing training as in the case in this current study. Lawless and Pellegrini (2007) also stressed out that efficient training could be provided to help teacher benefit from the use of technology at most. In another study by Gilmore (1995), the findings showed that technology training has a key role in teacher development.

FUTURE RESEARCH DIRECTIONS

In this study, the mobile technologies level of EFL instructors was investigated in terms of its effect on the online course overall. There is no information regarding which construct is more effective. However, for future studies, the mobile technologies level could be explored regarding its different constructs and which affects the most. That's to say, the constructs could be compared within each other.

Considering the workload of the instructors in this study, the online course was designed for 6 weeks to make attending this course less challenging for them. However, as there are two sections in some weeks in this course, they could be distributed to other weeks and the course could take 8 or 10 weeks by reducing the number of applications presented in each week.

In this study, the observation was conducted only after completing the online course. However, before starting to take the online course, the instructors could also be observed. Hence, in the future studies, the instructors might be observed before taking the online course to have a chance to compare and see the difference in to what extent they are using the mobile applications before and after taking the online course.

At the end of the online course, some participants were observed after completing the 6-week course. However, there is no information regarding how much these instructors are using or are able to use the target applications in their classes. Thus, some follow-up observations could be done in the further researches.

Furthermore, although the instructors were delighted with the online course in general, they stated they could have been provided with a sample technology-enhanced classroom video in the course. Hence, such a course could be designed in the future by including a sample classroom video in which technology is effectively integrated. Moreover, the instructors in this study also stated they could have a chance to observe each other's lessons while embedding technology into their classes. To this end, one or two weeks more could be added to such a training course and the instructors could have an opportunity to observe at least one or two colleagues while using mobile technologies in their teaching.

This study was designed regarding the needs of the instructors in the institution. Thus, the results might be context specific. However, the same online course could be offered to some other EFL-instructors in Turkey to see if there are any differences in terms of the results. In fact, the results could even be compared in state and privately funded universities.

Overall, regarding the technology integration into education, many studies focus on learners' perspectives and give little attention to teachers' roles as enhancing technologically advanced learning process. Further studies could be conducted on the integration of technology into teacher education programs as pre- and in-service trainings.

CONCLUSION

When the foreign language learners are regarded in this century, who are digital natives, the integration of technology into learning and teaching is a requirement so as to cater for the learners' needs better. Therefore, English language instructors, researchers and material designers should try to incorporate different technological tools into the courses or the materials. As regards with this point, curriculum design and assessment could also be integrated with technology.

This study proposes that skills considering digital technologies should be a part of any curriculum. Through technology integration, more student-centered language curriculum could be developed. This implication results in the needs of competent language teachers in technology enhanced teaching. To this end, technology courses could be integrated into the curriculum of English Language Teaching Departments in Turkey. When pre-service teachers study in their departments, they could be offered technology courses focusing on mobile learning.

After taking the online course, these instructors were more willing to use mobile technologies in their teaching and they felt mobile learning would be useful for their students in language learning process. From this point, a probable misconception that many instructors may refrain from the use of technology because they do not like it could be altered, as they seem to be willing to use technology in teaching, but they find their level of competency insufficient. In terms of the fact that they find mobile learning useful for students, it can be suggested that the incorporation of mobile learning into English language courses should be encouraged more as students are offered more outside class materials and more quality time is spent in class as students are being active learners.

As regards with the findings of the classroom observations conducted when the instructors completed the online course, the instructors were confident and competent in using technology in their classes. They could benefit from mobile learning to design more student-centered lessons. Based on this result, it could be recommended that with a structured technology training course in which mobile applications or ICT tools are presented, instructors might design a technology-enhanced lesson which increases student involvement in teaching and learning processes. Considering the interview results, it could be claimed that all the instructors were delighted with the online course content, the variety of the mobile applications presented and the guidelines and video tutorials. However, their major concern was that they could have been provided with a sample technology-enhanced classroom video in the online course.

When the findings of this study are scrutinized overall, it could be assumed that the instructors are aware of the fact that nowadays the foreign language learners are digital natives who were born with technology. Thus, the use of technology and mobile devices is an indispensable part of their daily lives. In order to reach them more and meet their needs better, the instructors feel mobile learning should be integrated into their learning process. Therefore, the institutions could try to provide technology courses for teachers to increase teaching and learning efficiency. On the other hand, there are also factors to consider before offering such a course in institutions. The first and utmost important point is the readiness of the teachers and their mobile technologies acceptance level. Hence, the institutional context and teachers' background should be taken into consideration.

As the results of this study suggest, the student involvement increases and they become active learners when their learning environment is arranged through mobile learning. Regarding this point, Blasszauer (2001) pointed out that teachers should adapt their teaching methods in relation to the needs and characteristics of the learners. In this way, we could help learners become lifelong learners. Yet, the online technology courses in this current study took 5 weeks and now the participants do not continue any other courses on technology although technology courses should be part of in-house training programs to be successful (Northrup & Little, 1996).

Finally, the instructors were those who volunteered to take the online course on mobile technologies. They are not normally provided with ICT courses for their professional development in the institution. Their use of mobile applications in teaching now may not reflect the effective use of technology across the institution. Hence, the other instructors could also be offered this course as part of their professional development process. As Samuel and Bakar (2006) put forward, to benefit from technology use fully, it is of importance to have the full cooperation with the school administration and offer ongoing training to update teachers' ICT skills.

Offering effective training to in-service teachers on how to integrate educational technologies into EFL classes is a neglected field, which this study aimed to investigate into. While acknowledging that constraints that may derive from the lack of competent personnel, time and financial resources in the institutions, bearing in mind the needs of the 21st century students, institutions might gain long term benefits from investing in courses as elaborated in this study.

ACKNOWLEDGMENT

This study is a part of my PhD thesis. I would like to express my deepest gratitude to my advisor Prof. Dr. Meral Aksu, who supported and guided me throughout my PhD thesis writing.

REFERENCES

Abu-Al-Aish, A. (2014). *Toward mobile learning deployment in higher education* (Doctoral dissertation). Brunel University, School of Information Systems, Computing and Mathematics.

Al-Fahad, F. N. (2009). Students' attitudes and perceptions towards the effectiveness of mobile learning in King Saud University. Academic Press.

Becker, H. J. (1999). *Internet use by teachers: Conditions of professional use and teacher-directed student use*. Center for Research on Information Technology and Organizations, the University of California, Irvine and the University of Minnesota.

Botzer, G., & Yerushalmy, M. (2007). Mobile Application for Mobile Learning. *Proceedings of the International Conference on Cognition and Exploratory Learning in the Digital Age.*

Cavus, N., & Ibrahim, D. (2009). M-learning: An Experiment in Using SMS to Support Learning New English Language Words. *British Journal of Educational Technology, 40*(1), 78–91. doi:10.1111/j.1467-8535.2007.00801.x

Chong, J., Chong, A. Y., Ooi, K., & Lin, B. (2011). An Empirical Analysis of the Adoption of M Learning in Malaysia. *International Journal of Mobile Communications, 9*(1), 1–18. doi:10.1504/IJMC.2011.037952

Dede, C. (2008). Technological Supports for Acquiring 21st Century Skills. Cambridge.

Denk, M., Weber, M., & Belfin, R. (2007). Mobile Learning-Challenges and potentials. *International Journal of Mobile and Organisation, 1*(2), 122–139. doi:10.1504/IJMLO.2007.012674

Duhaney, D. C. (2000). Technology and the educational process: Transforming Classroom Activities. *International Journal of Instructional Media*, 27.

Ertmer, P. A., & Ottenbreit-Leftwich, A. T. (2010). Teacher technology change: How knowledge, confidence, beliefs, and culture intersect. *Journal of Research on Technology in Education, 42*(3), 255–284. doi:10.1080/15391523.2010.10782551

Guenther, S., Winkler, T., Ilgner, K., & Herczeg, M. (2008). Mobile Learning with Moles: A Case Study for Enriching Cognitive Learning by Collaborative Learning in Real World Contexts. In *Proceedings of World Conference on Educational Multimedia, Hypermedia and Telecommunications 2008* (pp. 374-380). Chesapeake, VA: AACE.

Güneş, M. (2015). *A Study of Teachers' Attitudes Towards Computer Technology and Their Use of Technology at the Preparatory School of Ufuk University* (Unpublished Thesis). Ufuk University, Ankara.

Hampel, R. (2006). Rethinking task design for the digital age: A framework for language teaching and learning in a synchronous online environment. *ReCALL, 18*(1), 105–121. doi:10.1017/S0958344006000711

Hismanoglu, M. (2012a). The impact of a curricular innovation on prospective EFL teachers' attitudes towards ICT integration into language instruction. *International Journal of Instruction, 5*(1), 183–202.

Hismanoglu, M. (2012b). Prospective EFL teachers' perceptions of ICT integration: A study of Distance Higher Education in Turkey. *Journal of Educational Technology & Society, 15*(1), 185–196.

Ibrahim, R., & Jaafar, A. (2011). User Acceptance of Educational Games: A revised Unified Theory of Acceptance and Use of Technology (UTAUT). *World Academy of Science, Engineering and Technology, 53*, 551–557.

Ince, A. (2015). *English Language Teachers' Perspectives towards Blended Learning in English Language Teaching* (Master's thesis). Çağ Üniversitesi Sosyal Bilimler Enstitüsü.

Jairak, K., Praneetpolgrang, P., & Mekhabunchakij, K. (2009). An Acceptance of Mobile Learning for Higher Education Students in Thailand. *Proceedings of the 6th International Conference on E Learning from Knowledge-Based Society.*

Jayachandran, A. (2009). *Technology integration practices of foreign language pre-service teachers: A case study* (Unpublished doctoral dissertation). The University of Iowa.

Karakaya, K. (2010). *An investigation of English language teachers' attitudes toward computer technology and their use of technology in language teaching*. Academic Press.

Kurek, M., & Hauck, M. (2014). Closing the Digital Divide: A Framework for Multiliteracy Training. In J. Guikema & L. Williams (Eds.), *Digital Literacies in Foreign and Second Language Education* (pp. 119–140). San Marcos, TX: Calico.

Lee, J. W. (2010). Online Support Service Quality, Online Learning Acceptance, and Student Satisfaction. *The Internet and Higher Education, 13*(4), 277–283. doi:10.1016/j.iheduc.2010.08.002

Liu, Y., Li, H., & Carlsson, C. (2010). Factors Driving the Adoption of M-learning: An empirical study. *Computers & Education, 55*(3), 1211–1219. doi:10.1016/j.compedu.2010.05.018

OECD. (2010). *Inspired by Technology, Driven by Pedagogy: A systemic Approach to Technology-Based School Innovations*. Paris, France: OECD.

Özdemir, E. (2013). *Improving Pre-service English Language Teachers' ICT Skills and Developing Positive Attitudes Towards the Use of Technology in Language Teaching Through an Online Course* (Unpublished Thesis). Cukurova University.

Park, S. Y., Nam, M., & Cha, S. (2011). University Students" Behavioral Intention to Use Mobile Learning: Evaluating the technology acceptance model. *British Journal of Educational Technology, 43*(4), 592–605. doi:10.1111/j.1467-8535.2011.01229.x

Rogers, Y., Connelly, K., Hazlewood, W., & Tedesco, L. (2010). Enhancing learning: A study of how mobile devices can facilitate sense making. *Personal and Ubiquitous Computing, 14*(2), 111–124. doi:10.100700779-009-0250-7

Samuels, P. (2007). Mathematics Support and New Technologies. *MSOR Connections, 7*(1), 10–13. doi:10.11120/msor.2007.07010010

Simpson, E., & Stansberry, S. (2008). Video Games and Teacher Development: Bridging the Gap in the Classroom. In C. T. Miller (Ed.), *Games: Purpose and Potential Education*. New York: Springer.

Smith, P., & Ragan, T. (1999). *Instructional design* (2nd ed.). Toronto: John Wiley &Sons.

Song, Y. (2008). SMS enhanced vocabulary learning for mobile audiences. *International Journal of Mobile Learning and Organisation, 2*(1), 81–98. doi:10.1504/IJMLO.2008.018719

Stockwell, G. (2007). Vocabulary on the Move: Investigating an intelligent mobile phone-based vocabulary tutor. *Computer Assisted Language Learning, 20*(4), 365–383. doi:10.1080/09588220701745817

Vallance, M., & Martin, S. (2008). The Impact of Synchronous inter-networked teacher training in Information and Communication Technology Integration. *Computers & Education, 51*(1), 34–53. doi:10.1016/j.compedu.2007.04.001

Venkatesh, V., Morris, M. G., Davis, G. B., & Davis, F. D. (2003). User Acceptance of Information Technology: Toward a unified view. *Management Information Systems Quarterly*, *27*(3), 425–478. doi:10.2307/30036540

Wang, Y.S., Wu, M. & Wang, H. (2009). Investigating the Determinants and Age and Gender Differences in the Acceptance of Mobile Learning. *British Journal of Educational Technology*, *40*(1), 92-118.

Wilkins, D. A. (1972). *Linguistics in language teaching*. London: Edward Arnold.

Yasan, N. (2018). *The investigation of undergraduate students' mobile phone use in the academic environment: The Case of Middle East Technical University* (Unpublished doctoral dissertation). Middle East Technical University, Ankara.

Yuksel, G., & Kavanoz, S. (2011). In search of prospective EFL certificate teachers' attitudes towards technology. *Procedia Computer Science*, *3*, 666–671. doi:10.1016/j.procs.2010.12.111

ADDITIONAL READING

Attewell, J. (2005). *Mobile Technologies and Learning: A technology update and m-learning project summary*. London: Learning and Skills Development Agency.

Baek, Y. G., Jong, J., & Kim, B. (2008). What makes teachers use technology in the classroom? Exploring the factors affecting facilitation of technology with a Korean sample. *Computers & Education*, *50*(8), 224–234. doi:10.1016/j.compedu.2006.05.002

Barker, A., Krull, G., & Mallinson, B. (2005). A Proposed Theoretical Model for M- Learning Adoption in Developing Countries. *Proceedings of the 4th World Conference on mLearning, mLearn 2005*, October 25-28, Cape Town, South Africa, 1-10.

Becker, H. J. (1999). Internet use by teachers: Conditions of professional use and teacher directed student use. Center for Research on Information Technology and Organizations, the University of California, Irvine and the University of Minnesota.

Kainth, G. S., & Kaur, G. (2010). *Integration of ICT in teacher education.* Retrieved August 2, 2019 from: http://developmentcommunity.csdi.org/profiles/blogs/integration-of-ict-in-teacher-1

Park, S. Y., Nam, M., & Cha, S. (2011). University Students'' Behavioral Intention to Use Mobile Learning: Evaluating the technology acceptance model. *British Journal of Educational Technology*, *43*(4), 592–605. doi:10.1111/j.1467-8535.2011.01229.x

Rogers, Y., Connelly, K., Hazlewood, W., & Tedesco, L. (2010). Enhancing learning: A study of how mobile devices can facilitate sense making. *Personal and Ubiquitous Computing*, *14*(2), 111–124. doi:10.100700779-009-0250-7

Sanchez, R. A., & Hueros, A. D. (2010). Motivational factors that influence the acceptance of Moodle using TAM. *Computers in Human Behavior*, *26*(6), 1632–1640. doi:10.1016/j.chb.2010.06.011

Vallance, M., & Martin, S. (2008). The Impact of Synchronous inter-networked teacher training in Information and Communication Technology Integration. *Computers & Education*, *51*(1), 34–53. www.sciencedirect.com Retrieved April122012. doi:10.1016/j.compedu.2007.04.001

Venkatesh, V., Morris, M. G., Davis, G. B., & Davis, F. D. (2003). User Acceptance of Information Technology: Toward a unified view. *Management Information Systems Quarterly*, *27*(3), 425–478. doi:10.2307/30036540

Yuksel, G., & Kavanoz, S. (2011). In search of prospective EFL certificate teachers' attitudes towards technology. *Procedia Computer Science*, *3*, 666–671. doi:10.1016/j.procs.2010.12.111

KEY TERMS AND DEFINITIONS

Attitude: Attitude is a manner of acting, feeling or thinking. It is also the tendency to react a situation or concept positively or negatively.

ICT Skills: ICT stands for 'information communication technology'. The use of digital technology includes using a computer, tablet or mobile phone or send an email, which are examples of using basic ICT skills and technology. ICT skills help to develop the knowledge of technology and how it works as practical skills such as coding.

In-Service Training: It is the training given to teachers while they are working as full time. In-service training is what a teacher receives after he has entered to teaching profession and after he has had his education in a university.

Information Communication Technology (ICT): It is related to the technologies used for accessing, gathering, manipulating and presenting or communicating information and such technologies provide access to information through telecommunications.

Mobile Applications: The programs used for mobile devices such as iPad, tablets, etc. are called mobile applications. If students use online programs on computer, they are called web-based tools.

Mobile Devices: A mobile device is small and portable in order that it can be carried everywhere The examples of mobile devices are mobile phones, smart phones, iPad, tablets, personal digital assistants (PDAs), personal digital media players (iPods, etc.).

Mobile Learning: It is a mode of learning using content assisted by mobile devices like smart phones, IPad or tables.

Mobility of Learning: Mobile learning enables learners to use some mobile devices whenever and whenever they want. In this way, the information or the learning process could be carried wherever they go, which is mobility of learning.

Online Course: An online course is the delivery of a series of lessons on a web browser or mobile device, which can be accessed anytime and anyplace. It is designed as an online environment for convenient learning asynchronously.

Perception: Views or opinions stemming from experience and external factors acting on the individual.

Self-Efficacy: Self-efficacy is the belief that we have in our own abilities, to complete a task successfully It is generally related to the concept of self-control and the ability to modulate any behavior to achieve aims.

Chapter 13
A Digital Ecosystem for Teaching-Learning English in Higher Education:
A Qualitative Case Study

Ana María Pinto-Llorente
https://orcid.org/0000-0002-8538-9902
University of Salamanca, Spain

ABSTRACT

The aim of the research is to analyse pre-service teachers' perceptions about the effectiveness of the digital ecosystem implemented in the area of English morphosyntax in b-learning modality. Based on this goal, a qualitative research approach was adopted. One hundred forty-three learners were enrolled in the subject, and a total of 43 participated in the study. The instrument used to collect data was unstructured individual interviews. The findings suggested students' positive attitudes towards the implemented digital ecosystem. It highlighted that the students were active participants and knew how to manage their learning and how to collaborate with their classmates. The flexibility and accessibility provided by the technological tools available in the model allowed students to combine their personal and professional obligations with lifelong learning. It overcame all the spatial and temporal barriers and developed a kind of learning just-in-time, just-for-students, anytime and anywhere.

INTRODUCTION

In the last decades, the convergence of two teaching-learning approaches has been promoted. On the one hand, the traditional approach, in which all lessons and interactions are always carried out face-to-face, and, on the other hand, the e-learning training, in which some lessons and interactions are developed face-to-face and other ones virtually thanks to the affordances offered by new emerged technologies (Coaten, 2003; Graham, 2006; López & Matesanz, 2009).

DOI: 10.4018/978-1-7998-3062-7.ch013

This new approach, as Thorne (2003) points out, "represents a real opportunity to create learning experiences that can provide the right learning at the right time and in the right place for each and every individual, not just at work, but in schools, universities and even at home. In this context blended learning could become one of the most significant developments of the 21st century" (p.18). From these words, it can be deduced the relevant of this instruction to respond to the educational demands of the present society, since citizens need to carry out training to acquire the knowledge that allow them to keep job skills up-to-date according to the different situations and the changes in the present society (González et al., 2013).

Universities are trying to adapt to these new educational demands of knowledge society to compete and be successful in the changing economic and political dynamics of the modern world. Teachers are also trying to contribute to this through the design and implementation of innovative educational practices that allow learners to acquire a complete and solid training (González, 2008), and to be more involved in the construction of knowledge (Arteaga & Duarte, 2010; Pinto-Llorente, Sánchez-Gómez & García-Peñalvo, 2017).

This new technological blended instructional model can represent an alternative for the communicative language teaching (CLT) pedagogy, which focused on the development of the communicate competence, since it can eliminate the limits of the traditional face-to-face learning environments.

Applied linguists have contributed to the development of the concept of the communicative competence that was initially defined by Hymes (1972) as a competence not only as an inherent grammatical competence but also as the ability to use grammatical competence in a variety of situations. Savignon (1972) considered "the ability to function in a truly communicative setting, that is, in a dynamic exchange in which linguistic competence must adapt itself to the total informational input, both linguistic and paralinguistic, of one or more interlocutors" (p.8). A few years later Canale and Swain (1980) defined it as a concept comprised of three skills: grammatical competence (the mastery of the linguistic code: grammatical rules, morphological and syntactic rules, vocabulary, etc.), strategic competence (the knowledge of verbal and non-verbal communication strategies which allow learners to overcome difficulties when communication breakdowns and problems arise in the communication process) and sociolinguistic competence (the knowledge of the sociocultural code, the rules and conventions of language use in different sociocultural contexts). That definition was further elaborated by Canale (1983) who added another component, the discourse competence (the ability to combine language structures into different types of written texts or meaningful units of spoken language).

The current study deals with relevant aspects in the communicative language teaching (CLT) pedagogy, especially in the component of the communicative competence that refers to grammatical competence: grammatical rules, morphological and syntactic rules. It aims to explore the pre-service teachers' perceptions towards the effectiveness of the technological tools offered through the digital ecosystem implemented in blended learning modality.

The aim of the research was to find out pre-service teachers' perceptions on the effectiveness of the digital ecosystem implemented in the area of English Morphosyntax.

The study focused on these questions:

1. What are the benefits of transmissive, interactive and collaborative resources in learning English as a second language?
2. Do the participants consider that the e-activities provided them enough practice to achieve the goals of the course?

3. Do the implemented virtual environment and the instructional approach allow the participants to reinforce their autonomy and collaborative learning?

BACKGROUND

During the academic year 2003-2004, the Pontifical University of Salamanca started to implement blended learning modality. This modality was initially implemented in only two specialities of the degree in Primary Education: Special Education, and Audition and Language. A total of 348 students were enrolled in the 19 courses of both degrees.

Experts in technology evaluated different e-learning platforms, and they chose the platform UPC Plus. NEORIS Company was in charge of the training of the teachers that taught the degree courses mentioned above. During the development of that initial innovative experience, professors and experts evaluated the benefits and disadvantages of the platform to determinate its suitability for the blended learning modality.

The analysis carried out concluded that it was not the most appropriate e-learning platform due to the lack of versatility of its tools and resources, and the management of those tools. The results also emphasized that the use of the platform UPC Plus was complex because the university was not responsible for the overall management administration of the e-learning platform. As a result, when teachers wanted to update any of the materials, they could not do it directly, but it was necessary to communicate with the management center that was responsible for making any change. That eliminated the flexibility and freedom needed in that kind of instruction, since any change meant a great deal of time, and some of them were not even made. It was decided to evaluate other platforms, especially the open-source learning platform, Moodle.

After analyzing Moodle, experts concluded that the platform had a greater variety of technological tools than the previous platform. Besides, teachers were free to upload files in different formats, to design new activities, and to modify what they needed immediately.

These characteristics eliminated the two greater disadvantages of the UPC Plus, so the university decided to start using Moodle from the academic year 2004-2005. Moreover, the blended learning modality was implemented in more specific degrees in Primary Education (Special Education, Audition and Language, Physical Education, Music, Second Language: English, French, or German and Infant Education. There has been also a clear increase in the number of students enrolled in this modality, going from 348 in 2003-2004 to 1,470 during 2009-2010 and the rest of the academic years. The main conclusion drawn from the data is a clear increase in the number of students who demand this kind of education.

This study presents the results about the effectiveness of a digital ecosystem designed using Moodle and implemented in the area of English Morphosyntax in Primary Education (English) in blended learning modality. The flexibility of the platform, as Cole and Foster (2008) state, starts from the beginning, since it allows teachers to choose the visual organization of the course to show learners the materials. It was decided to choose the option topic format to organize the digital ecosystem around nineteen units that composed the course. Each unit included different didactic materials and tasks designed through the transmissive, interactive, and collaborative resources offered by the e-learning platform. As Gómez (2006) and Pérez et al., (2009) state, this division is due to two factors. On one hand, the degree of difficulty of the communication process, on the other hand, the pedagogical model in which they are based on.

Regarding transmissive resources, communication is one-way, and they reflect a more traditional teaching methodology (Gómez, 2006; Pérez et al., 2009). De la Torre (2006) states that they contain information that can be read or downloaded, so their main function is to transmit information. In the digital ecosystem, transmissive resources were files in different formats (PDF, PowerPoint and Word). The digital ecosystem also contains podcasts, videocast, and links to external websites. All transmissive resources could be downloaded to facilitate students' access to the contents of the subject and their practice in a multitude of situations, contexts and according to the participants' needs (Man-Man, 2006).

Referring to interactive resources, interaction is two-way although that communication only takes place between learners and computers, since they are done individually (Gómez, 2006; Pérez et al., 2009). The digital ecosystem contains different online test in each unit to carry out the continuous assessment of the learning process and allow participants to self-assess their progress. The rules of assessment and self-assessment tests were different. In the case of the assessment tests, it was decided to shuffle questions and answers randomly. The students only had one attempt, so the grading method was first attempt. Moreover, time was limited, there were applied penalties for incorrect answers, and review options were available after tests were closed. In the case of self-assessment tests, questions and answers were not shuffled randomly; time and the number of attempts were not limited; there was not any penalties for the incorrect answers; and review options were available immediately after each attempt. The purpose of the self-assessment tests was to help students to acquire the contents of the course, and to prepare them to do the assessment tests and the final exam.

Regarding collaborative resources, they promote a multidirectional communication and try to encourage learner participation. They also allow developing a collaborative work and permit the exchange of ideas, materials and knowledge between the participants of the digital ecosystem (Gómez, 2006; Pérez et al., 2009).

In the digital ecosystem there were two collaborative resources: wiki and forums. The wikis were used to carry out a group activity and the forums tried to facilitate the interaction between the participants. The design of the digital ecosystem contains two types of forums. On one hand, there were forums to encourage interaction among students to create a space where they were free to raise their concerns and where they could help each other. On the other hand, there were forums designed to help the learners to develop some tasks. The teacher assessed these forums in order to carry out a continuous assessment of the learners' progress and participation in the development of the activity.

The digital ecosystem was designed considering seven principles that could be identified in the structure, design, and organization of a constructivist-learning environment (Duffy & Cunningham, 1996; Honebein, 1996).

First, the design of the digital ecosystem tried to provide learners with an experience in the construction of knowledge. There were activities that learners were involved in the process to reflect on the solution of the activities, and to have enough independence to decide on resolutions.

Second, it must be an environment in which they are provided with different experiences and opportunities. Honebein (1996) considers that solving problems in real life does not usually have a single alternative, but there is a range of possibilities that depend on the perspective of how the problem is tackled. In a constructivist learning environment, learners must have the possibility of participating in activities that allow them to share and reflect on the different suggested solutions and to enrich their understanding. In the implemented digital ecosystem, there were tasks on which students must share their ideas and reflect on the best solution to do each activity. They had to share their views on the contents of the activities, and to determine the roles and functions of each member of the group.

Third, it is necessary to improve learning in real contexts which are relevant for students so that they can transfer what they learn in an academic context to everyday life, that is to say, they must relate learning to real practice (Gott, Lesgold & Kane, 1996; Payne, 2009; Willis, 2009). Morris, Bransford and Franks (1979) refer to the term *transfer appropriate processing* as learning that takes place in authentic and real conditions in which students have different opportunities to put it in practice in real contexts. In the digital ecosystem, the teacher tries to provide authentic materials adapted from different newspapers, magazines, television and radio programs. They also refer to real-life situations of communication on current topics that students can experience outside the academic context where they can practice their English. They develop group activities in the same way as they would be developed in real contexts. They share their opinions with others, define the problem, choose the resources, and achieve possible solutions. Specifically, they carry out activities using the same abilities and skills that are required in a real context outside the academic environment.

Fourth, a constructivist model is related to learner-centered pedagogy, since students are placed at the center of the teaching-learning process and take a principal role in the development of this. Thus, learners take an active role in their education and create knowledge (Allan, 2007; Grainger & Dunlap, 1996; Oliver, 2000). They put a great emphasis on the development of learning and on the skills for lifelong learning to reflect on their instruction, and take the initiative of their learning (Grabinger & Dunlap, 1996).

The implemented digital ecosystem tries to support learner-centered pedagogy, since the teacher act as a counsellor, facilitator, and guide (Blumberg, 2009; Gisbert, 2002). As Honebein (1996) points out, a key indicator in a learning-centered learning environment is the role of teachers. They promote autonomous learning through different individual activities, and collaborative learning by means of teamwork and debates (Lebow, 1993). There are also activities that help students acquire and develop learning competence, since they allow students to reflect on their progress, to develop a more active role, and to self-manage their learning.

Fifth, it is embedded learning in social experience in which takes place (Dunlap & Grabinger, 1996; Honebein, 1996; Lebow, 1993). Intellectual development is influenced by social interactions, collaboration between students and students, and students and teachers (Honebein, 1996). In the digital ecosystem, learning is embedded in social experience through the activities developed by means of asynchronous tools such as wikis and forums. These activities manage to eliminate loneliness and isolation that may occur as a result of the existing geographical distance between the participants, since they do not share the same physical space, but the same virtual space. They become members of a learning community through their contributions in these activities. It is tried to create a social virtual community, promoting social interactions between all the participants that are derived from the exchange of ideas, reflections, knowledge, and resources (Bell, 2009).

Sixth, it is the use of multiple modes of representation to meet the different learning styles of participants (Bersin, 2004; Kolb, 1984). In the digital ecosystem, they are combined with forms of transmitting knowledge.

Last, Honebein (1996) refers to the encouragement self-awareness of the knowledge construction process. That is the ability to analyze the construction of knowledge and its processes, as well as the ability to explain why or how to solve problems in a certain way. It is necessary to have learning activities that encourage students to reflect on their knowledge to defend their ideas and positions in solving of the problems. The model in this study presents several activities in which students must reflect on their knowledge and put them into practice. These activities are done through wikis and forums aiming to defend and share their ideas with others to solve problems in these activities.

MAIN FOCUS OF THE CHAPTER

According to the aim of the current study, a qualitative method was employed. The research is based on the Grounded Theory "a general methodology for developing theory that is grounded in data systematically gathered and analyzed. Theory develops and evolves during the research process due to the interplay between data collection and analysis phases." (Strauss & Corbin, 1994, p. 273).

It is relevant to emphasize that the process of the qualitative analysis is dynamic and creative, and two strategies can be distinguished. On one hand, the theoretical sampling that refers to the process of data collection, categorization and analyses, so data are collected and analyzed until theoretical saturation occurs (Glaser & Strauss, 1967). On the other hand, the constant comparison method that refers to the continuous comparative and reflection of the qualitative data to generate theory. According to Glaser and Strauss (2009) four phases can be differentiated 1) comparing incidents and data that are applicable to each category; 2) integrating these categories and their properties; 3) bounding the theory; and 4) setting out the theory.

Participants

Taking as a criterion the objective of our study, the population of the study was composed of a total of 143 pre-service teachers who were enrolled in the subject English Morphosyntax, 33 (23.1%) were men and 110 (76.9%) were women at first. However, the final number of students who participated in this study was 43 participants (25 women and 18 men). That subject is a compulsory area of the degree in Primary Education; students take this module for a semester that represents 150 hours of the student workload.

The participants were divided into three groups (ENG1, ENG2 & ENG3) and they studied the degree in Blended learning modality, having a compulsory face-to-face lesson of 50 minutes every month and two compulsory virtual lessons of 45 minutes every week during the whole semester (a total of 14 weeks). The lecturer used the Blackboard tool as an extended classroom. Apart from the face-to-face and virtual lessons, every group also had two optional and individual tutorials every week.

The qualitative sampling was purposeful sampling since "researchers intentionally select individuals to learn or understand the central phenomenon" (Creswell, 2012, p. 206). It was non-probabilistic, theoretical and cumulative, the necessary sample to reach data saturation and get enough information to meet the aim of the research. Glaser and Strauss (2017) define theoretical sampling as "the process of data collection for generating theory whereby the analyst jointly collects, codes, and analyses his data and decides what data to collect next and where to find them, in order to develop his theory as it emerges. This process of data collection is controlled by the emerging theory, whether substantive or formal." (p.45). They also stated, "saturation means that no additional data are being found" (p.61).

Instrument

The qualitative instrument used to collect data was an unstructured one-to-one interview. As Frances, Coughlan and Cronin (2009) and Creswell (2012) point out one-to-one interviews are more intense and foster intimacy, free expression and a more comprehensive and higher-quality approach of the individual discourse and the inner world of the interviewee. Moreover, this kind of interview may be more feasible and may allow an easier analysis.

On the other hand, as Creswell (2012) states unstructured interviews allow participants to express themselves freely and not to be conditioned by researchers. That means that the interviewer can control the rhythm, structure and content of the interview (Hernández et al., 2014).

Before collecting data, the researcher prepared a general guide for the issues related to the aim of the research. However, it was just a guide, so during the interviews necessary changes were made in each.

The external validity was guaranteed since coding was performed via consensus among 5 experts in educational research and English as a second language. It was calculated the Cohen's Kappa coefficient (k) to measure the agreement between coders in the category system, obtaining $k = 0.85$.

Regarding the internal validity, it was achieved through fulfilment of the recommendation suggested by Coleman and Unrau (2010) and Hernández et al. (2014).

Data Collection and Analyses

Qualitative data were collected at the Faculty of Education along with fifteen sessions carried out at the end of the first semester of 2016-2017 academic year.

The researcher carried out a total of 43 unstructured one-to-one interviews to reach theoretical saturation (Glaser & Strauss, 2017).

Before starting each interview, researchers explained participants the aim of the research and requested their consent to be recorded. Every session was recorded in order to facilitate subsequent transcription and increased its accuracy.

Qualitative data analysis was iterative and recurrent, performing with the help of the qualitative data analysis software NVivo12. As Flick (2004) states, "using software in qualitative research increases its quality, since it allows greater analytical consistency and rigour" (p. 266). The software was used to carry out the coding, storage, search and retrieval of data, as well as to analyze content.

For data analysis it was followed the scheme proposed by Miles and Huberman (1994) in which three phases are identified: data reduction, data display, and drawing and verifying conclusions, to process the data. First, the researcher carried out the separation of units according to thematic criteria. Next, the elements were identified and classified through categorizing and coding of data units to recognize their thematic components and classify them in a certain content category. Then, NVivo12 was used to carry out such categorization and codification. In the data display phase, data were arranged in figures to illustrate the results. Finally, in the last phase, the results were presented and interpreted, and the main conclusions of the research were driven.

RESULTS, SOLUTIONS AND RECOMMENDATIONS

The semantic analysis was carried out to find out the words or expressions that occurred more frequently in the individual semi-structured interviews. The word cloud (Figure 1) shows that ten terms appeared more often in the discourse which were: learning (579 references), English (559 references), education (551 references), knowledge (542 references), technology (541 references), innovation (528 references), community (526 references), activities (524 references), autonomous (514 references), lifelong (513 references), students (512 references), active (507 references), collaborative (505 references), teacher (504 references), grammar (502 references), skills (501 references), forums (492 references), roles (490 references), podcast (487 references), and videocast (482 references).

Figure 1. Word Cloud

Following the process of qualitative data analysis described previously, a series of categories and subcategories organized hierarchically (Figure 2) according to pre-service teachers' perceptions were determined. Regarding the aim of the research, a total of three categories with their subcategories emerged from the data analysis: 1. E-activities: 1.1. Innovation, 1.2. English, 1.3. Practice; 2. Learning: 2.1. Autonomous, 2.2. Collaborative; 2.3. Lifelong; 3. Roles: 3.1. Teacher, 3.2. Students.

Figure 2. Conceptual Map

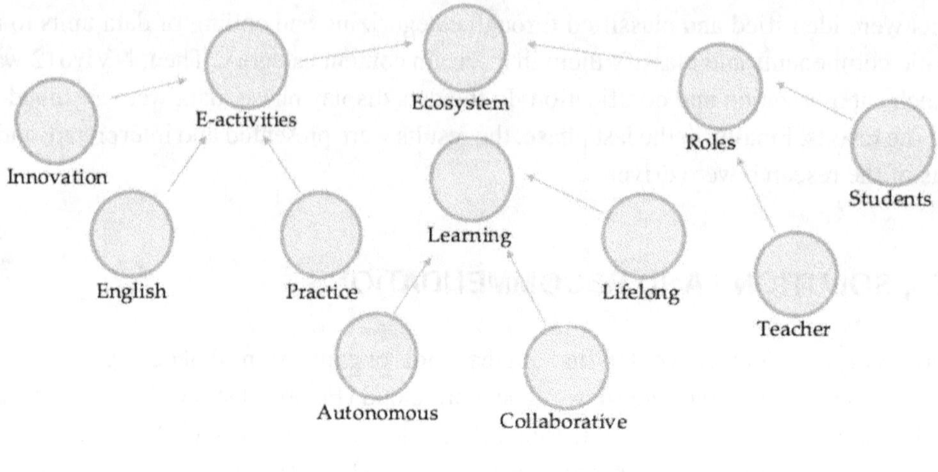

In the next sections, the researcher presents the findings of qualitative content analysis, including some verbatim quotes from the pre-service teachers' discourse.

Category 1. E-Activities

The analysis of the pre-service teachers' discourse revealed that the e-activities available in the digital ecosystem were very innovative. Participants directly related that aspect to the use of different asynchronous technological tools such as online tests, podcasts, videocasts, wikis or forums. According to the pre-service teachers' perceptions, it achieved a digital ecosystem that used technology with an educational purpose to help them to be successful and attained the aims of the course. Also, the qualitative results also emphasized how the e-activities were very efficient to improve their level of English and the achievement of the aims and contents of the subject English Morphosyntax. Based on the analysis of the discourse, participants might consider that there was a significant impact on their level of grammar competence, discourse competence and confidence in that second language (L2) through the development of the e-activities.

They referred to the digital ecosystem as a model in which the teacher provided a design, including diverse kinds of e-activities that helped them to gain or increase their confidence to use the second language. In line with findings of Jeffrey et al., (2014), the ecosystem helped the students to further improved their level by using the e-activities and technological tools used.

It was also highlighted the availability of the e-activities, since a great part of them could be done whenever they connected, adapting to their personal and professional obligations with an accessibility to 24 hours a day.

The pre-service teachers deemed that they had enough activities to learn the contents of the course and put them into practice in order to review and reinforce the concepts that could be more difficult. They believed that it would be impossible to pass assessment e-activities if they had not had enough practice. Moreover, they considered that they had done a lot of virtual work, and they valued positively that teacher had considered those tasks for their final mark. They also highlighted the importance of having self-assessment e-activities to know their progress in English, and to be conscious of their weaknesses and strengths. Also, the participants were actively involved in the learning process and managed their learning individually, and collaboratively as found by Yeh & Swinehart (2017).

The participants pointed that all that was possible because of the use of the asynchronous tools because they eliminated all the temporal and spatial barriers that could prevent it.

I think that the e-activities have been perfectly designed to improve our level of English. They have helped us to improve grammar, written skills... They have been perfect. (24-year-old man, participant 32)

We have had access to the development of different activities through technological tools that make the digital ecosystem highly innovative, using technological tools with an educational purpose. (42-year-old woman, participant 1)

I think that the activity developed through the technological tools has been quite appropriate to achieve the learning objectives. (27-year-old woman, participant 4)

I would like to say that the activity done has been very effective and we have had the opportunity to improve our written skills and English grammar. (32-year-old woman, participant 8)

I can really say that we have had many opportunities to improve, especially our writing skills. (43-year-old man, participant 7)

We have had the necessary activities to practice the contents of the course and improve our level of English. (25-year-old woman, participant 9)

There were different activities that have helped us to practice and learn the contents of the subject. (45-year-old woman, participant 16)

The resources and activities available in the digital ecosystem facilitated the acquisition of the contents. (31-year-old woman, participant 37)

I have definitely improved my level in English and I feel more confidence and motivated to carry on with my training as future primary education teacher. (29-year-old woman, participant 17)

We developed different activities through several technological tools that are always available. We have learned how to use tools such as forums and wiki in an educational context. It was a fully-equipped language model that was always available. (41-year-old woman, participant 25)

We have had a wide variety of self-assessment and assessment activities in each module which have helped us practice, review and consolidate English contents and skills. Blended learning is a modality that requires doing a lot of work, and teacher has valued it. (31-year-old woman, participant 42)

Category 2. Learning

The findings also indicated that the digital ecosystem implemented and the instructional approach behind it allowed the pre-service teachers to reinforce their autonomy and independence in learning, as well as the collaboration between them. These two ways of learning fit together well, since it was evident that they improved and developed autonomous learning skills as well as other skills such as positive and respectful attitudes, interpersonal skills, teamwork, task management and communication.

The participants' discourse pointed out that they had enough activities and resources to practice and the freedom to manage their pace of learning.

They considered that they were the main participants of the teaching-learning process, and that the instructional approach designed in the digital ecosystem implemented placed them in the center of all, what led to a personalized education and to an autonomous learning, successfully adjusting to the participants' different learning styles. That did not mean isolation on the part of the participants, and lack of collaborative learning, but they could decide their rhythm of learning, being aware of their strengths and weaknesses (Gómez, 2006; Pérez et al., 2009).

They learned to manage their own learning that is one of the strongest points of the European Higher Education Area (EHEA) and to reflect on what they were doing. They considered that that reflection helped them to acquire the skill of learning to learn which is essential to learn and improve in the acquisition of a L2, since the learning of any L2 implies a lifelong learning (Murphy et a., 2005). The results demonstrated that the design of the digital ecosystem was efficient for lifelong learning what permitted the pre-service teachers to carry out with their training. On the other hand, they highlighted that the digital ecosystem allowed them to participate in different tasks with their classmates, promoting collaborative learning, interaction and the creation of a learning community. They considered that it was possible because they had the necessary technological tools to promote collaborative learning regardless of wherever they are, the moment they connect to the digital ecosystem, and their personal and professional situation. They also emphasized how the collaborative virtual learning permitted them to help each other to achieve the learning objectives and the contents of the subject English Morphosyntax, to improve their knowledge in the second language.

The learning experience, as an interactive experience, was another of the main issue extracted from the content analysis. Most of the participants considered that the possibilities provided in the digital ecosystem for the interaction between the participants of the teaching-learning process were essential for the effectiveness of that learning. The pre-service teachers specifically emphasized how they could interact with their classmates during the development of the tasks as found by Hampel (2006) or when they wanted to solve some problems arise on the contents of the course, eliminating all the spatial and temporal barriers, and making the learning experience more dynamic.

I emphasize the planning and method of the digital ecosystem since it allows us to learn at our own pace. We have decided, considering our personal and professional duties and our free time, when we have connected to the virtual environment to use the materials or do the activities through different technological tools. In my opinion, I have felt that I have been part of a more personalized education. It has been designed an environment in which it has been considered the diversity of the participants studying this degree. It has adapted to the heterogeneity of us and to the needs of each one. (43-year-old man, participant 7)

This model allows us to be independent and manage our own time and learning. It permits us to decide what we do every day, what we need to study or devote more time. (23-year-old woman, participant 11)

This model allows us to be independent and manage our own time and learning. It permits us to decide what we do every day, what we need to study or devote more time. (22-year-old man, participant 43)

We have participated in an experience in which we could work individually acquiring the responsibility in a task in which we collaborated. It was a more effective learning process. (37-year-old woman, participant 22)

The way in which it has been designed has favored collaborative work in which we have learned together and have shared everything. (32-year-old man, participant 20)

I also highlight how the use of some technological tools allowed us to work as a team. For example, we have used different forums to share our ideas. All this has improved or promoted collaborative learning and teamwork. (37-year-old woman, participant 41)

Undoubtedly the digital ecosystem in which I have participated has been much more personalized than any other learning experience I have had. There have been used many technological tools to design the activities and different resources to provide the contents that have perfectly adapted to our needs and to the different types of learning. It has been a much more personalized education that it is centered in us, considering the personal characteristics of all of us, and our needs in the second language. The participants were not homogeneous, so it would have been a complete disaster to have tried to design and homogenous environment. (35-year-old man, participant 19)

The virtual environment has provided us different technological tools to develop the activities and work as a team, avoiding an individualistic learning. We have had, for example, the forums to work together and solve our problems on the content of the course, and the design and development of wikis of English grammar lessons or methodological ideas for teaching English. Both tools allowed us to communicate with our classmates with whom we have shared the virtual environment, and to work together. (27-year-old woman, participant 4)

The activities carried out with others have allowed us to have a fluid communication and participate more in the different tasks proposed in the digital ecosystem. We were pretty committed to the work developed in the community. (31-year-old woman, participant 37)

We have been actively involved in the development of the activities; we have taken the decisions and have assumed individual and group responsibilities. (31-year-old man, participant 24)

The fact that we could communicate through different technological tools available any day at any time have increased and have contributed to the possibilities to interact between us. (42-year-old man, participant 39)

Category 3. Roles

Regarding the roles of the participants of the teaching-learning process from the content analysis could gather that the teacher had a relevant role in the success of the course. The participants described that the teacher's role is not as a dominating trainer, as a primarily and only knowledge transmitter, but as a guide and facilitator of the learning and development of the tasks. They also highlighted the clarity and organization of the digital ecosystem. They considered that it was essential to have a digital ecosystem with a good organization in which everything was clearly specified, since they had few face-to-face lessons during the whole academic year, and the digital ecosystem became their classroom to which they connected daily to do the tasks, download the files, and participate in the different forums, etc. This was directly related to the involvement of the teacher in the process, since she decided the structure of the digital ecosystem, and planned the tasks, anticipating the difficulties that the students could have. She designed a digital ecosystem that did not lead itself to any mistake that prevented student from learning. The participants also pointed out that blended learning training required an intensive work on the part of the teachers and considered that the success or failure of a course in that modality depended on teacher's work.

On the other hand, the participants considered that they also had an active role in the learning process; they constructed knowledge, managed their own learning according to their personal situation, and reflected on their specific needs in the second language to achieve the learning objectives and contents of the course. They did not only download, read and memorized the contents of the course provided by the teacher, but they also analyzed them, planned the activities and their contents, collaborated in the development of the tasks, and helped each other. They were able to construct knowledge working in groups and exchanging their ideas on the different learning objectives and contents of the subject, and they kept an active role during the whole process.

The qualitative results demonstrated how the learning experience was engaging since the participants were involved in the development of the tasks. The fact of being an active and engaging learning experience increased their motivation and interest towards the contents of the course as found by Hampel and Hauck (2006). They felt that they were the protagonists of the teaching-learning process. That could mean that there was a shift in the kind of methodology from a tutor-centered instruction to a learner-centered one, and a change in the roles of teachers and students.

The role of the teacher is completely essential for the success of the virtual learning environment of this course. (27-year-old woman, participant 12)

The teacher is a fundamental key in this kind of education because she guides us. (41-year-old woman, participant 25)

I think the teacher makes a great effort because it is not easy to design all these e-activities and a digital ecosystem as the one we have used. (20-year-old man, participant 31)

The noun that best defines the digital ecosystem is clarity because the topics were well defined and organized. (22-year-old woman, participant 21)

I considered that the teacher has made a great effort in the previous design of the environment and during the development of the course. She has guided and has helped us during the whole process. (34-year-old woman, participant 40)

It was a well-designed digital ecosystem in which contents and e-activities were well defined and distributed, and technological tools were perfectly used. I am grateful that this digital ecosystem has been clear and has provided us all that we have needed to pass the course. (25-year-old man, participant 15)

The way in which was everything planned have engaged us and have encouraged our active participation during the course. (34-year-old man, participant 23)

The development of some e-activities through different technological tools have allowed us to participate more actively in the course, contribute to the construction of knowledge, and demonstrate what they had learned. (23-year-old woman, participant 28)

We have been actively involved in the learning process, in the development of the tasks and the creation of knowledge. We have taken decisions and assumed individual and group responsibilities. (42-year-old woman, participant 33)

I feel that I have been an active part of the teaching-learning process in which we have had access to all the resources and the tasks that we have been able to develop through the different technological tools. It is clear that this has increased my interest and motivation for the course. (37-year-old woman, participant 22)

FUTURE RESEARCH DIRECTIONS AND LIMITATION OF THE STUDY

The main limitations of the current research are, on one hand, the sample size since the researcher focused on a specific group of students, specifically they collected the data regarding the perspectives from 43 participants who were studying a second university degree. On the other hand, they focused on a specific University, on a specific degree and on a specific blended learning model or program. The results obtained in this study could probably vary if the sample was different or if the research was conducted in other grades and universities with different programs and different backgrounds, so it is recommended to carry out a similar study in different degrees and with a higher population to know or compare the results obtained in this previous study.

The current research suggests that blended learning modality and the new digital ecosystems represent a solid opportunity to offer students learning experiences that adapt to any personal or professional situation. Based on this perspective, it is possible to predict that blended learning modality will be an important instruction to respond to the educational demands of the present society. Besides, its current relevance will increase in the future since citizens of the 21st century need to train and keep their skills up-to-date.

The researchers conducted on blended learning and digital ecosystems in the future must focus not only on learners' formation but also on teachers' training. They will specifically focus on the acquisition of pedagogical and technological skills needed to carry out useful blended learning educational experiences. On the other hand, the future research must focus on how to support universities to implement these blended learning experiences providing them the necessary resources and materials.

CONCLUSION

To meet the goal of the study, researchers analyzed pre-service teachers' perspective on the effectiveness of the digital ecosystem implemented in the area of English Morphosyntax. The findings clearly confirmed the appropriateness of the digital ecosystem designed and implemented in blended learning modality to study a second language and achieve the aims and contents of the subject.

Regarding the results, it can be concluded that the efficiency of the model was due to the commitment of all the protagonist of the teaching-learning process, and the work developed by the participants and the teacher. The students were active participants and knew how to manage their learning, and to collaborate with their classmates (Yeh & Swinehart, 2017). On the other hand, the teacher achieved to design a well-organized model in which the participants had access to all the contents and information of the course and the necessary practice to meet the objectives of the subject. She properly guided the students in the development of the e-activities and the use of technological tools used (Jeffrey et al., 2014).

The flexibility and accessibility of the e-activities was provided thanks to the technological tools available in the digital ecosystem. That allowed the pre-service teachers to combine their personal and professional obligations with lifelong learning. Overcoming all the spatial and temporal barriers, and developing a kind of learning just-in-time, just-for-students, anytime, and anywhere were achieved, since the participants decided when they connected and carried out the e-activities at anyplace they were currently in, and determined their own pace. In short, the pre-service teachers managed their own learning, and were responsible for the progress in their level of English. All that was possible because the design of the digital ecosystem was compatible with any professional and personal situation, and with the possibility of continuing studying.

As it has been pointed out previously, the results demonstrated that the flexibility of the digital ecosystem was unquestionably linked to technology. Moreover, technological tools helped teacher to design individual, collaborative and innovative activities that enriched the teaching-learning process, and aided participants to study a second language.

The digital ecosystem created a favorable environment for learning and updating the participants' knowledge of different technological resources. The use of different technological tools permitted the digital literacy of the different generations. Although, at the beginning of the course, the use of these technologies could mean an extra effort on the part of the participants, the constant used allowed them to be updated with technologies and improve their confidence in them and their digital competence.

It was achieved that the participants had all the necessary resources and tools to be autonomous, independent, and self-manage their learning. At the same time, it was obtained a digital ecosystem that promoted a collaboration-based learning (Hampel, 2006), and the creation of a learning community (Lee, 2010; Pinto-Llorente, Sánchez-Gómez & García-Peñalvo, 2018; Twu, 2010), since some of the activities and the tools used allowed the pre-service teachers to solve their problems arise on the contents of the subject, share their ideas and create knowledge all together. Moreover, the technological tools and their asynchronicity contributed to the interaction and communication between the participants of the teaching-learning process, what it was essential to avoid isolation and loneliness.

The digital ecosystem model was adapted for different rhythms and learning styles, since the participants chose between a great multiplicity of files in different formats and decided their own pace, devoted more time to those contents that they considered more difficult.

According to Valiathan (2002) and his classification of blended learning models, it is possible to affirm that the digital ecosystem helps autonomous learning in which the participants decide their own pace, with the collaboration and support received by the teacher and the rest of classmates through different communicative and collaborative resources, as well as through tutorials and face-to-face lessons. It has been achieved to develop four different kind of learning: individual learning, collaborative learning, technological learning, and English learning.

The results of the current research proved the potential of the design of the digital ecosystem to study and practice a second language. The main limitation of the study was the sample size since the study focused on the perception of 43 pre-service teachers from one grade and a university. Although there are not evidences that the results obtained in the current research could vary. It could be possible that they were different if the sample size increased or if the study was conducted with different levels or universities.

REFERENCES

Allan, B. (2007). *Blended Learning tools for teaching and training*. London: Facet Publishing. doi:10.29085/9781856047845

Arteaga, R., & Duarte, A. (2010). Motivational factors that influence the acceptance of Moodle using TAM. *Computers in Human Behavior*, *26*(6), 1632–1640. doi:10.1016/j.chb.2010.06.011

Bell, G. (2009). *Building Social Web Applications*. Sebastopol, CA: O'Reilly Media.

Bersin, J. (2004). *The Blended Learning Book. Best Practices, Proven Methodologies, and Lessons Learned*. San Francisco: Pfeiffer.

Blumberg, P. (2009). *Developing Learner-Centered Teaching. A Practical Guide for Faculty*. San Francisco: John Wiley & Sons.

Canale, M. (1983). De la competencia comunicativa a la pedagogía comunicativa del lenguaje. In *Competencia comunicativa. Documentos básicos en la enseñanza de lenguas extranjeras* (pp. 63–83). Madrid: Edelsa.

Canale, M., & Swain, M. (1980). Theoretical Bases of Communicative Approaches to Second Language Teaching and Testing. *Applied Linguistics*, *1*(1), 1–47. doi:10.1093/applin/1.1.1

Coaten, N. (2003). Blended e-learning. *Educaweb, 69*. Retrieved from https://www.educaweb.com/esp/servicios/monografico/formacionvirtual/1181076.asp

Cole, J., & Foster, H. (2008). *Using Moodle. Teaching with the Popular Open Source Course Management System*. Sebastopol, CA: O'Reilly Media.

Coleman, H., & Unrau, Y. A. (2010). Qualitative Data Analysis. In R. M. Grinnell & Y. A. Unrau (Eds.), *Social Work: Research and Evaluation. Foundations of Evidence-Based Practice* (pp. 447–464). New York: Oxford University Press.

Creswell, J. (2012). *Educational Research: Planning, Conducting, and Evaluating Quantitative and Qualitative Research*. Boston: Pearson Education.

De la Torre, A. (2006). Web Educativa 2.0. *Edutec. Revista Electrónica de Tecnología Educativa*. Retrieved from https://www.uib.es/depart/gte/gte/edutec-e/revelec20/anibal20.htm

Duffy, T. M., & Cunningham, D. J. (1996). Constructivism: Implications for the Design and Delivery of Instruction. In D. H. Jonassen (Ed.), *Handbook of Research for Educational Communications and Technology* (pp. 170–198). New York: Macmillan Library Reference.

Dunlap, J. C., & Grabinger, R. S. (1996). Rich Environments for Active Learning in the Higher Education Classroom. In B. G. Wilson (Ed.), *Constructivist learning environments: Case studies in instructional design* (pp. 65–83). Englewood Cliffs, NJ: Educational Technology Publications.

Frances, R., Coughlan, M., & Cronin, P. (2009). Interviewing in qualitative research. *International Journal of Therapy and Rehabilitation*, *16*(6), 309–314. doi:10.12968/ijtr.2009.16.6.42433

Gisbert, M. (2002). El Nuevo rol del profesor en entornos tecnológicos. *Acción pedagógica, 11*(1), 48-59.

Glaser, B. G., & Strauss, A. L. (2017). *The Discovery of Grounded Theory: Strategies for Qualitative Research*. New York: Routledge. doi:10.4324/9780203793206

Gómez, J. (2006). *Moodle 1.5 Manual de Consulta. Propuesta Pedagógica*. Valladolid: GNU Press.

González, A. B., Rodríguez, M.-J., Olmos, S., Borham, M., & García, F. (2013). Experimental evaluation of the impact of b-learning methodologies on engineering students in Spain. *Computers in Human Behavior*, *29*(2), 370–377. doi:10.1016/j.chb.2012.02.003

González, J. C. (2008). TIC y la transformación de la práctica educativa en el contexto de las sociedades del conocimiento. *Revista de Universidad y Sociedad del Conocimiento, 5*(2). Retrieved from https://www.uoc.edu/rusc/5/2/dt/esp/gonzalez.pdf

Gott, S. P., Lesgold, A., & Kane, R. S. (1996). Tutoring for Transfer of Technical Competence. In B. G. Wilson (Ed.), *Constructivist learning environments: Case studies in instructional design* (pp. 33–48). Englewood Cliffs, NJ: Educational Technology Publications.

Grabinger, R. S., & Dunlap, J. C. (1996). Rich Environments for Active Learning in the Higher Education Classroom. In B. G. Wilson (Ed.), *Constructivist Learning Environments: Case Studies in Instructional Design* (pp. 65–81). Englewood Cliffs, NJ: Educational Technology Publications.

Graham, C. R. (2006). Blended Learning Systems. Definition, Current Trends, and Future Directions. In C. R. Graham & C. J. Bonk (Eds.), *The Handbook of Blended Learning. Global Perspectives, Local Design* (pp. 3–21). San Francisco: Pfeiffer.

Hampel, R. (2006). Rethinking task design for the digital age. *ReCALL, 18*(1), 105–121. doi:10.1017/S0958344006000711

Hampel, R., & Hauck, M. (2006). Computer-mediated language learning: Making meaning in multimodal virtual learning space. *The JALT CALL Journal*, *2*(2), 3–18.

Hernández, R., Fernández, C., & Baptista, P. (2014). *Metodología de la investigación*. McGraw Hill.

Honebein, P. C. (1996). Seven Goals for the Design of Constructivist Learning Environment. In B. G. Wilson (Ed.), *Constructivist learning environments: Case studies in instructional design* (pp. 11–24). Englewood Cliffs, NJ: Educational Technology Publications.

Hymes, D. (1972). On Communicative Competence. In J. Pride & J. Holmes (Eds.), *Sociolinguistics* (pp. 269–293). Harmondsworth, UK: Penguin.

Jeffrey, L. M., Milne, J., Suddaby, G., & Higgins, A. (2014). Blended learning: How teachers balance the blend of online and classroom components. *Journal of Information Technology Education, 13*, 121–140. doi:10.28945/1968

Kolb, D. A. (1984). *Experiential Learning: experience as the source of learning and development*. Prentice Hall.

Lebow, D. (1993). Constructivist Values for Instructional Systems Design: Five Principles toward a New Mindset. *Educational Technology Research and Development*, *41*(3), 4–16. doi:10.1007/BF02297354

Lee, L. (2010). Exploring wiki-mediated collaborative writing: A case-study in an elementary Spanish course. *CALICO Journal*, *27*(2), 260–276. doi:10.11139/cj.27.2.260-276

López, C., & Matesanz, M. (2009). *Las plataformas de aprendizaje. Del mito a la realidad.* Madrid: Editorial Biblioteca Nueva.

Man-Man, P. (2006). Developing Students' listening and speaking Skills Through ELT Podcasts. *Education Journal*, *34*(2), 115–134.

Miles, M. B., & Huberman, A. (1994). *Qualitative Data Analysis: An Expanded Sourcebook.* Newbury Park, CA: SAGE.

Morris, C. D., Bransford, J. D., & Franks, J. J. (1979). Levels of Processing versus Transfer Appropriate Processing. *Journal of Verbal Learning and Verbal Behavior*, *16*(5), 519–533. doi:10.1016/S0022-5371(77)80016-9

Murphy, L., Hauck, M., Nicolson, M., & Adams, H. (2005). Reflection and self-evaluation. In S. Hurd, & L. Murphy (Eds.), Success with Languages. Abingdon: Routledge in association with The Open University.

Oliver, R. (2000). When Teaching Meets Learning: Design, Principles and Strategies for Web-based Learning Environments that Support Knowledge Construction. In R. Sims, M. O'Reilly & S. Sawkins (Eds.), *Learning to Choose: Choosing to Learn. Proceedings of the 17th Annual ASCILITE Conference* (pp. 17-28). Lismore, Australia: Southern Cross University Press.

Payne, C. R. (2009). *Information Technology and Constructivism in Higher Education Progressive Learning Frameworks.* Hershey, PA: IGI Global. doi:10.4018/978-1-60566-654-9

Pérez, M. T. (2009). *Innovación en docencia universitaria con Moodle. Casos prácticos.* Alicante: Editorial Club Universitario.

Pinto-Llorente, A. M., Sánchez-Gómez, M. C., & García-Peñalvo, F. J. (2017). A Mixed Methods Research of Pre-service Teachers' Perceptions about the Benefits of Wiki-Based Tasks and Discussion Boards. In *Computer Supported Qualitative Research, Advances in Intelligent Systems and Computing* (pp. 260–276). Springer International Publishing.

Pinto-Llorente, A. M., Sánchez-Gómez, M. C., & García-Peñalvo, F. J. (2018). A Research on Students' Perceptions on a B-Learning English Environment to Improve Written Skills. In V. Ahuja & S. Rathore (Eds.), *Multidisciplinary Perspectives on Human Capital and Information Technology Professionals* (pp. 179–201). Hershey, PA: IGI Global. doi:10.4018/978-1-5225-5297-0.ch010

Savignon, S. J. (1972). *Communicative Competence: An experiment in foreign language teaching.* Philadelphia, PA: Center for Curriculum Development.

Strauss, A., & Corbin, J. (1994). Grounded Theory Methodology. An Overview. In N. K. Denzin & Y. S. Lincoln (Eds.), *Handbook of Qualitative Research* (pp. 273–285). Thousand Oaks: SAGE.

Thorne, K. (2003). *Blended Learning: How to integrate online and traditional learning*. London: Kogan.

Twu, H. (2010). A predictive study of Wiki interaction: Can attitude toward Wiki predict Wiki interaction in High-Context Cultures groups? *Journal of Educational Technology Development and Exchange*, *3*(1), 57–68. doi:10.18785/jetde.0301.05

Valiathan, P. (2002). *Designing a Blended Learning Solution*. Retrieved from http://www.docstoc.com/docs/2261631/Designing-a-Blended-Learning-Solution-What-is-Blended-Learning#

Willis, J. (2009). *Constructivist Instructional Design (C-ID). Foundations, Models, and Examples*. Charlotte, NC: Information Age Publishing.

Yeh, E., & Swinehart, N. (2017). A Learner-Centered Approach to Technology Integration: Online Geographical Tools in the ESL Classroom. In J. Keengwe & G. Onchwari (Eds.), Handbook of Research on Learner-Centered Pedagogy in Teacher Education and Professional Development (pp. 1-22). Hershey, PA: Information Science Reference, IGI Global.

ADDITIONAL READING

Cole, J., & Foster, H. (2008). *Using Moodle. Teaching with the Popular Open Source Course Management System*. Sebastopol, California: O'Reilly Media.

González, A. B., & … . (2013). Experimental evaluation of the impact of b-learning methodologies on engineering students in Spain. *Computers in Human Behavior*, *29*(2), 370–377.

Graham, C. R. (2006). Blended Learning Systems. Definition, Current Trends, and Future Directions. In C. R. Graham & C. J. Bonk (Eds.), *The Handbook of Blended Learning. Global Perspectives, Local Design* (pp. 3–21). San Francisco: Pfeiffer.

López, C., & Matesanz, M. (2009). *Las plataformas de aprendizaje. Del mito a la realidad*. Madrid: Editorial Biblioteca Nueva.

Pérez, M. T., & … . (2009). *Innovación en docencia universitaria con Moodle. Casos prácticos*. Alicante: Editorial Club Universitario.

Pinto-Llorente, A. M., Sánchez-Gómez, M. C., & García-Peñalvo, F. J. (2016). Students' perceptions and attitudes towards asynchronous technological tools in blended-learning training to improve grammatical competence in English as a second language. *Computers in Human Behavior*, *72*, 632–643.

Pinto-Llorente, A. M., Sánchez-Gómez, M. C., & García-Peñalvo, F. J. (2016). Assessing the Effectiveness of Interactive and Collaborative Resources to Improve Reading and Writing in English. *International Journal of Human Capital and Information Technology Professionals*, *7*(1), 66–85.

Pinto-Llorente, A. M., Sánchez-Gómez, M. C., & García-Peñalvo, F. J. (2017). Blended learning modality and English pronunciation: Findings from an ICT-supported model. *Revista de Educación a Distancia*, *52*, 1–29.

Pinto-Llorente, A. M., Sánchez-Gómez, M. C., & García-Peñalvo, F. J. (2018). Students Skills in a Blended Learning Environment: A Qualitative Research. In A. Borchers (Ed.), *Technology Management in Organizational and Societal Contexts* (pp. 249–280). Hershey, PA, USA: IGI Global.

Thorne, K. (2003). *Blended Learning: How to integrate online and traditional learning*. London: Kogan.

KEY TERMS AND DEFINITIONS

Active Learning: It is a type of learning in which teaching tries to involve learners in the learning process. Students are actively engaged in the development of the lessons, activities, etc., and improve skills such as reflection, problem solving and critical thinking, etc.

Autonomous Learning: It refers to a situation in which learners are responsible for their learning. They take charge of their own learning and are actively involved, taking individual decisions according to their necessities or preferences focused on the goals they need to achieve.

Blended Learning: A kind of education modality that combines both face-to-face and online lessons.

Collaborative Learning: It refers to a situation in which a group of students learn together and have an active role in creating and sharing knowledge.

Higher Education: It is the third level of education. It is beyond secondary education and is normally provided by universities or colleges.

Learner-Centered Pedagogy: It refers to a pedagogy that places students at the center of the teaching-learning process. Students are more active and participative, and the process turns knowledge into a negotiation between teachers and students. Furthermore, this pedagogy starts from students' interests and objectives, and it carries out a learning process based on real situations and materials, using the current technologies to favor this process.

Learning Community: It refers to a group of students who work collaboratively, share knowledge and have common learning objectives.

Qualitative Research: It is a methodological approach based on an interpretative perspective focused on the understanding of human behavior. The techniques used to collect qualitative data are observation, interviews (semi-structured interviews, unstructured interviews, structured interviews), group discussions, and evaluation of personal experiences, interaction with different communities, or recordings of life stories.

Section 3

ICT-Based Programs

Chapter 14
Effectiveness of Computer-Managed Instruction on Students' Performance in Tertiary Institutions

Salako E. Adekunle
FCT College of Education, Zuba, Nigeria

Solomon Adelowo Adepoju
https://orcid.org/0000-0002-1128-4753
Federal University of Technology, Minna, Nigeria

Garba Suleiman
https://orcid.org/0000-0001-7937-2816
FCT College of Education, Zuba, Nigeria

Muhammad Bashir Abdullahi
https://orcid.org/0000-0001-8200-2787
Federal University of Technology, Minna, Nigeria

ABSTRACT

The roles of information technology in the contemporary world cannot be over-emphasized considering its enormous usage in the educational sector. This chapter investigates the effectiveness of computer-managed instruction (CMI) on students' performance in tertiary institutions in the North-Central Geopolitical Zone of Nigeria. The control group was taught Computer Science using traditional lecture method (TLM) approach, and the experimental group was taught using CMI approach. A total of 360 students in colleges of education (COE), polytechnic, and university participated in the study by using multi-stage sampling procedures. The null hypotheses were tested using ANCOVA and ANOVA statistical analyses at 0.05 level of significance. Findings revealed that there was a statistical difference in the performance scores of students using CMI and TLM approaches. There was also a statistical difference between private and public tertiary institution students' performance. Additionally, the students from the university had the highest mean when compared with students from COE and polytechnics.

DOI: 10.4018/978-1-7998-3062-7.ch014

INTRODUCTION

The world has revolutionized with remarkable impacts of information and communication technologies (ICTs) in different spheres of life. The benefits of ICTs in Engineering, Science, Commerce, Energy, Health/Medicine, Communication, Manufacturing, Financial Institutions, Transportation and Agriculture have tremendously created a world of all possibilities. The field of education is not left behind in exploiting the significance of ICTs towards achieving the educational goals and objectives at all levels of education. The teaching and learning processes could be enhanced with the adoption of ICTs into the classroom's discussion by teachers and students. ICTs can be used for repetition of instructions until the specific learning objectives are achieved or mastered, preparation and presentation of ideas, and analysis among others. Educational packages such as Computer Assisted Instructions (CAI), Computer Based Training (CBT), Computer Managed Instruction (CMI) and Computer Assisted Learning (CAL) are available for use in the dissemination of educational instructions.

Therefore, this chapter intends to draw attention to the effectiveness of computer-managed instruction on students' performance in tertiary institutions in North-Central geopolitical zone of Nigeria. The main objective includes finding out the difference between computer-managed instruction and conventional lecture method in computer science in tertiary institutions. However, students get distracted with certain graphical information via the internet which later negatively affects the overall academic performance in a chosen course of study. The researchers stated that instructions which are not well managed and disseminated through the use of ICTs could endanger the academic performance of students at tertiary institutions in Nigeria. The causes of poor academic performance in computer science among students include poor teaching and learning techniques, infrastructures, instructional management, lack of conducive learning environment and non-availability of computers for studying and researching (Rozema, 2011).

The roles of tertiary institutions cannot be ignored in the development of individual and society at large. Tertiary institutions offer opportunities to a group of individuals to acquire skills, do research and develop human capacity. Regrettably, many tertiary institutions lack qualified lecturers and the few excellent lecturers they have in education are looking for a better career outside the teaching profession. However, when the tertiary institutions lack qualified lecturers to deliver their modules and do research effectively, then this will have a negative impact on improving the current education and the society at large. The fundamental responsibilities for future advancement and development of nations in the world lie on the youths and students in particular. Therefore, adequate attention is required to ensure that the students are provided with the required information and skills for intellectual capacity.

Significantly, ICT could be useful to enhance teaching and learning processes among the lecturers and students at tertiary institutions. A computer-based learning package can be provided to help teachers and students to share information and do research projects at the same time. According to Bada, Adewole and Olalekan (2009), the benefits of computer applications in education include the followings:

- Students could learn at their own pace
- Provision of suitable feedback
- Motivation towards learning
- Enhancement of personalized instruction through individualized reactions
- Provision of adequate control over learning
- Enhancement of self-assessment towards repetition of instructions until desired objectives are achieved.

For every student to achieve higher academic achievement in the twenty-first century, an integration of technology into the learning process cannot be neglected (Padma & Adi, 2000). The poor academic performance of students in the tertiary institutions has been an issue of concern to parents and educators. The students were asked to explain the causes of their poor academic performance in computer science. The finding revealed that poor teaching techniques were attributed to their poor academic performance (Emmanuel & Olusegun, 2015). Therefore, if computer-managed instructions can help students enhance and improve their learning at tertiary institutions, then to what extent would computer-managed instructions affect the academic performance or outcomes of students in computer science needs urgent attention before a full adoption into the classroom is recommended? The chapter presents empirical findings on the effectiveness of computer-managed instruction on students' performance in tertiary institutions in North-Central geopolitical zone of Nigeria. The following research questions were asked to guide the conduct of the research:

1. What is the difference between the performance scores of students taught computer science using computer managed instruction and traditional lecture method?
2. What is the difference in the performance of male and female students taught computer science using computer managed instruction?
3. What is the difference in the performance of public and private schools' students taught computer science using computer managed instruction?

As a follow up to the research questions, the following null hypotheses were postulated:

1. There is no significant difference in the mean performance score of students taught computer science using computer managed instruction and conventional lecture method.
2. There is no significant difference in the mean performance scores of students taught computer science using computer managed instruction based on institutions.

Specifically, the objectives of the research were to:

1. find out the difference in the performance scores of students taught computer science using computer managed instruction and conventional lecture method;
2. examine the difference in the performance of male and female students taught computer science using computer managed instruction;
3. observe the difference in the performance of public and private schools' students taught computer science using computer managed instruction;
4. investigate if there is a significant difference in the mean performance score of students taught computer science using computer managed instruction and conventional lecture method; and
5. investigate if there is a significant difference in the mean performance score of students taught computer science using computer managed instruction and the institutions.

BACKGROUND

A computer managed instruction is an application of a computer to deliver learning instructions to the learners and resources for achieving a specific set of objectives at the end of instructions. (Mee-chin, Abrizah, & Lip, 2012). Objectives such as students should be able to define computer and mention the basic hardware components of computer could be stated as objectives.

Computer managed instruction is referred to the instructional technique where learning instructions and assessment of specific objectives are carried out through the use of computer applications. In a computer-managed instruction environment, the learners might listen and watch computer animation to acquire specific knowledge. The teachers or instructors are not major active facilitators, rather; the learners are active because computer-managed instruction is a learner-centered technique. This implies that the learners could repeatedly learn specific instruction or acquire specific knowledge at their pace without over dependence on their teacher.

John and Harrison (2018) stated that CMI is an instructional strategy that uses a computer to deliver learning objectives, learning resources, and assessment of learner performance. Significantly, computer-managed instruction engages the learners to learn at their own pace and relieves the physical stress of teachers who would not actively involved in the teaching. (John & Harrison, 2018). Padma and Adi (2000) encouraged the teachers to integrate CMI technology in higher education for effectiveness in the teaching and learning process.

Bliss, Mark, Jonathan, Godwin and Justine (2017) investigated the effect of CAI on students' academic achievement in Mathematics. The finding showed that the CAI was effective on the acquisition of mathematical skills with little teachers' supervision or instructions. The research of Bliss et al. (2017) dealt with the effectiveness of using CAI on Mathematics. However, the current research focused on CMI and Computer Science as a subject. If CAI was effective on students' achievement in Mathematics, could CMI be effective on students' performance in Computer Science?

Imhanlahimi and Imhanlahimi (2008) investigated the effectiveness of traditional or expository and computer-assisted learning strategy of teaching biology. A true experimental design was used. The results indicated that the traditional method was better than the computer-assisted learning method in teaching biology. If a traditional method was better in teaching and learning Biology, would the application of CMI enhance the effectiveness of teaching Computer Science? This research focused on an empirical investigation that could assist the stakeholders in the tertiary institution on the adoption of computer-managed instruction into the teaching and learning of computer science.

Hammed (2015) discovered that CAI resulted in the significant achievement of secondary students at all levels in mathematics. However, the research of Hammed did not show any statistical difference between gender and academic performance in mathematics. In the selection of individuals into the positions of authorities, either male or female person could be voted. This implies that the academic performance of male and female students needs to be compered for future success in a chosen career. This current study investigated the performance of male and female students in Computer Science.

Chang and Bower (2016) carried a research on the effect of CAI on reading achievement. The researchers discovered CAI had a positive effect on reading performance of K–12 students. If CAI was effective in reading performance of students, would the application of CMI enhance the effectiveness of teaching Computer Science? The gap here was to investigate the effectiveness of CMI among the students of tertiary institutions in Computer Science, not K-12.

Kesan and Crow (2018) conducted a research on the effect of CAI on the achievement and students' attitudes towards mathematics. An experimental research design was adopted and findings indicated that the teaching of mathematics with the aid of CAI method increased students' performance in mathematics. More studies have been conducted on the effect of CAI in mathematics achievement. However, if a higher performance had been recorded in the mathematics achievement of students, could the same results be obtained when computer-managed instruction is introduced in computer science?

The impact of gender on students' academic performance is still under discussion among scholars. Hammed and Ola (2012) stated that electronic learning calls for active participation among male and female students. Likewise, Paul (2014) revealed there was no significant difference between male and female students in the aspects of examination scores, learning attitudes, and learning portfolios in computer managed instruction and traditional method. Yoohang (2014) reported that male students performed better than their female counterparts when taught using computer managed instruction.

Lilain and Musa (2017) investigated the use of CMI and its impact on students' performance in Chemistry. An experimental research design which involved control and experimental group was used and the finding showed a significant difference between male and female students who used CMI in learning Chemistry. However, the gap here was to investigate the effectiveness of CMI among the students of tertiary institutions in Computer Science not in Chemistry.

MAIN FOCUS OF THE CHAPTER

This section gives research methodology, such as research design, population, sample of the study, instruments and instruments validation, data collection and data analysis, and findings of the study presented in this chapter.

Research Design

The research design adopted for this study was experimental. The experimental design involved a group of students that received treatment, whereas the other group did not receive treatment. This research used a group called the experimental group (Computer Managed Instruction Approach, CMIA) and another group called control group (Traditional Learning Approach, TLA). The control group was taught computer science using traditional lecture method, while the experimental group was taught using CMIA.

In this study, the main independent variable was the categorical variable, methods (CMIA and TLA) while the dependent variable was the continuous variable, students' performance (scores). To determine the reference performance scores, the researcher with the assistance of computer lecturers in the tertiary institutions began the research by first measuring students' general performance on a selected topic in computer science with a set of questions titled Computer Science Assessment (CSA). The results of the pre-test were recorded on the Assessment Score (AS) and saved for reference at the end of the experiment.

Secondly, the control and experimental groups were taught the same topic in computer science, where students' general performance was evaluated, for three weeks under closed supervision of the researchers who are computer lecturers and experts with over ten years teaching experience. The same lecturers were used for the two groups to establish that the lecturers' years of teaching experience did not affect the students' performance score rather to investigate the effect of instruction methods either Computer Managed Instruction Approach (CMIA) or Traditional Learning Approach (TLA). The two groups were provided with a post-test after three weeks of instructions. The results of the post-test were recorded on a data collection sheet as carried out during the pre-test. The comparison was carried out on how the performance of both the control group and the experimental group changed from a pre-test to a post-test after being taught either with Computer Managed Instruction Approach (CMIA) or Traditional Learning Approach (TLA).

Population

The population of the study comprised of all the first-year students in Colleges of Education (COEs), Polytechnic (Poly) and University (Uni), North-Central geopolitical, Nigeria. There are six (6) states in the North-Central geopolitical, Nigeria namely, FCT-Abuja, Kogi, Nassarawa, Kwara, Niger and Plateau. The first-year students were used for the study because this is the first class in the tertiary institutions which requires effective learning towards excellent academic performance. A poor academic performance at the first-year examination could lead to an overall poor academic result at the final examination.

Sample of the Study

The research adopted a multi-stage sampling procedure. Firstly, a convenience sampling technique was used to select six Colleges of Education, four Polytechnic and six Universities from the public institutions while three Colleges of Education, two Polytechnic and three Universities were selected from the private institutions in North-Central geopolitical zone, Nigeria. According to Hamed (2016), a convenience sampling is a non-random sampling method that involves selecting participants because they are often readily and easily available for investigation. Secondly, a simple random sampling technique was used to select fifteen students from each institution. Thus, Table 1 showed the selected samples.

Table 1. Sample selected based on population

Institutions	COE	Polytechnic	University	Total
Public	90	60	90	240
Private	45	30	45	120
Total	135	90	135	360

Thirdly, purposive random sampling was used to select one hundred and eighty students for the experimental group and one hundred and eighty students for the control group. Therefore, a total of three hundred and sixty first-year students made-up the sample.

Instruments and Instruments Validation

The treatment instrument (Computer Managed Instruction Approach Package, CMIAP) and the test instrument (Computer Science Assessment, CSA) were used. The treatment instrument, CMIAP was developed by the researchers with the assistance of professionals such as system programmer, the instructional designers and educational technologists. A C# programming language was used to develop the package with other applications such as Microsoft Visual C# 2015. The sample of the package was presented to computer programmers and educational technology experts for validation. The contents of the package were validated by computer science specialists. Sample of the questions was presented to the experts in Educational Measurement and Evaluation for correction.

The contents of the package were validated by computer science specialists. The package had a topic selected from computer science and was subdivided into five lessons that covered three weeks. On the home page, there were Registration, Lesson: Modules, Exercise: Practice and Quit buttons. Each button on the Home page was linked to another page for a specific task. A student registered using the "Registration" button. On the Lesson: Modules, the students could acquire the instructions provided. The "Exercise: Practice" provided the opportunity for self-assessment. Lastly, the "Test/Examination" button was used to test the students' level of achievement in computer science based on the learning and acknowledge acquired using computer managed instruction, CMI.

Figure 1. Computer managed instruction approach package

Also, a test-retest method was used to determine the reliability coefficient of the test instrument and score sheet. One hundred students of Federal University of Technology, Akure in South West of Nigeria were used as a pilot sample. The instruments were administered during the pilot stage on two different occasions at four weeks' interval. A Cronbach's alpha statistical tool was used to determine the internal consistency of the instrument and 0.83 was obtained. Also, the Spearman correlation coefficient of 0.81 was obtained for the test instrument. These statistical values were considered reliable hence suitable for use in this research.

Data Collection

A correct answer provided by each participant had 1 mark. Nine hundred (900) copies of the Computer Science Assessment (CSA) were produced for pre-test and post-test. The performance scores at the pre-test stage were collected, collated, marked, recorded and kept for further analysis. The same questions were also distributed to the participants in both the control and experimental groups after the experiment (post-test). The performance scores at the post-test stage were collected, collated, marked, recorded and kept for comparison with the scores in the pre-test stage.

Data Analysis

There were twenty (20) objective-questions for a participant and one (1) mark for a correctly answered question. The maximum obtainable mark was twenty (20). The research questions were analyzed using mean and standard deviations while Analysis of Covariance (ANCOVA) and Analysis of Variance (ANOVA) statistical analysis were used to test the two null hypotheses postulated for the study at 0.05 level of significance. All the analyses were carried out in IBM Statistical Package for the Social Sciences (SPSS) 21.0 version.

Results

The three (3) research questions used for this study were analyzed, answered and presented as shown in the following subsections:

Research Question One: What is the difference in the performance scores of students taught computer science using computer managed instruction and traditional lecture method?

Table 2. Mean and standard deviation of students' performance in computer science using CMI and TLA methods

Group		Pre Score	Post Score	Difference
Control	Mean	6.72	7.09	0.37
	Std. Deviation	0.38	0.16	
	Minimum	3.00	5.00	
	Maximum	9.00	11.00	
Experimental	Mean	7.03	18.64	11.61
	Std. Deviation	0.31	0.03	
	Minimum	3.00	8.00	
	Maximum	12.00	19.00	
				11.24

Table 2 presents mean and standard deviation analysis of students' performance in computer science using computer-managed instruction (CMI) and traditional learning approach (TLA). Table 2 further showed that the scores of the participants in both experimental and control groups were relatively equivalent at the initial stage (pre-test) with means of 7.03 and 6.72 respectively and as illustrated in Figure 2. However, in the post-test, the experimental (using CMI) group had a mean of 18.64 while the mean of the control group (using TLA) was 7.09. Also, there was a statistical difference of 11.61 in the scores of students in the experimental group between the pre-test and post-test. Likewise, a statistical difference of 0.37 was recorded between the pre-test and post-test scores in the control group. Since the final score of 18.64 was greater than the initial score of 7.09 at the post-test, this implied that computer-managed instruction (CMI) was effective to learn computer science than the traditional learning approach (TLA). Therefore, there was a statistical difference of 11.24 in the performance scores of students taught computer science using computer-managed instruction (CMI) and the traditional learning approach (TLA).

Figure 2. Students' performance using CMI and TLA

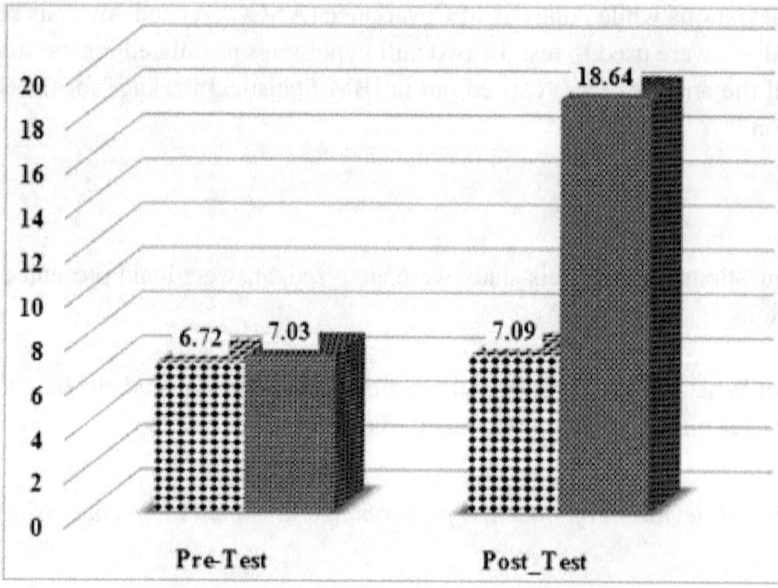

Research Question Two: What is the difference in the performance of male and female students taught computer science using computer managed instruction?

Table 3 indicates mean and standard deviation analysis of male and female students' performance in computer science using computer-managed instruction (CMI). Table 3 further showed that the scores of the participants at the initial stage (pre-test) were comparatively equivalent. The male and female participants had means of 10.33 and 9.64 respectively at the pre-test stage as illustrated in Figure 3. However, in the post-test, the male had a mean of 17.11 while the female had 12.34. In addition, there was a statistical difference of 6.78 in the scores of male students between the pre-test and post-test. Likewise, a statistical difference of 2.7 was recorded between pre-test and post-test scores of female students. The mean difference of male students was greater than the mean difference of female counterparts (6.78 > 2.7). This implied that the performance of male students was better than the performance of female students in computer science using computer-managed instruction. Therefore, there was a difference of 4.08 in the performance of male and female students taught computer science using computer-managed instruction. Statistically, at 0.05 level of significance, there was a significant difference ($0.05 > p < 0.001$) in the performance of male and female students taught computer science using computer-managed instruction.

Table 3. Mean and standard deviation of male and female students' performance in computer science using CMI

Gender		Pre Score	Post Score	Difference	Sig.
Male	Mean	10.33	17.11	6.78	
	Std. Deviation	0.25	0.13		
	Minimum	3.00	8.00		
	Maximum	12.00	19.00		
Female	Mean	9.64	12.34	2.7	<0.001
	Std. Deviation	0.44	0.91		
	Minimum	3.00	8.00		
	Maximum	12.00	19.00		
				4.08	

Figure 3. Students' gender performance using CMI

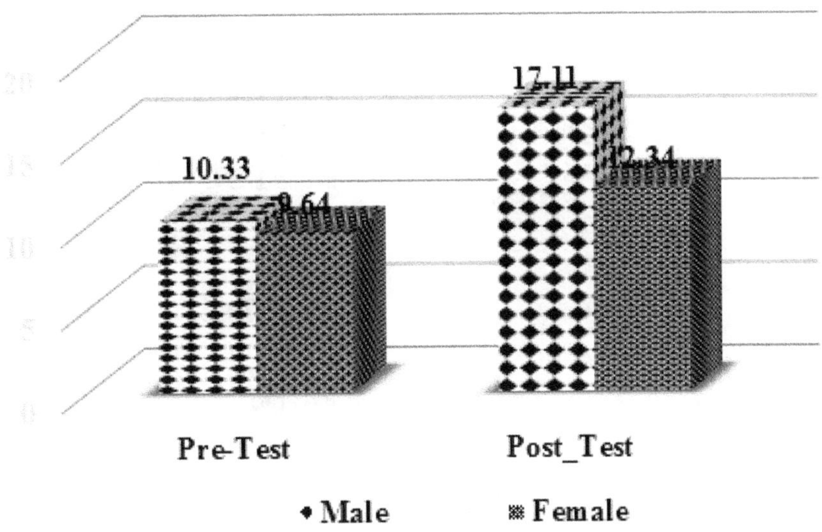

Research Question Three: What is the difference in the performance of public and private schools' students taught computer science using computer managed instruction?

Table 4. Mean and standard deviation of public and private students' performance in computer science using CMI

Institutions		Pre Score	Post Score	Difference	Sig.
Public	Mean	5.83	9.07	3.24	
	Std. Deviation	0.37	0.16		
	Minimum	3.00	8.00		
	Maximum	12.00	19.00		
Private	Mean	6.96	16.17	9.21	<0.001
	Std. Deviation	0.29	0.11		
	Minimum	3.00	8.00		
	Maximum	12.00	19.00		
				5.97	

Figure 4. Students' institutions performance using CMI

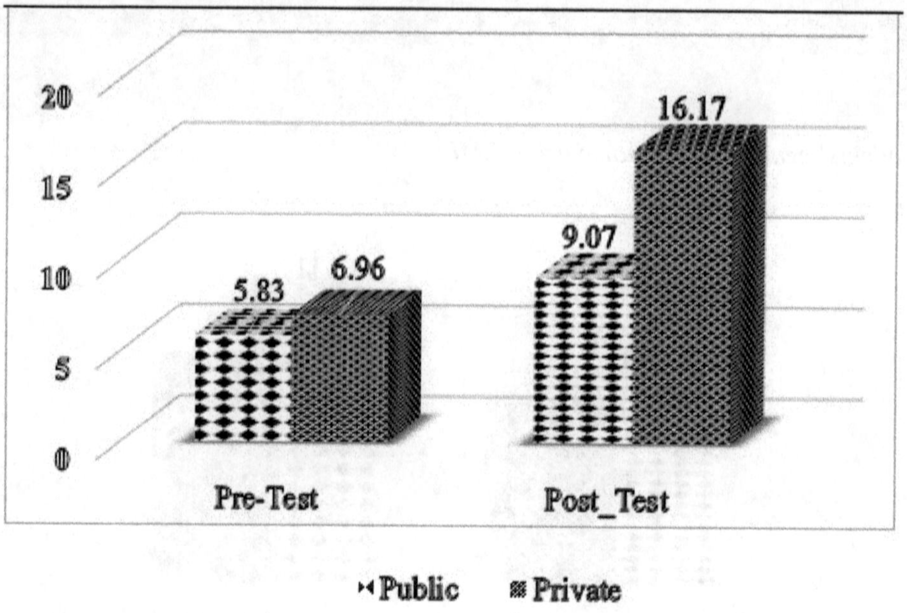

Table 4 showed mean and standard deviation analysis of public and private schools students' performance in computer science using computer-managed instruction (CMI). Table 4 further showed that the scores of the participants at the initial stage (pre-test) were fairly equivalent. The participants from public and private institutions had means of 5.83 and 6.96 respectively at the pre-test stage as graphically illustrated in Figure 4. However, in the post-test, the public institutions had a mean of 9.07 while the private institutions had 16.17. In addition, there was a statistical difference of 3.24 in the scores of students in the public institutions between the pre-test and post-test. Similarly, a statistical difference of 9.21 was noted between pre-test and post-test scores of students from private institutions. The mean difference of students from private tertiary institutions was greater than the mean difference of students from public tertiary institutions. (9.21 > 3.42). This implied that the performance of students in private institutions was better than the performance of students from public institutions in computer science using computer-managed instruction. Therefore, there was a difference of 5.97 in the performance of public and private schools' students taught computer science using computer-managed instruction. Statistically, at 0.05 level of significance, there was a significant difference ($0.05 > p < 0.001$) in the performance of public and private schools' students taught computer science using computer-managed instruction.

Testing Research Hypotheses

The null hypotheses postulated for this research were tested at 0.05 level of significance as given in the following subsections.

H_{01}: There is no significant difference in the mean performance score of students taught computer science using computer managed instruction and conventional lecture method.

Table 5. ANCOVA post-test on experimental (CMI) and control (TLA) groups

Source	Sum of Squares	Df	Mean Square	F	Sig.
Corrected Model	3.936	2	1.968	36.291	0.000
Intercept	321.943	1	321.94	5937.46	0.000
Post Score	0.116	1	0.116	2.140	0.144
Main Effect	3.797	1	3.797	70.020	0.000
Error	19.357	357	0.054		
Total	2356.040	360			
Corrected Total	23.293	359			

a. R Squared = 0.169 (Adjusted R Squared = 0.164)

Table 5 presents the Analysis of Covariance (ANCOVA) between experimental (CMI) and control (TLA) groups. The table further indicated a computed F-ratio for the main effect of the computer-managed instruction (CMI) and traditional learning approach (TLA) on the mean achievement of students was 70.020 which was significant at P-value of 0.000 (p-value $0.000 < 0.05$). This resulted in the rejection of the null hypothesis of no significant difference in the mean performance score of students taught computer science using computer managed instruction and conventional lecture method. In conclusion, there was a significant difference in the mean performance score of students taught computer science using computer managed instruction and conventional lecture method.

H_{02}: There is no significant difference in the mean performance score of students taught computer science using computer managed instruction based on institutions.

Table 6. Mean and standard deviation of students' performance in computer science using CMI and institutions

Institutions	N	Mean	Std. Deviation
COE	120	9.53	0.53
Poly	120	12.62	0.32
Uni	120	18.46	0.17

Table 6 shows mean and standard deviation analysis of students' performance in computer science using CMI and their respective institutions. The Colleges of Education (COE), Polytechnics (Poly) and University (Uni) had means of 9.53, 12.62 and 18.46 respectively in computer science. These statistical values revealed that the students from the University had the highest mean when compared with the scores of students from Colleges of Education and Polytechnics. However, to test if there is a significant difference between the students' performance in computer science using computer managed instruction and the institutions, the ANOVA statistical test was carried out.

Table 7. ANOVA analysis between students' performance in computer science and institutions

Source of Variation	Sum of Squares	df	Mean Square	F	Sig.
Between Groups	1.486	4	0.372	6.049	0.000
Within Groups	21.807	355	0.061		
Total	23.293	359			

Table 7 shows the Analysis of Variance (ANOVA) between students' performance score in computer science using computer-managed instruction (CMI) and the institutions. Table 7 further indicated the F-value of 6.049. The tested p-value of 0.05 was greater than the computed –p-value ($p<0.0001$). These statistical values led to the rejection of the postulated null hypothesis. Therefore, there was a significant difference in the mean performance score of students taught computer science using computer managed instruction based on institutions.

DISCUSSION

The analysis of the first research question revealed that the computer-managed instruction (CMI) was effective in learning computer science among the students of tertiary institutions in the North-central geopolitical zone of Nigeria than the traditional learning approach (TLA). It was discovered that there was a significant difference between the use of computer-managed instruction (CMI) and traditional learning approach (TLA) to learn computer science. This study has similar results with Adewole and Frank (2013), who discovered that the computer managed instruction was statistically more significant than the traditional teaching method with regard to students' performance in Physics. The cumulative performance score of students in the CMI group was higher than the performance score of students who did not use CMI to learn computer science. In addition, this finding further supported Adel (2015) that recorded higher scores for middle school students that used computer managed instruction to learn Computer Science in Saudi Arabia. The second research question focused on the difference in the performance of male and female students taught computer science using computer-managed instruction. The findings revealed that the performance of male students was higher than the performance of female students in computer science when computer-managed instruction was engaged. This result was akin to Okwuduba, Offiah and Madichie (2018) who recorded higher achievement for male students in chemistry than the mean achievement score of the female students using computer simulations. It was discovered that there was a statistical difference in the performance of male and female students taught computer science with the aid of computer-managed instruction. The third research question was on the difference in the performance of public and private schools' students taught computer science using computer-managed instruction. The researchers gathered that the performance of students in private institutions was higher than the performance of students from public institutions in computer science when computer-managed instruction was used. In Yildirim, Ozden and Aksu (2011), it was highlighted that private schools' students performed better than the public schools' students in Social Studies when computer-managed instruction was used to teach. This was an indication that the computer-managed instruction would be effective for the teachers and students at different levels of education and for different subjects of study, particular at the tertiary institutions.

In the testing of the null hypotheses postulated for the research, the findings revealed that there was a significant difference in the mean performance score of students taught computer science using computer managed instruction and conventional lecture method, the students from the University had the highest mean when compared with the scores of students from Colleges of Education and Polytechnics, and there was a significant difference in the mean performance score of students taught computer science using computer managed instruction and the institutions. The findings of this research agreed with that of Yoohang (2014), Andrew (2015), and Yerri and Henry (2016) which revealed that a group of students that used computer managed instruction was more successful in academic performance than their counterpart that used traditional teaching method in tertiary institutions.

FUTURE RESEARCH DIRECTIONS

The results of this research have strong implications for learning computer science in Nigeria and across the world at large using computer-managed instruction (CMI) approached. The ultimate consequence of this research was that CMI could make the performance scores of students in tertiary institutions to be higher and better than the traditional method of learning using chalkboard, papers and writing materials such as pencils, biro. Principally, the empirical findings and reports provided would serve as pieces of literature for scholarly examination and further investigations on the related subject matter.

Based on the findings of this research, the following recommendations were made:

i. Financial support to assist the institutions in procuring facilities such as computers, computer-managed instruction (CMI) software should be provided to the enhancement of students' academic performance.
ii. Qualified teachers that have deep knowledge of computer-managed instruction (CMI) to teach computer science should be employed to stimulate students' interest in learning.

iii. Standby generators should be provided to tackle the problem of power supply interruption during teaching and learning process.
iv. Technical support should be provided for the effective use of computer-managed instruction (CMI).
v. Adequate infrastructures such as buildings and laboratories should be provided in the institutions to facilitate the use of computer-managed instruction (CMI) in learning computer science.
vi. The effects of CMI on other courses in the tertiary institutions should be investigated towards promoting effective students' learning experiences.

CONCLUSION

The significance of computer-managed instruction (CMI) could not be over-emphasized. The effectiveness of computer-managed instruction on students' performance in tertiary institutions was investigated among the students of tertiary institutions in the North-central geopolitical zone of Nigeria. Students were selected from three types of tertiary institutions, Colleges of Education, Polytechnics and University. The students were grouped into experimental and control groups, tests were conducted and the results were analyzed. The researchers discovered that the computer-managed instruction (CMI) was effective in learning computer science among the students of tertiary institutions. The male students performed better than the female students in computer science when computer-managed instruction was engaged. It was highlighted that the performance of students in private institutions was higher than the performance of students from public institutions in computer science when computer-managed instruction was used. Conclusively, there was a significant difference in the mean performance score of students taught computer science using computer managed instruction and conventional lecture method, and the students from the University had the highest mean when compared with the scores of students from Colleges of Education and Polytechnics.

REFERENCES

Adewole, D. W., & Frank, L. P. (2013). Effects of computer managed instruction and traditional on students' academic performance in higher education. *Journal of Computer Assisted Learning*, *29*(3), 220–234.

Andrew, E. W. (2015). Computer managed instruction: Effect for tomorrow learning platform. *Journal of Learning and Technology*, *27*(3), 28–39.

Bada, T., Adewole, A., & Olalekan, O. (2009). Uses of computer and its relevance to teaching and learning in Nigerian educational system. *Educational Research Review*, *4*(10), 443–447.

Bliss, C. S., Mark, M., Jonathan, A. F., Godwin, A. K., & Justine, A. (2017). Effect of computer-assisted instruction (CAI) on senior high school students' achievement at pie chart and histogram in core mathematics. *Brock Journal of Education*, *5*(9), 45–68.

Chang, J. U., & Bower, P. A. (2016). Effect of computer-assisted instruction (CAI) on students' reading performance. *The American Psychologist*, *41*(2), 170–178.

Emmanuel, F. B., & Olusegun, O. B. (2015). Impediments on the implementation of computer science education curriculum in public secondary schools in Osun State Nigeria. *Asia Pacific Journal of Education. Arts and Sciences*, *2*(4), 12–17.

Hamed, T. (2016). Sampling methods in research methodology; how to choose a sampling technique for research. *International Journal of Academic Research in Management*, *5*(2), 18–27.

Hammed, A., & Ola, M. U. (2012). Assessment of students' satisfaction with computer managed instruction in a gender-segregated. *The Journal of Educational Research*, *5*(2), 94–103.

Hammed, T. U. (2015). A comparative study on computer-assisted instruction and its effect on secondary mathematics performance. *Dissertation Abstracts International*, *23*, 85–91.

Imhanlahimi, E. O., & Imhanlahimi, R. E. (2008). An Evaluation of the Effectiveness of Computer Assisted Learning Strategy and Expository Method of Teaching Biology: A Case Study of Lumen Christi International High School, Uromi, Nigeria. *Journal of Social Science*, *16*(3), 215–220.

John, N., & Harrison, W. T. (2018). The effects of drill-and-practice computer instruction on learning basic mathematics. *Journal of Computing in Childhood Education*, *6*, 349–356.

Kesan, C., & Crow, D. T. (2018). The effect of computer-assisted instruction on the achievement and attitudes towards mathematics of students in mathematics education. *International Journal of Global Education*, *1*(2), 50–57.

Lilian, C., & Musa, H. K. (2017). The attitudes on learning effects in computer managed instruction for Mathematics. *Journal of Technology and Computing*, *12*(3), 21-28.

Mee-chin, W., Abrizah, A., & Lip, Y. P. (2012). Computer-managed instruction (CMI)-based online forums. *Journal of Educational Computing Research*, *47*(2), 209–233. doi:10.2190/EC.47.2.e

Okwuduba, E. N., Offiah, F. C., & Madichie, C. J. (2018). Effect of computer simulations on secondary school students' academic achievement in chemistry in Anambra State. *Asian Journal of Education and Training*, *4*(4), 284–289. doi:10.20448/journal.522.2018.44.284.289

Padma, G. A., & Adi, Z. (2000). Computer managed instructions: Evaluation of alternate methods of technology integration in higher education. *Journal of Educational Technology & Society*, *3*(1), 84–87.

Paul, S. P. (2014). Student's academic performance and computer managed instruction. *Journal of Education*, *6*(2), 34–43.

Rozema, R. (2011). *Heart of darkness. WebQuest: Using technology to social studies*. Retrieved on 30th December, 2014 from http://www.edrs.com/WebQuest/hod/

Yerri, J., & Henry, D. (2016). A comparison of student knowledge between computer managed instruction and traditional method in a physical health education. *Journal of Educational Psychology*, *6*(2), 108–117.

Yildirim, Z. Y., Ozden, M., & Aksu, M. (2011). Comparison of public schools and private schools WebQuest-based learning of social studies. *The Journal of Educational Research*, *4*(4), 125–132.

Yoohang, H. T. (2014). Students' perceptions toward the use of the digital library in weekly computer managed instruction assignments portion of a hybrid programme. *Journal of Educational Technology, 42*, 712–725.

ADDITIONAL READING

Garba, S., & Salako, E. A. (2014). Appraisal of Secondary Schools Students on Computer Education in Abuja Municipal Area Council (AMAC) of FCT Abuja. *Nigerian Journal of Applied Arts and Science Federal Polytechnic Bida., 7*(1), 201–206.

Garba, S., Solomon, A. A., & John, K. A. (2015). Factors Militating against Successful Implementation of Computer Studies in 9 – Year Universal Basic Education (UBE) Programme. *International Journal of Modern Education and Computer Science., 7*(5), 50–58. doi:10.5815/ijmecs.2015.05.07

Hennessy, S., Onguko, B., Harrison, D., Ang'ondi, E. K., Namalefe, S., Naseem, A., & Wamakote, L. (2010). Developing the use of information and communication technology to enhance teaching and learning in East African schools: Review of the literature. *Centre for Commonwealth Education & Aga Khan University Institute for Educational Development–Eastern Africa Research Report, 1*.

Inoue, Y. (Ed.). (2009). *Cases on Online and Blended Learning Technologies in Higher Education: Concepts and Practices: Concepts and Practices*. IGI Global.

Oweis, T. I. (2018). Effects of Using a Blended Learning Method on Students' Achievement and Motivation to Learn English in Jordan: A Pilot Case Study. *Education Research International, 2018*, 2018. doi:10.1155/2018/7425924

Salako, E. A. (2018). A secured fingerprint biometric technique for curbing problem of examination impersonation. *Journal of Digital Innovations & Contemporary Research in Science. Engineering & Technology, 6*(1), 1–16. PMID:29682599

Salako, E. A., Solomon, A. A., & Muhammed, B. A. (2015). Perception of students on computer utilization and academic performance in the North-Central geopolitical zone of Nigeria. *International Journal of Modern Education and Computer Science, 7*(4), 53–60. doi:10.5815/ijmecs.2015.04.06

Serin, O. (2011). The Effects of the Computer-Based Instruction on the Achievement and Problem Solving Skills of the Science and Technology Students. *Turkish Online Journal of Educational Technology-TOJET, 10*(1), 183–201.

Yahaya, J., Abduraheem, O. U., & Garba, S. (2015). Globalization and the Role of Information and Communication Technology (ICT) in Teacher Education in Nigeria. *SLASS Multi-Disciplinary Journal of Educational Studies, 2*(1), 109–116.

KEY TERMS AND DEFINITIONS

Computer: An electronic device designed and implemented to sequentially accept, process and store data on the basis of a predefined set of instructions to produce valuable information.

Computer-Managed Instruction: This is a computer application software that is used the by learner to acquire relevant skills without depending on the instructions of teachers.

Effectiveness: The degree of attainment of stated objectives towards desired results.

Institutions: An organization where teaching and learning are experienced by the teachers and learners on specific areas of needs.

Performance: A measurement of completion of a task with specified knowledge, skills, and abilities.

Students: A group of learners enrolled in an institution for acquisition of specific learning experiences.

Tertiary: A higher institution of learning after post-secondary education.

Chapter 15
Factors Influencing Virtual Learning System Usage in Higher Education

Indira Padayachee
https://orcid.org/0000-0002-6838-7622
University of KwaZulu-Natal, South Africa

ABSTRACT

Virtual learning systems (VLSs), commonly referred to as learning or course management systems, have been formally adopted at many higher education institutions. However, knowledge of the actual usage of VLSs is limited in terms of what specific functional and non-functional characteristics are deemed useful and how this influences system usage. Furthermore, little is known about the role of other non-system-related factors related to VLS usage, such as pedagogic, organisational, and individual difference factors. This chapter proposes and describes the virtual learning system usage model (VLSUM), which represents the factors influencing VLS usage in higher education institutions. The VLSUM is based on a conceptual framework integrating multiple dimensions and is confirmed by the results of an empirical study. A mixed-methods research design was adopted in the development of the VSLUM. This model is valuable to educational technologists, instructional designers, and software designers for VLS implementation in higher education.

INTRODUCTION

The formal adoption of virtual learning systems (VLSs) in South African higher education is increasing and e-learning practices are becoming institutionalized. VLSs are a generic term that represents a class of software designed to support online education in universities (Gonella & Pantò 2008; Ozkan, Koseler & Baykal, 2009). VLSs are known as a number of different names, including course management systems, learning management systems (LMS), and virtual learning environments. Examples of well-known VLSs in use are Blackboard, Sakai, Moodle, Atutor, and Kewl (Ssekakubo, Suleman & Marsden, 2011; Unwin, et al., 2010). Despite being formally adopted for implementation by higher education institu-

DOI: 10.4018/978-1-7998-3062-7.ch015

tions, adoption rates of VLSs are uneven, and usage of system functions amongst educators is limited. A study conducted at universities in the Western Cape demonstrated limited usage of online interactive discussions, online assessment, online grading and more advanced VLS functions (Mlitwa & Van Belle 2011), as did a multi-institutional study conducted in Ireland (Cosgrave, et al., 2011) and a study conducted by EDUCAUSE Center for Analysis and Research (ECAR) with 151 universities across 13 countries (Dahlstrom, Brooks & Bichsel, 2014). Similarly, Mtebe (2015) reported that while there was increased adoption of VLS in the Sub-Saharan Africa, the actual usage was low. In another study, findings concur that most academic staff at the University of Dar es Salaam in Tanzania use the VLS (referred to as LMS) for uploading content and files only (South Africa Institute of Distance Education, 2013).

Much of the research on VLSs has focused on studies evaluating e-learning systems (Ozkan & Koseler, 2009), measuring VLS/LMS success using an adapted version of the DeLone and McLean Model (Mtebe, 2015), or studies of adoption based on existing models such as the technology acceptance model (TAM) (Davis, 1989), TAM extensions (Tarhini, Hone, Liu & Tarhini. 2017), the unified theory of acceptance and use of technology (UTAUT) (Venkatesh, Morris, Davis & Davis, 2004) and its extension UTAUT2 (El-Masri & Tarhini, 2017). There has been limited research on an integrated approach to studying the problem of limited or uneven VLS usage in higher education from a multidimensional perspective.

The research reported on in this chapter addresses the gap in research on the limited or uneven VLS usage in South Africa with the goal of designing a comprehensive integrated model that specifically addresses VLS usage from a multi-dimensional perspective, taking the lessons learnt from technology adoption and usage models into consideration. Consequently, the questions focused and reported on in this chapter are:

1) What are the multi-dimensional factors that influence VLS usage in South African higher education institutions?
2) How can these factors and their relationships be represented in a model of VLS usage?

A technology usage model can be utilized by educational technologists and instructional designers to implement strategies to optimize usage of VLSs in higher education. This model can also be beneficial to designers by guiding the future design of VLSs. Therefore, this chapter covers the multi-dimensional factors that influence VLS usage in South African higher education institutions, culminating in a model of VLS usage.

BACKGROUND

VLSs are web-based applications designed to support a model of online teaching and learning based on readings, lecture material, discussion forums, activities and associated communication and management (Gonella & Pantò, 2008; Klobas, & McGill, 2010). VLSs comprise a range of tools to support educational practices, including tools for communication and collaboration, student productivity and involvement, course administration/management, assessment and content (Elabnody, 2016; Wcet, n.d.).

Higher education (or tertiary education) in the South African context encompasses "all learning programs leading to qualifications higher than Grade 12 or its equivalent in terms of the National Qualifications Framework as contemplated in the South African Qualifications Authority Act, 1995 (Act 58 of 1995), and includes tertiary education as contemplated in Schedule 4 of the Constitution" (South

Africa, 2001:8). Higher education institutions refer to any institution that provides higher education on a full-time, part-time or distance teaching basis.

The South African government has emphasized the importance of information and communication technologies (ICTs) in transforming teaching and learning environments into an inclusive and integrated practice, where learners study collaboratively, engage in meaningful contexts and develop creative thinking and problem-solving skills (South African Government, 2004).

The perspectives in studying VLSs in the past was, however, mostly from a singular perspective. There has been limited research on the factors that influence usage of VLSs from a multi-dimensional perspective encompassing, for example, system features, pedagogic aspects/features, organizational support for online teaching and learning, users' characteristics and demographic aspects. There is thus evidence that a multi-dimensional perspective or view is needed that will incorporate the various individual perspectives.

Perspectives of VLS Usage

Through a comprehensive literature review on VLS usage, five significant perspectives were identified, namely systems (Myers & Avison, 2002), pedagogic (Kaur, 2013), organizational (Al-Busaidi & Al-Shihi, 2010), individual or user differences (Burton-Jones & Hubona, 2005), and demographics. Each of these perspectives is briefly discussed below.

Systems Perspective

Functional characteristics represent the functions that satisfy stated or implied needs in the system. Non-functional characteristics refer to desired characteristics that a system must possess that may not be related to a specific function such as security or usability. A systems perspective to studying the problem of VLS usage in higher education involves exploring the role of functional and non-functional VLS characteristics on actual system usage. The functional VLS characteristics considered were:

- Communication via discussion forums, internal mail and real-time chat tools (Augar, Raitman & Zhou, 2006; Cole & Foster, 2007; Disbrow, 2008; Elabnody, 2016; Radwan, Senousy & Riad, 2014; Wcet, n.d.).
- Student productivity using bookmarks, calendars, searching and synchronize tools (Blackboard Inc. 2006; Kasim & Khalid, 2016; Vipond & Clarey, 2018; Wcet, n.d.).
- Student involvement via group work, community networking, and student profile tools (Botturi, 2004; Wcet, n.d.).
- Course management via authentication, course authorization, registration integration, user access, multiple roles and management tools (Brooks, Kettel & Hansen, 2005; Kasim & Khalid, 2016; Wcet, n.d.).
- Assessment using online testing, marking, grade book and assignment tools (Brown & Peterson, 2008; Elabnody, 2016; Kasim & Khalid, 2016; Radwan, Senousy & Riad, 2014; Sachan, et al., 2006; Wcet, n.d.).
- Student activity and progress tracking tools (Radwan, Senousy & Riad, 2014; Vipond & Clarey, 2018; Wcet, n.d.).

- Content via authoring, delivery and file management tools (Elementk, 2003; Vipond & Clarey, 2018; Wcet, n.d.).

The non-functional VLS characteristics considered were:

- Usability comprising criteria such as ease of use, a familiar look and feel, ability to capably operate the system, a well-designed interface, where users do not become confused, lost or annoyed, with unambiguous menus, buttons or links; navigation and feedback (Ardito, et al., 2005; Gamage, Fernando & Perera, 2014; Kasim, & Khalid, 2016; Radwan, Senousy & Riad, 2014);
- Security involving aspects such as unique IDs and passwords with secure distribution, secure socket layer (SSL) for encrypting data exchanged over the Internet, a set of user privileges with accompanying permission levels, activity logs for review purposes (Elementk, 2003; Radwan, Senousy & Riad, 2014);
- Reliability covering aspects that should be avoided or minimized, such as computer freezes, browser crashes, an overwhelmed server, and disruption/downtime; 24/7 availability (Horton & Horton, 2003; Radwan, Senousy & Riad, 2014);
- Efficiency encompassing attributes such as efficient response time performance, keyboard shortcuts, importing of registered students in one operation, and performing operations on multiple objects (Kalinga, 2008; Radwan, Senousy & Riad, 2014);
- Flexibility including ability to add/remove resources (content) and processes to/from the course structure, adjust topic-related learning activities according to the needs of a learner or sub-group, availability of discussion tools within topic areas, and individual or collective document writing (Elementk, 2003; Kasim, & Khalid, 2016; Radwan, Senousy & Riad, 2014; Vipond & Clarey, 2018); and
- Standards such as compliance with the sharable content object reference model (SCORM) (Adlnet, n.d.), which is a content packaging standard to allow VLSs to function on multiple platforms (Adlnet, n.d.; Blinco, Mason, McLean & Wilson, 2004; Kasim, & Khalid, 2016).

Pedagogic Perspective

A pedagogic perspective to studying the problem of VLS usage in higher education involves exploring the role of pedagogical aspects and online teaching characteristics in VLS usage. The following pedagogical aspects of VLSs were identified:

- Personalized e-learning (Radwan, Senousy & Riad, 2014;Wan, Zhao, Liu, & Sun, 2005);
- Differentiated instruction (Sallam & Alzouebi, 2014);
- Access to digital learning resources and assessment feedback (Neal & Miller, 2005);
- Online learning activities (Oliver, 2001; Vipond & Clarey, 2018);
- Links to online databases/journals (Barron, 2003);
- "Scaffolding and assisted learning" (Egert, Jacobs & Barnes, 2009, p.454); and
- Student interaction with faculty/students (Gamage, Fernando & Perera, 2014).

In addition, the following characteristics of online teaching were identified:

- Flexible teaching and learning (Martin, 2008; Sallam & Alzouebi, 2014);
- Effectiveness of online tools (Barron, 2003; Neal & Miller, 2005; Vipond & Clarey, 2018);
- Convenience (Song, Singleton, Hill & Koh, 2004) and
- Enhanced communication, coordination and additional effort (McGill & Klobas, 2009; Vipond & Clarey, 2018).

Organizational Perspective

An organizational perspective to studying the problem of VLS usage in higher education involves determining the role of institutional support in VLS usage. Based on the literature review, the following organizational aspects were identified:

- Technical and administrative support, funding, facilities, and training in the use of tools (Al-Busaidi & Al-Shihi, 2010; Buabeng-Andoh, 2012; Morgan, 2003; Mtebe, 2015; Radwan, Senousy & Riad, 2014; Selim, 2007);
- Professional development for academics (Britain & Liber, 2004);
- Instructional designer support (McGee & Green, 2008);
- Stable and reliable university information technology infrastructure (Selim, 2007); and
- Information security policy and institutional eLearning policy (Liu, Huang & Lin, 2012; Mtebe, 2015).

Individual Difference Perspective

An individual difference perspective to studying the problem of VLS usage in higher education involves determining the role of individual differences in VLS usage. Some of the individual difference variables cited were:

- Computer self-efficacy, defined as "individuals' self-assessment of their ability to apply computer skills to accomplish their tasks" (Al-Busaidi & Al-Shihi, 2010, p.4);
- End users' computer literacy (Goodhue, 2009; Selim, 2007);
- Comfort with online technologies (Song et al., 2004);
- Online instructor effort (Masrom, Zainon & Rahiman, 2008);
- Effectiveness of the educational process and improved communication (Cavus & Momani, 2009);
- Teaching style (Al-Busaidi & Al-Shihi, 2010; Selim, 2007).

Demographic Perspective: System Experience

A demographic perspective involves examining the role of Experience with the Use of Technology (EUT) on VLS usage. According to Al-Busaidi and Al-Shihi (2010), Buabeng-Andoh, (2012) and Oliver and Moore (2008), EUT plays an important role in the use of web tools by academic staff members.

It is envisaged that a multi-dimensional perspective for studying the problem of VLS usage in higher education would contribute to identifying the components of an overall conceptual model representing factors that influence VLS usage in higher education. The outcome of the literature review formed the foundation for the conceptual framework described in the following section.

Conceptual Model

While there are several models to study technology usage, this article explored the use of specific constructs/categorical variables/factors from three of the technology adoption/usage models, namely the technology acceptance model (TAM), utilization of information system and the model of factors relating to eLearning adoption, which were synthesized to study the problem of VLS usage in higher education from a multi-dimensional perspective.

The key constructs of perceived usefulness (PU) and perceived ease of use from TAM were adapted to study the systems perspective. The study by Trice and Treacy (1988, p.13) discussed the relationship between individual utilization of an information system and four types of independent categorical variables, namely "design and implementation process variables, information system characteristics, individual differences, and task characteristics". The task characteristics from this framework were adapted to fit the concepts of the pedagogic perspective. Nanayakkara (2007) proposed a model of factors relating to eLearning adoption that was centered on key individual, system and organizational factors. The individual factors were adapted to fit the concepts of the individual/user difference perspective. The organizational factors were adapted to fit the concepts of the organization perspective. The demographic concept of EUT was included in the conceptual model.

Figure 1 represents the conceptual framework comprising the independent constructs/categorical variables/factors selected from the technology adoption/usage models discussed above to study the problem of limited or uneven VLS usage. The conceptual framework was designed to assess the role of the system, organizational, pedagogic, user difference and systems experience categories on actual system usage. This conceptual framework was empirically tested in the context of two universities in KwaZulu-Natal in South Africa, and the results are discussed in the next section.

Figure 1. Conceptual Framework

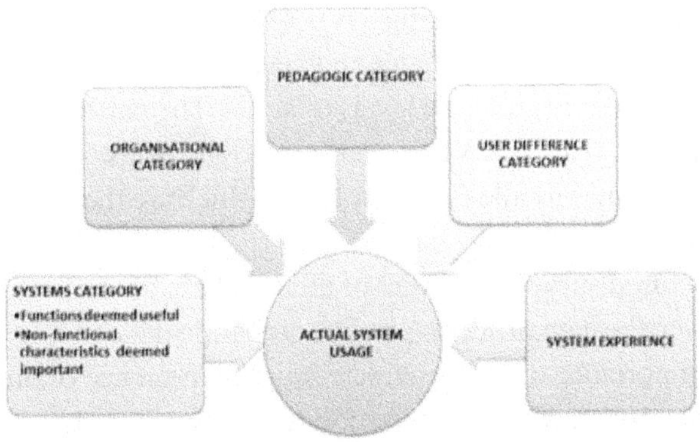

FACTORS INFLUENCING VLS USAGE IN HIGHER EDUCATION

This chapter reports on a study at two higher education institutions, situated in the KwaZulu-Natal province of South Africa, offering full-time, campus-based higher education. The institutions are the University of KwaZulu-Natal (UKZN) and the Durban University of Technology (DUT). A mixed-methods design using both qualitative and quantitative approaches was used during data collection and analysis.

Data Collection Instruments

The interview schedule and structured survey were the two research instruments designed for the purpose of collecting primary data to answer the first research question: "What are the multi-dimensional factors that influence VLS usage in higher education?"

The interview schedule comprised questions in the following six categories: demographic details, VLS functional and non-functional characteristics, pedagogic aspects for online teaching with a VLS, institutional e-learning capabilities, and e-learning challenges. Each of these categories were used to assess the role of the five perspectives of system, organizational, pedagogic, user difference and systems experience on VLS usage, as well as to determine the challenges of online teaching and learning in the two higher educational institutions in South Africa.

The questionnaire used for the surveys comprised questions in the following nine categories: demographics, characteristics of online teaching, experience of online teaching, pedagogic aspects required, nature and extent of VLS utilization, functions deemed useful for online teaching and learning, importance of non-functional characteristics for a VLS, institutional support for online education, and challenges of online education. A comprehensive set of unique questions were designed for each of the nine categories to determine educators' perceptions of the factors and sub-factors influencing VLS usage in South African higher educational institutions.

Participants

Two target institutions of higher education, namely the University of KwaZulu-Natal (UKZN) and Durban University of Technology (DUT) were selected for the purpose of this study. These institutions were selected as they had formally adopted a VLS and fell within the Province of KwaZulu-Natal, in South Africa, which was the location for the study.

A purposive sampling technique was used to select potential participants for the interviews based on their knowledge of and experience with using a VLS for teaching. The interviewees comprised five females and five males from DUT, and seven males and nine females from UKZN. Educators interviewed taught at both undergraduate and postgraduate levels of study. The participants had at that time been using VLSs for a minimum of one year. The VLSs that formed the basis of this research were Blackboard (Enterprise and Basic edition) and Moodle (Version 1.9x), which are the official VLSs formally adopted by DUT and UKZN respectively.

The sample for the structured survey consisted of all members of staff currently using a VLS at both UKZN and DUT, as they were best qualified to provide authentic data on VLS usage patterns, perceived usefulness and perceived importance of VLS characteristics, experience of online teaching, institutional support and challenges encountered. This included 358 lecturers using Moodle at UKZN and 221 lecturers using Blackboard at DUT. All 579 staff members were contacted via e-mail and invited to participate in the research by clicking on a link to complete the web-based questionnaire. Educators that completed the survey were from diverse faculties in both institutions.

Data Analysis

Twenty-six interviews were conducted, 10 at DUT and 16 at UKZN, which were recorded and transcribed before being imported into the NVivo (QSRInternational n.d.) software analysis tool. Thematic analysis was used to analyze the qualitative data and to identify categories or themes. A confirmatory approach to qualitative data analysis (Guest, MacQueen & Namey, 2012) was followed, where specific codes or analytic categories were predetermined from the conceptual framework depicted in Figure 1. A total of 108 responses to the online survey were received from educators, 36 from DUT and 72 from UKZN, yielding a response rate of 19%. The low response rate did not affect the quality of the survey or the data collected, as the respondents were representative of the population of interest.

The quantitative data were statistically analyzed using SPSS Version 17. Descriptive and inferential statistics were used to analyze the quantitative data obtained from the survey administered at DUT and UKZN.

Findings

This section describes the qualitative and quantitative results of the empirical study, which was used as a basis to propose the Virtual Learning System Usage Model (VLSUM).

Qualitative Results

The first category identified represented participants' actual system usage of VLS tools for blended education. Interview findings revealed that the common uses of a VLS were for content delivery, communication, administration and online assessment. There was less emphasis on the use of VLSs for student tracking and student productivity and involvement.

The user difference category revealed the following subcategories related to the theme of actual system usage: computer comfort level, teaching style preference, and experience of online teaching. Educators from both DUT and UKZN reported that they were comfortable with using computer applications, preferred a blended teaching style, found online delivery effective but time-consuming, and work intensive. Data excerpts relating to the theme of teaching style were:

- *Cannot get rid of face-to-face altogether as people like to relate to each other;*
- *Face-to-face learning and e-learning should complement one another.*

Data excerpts relating to the theme of experience of online teaching were:

- *I think a lot of lecturers shy away from creating quizzes because it takes hours of work;*
- *You can do so much more in terms of keeping their interest and keeping the interaction alive through the discussions and mail;*
- *You do not realize how easy the system makes your job unless you do it.*

The subcategories that emerged for the pedagogic category included pedagogic aspects and characteristics of the online classroom. Educators agreed on the following characteristics of online teaching: flexibility, learner-centeredness, collaborative learning, student tracking, improved course management, as well as diverse teaching and learning styles. Data excerpts related to this theme of characteristics of the online classroom were:

- *Students could work at different paces;*

- *Students can access course material asynchronously;*
- *More student-focused approach to learning;*
- *I think the new way of teaching and learning is that students learn more from each other;*
- *It's easy to track students' contributions;*
- *The administration load is decreased by so much;*
- *I found I could use the tool to accommodate my different approaches.*

The pedagogic aspects identified for support in VLSs were teaching approaches, learning strategies and instructional design strategies. Data excerpts relating to the theme of pedagogic aspects were:

- *Teaching approaches: a combination of learning theories, social constructivist approach, communities of learning, and constructivism are used;*
- *Learning strategies: peer review of assignments at higher levels; quizzes and other forms of self-assessment; threaded discussion for collaborative learning;*
- *Instructional design strategies: designing different classrooms to cater for groups of students with different levels of computer skills; structured and guided teaching as students are not independent learners at first level.*

The system experience category was measured by the length of VLS usage in years and the distinct number of online/hybrid courses taught.

The VLS functions deemed useful included the following subcategories: Communication, student involvement, course management, assessment, student tracking, and course content. System challenges raised were the challenge of inflexible discussion forums; operating system compatibility issues; missing functions in assessment, content, communication, and management; inflexible design; and rigid architecture. Data excerpts relating to sub categories of this theme were:

- *Communication: able to upload images to posts; keeps a record of chat sessions; announcements allow you to keep contact with students; email used to communicate new deadlines or new arrangements; blogs are important as they support communication; wikis support collaborative work;*
- *Course management: you can edit, archive and backup courses;*
- *Student involvement: students should have personal calendars to manage their own learning;*
- *Assessment: allows you to randomize your test questions and answers;*
- *Tracking: you can track students' contributions to discussions;*
- *Course content: you can create lessons, quizzes, tests, learning objects, glossary definitions, websites, and dynamic web pages.*

The non-functional VLS characteristics deemed important included the following subcategories: Usability, Security, Reliability, Robustness, Customizability, Efficiency, Flexibility, Interoperability, Extensibility, and Standards compliance. In addition, non-functional system challenges were identified, for example the usability challenge of VLS functionality not being self-evident. Data excerpts relating to the subcategories of this theme were:

- *Usability: it is easy to learn how to operate the tool mechanically;*
- *Security: students should not be able to view or change other student's marks;*
- *Reliability: twenty-four hours a day, seven days a week availability;*
- *Robustness: the software rarely crashes;*
- *Customizability: has the facility to structure and organize your courses;*
- *Efficiency: minimum number of steps to perform tasks;*
- *Flexibility: access tools directly or access via links;*
- *Interoperability: importing and exporting data like class lists;*
- *Extensibility: integrating third party tools;*
- *Standards: SCORM compliant.*

The subcategory identified under the organizational category was institutional support for e- Learning. In both institutions, the basic themes associated with the subtheme of institutional support for e-Learning were similar, covering training and workshops, policy and guidelines, physical resources and user support. Data excerpts relating to the theme of institutional support were:

- *Organizational and technical support: core institutional support and technical assistance;*
- *Instructional design and development support: professional training to understand the pedagogy and the functionality to adapt the teaching approach;*
- *Physical Resources: hot spots Wi-Fi areas; more bandwidth for faster speeds.*
- *Management support: policy or guidelines that supports a framework for online teaching and learning.*

The qualitative results confirmed the categories and subcategories that influence VLS usage, based on the conceptual framework, and identified additional subcategories for each of the categories.

Quantitative Results

This section describes the findings and analysis of the data from the structured survey administered at DUT and UKZN. The goal of the surveys was to identify the factors that influence VLS usage in higher education.

The majority of the respondents were lecturers (46%), followed by the academic ranks of senior lecturer (18%), associate professor (11%), professor (6%) and other (19%).

The Cronbach alpha technique was used to measure the reliability of constructs grouped together under system factors, pedagogic factors, organizational factors and user difference factors, which were all >0.7, thereby permitting analysis.

The descriptive statistics used for the factors comprising the whole sample are depicted in Table 1.

Table 1. Descriptive statistics for factors of whole sample DUT and UKZN

	System Factors_ Perceived usefulness (PU) of functions	System Factors_ Perceived Importance (PI) of non-functional characteristics	Pedagogic Factors	Organizational Factors_ eLearning support	User Difference Factors_ Experience of online teaching
N	108	108	108	108	108
Mean	4.14	4.46	4.02	4.50	3.18
Std. Deviation	.469	.436	.353	.512	.588

Table 2. Correlations among factors for DUT and UKZN and total system usage

		System Factors_ Perceived usefulness (PU) of functions	System Factors_ Perceived Importance (PI) of non-functional characteristics	Pedagogic Factors	Organizational Factors_ eLearning support	User Difference Factors_ Experience of online teaching	Total system usage
System Factors_ Perceived usefulness (PU) of functions	Pearson Correlation	1	.606**	.585**	.389**	.071	.321**
	Sig. (2-tailed)		.000	.000	.000	.466	.001
	N	108	108	108	108	108	108
System Factors_ Perceived Importance (PI) of non-functional characteristics	Pearson Correlation	.606**	1	.481**	.700**	-.076	.062
	Sig. (2-tailed)	.000		.000	.000	.433	.521
	N	108	108	108	108	108	108
Pedagogic Factors	Pearson Correlation	.585**	.481**	1	.644**	.180	.241*
	Sig. (2-tailed)	.000	.000		.000	.062	.012
	N	108	108	108	108	108	108
Organisational Factors_ eLearning support	Pearson Correlation	.389**	.700**	.644**	1	.034	.077
	Sig. (2-tailed)	.000	.000	.000		.726	.426
	N	108	108	108	108	108	108
User Difference Factors_ Experience of online teaching	Pearson Correlation	.071	-.076	.180	.034	1	.316**
	Sig. (2-tailed)	.466	.433	.062	.726		.001
	N	108	108	108	108	108	108
Total system usage	Pearson Correlation	.321**	.062	.241*	.077	.316**	1
	Sig. (2-tailed)	.001	.521	.012	.426	.001	
	N	108	108	108	108	108	108

**. Correlation is significant at the 0.05 level (2-tailed).*
***. Correlation is significant at the 0.01 level (2-tailed).*

Analysis of the survey findings depicted in Table 1 revealed mean scores of 4.14 for system factors – perceived usefulness (PU) of functions and 4.46 for system factors – perceived importance (PI) of non-functional characteristics, as well as mean scores of 4.02, 4.50, and 3.18 for pedagogic factors, organizational factors – e-learning support and user difference factors – experience of online teaching respectively. These means were significantly above a neutral score of 3, demonstrating that there was significant agreement amongst educators on the independent factors.

The findings of the correlations of five main factors, namely system, pedagogic, organizational, user difference and demographic factors with total system usage and inter-correlations among the factors are described in the following sub-sections.

Correlations Between Total System Usage and System Factors

There was an overall positive correlation (r=0.321), as depicted in Table 2, between system factors perceived usefulness (PU) of functional characteristics and total system usage, demonstrating that PU of the functions has a positive influence on total system usage. This finding supports those of Barron (2003), Botturi (2004), Coleman and Mtshazi (2017) and Martin (2008). According to McGill and Klobas (2009), factors such as PU have been found to influence VLS use. However, the Pearson product correlation analysis of the survey findings did not confirm a positive correlation (r=0.062) between system factors perceived importance (PI) of non-functional characteristics and total system usage. This finding did not support that of McGill and Klobas (2009), who reported that system characteristics strongly influenced use and that of Coleman and Mtshazi (2017), who reported that system characteristics such as reliability and perceived ease of use influenced use among academic staff.

Correlations Between Total System Usage and Pedagogic Factors

There was an overall positive correlation (0.241), depicted in Table 2, between the pedagogic factors characteristics of online teaching and total system usage, demonstrating that pedagogic factors influenced total system usage. This finding is supported by those of previous studies on flexible teaching and learning (Martin, 2008), convenience (Coleman & Mtshazi, 2017; Song et al., 2004), enhanced communication, coordination and more work (Coleman & Mtshazi, 2017; McGill & Klobas, 2009), as well as effectiveness of online tools (Barron, 2003; Neal & Miller, 2005; Vipond & Clarey, 2018).

Correlations Between Total System Usage and Organizational Factors

Organizational factors, however, were not directly correlated (r=0.077) with total system usage, as depicted in Table 2. The finding of no overall positive correlation between organizational factors – e-learning support and total system usage is supported by McGill and Klobas (2009, p.499), who reported that facilitating conditions did not influence use, even though it was considered important for the success of e-learning. According to McGill, Klobas and Renzi (2008, p.653), "support services have little effect on the ways in which university teachers incorporate" VLS into their teaching. The finding refuted the findings of a study by Coleman and Mtshazi (2017), who reported that technical support influences usage of LMSs/ VLSs. The authors, however, cited inadequate training as a factor contributing to non-usage of VLSs.

Correlations Between Total System Usage and User Difference Factors

The finding of a positive correlation (r= 0.316) between user difference factors – experience of online teaching and total system usage is depicted in Table 2. This relationship means that the experience of online teaching construct of user difference factors influences total system usage.

The Mann-Whitney test was used to establish a correlation between total system usage and the comfortable with computer applications construct of user difference factors, since the data did not follow a normal distribution. The respondents who used spreadsheet software were found to have significantly higher total system usage (Mann-Whitney test statistic = 258; p = 0.016). In addition, the respondents from UKZN who wrote computer programs were found to have higher total system usage (Mann-Whitney test statistic = 355; p = 0.024). The finding related to comfort with computer applications was supported by Al-Busaidi and Al-Shihi (2010), who reported a significant effect of computer self-efficacy on instructors' acceptance of an e-learning system. Similarly, Coleman and Mtshazi (2017) reported that possession of a formal qualification in computing or experience influenced academic staff use of an LMS/VLS.

The Chi-Square test results depicted a significant correlation between total system usage and the teaching style construct of user difference factors (Chi-Square value = 14.804, df=2, asymptotic significance = 0.001). The average system usage for those preferring a blended and online teaching style was significantly higher than for those favouring a traditional teaching style. The role of the instructor's teaching style was also found to be a determining factor in system usage, as discussed by Al-Busaidi and Al-Shihi (2010) and Coleman and Mtshazi (2017).

Correlations Between Total System Usage and Demographic Factors

Demographic factors comprised the length of VLS usage, the number of blended courses taught, the level of study taught, and academic rank. There was a positive correlation (r = 0.323, p = 0.001) between total system usage and demographic factors –length of use for the whole sample comprising DUT and UKZN respondents. There was a positive correlation (r = 0.300, p = 0.002) between total system usage and demographic factors – the number of courses taught for the whole sample comprising DUT and UKZN respondents. The demographic factors, namely the length of use and the number of courses taught, collectively measured how the system experience of educators influenced total system usage.

A correlation was found between total system usage and the demographic factors – level of study by applying the Kruskal Wallis test to the whole sample (Chi-square value = 14.758, degrees of freedom (df) = 3, p = 0.002). This finding indicates that those educators who mainly lectured postgraduates (and some undergraduates) had a higher usage than those who mostly lectured undergraduates (and some postgraduates) as well as those who lectured only undergraduates. There was no significant correlation between total system usage and the demographic factors – academic rank.

This finding was supported by Oliver and Moore (2008), who reported that experience may play an important role in the web tools that faculty members employ, as the faculty trend was to add tools to their repertoire. This was confirmed in other studies, where EUT was found to play a major role in the acceptance of technology (Al-Busaidi & Al-Shihi, 2010;Coleman & Mtshazi, 2017).

Actual VLS Usage

In considering VLS usage in higher education, the total system usage, the extent and frequency of feature usage, as well as usage clusters were identified. The average frequency usage score of all functions surveyed in this research was used to measure the total system usage. Function usage extent referred to actual system usage from a function-centered perspective, which included 26 functions from the system category with frequency levels ranging from 'not at all', scored at 1, to 'usually', scored at 5. High-frequency usage of functions was associated with a 'total score' above the neutral score of 3. Low-frequency usage of functions was associated with a 'total score' below the neutral score of 3. The percentage of functions that displayed high-frequency usage was 38.5% (i.e. 10 out of 26), while 61.5% (i.e. 16 out of 26) displayed low-frequency usage for the institution DUT. The percentage of functions that displayed high-frequency usage was 19.2% (i.e. 5 out of 26), while 80.8% (i.e. 21 out of 26) displayed low-frequency usage for the institution UKZN.

The usage clusters were derived from the survey findings of function usage items using Cronbach's alpha, which tested for the internal consistency or reliability of items. The communication usage cluster with a Cronbach's alpha value of 0.762 included e-mail, real-time chat, threaded discussion forum, whiteboard, blogs, announcement/notices, calendar, file exchanges and student online journals. The management usage cluster with a Cronbach's alpha value of 0.772 included tracking student participation, online surveys and online polls. The pedagogic usage cluster with a Cronbach's alpha value of 0.874 included wikis, online glossary, online quizzes, online tests, online assignment submission, online marking, peer reviews of student assignments, grading of peer reviews, and grading of student participation in online discussion. The content usage cluster with a Cronbach's alpha value of 0.822 included uploading course information and content. The content cluster was used more than the other clusters at both DUT and UKZN, indicating that content functions enjoyed high usage by educators at both institutions. An analysis using an independent samples t-test showed that average system usage for DUT (2.6) of the pedagogic cluster was significantly greater than that of UKZN (2.0) ($p = 0.007$), meaning that educators at DUT were using more of the pedagogic functions than their counterparts at UKZN. A rounded-off average score of 3 for the communication cluster meant that educators at both DUT and UKZN were making moderate usage of communication functions. Average scores of 2.2 and 2.1 obtained for DUT and UKZN respectively implied that management functions enjoyed lower frequency of usage.

The results presented in this chapter represent only a snapshot of all the statistical analysis performed. It is beyond the scope of this chapter to show all detailed statistics of frequency of all functions, as well as correlations between factors and usage clusters.

Inter-Factor Correlations

Table 2 illustrates that total system usage is positively and directly correlated with the following factors: system factors – PU of functions, pedagogic factors – characteristics of online teaching, and user difference factors – experience of online teaching. In addition, total system usage is correlated with demographic factors – length of use, demographic factors – number of courses taught, and demographic factors – level of study. The inter-factor correlations illustrated in Table 2 are between:

- System factors – PI of non-functional characteristics and PU of functions (r= 0.606).
- Pedagogic factors – characteristics of online teaching, and system factors – PU of functions (r=0.585).
- Pedagogic factors – characteristics of online teaching and system factors – PI of non-functional characteristics (r=0.481).
- Organizational factors – e-learning support and system factors – PU of functions (r= 0.389).
- Organizational factors – e-learning support and system factors – PI of non-functional characteristics (r= 0.700).
- Organizational factors – e-learning support and pedagogic factors – characteristics of online teaching (r=0.644).

In addition, the following inter-factor correlations, between demographic factors and user difference factors, is evident from the following:

- The average user difference factors – experience of online teaching score for 'less than 1 year' (2.733) is significantly less than the user experience score for '1–3 years' (3.248) and '5+ years' (3.317) (p = 0.019; f = 3.473; df = 3.104).
- The average user difference factors – experience of online teaching score for 'greater than 6' (3.488) is significantly more than the user experience score for '1–3' (3.039) (p = 0.002; f =6.692; df = 2.103).

In summary, the findings answer the first research question: What are the multi-dimensional factors that influence VLS usage in South African higher educational institutions? The factors that directly influence VLS usage in South African higher educational institutions are perceived usefulness of functional characteristics within System Factors, Pedagogic Factors, User Difference Factors and Demographic Factors. It is now possible to provide a complete representation of the factors that influence VLS usage and their relationships (illustrated by inter-factor correlations), which answers the second research question presented in the next section.

The Virtual Learning System Usage Model (VLSUM)

This section presents a depiction of the VLSUM, which was based on the conceptual framework described in Figure 1 and the empirical results. Figure 2 depicts the components, the factors influencing VLS usage, and the inter-relationships among the factors and the components. The three main distinguishing components of the VLSUM, as depicted in Figure 2, are the system factors, influential factors, and actual system usage.

The *System Factors* component consists of *Functions/Features, Non-functional Characteristics* and *Challenges*. The *Functions/Features* of VLS tools included that of Assessment tools, Content tools, Administration/management tools, Communication tools, Student productivity and involvement tools and the Student tracking tool. The *Non-functional Characteristics* included flexibility, compliance to standards (e.g. SCORM compliancy), security, reliability, usability (e.g., easy to learn and use, user friendliness) and efficiency. The *Challenges,* identified from the qualitative data analysis are as follows: interoperability issues, missing functions/properties particularly in course assessment, inadequate train-

Figure 2. The Virtual Learning System Model (VLSUM).

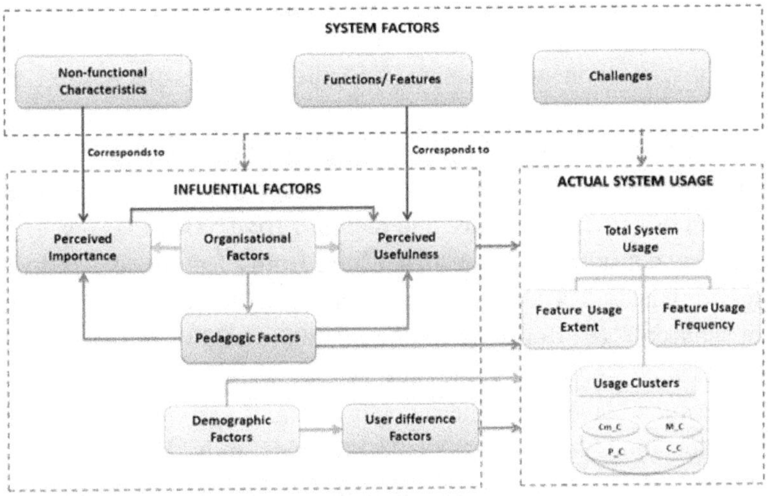

ing in using advanced functionality of VLS, lack of integration with social media as a learning platform, discussion forums that were too formal and cumbersome, inflexible design, and rigid architecture.

The *Influential Factors* component, as depicted in Figure 2, represents the following factors having an influence on the VLS usage.

- *Perceived Usefulness* refers to the extent to which a person believes that the use of a specific system would improve job performance (Davis, 1989).
- *Perceived Importance* refers to the degree to which a person believes that the non-functional characteristics of the VLS will enhance usage.
- *Pedagogic Factors* refer to users' perception of factors corresponding to the profession of teaching that are related to VLS usage. The sub-factors herein are the pedagogic aspects/features covering support for online teaching approaches underpinned by learning theories as well as instructional design activities. The characteristics of online teaching comprises flexible delivery, better course planning, more learner centered, more collaborative learning, better tracking of students' progress, more teaching or instructional strategies, and better course management. The challenges that merit consideration include distance mediation, discussion forums, prior learning and discipline specific issues.
- *Organizational Factors* refer to factors that support or impede VLS usage to integrate e-learning within the organization. Sub-factors that are included are e-learning support comprising infrastructure, instructional design and development support, user support, resources support, and policy/guidelines and other challenges that relate to the organization.
- *User Difference Factors* refer to differences in user characteristics that impact on VLS usage to integrate e-learning. The sub-factors that are included are computer comfort level, teaching style preference, experience of online teaching (comfort, effectiveness, effort, and communication ease) and challenges.
- *Demographic Factors* refer to the participants' profiles that influence VLS usage to integrate e-learning. The sub-factors include system experience and level of study.

According to Petter, DeLone and McLean (2008, p.239), system use refers to the "degree and manner in which staff and customers utilize the capabilities of an information system, for example the amount of use, frequency of use, nature of use, appropriateness of use, extent of use, and purpose of use".

The *Actual System Usage* component, as depicted in Figure 2, consists of four sub-components, namely:

- *Total System Usage* considers *Actual System Usage* from a system perspective (Chang, Lie, & Fan, 2010) comprising all functions/features. The average frequency usage score of all functions/features surveyed in this research was used to measure *Total System Usage.*
- *Feature Usage Extent* considers *Actual System Usage* from a feature-centered perspective. The extent to which a system is used is defined as "breadth of use (number of features)" and as "variety of use (number of subtasks)" (Burton-Jones & Straub, 2006, p.233). A total of 26 functions/features surveyed in this research were used to measure *Feature Usage Extent.*
- *Feature Usage Frequency* measures the number of times system is used (periods were: daily, weekly, etc.) (Burton-Jones & Straub, 2006:230). In this study, *Feature Usage Frequency* refers to how often individual *Functions/Features System Factors* were used, measured on a five-point scale from highest level of usage measured as 'usually' (5) to non-usage 'not at all' (1). The average frequency score was used to measure *Feature Usage Frequency.*
- *Usage Clusters* refers to groupings or patterns of *Actual System Usage* (Chang et al., 2010; Dutton, Cheong, & Park, 2004). The *Usage Clusters* include Communication cluster (*Cm_C*), Management cluster (*M_C*), Pedagogic cluster (*P_C*) and Content cluster (*C_C*). The *Usage Clusters* are a subset of the *Functions/Features* in the *System Factors* component.

The relationships described in this section refer to the various components and sub-components of VLSUM, as depicted in Figure 2. The solid arrows on the graphical model of VLSUM represent correspondence relationships and correlation relationships. The correspondence relationships are labelled 'Corresponds to'. The unlabeled solid arrows in VLSUM are correlation relationships. The correlation relationships in VLSUM are based on the correlations illustrated in Table 2. Dashed arrows between components refer to underlying relationships that have not been statistically tested. For example, the dashed arrow between the *System Factors* component and the *Influential Factors* component refer to the fact that *System Factors* are the underlying component, or the point of reference, for the *Influential Factors*. The dashed arrows between the *System Factors* component and the *Actual System Usage* component depict the relationships between the concept 'usage' and the 'system' referenced. The representation and description of the virtual learning system usage model (VLSUM) in Figure 2 answers the second research question.

SOLUTIONS AND RECOMMENDATIONS

The research reported on in this chapter covered the design of a comprehensive integrated model that specifically addresses the problem of VLS usage from a multi-dimensional perspective. The VLSUM suggests that systems factors, pedagogic factors, user difference factors and demographic factors are direct determinants of VLS usage. Studying the phenomenon from a multi-dimensional perspective allows academic managers and educational technologists to tackle the problem of VLS usage holistically when implementing strategies. The following are recommended by the challenges reported in the empirical findings:

Modelling Discussion Forums Around Social Media

Challenges with VLS discussion forums and the need to emulate or incorporate a social media platform is supported by studies conducted by Coleman and Mtshazi (2017); Egert et al., (2009); Tarade and Singh (2014) and Thomas and Thomas (2012). Egert et al., (2009) reported that students did not think that a VLS created a social network similar to social media systems they used. Thomas and Thomas (2012) argued that the rise in the status of social media and Web 2.0 technologies such as forums, microblogging, social networking, social bookmarking and wikis has changed the way people communicate. Tarade and Singh (2014) proposed the use of social media tools to enhance teaching and collaboration among academics and students as well as to increase professional collaboration between educators. Coleman and Mtshazi (2017) reported challenges with VLS/LMS citing poor student uptake of the online discussion forum and complex management of online threaded discussions in large classes.

Improving Interoperability Between Tools

The need for web services and interoperability specifications is supported by Conde et al. (2012), who argued that systems should interoperate where there are different learning platforms, repositories, tools, types of content, etc. so as to provide improved learning services to students and educators.

Creating a Flexible Design for Future Iterations of VLSs

The need for creating a flexible design for future versions of VLSs is supported by García-Peñalvo. and Forment (2014), who argued that a VLS should evolve from a silo used by institutions into an adaptable and flexible framework by incorporating new tools and processes to support learner needs. This view was further supported by Coleman and Mtshazi (2017) who reported that lack of optimized usage was due to poorly designed features of the VLS/LMS, which did not meet the needs of lecturers.

Incorporating Added Functionality to Assessment Tools

The limitations of current online assessment and the need for incorporating additional capability to assessment tools are supported by Chiheb, Faizi and Afia (2005), who argued that assessment tools should provide opportunities for further learning, and embrace other assessment techniques testing a wider range of intellectual proficiency and by Appana (2008) who argued that there should not be an over reliance on multiple choice/true/false/ responses, as it is insufficient to assess students' depth of knowledge and skills.

Complementing the Use of VLSs With Social Applications for Teaching and Learning

The complementary use of social applications in conjunction with a VLS was supported by Junco (2012), who recommended integrating Web technology 20 tools for teaching and learning as students preferred to communicate with their fellow students by means of their cellular phones and social networks. Exter, Rowe, Boyd and Lloyd (2012) concurred by arguing that Web 2.0 tools usage in higher education improves student engagement, provides a social platform where students can interact with their peers, develop a better understanding of content and learn collaboratively by working in groups.

Offering Training to Educators on More Advanced Functions of VLSs

The need to offer training to educators on more advanced VLS features is supported by Nanayakkara, (2007) who argued that institutions should be equipped with a learning technologies unit offering instructional development services such as training staff members to use e-learning software, assisting them in understanding online pedagogy, assisting them with instructional design, and helping them develop courses. A major finding from the Coleman and Mtshazi (2017) study was that the lack of effective use of the VLS was due to inadequate training.

FUTURE RESERCH DIRECTIONS

Further research can be conducted on the VLSUM by testing for implementation and management variables that influence actual system usage in higher education, or information systems success by studying the impact of actual system usage on individuals or the organization. Future research can consider the role of gamification as a feature in VLSs. In addition, the role of mobile learning application and complementing VLS with social applications should be examined for teaching and learning purposes. Future research endeavors could also address the limitations of the current study by surveying a broader target population, comprising educators and learners from universities in other provinces of South Africa and examining the functional and non-functional features of other VLSs deployed in higher universities.

CONCLUSION

The main contribution of this study is the development of a VLSUM representing the multi-dimensional factors that influence VLS usage in higher education, based on the beliefs and perceptions of educators in higher education. The model is different from other technology models, in that it focuses on post-adoptive usage behavior, and the participants in this research had been using the target software for over a year. The VLSUM has advanced the current state of models in the field of VLS usage in higher education by drawing on research from systems design, pedagogy, user characteristics and management information systems. This research extended the work of McGill et al. (2008) on VLS utilization as a dependent variable, by examining the extent and frequency of educator utilization of individual VLS functions for online teaching. In addition, the research modelled task requirements for teaching with the functions of VLSs by analyzing instructors' perceptions of the perceived usefulness of the individual functions.

REFERENCES

Adlnet. (n.d.). Advanced Distributed Learning. *SCORM*. Retrieved November 8, 2012, from https://www.adlnet.gov/capabilities/scorm

Al-Busaidi, K.A. & Al-Shihi, H. (2010). Instructors' Acceptance of Learning Management Systems: A Theoretical Framework. *Communications of the IBIMA*, 1-10. doi:10.5171/2010.862128

Appana, S. (2008). A Review of Benefits and Limitations of Online Learning in the Context of the Student, the Instructor, and the Tenured Faculty. *International Journal on E-Learning*, *7*(1), 5–22.

Ardito, C., Costabile, M. F., De Marsico, M., Lanzilotti, R., Levialdi, S., Roselli, T., & Rossano, V. (2005). An approach to usability evaluation of e-learning applications. *Universal Access in the Information Society*, *4*(3), 270–283. doi:10.100710209-005-0008-6

Augar, N., Raitman, R., & Zhou, W. (2006). Wikis: Collaborative Virtual Learning Environments. In *The International Handbook of Virtual Learning Environments* (pp. 1251–1269). doi:10.1007/978-1-4020-3803-7_52

Barron, A. E. (2003). Course management systems and online teaching. *Journal of Computing in Higher Education*, *15*(1), 128–142. doi:10.1007/BF02940856

Blackboard Inc. (2006). *Blackboard Learning System™ Designer and Instructor Reference*. Blackboard Inc.

Blinco, K., Mason, J., McLean, N., & Wilson, S. (2004). *Trends and Issues in E-learning Infrastructure development*. A White Paper for alt-i-lab. Redwood City, CA: Altilab04. Retrieved October 24, 2012, from http://scholar.google.com/scholar?hl=en&btnG=Search&q=intitle:Trends+and+Issues+in+E-learning+Infrastructure+Development#0

Botturi, L. (2004). *Functional Assessment of some Open-Source LMS*. Unpublished Manuscript. Retrieved September 12, 2012, from www.istituti.usilu.net/botturil/web/publications/OS_review_Nov2004.pdf

Britain, S., & Liber, O. (2004). *A Framework for the Pedagogical Evaluation of eLearning Environments*. Retrieved November 8, 2012, from https://www.jisc.ac.uk/uploaded_documents/jtap-041.doc

Brooks, C., Kettel, L., & Hansen, C. (2005). Building a Learning Object Content Management System E-learning Specifications. *eLearnMagazine*. Retrieved June 6, 2013, from https://pdfs.semanticscholar.org/ea53/6da43b5e5ca7f44b5247bbe463f16c83c9e7.pdf

Brown, G., & Peterson, N. (2008). The LMS Mirror: School as We Know IT versus School as We Need IT and the Triumph of the Custodial Class. *Journal of Online Learning and Teaching*, *4*(2), 190–197.

Buabeng-Andoh, C. (2012). Factors influencing teachers ' adoption and integration of information and communication technology into teaching: A review of the literature. *International Journal of Education and Development Using Information and Communication Technology*, *8*(1), 136–155.

Burton-Jones, A., & Hubona, G. (2005). Individual differences and usage behavior: revisiting a technology acceptance model assumption. *ACM SIGMIS Database*, *36*(2), 58–77. Retrieved August 18, 2013, from https://dl.acm.org/citation.cfm?id=1066155

Cavus, N., & Momani, A. M. (2009). Computer aided evaluation of learning management systems. *Procedia: Social and Behavioral Sciences*, *1*(1), 426–430. doi:10.1016/j.sbspro.2009.01.076

Chiheb, R., Faizi, R., & Afia, A. E. L. (2005). *Using Objective Online Testing Tools to Assess Students' Learning: Potentials and Limitations*. Retrieved September 20, 2013, from http://www.jatit.org/volumes/research-papers/Vol24No1/8Vol24No1.pdf

Cole, J., & Foster, H. (2007). Using Moodle: teaching with the popular open source course management system. *O'Reilly Media, Inc.* Retrieved October 23, 2012, from https://books.google.com/books?hl=en&lr=&id=wfPPb1m0G6EC&oi=fnd&pg=PR5&dq=Using+Moodle+Teaching+with+the+Popular+Open+Source+Course+Management+System&ots=vQBiCk0BQy&sig=y1AV_mAH776UCLis-FliArlzXHMY

Coleman, E., & Mtshazi, S. (2017). Factors affecting the use and non-use of Learning Management Systems (LMS) by academic staff. *South African Computer Journal*, *29*(3). doi:10.18489acj.v29i3.459

Conde, M. A., García-Peñalvo, F. J., Piguillem, J., Casany, M. J., & Alier, M. (2012). *Interoperability in eLearning Contexts. Interaction Between LMS and PLE.* Paper presented at the 1st Symposium on Languages, Applications and Technologies (SLATE 2012), Braga, Portugal.

Cosgrave, R., Rísquez, A., Logan-phelan, T., Farrelly, T., Costello, E., & Palmer, M. (2011). Usage And Uptake Of Virtual Learning Environments In Ireland : Findings From A Multi Institutional Study. *Aishe-J*, *3*(1), 1–14.

Dahlstrom, E., Christopher, D. B., & Jacqueline, B. (2014). The Current Ecosystem of Learning Management Systems in Higher Education: Student, Faculty, and IT Perspectives. *EDUCAUSE Research Report*, 27. https://www.educause.edu/ecar

Davis, F. D. (1989). Perceived Usefulness, Perceived Ease of Use, and User Acceptance of Information Technology. *Management Information Systems Quarterly*, *13*(3), 319–340. doi:10.2307/249008

Disbrow, L. M. (2008). The Overall Effect of Online Audio Conferencing in Communication Courses: What do Students Really Think? *Journal of Online Learning and Teaching*, *4*(2).

Egert, C. A., Jacobs, S., & Barnes, S. B. (2009). When Social Worlds Collide : Charting the Intersection of Social Media and Courseware / Course Management Systems. In P. Zaphiris & A. A. Ozok (Eds.), *Online Communities, LNCS 5621* (pp. 452–461). Berlin: Springer-Verlag. doi:10.1007/978-3-642-02774-1_49

El-Masri, M., & Tarhini, A. (2017). Erratum to: Factors affecting the adoption of e-learning systems in Qatar and USA: Extending the Unified Theory of Acceptance and Use of Technology 2 (UTAUT2). *Educational Technology Research and Development*, *65*(3), 765–767. doi:10.100711423-017-9526-1

Elabnody, M. E. (2016). A Survey of Top 10 Open Source Learning Management Systems. *International Journal of Scientific & Technology Research,* 5(9).

Elementk. (2003). *Learning Management Systems in the Work Environment: Practical considerations for the selection and and implementation of an e-Learning platform*. Author.

Exter, K. D., Rowe, S., Boyd, W., & Lloyd, D. (2012). Using Web 2.0 Technologies for Collaborative Learning in Distance Education—Case Studies from an Australian University. *Future Internet, 4*(1), 216–237. doi:10.3390/fi4010216

Gamage, D., Fernando, S., & Perera, I. (2014). Factors affecting to effective eLearning: Learners Perspective. *Scientific Research Journal, 2*(5), 42–48. Retrieved October 18, 2015, from http://www.scirj.org

García-Peñalvo, F. J., & Forment, M. A. (2014). Learning management system: Evolving from silos to structures. *Interactive Learning Environments, 22*(2), 143–145. doi:10.1080/10494820.2014.884790

Gonella, L. & Pantò, E. (2008). Didactic architectures and organization models: a process of mutual adaptation. *eLearning Papers, 9*, 1–12.

Goodhue, D. L. (2009). Understanding User Evaluations of Information Systems. *Management Science, 41*(12), 1827–1844. doi:10.1287/mnsc.41.12.1827

Guest, G., MacQueen, K. M., & Namey, E. E. (2012). *Applied thematic analysis.* Los Angeles: Sage Publications. doi:10.4135/9781483384436

Horton, W., & Horton, K. (2003). *E-learning Tools and Technologies: A consumer's guide for trainers, teachers, educators, and instructional designers*. Chichester: Wiley.

Junco, R. (2012). *College students prefer to use Facebook in their courses.* Retrieved March 12, 2014, from http://blog.reyjunco.com/college-students-prefer-to-use-facebook-in-their-courses

Kalinga, E. A. (2008). *Development of an Interactive eTlearning Management System (eTLMS) for Tanzanian Secondary Schools.* Retrieved October 22, 2012, from https://www.bth.se/fou/forskinfo.nsf/alfs/078658eaeb62ee0ec12574570033056b/$file/Kalinga_lic.pdf

Kasim, N. N. M., & Khalid, F. (2016). Choosing the Right Learning Management System (LMS) for the Higher Education Institution Context: A Systematic Review. *iJET, 11*(6), 55-61. Retrieved March 25, 2019, from http://www.i-jet.org

Kaur, M. (2013). Blended learning - its challenges and future. *Procedia: Social and Behavioral Sciences, 93*, 612–617. doi:10.1016/j.sbspro.2013.09.248

Klobas, J., & McGill, T. (2010). The role of involvement in learning management system success. *Journal of Computing in Higher Education, 22*(2), 114–134. doi:10.100712528-010-9032-5

Liu, Y. C., Huang, Y., & Lin, C. (2012). Organizational factors' effects on the success of e-learning systems and organizational benefits: An empirical study in Taiwan. *The International Review of Research in Open and Distributed Learning*. Retrieved April 2, 2015, from http://www.irrodl.org/index.php/irrodl/article/view/1203/2302

Martin, F. (2008). Blackboard as the learning management system of a computer literacy course. *Journal of Online Learning and Teaching, 4*(2), 138–145. http://libres.uncg.edu/ir/uncw/f/martinf2008-1.pdf

Masrom, M., Zainon, O., & Rahiman, R. (2008). Critical success in e-learning: An examination of technological and institutional support factors. *International Journal of Cyber Society and Education, 1*(2), 131–142. http://eprints.utm.my/6952/

Mcgee, P., & Green, M. (2008). Lifelong learning and systems: A postFordist analysis. *Journal of Online Learning and Teaching*, *4*(2), 146–157.

McGill, T., Klobas, J. E., & Renz, S. (2008). The Relationship between LMS Use and Teacher Performance The Role of Task-Technology Fit. *19th Australasian Conference on Information Systems*, 648–657.

McGill, T. J., & Klobas, J. (2009). A task–technology fit view of learning management system impact. *Computers & Education*, *52*(2), 496–508. doi:10.1016/j.compedu.2008.10.002

Mlitwa, N. B. W., & Van Belle, J. P. W. (2011). Mediators for Lecturer Perspectives on Learning Management Systems at Universities in The Western Cape, South Africa. In *Pacific Asia Conference on Information Systems, PACIS 2011: Quality Research in Pacific Asia, Brisbane, Queensland, Australia*, 7-11.

Morgan, G. (2003). *Faculty use of course management systems*. Retrieved November 10, 2012, from https://www.educause.edu/ir/library/pdf/EKF/ekf0302.pdf

Mtebe, J.S. (2015). Learning Management System success: Increasing Learning Management System usage in higher education in sub-Saharan Africa. *International Journal of Education and Development using Information and Communication Technology, 11*(2), 51-64.

Myers, M., & Avison, D. (2002). *Qualitative research in information systems: a reader*. London: Sage Publications. Retrieved December 6, 2012, from http://en.scientificcommons.org/8816846

Nanayakkara, C. (2007). A model of user acceptance of learning management systems: a study within tertiary institutions in New Zealand. *The International Journal of Learning*. Retrieved November 7, 2012, from https://www.caudit.edu.au/educauseaustralasia07/authors_papers/Nanayakkara-361.pdf

Neal, L., & Miller, D. (2005). ACM Digital Library Communications of the ACM Human Factors. *eLearn Magazine Education and Technology in Perspective*. https://elearnmag.acm.org/index.cfm

Oliver, K. (2001). Recommendations for Student Tools in Online Course Management Systems. *Journal of Computing in Higher Education*, *13*(1), 47–70. doi:10.1007/BF02940944

Oliver, K., & Moore, J. (2008). Faculty Recommendations for Web Management Systems. *Journal of Computing in Higher Education*, *19*(2), 3–24. doi:10.1007/BF03033424

Ozkan, S., & Koseler, R. (2009). Multi-dimensional students' evaluation of e-learning systems in the higher education context: An empirical investigation. *Computers & Education*, *53*(4), 1285–1296. doi:10.1016/j.compedu.2009.06.011

Ozkan, S., Koseler, R., & Baykal, N. (2009). Evaluating learning management systems. *Transforming Government: People. Process and Policy*, *3*(2), 111–130. doi:10.1108/17506160910960522

QSRInternational. (n.d.). *NVivo 10 research software for analysis and insight*. Retrieved October 5, 2012, from http://www.qsrinternational.com/products_nvivo.aspx

Radwan, N. M., Senousy, M. B., & Riad, A. E. D. M. (2014). Current Trends and Challenges of Developing and Evaluating Learning Management Systems. *International Journal of e-Education, e-Business, e-. Management Learning*, *4*(5), 361–375.

Sachan, A., Agarwal, A., Rai, A., Sharma, S., Verma, J., & Mishra, M. (2006). *Software Requirement Specification (SRS) Learning Course Management System* (Version 1). Academic Press.

Sallam, N., & Alzouebi, K. (2014). Teacher Perceptions of the Use of Moodle to Enhance the Quality of Teaching and Learning in a K-12 Private School in the United Arab Emirates. *J. Tea. Tea. Edu.*, 2(2), 93–101. doi:10.12785/jtte/020202

Selim, H. M. (2007). Critical success factors for e-learning acceptance: Confirmatory factor models. *Computers & Education, 49*(2), 396–413. doi:10.1016/j.compedu.2005.09.004

Song, L., Singleton, E. S., Hill, J. R., & Koh, M. H. (2004). Improving online learning: Student perceptions of useful and challenging characteristics. *The Internet and Higher Education, 7*(1), 59–70. Retrieved October292012. doi:10.1016/j.iheduc.2003.11.003

South Africa. (2001). Higher Education Act 101. Pretoria: Academic Press.

South African Government. (2004). *Government Gazette* (Vol. 470). Pretoria: Government Printer.

South Africa Institute of Distance Education. (2013). *The use of Moodle to support teaching and learning at the university of Dar es salaam.* Tanzania: Author.

Ssekakubo, G., Suleman, H., & Marsden, G. (2011). Issues of adoption: Have e-Learning Management Systems fulfilled their potential in developing countries? In *Proceedings of the South African Institute of Computer Scientists and Information Technologists Conference on Knowledge, Innovation and Leadership in a Diverse, Multidisciplinary Environment.* Cape Town, South Africa.: ACM.

Oloo, L. M. (2010). Digital learning management systems in Africa: myths and realities. *OpenLearning: The Journal of Open and Distance Learning, 25*(1), 5–23. Retrieved May 6, 2012, from http://www.informaworld.com/openurl?genre=article&doi=10.1080/02680510903482033&magic=crossref||D404A21C5BB053405B1A640AFFD44AE3

Tarade, R. S., & Singh, N. (2014). Significance of Web 2.0 Technology and its Application in Academic Libraries. *International Journal of Computer Trends and Technology, 10*(5). doi:10.14445/22312803/IJCTT-V10P143

Tarhini, A., Hone, K., Liu, X., & Tarhini, T. (2017). Examining the moderating effect of individual level cultural values on users' acceptance of Elearning in developing countries: a structural equation modeling of an extended technology acceptance model. *Interactive Learning Environments.*

Thomas, M., & Thomas, H. (2012). Using new social media and Web 2.0 technologies in business school teaching and learning. *Journal of Management Development, 31*(4), 358–367. doi:10.1108/02621711211219013

Trice, A. W., & Treacy, M. E. (1988). Utilization as a dependent variable in MIS research. *ACM SIGMIS Database.* Retrieved October 23, 2012, from https://dl.acm.org/citation.cfm?id=65771

Venkatesh, V., Morris, M. G., Davis, G. B., & Davis, F. D. (2004). User Acceptance of Information Technology: Toward a unified view. *MIS Quarterly, 27*(3), 425–478. Retrieved November 1, 2012, from http://onlinelibrary.wiley.com/doi/10.1002/cbdv.200490137/abstract

Vipond, S., & Clarey, J. (2018). Academic Learning Management Systems. *Research from the Elearning Guild and Adobe Systems.* www.eLearningGuild.com

Wan, L., Zhao, C., Liu, Q., & Sun, J. (2005). Work in progress-an evaluation model for learning content management systems: from a perspective of knowledge management. In *Frontiers in Education, FIE' 05. Proceedings 35th Annual Conference*. IEEE. Retrieved November 1, 2012, from. https://ieeexplore.ieee.org/xpls/abs_all.jsp?arnumber=1612111

WCET. (n.d.). EduTools. *CMS: Product Comparison System*. Retrieved October 8, 2015, from https://wcet.wiche.edu/sites/default/files/docs/resources/OldEdutoolsCMSFeaturesandCriteriaRev041513.docx

ADDITIONAL READING

Coleman, E., & Mtshazi, S. (2017). Factors affecting the use and non-use of Learning Management Systems (LMS) by academic staff. *South African Computer Journal, 29*(3). doi:10.18489acj.v29i3.459

Hubackova, S., & Semradova, I. (2016). Evaluation of Blended Learning. *Procedia: Social and Behavioral Sciences, 217*, 551–557. doi:10.1016/j.sbspro.2016.02.044

Padayachee, I., van der Merwe, A., & Kotzé, P. (2015). Virtual learning system usage in Higher Education—A study at two South African institutions. *South African Computer Journal, 57*(57), 32–57. doi:10.18489acj.v0i57.324

KEY TERMS AND DEFINITIONS

Efficiency: It falls under the category of non-functional characteristics that refers to the capability of the system to provide the required performance in terms of amount of resources used and acceptable response time.

Flexibility: A non-functional characteristic that refers to seamless integration or links to other systems, as well as the ability to import content from and supply content to digital libraries and other e-Learning systems.

Functional Characteristics: Functional characteristics in a VLS typically comprise communication, student productivity and involvement, course administration and management, assessment, student tracking and content functions to support educational practices.

Non-Functional Characteristics: They refer to desired characteristics that a system must possess that may not be related to a specific function such as security or usability.

Pedagogy: A discipline that deals with the theory and practice of education. Examples of pedagogy include the use of simulation, case study, assignment, modelling, video, role play, tutorial, lecture, project, power point, quiz, and so on.

Reliability: A non-functional characteristic that refers to the capability of the system to retain its performance level. It also implies little or no disruption/system downtime.

Security: A non-functional characteristic that refers to the ability to prevent unauthorized access to software and data.

Standards: Rules which are set by national or international bodies to ensure compliance in the design of systems.

Usability: A non-functional characteristic that refers to capability of the system to be understood, learnt, used and liked by users.

Virtual Learning System (VLS): A generic term used to describe the class of software designed to support a model of online teaching and learning in higher education. Examples of VLSs in use are Blackboard, Sakai, and Moodle.

Chapter 16
Technology Integration Into Instruction in the United States: A Policy Brief on Accountability in Higher Education

Ibrahim M. Karkouti
https://orcid.org/0000-0001-5900-2682
The American University in Cairo, Egypt

ABSTRACT

Technology integration into higher education is considered essential in terms of achieving accountability performance measures that qualify institutions to receive federal grants. The policy presented in this chapter focuses on technology integration into curricula and instruction as a means to enhance student outcomes. This chapter describes the problems that prevent higher education institutions from integrating technology effectively into their educational systems, tracks the implementation of America's Higher Education Opportunity Act of 2008, and measures the progress of Section 204, Part G of the law. The chapter also proposes key solutions in an effort to better integrate technology into higher education classrooms.

INTRODUCTION

Technology integration, which is a process that aims at supporting teaching and learning at schools (Young, 2003), can be defined as effective educational technology implementation and practices to improve teaching methodologies, achieve learning outcomes, and increase students' motivation towards learning (Davies, Sprague, & New, 2008; Koruyan, 2016). In addition to improving the quality of education, increasing accessibility, and enhancing cost-efficiency, technology integration helps learners to face the challenges of globalization (Albirini, 2006). According to Jung (2005), implementing technology into education has become a necessity to decrease postsecondary institutions' financial expenditures while enhancing the quality of their educational systems.

DOI: 10.4018/978-1-7998-3062-7.ch016

Technology integration has been affecting higher education since the successful introduction of microcomputers (e.g., Commodore Educator 64) in the early 1980s (Haran, 2015; Wang & Reeves, 2004). Nevertheless, the integration of technology into curricula and instruction has been plagued by many barriers inhibiting the implementation of this initiative (Faudler, 2011; Surry, Ensminger, & Haab, 2005). One of the problems is the lack of sufficient and efficient technology training, which in turn, prevents faculty from professionally integrating technology into their teaching practices. Students and teachers need adequate training to use technology effectively for learning purposes (Gönen & Akbarov, 2015).

Researchers have identified the reasons why technology integration into curricula and instruction seems to be essential today. One key reason is the rising financial burdens confronting higher education that has focused the attention on technology integration as a means to improve the quality of learning and enhance student outcomes, while significantly reducing instructional costs (Green & Gilbert, 1995; Selingo, 2013). For example, online learning costs 41% less than traditional learning, and the total cost of a student enrolled in an online program is 57% less than traditional face-to-face instruction (Jung, 2005). As such, investing in technology decreases the cost per student, which in turn increases higher education institutions' financial capacity. Jones and Mathews (2002) and Christensen and Eyering (2011) stated that the main reason why states and higher education institutions are interested in greater use of technology into their educational systems is that education practitioners and policymakers believe that information technology is now essential to the global economy and has transformed the majority of U.S. industries except education.

According to Prensky (2005), the issue of technology integration asserts itself because students today seem to come to class with a technological expertise that disturbs some teachers and appear to go untapped. Prensky (2001) proposes the concept of 'digital natives' who have grown up with technology and rely on it. Students have spent their entire lives surrounded by and using computers, videogames, digital music players, cell phones and all the other toys and tools of the digital age, and they are naturally skilled at using new and emerging technologies (Prensky, 2001). Therefore, educators should embrace technology and adopt approaches that enable students to take an active role in the learning process.

In addition, the globalized impacts of fast-paced technological changes necessitate the development of new higher education models that integrate technology into curricula and instruction (U.S. Department of Education, 2017). Therefore, this chapter aims to investigate the factors that obstruct and facilitate the integration of technology into curricula and instruction and highlights the policy that mandates the incorporation of technology into higher education. Simply put, the chapter seeks to answer the following research question: How can educational leaders enhance the use of technology for teaching and learning purposes?

First, this chapter addresses the importance of integrating technology into higher education, identifies the policy that governs its implementation, and describes the factors that obstruct technology use inside the classroom. It then offers recommendations and solutions to improve the use of technology inside the classroom based on a systematic review that was conducted for this specific purpose.

BACKGROUND

This section gives information about the policy details. On July 31, 2008, the U.S. Congress passed the Higher Education Opportunity Act (2008). President Obama signed the Act into law on August 14, 2008. Section 204, Part G of the law, "Accountability and Evaluation" (p. 70), specifically addresses the issue of technology integration into curricula and instruction. The policy addressing this issue enhances higher education institutions' accountability mechanisms by connecting federal grants to the degree of technology integration into their curricula and instruction. Therefore, universities and colleges are required to submit an evaluation plan that includes adequate and measurable performance indicators that assess the percentage-rate of teachers trained to integrate technology effectively into curricula and instruction in order to be eligible for federal grants. In summary, the policy represents a meaningful financial incentive for institutions trying to improve the quality of education through connecting their performance to federal grants.

Section 204, Part G of the Higher Education Opportunity Act (2008) also accounts for students' academic achievement. The evaluation plan that qualifies higher education institutions for federal grants requires assessment of the percentage-rate of instructors trained on using technology effectively to collect, manage, and analyze data to improve students' academic performance. The importance of this policy does not solely depend on technology integration as a means to improve the quality of education and students' academic achievement, but also stresses the importance of data-driven decision making in higher education, which in turn influences policymaking based on data and evidence.

The Higher Education Opportunity Act (2008) is a federal law enacted by the U.S. Congress and it reauthorized the Higher Education Act of 1965 (Stephanie, 2009). The Act enforces new reporting and disclosure requirements on higher education institutions that participate in Title IV federal student financial aid programs. Therefore, public and private higher education institutions should implement new policies in order to receive adequate federal financial support. Furthermore, governing boards need to track their institutional progress and compliance with the law in order to receive sufficient resources and sustain federal financial support.

In addition to improving education and strengthening accountability measures, the Higher Education Opportunity Act (2008) also empowers the American socioeconomic system through enhancing the development of innovative educational curricula that prepare fresh graduates for the challenges of the modern economy. In summary, this policy engages university governing boards, faculty, staff, students, researchers, and policymakers into the process of building effective and efficient educational systems that eventually lead to the development of a strong sustainable economy conducive to high levels of employment growth.

Resolving the issues that prevent technology integration into education is essential for higher education institutions and a basic requirement of Section 204 of the Higher Education Opportunity Act (2008). Institutions are required to continuously report their progress on this policy to the Department of Education in order to be eligible for federal grants. The secretary will then determine whether eligible partnerships receiving a grant are accomplishing the objectives and measures of the grant or not. Failure to do so can lead to serious consequences including federal fiscal penalties such as the cancellation of federal grants. According to Tandberg (2010), higher education institutions balance their budget deficits by increasing their tuition fees when they fail to compete for adequate governmental financial support. Thus, incompliance with the policy requirements will increase the financial burden of undergraduate students because costs are passed on to them and this, in turn, could impact enrollment rates.

MAIN FOCUS OF THE CHAPTER

This chapter draws policymakers' attention towards the current status of technology integration at higher education institutions in the United States by examining the factors that facilitate and obstruct the integration of technology into curricula and instruction. In order to achieve this, a systematic review of three electronic databases (i.e., ERIC, Google Scholar, and EBSCOhost) was conducted to identify empirical studies that (a) focus on the implementation of technology in higher education and (b) unveil the factors that enhance and prevent the use of technology in education. These studies were included to support the chapter's argument and add depth and breadth to its content.

Factors Preventing Policy Implementation

Technology has transformed higher education processes and practices (Selingo, 2013). Although it has become a necessity in all aspects of people's lives, research suggests that technology resistance still exists in the higher education arena (Lofstrom & Nevgi, 2007). Research addressed the issues that are limiting the integration of technology into the teaching and learning process. Mills and Tincher (2003) and Elmes (2017) indicated that the issue facing higher education institutions is no longer whether students and faculty will use technology, but how technology can be used to enhance teaching and improve student outcomes. In other words, merely by providing technological tools, learning will not occur on its own (Healey, 1999), but rather, as Motteram (2013) suggests, how to deploy those technologies in classroom practice and "how they mediate that practice" (p. 182) are more important. Therefore, training both teachers and students is essential for learners trying to benefit from the use of technology in this digital age. The literature (e.g. Hauck, 2007; Hampel, 2006; Hauck & Youngs, 2008) on technology and its affordances, language learning and teaching in particular also warns that the use of technology needs to be informed by pedagogy rather than simply being technology-driven. This means that technology should be part of a comprehensive pedagogical framework. In other words, instructors should never ignore the importance of aligning specific technology tools with learning objectives, course content, and student learning outcomes (Okojie, Olinzock, & Okojie-Boulder, 2006).

Similarly, Ertmer (1999) and Islim and Cirak (2017) concluded that there is a distinction between the personal use of technology, professional use of technology, and technology integration into instruction in higher education institutions. Thus, it is essential to establish performance indicators that can adequately evaluate the effectiveness of technology integration on faculty performance and student outcomes. Further, it is also important to determine the actions that will lead higher education institutions towards implementing the whole process of technology integration. Green and Gilbert (1995) and Jones (2015) explained that the process of technology infusion into learning requires years, not weeks or months.

In a recent study that examined the current state of technology integration in Texas higher education system, Martirosyan, Kennon, Saxon, Edmonson, and Skidmore (2017) identified various barriers preventing the integration process. These barriers include lack of professional development programs, insufficient technology skills, and disbelief of the benefits of technology. Table 1 summarizes these barriers.

Table 1. Forms of Barriers (Martirosyan et al., 2017)

Types of Barriers	Description of Barriers
Professional Development and Training	Insufficient professional development and training programs that are aimed at enhancing faculty technology skills.
Faculty Technology Expertise	Faculty not knowing how to use technology to enhance teaching and learning inside the classroom.
Students' Technology Skills	Students lacking technology skills and competencies needed for learning purposes.
Faculty Beliefs and Self-Efficacy	Faculty not envisioning the benefits of technology and the positive impact it has on the overall quality of their courses and student learning.

It is evident from the review of the literature that faculty beliefs about technology, instructors' lack of expertise, and insufficient training are the main problems that inhibit the implementation of technology integration into curricula and instruction at higher education institutions (e.g., Fabry & Higgs, 1999; Karkouti, 2016; Martirosyan et al., 2017). The next section presents a review of five studies at different U.S. institutions that examined the impact of training on technology integration into curricula and instruction.

Selected Research Related to the Effects of Faculty Training on Technology Integration into Higher Education

Covering over 15 years of research, the following investigations are chronologically ordered and representative of the published empirical studies on the topic (Brown, 2016; Fathema, Shannon, & Ross, 2015; Dempsey, Fisher, Wright, & Anderton, 2008; Georgina & Olson, 2007; Vannatta & Beyerbach, 2000). These studies show how professional development programs increase the use of technology inside the classroom and were therefore included for reasons including appropriateness, significance, and relevance to the examined topic. The results revealed that technology workshops, training sessions, and professional development programs were essentially vital for improving faculty technology skills and enhancing the integration of technology into curricula and instruction.

In an effort to understand the impact of faculty training on technology integration into curricula and instruction, Vannatta and Beyerbach (2000) examined the relationships between training programs and technology infusion into education through conducting a technology integration project. The project aimed to prepare higher education faculty, K-12 teachers, and pre-service teachers to integrate technology into instruction in order to facilitate teaching and learning. The study described year two of the project where four teams participated in the training activities from May 1998 to May 1999. The sample of the study consisted of eight higher education faculty members, eight K-12 teachers, and 300 pre-service teachers. The study was conducted at the State University of New York at Oswego. The research was funded by a grant that supports technology integration project and sought to increase technology skills among higher education faculty, K-12 teachers, and pre-service teachers.

Vannatta and Beyerbach (2000) conducted a mixed methods research to fully understand the project and its effects on participants. The researchers collected data using pre- and post-treatment surveys and focus group interviews. The project directors developed the interview questions, while the questionnaire packages included the Faculty Technology Survey and the Pre-service Teacher Technology Survey (as cited in Vannatta & Beyerbach, 2000). The researchers found that training activities enhanced proficiency in technology applications and instructional methods among all participants. The results also indicated a significant increase in faculty integration of technology into education courses. Furthermore, higher education faculty members reported that the training program enabled them to use technology as an instructional tool that facilitates learning. More importantly, the percentage of faculty reporting moderate to high proficiency in the area of instructional methods of technology integration increased from 33.4% to 93.3% after the training program.

Georgina and Olson (2007) conducted a correlation study to explore how faculty technology literacy and technology training affected their pedagogy. This required an evaluation of how faculty digital literacy skills related to their pedagogical practice (technology integration into instruction), while controlling for the training variable. The sample consisted of 1,115 higher education faculty members recruited from the Colleges of Education of 15 universities that are considered peer institutions to the University of North Dakota. The researchers emailed each participant a unique URL for the online survey. The total number of respondents who completed the online survey represented a rate of 21.2%. Female responses accounted for 65.4% of the survey, while male responses accounted for 34.6%. The participants for this study were randomly sampled to complete an online survey with three questions. The first question on self-perception was scored using a Likert-based scale of proficiency, while the remaining two questions were open-ended. Data analysis relied exclusively on the information derived from the administered online survey. The results indicated a significant correlation ($p<.001$) between technology proficiency and pedagogical practice integration. Furthermore, the study revealed that if an instructor had the technological skills needed to integrate technology into instruction, then, according to the collected data, it was very likely that the instructor would integrate technology into pedagogical practices. The results also indicated that faculty technology training might be maximized for the integration of pedagogy by using a technology training strategy that emphasized small group faculty forums with a trainer.

Similarly, Dempsey et al. (2008) examined the effects of faculty and student training and support on the utilization of online library resources. The study also focused on enhancing traditional classes by integrating the internet into courses. Data were collected from six groups that comprised of 140 faculty members and 707 students. The sampled population participated entirely in online courses, web-enhanced courses, and traditional classroom courses. The study was conducted at a university located in the southeastern United States that employs the use of both online and web-based courses. Dempsey et al. conducted six separate surveys via internet and telephone. The questions ranged from 53 items for faculty and students participating in online courses to 27 items for those participating in traditional classroom courses. The questions aimed to identify faculty reports regarding the types of training they perceive as the most important, and students' reports regarding their technical skills that require additional training. Overall, 77% of all faculty surveyed reported that formal training opportunities were perceived as the most important, and 90% of all surveyed students reported a high level of expertise in information technology and computer tools. Dempsey et al. (2008) found that formal training opportunities were very important to faculty members and that online learning instructors should be professionally trained in the use of the medium. Faculty members in this study looked first for pedagogical assistance from their peers and second from the university and software company assistance mechanisms in order to effectively and efficiently integrate technology into curricula and instruction. Surprisingly, the study revealed that both faculty and students involved in traditional classroom courses reported more use of online resources than faculty and students who participated in other courses that incorporated educational technology.

Using Davis's (1989) technology acceptance model which was developed to explain individuals' behaviors and attitudes towards using technology systems, Fathema et al. (2015) conducted a quantitative study that examined the factors that helped instructors use learning management systems (LMS) for teaching and learning purposes. The sample for this study consisted of 560 faculty members drawn from two public research universities in the United States. The researchers emailed 2,330 faculty members and graduate assistants a web-based survey link and received an average response rate of 24%. Out of the 560 participants who completed the survey in due course, 298 (53.21%) were male, and 262 (46.79%) were female instructors. The majority of the participants (30.18%) were aged between 51 and 60. Findings from this study showed that providing instructors with adequate training, workshops, and online support enhanced the use of LMS for educational purposes. Furthermore, the study revealed that a lack of professional development and training programs would not only degrade teaching performance, but also decrease faculty acceptance of similar technological systems in the future. The study concluded that increasing faculty use of technology and LMS inside the classroom required periodic training programs and extended online help for LMS use. According to Fathema et al. (2015), offering professional development programs and on time technical support provide faculty members with hands-on experiences which improve their technology proficiency, enhance their LMS use inside the classroom, and increase the likelihood of technology integration into learning and instruction.

Equally important, Brown (2016) reviewed a significant body of literature on the factors that influence faculty members' adoption of online technology tools for face-to-face teaching. More specifically, the author reviewed 58 articles on hybrid learning and blended instruction at higher education institutions in the United States where faculty members were the unit of analysis and instructional practice was the outcome. The result of the review generated six different themes that influence faculty use of online technology tools for teaching and learning purposes. These themes were identified as faculty members' interactions with technology, academic workload, interactions with students, institutional environment, instructors' beliefs and attitudes towards teaching, and professional development opportunities. For the purposes of this chapter, opportunities for professional development were only examined. Findings from Brown's (2016) literature review showed that institutional support and professional development opportunities were the primary sources of assistance that helped faculty learn how to use online technology tools and navigate the learning process. Training programs that provide faculty with advanced technological experiences enhanced faculty members' technological literacy, which in turn increased their intention to utilize online technology tools in the classroom. Participation in technology seminars with hands-on technical training helped faculty overcome technological anxiety. Finally, hands-on training dissipated faculty members' concerns regarding the quality of teaching that can be accomplished using online technology tools.

The results suggest that even though this is a digital era and some, or maybe the majority, of faculty and students have access to gadgets such as mobile phones, PCs and/or laptops and use social media, they still need training on how to use technology for learning (Gönen & Akbarov, 2015).

SOLUTIONS AND RECOMMENDATIONS FOR POLICY

This section critiques the policy, offers recommendations that support higher education institutions to meet the policy requirements, and proposes an assessment plan that evaluates the effects of the recommended solutions. Both recommendations and assessment plan relate directly to faculty technology expertise and include suggestions on how to implement them.

Section 204, Part G of the Higher Education Opportunity Act (2008) clearly articulates the requirements for federal grants, but does not clarify any means of support for institutions willing to engage in this initiative. It would have been more helpful if the policy included guidelines that aid higher education institutions in overcoming implementation difficulties. Furthermore, the policy would have been more comprehensive and precise if it clarified the standards and performance objectives that should be fulfilled.

The process of increasing the percentage of faculty trained to integrate technology effectively into teaching and learning faces major barriers including resistive behaviors (Becker et al., 2018). The absence of professional incentives and rewards constitute a major obstacle that faces the development of faculty technology skills (Dempsey et al., 2008). Thus, it is essential to reward faculty for their extra efforts in order to motivate them to participate in professional development programs. In order to enhance faculty technology literacy and enable them to effectively integrate technology into curricula and instruction, higher education institutions are required to apply the following:

1. Assess faculty technology literacy by employing multiple data collection tools.
2. Develop professional development programs that address faculty skill deficiencies and help them envision the benefits of technology. Faculty professional development programs should adhere to the Department of Education performance standards.
3. Conduct professional development programs and track faculty progress.
4. Revaluate faculty technology skills to assess the extent to which technology is used inside the classroom. If professional development programs were ineffective, educational leaders are required to identify and address deficiencies through action research.

Universities and colleges should also consider that active leadership at the highest level and long-term institutional support facilitate a successful technology integration project (Rogers, 2000). A successful technology integration project should engage faculty members as active learners, adequately allocate resources, emphasize trial and error learning style, provide online resources, encourage all types of assistance including software and hardware company assistance mechanisms, constantly organize training workshops, and support partnerships with other institutions of similar interests. Moreover, higher education institutions should address technology integration in their education programs, such that several education courses provide students with practical technology experiences.

Installing an advanced technological infrastructure is of great importance for universities trying to secure federal financial assistance (Higher Education Opportunity Act, 2008). Therefore, it becomes essential to install basic technology equipment such as computers, peripherals, software, hardware, internet connection, and media systems. Setting up this type of infrastructure has always been expensive (Christensen, 2019). In fact, one of the main financial burdens that overwhelm institutions and organizations is how expensive these setups may cost, and insufficient resources make it difficult to implement technology in the classroom. Costs include hardware, software, technical support, maintenance, professional development, and connectivity. Nevertheless, many educational software and teaching packages can be found online for little or free cost. Today, it is easy to secure funding from different sources such as:

1. Private funding from organizations and investors
2. Loans from banks or other financial institutions
3. Fundraising, donations, and sponsorships
4. Partnerships with other universities and relevant organizations

FUTURE RESEARCH DIRECTIONS

Since technology integration reflects a major accountability mechanism, researchers are required to inform policymaking through examining the effects of technology integration into education on degree attainment rates. Furthermore, higher education institutions must comply with the policy requirements in order to compete for adequate financial resources, decrease the disparity between colleges and wealthier universities, and reduce the inequality between underrepresented minorities and other social classes through offering students of lower socioeconomic status affordable online learning opportunities (Rabovsky, 2012).

Today, more than ever, researchers are required to examine, review, and improve current existing policies that govern technology integration at higher education institutions in the United States. More importantly, researchers should investigate (a) how technology integration into curricula and instruction enhances accountability mechanisms within the higher education arena, (b) the extent to which educational technology helps disadvantaged students attain postsecondary education, (c) the factors that facilitate the integration of technology into higher education and enhance the use of technology for teaching and learning purposes, and (d) the impact of faculty professional development on the integration of technology into curricula and instruction. Failure to address this pressing issue through research and practice will not only diminish postsecondary institutions' accountability and hinder promising attempts to reduce higher education costs, but also slash learning opportunities for students seeking lower tuition fees.

CONCLUSION

In summary, conducting a systematic review of the literature related to technology integration into tertiary and postsecondary education proved to be timely and important because faculty members in the United States still resist the implementation of technology in education (e.g., Martirosyan et al., 2017). More specifically, the results of the examined studies (Dempsey et al., 2008; Brown, 2016; Fathema et al., 2015; Georgina & Olson, 2007; Vannatta & Beyerbach, 2000) showed that integrating technology into teaching and learning necessitates technology workshops, training sessions, and professional development programs that not only enhance the use of technology inside the classroom, but also help faculty envision the educational benefits of technology.

Finally, in order to attain the benefits of the above described policy and facilitate the use of technology for teaching and learning purposes, policymakers and educational leaders are required to generate context specific policies, recommendations, and practices that establish the fundamental link between technology, learning, and student success. This will help faculty members envision the benefits of educational technology, which in turn motivates them to integrate technology into every aspect of their work. Along with instructors, administrators and institutional leaders must also join efforts and learn how to apply these tools within their own institutions. Once faculty and administrators believe that technology is the 21st century's educational and employability requirement, higher education institutions will then have a competitive edge in the new millennium.

REFERENCES

Albirini, A. (2006). Teachers' attitudes toward information and communication technologies: The case of Syrian EFL teachers. *Computers & Education*, *47*(4), 373–398. doi:10.1016/j.compedu.2004.10.013

Becker, S. A., Brown, M., Dahlstrom, E., Davis, A., DePaul, K., Diaz, V., & Pomerantz, J. (2018). *NMC Horizon Report: 2018 higher education edition*. Louisville, CO: EDUCAUSE.

Brown, M. G. (2016). Blended instructional practice: A review of the empirical literature on instructors' adoption and use of online tools in face-to-face teaching. *Internet and Higher Education*, *38*, 1–10. doi:10.1016/j.iheduc.2016.05.001

Christensen, C., & Eyering, H. (2011). *The innovative university: Changing the DNA of higher education from the inside out*. San Francisco, CA: Jossey-Bass.

Christensen, D. (2019). *What is the real cost of technology in education?* Retrieved from https://www.classcraft.com/blog/features/cost-of-technology-in-education/

Davies, R., Sprague, C., & New, C. (2008). Integrating technology into a science classroom: An evaluation of inquiry-based technology integration. In D. W. Sunal, E. L. Wright, & C. Sundberg (Eds.), *The impact of technology and the laboratory on K-16 science learning series: Research in science education* (pp. 207–237). Charlotte, NC: Information Age Publishing.

Davis, F. D. (1989). Perceived usefulness, perceived ease of use, and user acceptance of information technology. *Management Information Systems Quarterly*, *13*(3), 319–340. doi:10.2307/249008

Dempsey, J. V., Fisher, S. F., Wright, D. E., & Anderton, E. (2008). Training and support, obstacles, and library impacts on elearning activities. *College Student Journal*, *42*(2), 630–636.

Elmes, J. (2017). *Six significant challenges for technology in higher education in 2017*. Retrieved from https://www.timeshighereducation.com/features/six-significant-challenges-technology-higher-education-2017#survey-answer

Ertmer, P. A. (1999). Addressing first and second-order barriers to change: Strategies for technology integration. *Educational Technology Research and Development*, *47*(4), 47–61. doi:10.1007/BF02299597

Fabry, D. L., & Higgs, J. R. (1997). Barriers to the effective use of technology in education: Current status. *Journal of Educational Computing Research*, *17*(4), 385–395. doi:10.2190/C770-AWA1-CMQR-YTYV

Fathema, N., Shannon, D., & Ross, M. (2015). Expanding the technology acceptance model (TAM) to examine faculty use of learning management systems in higher education institutions. *Journal of Online Learning and Teaching*, *11*(2), 210–232.

Faudler, T. R. (2011). *Technology integration: A research-based professional development program* (Unpublished master's thesis). Cedarville University, Cedarville, OH.

Georgina, D. A., & Olson, M. R. (2007). Integration of technology in higher education: A review of faculty self-perceptions. *The Internet and Higher Education*, *11*(1), 1–8. doi:10.1016/j.iheduc.2007.11.002

Gönen, K., & Akbarov, A. (2015). Digital Natives in Higher Education Related to Language Learning. *Journal of Foreign Language Teaching and Applied Linguistics*. Available at www.j-fltal.org/storage/j-fltal-12.pdf

Green, K. C., & Gilbert, S. W. (1995). Great expectations: Content, communications, productivity, and the role of information technology in higher education. *Change, 27*(2), 8–29. doi:10.1080/00091383.1995.9937733

Hampel, R. (2006). Rethinking task design for the digital age. *ReCALL, 18*(1), 105–121. doi:10.1017/S0958344006000711

Haran, M. (2015). *A history of higher education*. Retrieved from http://institute-of-progressive-education-and-learning.org/a-history-of-education-technology/

Hauck, M., & Youngs, B. (2008). Telecollaboration in multimodal environments: The impact on task design and learner interaction. *CALL, 21*(2), 87–124. doi:10.1080/09588220801943510

Healey, D. (1999). Theory and research: autonomy in language learning. In J. Egbert & E. Hanson-Smith (Eds.), *CALL Environments: Research, Practice and Critical Issues* (pp. 391–402). TESOL.

Higher Education Opportunity Act (2008). *Higher Education Opportunity Act of 2008*. Pub. L. No. 110-315, § 204, 122 Stat. 70.

Islim, O. F., & Cirak, N. S. (2017). Technology and college students: What faculty members think about the use of technology in higher education. *Malaysian Online Journal of Educational Technology, 5*(2), 51–67.

Jones, D., & Matthews, D. (2002). *The transformation of instruction by information technology: Implications for state higher education policy*. Retrieved from https://wcet.wiche.edu/wcet/docs/whitepapers/Transformation_of_Instruction_by_IT_White_Paper.pdf

Jones, R. (2015). *Technology integration and higher education*. Retrieved from https://www.linkedin.com/pulse/technology-integration-higher-education-ronnie-jones/

Jung, I. (2005). Cost-effectiveness of online teacher training. *Open Learning, 20*(2), 131–146. doi:10.1080/02680510500094140

Karkouti, I. M. (2016). *University faculty members' perceptions of the factors that facilitate technology integration into their instruction: An exploratory case study in Qatar* (Unpublished doctoral dissertation). University of Hartford, West Hartford, CT.

Koruyan, K. (2016). *The influence of technology-enhanced task design on the development of language learner autonomy and motivation in an Anatolian high school; A case study* (Unpublished Doctoral dissertation). Open university, Milton Keynes, UK.

Lofstrom, E., & Nevgi, A. (2007). From strategic planning to meaningful learning: Diverse perspectives on the development of web-based teaching and learning in higher education. *British Journal of Educational Technology, 38*(2), 312–324. doi:10.1111/j.1467-8535.2006.00625.x

Martirosyan, N. M., Kennon, J. L., Saxon, D. P., Edmonson, S. L., & Skidmore, S. T. (2017). Instructional technology practices in developmental education in Texas. *Journal of College Reading and Learning, 47*(1), 3–25. doi:10.1080/10790195.2016.1218806

Mills, S. C., & Tincher, R. C. (2005). Be the technology: A developmental model for evaluating technology integration. *Journal of Research on Technology in Education, 35*(3), 382–401. doi:10.1080/15391523.2003.10782392

Motteram, G. (2013). *Innovations in learning technologies for English language teaching*. London, UK: The British Council.

Okojie, M. C., Olinzock, A. A., & Okojie-Boulder, T. C. (2006). The pedagogy of technology integration. *The Journal of Technology Studies, 32*(2), 66–71. doi:10.21061/jots.v32i2.a.1

Prensky, M. (2001). Digital natives, digital immigrants. *On the Horizon, 9*(5), 1–6. doi:10.1108/10748120110424816

Prensky, M. (2005). Engage me or enrage me: What today's learners demand. *EDUCAUSE Review, 40*(5), 60–65.

Rabovsky, T. M. (2012). Accountability in Higher Education: Exploring impacts on state budgets and institutional spending patters. Oxford University Press. doi:10.1093/jopart/mur069

Rogers, D. L. (2000). A paradigm shift: Technology integration for higher education in the new millennium. *Educational Technology Review, 1*(13), 19–33.

Selingo, J. J. (2013). *College (un)bound: The future of higher education and what it means for students*. Las Vegas, NV: Amazon Publishing.

Stephanie, L. (2009). *Overview of the Federal Higher Education Opportunity Act*. Boston, MA: Institute for Community Inclusion.

Surry, D. W., Ensminger, D. C., & Haab, M. (2005). A model for integrating instructional technology into higher education. *British Journal of Educational Technology, 36*(2), 327–329. doi:10.1111/j.1467-8535.2005.00461.x

Tandberg, D. A. (2010). Politics, interest groups and state funding of public higher education. *Research in Higher Education, 51*(5), 416–450. doi:10.100711162-010-9164-5

U.S. Department of Education. (2017). *Reimagining the role of technology in education: 2017 national education technology plan update*. Retrieved from https://tech.ed.gov/files/2017/01/NETP17.pdf

Vannatta, R. A., & Beyerbach, B. (2000). Facilitating a constructivist vision of technology integration among education faculty and preservice teachers. *Journal of Research on Computing in Education, 33*(2), 132–148. doi:10.1080/08886504.2000.10782305

Wang, F., & Reeves, T. C. (2003). Why do teachers need to use technology in their classrooms? Issues, problems, and solutions. *Computers in the Schools, 20*(4), 49–65. doi:10.1300/J025v20n04_05

Young, S. C. (2003). Integrating ICT into second language education in a vocational high school. *Journal of Computer Assisted Learning, 19*(4), 447–461. doi:10.1046/j.0266-4909.2003.00049.x

ADDITIONAL READING

Adams, N. B. (2002). Educational computing concerns of postsecondary faculty. *Journal of Research on Technology in Education, 34*(3), 285–303. doi:10.1080/15391523.2002.10782350

Anderson, B., & Horn, R. (2012). Community colleges in the information age: Gains associated with students' use of computer technology. *Journal of Educational Computing Research, 47*(1), 51–65. doi:10.2190/EC.47.1.c

Bates, T. A. W., & Sangra, A. (2011). *Managing technology in higher education: Strategies for transforming teaching and learning*. San Francisco, CA: Jossey-Bass.

Bowen, W. G. (2015). *Higher education in the digital age*. Princeton, NJ: Princeton University Press. doi:10.1515/9781400866137

Georgina, D. A., & Hosford, C. C. (2009). Higher education faculty percpetions on technology integration and training. *Teaching and Teacher Education, 25*(5), 690–696. doi:10.1016/j.tate.2008.11.004

Keengwe, J., & Kidd, T. T. (2010). Towards best practices in online learning and teaching in higher education. *Journal of Online Learning and Teaching, 6*(2), 533–541.

Kim, C., Kim, M. K., Lee, C., Spector, J. M., & DeMeester, K. (2013). Teacher beliefs and technology integration. *Teaching and Teacher Education, 29*, 76–85. doi:10.1016/j.tate.2012.08.005

Kumpulainen, K. (2007). *Educational technology: Opportunities and challenges*. Oulu, Finland: University of Oulu.

Lu, J., Yu, C. S., Lui, C., & Yao, J. E. (2003). Technology acceptance model for wireless Internet. *Internet Research, 13*(3), 206–222. doi:10.1108/10662240310478222

McIntyre, P., Fulton, J., Paton, E., Kerrigan, S., & Meany, M. (2018). *Educating for creativity within higher education: Integration of research into media practice*. London, UK: Palgrave Macmillan. doi:10.1007/978-3-319-90674-4

McLoughlin, J. A., Wang, L.-C. C., & Beasley, W. A. (2008). Transforming the college through technology: A change of culture. *Innovative Higher Education, 33*(2), 99–109. doi:10.100710755-008-9065-0

Mikre, F. (2011). The roles of information communication technologies in education: Review article with emphasis to the computer and Internet. *Ethiopian Journal of Education and Sciences, 6*(2), 109–126.

Moeller, B., & Reitzes, T. (2011). *Integrating technology with student-centered learning*. Quincy, MA: The Nellie Mae Education Foundation.

Parra, J., Raynor, C., Osanloo, A., & Guillame, R. O. (2019). (Re)imagining an undergraduate integrating technology with teaching course. *TechTrends, 63*(1), 68–78. doi:10.100711528-018-0362-x

Roblyer, A. D., & Hughes, J. E. (2019). *Integrating educational technology into teaching: Transforming learning across disciplines* (8th ed.). Boston, MA: Pearson.

Rogaten, J., Rienties, B., Sharpe, R., Cross, S., Whitelock, D., Lygo-Baker, S., & Littlejohn, A. (2019). Reviewing affective, behavioural and cognitive learning gains in higher education. *Assessment & Evaluation in Higher Education*, *44*(3), 321–337. doi:10.1080/02602938.2018.1504277

Skorton, D., & Bear, A. (2018). *The integration of the humanities and arts with sciences, engineering, and medicine in higher education: Branches from the same tree*. Washington, DC: The National Academies Press. doi:10.17226/24988

KEY TERMS AND DEFINITIONS

Accountability: The state of being responsible for the actions, choices, and decisions one makes.

Education Policy: A set of guidelines or rules that aims at improving the quality of education and the performance of teachers at schools, colleges, and universities.

Educational Technology: The process of improving teaching and learning through the optimal use of technological resources inside the classroom.

Higher Education: Institutions of higher learning that provide students with post-secondary education that is geared towards a degree-level diploma.

Higher Education Opportunity Act: A legislation that was enacted into law on August 14, 2008 to improve the quality of postsecondary education and enhance disadvantaged students' accessibility to colleges and universities in the United States of America.

Technology Integration: The incorporation of technological resources and processes into the daily practices of schools.

Chapter 17
Silent Observation

Mohd Javed Khan
https://orcid.org/0000-0002-6742-3038
Jamia Millia Islamia, India

ABSTRACT

With the growth of information communication technology, new technologies are emerging, and their applications in learning are increasing. Emerging technologies that may produce effective learning outcomes include 5G technology to have efficient and effective learning, artificial intelligence – imitating human-like behaviour, voice searches, augmented reality (AR), virtual reality (VR), and mixed reality (MR). Research in the field of emerging technologies reflects that they are able to engage learners and grab their attention. Learners must be assessed to measure learning gains. Learner assessment using Bloom's taxonomy has been proved effective. Algorithm "Silent Observation," proposed to assess learners, is found to be effective in its idea of conception stage. The algorithm has sound footing in micro-research findings on formative assessment and emerging technologies. Assessment using this algorithm will be an iterative process and will refine itself using AI techniques. "Silent Observation" has a strong pedagogical framework interweaving emerging technologies.

INTRODUCTION

Information communication technology (ICT) came into existence around 1980. As research in ICT evolved, it led to the improvement of old technology and the birth of new technology. These technologies are used in primary, secondary, tertiary and quaternary industries. Technologies based on ICT endorse unified communication. Unified communication is possible by building a robust computer network by storing, retrieving, manipulating, transmitting or receiving information in digital form and merging it with the telecommunication network. Transfer of information in digital form has been possible with the introduction of the internet in 1960 (Bill Stewart, 2000). With the horizontal and vertical growth of research in the domain of computer network and telecommunication technology, the internet improved its capability to support a more robust network that can support high-speed data transfer. As the network became capable of transferring high-speed data, emerging technologies came into existence.

DOI: 10.4018/978-1-7998-3062-7.ch017

Research can be categorized into Foundation research, Application research and Theory Building research (Spector, Merrill, Merrienboer, & Driscoll, 2008). *Foundation research* is carried-out in Psychology, Computer Science, Information Management and Engineering; *Application research* is carried-out in Education Technology and Instructional Design; and *Theory Building research* is carried-out in learning sciences. Foundation research often focuses on developing a fundamental understanding of the affective aspects of technology in use and motivates its users during its use to achieve the desired objective effectively (Spector et al., 2008). To measure the degree of effectiveness of achieved desired objectives, Application research is carried out.

Application research explores user interaction with innovative research. Users carry out procedures to find the effectiveness of innovative research using different state of variables. This process is known as Theory Building. Theory Building develops an understanding of innovative research and lays the foundation for Emerging Technologies (Spector et al., 2008). Thus, Foundation Research, Application Research, and Theory Building develop Emerging Technologies (*see* Figure 1).

Figure 1. Researches and Theory Building

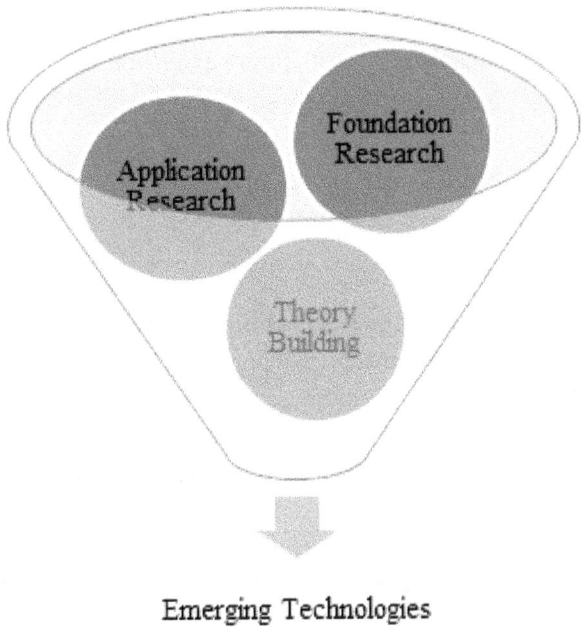

Emerging technologies are used to develop tools of personalized inquiry from typed text to computer-aided virtual environments. Learners of today at the tertiary level must be aware of the potential effectiveness of these new technologies and their use in learning. Emerging technology that may produce effective learning outcome includes 5G technology to have efficient and effective learning, Artificial Intelligence (AI) – imitating human-like behaviour, Voice Searches, and Augmented Reality (AR), Virtual Reality (VR) and Mixed Reality (MR) (Hogle, 2019).

Furthermore, tertiary learners must develop a fundamental understanding of emerging technologies. They must know how to interact with them and how to use them to achieve learning gains and develop an understanding of known principles and processes of emerging technology for decision making. Also, they must know how to use tools based on emerging technologies to achieve learning gains. Emerging technology such as AI is used in Intelligent Tutoring Systems (ITS) in an efficient manner to act on learners. AI algorithms interact with learner data and generate decision-making rules. However, there is a research gap in understanding the literature on emerging technologies. Therefore, this chapter looks at emerging technologies to harness its pedagogical potential. Based on the systematic review of the related literature, it aims to answer the following research questions:

1. What are the emerging technologies that have been used in ITS?
2. Which AI techniques have been used most?
3. What are the Instructional Strategies/Methods that have been used in ITS?
4. What is the ergonomics of the learning interface of ITS?
5. What are the assessment methods that are used in ITS?
6. What are the components of an effective pedagogical framework?

This chapter first introduces emerging technologies and Artificial Intelligence (AI) in education. Then, it delivers a relational study on AI and pedagogical framework. Next, it evaluates the Intelligent Tutoring Systems (ITS). Using these studies, this chapter lays the foundation for developing an algorithm "*Silent Observation*" and makes suggestions for its future extension studies.

BACKGROUND

Emerging Technologies

Emerging technologies have a direct impact on learner thinking and balance of senses. Emerging technology such as 5G is required by a network having high data traffic. 5G in the coming years will provide high-speed broadband with fixed, wireless, smooth and cost-effective internet access. 5G possesses the capability of providing a resilient, secure and high-speed data transfer rates. High-speed data transfer rate is required in Automation, Non-Cellular, Advanced Data Analytics, and Manufacturing industries (Fortier et al., 2019). Different industries require different data transfer rates, and during peak hours, high data transfer rate is required. Industries that produce voluminous video content requires 220 Kbytes/s with a session interval time of 3600 seconds. Bandwidth requirement increases when the video is combined with text messages. Using 5G high-quality real-time video can be delivered to a large set of devices. 5G provides evolving ground to time-critical operations and help in developing Augmented Reality (AR)/ Virtual Reality (VR). Mixed reality content having an application of AR/VR requires the support of the 5G network. AR/VR based learning solutions enable learners to understand concepts using psychomotor skills like touch, pinching and zooming. AR/VR combined with Artificial Intelligence (AI) produces real-time data, 5G has the capability of supporting real-time data. AI can deliver real-time feedback to learners to improve problem-solving capability. Timely feedback may change learner behavior. Feedback is an essential part of AI-based robotic applications.

AI helps in making decisions based on - data, speech-driven actions and language translations. AI is data-dependent and suffers from a cold-start problem. To avoid cold-start problem, data collected from user activity is used along with anonymized data. As users use internet searches, online industries that include - marketing, accounting, banking, aviation, education and government sectors use this user interaction data to act as an input into AI processing engine to make decisive actions on it. In addition to industries, AI is used in online learning and in several immersive technologies, like Augmented Reality (AR)/Virtual Reality (VR) and Mixed Reality (MR). AR, VR and MR merge virtual and physical worlds. They are also interrelated. For instance, AR can be further enhanced using Virtual Reality (VR). VR can simulate human motions for a process to provide alternative actions. AI using natural language processing helps in building Voice Search techniques, in which query strings are generated using voice and fired against data repositories. The search engine processes voice search queries on predetermined lexicon words and returns results. Voice searches have also made a noticeable presence in AR/VR based applications. Voice assistants using voice-search techniques in AR/VR based applications are seen as an integral inseparable part of the future AR gear.

Artificial Intelligence (AI) and Education

In education, AI is used to model student knowledge, learning topics and teaching/learning strategies. AI-based computer-assisted instructions are used to improve learning and implemented by Intelligent Tutoring Systems (ITSs). ITSs model learner behavior and act on learner activity. Most of the ITS use conceptions and misconceptions to model learners and their cognition, learning style and interactive styles (Abyaa, Khalidi, & Bennani, 2019). AI bots in ITS provide scaffolding to work on well-designed learning paths. AI bots use an algorithm such as Reinforcement learning, Bayesian networks, etc., to predict the occurrence of learner actions and forecast the next instructional material to study (Smith, Min, Mott, & Lester, 2015). AI algorithms also play a significant role in the formative assessment of learners. Thus, AI augments education by building highly individualized and pedagogically sound educational material supporting multiple teaching strategies such as collaboration, inquiry and dialogue (Chen, 2008).

Teaching must be effective, and efforts must be made to improvise teaching methods. Different teaching methods are used to deliver instructional materials. Learners learn using instructional material and exhibit the degree of learning by acquiring grades in learning examination. Ineffective teaching methods often result in low grades in learning assessments. To improve learner performance and make them attain high learning grades, teaching methods are improved using information technology. Information technology has a significant influence on teaching and learning and is able to produce a one-to-one tutoring effect (Krathwohl, 2002). Instructional material generated using Information Technology is more effective and aids in achieving the learning objectives (Kulik & Fletcher, 2015).

AI makes difficult concepts easier by building simulations, game-based learning scenarios, a virtual reality system or group collaboration. AI-based tutoring system represents learning topics in a systematic and organized manner, tracks learner performance and adapts to learner needs (Abyaa et al., 2019). The next section describes Intelligent Tutoring Systems, evaluating them on AI algorithms and Learning Theories. The outcome of the section will clearly state-specific AI algorithm that has the highest frequency in terms of its use and learning domain influenced by it. The outcome of the survey will be used to develop the pedagogical framework.

Artificial Intelligence (AI) and Pedagogical Framework

AI algorithm works on data collected from user activity. In any education system, data is learner action taken during learning. This data is recorded and fed in an AI algorithm to make future decisions. AI agents observe learner behavior and help them in the decision-making process. The decision-making process is further improved when the learner uses prior-knowledge to develop new theories on it. The validity of the decision is evaluated using learner assessment strategies (Albacete & Vanlehn, 2000). Different assessment strategies are employed by ITS to evaluate learners. An effective ITS mimics a human tutor to assess the learner. ITS can infer learner conceptions, misconceptions, false beliefs and efficiency of acquired skills. As teaching progresses ITS virtual assistants/classroom teachers can ask questions to diagnose misconceptions (Chi, Siler, Jeong, Yamauchi, & Hausmann, 2001). Based on learner response difficulty level of instructional material is either raised or lowered with the flow of teaching. To diagnose learner conception/misconception following strategies may be used (Watanabe-Crockett, 2019): *strategic questioning, exit ticket, classroom polls* and *making learners write the name of the topic that they found most confusing*.

To make learners focus on learning activities, Task Selection is important. The selected tasks must align with the learning objectives. Learning activities that comprise tasks must be presented in increasing order of their complexity. Learner performance in accomplishing learning activity may be improved by opting for punishment-reward strategies and making them indulge in dialogues on learning topics. Tutor learner dialogues include discussion on prerequisites to understand concepts, and these discussions motivate learners. Motivated learners exert more efforts to build cognitive thinking and achieve learning objectives. Learners are further motivated by providing appropriate feedback. Feedback must be delivered to corner misconceptions and relearn selected topics. In ITS, feedback is delivered to learners as the sign of misconception is emerged. The strength of feedback is decided by the level of misconceptions, and feedback is iterated to improve learning. Feedback must be supported by scaffolding. Through scaffolding, learners are directed to correct the learning path to attain the desired learning objectives (Cade, Copeland, Person, & Mello, 2008).

The past few years have seen considerable use of AI to mimic human tutors. ITS is an adaptive instructional system that has the ability to take the decision on learner activity and select instructional strategies that are best suited for the learner (Millán, Loboda, & Pérez-de-la-Cruz, 2010). The architecture of ITS consists of Expert model, Student model, Pedagogical model, and User Interface model (Nkambou & Bourdeau, 2010). *The expert model* delivers domain knowledge to the learner and keeps track of learner activities in the learning process, whereas *Student model* records learner prior knowledge, activities, responses, learning styles and misconceptions, and *Pedagogical model* decides instructional strategies and last is *Interface model* controlling the interaction between user and tutoring system (Nkambou & Bourdeau, 2010).

ITSs must match learner needs by delivering alternative representation of content and learning paths. ITSs should produce pedagogically sound instructional material. ITSs are mostly based on the algorithm of AI, Cognitive Science and Education Theories. The first ITS named GUIDON was developed by William Clancey (Clancey, 1979). Since then, different categories of ITS have come into existence from simulation-based systems, game-based systems, virtual reality systems, and group collaborative systems. Thus, a systematic review must be carried out to answer the posed research questions in the Introduction.

MAIN FOCUS OF THE CHAPTER

Method

A systematic review of developed ITS was conducted based on guidelines for systematic reviews proposed by Silva and Neiva (2016). Research papers from Taylor and Francis, ProQuest, Elsevier, Springer, Web of Science, Google Scholar, Scopus, PubMed were searched from 1996 to 2019. Search strings were designed on the guidelines of Silva and Neiva (2016). Search results were filtered and English language original research papers in ITS were undertaken for analysis. Educational Systems lacking in intelligence were excluded from the study. In the initial phase, Titles and Abstract were read by reviewers working in the domain of ITS. Thus, the selection of research articles went through three phases.

In phase – I, research articles on ITS were included for study. In phase – II, research articles on the educational system having 30 to 60 percent intelligent components were undertaken for the study. Phase-III included research articles having 10 to 20 percent intelligent components. These research articles were screened against twelve variables, description of these variables are as follows in Table 1:

Table 1. Variables used to filter research paper

Name of the System:	Gives Title and Author Details of the research article.
Population:	Gives detail about the experimental set (sample on which ITS prototype was tested).
Educational Field:	Educational domain on which ITS was developed.
Emerging Technologies:	Technologies that are in their developmental stage and are still in their frenzy of practical applications. These include Augmented/Virtual/Mixed Reality, Artificial Intelligence, and Voice Search.
Learning Domain Influenced:	Influence of ITS on Cognitive, Affective and Psychomotor domain.
Instructional Strategies Used:	Instructional strategies include methods such as Visualization, Cooperative learning and technology used to deliver instructions etc.
Ergonomics of learning interface:	Design of learning interface to deliver instructions.
Assessment method used:	Type of Assessment used such as Formative/Summative assessment.
Assessment strategies used:	Techniques used for Formative/Summative assessment.
Methodology opted to evaluate the effectiveness of ITS:	Evaluation of Pre-test and Post-test.
Statistics Employed:	The statistical methods used to validate results.
Outcome:	The outcome of statistical methods employed revealing the effectiveness of ITS.

Evaluation of ITS

Based on the systematic review of fifty research studies on ITSs (*as given in*, Table 2), research questions posed in Introduction were answered considering above mentioned twelve variables. Research questions posed in the Introduction have been answered in this section.

Table 2. ITS taken under study

Sr. No	Year	Name of the study
1	1996	Intelligent Algebraic Tutoring Based on Student Misconceptions (Grossman, 1996).
2	2001	Intelligent Tutoring Systems with Conversational Dialogue (Graesser, Vanlehn, Rosé, Jordan, & Harter, 2001).
3	2007	An Experimental Evaluation of *Logiocando*, an Intelligent Tutoring Hypermedia System (Lanzilotti & Roselli, 2007).
4	2008	LIA: An Intelligent Advisor for e-Learning (Capuano, Gaeta, Miranda, & Orciuoli, 2008).
5	2008	A Natural Language Intelligent Tutoring System for Training Pathologists – Implementation and Evaluation (Saadawi et al., 2008).
6	2008	I-MINDS: A Multiagent System for Intelligent Computer-Supported Collaborative Learning and Classroom Management (Soh, Khandaker, & Jiang, 2008)
7	2008	Diagnosis Mechanism and Feedback System to Accomplish the Full-Loop Learning Architecture (Heh, Li, Chang, Chang, & Liu, 2008)
8	2008	Intelligent web-based learning system with personalized learning path guidance (Chen, 2008)
9	2009	ZOSMAT: Web-based intelligent tutoring system for the teaching-learning process (Keles, Ocak, Keles, & Gulcu, 2009)
10	2009	Evaluating an Intelligent Tutoring System for Design Patterns: the DEPTHS Experience (Jeremi, Jovanovi, & Gaševi, 2009)
11	2009	The Adaptive Intelligent Personalised Learning Environment (Costello & Mundy, 2009)
12	2010	Intelligent E-Learning Systems for Evaluation of User's Knowledge and Skills with Efficient Information Processing (Kacalak, Majewski, & Zurada, 2010)
13	2010	Adaptive E-Learning using ECpAA Rules, Bayesian Networks, and Group Profile And Performance Data (Jeon, 2010)
14	2010	Towards Intelligent Tutoring with Erroneous Examples: A Taxonomy of Decimal Misconceptions (Isotani, Mclaren, & Altman, 2010)
15	2012	Using The Rasch Model To Assess Examination Beyond Students Scores (Ibrahim, Aziz, Zubairi, & Zaharim, 2012)
16	2012	Using Edit Distance to Analyse Errors in a Natural Language to Logic Translation Corpus (Plummer, Dale, & Cox, 2012)
17	2012	Evaluating the integration of fuzzy logic into the student model of a web-based learning environment (Chrysafiadi & Virvou, 2012)
18	2012	Employing UMLS for generating hints in a tutoring system for medical problem-based learning (Kazi, Haddawy, & Suebnukarn, 2012)
19	2012	BeSocratic: An Intelligent Tutoring System for the Recognition, Evaluation, and Analysis of Free-form Student Input (Bryfczynski, 2012)
20	2013	A Web-Based Intelligent Tutoring System for a Basic Control Course (Ozek, Akpolat, & Orphan, 2013)
21	2013	An empirically-based, tutorial dialogue system: design, implementation and evaluation in a first-year health sciences course (Mcdonald, Knott, Stein, & Zeng, 2013)
22	2013	Sequential Patterns of Affective States of Novice Programmers (Bosch & D'Mello, 2013)
23	2013	Teaching AI Search Algorithms In A Web-Based Educational System (Grivokostopoulou & Hatzilygeroudis, 2013)
24	2013	Setting the Standard for Project Design course using the Rasch Measurement Model (Khatimin, Aziz, Zaharim, Sahari, & Rahmat, 2013)
25	2013	Semantic Rule-based Approach for Supporting Personalised Adaptive E-Learning (Yarandi, 2013)
26	2013	Abdullah: An Intelligent Arabic Conversational Tutoring System for Modern Islamic Education (Alobaidi, Smieee, Mieee, & Jarad, 2013)
27	2014	Analyzing Student Programs in the PHP Intelligent Tutoring System (Weragama & Reye, 2014)
28	2014	Adaptive Intelligent Support to Improve Peer Tutoring in Algebra (Walker, Rummel, & Koedinger, 2014)
29	2014	Framework for Instructional Technology: Methods of Implementing Adaptive Training and Education (Durlach & Randall, 2014)
30	2014	BEETLE II: Deep Natural Language Understanding and Automatic Feedback Generation for Intelligent Tutoring in Basic Electricity and Electronics (Dzikovska, Steinhauser, Farrow, Moore, & Campbell, 2014)
31	2014	Context-aware adaptive and personalized mobile learning delivery supported by UoLmP (Gomez, Zervas, Sampson, & Fabregat, 2014)
32	2014	Building intelligent tutoring systems immersed in repositories of e-learning content (Marciniak, 2014)
33	2014	Reasoning Mind Genie 2: An Intelligent Tutoring System as a Vehicle for International Transfer of Instructional Methods in Mathematics (Khachatryan et al., 2014)
34	2014	An Intelligent Debugging Tutor For Novice Computer Science Students (Carter, 2014)
35	2014	Algorithm and intelligent tutoring system design for programmable controller programming (Hsieh & Cheng, 2014)
36	2015	BopoNoto: An Intelligent Sketch Education Application for Learning Zhuyin Phonetic Script (Taele & Hammond, 2015)
37	2015	Mirroring Teachers ' Assessment of Novice Students ' Presentations Through an Intelligent Tutor System (Echeverr & Chiluiza, 2015)
38	2015	Evaluating Students ' Need in Using Computer-Aided Software in Landscape Design Course (Abdullah, Yaakub, & Wahil, 2015)
39	2015	Dynamic Cultural Contextualisation of Educational Content in Intelligent Learning Environments using ICON (Mohammed & Mohan, 2015)
40	2015	Diagrammatic Student Models: Modelling Student Drawing Performance with Deep Learning (Smith et al., 2015)
41	2015	Cluster analysis of student activity in a web-based intelligent tutoring system (Jugo, Kovačić, & Tijan, 2015)
42	2015	Adapting Methods of Student Evaluation and Grading in Electrical Power Engineering (Vuc, Baloi, & Litcanu, 2015)
43	2015	A flowchart-based intelligent tutoring system for improving problem-solving skills of novice programmers (Hooshyar, Ahmad, Yousefi, Yusop, & Horng, 2015)
44	2015	A Multi-Componential Analysis of Emotions during Complex Learning with an Intelligent Multi-Agent System (Harley, Bouchet, Hussain, Azevedo, & Calvo, 2015)
45	2016	Users-Centric Adaptive Learning System Based On Interval Type-2 Fuzzy Logic For Massively Crowded E-Learning Platforms (Almohammadi, Hagras, Alghazzawi, & Aldabbagh, 2016)
46	2016	Affecting Off-Task Behaviour: How Affect-aware Feedback Can Improve Student Learning (Grawemeyer, Holmes, Gutierrez-santos, & Wiedmann, 2016)
47	2017	Solving Optimization Problems via Vortex Optimization Algorithm and Cognitive Development Optimization Algorithm (Demir & Kosse, 2017)
48	2017	Analyzing the Outcome of a Learning Process Conducted Within the System ALS _ CORR [LP] (Ghouch, Mokhtar, & Seghroucheni, 2017)
49	2019	Rule-based adaptive user interface for adaptive E-learning system (Kolekar, M Pai, & Pai M M, 2019)
50	2019	The effectiveness of an online learning system based on aptitude scores: An effort to improve students ' brain activation (Eldenfria & Al-samarraie, 2019)

Research Question 1: What are the emerging technologies that have been used in ITS?

From the analysis, it was found that Artificial Intelligent and Machine Learning techniques were used most in ITS. These techniques were used to maintain a dialogue with the learner, track learner activity, sequence learning path, sequence instructional material, maintain activity log to handle misconceptions etc., It was revealed that Augmented Reality/Virtual Reality/Mixed Reality and Voice Searches were not used. Figure 2 gives a graphical representation of the Frequency of techniques used.

Figure 2. Frequency of techniques used

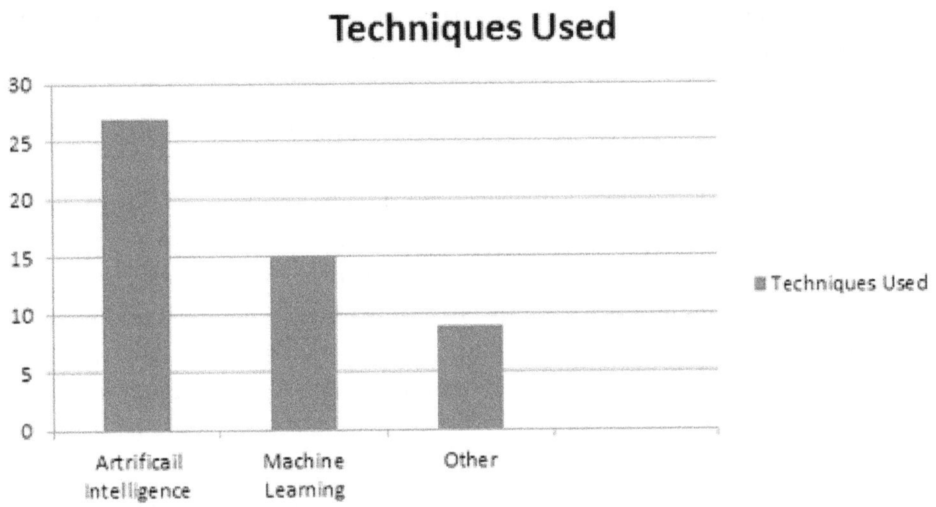

Artificial Intelligence techniques include – *Semantic Network, Concept Graph, Natural Language Processing, Bayesian network, Fuzzy Logic, Markov Model, Ontology and other AI techniques*. Machine Learning that was used is – *Classification Algorithm, Genetic Algorithm, Rule-Based Reasoning, Neural Network, Rule-Based Algorithm, Case-Based Reasoning, k-means, Automatic Facial Recognition, Vortex Optimization Algorithm and Epic Emotive, Computer EEG Tool.* Other techniques that were used in ITS are - *If-Than-Else logic, Finite State Automata, Rasch Model, Retrospective Judgement Protocol and Gauss Distribution.*

Research Question 2: Which AI Techniques Have Been Used Most?

Artificial Intelligence (AI) techniques have been used in 27 ITSs. It was found that the Bayesian Model having a frequency count of 9 is the most utilized AI technique followed by Natural Language Processing (NLP) techniques. After AI, the next most used technology is Machine Learning. It was revealed that Case Base Reasoning (CBR), one of the Machine Learning Technique, is used to achieve adaptive features in ITSs. Research evidence exists about the use of CBR for problem-solving and decision-making processes. CBR can filter out similar problems according to learner requirements. It was found that only two systems (Grawemeyer et al., 2016; Kacalak et al., 2010) have integrated Voice Search techniques. Voice Search Techniques were appreciated by learners as it provided easy access to the desired information. Further, out of 50 systems, no system employed Augmented Reality/Virtual Reality/Mixed Reality, hence their influence on ITS cannot be inferred.

On the baises of analysis, it was found that the "Bayesian Network" is the most used AI technique. Bayesian network use probability to draw inference hence possess the ability to find misconceptions, make decisions based on learner activities, suggest instructional material based on learner knowledge level etc. Bayesian network in association with Classification algorithm can be used to classify learners and instructional materials. It has been used in many developed ITSs (Gomez et al., 2014; Soh et al., 2008; Walker et al., 2014). Research analysis revealed that Bayesian Network has a wide application in Formative Assessment. Method of formative assessment diagnoses learners and structure instructional material using Bayesian Networks. It was expressed that Bayesian Network possesses such properties as forward and backward chaining, evidence-based propagation algorithm, and provable inference mechanism (Ramírez-Noriega, Juárez-Ramírez, & Martínez-Ramírez, 2017).

Research Question 3: What are the Instructional Strategies/Methods that have been used in ITS?

Instructional Strategies have the most significant impact on learner success. Instructional strategies decided on techniques of delivering instructions. Instructional strategies must possess the capability to engage the learner in the learning process and direct learners to learning objectives. There exists a variety of instructional strategies to make learning environments more interactive. Instructional strategies that have been used most in ITS and found to be effective are: *Feedback, Quizzes, Text Direction, Talking Head, Pictures, Animations, Game-based learning, Video Clip, Simulation, Fill-in-the-blank and True oe Fasle.*

Research Question 4: What is the Ergonomics of the Learning Interface of ITS?

Ergonomics provides a set of guiding principles to develop an aesthetically pleasing interface. Aesthetics evoke immediate responses. *Balance*, *Proportion*, *Unity* and *Sequence* are some of the ergonomic principles that may be used to develop an aesthetically pleasing learning interface (Altaboli & Lin, 2011). An analytical study conducted on ITS given in Table 2 revealed that ergonomic guiding principles were not considered to the extent that it influences learners in engaging them in learning. Visually pleasing learning interface displays a high degree of usability and learner engagement (Kurosu & Kashimura, 1995; Moshagen, Musch, & Göritz, 2009). Learning interface rich in ergonomic principles enhances the transfer of information and motivates learners (Szabo & Kanuka, 1998; Zain, Tey, & Goh, 2007). A detailed study of ergonomic principles and guidelines that can be used to develop a learning interface is provided in Khan and Mustafa (2019).

Research Question 5: What are the Assessment Methods that are used in ITS?

Learning must be measured to judge the effectiveness of instructional strategies. Learning is measured using assessment strategies. Assessment is an integral part of learning and it can be summative or formative. A summative assessment is carried out to measure positive or negative learning gains. The negativity of learning gains may be reduced by diagnosing and reducing learner misconceptions using formative assessment. Summative assessment evaluates learners to grade learning. It is usually conducted at the end of the learning session. It is an evaluative process rather than a diagnostic process. Through

Summative Assessment effectiveness of instructional material is judged and learning gains are measured through grade, scores or percentage. Obtained grade, scores or percentages are statistically analyzed.

Formative assessment is often carried out to measure the gap between the actual level of learning and the desired level of learning. Formative assessment is conducted by using *Rhetorical Question, Quizzes, Time-bound learning activities* etc. From the analytical study carried out on ITS, it was found that twenty-nine (29) systems implemented summative assessment and twenty-one (21) systems implemented formative assessment. Formative assessment is procedural and finds learner misconceptions. ITSs are developed using AI techniques to diagnosis learner misconceptions during learning. These misconceptions are then used to deliver instructional material to improve learner understanding level. Formative assessment is an ongoing process and carried out as learning progress. It was found in research studies that AI or Machine Learning Techniques are mostly used to conduct the formative assessment. Other techniques that are used include – *why, how and what-if questions, feedback on learner actions* and using *type-2 fuzzy sets.*

Research Questions 6: What are the Components of an Effective Pedagogical Framework?

The pedagogical framework supports learning. An effective pedagogical framework maximizes positive learning gains. Components of the pedagogical framework are critical. Based on the systematic review of studies given in Table 2, an effective pedagogical framework consists of learner engaging, assess misconceptions, link new and existing knowledge, multi-modal representation of information, an in-depth explanation of the learning topic, and motivate and provide feedback.

Developing Pedagogical Framework

In technology-enhanced learning, the pedagogical framework supports in delivering instructional material to maximize learning gains. Components of the pedagogical framework are critical for attaining higher learning gains. An exhaustive literature survey was conducted to find critical components of the pedagogical framework. From the survey, it was exposed that the pedagogical framework must be *"Learner Engaging"*, it should provide opportunities for *"Self-Assessment of Misconceptions"*. Constructivism should be an essential part of the pedagogical framework in which learners must be able to *"Link new and existing knowledge"*, and the pedagogical framework must support the *"Multi-modal representation of Information"* to provide an *"In-depth explanation of learning topic"* and develop a better understanding. To judge the understanding level of learners, they must be assessed using well designed *"Assessment and Feedback"* rubric. The selection of appropriate *"Assessment and Feedback"* strategies must be based on the outcome of analysis conducted on empirical studies. Feedback also acts as a motivator. The degree of grasping of concepts of motivated learners is much high as compared to de-motivated learners (Keller, 1987). Thus, *"Motivation"* should be an essential component of the pedagogical framework.

Modelling a pedagogical framework is a laborious and complex task. From the literature survey, critical components of the pedagogical framework to attain high learning gains are given in Table 3. These components have been tested empirically and have a track of producing positive learning gains as inferred from analytical study conducted on ITS given in Table 2. Thus, the probability of attaining learning objectives by incorporating these components in the pedagogical framework is high.

Table 3. Framework Ingredients

Learner Engaging	Tapping prior knowledge
	Discussions
	Multi-modal representation of instructional material
	Competitive exercises
	Feedback
Misconceptions	Having open access and debate ideas
	State-predict exercises
	Predict-Observe-Explain
	Investigable questions
	Activities to be carried out by applying principles learned
Connecting Knowledge	Think sheets
	Quizzes
	One-minute test
	Naming exercises
	Application cards
	Opinion Polls on learning topics
	Concept Maps that provide graphical representation of learning topic
Multi-Model Representation	Text
	Audio
	Video
	Graphics
	Images
	Animations
	Simulations
	Demonstration
	Illustration
	Educational Game
	2D Charts
	Heat Maps
	Activity Charts
	Zoom-in/out
	Jumbled Sentences
In-depth explanation	Provide Definition
	Provide Example and Non-Examples
	Provide Analogies
Assessment	Test/Questionnaire/Quizzes at the end of learning topic in case of Summative Assessment
	For Formative Assessment use: *Rhetorical Question, provide feedback on learner actions, misconceptions*
Feedback & Motivation	Color cues
	Hints
	Time-bound activities
	Metaphors
	Beep Sound
	Meaningful Images
	Animations at an interval to grab attention

Ingredients given in Table 3 may act as a building block of a pedagogical framework having its roots in learning theories. Cognitivism which is an information-processing learning theory influencse the degree of learner engagement. Cognitivism supports investigative and problem-solving learning which engages learners (Bower & Hilgard, 1948). Grabbing learner attention is an essential part of learning and is an integral component of cognitive development. As learner pays attention, it gets involved in learning termed as "Learner Engaging Learning". Thus, learner engagement is an essential part of the pedagogical framework. The degree of learner engagement is improved by providing feedback during learning. Feedback is delivered to change learner behavior and attain learning objectives. Feedback is an essential part of reinforcement learning drawn from the theory of Behaviourism (Kulhavy, 1977). Learning involves both Cognitivist and Behaviourist approach and linking prior knowledge with new knowledge.

A learning objective is attained by constructing knowledge. Knowledge is constructed by linking prior knowledge with the knowledge to be learned. This principle of knowledge linking comes down from the theory of Constructivism. Vygotsky's social development theory is one of the founding principle constructivism (Duffy & Cunningham, 1996). Framework ingredients *Connecting Knowledge, Judging Misconceptions* (as given in Table 3) come from the theory of Constructivism. Constructivism promotes learning through observation and scientific study. "*Questioning*", "*Performing Experiments*", and "*Inquiry-based learning*" are the major tools of constructivism to transform learning from novice learners to expert learners. These tools must be an essential part of the pedagogical framework to promote learning. Instructional strategies based on constructivism that engages learners and promotes learning include – "*Cause and Effect relationships*", "*Models and Theories*", "*Predictions and Time-Scale activities*".

Learning is not just a cognitive and constructivist process, but it does involve learner attitude towards learning. Learner feelings, emotions, and attitudes are involved in learning. Learner having positive feelings, emotions and attitudes pays attention to phenomena and actively participates in learning by associating values, information and ideas. Attentive learners receive positive learning gains and learner attentiveness is influenced by learner satisfaction level and motivation level. Thus, learner affective states increase the degree of learner engagement in the learning activity and improving the cognition level of learners. Hence, maintaining an effective state of learners is one of the critical components of the pedagogical framework.

Different levels of human cognition may be judged by Bloom's taxonomy named after Benjamin Bloom an American Educational Psychologists (Morshead, 1965). Human cognition relates to learning objectives. Bloom classification of learning objectives includes:

- *Remembering:* Recall and Recognize relevant knowledge.
- *Understanding:* Interpreting and Inferring understanding of concepts.
- *Applying:* Implementing learning procedures.
- *Analyzing:* Systematic organization of learned information to develop logical understanding.
- *Evaluating:* Using Criteria and Standards to evaluate learned concepts.
- *Creating:* Learned patterns are organized, planned and produced by putting them together.

These learning objectives generate learning paths capable of achieving the desired learning outcome in the cognitive domain. To measure the degree of learning gains Bloom taxonomy provides a set of verbs that may be used to develop test items (Krathwohl, 2002). Bloom taxonomy defines three learning domains – cognitive, affective and psychomotor domains. These three domains are used to measure learning gains. For each domain, Bloom defined verbs that may be used in the questionnaire to measure learning. Verbs that may be used to measure learning in the cognitive domain are given in Table 4 (Emporia State University, 2019).

Table 4. Verbs to measure learning in Cognitive Domain

Remember	Understand	Apply	Analyze	Evaluate	Create
Arrange	Abstract	Apply	Analyze	Argue	Build
Cite	Associate	Carry Out	Assess	Assess	Combine
Choose	Categorize	Demonstrate	Check	Coordinate	Compose
Count	Clarify	Determine	Conclude	Detect	Construct
Define	Compare	Develop	Coordinate	Evaluate	Create
Identify	Contrast	Execute	Criticize	Justify	Formulate
List	Compare	Implement	Evaluate	Prioritize	Integrate
Recall	Conclude	Operate	Justify	Rank	Plan
Repeat	Exemplify	Solve	Rank	Recommend	Produce

These variables may be used to develop formative and summative assessments to assess logical thinking in cognitive domain. Logical thinking in cognitive domain is further made stronger by developing psychomotor skills. Psychomotor skills are measured in the psychomotor domain. Psychomotor skills may be measured using "*Observe and Learn*" learning activities. Verbs that can be used to measure the psychomotor domain are given in Table 5 (Emporia State University, 2019).

Table 5. Verbs to measure learning in Psychomotor Domain

Imitation	*Manipulation*	*Precision*	*Articulation*	*Naturalization*
Copy	Build	Complete	Adapt Combine	Design
Follow	Execute	Control	Construct	Invent
Repeat	Implement	Demonstrate	Coordinate	Manage
Replicate	Perform	Perfect	Develop	Project
	Recreate	Show	Formulate	Specify
			Integrate	

Learning gains can be increased using the affective domain. If the learner's emotional state is strong, then it may readily accept new information (The Peak Performance Center, 2019). Table 6 provide verbs that can be used to measure learning in the Affective Domain.

Verbs listed in Tables 4, Table 5 and Table 6 can be used to develop formative and summative assessments. Assessment is an integral part of the pedagogical framework.

The sequencing of instructional material is the next critical component to be considered in developing a pedagogical framework. Instructional materials are sequenced to achieve learning objectives. Well

Table 6. Verbs to measure Affective Domain

Receiving	Responding	Valuing	Organizing
Watching	Conversation	Team Work	Spending Time
Listening	Participation	Supporting Ideas	Recognizing need
	Group Discussion	Improving Proficiency	Prioritizing time
	Follow Directions	Informing about possible issues	

sequenced instructional material can achieve three components of the pedagogical framework – *firstly*, it can engage learners, *secondly*, it is able to find misconceptions and *thirdly*, it can connect prior and new knowledge. Bloom taxonomy may be used as a guideline to sequence instructional material. The sequencing of instructional material may be done using learner prior knowledge level or by using machine learning techniques such as Naïve Bayes Classifier (Nafa, Othman, & Khan, 2016). In a similar approach, Nafa and Khan (2015) presented a classification algorithm to classify learning concepts into varied Bloom Taxonomy levels. This classification strategy was able to measure learning gains. Learning gain may be measured using formative or summative assessment strategies combined with intelligent feedback (intelligent feedback motivates learners) (Mcdonald et al., 2013). Formative assessment was conducted using the TuTalk dialogue engine by Mcdonald et al. (2013). TuTalk dialogue engine classifies learner responses using Natural Language Processing technique and provides appropriate feedback. The Framework for Instructional Technology (FIT) supported the use of formative assessment and delivered on-going adaptation using it (Durlach & Spain, 2014). Hence, formative assessment is one of the critical components of the pedagogical framework.

Developing Silent Observation: An Algorithm

Silent Observation is based on efficient use of emerging technologies, presentation of learning content and formative assessment with inbuilt intelligent feedback. Formative assessment is developed on Bloom Taxonomy. Algorithm "*Silent Observation*" draws from a similar approach adopted in Ramírez-Noriega et al. (2017).

Silent Observation given in Table 7 uses "Augmented Reality" and "Bayesian Network" as Emerging Technology. From the discussion made so far in this chapter, it was revealed that ITS can produce effective learning outcomes and support formative assessment. Most of the ITS cited in Table 2 use the "Bayesian Network" to develop learner model and had a major impact on cognitive domain followed by psychomotor domain and then on affective domain (cognitive domain>psychomotor domain>affective domain). The effectiveness of these ITS was evaluated using the Summative Assessment as a tool to assess learners. Results of summative assessment will be analyzed using *Mean, Standard Deviation, t*-Test, and *f*-Test statistics as these statistical methods were found to be efficient in most of the ITS given in Table 2. It was revealed in the analyses that instructional material presented in these ITS was not delivered using well-developed research guidelines on ergonomics. "*Silent Observation*" is an attempt to provide a solution to this shortcoming by using Khan and Mustafa (2019). In "*Silent Observation*", instructional material will be delivered on the guidelines given in Khan and Mustafa (2019), Krathwohl (2002) and Nafa et al. (2016) and will follow the order given in Table 8:

Table 7. Algorithm "Silent Observation"

Phase – I	
Initialization Phase (IP): IP 1: Calculate the prior knowledge level of learners using Pre-Test. IP 2: Compute the probability of correct answer using prior knowledge level of learners. Formula to Calculate probability: Prior-knowledge level * (Correct option for a question / total number of options in question) IP 3: Construct Bayesian Network (to diagnose the cause of Incorrect Answer) using stage IP 2 and Phase - II. IP4: Use Augmented Reality to provide dynamic feedback and perform a diagnostic evaluation. IP 5: Display hints to be followed by learners. IP 6: To check the correctness of the answer use algorithm given by (Mcdonald et al., 2013). IP7: Display Rhetorical questions inquiring about the satisfaction level of learners related to the presentation. IP 8: If the probability of delivering incorrect answer due to presentation is high than *goto* Phase – II	
Phase – II	
1.0 Remember 1.1 Ask question containing verbs "Recognize" and "Recall" *goto 1.2* 1.2 If the answer to questions in *1.1* is correct *goto 2.0* otherwise *goto 1.3* 1.3 Ask question containing verbs "Choose" and "Identify" *goto 1.4* 1.4 If the answer to questions in 1.3 is correct *goto 2.0* otherwise *goto 1.5* 1.5 Ask question containing verbs "Define" and "List" *goto 1.6* 1.6 If the answer to questions in 1.5 is correct than goto 2.0 otherwise set *tag*: = *R1 goto OF1*.	OF1: Overview and Fact OF1.1 If *tag* not equal to *R1* than *goto* OF1.1.1 otherwise *goto* OF1.1.2 OF1.1.1 Deliver Instructional material as per guidelines on Content Presentation Model (Khan & Mustafa, 2019). OF1.1.2 Change presentation of Instructional Material by using guidelines of Content Presentation Model (Khan & Mustafa, 2019) that is different from that used in OF1.1.1 OF1.1.3 Update Bayesian Network using 1.0 Remember.
2.0 Understand 2.1 Ask question containing verbs "Interpreting" and "Inferring" *goto 2.2* 2.2 If the answer to questions in 2.1 is correct than *goto 3.0* otherwise *goto 2.3* 2.3 Ask questions containing verbs "Compare" and "Contrast" than goto 2.4 2.4 If the answer to questions in 2.3 is correct than *goto 3.0* otherwise *goto 2.5* 2.5 Ask question containing verbs "Categorize" and "Classify" goto 2.6 2.6 If the answer to questions in 2.5 is correct than goto 3.0 otherwise set *tag*: = U2 goto C2	C2: Concept C2.1 If *tag* not equal to U2 than *goto* C2.2 otherwise *goto* C2.3 C2.2 Deliver Instructional material as per the guidelines are given in the Content Presentation Model (Khan & Mustafa, 2019) C2.3 Change presentation of instructional material, use guidelines of Content Presentation Model (Khan & Mustafa, 2019) different from that used in C2.2 C2.3 Update Bayesian Network using 2.0 Understand.
3.0 Apply 3.1 Ask questions containing the verb "Executing" and "Implementing" *goto 3.2* 3.2 If the answer to questions in 3.1 is correct than goto 4.0(Analyse) otherwise goto 3.3 3.3 Ask questions containing verbs "Demonstrate" and "Determine" *goto 3.4* 3.4 If the answer to questions in 3.3 is correct than goto 4.0 (Analyse) otherwise goto 3.5 3.5 Ask question containing the verbs "Operate" and "Solve" *goto 3.6* 3.6 If the answer to questions in 3.5 is correct than goto 1.0(Remember) otherwise set tag: = A3 goto A3	A3 Procedure A3.1 If *tag* not equal to A3 than *goto* A3.2 otherwise *goto* A3.3 A3.2 Deliver Instructional material as per the guidelines are given in the Content Presentation Model(Khan & Mustafa, 2019) A3.3 Change presentation of instructional material, use guidelines of Content Presentation Model(Khan & Mustafa, 2019) different from that used in A3.2 A3.4 Update Bayesian Model using results of 3.0 Apply.

Table 8. Bloom taxonomy tags for Instructional Materials

Bloom Taxonomy Tag	*Order of Instructional Material (Khan & Mustafa, 2019)*
Remember	Overview and Fact
Understand	Concept
Apply	Procedure
Analyze	Principle
Evaluate	Assessment
Create	Feedback and Motivation

Content Presentation Model given in Khan and Mustafa (2019) produces guidelines on appropriate utilization of Media, Ergonomics and Navigation structures. "*Silent Observation*" improves the Content Presentation Model (Khan & Mustafa, 2019) by enriching it with Assessment Model based on Bloom Taxonomy and Bayesian Network. The proposed algorithm given in Table 7 will begin by setting the OF1 tag to Null (*tag: = Null*). As "Remember", "Understand", "Apply" parameters of Bloom Taxonomy are modelled in "*Silent Observation*" remaining parameters ("Analyse", "Evaluate" and "Create") will be modelled. The proposed algorithm will provide intelligent feedback and conduct formative assessment based on learner actions. Diagnositic capability of formative assessment will improve Bayesian Network and will deliver intelligent feedback using Augmented Reality.

SOLUTIONS AND RECOMMENDATIONS

Since 1980, Information Communication Technologies (ICTs) have been being used in education by academic researchers. With the evolution of ICTs, new technologies have emerged, and in turn, their application in learning is increasing. Learners of the tertiary level must be aware of the potential effectiveness of these new technologies and their use in learning. Learners proficient in using emerging technologies and tools developed on these technologies may produce effective learning outcomes. Substantial research evidence exists in support of attaining positive learning gains by the use of emerging technologies and tools developed on it. Thus, it became the need of the time to further strengthen the impact of emerging technologies on learning and harness their pedagogical potential.

In the quest of finding the impact of emerging technologies, a detailed study was carried out, and this chapter has an imprint of this research study. From the study, it was revealed that AI has a significant influence on online learning. Using AI learner emotions, cognitive level and psychomotor skills may be judged and may be used in decision-making processes. This chapter brought forward the impact of AI on mimicking human tutor and its use in developing a strong pedagogical framework.

An effective and efficient pedagogical framework must have ICT as a medium to transfer learning. A pedagogical principle such as Operant Conditioning is used to modify learner behavior by reinforcement or punishment and implemented using ICT. Feedback and Motivation is an example of Operant Conditioning and can be implemented using ICT based instructional strategies given in Table 3. Feedback is provided to learners to rectify or improve their learner behavior and achieve positive learning gains. Change in learner behavior is a pedagogical principle given by Edward Thorndike in 1988 under the theory of Behaviourism. Behaviourism is used to predict learner behavior in a specific situation, so this principle is often implemented using ICT based on AR/VR/MR technologies.

The change in learner behavior is possible when the learner diverts attention to the stimulus provided. Gaining attention is the most critical component of an effective pedagogical framework. When learner attention is achieved, the degree of learning outcome is improved. Professor A J Romiszowski has done considerable work on gaining learner attention and efficient and effective use of instructional media. According to Romiszowski, instructional media can effectively be used for the process of planned instruction (Romiszowski, 1988). Romiszowski has categorized instructions into Intent, Consent, and Coding (*see* Table 9). Based on this categorization he has given detail study about the use of instructional media and its categorization. Romiszowski appreciated the work of Skinner, Gilbert, Pressey and Bloom laying the foundation to develop the technology of instructional media. Instructional media supports the discovery learning of Jerome Bruner. Jerome Bruner's (Bruner, 1961) discovery learning has been used in mathematical education. Many ITSs have been developed in Mathematics based on Bruner's discovery learning. Bruner's discovery learning builds cognitive structures.

Table 9. Factors on which Instructions depend (Instructional messages: three categories of design factors (Romiszowski, 1988)

Messages may be designed by paying attention to three types of factors				
Intent	**Consent**		**Coding**	
What we hope to achieve by communicating the message	The information is to be communicated		The symbol-system by which the message will be communicated	
To entertain/interest	Class	Complexity	Concrete	Defined
To motivate/influence	Factual (facts, procedures)	Discrete (single, simple items)	Sensory (direct communication)	Verbal (language) communication
To inform/enlighten	Conceptual (concepts, principles)	Structured (complex ideas)	Non-verbal signs/ conventions	Formal symbolic codes/ conventions

Bloom taxonomy (Krathwohl, Bloom, & Masia, 1956) encouraged rote or meaningful learning to build cognitive structures. Bloom taxonomy is well supported by David Ausubel (Koscianski & Farago, 2014), who used it to develop educational multimedia software. Most of the Educational multimedia Softwares did not fragment learning content and presented them as a big chunk. Ergonomic principles avoid the use of a big chunk of learning content as it distracts learners. To overcome this difficulty, a significant extension to Skinner, Gilbert, Pressey, Bloom and Ausubel's theory of instruction design has come out as Component Display Theory (Merrill, 1983). Component Display Theory has given multimodal representation of instructions and has categorized learning content into Facts, Concepts, Procedures, and Principles. Component Display Theory may be used at the macro level to develop an ICT integrated curriculum and at a micro level to develop a multimodal multimedia representation of exercises and material. Curriculum design at the macro level decides sequencing of instruction and the use of media to generate instruction. Media at the macro level may be extended to generate instruction at micro level.

This chapter recommends to further extend approaches given in the Component Display Theory to design instructions. The selection and use of media must act as an instrument to frame learning theories to design instructions. Thus, media, learning theories and emerging technologies must be intertwined to build a strong pedagogical framework. "*Silent Observation*" is an attempt to provide a solution and recommendation to achieve positive learning gains using ICT at the tertiary level.

FUTURE RESEARCH DIRECTIONS

The United Nations Educational, Scientific and Cultural Organization (UNESCO), a division of the United Nations has integrated ICT into education. With the growth of Communication Technology, new technology is emerging and their application in learning is increasing. Emerging technologies that may produce effective learning outcomes include - *5G technology to have efficient and effective learning, Artificial Intelligence, Voice Searches, Augmented Reality (AR), Virtual Reality (VR) and Mixed Reality (MR).* These emerging technologies must be interwoven with pedagogical principles to produce effective and efficient instructions. Operant Conditioning implemented using ICT is used to modify learner behavior by reinforcement or punishment. ICT is often used to implement Behaviourism, Cognitivism, and Constructivism to accomplish a learning task. A Learning outcome is decided by the task to be carried out. A task is a goal-oriented activity and it can be - a problem-solving task, puzzle-solving task, comparing exercises, 'discovery' learning activity, question-and-answer practice, information-gap activities, problem-solving activities or conducting discussion/explanation on a topic. Tasks can be initiated through written text, visual data or dwelling on learner experiences or demonstration or combination of these. The task must be designed to improve the learner's cognitive level. Implementing tasks is a major issue to be considered. On conducting a literature survey on Task implementation, it was revealed that tasks are implemented using three major stages, these stages are given Table 9 adopted from (Skehan, 1996). From research studies, it was found that there exists a correlation between task and Merrill 1983 Component Display Theory, that classifies a topic into "*Fact*", "*Concept*", "*Procedure*", and "*Principles*". Thus, "*Fact*", "*Concept*", "*Procedure*", and "*Principles*" in Component Display Theory is a task and can be implemented using emerging technologies and guidelines given in (Khan & Mustafa, 2019). Factors that need to be considered in task implementation are provided in Table 10.

According to the author, future research can develop "*Silent Observation*" into a model by incorporating Component Display Theory. Component Display Theory has been used to develop an instructional model by Khan and Mustafa (2019) this model should be used to develop a robust algorithm of "*Silent Observation*". "*Silent Observation*" uses Bloom Taxonomy to assess learners and change the presentation of instructional material using an algorithm proposed by Khan and Mustafa (2019). "*Silent Observation*" is still in its birth stage and will undergo changes to integrate learning theories into emerging technologies. The proposed algorithm will be based on the pedagogical framework that will asses learners using formative assessment. The degree of the robustness of "*Silent Observation*" may be improved by the intelligent use of summative assessment and by exploring its theoretical aspect. Thus, exploring the theoretical aspect of "*Silent Observation*" is the most probable future research direction.

Table 10. Factors influencing task implementation

Stage Goal	Code complexity	Stress	Cognitive complexity
1. Pre-emptive Restructuring:			
• Establish the target language • Reduce cognitive load	Pre-tech Consciousness-raising Practice: • conventional • parallel tasks • rehearsal of elements	-	It includes: • Processing • Observe • Solve similar tasks Plan: a) Cognitively b) linguistically • Familiarity • Activate
2. During			
• Mediating accuracy and fluency		Factors that influence communicative stress:	
	• Accuracy focus • Conformity pressure	• Time	• Support available surprise elements by providing:
		• Modality	a) Additional elements
		• Scale	b) Conflicting elements
		• Stakes	
		• Control	
3. Post-task Activities			
Post 1			
• Increase accuracy	• Public performance in front of:		
• Encourage restructuring	a) Teacher b) group c) camera		
• Discourage excessive synthesis	• Increase Degree of analysis & testing		
Post 2			
• The cycle of task synthesis and analysis	Conduct task sequencing by: • Repeating tasks • Introducing parallel tasks • Selecting tasks from task families		

CONCLUSION

Silent Observation is an attempt to develop a pedagogical framework to deliver instructional material using Emerging Technologies. Instructional strategies to deliver instructions that may be used are given in Table 3. These instructional strategies are based on learning theories of Behaviourism, Cognitivism, and Constructivism. Table 2 *ITS taken under study* provides a list of ITS used to develop pedagogical framework. Most of the ITS had a noticeable impact on cognitive domain. The pedagogical framework of most of the ITS given in Table 2 is based on learning theories of Cognitivism blended with the theories of Behaviourism and Constructivism. Focus on cognitive domain evolve learner thinking, but ITS such as (Jugo et al., 2015; Smith et al., 2015) provided Visualization reflecting its influence on psychomotor domain. This chapter has discussed a detailed analysis of ITS and its influence on the learning domains. Visualization can be enhanced using Emerging Technologies. Emerging Technologies help in grabbing learner attention. Better learner attention produces positive learning outcomes. Emerging technology such as Augmented Reality (AR)/Virtual Reality (VR) is a boon in gaining learner attention. The impact of AR/VR can be seen on learners (Workers) of Manufacturing Industry, Automotive Industry and Utility Industry (Cohen et al., 2018), learners of this industries reported that use of AR/VR will save time, increase efficiency and reduce complexity.

It was revealed in scientific research studies that learner knowledge level can be evaluated using Bloom Taxonomy. Bloom Taxonomy provides verbs that will be used to measure learning in cognitive, affective and psychomotor domains (given in *Table 4, Table 5 & Table 6*). This curated set of verbs may be used to assess learning according to different learning objectives. Thus, designing learner assessment based on Bloom Taxonomy helps in assessing learning in cognitive, affective and psychomotor domains. The proposed algorithm "*Silent Observation*" uses Bloom Taxonomy to assess learners, deliver dynamic feedback using Augmented Reality and represent instructional material using (Khan & Mustafa, 2019; Mcdonald et al., 2013). "*Silent Observation*" is made stronger by building and improving the Bayesian Network based on the outcome of learner assessment (Ramírez-Noriega et al., 2017; Vanlehn et al., 2005).

Guidelines to develop pedagogical framework and algorithm "*Silent Observation*" proposed in this chapter needs to be integrated into an educational software application. The developed application will be evaluated by a set of experts in the domain of instructional technology. The results of the rigorous evaluation will be statistically evaluated using Mean, Standard Deviation, *t*-Test, and *f*-Test.

REFERENCES

Abdullah, S. A., Yaakub, A., & Wahil, Z. (2015). Evaluating Students ' Need in Using Computer Aided Software in Landscape Design Course. *Procedia: Social and Behavioral Sciences, 195*, 828–836. doi:10.1016/j.sbspro.2015.06.188

Abyaa, A., Khalidi, M., & Bennani, S. (2019). Learner modelling : Systematic review of the literature from the last 5 years. *Educational Technology Research and Development, 67*(5), 1–39. doi:10.1007/s11423-018-09644-1

Albacete, P. L., & Vanlehn, K. A. (2000). Evaluating the Effectiveness of a Cognitive Tutor for Fundamental Physics Concepts. *Annual Meeting of the Cognitive Science Society.*

Almohammadi, K., Hagras, H., Alghazzawi, D., & Aldabbagh, G. (2016). Users-Centric Adaptive Learning System Based On Interval Type-2 Fuzzy Logic For Massively Crowded E-Learning Platforms. *Journal of Artificial Intelligence and Soft Computing Research, 6*(2), 81–101. doi:10.1515/jaiscr-2016-0008

Alobaidi, O. G., Smieee, K. A. C., Mieee, J. D. O. S., & Jarad, T. M. (2013). Abdullah : An Intelligent Arabic Conversational Tutoring System for Modern Islamic Education. In *Proceedings of the World Congress on Engineering* (Vol. 2). London, UK: Academic Press.

Altaboli, A., & Lin, Y. (2011). Investigating Effects of Screen Layout Elements on Interface and Screen Design Aesthetics. Advances in Human-Computer Interaction, 2011(5), 1–10. doi:10.1155/2011/659758

Bosch, N., & D'Mello, S. (2013). Sequential Patterns of Affective States of Novice Programmers. In AIED 2013 Workshops Proceedings (Vol. 9). Academic Press.

Bower, G. H., & Hilgard, E. R. (1948). *Theories of Learning* (Vol. 3). Academic Press.

Bruner, J. S. (1961). The act of discovery. *Harvard Educational Review*.

Bryfczynski, S. (2012). BeSocratic : An Intelligent Tutoring System for the Recognition, Evaluation, and Analysis of Free-form Student Input. Clemson Univeristy. Retrieved from https://tigerprints.clemson.edu/all_dissertations/1053

Cade, W. L., Copeland, J. L., Person, N. K., & Mello, S. K. D. (2008). Dialogue Modes in Expert Tutoring. In International Conference on Intelligent Tutoring Systems (pp. 470–471). doi:10.1007/978-3-540-69132-7_50

Capuano, N., Gaeta, M., Miranda, S., & Orciuoli, F. (2008). LIA : An Intelligent Advisor for e-Learning. In *WSKS 2008* (pp. 187–196). Berlin: Springer-Verlag.

Carter, E. E. (2014). *An Intelligent Debugging Tutor For Novice Computer Science Students*. Lehigh Univeristy.

Chen, C. (2008). Intelligent web-based learning system with personalized learning path guidance. *Computers & Education, 51*(2), 787–814. doi:10.1016/j.compedu.2007.08.004

Chi, M. T. H., Siler, S. A., Jeong, H., Yamauchi, T., & Hausmann, R. G. (2001). Learning from human tutoring. *Cognitive Science, 25*(4), 471–533. doi:10.1207/s15516709cog2504_1 PubMed

Chrysafiadi, K., & Virvou, M. (2012). Evaluating the integration of fuzzy logic into the student model of a web-based learning environment. *Expert Systems with Applications, 39*(18), 13127–13134. doi:10.1016/j.eswa.2012.05.089

Clancey, W. J. (1979). *Transfer of rule-based expertise through a tutorial dialogue*. Stanford University.

Cohen, L., Duboe, P., Buvat, J., Melton, D., Khadikar, A., & Shah, H. (2018). *Augmented and Virtual Reality in Operations*. Academic Press.

Costello, R., & Mundy, D. P. (2009). The Adaptive Intelligent Personalised Learning Environment. *IEEE International Conference on Advanced Learning Technologies*. 10.1109/ICALT.2009.38

Demir, A., & Kosse, U. (2017). Solving Optimization Problems via Vortex Optimization Algorithm and Cognitive Development Optimization Algorithm. *Broad Research in Artificial Intelligence and Neuroscience, 7*(4), 23–42.

Duffy, T. M., & Cunningham, D. J. (1996). Constructivism: Implications for the design and delivery of instruction. In *Handbook of research for educational communications and technology* (pp. 1–31). New York: Macmillan Library Reference.

Durlach, P. J., & Randall, D. S. (2014). *Framework for Instructional Technology : Methods of Implementing Adaptive Training and Education*. Academic Press.

Dzikovska, M., Steinhauser, N., Farrow, E., Moore, J., & Campbell, G. (2014). BEETLE II : Deep Natural Language Understanding and Automatic Feedback Generation for Intelligent Tutoring in Basic Electricity and Electronics. *International Journal of Artificial Intelligence in Education*, *24*(3), 284–332. doi:10.1007/s40593-014-0017-9

Echeverr, V., & Chiluiza, K. (2015). Mirroring Teachers ' Assessment of Novice Students ' Presentations Through an Intelligent Tutor System. In Asia-Pacific Conference on Computer Aided System Enginnering (pp. 264–269). doi:10.1109/APCASE.2015.53

El Ghouch, N., Mokhtar, E., & Seghroucheni, Y. Z. (2017). Analysing the Outcome of a Learning Process Conducted Within the System ALS _ CORR. *International Journal of Emerging Technologies in Learning*, *12*(3), 43–56. doi:10.3991/ijet.v12i03.6377

Eldenfria, A., & Al-samarraie, H. (2019). The effectiveness of an online learning system based on aptitude scores : An effort to improve students ' brain activation. *Education and Information Technologies*, *24*(5), 1–15. doi:10.1007/s10639-019-09895-2

Emporia State University. (2019). Learning Domains. Retrieved October 27, 2019, from https://www.emporia.edu/studentlife/learning-and-assessment/guide/domains.html

Fortier, P., Mindala-Freeman, M. M., Bagnon, P., Tignon, M., Larsson, T., & Buvat, J. … Gosh, A. (2019). 5G in industrial operations How telcos and industrial companies stand to benefit. Paris, France: Academic Press.

Gomez, S., Zervas, P., Sampson, D. G., & Fabregat, R. (2014). Context-aware adaptive and personalized mobile learning delivery supported by UoLmP. *International Journal of Computational Science*, *26*(1), 47–61. doi:10.1016/j.jksuci.2013.10.008

Graesser, A. C., Vanlehn, K., Rosé, C. P., Jordan, P. W., & Harter, D. (2001). Intelligent Tutoring Systems with Conversational Dialogue. In American Association for Artificial Intelligence (pp. 39–52). Academic Press.

Grawemeyer, B., Holmes, W., Gutierrez-santos, S., & Wiedmann, M. (2016). Affecting Off-Task Behaviour : How Affect-aware Feedback Can Improve Student Learning. In Sixth International conference on learning analytics & knowledge (pp. 104–113). doi:10.1145/2883851.2883936

Grivokostopoulou, F., & Hatzilygeroudis, I. (2013). Teaching AI Search Algorithms In A Web-Based Eeducational System. IADIS International Conference e-Learning.

Grossman, B. (1996). *Intelligent Algebraic Tutoring Based on Student Misconceptions*. Massachusetts Institute of Technology.

Harley, J. M., Bouchet, F., Hussain, S. M., Azevedo, R., & Calvo, R. A. (2015). A Multi-Componential Analysis of Emotions during Complex Learning with an Intelligent Multi-Agent System. *Computers in Human Behavior*, *48*, 615–625. doi:10.1016/j.chb.2015.02.013

Heh, J. S., Li, S. C., Chang, A., Chang, M., & Liu, T. C. (2008). Diagnosis Mechanism and Feedback System to Accomplish the Full-Loop Learning Architecture. *Journal of Educational Technology & Society*, *11*, 29–44.

Hogle, P. S. (2019). Emerging Technology (S. Jacobs, Ed.). Santa Rosa, CA: The eLearning Guild. Retrieved from www.elearningGuild.com

Hooshyar, D., Ahmad, R. B., Yousefi, M., Yusop, F. D., & Horng, S. (2015). A flowchart-based intelligent tutoring system for improving problem-solving skills of novice programmers. *Journal of Computer Assisted Learning*, *31*(4), 1–17. doi:10.1111/jcal.12099

Hsieh, S., & Cheng, Y.-T. (2014). Algorithm and intelligent tutoring system design for programmable controller programming. *International Journal of Advanced Manufacturing Technology*, *71*(5-8), 1099–1100. doi:10.1007/s00170-013-5539-z

Ibrahim, F. M., Aziz, A. A., Zubairi, Y. Z., & Zaharim, A. (2012). Using The Rasch Model To Assess Examination Beyond Students Scores. *IEEE Global Engineering Education Conference*.

Isotani, S., Mclaren, B. M., & Altman, M. (2010). *Towards Intelligent Tutoring with Erroneous Examples : A Taxonomy of Decimal Misconceptions. In 10th International Conference on Intelligent Tutoring Systems* (Vol. 6094, pp. 346–348). Berlin: Springer; doi:10.1007/978-3-642-13437-1_66.

Jeon, S. S. (2010). *Adaptive E-Learning using ECpAA Rules*. Bayesian Networks and Group Profile And Performance Data. Univeristy of Florida.

Jeremi, Z., Jovanovi, J., & Gaševi, D. (2009). Evaluating an Intelligent Tutoring System for Design Patterns : The DEPTHS Experience. *Journal of Educational Technology & Society*, *12*, 111–130.

Jugo, I., Kovačić, B., & Tijan, E. (2015). Cluster analysis of student activity in a web-based intelligent tutoring system. *Scientifc Journal of Maritime Research*, *29*, 75–83.

Kacalak, W., Majewski, M., & Zurada, J. M. (2010). Intelligent E-Learning Systems for Evaluation of User ' s Knowledge and Skills with Efficient Information Processing. In *International Conference on Artificial Intelligence and Soft Computing* (pp. 508–515). Springer.

Kazi, H., Haddawy, P., & Suebnukarn, S. (2012). Employing UMLS for generating hints in a tutoring system for medical problem-based learning. *Journal of Biomedical Informatics*, *45*(3), 557–565. doi:10.1016/j.jbi.2012.02.010 PubMed

Keles, A., Ocak, R., Keles, A., & Gulcu, A. (2009). ZOSMAT : Web-based intelligent tutoring system for teaching – learning process. *Expert Systems with Applications*, *36*(2), 1229–1239. doi:10.1016/j.eswa.2007.11.064

Keller, J. M. (1987). Development and Use of the ARCS Model of Instructional Design. *Journal of Instrcutional Development*, *10*(3), 2–10. doi:10.1007/BF02905780

Khachatryan, G. A., Romashov, A. V., Khachatryan, A. R., Gaudino, S. J., Khachatryan, J. M., Guarian, K. R., & Yufa, N. V. (2014). Reasoning Mind Genie 2 : An Intelligent Tutoring System as a Vehicle for International Transfer of Instructional Methods in Mathematics. *International Journal of Artificial Intelligence in Education*, *24*(3), 333–382. doi:10.1007/s40593-014-0019-7

Khan, M. J., & Mustafa, K. (2019). Adaptive hypermedia instructional system (AHIS): A model. *Education and Information Technologies, 24*(6), 3329–3392. doi:10.1007/s10639-019-09927-x

Khatimin, N., Aziz, A. A., Zaharim, A., Sahari, J., & Rahmat, A. O. K. (2013). Setting the Standard for Project Design course using Rasch Measurement Model. In *IEEE Global Engineering Education Conference* (pp. 1062–1065). Berlin, Germany: IEEE; doi:10.1109/EduCon.2013.6530239.

Kolekar, S. V. M., Pai, R., & Pai, M. M. M. (2019). Rule based adaptive user interface for adaptive E-learning system. *Education and Information Technologies, 24*(1), 613–641. doi:10.1007/s10639-018-9788-1

Koscianski, A., & Farago, D. (2014). A Design Model for Educational Multimedia Software. Creative Education, 05(23), 5. doi:10.4236/ce.2014.523224

Krathwohl, D. R. (2002). A Revision of Bloom's Taxonomy: An Overview. *Theory into Practice, 41*(1), 212–218. doi:10.1207/s15430421tip4104_2

Krathwohl, D. R., Bloom, B. S., & Masia, B. B. (1956). Taxnomy of Educational Objectives: The Classification of Eucational Goals. In *Handbook II*. Affective Domain. David McKay Company, Incorporated.

Kulhavy, R. W. (1977). Feedback in Written Instruction. *American Educational Reserach Association, 47*(2), 211–232.

Kulik, J. A., & Fletcher, J. D. (2015). Effectiveness of Intelligent Tutoring Systems: A Meta-Analytic Review. *Review of Educational Research, 37*, 1–37. doi:10.3102/0034654315581420

Kurosu, M., & Kashimura, K. (1995). Apparent Usability vs. Inherent Usability. In CHI 95 Mosaic Of Creativity (pp. 1–2). doi:10.1145/223355.223680

Lanzilotti, R., & Roselli, T. (2007). An Experimental Evaluation of Logiocando, an Intelligent Tutoring Hypermedia System. *International Journal of Artificial Intelligence in Education, 17*(1), 41–56.

Marciniak, J. (2014). Building intelligent tutoring systems immersed in repositories of e-learning content. *Procedia Computer Science, 35*, 541–550. doi:10.1016/j.procs.2014.08.135

Mcdonald, J., Knott, A., Stein, S., & Zeng, R. (2013). An empirically-based, tutorial dialogue system: design, implementation and evaluation in a first year health sciences course. 30th ascilite Conference.

Merrill, M. D. (1983). Component Diaply Theory. In Instructional Design Theories and Models: An overview of their current status (pp. 282–333). Academic Press.

Millán, E., Loboda, T., & Pérez-de-la-Cruz, J. L. (2010). Bayesian networks for student model engineering. *Computers & Education, 55*(4), 1663–1683. doi:10.1016/j.compedu.2010.07.010

Mohammed, P., & Mohan, P. (2015). Dynamic Cultural Contextualisation of Educational Content in Intelligent Learning Environments using ICON. *International Journal of Artificial Intelligence in Education, 25*(2), 249–270. doi:10.1007/s40593-014-0033-9

Morshead, R. W. (1965). Taxonomy of Educational Objectives HandBook II : Affective Domain. In Studies in Phiolosophy and Education (pp. 164–170). Academic Press.

Moshagen, M., Musch, J., & Göritz, A. S. (2009). A blessing, not a curse : Experimental evidence for beneficial effects of visual aesthetics on performance. *Ergonomics, 52*(10), 1311–1311. doi:10.1080/00140130903061717 PubMed

Nafa, F., & Khan, J. (2015). Conceptualize the Domain Knowledge Space in the Light of Cognitive Skills. CSEDU 2015 - 7th International Conference on Computer Supported Education. *Proceedings, 1*, 285–295. doi:10.5220/0005441602850295

Nafa, F., Othman, S., & Khan, J. (2016). Automatic Concepts Classification based on Bloom's Taxonomy using Text Analysis and the Naïve Bayes Classifier Method. CSEDU 2016 - Proceedings of the 8th International Conference on Computer Supported Education, 1, 391–396. 10.5220/0005813303910396

Nkambou, R., & Bourdeau, J. (2010). Building Intelligent Tutoring Systems : An Overview. In Advances in Intelligent Tutoring Systems (pp. 361–375). Academic Press.

Ozek, M., Akpolat, Z. H., & Orphan, A. (2013). A Web-Based Intelligent Tutoring System for a Basic Control Course. *Computer Applications in Engineering Education, 21*(3), 561–571. doi:10.1002/cae.20501

Plummer, D. B., Dale, R., & Cox, R. (2012). Using Edit Distance to Analyse Errors in a Natural Language to Logic Translation Corpus. Retrieved from https://sro.sussex.ac.uk

Ramírez-Noriega, A., Juárez-Ramírez, R., & Martínez-Ramírez, Y. (2017). Evaluation module based on Bayesian networks to Intelligent Tutoring Systems. *International Journal of Information Management, 37*(1), 1488–1498. doi:10.1016/j.ijinfomgt.2016.05.007

Romiszowski, A. J. (1988). *The Selection and Use of Instructional Media*. Kogan Page Ltd.

Saadawi, G. M., Tseytlin, E., Jukic, D., Castline, M., Gormley, R., & Crowley, R. S. (2008). A Natural Language Intelligent Tutoring System for Training Pathologists - Implementation and Evaluation. *Advances in Health Sciences Education : Theory and Practice, 13*(5), 709–722. doi:10.1007/s10459-007-9081-3 PubMed

Silva, R. L. S., & Neiva, F. W. (2016). Systematic Literature Review in Computer Science - A Practical Guide. doi:10.13140/RG.2.2.35453.87524

Skehan, P. (1996). A Framework for the implementation of task-based instruction. *Applied Linguistics, 17*(1), 38–62. doi:10.1093/applin/17.1.38

Smith, A., Min, W., Mott, B. W., & Lester, J. C. (2015). Diagrammatic Student Models: Modeling Student Drawing Performance with Deep Learning. International Conference on User Modelling, Adaptation and Personalization, 2016–2227. doi:10.1007/978-3-319-20267-9_18

Soh, L., Khandaker, N., & Jiang, H. (2008). I-MINDS : A Multiagent System for Intelligent Computer-Supported Collaborative Learning and Classroom Management. Computer Science and Engineering Journal. Retrieved from https://digitalcommons.unl.edu/csearticles

Spector, J. M., Merrill, M. D., van Merrienboer, J., & Driscoll, M. P. (2008). *HandBook Of Research On Educational Communications And Technology*. New York, NY: Taylor & Francis.

Stewart, B. (2000). IPTO - Information Processing Techniques Office. Retrieved August 10, 2019, from https://www.livinginternet.com/i/ii_ipto.htm

Szabo, M., & Kanuka, H. (1998). Effects of Violating Screen Design Principles of Balance, Unity, and Focus on Recall Learning, Study Time, and Completion Rate. *Journal of Educational Multimedia and Hypermedia*, *8*(1), 23–42.

Taele, P., & Hammond, T. (2015). BopoNoto : An Intelligent Sketch Education Application for Learning Zhuyin Phonetic Script. DMS, 101–107.

The Peak Performance Center. (2019). *Bloom's Affective Domain*. Author.

Vanlehn, K., Lynch, C., Schulze, K., Shapiro, J. A., Shelby, R., Taylor, L., ... Wintersgill, M. (2005). The Andes Physics Tutoring System : Lessons Learned. *International Journal of Artificial Intelligence in Education*, *15*(3), 1–47.

Vuc, G., Baloi, F., & Litcanu, M. (2015). Adapting Methods of Student Evaluation and Grading in Electrical Power Engineering. *Procedia: Social and Behavioral Sciences*, *191*, 147–151. doi:10.1016/j.sbspro.2015.04.366

Walker, E., Rummel, N., & Koedinger, K. R. (2014). Adaptive Intelligent Support to Improve Peer Tutoring in Algebra. *International Journal of Artificial Intelligence in Education*, *24*(1), 33–61. doi:10.1007/s40593-013-0001-9

Watanabe-Crockett, L. (2019). 10 Innovative Formative Assessment Examples for Teachers to Know. Retrieved January 30, 2020, from https://www.wabisabilearning.com/blog/formative-assessment-examples

Weragama, D., & Reye, J. (2014). Analysing Student Programs in the PHP Intelligent Tutoring System. *International Journal of Artificial Intelligence in Education*, *24*(2), 162–188. doi:10.1007/s40593-014-0014-z

Yarandi, M. (2013). Semantic Rule-based Approach for Supporting Personalised Adaptive E-Learning. Univeristy of East London.

Zain, J. M., Tey, M., & Goh, Y. (2007). Does Aesthetics of Web Page Interface Matters to Mandarin Learning? *Journal of Computer Science and Netwrok Security*, *7*(8), 43–51.

ADDITIONAL READING

Black, P., & Wiliam, D. (2009). Developing the theory of formative assessment. *Educational Assessment, Evaluation and Accountability*, *21*(1), 5–31. doi:10.1007/s11092-008-9068-5

Francis, D., & Stephens, A. (2018). *English Learners in STEM Subjects: Transforming Classrooms, Schools and Lives. The National Academies of Science Engineering Medicine*. Washington, DC: The National Academies Press; doi:10.17226/25182.

Godinez, J. E., & Jamil, H. M. (2019). Meet Cyrus - The query by voice mobile assistant for the tutoring and formative assessment of SQL learners. Proceedings of the 34th ACM/SIGAPP Symposium on Applied Computing, 2461–2468. doi:10.1145/3297280.3297523

Hilton, M. (2002). Enhancing Undergraduate Learning with Information Technology: A Workshop Summary. The National Academies of Science Engineering Medicine. Washington, D.C.: The National Academies Press. 10.17226/10270

Peat, M., & Franklin, S. (2002). Supporting student learning: The use of computer-based formative assessment modules. *British Journal of Educational Technology*, *33*(5), 515–523. doi:10.1111/1467-8535.00288

Pools-m. (2019). Task Based Learning. Retrieved December 24, 2019, from https://www.languages.dk/archive/pools-m/manuals/final/taskuk.pdf

Rakoczy, K., Pinger, P., Hochweber, J., Klieme, E., Schütze, B., & Besser, M. (2019). Formative assessment in mathematics: Mediated by feedback's perceived usefulness and students' self-efficacy. *Learning and Instruction*, *60*, 154–165. doi:10.1016/j.learninstruc.2018.01.004

Russell, S. J., & Norvig, P. (2016). *Artificial Intelligence A Mordern Approach* (S. Russell & P. Norvig, Eds.). Prentice Hall.

Willis, J. (1996). *A Framework For Task-based Learning*. Harlow: Longman.

KEY TERMS AND DEFINITIONS

Andragogy: Delivering learning instructions on empirical guidelines to maximize learning gains.
Epistemology: The theory of knowledge, with regards to its methods, validity, and scope.
Formative Assessment: Diagnosing learners for there misconceptions.
Heutagogy: Self-determined learning.
Pedagogy: It provide guidelines to be followed to deliver learning instructions to learners.
Task-Based Learning: Learning activities undertaken to attain desired learning objective.
Tertiary Education: It is the process of providing occupation specific learning.

Chapter 18
Evaluation of Moodle, Canvas, Blackboard, and Open EdX

Yunus Emre Öztürk
https://orcid.org/0000-0001-5109-5378
EdTech Center, Ubion Co. Ltd., South Korea

İsmail Gürler
https://orcid.org/0000-0002-6394-782X
Agri Ibrahim Cecen University, Turkey

ABSTRACT

The digital world abolishing all the limitations to reach knowledge and removing the borders of the countries and even continents serves as a facilitator for everyone who wants to learn and reach knowledge. The growing demand for knowledge throughout the world also increases the need for a variety of courses from highly appreciated institutions and instructors in the most effective educational methods and techniques. Therefore, deciding which substructure or platform to be chosen by both enterprises to make a profit and learners to acquire knowledge in the most suitable way is becoming a more challenging issue for both counterparts of teaching and learning. In order to make this selection process easy, based on the document analysis method, this chapter presents an evaluative report on globally popular e-learning platforms including Canvas, Blackboard, Moodle, and Open edX in terms of their market share, user interface, feature strengths and weaknesses, and it reaches a conclusion by comparing and contrasting their differences and similarities.

INTRODUCTION

Ford (2015), who emphasizes the dazzling development in technology based on Moore's law in the mid-60s, indicates that every couple of years the speed and the power of processors double and their cost is halved. Accordingly, e-learning platforms and their usage are increasing day by day at an incredible speed everywhere in the world. This increasing speed of technology and the demand for knowledge demonstrate the need for facilitating factors to access any kind of knowledge via the internet. Today, "distance" has

DOI: 10.4018/978-1-7998-3062-7.ch018

little meaning when there is an internet connection in our globalizing world. Web-based learning has been gaining more importance in the learning environment that allows both learners and instructors to learn and teach respectively without time or space limitation. The Internet and related web technologies do offer great solutions for presenting, publishing and sharing learning content and information, as is the case in many other areas (Cavus, 2010; Ramesh & Ramanathan, 2013).

Rapid changes and innovations in technology and technology-mediated instruction have removed the barriers of traditional teaching and learning, and by discarding the four-wall concept of traditional classrooms and schools. Nowadays, special-designed software environments are enabling teachers to extend the classroom beyond its traditional boundaries of time and space and can be used to supplement a conventional course experience. The success of the e-learning paradigm has led to the development of a great number of either commercial or open-source learning environments (Pecheanu, Stefanescu, Dumitriu, & Segal, 2011). In accordance with the developments of such kind software, the increasing adaptation skills of the learners to these kinds of technologies force institutions to make a choice whether to offer web-based instruction facilities to learners all over the world.

There are currently over 250 e-learning platforms (Al-Ajlan & Zedan, 2008) and those platforms bring selection issues among various software packages from the providers. The existing literature focuses on LMS platforms and MOOC platforms separately. However, this chapter compares MOOC and LMS platforms selecting the most valued and preferred e-learning platforms throughout the world.

This chapter aims to make the selection of suitable e-learning platforms easy for both the enterprises and learners in higher education. Therefore, it provides an overall evaluation of the four different e-learning platforms and tries to answer the following research questions:

1. What are the differences between Canvas, Blackboard, Moodle and edX in terms of user interface and user experience?
2. What are the differences between Canvas, Blackboard, Moodle and edX in terms of features?
3. What are the strengths and weaknesses of Canvas, Blackboard, Moodle and edX?

This chapter provides detailed information on how to select the optimum e-learning platform for higher education institutions by analyzing and comparing the most widely used e-learning platforms in the world including Canvas, Blackboard, Moodle and Open Edx and by making the SWOT analysis of the potential candidate platforms. Based on this analysis, this chapter deals with the current issues of mostly used e-learning platforms.

First, this chapter briefly describes what online learning platforms are, and covers major Learning Management Systems (LMS), including their market data, brief introduction, user interfaces and feature comparison. Next, it encompasses four e-learning platforms such as Canvas, Blackboard, Moodle and Open Edx. Finally, it seeks out the potential requirements of the system that is desired followed by some suggestions about adopting platforms for educational platforms by providing their SWOT analysis data.

BACKGROUND

There is various web-based software developed to enhance learners' diversity both in learning management systems (LMSs) such as Angel, Blackboard, Canvas, Desire2Learn, Moodle, Sakai and in massive open online courses (MOOCs) platforms such as Coursera, EdX, XuetangX, FutureLearn and Udacity.

There is overabundance on LMS providers with the number of stretching over 250 (Al-Ajlan & Zedan, 2008). They facilitate streamline, efficient delivery of courses; help to standardize e-learning content; and manage creation, delivery and management of content and assessment (Ramesh & Ramanathan, 2013). There are various advantages of using such kinds of e-learning platforms that enable both instructor and learners to share, reuse and develop the education content. Contents being ubiquitous make it easy for learners to manage their time, increase their level of readiness for the instruction and enhance the level of understanding. These platforms also have pedagogical and administrative ease and benefits (Scalter, 2008). Getting used to employing e-learning platforms is hard for instructors at first, but this one-time effort is beneficial in terms of administering the courses, helping instructors save time and developing contents easily.

The number of various e-learning platforms and the repertoire of different options for any future planners have a question in mind as which one to choose and adopt. Selecting and evaluating the existing application are another challenging factor for the learners. There are growing demands in organizations to produce a variety of software packages that can be customized according to the specific requirements for organizations' demand (Cavus, 2011; Jadhay & Sonar, 2011). No matter how important it is to use e-learning platforms to disseminate information and make learning feasible, choosing and selecting inappropriate e-learning software will adversely affect the business process and functions of the organization (Abdullateef, Elias, Mohamed, Zaidan, & Zaidan, 2016). The process of selecting a suitable LMS-MOOC packages has been becoming more complex, since there are large number of software package options on the market, the continuing development in the field, the technology and inexperienced decision makers (Cavus, 2010; Jadhav & Sonar, 2009a; Lin, Hsu & Sheen, 2007).

To ease the complex characteristics of choosing a suitable e-learning platform, there have been some studies conducted on evaluation and selection of the suitable packages of e-learning platforms (Abdullateef et al., 2016; Al- Ajlan, 2008; Al-Ajlan, 2012; Cavus, 2010; Gañán, Caballé, Clarisó & Conesa, 2016; Leba, Ionica & Edelhauser, 2013; Pecheanu, Stefanescu, Dumitriu & Segal, 2011; Ramesh & Ramanathan, 2013). In order to choose the most suitable VLE (virtual learning environment) platform to meet some university requirements, Al- Ajlan (2012) conducted a comparative study by comparing the specifications of Moodle and nine VLE platforms through features, capabilities, and their technical aspects. The study reached a conclusion that the best suitable e-learning platforms to meet the demands of their university are Moodle and Sakai. This study also generalized that the optimum VLE platform for all universities and Qassim University in particular is Moodle, which missed just two out of forty features the predetermined checklist. In the evaluation study, Abdullateef et al. (2016) presented a comprehensive insight on evaluation and selection of e-learning platforms. The study was based on three phases: The first one is to make certain available platforms according to the published papers. The second one is to establish criteria to evaluate considering the existing assessment criteria and its selection problems. The third one is to determine the abilities to solve the evaluation problems. The results reveal that the list of active LMS packages, the gap on the evaluation criteria on LMS and other problems, the use of multi-attribute or multi-criteria decision-making techniques for evaluation and selection of the Opens Source Software (OSS) in education are recommended as potential solutions (p.1). There are various online learning platforms for different purposes. In order to decide which platform is the best, it is necessary to understand what they are. Based on the related literature and studies, the current chapter seeks out to evaluate four mostly used e-learning platforms.

E-Learning Platforms

The first generation of e-learning platforms mainly comprises learning management systems (LMS) that have a strong focus on creating and standardizing learning content, distributing materials to learners and providing functionalities for self-assessment exercises and examination purposes. Driven by various factors like increasing number of students in higher education settings, the need for competency and outcome-oriented teaching (cf. Bologna Process), novel insights from research, and other influences and new requirements for e-learning technologies arose and led to an evolution of LMSs which are complex software systems that enable didactically enriched learning experience, which is called e-learning platforms. Therefore, in this study, the term "e-learning platform" is used as a comprehensive word to imply both LMS and MOOC platforms.

A learning management system (LMS) is a web based software application for the organization, implementation, and evaluation of education. LMS packages provide online learning material, evaluation, and collaborative learning environment (Abdullateef, Elias, Mohamed, Zaidan, & Zaidan, 2016). The main features of this system are user (student & teacher) registration & management, course management, online assessment (e.g., quiz), and reporting (Site & course reporting). They are mostly used by universities and corporations. Major LMSs are Canvas, Blackboard and MOODLE.

MOOC platforms are used to offer MOOC courses. The courses in those platforms are performed 100% online. The target learners of these platforms can be anyone, a university student, a child, a worker, or a retiree. Learners might obtain a certificate after completing a MOOC course. Also, most MOOC courses have a huge number of learners. Major MOOC platforms are edX, Coursera and Udacity. While an LMS is typically used by a single institution with a limited number of enrolments, a MOOC is used by many institutions and tends to have enrolments in the tens of thousands.

Introduction of Major LMS: Canvas, Blackboard and Moodle

This section introduces major LMS platforms such as Canvas, Blackboard and Moodle and gives general information on their market, user interface (UI) and user experience (UX), comparison of their main features and analysis of Canvas, Blackboard, and Moodle reflecting their strengths.

Canvas was developed and launched in 2011 by Instructure Inc. It is used by more than 3000 universities and institutions. It is also open-source and free. However, the cloud version is paid (commercialized by Instructure Inc.) It is popular especially in North America (the leader of Higher Education LMS Market in North America since June 2018). Due to its high usability and intrinsic User Interface, it is the hottest LMS in the market.

Blackboard was developed in 1998 by Blackboard Inc., which was founded in 1997 (the oldest LMS company). Blackboard has been the leader of the Higher Education in LMS Market in North America for the last 20 years. It is the oldest and most reliable platform of LMS, but it has only one version, paid one.

Moodle was developed in 2002 by Martin Dougiamas and it is the most widely-known and the most used platform of LMS across the world and it is an open-source and free. It is used in 200 countries and translated into 87 languages with its extensible features with 3rd party plugins having the biggest community in the world.

LMS Markets: Global and Regional Differences

Figure 1 shows differences in the market share of LMS platforms according to regions and countries. The following data reflect the most common LMS platforms and their acceptance ratio from region to region.

Figure 1. Higher Education LMS Market by Continents (Hill, 2017)

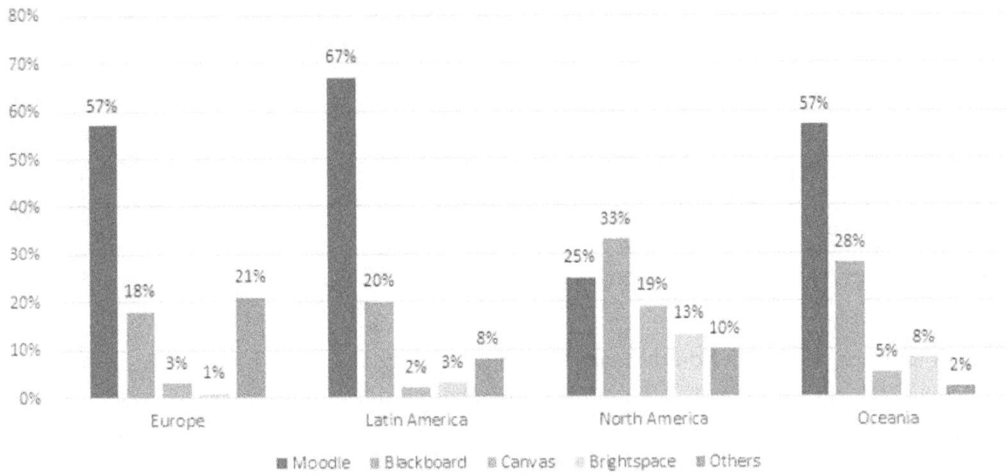

According to Figure 1, except North America, the highest LMS platform used is Moodle all over the world. In North America, Blackboard and Canvas have the biggest share. Blackboard and Canvas are used as cloud services. However, Moodle is preferred when there is a need for great personalization, which requires customizations.

However, in the LMS market, the most active and changing market is the US Market. Therefore, it is required to follow the US Market to understand LMS trends. Blackboard was the leader of Higher Education (HE) amongst the LMS platforms in the US until recently. But Canvas, which is the newest and youngest player of the LMS platform, has surpassed Blackboard since Spring 2019. As 2020 data shows, 33.4% of US universities use Canvas while 28.4% use Blackboard as an LMS system. On the other side, Moodle users are less than 17% in the US universities (edutechnica, 2020).

Top MOOC Platforms

To find out the top MOOC platforms, one should look at the number of the users and courses given using these platforms. Table 1 shows the top five MOOC platforms according to the number of registered users and courses delivered.

The most popular MOOC providers in the world are Coursera, edX, Udacity, FutureLearn and Swayam. Among them, edX uses an open source platform named "open edX" platform. Anyone can create an online learning environment by utilizing open edX platform for free. Therefore, this study examines open edX platform in terms of its features, user interface and applicability.

Open edX was developed by MIT & Harvard in 2013 and it is a free and open source course management system (CMS). It is used for Massive Open Online Courses (MOOCs) as well as smaller classes

Table 1. World's Top-5 MOOC Providers (Shah, 2018)

MOOC platform	Country of Origin	Year of Launch	Number of registered Users	Number of Courses
Coursera	USA	2012	45 Million	3,800
edX	USA	2012	24 Million	2,640
Udacity	USA	2012	11.5 Million	200
FutureLearn	UK	2012	10 Million	880
Swayam	India	2017	10 Million	1,000

and training modules. Various universities and institutions around the world provide MOOC services based on open edX platform. The architecture of Open edX is a scalable system through plugins.

MAIN FOCUS OF THE CHAPTER

This section covers the findings of documentation analysis by giving user interface and user experience results of Canvas, Blackboard, Moodle and Open edx after giving the research method. A general comparison of main features is also made. Some extra details of these e-learning platforms are also presented through their distinctive features and strengths.

Research Method

Document analysis can be implemented by either as a stand-alone study or a component of larger mixed method studies or qualitative studies (Gross, 2018). In general, document analysis is defined as a systematic procedure to be followed to review or evaluate the documents from sources such as printed, computer-based and internet-transmitted materials (Bowen, 2009). There are a variety of documents from advertisements to meeting minutes, manuals to diaries, books to newspapers, radio and television programs to maps and pictures. Whereas documentary analysis is stated as a part of larger studies, this method is also used as stand-alone. It is also less time-consuming that allows researchers to select rather than to collect data. Selection of the required data from the available sources also makes this method cost-effective. Documents, unlike other data, are stable and exact having no reaction that differs from a researcher to another researcher. However, they lack sufficient detail as secondary data are not collected for the same research purpose, and access to some kind of documents is difficult or sometimes impossible as they are blocked which might be top secret documents that authority ban them because of their contents (Bowen, 2009). This lack was aimed to be overcome by conducting SWOT analysis. While implementing SWOT analysis to see and identify the weaknesses and strengths of e-learning platforms and analyze the opportunities and threats, both researchers consider the distinctive features of each platform. In order to find the strength sides of the platform, the advantages, values and specifications that the others do not have are taken into account. While determining the weak sides of the platform, the features that the platform does not have while others have are considered as weaknesses. What the platforms offer for users and what features to be developed are seen as the opportunities. The obstacles, competing factors and changing user needs were thought as threats.

In this study, document analysis method, which involves skimming, reading and interpretation, was used to analyze documentary evidence and find answers to the research questions as a stand-alone research method. In the analysis process, even though coding, categorizing and interpretation can be used (Gross, 2018), only content and thematic analyses were used in accordance with the research questions (Bowen, 2009). In content analysis, the researchers tried to organize the gathered information into categories related to the main topics of the study. In thematic analysis, the researchers focused on re-reading and reviewing the data to emerge themes into categories to analyze and interpret data effectively.

In order to provide validity, two different coders who have had the expertise in the field for nearly a decade were asked to evaluate content through existing literature. In order to be sure about the consistency of the results, one coder made another coding after 2-3 months later. Firstly, all related studies were scanned from different databases, and then the collected literature was categorized according to their topics. Considering the previous findings of the existing literature and through the coders' experience, the e-learning platforms were evaluated according to different themes. The intercoder reliability was assured ensuring that the agreement on coded themes is 80%.

Findings From Documentation Analysis of Canvas, Blackboard, Moodle and Open edX

As a response to the first research question, this section aims to provide a general analysis and evaluation of Canvas, Blackboard, Moodle and open edX in terms of user interface and user experience.

User Interface (UI) and User Experience (UX)

UI/UX is a significant criterion for the successful implementation of any software, including an LMS. UI/UX of an LMS should be intuitive, simple and easy-to-use, so that learners and instructors will rapidly get used to the LMS. It is believed that one of the reasons for Canvas's success is its distinctive UI & UX. Therefore, this section is going to give information about the UI/UX of Canvas, Blackboard and Moodle, firstly about their homepages, and then their course homepages.

Canvas UI and UX

Canvas' homepage has a card-based design that is able to put images for the courses, and it includes the most important information for users: Enrolled courses, calendar, to-do activities and recent feedback. Users can also see the main menu and its subtitles: User Account, Dashboard, Courses, Calendar, Inbox (Messages), Commons, and Help. On the homepage of Canvas, one can easily see the enrolled courses, calendar, to-do list and recent feedback as separate titles.

Homepage of a Canvas course can be seen under the title of Module page, Syllabus, Course Activity Stream, Assignment list or any page designed by the user. It has (1) Course menu: Assignments, Quizzes, Forums/Discussions, Grades, Participants, Modules (teacher can disable any item in course menu); (2) Module page (where the activities and resources are arranged by weeks/chapters) that has a modern interface and look, and it also has features such as dragging & dropping to move items and it provides checklist to create an optimum Canvas course.

Blackboard UI and UX

In the Blackboard homepage, one can easily see (1) Main course menu and course management menu (2) Course tools: announcement, blogs, rubrics, wikis, etc. (3) Course-related items: course activities & materials, course management options, schedule, notifications, announcement, to-do, early warning system, etc. However, there are countless items in menus, everything is in one place so it serves a complicated UI, users need time to get used to UI and users cannot change the style of course homepage.

Moodle UI and UX

Moodle for its users presents the card-based design, in which each card represents a course in the homepage which is a simple and clear design. It also allows its users to modify the homepage and its menus according to the users' desires in its flexible structure. One can easily see (1) Main menu: All courses, calendar, User files, (2) Enrolled courses, (3) User navigation bar, and (4) Announcements, to-do list, etc.

Course homepage in Moodle contains the following items: (1) Course menu which has Participants, Grades, Resources and Pages. (2) Core menu. (3) User navigation bar (4) The contents of the course (course activities and resources are arranged as Modules). Moreover, the items of course homepage can also be changed.

Open edX UI and UX

Course page in Open edX platform consists of (1) main menu of course, (2) course activities and resources which are in an organized form (by chapters/ weeks), (3) Inside of a course activity.

Comparison of Main Features

The second research question deals with the difference of Canvas, Blackboard, Moodle and edX n terms of features. While comparing the features of these LMS platforms, such main features as instruction support, content development and management, administration support and some other features like 3rd party tool integration and their being free or commercial were considered within some detailed subsections. Table 2 shows their comparison of main features.

When looking at the table in general, it can be seen that there is no big difference among e-learning platforms in terms of features. They also utilize third part tools if they do not have a specific feature. For example, normally Moodle and Canvas do not have a plagiarism checking tool, but third-party tools can be easily integrated.

The third research question is about the strengths and weaknesses of the e-learning platforms, there the next two section with deal with it.

Strengths of Canvas

Simple UI

The biggest strength and distinctive feature of Canvas is its UI/UX. Compared to other LMS systems, Canvas has the simplest, easy-to-use and intrinsic UI/UX. Therefore, users (teachers & students) need

Table 2. Comparison of the features of Blackboard, Moodle, Canvas and Open edX

Features with Categories	Blackboard	Moodle	Canvas	Open edX
Instruction Support				
Course Development & Management				
Course and Subject Development	○	○	○	○
Course Construction & Time Mgmt.	○	○	○	○
Course announcement and information	○	○	○	○
Learning Management				
Learning Progress Check and Mgmt.	○	○	○	○
Learning Analytics	○	○	○	○
E-portfolio development and mgmt..	○	△(Third party)	○	x
Content provision according to learner level	○	△(Third party)	○	x
Evaluation & Grading				
Exam/Test Development and Mgmt.	○	○	○	○
Assignment Development and Mgmt.	○	○	○	○
Automatic Grading	○	○	○	○
Multimedia Feedback (text, audio, video)	x	x	○	x
Anonymous evaluation	○	○	○	x
Rubric Development	○	○	○	○
Plagiarism Checker	○	△(Third party	△(Third party	x
Self-assessment	○	x	x	○
Peer assessment	○	○	○	○
Communication				
Discussion Board / Forum	○	○	○	○
Voting and Survey	○	○	○	○
Real-time Chatting	○	○	○	x
e-mail & message	○	○	○	○
Collaborative Learning				
Group work (Wiki, Google Docs)	x	○	○	x
Team Project Support	○	○	○	○
Group & Learning Community Dev.	○	○	○	○
Content Development & Management				
Video Development & Management				
Video Creation and Development	○	○	○	△(Third party)
Video Speed Control & Section Move	△Section move possible	△Section move possible	△Section move possible	○
Video Resolution Control	x	x	x	○
Video Subtitle	○	○	○	○
Content Structure & Director Mgmt.	○	○	○	×
Video Database Build	○	○	○	×
Metadata Sharing	×	○	○	×
Learning Material Development & Management				
Various Learning Material Development	○	○	○	○
Various formatted material download	○	○	○	○
Material Database Build	○	○	○	○
Sharing to the out of platform	○	○	○	○
Administration Support				
User Management				
Add Contact Info	○	○	○	○
User Rights & Authorization Mgmt.	○	○	○	○
Certification Management				
Badge	○	○	○	○
Certification	○	○	○	○
Course Administration Support				
Alarms (Email, message, etc.)	○	○	○	○
Schedule Management (Calendar, etc.)	○	○	○	○
Announcement	○	○	○	○
Others				
3rd party tool integration	○	○	○	○
Free/Commercial	Commercial	Commercial /Free	Commercial/Free	Commercial/Free

less time to get used to it. Thus, even some users who might have difficulties in using technology are able to use Canvas.

Easy Integration With Third Party Tools

Canvas can be easily integrated with external tools such as YouTube, Turnitin, Twitter, MS OneNote, Wikipedia, Portfolium, OpenEd and Dropbox. Thus, it is possible to extend Canvas features. Canvas operates a website (see Eduappcenter, 2019) to introduce the external tools/platforms that can be integrated in Canvas. It gives detailed instructions/guidelines about how to integrate these tools within Canvas.

Some external tools: YouTube, Twitter, OpenEd, OneNote, One Drive, Portfolium (a portfolio tool), ALEKS (an adaptive learning platform), Turnitin (a plagiarism checker tool), Office Mix, OER Commons and BadgeStack (a badge tool).

The tools/platforms in Eduappcenter can be filtered by the followings:

- Categories: assessment, community, content, open content, plagiarism, free
- Grade levels: primary school, secondary school, university
- Platforms: Canvas, Blackboard, Moodle, Sakai
- Access: Open access, authenticated

Online Assignment Grading

Canvas provides various evaluation/feedback methods for the submitted assignments. A teacher can give feedback to students by using the following methods:

- Note taking on the paper
- Highlighting
- Annotations
- Strikeout
- Multimedia feedback (voice & video recording)
- File attachment
- Comment writing
- Rubrics

Global Share (Canvas Commons)

Canvas provides a global share environment called Commons. Users are able to share or utilize learning resources and activities which are developed by other Canvas users. Users can share learning resources and activities which they create by storing metadata and making copyright settings. Users can download other learning resources and activities and bring them to their own Canvas environment.

Users also can filter the contents in several ways:

- Content type: courses, modules, assignments, quizzes, discussions, pages, documents, videos, audios, images
- Institution type: Pre-school, Elementary school, High school, University, Graduate school

Learning Mastery

Learning Mastery feature enables to measure learners' performance based on classroom standards, or outcomes whose scores are tied to assignments and other items throughout Canvas. This feature is used especially for mastering learning. The aim is to make students master a specific skill in this feature. This system is especially used for elementary and high schools where there are national standards.

The method of learning mastery is shown in Figure 2.

Figure 2. Method of Learning Mastery

Social Media Integration

Canvas can be integrated with various social media platforms such as Twitter. With Twitter integration into Canvas, you can connect with your own Twitter account to:

- get course notifications,
- display your Twitter feeds in Canvas,
- follow others' tweets,
- follow specific hashtags, and
- follow a group on Twitter accounts (e.g.: your students' tweets)

Built-In Video Recording

Users can record video or audio with Canvas without using any other external tool and upload it to anyplace in Canvas. Thus, users can use their recorded videos and audios as course materials or feedback for assignments.

Strengths of Blackboard

Retention Center

One of the most distinctive features of Blackboard is Retention Center, which is a learning analytics tool. With the Retention Center, you can detect the students who are at-risk of failing the course. This means that if there is a student who studies less than the expected and will fail if she/he continues to study like this, the Retention Center detects him/her early and notify the instructor. Thus, the instructor can find out the student who falls behind the class and sends a message/warning/notification to them. The system categorizes students who are at risk based on four factors: missed deadlines, grades, course activity and course access data.

Blackboard Collaborate

Another strength of Blackboard is its video conferencing tool. Blackboard has a great powerful video conferencing tool named Collaborate. Collaborate has the all required features for an online learning environment. Blackboard sells this Collaborate platform separately.

Strengths of Moodle

Free and Open-Source Platform

Moodle is free and open source. Therefore, anyone can use it. Since Moodle is one of the oldest platforms of LMS, it has a very big global community. This community develops and provides various additional features in plug-in form for free or premium to the Moodle users all over the world. Anyone can search and download Moodle plugins in the Moodle plugin page (see Moodle, 2020a).

Having a Huge Global Community

Moodle is the most used LMS in the world and has a huge global community. This community not only develops new features, but also provides additional help and guidance on the technical and other issues related to Moodle. Moodle has a seperate website for this community (see Moodle, 2020b).

Strengths of Open edX

edX Insights

edx Insights is a comprehensive analytics tool developed for open edX. It allows computing and displaying detailed and visual representation of the learners population, its level of engagement, and its performance, both aggregated per course and also per learner. In other words, edX Insights enables to view video data of learners, enrollment numbers and activities, weekly engagement data of learners and demographic and geographic information of learners.

Open-Source and Expandability

Open edX platform is completely open source and has a wide community of contributors consisting of developers, research teams, users, and other partners. Since it is open-source, anyone can change or modify its code. Also, open edX platform contains XBlocks allowing users to easily add new features to customize open edX according to the needs.

Modern User Interface

Open edX has a modern, intuitive user interface for users. This allows users to learn the system quickly and use it efficiently. Thus, learners do not have to spend time on learning the system itself and focus on just learning.

SWOT Analysis

SWOT analysis is a strategic planning technique to determine the strengths, weakness, opportunities and threats related to the project planning. This section provides SWOT analysis results for the e-learning platforms in order to answer the third research question. Data will be given in tables for each e-learning platform.

SWOT for Canvas

Table 3 presents SWOT analysis for Canvas along with its strengths and weaknesses.

Table 3. SWOT analysis for Canvas

Strengths	Weakness
● Simple, modern & intuitive User Interface ● Easy-to-use ● High usability ● Great features such as social media and built-in video recorder features ● Compatible for both offline and online learning ● Need less work to modify for ● Extendable in terms of features	
Opportunities	**Threat**
● Increase number of users registered to the e-learning platform ● Promote learning opportunities & activities online ● Increase the time spent by users on the e-learning platform	● Need a software engineer specialized on Ruby on Rail to modify Canvas

SWOT for Blackboard

Table 4 presents SWOT analysis for Blackboard including its strengths and weaknesses.

Table 4. SWOT analysis for Blackboard

Strengths	Weakness
● Tenured leadership in LMS market ● Cloud-based ● Equipped with pre-configured analytics software allowing teachers to track students' activities. ● Effective video-conferencing tool	● Commercial product (high cost) ● Not possible to integrate with the external tools by the user ● User dissatisfaction on user interface and usability ● Not customizable to create a personal learning environment
Opportunities	**Threat**
● Longevity in the e-learning environment ● Growing international customers	● High switching costs for prospective clients ● Competition from open-source products ● Slow to respond to changing learners' needs

SWOT for edX

Table 5 demonstrates SWOT analysis for edX considering its strengths and weaknesses.

Table 5. SWOT analysis for edX

Strengths	Weakness
● Simple & modern User Interface ● Best suitable for 100% online learning ● Restrict user actions on an online course ● Need less work to modify to match with the requirements	● Having less features comparing to other platforms
Opportunities	**Threat**
● Increase time spent by users on the e-learning platform	● Need a software engineer specialized in PHP and Django.

SWOT for Moodle

Table 6 shows SWOT analysis for Moodle stating its strengths and weaknesses.

Table 6. SWOT analysis for Moodle

Strengths	Weakness
● Simple User Interface ● Easy-to-use ● Provide a variety of features ● Compatible for both offline and online learning ● Extendable in terms of features ● Having a huge global community to solve problems/issues, develop new features and make updates	● Old-style user interface
Opportunities	**Threat**
● Promote learning opportunities & activities online	● Decrease of the number of users within time due to its old-style User Interface ● Need a software engineer specialized on PHP ● Need a great work to modify for

SOLUTIONS AND RECOMMENDATIONS

The study in this chapter has analyzed popular e-learning platforms including Canvas, Moodle, Blackboard and Open edX in terms of features and user interface. Our analysis relieved that LMS systems show similarities in terms of functionality though there are some differences with respect to UI/UX and system extendibility.

Function Issue

Now is the peak point for e-learning platforms in terms of functions. All of the platforms analyzed in this study have basic e-learning functions including course development and management, content development and provision, learning progress check, grading and evaluation tools such as quiz and assignment, discussion forum and certification/badge management. Besides, it is not a big deal to develop a feature/function if an e-learning platform does not have it. Another way to acquire a new feature/function for an e-learning platform is to utilize third party tools (external tools). Many e-learning platforms can be integrated with third party tools so that they are able to improve their abilities. For instance, when you integrate Canvas with Microsoft OneNote, you will be able to do all OneNote activities in your Canvas LMS. You can also integrate with YouTube so that you will easily bring all YouTube videos into your Canvas LMS environment. Then, if all e-learning platforms have similar features or are able to acquire new features easily, what makes e-learning platforms different from each other?

UI/UX Issue

One crucial distinction of e-learning systems is user interface (UI) and user experience (UX). E-learning platforms should provide effective UI/UX for users, since these platforms are software and UI/UX design has an impact on the use of a software. Then, what is the effective UI/UX for e-learning platforms? This study recommends examining Canvas to answer this question because Canvas's UI/UX gets praise from all users including students and teachers. Many case studies evaluating e-learning platforms show that even if Canvas has similar features to Moodle and Blackboard, one main reason that universities selecting Canvas is its modern, simple and intuitive UI and its great UX. Such universities are Missouri University of Science and Technology (Cudney et al., 2017), University of Washington (Fournier et al., 2017), California State University Stanislaus (Pillsbury, 2019), Indiana University (Pionte & Morrone, 2013). Since Canvas provides an easy use platform, the users who have the first experience using Canvas for the first time can get used to Canvas in a short time when compared to other platforms. This provides users not to waste time on learning the e-learning platform itself. Therefore, e-learning platforms should provide modern, simple, easy-to-use, intuitive UI/UX to the users.

New Requirements

Recently, new requirements have emerged for future e-learning platforms. Future-oriented e-learning platforms should also consider social media integration, interaction among stakeholders and interoperability and personalization.

In this post-modern, technology-oriented century, social media has become one of the most indispensable parts of our daily lives and there are various studies revealing the positive effect of social media on learning performance and motivation. Thanks to social media, formal learning can be extended with informal and non-formal learning environments, where learners are the owners of their learning. Therefore, any e-learning platform should be linked with social media platforms such as Facebook and Twitter. There are such platforms, such as Canvas. Canvas can be integrated with Twitter. With Twitter integration into Canvas, you can 1) connect with your own Twitter account in order to get course notifications and display your Twitter feeds in Canvas, follow others' tweets, follow specific hashtags and, follow a group of Twitter accounts (e.g.: your students' tweets).

Another requirement is to promote interaction among stakeholders. There are various studies proving the positive impact of interaction on learning performance (Sher, 2009; Zimmerman, 2012). Interaction in a learning environment occurs in three ways: 1) Interaction between student-student; 2) Interaction between student-teach; 3) Interaction between student-content (Moore, 1993). Many e-learning platforms have tools to support interaction. However, these tools/features need to be improved. An e-learning platform can promote interaction in the following ways. To promote student-student and student-teacher interaction, it should provide discussion forums, chatting, messaging & mailing tools as well as integration with Social Media such as Facebook and Twitter. To support student-content interaction, an e-learning platform should not only enable to share contents like videos, audios, images and files like WORD, PDF, PPT and XLS, but also provide advanced video-based learning environments. Such video-watching environments might have the following features: personal/public memo, personal/public bookmark, section highlighting, commenting at a specific time, putting quizzes/texts into videos, and so on (Kim et al., 2014; Kleftodimos & Evangelidis, 2016; Chatti et al., 2016). Thus, learners will be able to utilize much more interactive videos by enabling interaction not only between learner and learner, but also between learner and instructor in a content-based learning environment. There are some popular platforms like Vizia (see Vizia, 2020), Playplosit (see Playposit, 2020) and Edpuzzle (see Edpuzzle, 2020) enabling to integrate quizzes/texts/pools with videos. Besides, some of these tools can be integrated with e-learning platforms such as Moodle and Canvas.

Another significant requirement for the future e-learning platforms is interoperability and personalization, as mentioned by an EDUCAUSE report (Brown et al., 2015). Modern e-learning platforms do not have to do all things and even it is quite difficult to accomplish it. It might be enough if an e-learning platform has a technological environment enabling to integrate with external tools which are already perfect and various to enhance the capability of e-learning platforms.

External tools can bring different features/tools that are new or advanced ones into an e-learning platform, as we download a chatting app from an app store even if the smartphone has the same function itself. Moreover, external tools can bring various content providers such as YouTube, Vimeo and OER sources into e-learning platforms.

Another advantage of external tool integration is to enable personalization for the institute, course or users. By integrating the same e-learning platform with different external tools, it is available to create completely different learning environments for a specific educational institution, course, and a teacher. LMS companies already provide information about what external tools can be integrated with themselves. Canvas operates Eduappcenter website to provide the list of external tools/websites integrated with Canvas LMS along with the guidelines on how to integrate. Similarly, Moodle has a website presenting external tool directory.

FUTURE RESEARCH DIRECTIONS AND LIMITATIONS OF THE STUDY

This study evaluated e-learning platforms embracing only a document analysis method. Further studies can implement other data collection tools and research methods such as surveys, interviews and focus groups in order to evaluate e-learning platforms. Another limitation of this research is that it focused on only 4 e-learning platforms due to their popularity worldwide. There are other platforms which might have unique features and characteristics needed to get attention. Therefore, the future studies can focus on the other e-learning platforms such as Desire2Learn and Sakai. A further study can also look at users' actions in e-learning platforms by interviewing and observing them, which can contribute to the related field, the strengths and weaknesses of e-learning platforms in terms of the users' experiences.

CONCLUSION

This study has analyzed and compared four mostly used e-learning platforms including Canvas, Moodle, Blackboard and open edX. All these systems have similar functions like course development and management, learning management, evaluation and assessment, communication and collaboration, content development and management and administration support tools. However, there are some differences with respect to use purpose, availability, UI/UX and extendibility. First, in terms of use purpose, open edX shows notable differences than the others. While open edX is suitable only for 100% online learning, other platforms are adaptable not only for online learning but also for offline and blended learning environments. Another visible difference is that Canvas, Moodle and open edX are open source, whereas Blackboard is a paid product. With respect to UI/UX, Canvas provides much more simple, modern and intuitive user interface, and has a higher usability, which makes Canvas superior to other systems and top in the US. LMS market. One of the considerable reasons for universities for choosing Canvas as their LMS system is its high usability and effective UI/UX. Lastly, since Canvas, Moodle and open edX are open-source, these platforms can be extended in terms of functionality by integrating with external tools or plugins according to the user needs. While Moodle has a huge global community developing new plugins for Moodle, Canvas has a website providing free information and paid external/third party tools that can be integrated with Canvas LMS.

REFERENCES

Abdullateef, B. N., Elias, N., Mohamed, H., Zaidan, A., & Zaidan, B. (2016). An evaluation and selection problems. *SpringerPlus*, *5*(248), 2–35. doi:10.118640064-016-1828-y PMID:27064567

Ajlan, S. (2012). A Comparative Study Between E-Learning Features, Methodologies, Tools and New Developments for E-Learning. *InTech*. Available from: https://www.intechopen.com/books/methodologies-tools-and-new-developments-for-e-learning/a-comparativestudy-between-e-learning-features

Al-Ajlan, A., & Zedan, H. (2008). Why Moodle. In *12th IEEE International Workshop on Future Trends of Distributed Computing Systems* (pp. 58-64). Kunming, China: IEEE. 10.1109/FTDCS.2008.22

Bowen, G. A. (2009). Document analysis as a qualitative research method. *Qualitative Research Journal*, *9*(2), 27–40. doi:10.3316/QRJ0902027

Brown, M., Dehoney, J., & Millichap, N. (2015). *The next generation digital learning environment. A Report on Research. ELI Paper*. Louisville, CO: Educause April.

Cavus, N. (2010). The evaluation of learning management systems using an artificial intelligence fuzzy logic algorithm. *Advances in Engineering Software*, *41*(2), 248–254. doi:10.1016/j.advengsoft.2009.07.009

Cavus, N. (2011). The application of a multi-attribute decision-making algorithm to learning management systems evaluation. *British Journal of Educational Technology*, *42*(1), 19–30. doi:10.1111/j.1467-8535.2009.01033.x

Chatti, M. A., Marinov, M., Sabov, O., Laksono, R., Sofyan, Z., Yousef, A. M. F., & Schroeder, U. (2016). Video annotation and analytics in CourseMapper. *Smart Learning Environments*, *3*(1), 1–21. doi:10.118640561-016-0035-1

Cudney, E. A., Murray, S. L., Groner, B., & Kaczmarek, K. M. (2017). Using the Voice of the Student to Evaluate Learning Management Systems. In *Proceedings of the 2017 ASEE Annual Conference & Exposition*. American Society for Engineering Education. 10.18260/1-2--29091

Edpuzzle. (2020). Retrieved from www.edpuzzle.com

Eduappcenter. (2019). Retrieved from www.eduappcenter.com

Edutechnica. (2020). *LMS Data- Spring 2020.* Retrieved from https://edutechnica.com/

Fitzgerald, T. (2007). Documents and documentary analysis: Reading between the lines. In A. R. Briggs & M. Coleman (Eds.), *Research methods in educational leadership and management* (2nd ed., pp. 278–294). Thousand Oaks, CA: Sage.

Ford, M. (2015). *Rise of the Robots: Technology and the Threat of a Jobless Future*. New York: Basic Books.

Fournier, J., Cruz, S., & Roberts, K. (2017). *Canvas 2017: Evaluation Report.* Retrieved from https://itconnect.uw.edu/wp-content/uploads/2018/07/Canvas2017EvaluationReport.pdf

Gross, J. M. (2018). *Document Analysis. In The SAGE Encyclopedia of Educational Research, Measurement, and Evaluation* (pp. 545–548). Thousand Oaks: SAGE Publications, Inc.

Hill, P. (2017). *Academic LMS market share: A view across four global regions*. Retrieved from https://eliterate.us/academic-lms-market-share-view-across-four-global-regions/

Jadhav, A. S., & Sonar, R. M. (2011). Framework for evaluation and selection of the software packages: A hybrid knowledge based system approach. *Journal of Systems and Software*, *84*(8), 1394–1407. doi:10.1016/j.jss.2011.03.034

Kim, J., Guo, P. J., Cai, C. J., Li, S. W., Gajos, K. Z., & Miller, R. C. (2014, October). Data-driven interaction techniques for improving navigation of educational videos. In *Proceedings of the 27th annual ACM symposium on User interface software and technology* (pp. 563-572). 10.1145/2642918.2647389

Kleftodimos, A., & Evangelidis, G. (2016). Using open source technologies and open internet resources for building an interactive video based learning environment that supports learning analytics. *Smart Learning Environments*, *3*(9), 1–23. doi:10.118640561-016-0032-4

Lim, C., Han, H., Jung, D., Ozturk, Y. E., Hong, J., Kim, K., & Kwon, H. (2017). Exploring an e-learning platform prototype for supporting learning design. *Journal of Educational Technology*, *33*(4), 799–837. doi:10.17232/KSET.33.4.799

Lin, H.-Y., Hsu, P.-Y., & Sheen, G.-J. (2007). A fuzzy-based decision-making procedure for data warehouse system selection. *Expert Systems with Applications*, *32*(3), 939–953. doi:10.1016/j.eswa.2006.01.031

Moodle. (2020a). Retrieved from https://moodle.org/plugins/

Moodle. (2020b). Retrieved from https://moodle.com/community/

Moore, M. G. (1993). Three types of interaction. In K. Harry, M. Hohn, & D. Keegan (Eds.), *Distance education: New perspectives* (pp. 12–24). London: Routledge.

Pecheanu, E., Stefanescu, D., Dumitriu, L., & Segal, C. (2011). Methods to evaluate open source learning platforms. In *Proceedings of Global Engineering Education Conference (EDUCON)*, 2011 *IEEE* (pp. 1152-1161). IEEE. 10.1109/EDUCON.2011.5773292

Pillsbury, G. (2019). *2018-19 LMS Evaluation - Phase II, Part 1: Canvas.* Retrieved from https://www.csustan.edu/sites/default/files/groups/Office%20of%20Information%20Technology/documents/2018_canvas_evaluation_summary.pdf

Piontek, M., & Morrone, A. (2013). *Evaluation of the Pilot of the Canvas Learning Management System Implemented in Academic Year 2012-2013.* Retrieved from https://assets.uits.iu.edu/pdf/Faculty%20and%20Student%20Evaluation%20of%20Instructure%20Canvas.pdf

Playposit. (2020). Retrieved from www.playposit.com

Ramesh, V. M., & Ramanathan, C. (2013). A rubric to Evaluate Learning Management Systems. In Proceedings of Teaching, Assessment and Learning for Engineering (TALE), 2013 IEEE (pp. 73-77). IEEE. doi:10.1109/TALE.2013.6654402

Scalter, N. (2008, June 24). Web 2.0, Personal Learning Environments, and the Future of Learning Management Systems. *Educause Center for Applied Research Bulletin*, *2008*(13), 2–13.

Shah, D. (2018). *By the numbers: MOOCs in 2018.* Retrieved from https://www.classcentral.com/report/mooc-stats-2018/

Vizia. (2020). Retrieved from www.vizia.co

Zimmerman, T. D. (2012). Exploring learner to content interaction as a success factor in online courses. *The International Review of Research in Open and Distributed Learning*, *13*(4), 152–165. doi:10.19173/irrodl.v13i4.1302

ADDITIONAL READING

Andergassen, M., Ernst, G., Guerra, V., Mödritscher, F., Moser, M., Neumann, G., & Renner, T. (2015). *The evolution of e-learning platforms from content to activity based learning.* In *Proceedings of 2015 International Conference on Interactive Collaborative Learning (ICL)*, IEEE (pp. 779-784). Florence, Italy. 10.1109/ICL.2015.7318127

Ellis, R. K. (2009). *Field Guide to Learning Management Systems. Alexandria*. VA: American Society for Training & Development.

Gañán, D., Caballé, S., Clarisó, R., & Conesa, J. (2016). *Evaluation of an e-learning platform featuring learning analytics and gamification*. In Proceedings of International Conference on P2P, Parallel, Grid, Cloud and Internet Computing (pp. 947-959). Springer International Publishing.

Garmendía, A., & Cobos, R. (2013). *Towards the extension of a LMS with Social Media services*. In Y. Luo (Ed.) *International Conference on Cooperative Design, Visualization and Engineering* (pp. 67-72). Springer, Berlin, Heidelberg. 10.1007/978-3-642-40840-3_11

Hill, P. (2017). *State of higher Ed LMS market for US and Canada: Spring 2017 edition*. Retrieved from http://mfeldstein.com/state-higher-ed-lms-market-us-canada-spring-2017-edition/

Ho, W. S., Ng, A., Leung, K., Wang, F. L., & Wong, L. P. (2015). A teachers' survey on the effectiveness of e-learning platform in a higher education institution. In *proceedings of International Conference on Technology in Education* (pp. 284-291). Springer, Berlin, Heidelberg 10.1007/978-3-662-48978-9_26

KEY TERMS AND DEFINITIONS

E-Learning: It is web-based training, learning, and information management activities carried out through internet technologies. E-learning makes life easier for institutions and employees. It facilitates the internal training processes of the institutions and supports the dynamic corporate culture.

Learning Management Systems (LMS): A learning management system (LMS) is a computer software providing management of a distance education system, documentation and reporting processes, educator-student, student-student communication, publishing of course content and remote assessment evaluation functions.

Learning Mastery: Learning Mastery feature enables to measure learners' performance based on classroom standards or outcomes. The method of learning master includes outcomes, rubrics, assignments, and grades.

Massive Open Online Course (MOOC): It is a result of the openness movement, which has emerged as an extension of the distance education approach, offered to lifelong learners in a pedagogical context. "Massive" represents the number of people who can take the lesson at the same time may be more than usual and the diversity; The word "open" means the removal of obstacles to access to learning, the word "online" means the learning approach based on computer networks, and the word "course" means the teaching content to be given with a specific pedagogical approach.

Third Party Tools: These are the tools of an e-learning that help users indirectly to operate or use the systems. Users can bring materials outside such as video, quiz, textbooks, e-books, assignments, etc. and bring new features outside such as Google Docs, Facebook, Twitter, Office Mix etc.

User Experience (UX): UX expresses the feelings and behaviors of people when using a product, system or service. It covers the practical, experimental, affective, meaningful and valuable aspects of human-computer interaction.

User Interface (UI): It is the name given to the combination of methods that enable people to interact with a machine, device, computer program or complex tools. The user interface makes it possible for users to change the operation of systems (input) and its results (output).

Compilation of References

Abdelaziz, A. (2018). *Developing Employability and Job-Related Skills at Mobile Learning Environments: a case study at an industrial training centre*. Lancaster: Lancaster University.

Abdous, M., Camarena, M. M., & Facer, B. R. (2009). MALL Technology: Use of Academic Podcasting in the Foreign Language Classroom. *ReCALL, 21*(1), 76–95. doi:10.1017/S0958344009000020

Abdullah, S. A., Yaakub, A., & Wahil, Z. (2015). Evaluating Students ' Need in Using Computer Aided Software in Landscape Design Course. *Procedia: Social and Behavioral Sciences, 195*, 828–836. doi:10.1016/j.sbspro.2015.06.188

Abdullateef, B. N., Elias, N., Mohamed, H., Zaidan, A., & Zaidan, B. (2016). An evaluation and selection problems. *SpringerPlus, 5*(248), 2–35. doi:10.118640064-016-1828-y PMID:27064567

Abdul-Razak, Z. N. (2000). *Motivational Factors and Learners' Strategies in the English as a Second Language Classroom at Universiti Technology Malaysia with Special Reference to Computer Assisted Language Learning* (Unpublished PhD thesis). University of Stirling.

Abu-Al-Aish, A. (2014). *Toward mobile learning deployment in higher education* (Doctoral dissertation). Brunel University, School of Information Systems, Computing and Mathematics.

Abyaa, A., Khalidi, M., & Bennani, S. (2019). Learner modelling : Systematic review of the literature from the last 5 years. *Educational Technology Research and Development, 67*(5), 1–39. doi:10.1007/s11423-018-09644-1

Adewole, D. W., & Frank, L. P. (2013). Effects of computer managed instruction and traditional on students' academic performance in higher education. *Journal of Computer Assisted Learning, 29*(3), 220–234.

Adlnet. (n.d.). Advanced Distributed Learning. *SCORM*. Retrieved November 8, 2012, from https://www.adlnet.gov/capabilities/scorm

Afrin, S. (2016). Writing Problems of Non-English Major Undergraduate Students in Bangladesh: An Observation. Open Journal of Social Sciences, 4(3), 104–115. doi:10.4236/jss.2016.43016

Agustin-Llach, M. P., & Jiménez-Catalán, R. M. (2018). Teasing out the role of age and exposure in EFL learners' lexical profiles: A comparison of children and adults. *International Review of Applied Linguistics in Language Teaching, 56*(1), 25–43. doi:10.1515/iral-2015-0075

Ahmad, J. (2016). Technology assisted Language learning is a silver bullet for enhancing language competence and performance : A case study. *International Journal of Applied Linguistics and English Literature, 5*(7), 118–113. doi:10.7575/aiac.ijalel.v.5n.7p.118

Ahmed, R., Al-kadi, A., & Hagar, T. (2020). Preface. In A. Rashad, A. Al-kadi, & T. Hagar (Eds.), *Enhancements and limitations to ICT-based informal language learning: Emerging research and opportunities* (pp. xii–xx). Hershey, PA: IGI Global. doi:10.4018/978-1-7998-2116-8

AJE. (2019). Available online: https://www.aje.com/

Ajlan, S. (2012). A Comparative Study Between E-Learning Features, Methodologies, Tools and New Developments for E-Learning. *InTech.* Available from: https://www.intechopen.com/books/methodologies-tools-and-new-developments-for-e-learning/a-comparativestudy-between-e-learning-features

Al Kaboody, M. (2013). Second language motivation; the role of teachers in learners' motivation. *Journal of Academic and Applied Studies*, *3*(4), 45–54.

Al-Ahdal, A. A. M. H. (2013). Integration of information and communication technology (ICT) into the education system of Yemen: The need of the hour. *International Journal of Social Sciences & Education*, *3*(1), 40–47.

Al-Ajlan, A., & Zedan, H. (2008). Why Moodle. In *12th IEEE International Workshop on Future Trends of Distributed Computing Systems* (pp. 58-64). Kunming, China: IEEE. 10.1109/FTDCS.2008.22

Albacete, P. L., & Vanlehn, K. A. (2000). Evaluating the Effectiveness of a Cognitive Tutor for Fundamental Physics Concepts. *Annual Meeting of the Cognitive Science Society.*

Albirini, A. (2006). Teachers' attitudes toward information and communication technologies: The case of Syrian EFL teachers. *Computers & Education*, *47*(4), 373–398. doi:10.1016/j.compedu.2004.10.013

Al-Buainain, H. (2010). Language learning strategies employed by English majors at Qatar University: Questions and queries. *ASIATIC*, *4*(2), 92–120.

Al-Busaidi, K.A. & Al-Shihi, H. (2010). Instructors' Acceptance of Learning Management Systems: A Theoretical Framework. *Communications of the IBIMA*, 1-10. doi:10.5171/2010.862128

Al-Fahad, F. N. (2009). Students' attitudes and perceptions towards the effectiveness of mobile learning in King Saud University. Academic Press.

Alhaisoni, E. (2017). Language learning strategy use of Saudi EFL students in an intensive English learning context. *Asian Social Science*, *8*(13), 115–127. doi:10.5539/ass.v8n13p115

Alhaysony, M. (2017). Language learning strategies use by Saudi EFL students: The effect of duration of English language study and gender. *Theory and Practice in Language Studies*, *7*(1), 18–28. doi:10.17507/tpls.0701.03

Al-Hazmi, S. (2003). EFL teacher preparation programs in Saudi Arabia: Trends and challenges. *TESOL Quarterly*, *37*(2), 341–344. doi:10.2307/3588509

Ali, J.K.M., & Bin-Hady, W. R. A. (2019). A study of EFL students' attitudes, motivation and anxiety towards WhatsApp as a language learning tool. *Arab World English Journal,* (5), 289-298. Doi:10.24093/awej/call5.19

Ali, S. (2016). Towards the development of a comprehensive pedagogical framework for pronunciation training based on adapted automatic speech recognition systems. In S. Papadima-Sophocleous, L. Bradley & S. Thouësny (Eds.), CALL communities and culture – short papers from EUROCALL 2016 (pp. 7-13). Research-publishing.net. doi:10.14705/rpnet.2016.eurocall2016.530

Aljuaid, H. (2010). Language learning strategies: Perceptions of female Saudi EFL learners. In *Papers from the Lancaster University Postgraduate Conference in Linguistics & Language Teaching, 2010*, 2–24.

Al-Kadi, A. (2018). Towards humanizing ELT: Revisiting the need for English in the medical context in Yemen. *Eric database* (ERIC Number: ED591138).

Alkahtani, M., Ahmad, A., Darmoul, S., Samman, S., Al-zabidi, A., & Matraf, K. B. (2016). Multitasking Trends and Impact on Education: A Literature Review. *World Academy of Science. Engineering and Technology International Journal of Educational and Pedagogical Sciences, 10*(3), 1006–1012.

Allan, B. (2007). *Blended Learning tools for teaching and training*. London: Facet Publishing. doi:10.29085/9781856047845

Al-Maktary, H. (2018). A cross-sectional study of oral communication strategies by successful EFL learners. *International Journal of Foreign Language Teaching & Research, 6*(24), 23–37. http://jfl.iaun.ac.ir/article_611572.html

Almerich, G., Orellana, N., Rodríguez, J., & García, I. (2016). Teachers' information and communication technology competences: A structural approach. *Computers & Education, 100*, 110–125. doi:10.1016/j.compedu.2016.05.002

Almohammadi, K., Hagras, H., Alghazzawi, D., & Aldabbagh, G. (2016). Users-Centric Adaptive Learning System Based On Interval Type-2 Fuzzy Logic For Massively Crowded E-Learning Platforms. *Journal of Artificial Intelligence and Soft Computing Research, 6*(2), 81–101. doi:10.1515/jaiscr-2016-0008

Alobaidi, O. G., Smieee, K. A. C., Mieee, J. D. O. S., & Jarad, T. M. (2013). Abdullah : An Intelligent Arabic Conversational Tutoring System for Modern Islamic Education. In *Proceedings of the World Congress on Engineering* (Vol. 2). London, UK: Academic Press.

Al-Qahtani, A., & Higgins, S. (2013). Effects of traditional, blended and e-learning on students' achievement in higher education. *Journal of Computer Assisted Learning, 29*(3), 220–234. doi:10.1111/j.1365-2729.2012.00490.x

Alqasham, F. H. (2018). Exploring Saudi EFL learners' agency toward the use of WhatsApp for English learning at Qassim University. *International Journal of Linguistics, 10*(6), 10–43. doi:10.5296/ijl.v10i6.13857

Alsamadani, H. A. (2017). The Effectiveness of Using Online Blogging for Students' Individual and Group Writing. *International Education Studies, 11*(1), 44. doi:10.5539/ies.v11n1p44

Al-Shammari, M. H. (2007). *Turkish English as a Foreign Language: Learners' Attitudes toward Computer Assisted Language Learning* (Unpublished PhD thesis). West Virginia University.

Al-Sohbani, Y. A. Y. (2016). An investigation of the reasons behind the weaknesses in English among public secondary school leavers. *Journal of Teaching and Teacher Education, 4*(2), 41-51.

Altaboli, A., & Lin, Y. (2011). Investigating Effects of Screen Layout Elements on Interface and Screen Design Aesthetics. Advances in Human-Computer Interaction, 2011(5), 1–10. doi:10.1155/2011/659758

Altanopoulou, P., Tselios, N., Katsanos, C., & Georgoutsou, M. (2015). Wiki-Mediated Activities in Higher Education: Evidence-Based Analysis of Learning Effectiveness Across Three Studies. *Journal of Educational Technology & Society, 18*(4), 511–522.

Altanopoulou, P., Tselios, N., Katsanos, C., Georgoutsou, M., & Panagiotaki, M. (2015). Wiki-Mediated Activities in Higher Education. *Evidence-Based Analysis of Learning Effectiveness Across Three Studies, 18*, 511–522.

Altınyelken, H. K. (2010). Pedagogical renewal in sub-Saharan Africa: The case of Uganda. *Comparative Education, 46*(2), 151–171. doi:10.1080/03050061003775454

Alzubi, A. A. F. (2019). *The effects of smartphones mediated language learning strategies on the learner autonomy of Saudi Arabian undergraduates* (Unpublished Ph.D. thesis). Universiti Sains Malaysia.

Alzubi, A. A. F., & Singh, M. K. M. (2017). The use of language learning strategies through smartphones in improving learner autonomy in EFL reading among undergraduates in Saudi Arabia. *International Journal of English Linguistics, 7*(6), 59–72. doi:10.5539/ijel.v7n6p59

Andrew, E. W. (2015). Computer managed instruction: Effect for tomorrow learning platform. *Journal of Learning and Technology, 27*(3), 28–39.

Angeli, C., & Valanides, N. (2009). Epistemological and methodological issues for the conceptualization, development, and assessment of ICT-TPCK: Advances in technological pedagogical content knowledge (TPCK). *Computers & Education, 52*(1), 154–168. doi:10.1016/j.compedu.2008.07.006

Appana, S. (2008). A Review of Benefits and Limitations of Online Learning in the Context of the Student, the Instructor, and the Tenured Faculty. *International Journal on E-Learning, 7*(1), 5–22.

Ardito, C., Costabile, M. F., De Marsico, M., Lanzilotti, R., Levialdi, S., Roselli, T., & Rossano, V. (2005). An approach to usability evaluation of e-learning applications. *Universal Access in the Information Society, 4*(3), 270–283. doi:10.100710209-005-0008-6

Arnal, J., Rincón, D., & Latorre, A. (1994). *Investigación educativa. Fundamentos y metodología.* Barcelona: Labor.

Arslan, M., & Akbarov, A. (2010). Türkiye'de yabancı dil öğretiminde motivasyon - yöntem sorunu ve çözüm önerileri. *Selçuk Üniversitesi Edebiyat Fakültesi Dergisi, 24*, 179–191.

Arteaga, R., & Duarte, A. (2010). Motivational factors that influence the acceptance of Moodle using TAM. *Computers in Human Behavior, 26*(6), 1632–1640. doi:10.1016/j.chb.2010.06.011

Aryadoust, V., & Riazi, M. (2017). Role of assessment in second language writing research and pedagogy. *Educational Psychology, 37*(1), 1–7. doi:10.1080/01443410.2016.1227089

Ary, D., Jacobs, L., & Razavieh, A. (2010). *Introduction to research in education.* New York: Holt, Rinehart and Winston.

Asbhy, M. (2008). New directions in learning teaching and assessment for phonetics. *Estudios de Fonética Experimental, 17*, 17-44.

Ashworth, P., & Lucas, U. (2000). Achieving Empathy and Engagement: A practical approach to the design, conduct and reporting of phenomenographic research. *Studies in Higher Education, 25*(3), 295–308. doi:10.1080/713696153

Atay, D. (2004). İngilizce öğretmenlerinin motivasyon stratejileri. *HAYEF: Journal of Education, 1*(1), 99–108.

Attali, Y., & Burstein, J. (2006). Automated essay scoring with e-rater V. 2. *The Journal of Technology, Learning, and Assessment, 4*. Retrieved from http://www.jtla.org

Augar, N., Raitman, R., & Zhou, W. (2006). Wikis: Collaborative Virtual Learning Environments. In *The International Handbook of Virtual Learning Environments* (pp. 1251–1269). doi:10.1007/978-1-4020-3803-7_52

Bacanak, A., Karamustafaoğlu, O., & Köse, S. (2003). Yeni bir bakış: Eğitimde teknoloji okuryazarlığı. *Pamukkale Üniversitesi Eğitim Fakültesi Dergisi, 14*(14), 191–196.

Bada, T., Adewole, A., & Olalekan, O. (2009). Uses of computer and its relevance to teaching and learning in Nigerian educational system. *Educational Research Review, 4*(10), 443–447.

Bai, L., & Hu, G. (2017). In the face of fallible AWE feedback: How do students respond? *Educational Psychology, 37*(1), 67–81. doi:10.1080/01443410.2016.1223275

Baker, J., & Gossman, P. (2013). The learning impact of a virtual learning environment: Students' views. *Teacher Education Advancement Network Journal, 5*(2), 19–38.

Balçıkanlı, C. (2010). Learner Autonomy in Language Learning: Student Teachers' Beliefs. *The Australian Journal of Teacher Education, 35*(1). doi:10.14221/ajte.2010v35n1.8

Baleni, Z. (2015). Online formative assessment in higher education: Its pros and cons. *The Electronic Journal of e-Learning, 13*(4), 228-236.

Barker, A., Krull, G., & Mallinson, B. (2005). A proposed theoretical model for m-learning adoption in developing countries. Proceedings of mLearn, 2005(4), 1-10.

Barron, A. E. (2003). Course management systems and online teaching. *Journal of Computing in Higher Education, 15*(1), 128–142. doi:10.1007/BF02940856

Bartolí, M. (2005). La pronunciación en la clase de lenguas extranjeras. *Phonica, 1*, 1–27.

Bates, A. W. (2019). *Teaching in a Digital Age – Second Edition.* Vancouver: Tony Bates Associates Ltd. Retrieved 23 January 2019 from https://pressbooks.bccampus.ca/teachinginadigitalagev2/

Baxter, P., & Jack, S. (2008). Qualitative Case Study Methodology: Study Design and Implementation for Novice Researchers. *Qualitative Report, 13*(4), 544–559. Retrieved from https://nsuworks.nova.edu/tqr/vol13/iss4/2

Bayat, A., Jamshidipour, A., & Hashemi, M. (2017). The beneficial impacts of applying formative assessment on Iranian university students' anxiety reduction and listening efficacy. *Online Submission, 5*(2), 1–11. doi:10.18298/ijlet.1740

Becker, H. J. (1999). *Internet use by teachers: Conditions of professional use and teacher-directed student use.* Center for Research on Information Technology and Organizations, the University of California, Irvine and the University of Minnesota.

Becker, S. A., Brown, M., Dahlstrom, E., Davis, A., DePaul, K., Diaz, V., & Pomerantz, J. (2018). *NMC Horizon Report: 2018 higher education edition.* Louisville, CO: EDUCAUSE.

Bekleyen, N., & Hayta, F. (2015). Language learning in new era: Do mobile phones help? In A. Akbarov (Ed.), *The practice of foreign language teaching: Theories and applications* (pp. 434–445). New Castle, UK: Cambridge Scholars Publishing.

Belet, Ş., & Yaşar, Ş. (2007). Öğrenme stratejilerinin okuduğunu anlama ve yazma becerileri ile Türkçe dersine ilişkin tutumlara etkisi. *Eğitimde Kuram ve Uygulama, 3*(1), 69–86.

Bell, G. (2009). *Building Social Web Applications.* Sebastopol, CA: O'Reilly Media.

Bender, D. A. (2003). MCQ, EMSQ or multiple true/false questions? *Bioscience Education, 2*(1), 1–3. doi:10.3108/beej.2003.02000009

Bennett, R. E. (2002a). *Inexorable and inevitable: the continuing story of technology and assessment.* Paper presented at 28th Conference of the International Association for Educational Assessment, Hong Kong.

Bennett, R. E. (2008). *Technology for large-scale assessment.* ETS Report No. RM-08-10. Princeton, NJ: Educational Testing Service.

Bennett, R. E. (2002b). Using electronic assessment to measure student performance (Issue Brief); partly based on: How the Internet will help large-scale assessment reinvent itself. *Education Policy Analysis Archives, 9*(5).

Bennett, R. E. (2015). The changing nature of educational assessment. *Review of Research in Education, 39*(1), 370–407. doi:10.3102/0091732X14554179

Benson, P. (1996). Concepts of autonomy in language learning. In R. Pemberton, E. S. L. Li, W. W. F. Or, & H. Pierson (Eds.), *Taking Control: Autonomy in Language Learning* (pp. 27–34). Hong Kong: Hong Kong University Press.

Benson, P. (2001). *Teaching and researching autonomy in language learning*. London: Longman.

Benson, P. (2001). *Teaching and Researching Autonomy in Language Learning*. London: Longman.

Benson, P. (2007a). Autonomy in language teaching and learning. *Language Teaching, 40*(1), 21–40. doi:10.1017/S0261444806003958

Benson, P. (2010). Measuring autonomy: Should we put our ability to the test? In A. Paran & L. Sercu (Eds.), *Testing the Untestable in Language Education* (pp. 77–97). Bristol: Multilingual Matters. doi:10.21832/9781847692672-007

Benson, P. (2011). *Teaching and researching autonomy* (2nd ed.). London: Pearson Education.

Benson, P. (2011). *Teaching and Researching Autonomy*. Harlow: Pearson.

Benson, P. (Ed.). (2007b). *Learner autonomy 8: Teacher and learner perspectives*. Dublin: Authentik.

Benson, P., & Cooker, L. (2013). The social and the individual in applied linguistics research. In P. Benson & L. Cooker (Eds.), *The Applied Linguistic Individual- Sociocultural Approaches to Identity, Agency and Autonomy* (pp. 1–16). Sheffield: Equinox Publishing Ltd.

Benson, P., & Voller, P. (Eds.). (1997). *Autonomy and Independence in Language Learning*. London: Longman.

Bersin, J. (2004). *The Blended Learning Book. Best Practices, Proven Methodologies, and Lessons Learned*. San Francisco: Pfeiffer.

Biasutti, M. (2017). A comparative analysis of forums and wikis as tools for online collaborative learning. *Computers & Education, 111*, 158–171. doi:10.1016/j.compedu.2017.04.006

Biasutti, M., & El-Deghaidy, H. (2012). Using Wiki in teacher education: Impact on knowledge management processes and student satisfaction. *Computers & Education, 59*(3), 861–872. doi:10.1016/j.compedu.2012.04.009

Bikowski, D. (2015). The pedagogy of collaboration: Teaching effectively within an evolving technology landscape. In G. Pickering & P. Gunashekar (Eds.), *Innovation in English Language Teacher Education* (pp. 223–231). New Delhi, India: British Council.

Bilici, S., Guzey, S., & Yamak, H. (2016). Assessing pre-service science teachers' technological pedagogical content knowledge (TPACK) through observations and lesson plans. *Research in Science & Technological Education, 5143*(April), 1–15. doi:10.1080/02635143.2016.1144050

Bin-Hady, W. R. A. (2016). *Communicative competence in teaching English at secondary schools: A critical investigation in Yaff'ae district of Yemen*. GRIN Verlag. doi:10.13140/RG.2.2.17234.40645

Bishop, J., & Elen, J. (2014). Emerging Technologies. In M. Spector, M. Merrill, M. Bishop, & J. Elen (Eds.), *Handbook of Research on Educational Communications and Technology* (pp. 673–674). New York, NY: Academic Press.

Blackboard Inc. (2006). *Blackboard Learning System™ Designer and Instructor Reference*. Blackboard Inc.

Black, P., & Wiliam, D. (1998). Assessment and classroom learning. *Assessment in Education: Principles, Policy & Practice, 5*(1), 7–74. doi:10.1080/0969595980050102

Blake, R., Wilson, N. L., Cetto, M., & Pardo-Ballester, C. (2008). Measuring oral proficiency in distance, face-to-face, and blended classrooms. *Language Learning & Technology, 12*(3), 114–127.

Blinco, K., Mason, J., McLean, N., & Wilson, S. (2004). *Trends and Issues in E-learning Infrastructure development.* A White Paper for alt-i-lab. Redwood City, CA: Altilab04. Retrieved October 24, 2012, from http://scholar.google.com/scholar?hl=en&btnG=Search&q=intitle:Trends+and+Issues+in+E-learning+Infrastructure+Development#0

Blin, F. (1999). CALL and the development of learner autonomy. In R. Debski & M. Levy (Eds.), *WORLDCALL: Global Perspectives on Computer-assisted Language Learning* (pp. 133–149). Lisse: Swets & Zeitlinger.

Bliss, C. S., Mark, M., Jonathan, A. F., Godwin, A. K., & Justine, A. (2017). Effect of computer-assisted instruction (CAI) on senior high school students' achievement at pie chart and histogram in core mathematics. *Brock Journal of Education, 5*(9), 45–68.

Bloom, B. S., Engelhart, M. D., Furst, E. J., Hill, W. H., & Krathwohl, D. R. (1956). *Taxonomy of Educational Objectives: The Classification of Educational Goals.* New York: David McKay.

Blumberg, P. (2009). *Developing Learner-Centered Teaching. A Practical Guide for Faculty.* San Francisco: John Wiley & Sons.

Borg, S., & Al-Busaidi, S. (2012). *Learner Autonomy: English Language Teachers" Beliefs and Practices.* London: The British Council.

Bosch, N., & D'Mello, S. (2013). Sequential Patterns of Affective States of Novice Programmers. In AIED 2013 Workshops Proceedings (Vol. 9). Academic Press.

Botturi, L. (2004). *Functional Assessment of some Open-Source LMS.* Unpublished Manuscript. Retrieved September 12, 2012, from www.istituti.usilu.net/botturil/web/publications/OS_review_Nov2004.pdf

Botzer, G., & Yerushalmy, M. (2007). Mobile Application for Mobile Learning. *Proceedings of the International Conference on Cognition and Exploratory Learning in the Digital Age.*

Bowen, G. A. (2009). Document analysis as a qualitative research method. *Qualitative Research Journal, 9*(2), 27–40. doi:10.3316/QRJ0902027

Bower, M., Sturman, D., & Alvarez, V. (2016). Perceived utility and feasibility of wearable technologies in higher education. *Mobile Learning Futures–Sustaining Quality Research and Practice in Mobile Learning, 15th World Conference on Mobile and Contextual Learning, mLearn 2016 Sydney, Australia, October 24-26, 2016 Proceedings.*

Bower, G. H., & Hilgard, E. R. (1948). *Theories of Learning* (Vol. 3). Academic Press.

Bower, M. (2016). Deriving a typology of Web 2.0 learning technologies. *British Journal of Educational Technology, 47*(4), 763–777. doi:10.1111/bjet.12344

Boylu, E. (2015). *Yabancı dil olarak türkçe öğrenenlerin dil öğrenme stratejilerini kullanma düzeyleri.* Ankara: Yayımlanmamış Yüksek Lisans Tezi. Gazi Üniversitesi.

Boyno, M. (2011). *An Analysis of the Factors Influencing Learner Autonomy in the Turkish EFL Context* (Unpublished PhD thesis). Çukurova University.

Božinović, N., & Sindik, J. (2011). Gender differences in the use of learning strategies in adult foreign language learners. *Metodički obzori: časopis za odgojno-obrazovnu teoriju i praksu, 6*(11), 5-20.

Brantmeier, C., & Vanderplank, R. (2008). Descriptive and criterion-referenced self-assessment with L2 readers. *System, 36*(3), 456–477. doi:10.1016/j.system.2008.03.001

Brindley, G. (1998). Assessing listening abilities. *Annual Review of Applied Linguistics, 18*, 171–191. doi:10.1017/S0267190500003536

Britain, S., & Liber, O. (2004). *A Framework for the Pedagogical Evaluation of eLearning Environments*. Retrieved November 8, 2012, from https://www.jisc.ac.uk/uploaded_documents/jtap-041.doc

Bromberg, N. R., Techatassanasoontorn, A. A., & Andrade, A. D. (2013). Engaging students: Digital storytelling in information systems learning. *Pacific Asia Journal of the Association for Information Systems*, *5*(1), 1–22. doi:10.17705/1pais.05101

Brooks, C., Kettel, L., & Hansen, C. (2005). Building a Learning Object Content Management System E-learning Specifications. *eLearnMagazine*. Retrieved June 6, 2013, from https://pdfs.semanticscholar.org/ea53/6da43b5e5ca7f44b5247bbe463f16c83c9e7.pdf

Brophy, J. (2004). *Motivating students to learn*. Lawrence Erlbaum Associates. doi:10.4324/9781410610218

Brown, G. (2017). Teaching listening comprehension. In G. Brown (Ed.), *Listening to Spoken English* (pp. 158–186). London, UK: Routledge. doi:10.4324/9781315538518

Brown, G., & Peterson, N. (2008). The LMS Mirror: School as We Know IT versus School as We Need IT and the Triumph of the Custodial Class. *Journal of Online Learning and Teaching*, *4*(2), 190–197.

Brown, H. D., & Lee, H. (2015). *Teaching by principles: An interactive approach to language pedagogy*. White Plains, NY: Pearson Education.

Brown, M. G. (2016). Blended instructional practice: A review of the empirical literature on instructors' adoption and use of online tools in face-to-face teaching. *Internet and Higher Education*, *38*, 1–10. doi:10.1016/j.iheduc.2016.05.001

Brown, M., Dehoney, J., & Millichap, N. (2015). *The next generation digital learning environment. A Report on Research. ELI Paper*. Louisville, CO: Educause April.

Bruner, J. S. (1961). The act of discovery. *Harvard Educational Review*.

Bryfczynski, S. (2012). BeSocratic : An Intelligent Tutoring System for the Recognition, Evaluation, and Analysis of Free-form Student Input. Clemson Univeristy. Retrieved from https://tigerprints.clemson.edu/all_dissertations/1053

Buabeng-Andoh, C. (2012). Factors influencing teachers ' adoption and integration of information and communication technology into teaching: A review of the literature. *International Journal of Education and Development Using Information and Communication Technology*, *8*(1), 136–155.

Buendía, L., Colás, P., & Hernández, F. (1997). *Métodos de investigación en psicopedagogía*. Madrid: McGraw-Hill.

Bülbül, S., Mısırlıoğlu, E., Ceyhun, G., Araz, N., & Altuğ, U. (2014). Factors affecting reading habit and media follow-up in Turkey. *Türkiye Atletizim Federasyonu Preventive Medicine Bulletin*, *13*(1), 47–56. doi:10.5455/pmb.1-1361624478

Burden, K., & Kearney, M. (2016). Conceptualising authentic mobile learning. In D. Churchill, J. Lu, T. Chiu, & B. Fox (Eds.), *Mobile learning design: Theories and application* (pp. 27–42). Singapore: Springer. doi:10.1007/978-981-10-0027-0_2

Burstein, J., Chodorow, M., & Leacock, C. (2004). Automated essay evaluation: The Criterion online writing system. *AI Magazine*, *25*, 27–36.

Burton, D. (2000). *Research Training for Social Scientists*. London: Sage. doi:10.4135/9780857028051

Burton-Jones, A., & Hubona, G. (2005). Individual differences and usage behavior: revisiting a technology acceptance model assumption. *ACM SIGMIS Database, 36*(2), 58–77. Retrieved August 18, 2013, from https://dl.acm.org/citation.cfm?id=1066155

Büyükkantarcıoğlu, N. (2004). A sociolinguistic analysis of the present dimensions of English as a foreign language in Turkey. *International Journal of the Sociology of Language, 165*(165), 33–58. doi:10.1515/ijsl.2004.006

Büyüköztürk, Ş. (2007). Sosyal bilimler için veri analizi el kitabi (7. Bs). Ankara: Pegem Akademi.

Büyüköztürk, Ş., Kılıç Çakmak, E., Akgün, Ö. E., Karadeniz, Ş., & Demirel, F. (2018). Bilimsel araştırma yöntemleri (24. Bs.). Ankara: Pegem Akademi.

Büyüköztürk, Ş., Akgün, Ö. E., Özkahveci, Ö., & Demirel, F. (2004). The validity and reliability study of the turkish version of the motivated strategies for learning questionnaire. *Educational Sciences: Theory and Practice, 4*(2), 231–239.

Cade, W. L., Copeland, J. L., Person, N. K., & Mello, S. K. D. (2008). Dialogue Modes in Expert Tutoring. In International Conference on Intelligent Tutoring Systems (pp. 470–471). doi:10.1007/978-3-540-69132-7_50

Çakır, R., & Yıldırım, S. (2009). What do computer teachers think about the factors affecting technology integration in schools? *İlköğretim Online, 8*(3), 952-964.

Çalışkan, M. (2016). Öğrenme sürecine etkin katilma: Öğrenme stratejileri ve yürütücü biliş. In M. Yavuz (Ed.), Yeni nesil okul-araştıran okul içinde (pp. 37-76). Konya: Eğitim Yayınevi.

Campbell, T. A. (2012). Digital storytelling in an elementary classroom: Going beyond entertainment. *Procedia: Social and Behavioral Sciences, 69*, 385–393. doi:10.1016/j.sbspro.2012.11.424

Canale, M. (1983). De la competencia comunicativa a la pedagogía comunicativa del lenguaje. In *Competencia comunicativa. Documentos básicos en la enseñanza de lenguas extranjeras* (pp. 63–83). Madrid: Edelsa.

Canale, M., & Swain, M. (1980). Theoretical Bases of Communicative Approaches to Second Language Teaching and Testing. *Applied Linguistics, 1*(1), 1–47. doi:10.1093/applin/1.1.1

Capper, C. A., & Frattura, E. M. (2009). *Meeting the needs of students of all abilities: How leaders go beyond inclusion.* Thousand Oaks, CA: Corwin Press.

Capuano, N., Gaeta, M., Miranda, S., & Orciuoli, F. (2008). LIA : An Intelligent Advisor for e-Learning. In *WSKS 2008* (pp. 187–196). Berlin: Springer-Verlag.

Carter, E. E. (2014). *An Intelligent Debugging Tutor For Novice Computer Science Students.* Lehigh Univeristy.

Caruso, M., Gadd Colombi, A., & Tebbit, S. (2017). Teaching how to Listen. Blended Learning for the Development and Assessment of Listening Skills in a Second Language. *Journal of University Teaching & Learning Practice, 14*(1), 14.

Cavus, N. (2010). The evaluation of learning management systems using an artificial intelligence fuzzy logic algorithm. *Advances in Engineering Software, 41*(2), 248–254. doi:10.1016/j.advengsoft.2009.07.009

Cavus, N. (2011). The application of a multi-attribute decision-making algorithm to learning management systems evaluation. *British Journal of Educational Technology, 42*(1), 19–30. doi:10.1111/j.1467-8535.2009.01033.x

Cavus, N., & Ibrahim, D. (2009). M-learning: An Experiment in Using SMS to Support Learning New English Language Words. *British Journal of Educational Technology, 40*(1), 78–91. doi:10.1111/j.1467-8535.2007.00801.x

Cavus, N., & Momani, A. M. (2009). Computer aided evaluation of learning management systems. *Procedia: Social and Behavioral Sciences, 1*(1), 426–430. doi:10.1016/j.sbspro.2009.01.076

Çelik, M. (2013). Interest-based language teaching to increase motivation and output in Turkey. *Sosyal ve Beşeri Bilimler Araştırmaları Dergisi, 24*, 29–44.

Center for Digital Storytelling. (2005). *Seven elements of digital storytelling*. https://www.storycenter.org/history.html

Cevdet, Y. Õ. (2010). The relationship between language learning strategies, gender, proficiency and self-efficacy beliefs: A study of ELT learners in. *Procedia: Social and Behavioral Sciences, 2*(2), 682–687. doi:10.1016/j.sbspro.2010.03.084

Chacón, C., & Pérez, C. (2011). El podcast como innovación en la enseñanza del inglés como lengua extranjera. *Pixel-Bit. Revista de Medios y Educación, 39*, 41–54.

Chalhoub-Deville, M. (2001). Language testing and technology: Past and future. *Language Learning & Technology, 5*(2), 95–98.

Champagne, M. F., Clayton, T., Dimmitt, N., Laszewski, M., Savage, W., Shaw, J., ... Walter, P. (2001). The assessment of learner autonomy and language learning. *AILA Review, 15*, 45–55.

Chan, S., Bax, S., & Weir, C. (2017). *Researching participants taking IELTS Academic Writing Task 2 (AWT2) in paper mode and in computer mode in terms of score equivalence, cognitive validity and other factors*. IELTS Research Reports Online Series 2017/14. British Council/Cambridge English Language Assessment/IDP: IELTS Australia. Retrieved from https://www.ielts.org/-/media/research-reports/ielts_online_rr_2017-4.ashx

Chang, C.-C., Warden, C. A., Liang, C., & Chou, P.-N. (2018). Performance, cognitive load, and behaviour of technology-assisted English listening learning: From CALL to MALL. *Journal of Computer Assisted Learning, 34*(2), 105–114. doi:10.1111/jcal.12218

Chang, J. U., & Bower, P. A. (2016). Effect of computer-assisted instruction (CAI) on students' reading performance. *The American Psychologist, 41*(2), 170–178.

Chan, V. (2001). Readiness for Learner Autonomy: What do our learners tell us? *Teaching in Higher Education, 6*(4), 505–518. doi:10.1080/13562510120078045

Chao, I., & Liu, E. (2017). Developing an automated essay scoring and feedback system for learners of English in Taiwan. In *4th Annual International Conference of the Asian Association for Language Assessment*. Taipei, Taiwan: The Language Training and Testing Center.

Chapelle, C. (2000). Innovative language learning: Achieving the vision. *ReCALL, 13*(1), 3–14. doi:10.1017/S0958344001000210

Chapelle, C. A. (2008). Utilizing technology in language assessment. In *Encyclopedia of Language and Education: Language Testing and Assessment*. Heidelberg: Springer Verlag.

Chapelle, C. A., & Douglas, D. (2006). *Assessing language through computer technology*. Cambridge, UK: Cambridge University Press. doi:10.1017/CBO9780511733116

Chapelle, C. A., & Voss, E. (2016). 20 years of technology and language assessment in Language Learning &Technology. *Language Learning & Technology, 20*(2), 116–128.

Chapelle, C., & Jamieson, J. (2008). *Tips for Teaching with CALL: Practical Approaches to Computer-assisted Language Learning*. New York: Pearson-Longman.

Chatti, M. A., Marinov, M., Sabov, O., Laksono, R., Sofyan, Z., Yousef, A. M. F., & Schroeder, U. (2016). Video annotation and analytics in CourseMapper. *Smart Learning Environments, 3*(1), 1–21. doi:10.118640561-016-0035-1

Chen, C. (2008). Intelligent web-based learning system with personalized learning path guidance. *Computers & Education, 51*(2), 787–814. doi:10.1016/j.compedu.2007.08.004

Chen, C.-F. E., & Cheng, W.-Y. E. (2008). Beyond the design of automated writing evaluation: Pedagogical practices and perceived learning effectiveness in EFL writing classes. *Language Learning & Technology, 12*(2), 94–112.

Cheng, H. F., & Dörnyei, Z. (2007). The use of motivational strategies in language instruction: The case of EFL teaching in Taiwan. *International Journal of Innovation in Language Learning and Teaching, 1*(1), 153–174. doi:10.2167/illt048.0

Chen, N., & Hsieh, S., & Kinshuk. (2008). Effects of Short-Term Memory and Content Representation Type on Mobile Language Learning. *Language Learning & Technology, 12*(3), 93–113.

Chen, R. T.-H. (2015). L2 Blogging: Who Thrives and Who Does Not? *Language Learning & Technology, 19*(192), 177–196. Retrieved from http://llt.msu.edu/issues/june2015/chen.pdf

Chen, W. (2019). An Exploratory Study on the Role of L2 Collaborative Writing on Learners' Subsequent Individually Composed Texts. *The Asia-Pacific Education Researcher, 28*(6), 563–573. doi:10.1007/s40299-019-00455-3

Chen, W., & Yu, S. (2019). Implementing collaborative writing in teacher-centered classroom contexts: Student beliefs and perceptions. *Language Awareness, 28*(4), 247–267. doi:10.1080/09658416.2019.1675680

Cheung, R., & Vogel, D. (2013). Predicting user acceptance of collaborative technologies: An extension of the technology acceptance model for e-learning. *Computers & Education, 63*, 160–175. doi:10.1016/j.compedu.2012.12.003

Chiheb, R., Faizi, R., & Afia, A. E. L. (2005). *Using Objective Online Testing Tools to Assess Students' Learning: Potentials and Limitations.* Retrieved September 20, 2013, from http://www.jatit.org/volumes/research-papers/Vol24No1/8Vol24No1.pdf

Chi, M. T. H., Siler, S. A., Jeong, H., Yamauchi, T., & Hausmann, R. G. (2001). Learning from human tutoring. *Cognitive Science, 25*(4), 471–533. doi:10.1207/s15516709cog2504_1 PubMed

Chong, J., Chong, A. Y., Ooi, K., & Lin, B. (2011). An Empirical Analysis of the Adoption of M Learning in Malaysia. *International Journal of Mobile Communications, 9*(1), 1–18. doi:10.1504/IJMC.2011.037952

Christensen, D. (2019). *What is the real cost of technology in education?* Retrieved from https://www.classcraft.com/blog/features/cost-of-technology-in-education/

Christensen, C., & Eyering, H. (2011). *The innovative university: Changing the DNA of higher education from the inside out.* San Francisco, CA: Jossey-Bass.

Chrysafiadi, K., & Virvou, M. (2012). Evaluating the integration of fuzzy logic into the student model of a web-based learning environment. *Expert Systems with Applications, 39*(18), 13127–13134. doi:10.1016/j.eswa.2012.05.089

Chung, S. K. (2006). Digital storytelling in integrated arts education. *The International Journal of Arts Education, 4*(1), 33–50.

Churches, A. (2010). *Bloom's digital taxonomy.* Retrieved from http://burtonslifelearning.pbworks.com/f/BloomDigitalTaxonomy2001.pdf

Churchill, D. (2011). Web 2.0 in education: A study of the explorative use of blogs with a postgraduate class. *Innovations in Education and Teaching International, 48*(2), 149–158. doi:10.1080/14703297.2011.564009

Ciğerci, F. M., & Gültekin, M. (2017). Use of digital stories to develop listening comprehension skills. *Issues in Educational Research, 27*(2), 252–268.

Çıralı, H. (2014). *Dijital hikâye anlatımının görsel bellek ve yazma becerisi üzerine etkisi*. Ankara: Yüksek Lisans Tezi. Hacettepe Üniversitesi.

Clancey, W. J. (1979). *Transfer of rule-based expertise through a tutorial dialogue*. Stanford University.

Clarke, B., & Svanaes, S. (2014). *Tablets for Schools: An Updated Literature Review on the Use of Tablets in Education*. Retrieved 16 Apr. 2015 from: http://www.e-learningfoundation.com/Websites/elearningfoundation/images/PDF%20 Documents/T4S-Use-of-Tablets-in-Education.pdf

Coaten, N. (2003). Blended e-learning. *Educaweb, 69*. Retrieved from https://www.educaweb.com/esp/servicios/monografico/formacionvirtual/1181076.asp

Coffey, J., Hammer, D., Levin, D., & Grant, T. (2011). The missing disciplinary substance of formative assessment. *Journal of Research in Science Teaching*, *48*(10), 1109–1136. doi:10.1002/tea.20440

Cohen, L., Duboe, P., Buvat, J., Melton, D., Khadikar, A., & Shah, H. (2018). *Augmented and Virtual Reality in Operations*. Academic Press.

Cohen, L., Manion, L., & Morrison, K. (2007). *Research Methods in Education* (6th ed.). London: Routledge. doi:10.4324/9780203029053

Cole, J., & Foster, H. (2007). Using Moodle: teaching with the popular open source course management system. *O'Reilly Media, Inc*. Retrieved October 23, 2012, from https://books.google.com/books?hl=en&lr=&id=wfPPb1m0G6EC&oi=fnd&pg=PR5&dq=Using+Moodle+Teaching+with+the+Popular+Open+Source+Course+Management+System&ots=vQBiCk0BQy&sig=y1AV_mAH776UCLisFliArlzXHMY

Cole, J., & Foster, H. (2008). *Using Moodle. Teaching with the Popular Open Source Course Management System*. Sebastopol, California: O'Reilly Media.

Coleman, E., & Mtshazi, S. (2017). Factors affecting the use and non-use of Learning Management Systems (LMS) by academic staff. *South African Computer Journal*, *29*(3). doi:10.18489acj.v29i3.459

Coleman, H., & Unrau, Y. A. (2010). Qualitative Data Analysis. In R. M. Grinnell & Y. A. Unrau (Eds.), *Social Work: Research and Evaluation. Foundations of Evidence-Based Practice* (pp. 447–464). New York: Oxford University Press.

Conde, M. A., García-Peñalvo, F. J., Piguillem, J., Casany, M. J., & Alier, M. (2012). *Interoperability in eLearning Contexts. Interaction Between LMS and PLE*. Paper presented at the 1st Symposium on Languages, Applications and Technologies (SLATE 2012), Braga, Portugal.

Confessor, G. J., & Park, E. M. (2004). Factor validation of the learner autonomy profile (Version 3.0) and extraction of the short form. *International Journal of Self-Directed Learning*, *1*(1), 39–58.

Cooker, L. (2012). *Formative (self-) assessment as autonomous language learning* (Unpublished PhD dissertation). University of Nottingham, Nottingham, UK.

Cortés, M. (2002). *Didáctica de la prosodia del español: la acentuación y la entonación*. Barcelona: Edinumen.

Cosgrave, R., Rísquez, A., Logan-phelan, T., Farrelly, T., Costello, E., & Palmer, M. (2011). Usage And Uptake Of Virtual Learning Environments In Ireland : Findings From A Multi Institutional Study. *Aishe-J*, *3*(1), 1–14.

Costello, R., & Mundy, D. P. (2009). The Adaptive Intelligent Personalised Learning Environment. *IEEE International Conference on Advanced Learning Technologies*. 10.1109/ICALT.2009.38

Cotos, E. (2011). Potential of automated writing evaluation feedback. *CALICO Journal*, *28*(2), 420–459. doi:10.11139/cj.28.2.420-459

Cotterall, S. (1995a). Readiness for Autonomy: Investigating Learner Beliefs. *System, 23*(2), 195–205. doi:10.1016/0346-251X(95)00008-8

Cotterall, S., & Malcolm, D. (2015). Epilogue. In C. J. Everhard & L. Murphy (Eds.), *Assessment and autonomy in language learning* (pp. 167–175). Basingstoke, UK: Palgrave Macmillan. doi:10.1057/9781137414380_8

Council of Europe. (2001). *Common European Framework of Reference for Languages: Learning, teaching, assessment.* Cambridge: Cambridge University Press.

Course, S. (2014). Critical reading in EFL in a Turkish high school context. *International Journal of Language Academy, 2*(3), 133–156. doi:10.18033/ijla.108

Craig, D. A., & Kim, J. (2010). Anxiety and performance in video-conferenced and face-to-face oral interviews. *Multimedia-Assisted Language Learning, 13*(3), 9–32. doi:10.15702/mall.2010.13.3.9

Creswell, J. (2012). *Educational Research: Planning, Conducting, and Evaluating Quantitative and Qualitative Research.* Boston: Pearson Education.

Creswell, J. W. (2012). *Educational research: planning, conducting, and evaluating quantitative and qualitative research* (4th ed.). Boston: Pearson Education.

Creswell, J. W. (2013). *Qualitative inquiry & research design: Choosing among five approaches.* Los Angeles, CA: Sage.

Crompton, H. (2013). A Historical overview of m-Learning: Toward Learner-Centered Education. In Z. Berge & L. Muilenburg (Eds.), *Handbook of mobile learning.* New York: Routledge.

Crompton, H., Burke, D., Gregory, K. H., & Gräbe, C. (2016). The use of mobile learning in science: A systematic review. *Journal of Science Education and Technology, 25*(2), 149–160. doi:10.100710956-015-9597-x

Crookes, G., & Schmidt, R. (1991). Motivation: Reopening the research agenda. *Language Learning, 41*(4), 469–512. doi:10.1111/j.1467-1770.1991.tb00690.x

Cudney, E. A., Murray, S. L., Groner, B., & Kaczmarek, K. M. (2017). Using the Voice of the Student to Evaluate Learning Management Systems. In *Proceedings of the 2017 ASEE Annual Conference & Exposition.* American Society for Engineering Education. 10.18260/1-2--29091

Dahlstrom, E., Christopher, D. B., & Jacqueline, B. (2014). The Current Ecosystem of Learning Management Systems in Higher Education: Student, Faculty, and IT Perspectives. *EDUCAUSE Research Report*, 27. https://www.educause.edu/ecar

Dam, L., Eriksson, R., Little, D., Miliander, J., & Trebbi, T. (1990). Towards a definition of Autonomy. In T. Trebbi (Ed.), *Third Nordic Workshop on Developing Autonomous Learning in the FL Classroom.* Bergen, Norway: Institute for praktisk pedagogikk, University of Bergen. http://www.warwick.ac.uk/go/dahla/archive/trebbi_1990

Dam, L. (1995). *Learner Autonomy 3: From Theory to Classroom Practice.* Dublin: Authentic.

Dam, L. (2011). Developing learner autonomy with school kids: principles, practices, results. In D. Gardner (Ed.), *Fostering Autonomy in Language Learning* (pp. 40–51). Gaziantep. Available at http://ilac2010.zirve.edu.tr/Fostering_Autonomy.pdf

Dam, L., & Legenhausen, L. (2010). Learners reflecting on learning: Evaluation versus testing in autonomous language learning. In A. Paran & L. Sercu (Eds.), *Testing the Untestable in Language Education* (pp. 120–138). Bristol, UK: Multilingual Matters. doi:10.21832/9781847692672-009

Dar, M. F., & Khan, I. (2015). Writing anxiety among public and private sectors Pakistani undergraduate university students. *Pakistan Journal of Gender Studies, 10*(1), 121–136.

Davidson, R. (2012). Wiki use that increases communication and collaboration motivation. *Journal of Learning Design*, *5*(2), 38–49. doi:10.5204/jld.v5i2.110

Davies, R., Sprague, C., & New, C. (2008). Integrating technology into a science classroom: An evaluation of inquiry-based technology integration. In D. W. Sunal, E. L. Wright, & C. Sundberg (Eds.), *The impact of technology and the laboratory on K-16 science learning series: Research in science education* (pp. 207–237). Charlotte, NC: Information Age Publishing.

Davis, F. D. (1989). Perceived Usefulness, Perceived Ease of Use, and User Acceptance of Information Technology. *Management Information Systems Quarterly*, *13*(3), 319–340. doi:10.2307/249008

De la Torre, A. (2006). Web Educativa 2.0. *Edutec. Revista Electrónica de Tecnología Educativa*. Retrieved from https://www.uib.es/depart/gte/gte/edutec-e/revelec20/anibal20.htm

De Wever, B., Van Keer, H., Schellens, T., & Valcke, M. (2010). Roles as a structuring tool in online discussion groups: The differential impact of different roles on social knowledge construction. *Computers in Human Behavior*, *26*(4), 516–523. doi:10.1016/j.chb.2009.08.008

De Wever, V. K., Van Keer, H., Schellens, T., & Valcke, M. (2009). Structuring asynchronous discussion groups: The impact of role assignment and self-assessment on students' levels of knowledge construction through social negotiation. *Journal of Computer Assisted Learning*, *25*(2), 177–188. doi:10.1111/j.1365-2729.2008.00292.x

Deci, E. L., & Flaste, R. (1995). *Why We Do What We Do*. New York: Penguin Books.

Deci, E. L., & Ryan, R. M. (1985). *Intrinsic Motivation and Self-determination in Human Behavior*. New York: Plenum. doi:10.1007/978-1-4899-2271-7

Deci, E. L., & Ryan, R. M. (2000). Intrinsic and extrinsic motivations: Classic definitions and new directions. *Contemporary Educational Psychology*, *25*(1), 54–67. doi:10.1006/ceps.1999.1020 PMID:10620381

Dede, C. (2008). Technological Supports for Acquiring 21st Century Skills. Cambridge.

Dede, C., Salzman, M., Loftin, R. B., & Ash, K. (2000). The design of immersive virtual learning environments: Fostering deep understandings of complex scientific knowledge. In J. M. Jacobson & R. B. Kozma (Eds.), *Innovations in science and mathematics education: Advanced designs for technologies of learning* (pp. 361–413). Mahwah, NJ: Lawrence Erlbaum Associates.

Demir, A., & Kosse, U. (2017). Solving Optimization Problems via Vortex Optimization Algorithm and Cognitive Development Optimization Algorithm. *Broad Research in Artificial Intelligence and Neuroscience*, *7*(4), 23–42.

Demirer, V. (2013). *İlköğretimde e-öyküleme kullanımı ve etkileri*. Konya: Yayınlanmamış Doktora Tezi. Necmettin Erbakan Üniversitesi.

Dempsey, J. V., Fisher, S. F., Wright, D. E., & Anderton, E. (2008). Training and support, obstacles, and library impacts on elearning activities. *College Student Journal*, *42*(2), 630–636.

Deng, C., & Carless, D. (2010). Examination preparation or effective teaching: Conflicting priorities in the implementation of a pedagogic innovation. *Language Assessment Quarterly*, *7*(4), 285–302. doi:10.1080/15434303.2010.510899

Denk, M., Weber, M., & Belfin, R. (2007). Mobile Learning-Challenges and potentials. *International Journal of Mobile and Organisation*, *1*(2), 122–139. doi:10.1504/IJMLO.2007.012674

Denzin, N. K. (1978). *The Research Act: A Theoretical Introduction to Sociological Methods*. Englewood Cliffs, NJ: Prentice Hall.

Derwing, T. M., & Munro, M. (2005). Second Language Accent and Pronunciation Teaching: A Research-Based Approach. *TESOL Quarterly*, *39*(3), 379–397. doi:10.2307/3588486

DeWitt, D., Alias, N., & Siraj, S. (2014). The design and development of a Collaborative mLearning prototype for Malaysian secondary school science. *Educational Technology Research and Development*, *62*(4), 461–480. doi:10.1007/s11423-014-9340-y

Dewitt, D., Alias, N., & Siraj, S. (2015). Collaborative learning: Interactive debates using Padlet in a higher education institution. *The Turkish Online Journal of Educational Technology*, *2015*, 88–95.

Dickinson, L. (1987). *Self-instruction in Language Learning*. Cambridge: Cambridge University Press.

Dikbaş, Y., & Hasırcı, Ö. K. (2008). Öğrenme stratejileri öğretiminin ve ders işlenişinde kullanımının öğrencilerin akademik başarılarına ve tutumlarına etkisi. *Ahi Evran Üniversitesi Kırşehir Eğitim Fakültesi Dergisi*, *9*(2), 69–76.

Dikli, S., & Bleyle, S. (2014). Automated essay scoring feedback for second language writers: How does it compare to instructor feedback? *Assessing Writing*, *22*, 1–17. doi:10.1016/j.asw.2014.03.006

Dillenbourg, P., Baker, M., Blaye, A., & O'Malley, C. (1996). The evolution of research on collaborative learning. In H. Spada & P. Reimann (Eds.), *Learning in humans and machines* (pp. 189–211). Oxford: Elsevier Science.

Disbrow, L. M. (2008). The Overall Effect of Online Audio Conferencing in Communication Courses: What do Students Really Think? *Journal of Online Learning and Teaching*, *4*(2).

Dixon, D. (2011). *Measuring language learner autonomy in tertiary-level learners of English* (Unpublished PhD dissertation). University of Warwick, UK.

Dogan, B., & Robin, B. (2008). Implementation of digital storytelling in the classroom by teachers trained in a digital storytelling workshop. In *Society for Information Technology & Teacher Education International Conference* (pp. 902-907). Association for the Advancement of Computing in Education (AACE).

Doğan, Ö. (2009). *İngilizce hazırlık okuyan öğrencilerin motivasyon düzeyleri*. Eskişehir: Yüksek Lisans Tezi. Osmangazi Üniversitesi.

Dolgunsöz, E. (2016). Using eye-tracking to measure lexical inferences and its effects on reading rate during EFL reading. *Dil ve Dilbilimi Çalışmaları Dergisi*, *12*(1), 63–78.

Dooly, M., & Sadler, R. (2016). Becoming little scientists: Technologically-enhanced project-based language learning. *Language Learning & Technology*, *20*(1), 54–78.

Dörnyei, Z. (2005). The psychology of the language learners: Individual differences in second language acquisition. In Annual Review of Psychology. London: Lawrence Erlbaum.

Dörnyei, Z., & Ottó, I. (1998). *Motivation in action: a process model of L2 motivation*. Working Papers in Applied Linguistics 4. London: Thames Valley University.

Dörnyei, Z. (1994). Motivation and motivating in the foreign language classroom. *Modern Language Journal*, *78*(3), 273–284. doi:10.1111/j.1540-4781.1994.tb02042.x

Dörnyei, Z. (1998). Motivation in second and foreign language learning. *Language Teaching*, *31*(3), 117–135. doi:10.1017/S026144480001315X

Dörnyei, Z. (2007). *Research methods in applied linguistics*. New York: Oxford University Press.

Dörnyei, Z. (2007). *Research Methods in Applied Linguistics: Quantitative, Qualitative, and Mixed Methodologies.* Oxford: Oxford University Press.

Dörnyei, Z., & Ushioda, E. (2011). *Teaching and Researching Motivation* (2nd ed.). Harlow: Longman.

Dörnyei, Z., & Ushioda, E. (2011). *Teaching and researching: Motivation.* Harlow, England: Pearson Education.

Dreon, O., Kerper, R. M., & Landis, J. (2011). Digital storytelling: A tool for teaching and learning in the youtube generation. *Middle School Journal, 42*(5), 4–10. doi:10.1080/00940771.2011.11461777

Ducate, L., & Lomicka, L. (2013). Going Mobile: Language Learning with an iPod Touch in Intermediate French and German Classes. *Foreign Language Annals, 26*(3), 45–468. doi:10.1111/flan.12043

Dudeney, G., & Hockly, N. (2007). *How to Teach English with Technology.* Pearson Education Limited.

Duffy, T. M., & Cunningham, D. J. (1996). Constructivism: Implications for the design and delivery of instruction. In *Handbook of research for educational communications and technology* (pp. 1–31). New York: Macmillan Library Reference.

Duffy, T. M., & Cunningham, D. J. (1996). Constructivism: Implications for the Design and Delivery of Instruction. In D. H. Jonassen (Ed.), *Handbook of Research for Educational Communications and Technology* (pp. 170–198). New York: Macmillan Library Reference.

Duhaney, D. C. (2000). Technology and the educational process: Transforming Classroom Activities. *International Journal of Instructional Media*, 27.

Dunlap, J. C., & Grabinger, R. S. (1996). Rich Environments for Active Learning in the Higher Education Classroom. In B. G. Wilson (Ed.), *Constructivist learning environments: Case studies in instructional design* (pp. 65–83). Englewood Cliffs, NJ: Educational Technology Publications.

Durlach, P. J., & Randall, D. S. (2014). *Framework for Instructional Technology : Methods of Implementing Adaptive Training and Education.* Academic Press.

Dzikovska, M., Steinhauser, N., Farrow, E., Moore, J., & Campbell, G. (2014). BEETLE II : Deep Natural Language Understanding and Automatic Feedback Generation for Intelligent Tutoring in Basic Electricity and Electronics. *International Journal of Artificial Intelligence in Education, 24*(3), 284–332. doi:10.1007/s40593-014-0017-9

Early, P., & Swanson, P. B. (2008). Technology for oral assessment. In C. M. Cherry & C. Wilkerson (Eds.), *Dimension* (pp. 39–48). Valdosta, GA: SCOLT Publications.

Echeverr, V., & Chiluiza, K. (2015). Mirroring Teachers ' Assessment of Novice Students ' Presentations Through an Intelligent Tutor System. In Asia-Pacific Conference on Computer Aided System Enginnering (pp. 264–269). doi:10.1109/APCASE.2015.53

Edmodo. (2019). Available online: https://www.edmodo.com

Edpuzzle. (2020). Retrieved from www.edpuzzle.com

Eduappcenter. (2019). Retrieved from www.eduappcenter.com

Edutechnica. (2020). *LMS Data- Spring 2020.* Retrieved from https://edutechnica.com/

Egbert, J. (2005). *CALL essentials: Principles and practice in CALL classrooms.* Alexandria, VA: TESOL.

Egbert, J., Akasha, O., Huff, L., & Lee, H. (2011). Moving forward: Anecdotes and evidence guiding the next generation of CALL. *International Journal of Computer-Assisted Language Learning and Teaching, 1*(1), 1–15. doi:10.4018/ijcallt.2011010101

Egbert, J., & Hanson-Smith, E. (Eds.). (2007). *CALL environments: Research, practice, and critical issues* (2nd ed.). Alexandria, VA: TESOL.

Egert, C. A., Jacobs, S., & Barnes, S. B. (2009). When Social Worlds Collide : Charting the Intersection of Social Media and Courseware / Course Management Systems. In P. Zaphiris & A. A. Ozok (Eds.), *Online Communities, LNCS 5621* (pp. 452–461). Berlin: Springer-Verlag. doi:10.1007/978-3-642-02774-1_49

El Ebyary, K., & Windeatt, S. (2019). Eye tracking analysis of EAP students' regions of interest in omputer-based feedback on grammar, usage, mechanics, style and organization and development. *System, 83*, 36–49. doi:10.1016/j.system.2019.03.007

El Ghouch, N., Mokhtar, E., & Seghroucheni, Y. Z. (2017). Analysing the Outcome of a Learning Process Conducted Within the System ALS _ CORR. *International Journal of Emerging Technologies in Learning, 12*(3), 43–56. doi:10.3991/ijet.v12i03.6377

Elabnody, M. E. (2016). A Survey of Top 10 Open Source Learning Management Systems. *International Journal of Scientific & Technology Research,* 5(9).

Eldenfria, A., & Al-samarraie, H. (2019). The effectiveness of an online learning system based on aptitude scores : An effort to improve students ' brain activation. *Education and Information Technologies, 24*(5), 1–15. doi:10.1007/s10639-019-09895-2

Elementk. (2003). *Learning Management Systems in the Work Environment: Practical considerations for the selection and and implementation of an e-Learning platform*. Author.

Ellis, R. (2000). Task-based research and language pedagogy. *Language Teaching Research, 4*(3), 193–220. doi:10.1177/136216880000400302

Ellis, R. (2003). *The Study of Second Language Acquisition*. Oxford: OUP.

Ellis, R. (2015). *Understanding second language acquisition* (2nd ed.). Oxford, UK: Oxford University Press.

Ellis, R. (2018). *Reflections on task-based language teaching*. Multilingual Matters.

El-Masri, M., & Tarhini, A. (2017). Erratum to: Factors affecting the adoption of e-learning systems in Qatar and USA: Extending the Unified Theory of Acceptance and Use of Technology 2 (UTAUT2). *Educational Technology Research and Development, 65*(3), 765–767. doi:10.100711423-017-9526-1

Elmes, J. (2017). *Six significant challenges for technology in higher education in 2017*. Retrieved from https://www.timeshighereducation.com/features/six-significant-challenges-technology-higher-education-2017#survey-answer

Elola, I., & Oskoz, A. (2010). Collaborative writing: Fostering foreign language and writing conventions development. *Language Learning & Technology, 14*(3), 51–71.

Elyas, T., & Picard, M. (2010). Saudi Arabian educational history: Impacts on language teaching. *Education, Business and Society, 3*(2), 136–145. doi:10.1108/17537981011047961

Emmanuel, F. B., & Olusegun, O. B. (2015). Impediments on the implementation of computer science education curriculum in public secondary schools in Osun State Nigeria. *Asia Pacific Journal of Education. Arts and Sciences, 2*(4), 12–17.

Emporia State University. (2019). Learning Domains. Retrieved October 27, 2019, from https://www.emporia.edu/studentlife/learning-and-assessment/guide/domains.html

Ertmer, P. A. (1999). Addressing first and second-order barriers to change: Strategies for technology integration. *Educational Technology Research and Development, 47*(4), 47–61. doi:10.1007/BF02299597

Ertmer, P. A., & Ottenbreit-Leftwich, A. T. (2010). Teacher technology change: How knowledge, confidence, beliefs, and culture intersect. *Journal of Research on Technology in Education*, *42*(3), 255–284. doi:10.1080/15391523.2010.10782551

Erzberger, C., & Kelle, U. (2003). Making inferences in mixed methods: the rules of integration. In A. Tashakkori & C. Teddlie (Eds.), *Handbook of Mixed Methods in Social and Behavioral Research*. Thousand Oaks, CA: Sage.

Esch, E. (1997). Learner training for autonomous language learning. In P. Benson & P. Voller (Eds.), *Autonomy and Independence in Language Learning* (pp. 164–176). London: Longman.

Evangelidou, F. (2017). Kavala's 6th Graders towards Mastering Mathematics: A Blended Learning Proposal at Disabled Students' Side. In A. Palalas & P. Pawluk (Eds.), *Blended Learning Theory and Practice Proceedings of the 2nd World Conference on Blended Learning (IABL2017)* (pp. 79-84). Toronto: International Association for Blended Learning and George Brown College.

Everhard, C. J. (2006). The elusiveness of autonomy. *Independence. Newsletter of the IATEFL Learner Autonomy Special Interest Group*, *38*, 9–13.

Everhard, C. J. (2015a). The assessment-autonomy relationship. In C. J. Everhard & L. Murphy (Eds.), *Assessment and Autonomy in Language Learning* (pp. 8–34). Basingstoke, UK: Palgrave Macmillan. doi:10.1057/9781137414380_2

Everhard, C. J. (2015b). Investigating peer- and self-assessment of oral skills as steppingstones to autonomy in EFL higher education. In C. J. Everhard & L. Murphy (Eds.), *Assessment and Autonomy in Language Learning* (pp. 114–142). Basingstoke, UK: Palgrave Macmillan. doi:10.1057/9781137414380_6

Everhard, C. J., & Murphy, L. (Eds.). (2015). *Assessment and autonomy in language learning*. Basingstoke, UK: Palgrave Macmillan. doi:10.1057/9781137414380

Exter, K. D., Rowe, S., Boyd, W., & Lloyd, D. (2012). Using Web 2.0 Technologies for Collaborative Learning in Distance Education—Case Studies from an Australian University. *Future Internet*, *4*(1), 216–237. doi:10.3390/fi4010216

Fabera, J.M., & Visscherb, A.J. (2018). The effects of a digital formative assessment tool on spelling achievement: Results of a randomized experiment. *Computers & Education.*

Fabry, D. L., & Higgs, J. R. (1997). Barriers to the effective use of technology in education: Current status. *Journal of Educational Computing Research*, *17*(4), 385–395. doi:10.2190/C770-AWA1-CMQR-YTYV

Fang, B. (2009). From distraction to engagement: Wireless devices in the classroom. *EDUCAUSE Quarterly*, *32*(4), 4–9.

Farangi, M. R., & Kheradmand Saadi, Z. (2017). Dynamic assessment or schema theory: The case of listening comprehension. *Cogent Education*, *4*(1), 1312078. doi:10.1080/2331186X.2017.1312078

Fareed, M., Ashraf, A., & Bilal, M. (2016). ESL Learners' Writing Skills: Problems, Factors and Suggestions. *Journal of Education & Social Sciences*, *4*(2), 83–94. doi:10.20547/jess0421604201

Fathema, N., Shannon, D., & Ross, M. (2015). Expanding the technology acceptance model (TAM) to examine faculty use of learning management systems in higher education institutions. *Journal of Online Learning and Teaching*, *11*(2), 210–232.

Faudler, T. R. (2011). *Technology integration: A research-based professional development program* (Unpublished master's thesis). Cedarville University, Cedarville, OH.

Fereday, J., & Muir-Cochrane, E. (2006). Demonstrating rigor using thematic analysis: A hybrid approach of inductive and deductive coding and theme development. *International Journal of Qualitative Methods*, *5*(1), 80–92. doi:10.1177/160940690600500107

Ferris, D. (1999). The case for grammar correction in L2 writing classes: A response to Truscott (1996). *Journal of Second Language Writing, 8*(1), 1–11. doi:10.1016/S1060-3743(99)80110-6

Fırat, E. A., & Koksal, M. S. (2017). The relationship between use of Web 2.0 tools by prospective science teachers and their biotechnology literacy. *Computers in Human Behavior, 70*, 44–50. doi:10.1016/j.chb.2016.12.067

Fitzgerald, T. (2007). Documents and documentary analysis: Reading between the lines. In A. R. Briggs & M. Coleman (Eds.), *Research methods in educational leadership and management* (2nd ed., pp. 278–294). Thousand Oaks, CA: Sage.

Flick. (2009). *An introduction to qualitative research.* London: Sage.

Flipgrid. (2019). Available online: https://info.flipgrid.com/

Ford, M. (2015). *Rise of the Robots: Technology and the Threat of a Jobless Future.* New York: Basic Books.

Fortier, P., Mindala-Freeman, M. M., Bagnon, P., Tignon, M., Larsson, T., & Buvat, J. … Gosh, A. (2019). 5G in industrial operations How telcos and industrial companies stand to benefit. Paris, France: Academic Press.

Fourie, S., Summers, B., & Zweygarth, M. (2010). Difficulty and discrimination indices as quality assurance tools for assessments in a South African problem-based pharmacy programme. *Pharmacy Education*, 10.

Fournier, J., Cruz, S., & Roberts, K. (2017). *Canvas 2017: Evaluation Report.* Retrieved from https://itconnect.uw.edu/wp-content/uploads/2018/07/Canvas2017EvaluationReport.pdf

Fox, A. B., Rosen, J., & Crawford, M. (2009). Distractions, distractions: Does instant messaging affect college students' performance on a concurrent reading comprehension task? *Cyberpsychology & Behavior, 12*(1), 51–53. doi:10.1089/cpb.2008.0107 PMID:19006461

Frances, R., Coughlan, M., & Cronin, P. (2009). Interviewing in qualitative research. *International Journal of Therapy and Rehabilitation, 16*(6), 309–314. doi:10.12968/ijtr.2009.16.6.42433

Fried, C. B. (2008). In-class laptop use and its effects on student learning. *Computers & Education, 50*(3), 906–914. doi:10.1016/j.compedu.2006.09.006

Gale, N. K., Heath, G., Cameron, E., Rashid, S., & Redwood, S. (2013). Using the framework method for the analysis of qualitative data in multi-disciplinary health research. *BMC Medical Research Methodology, 13*(1), 117. doi:10.1186/1471-2288-13-117 PMID:24047204

Gallegos, C., & Nakashima, H. (2018). Mobile Devices: A Distraction, or a Useful Tool to Engage Nursing Students? *The Journal of Nursing Education, 57*(3), 170–173. doi:10.3928/01484834-20180221-09 PMID:29505077

Gamage, D., Fernando, S., & Perera, I. (2014). Factors affecting to effective eLearning: Learners Perspective. *Scientific Research Journal, 2*(5), 42–48. Retrieved October 18, 2015, from http://www.scirj.org

Gan, B., Menkhoff, T., & Smith, R. (2015). Enhancing students' learning process through interactive digital media: new opportunities for collaborative learning. *Computers in Human Behavior, 51*(B), 652-663.

García Laborda, J. (2007). On the net: Introducing standardized EFL/ESL exams. *Language Learning & Technology, 11*(2), 3–9.

Garcia, E., Elbeltagi, I., Brown, M., & Dungay, K. (2015). The implications of a connectivist learning blog model and the changing role of teaching and learning. *British Journal of Educational Technology, 46*(4), 877–894. doi:10.1111/bjet.12184

García-Peñalvo, F. J., & Forment, M. A. (2014). Learning management system: Evolving from silos to structures. *Interactive Learning Environments, 22*(2), 143–145. doi:10.1080/10494820.2014.884790

Gardner, R. (1985). *Social Psychology and Second Language Learning: The Role of Attitudes and Motivation*. London: Edward Arnold.

Gardner, R., & Lambert, W. E. (1959). Motivational variables in second language acquisition. *Canadian Journal of Psychology, 13*(4), 266–272. doi:10.1037/h0083787 PMID:13855818

Garrett, N. (2009). Computer-assisted language learning trends and issues revisited: Integrating innovation. *Modern Language Journal, 93*(S1), 719–740. doi:10.1111/j.1540-4781.2009.00969.x

Gass, S., & Mackey, A. (2007). Input, interaction, and output in second language acquisition. In J. Williams & B. VanPatten (Eds.), *Theories in second language acquisition: An introduction* (pp. 175–199). Mahwah, NJ: Lawrence Erlbaum.

Georgina, D. A., & Olson, M. R. (2007). Integration of technology in higher education: A review of faculty self-perceptions. *The Internet and Higher Education, 11*(1), 1–8. doi:10.1016/j.iheduc.2007.11.002

Gikandi, J. W., Morrow, D., & Davis, N. E. (2011). Online formative assessment in higher education: A review of the literature. *Computers & Education, 57*(4), 2333–2351. doi:10.1016/j.compedu.2011.06.004

Gikas, J., & Grant, M. M. (2013). Mobile computing devices in higher education: Student perspectives on learning with cellphones, smartphones & social media. *Internet and Higher Education, 19*, 18–26. doi:10.1016/j.iheduc.2013.06.002

Gils, F. V. (2005). Potential applications of digital storytelling in education. In *3rd Twente Student Conference on IT* (Vol.7). University of Twente, Faculty of Electrical Engineering, Mathematics and Computer Science Enschede.

Gipps, C. V. (2005). What is the role for ICT-based assessment in universities? *Studies in Higher Education, 30*(2), 171–180. doi:10.1080/03075070500043176

Gisbert, M. (2002). El Nuevo rol del profesor en entornos tecnológicos. *Acción pedagógica, 11*(1), 48-59.

Glaser, B. G., & Strauss, A. L. (2017). *The Discovery of Grounded Theory: Strategies for Qualitative Research*. New York: Routledge. doi:10.4324/9780203793206

GoClass. (2019). Available online: https://www.goclass.com/

Godwin-Jones, R. (2008). Web-writing 2.0: Enabling, documenting, and assessing writing online. *Language Learning & Technology, 12*(2), 7–13.

Gómez, J. (2006). *Moodle 1.5 Manual de Consulta. Propuesta Pedagógica*. Valladolid: GNU Press.

Gomez, S., Zervas, P., Sampson, D. G., & Fabregat, R. (2014). Context-aware adaptive and personalized mobile learning delivery supported by UoLmP. *International Journal of Computational Science, 26*(1), 47–61. doi:10.1016/j.jksuci.2013.10.008

Gömleksiz, M. N., & Pullu, E. K. (2017). Toondoo ile dijital hikâyeler oluşturmanın öğrenci başarısına ve tutumlarına etkisi. *Electronic Turkish Studies, 12*(32), 95–110. doi:10.7827/TurkishStudies.12717

Gonella, L. & Pantò, E. (2008). Didactic architectures and organization models: a process of mutual adaptation. *eLearning Papers, 9*, 1–12.

Gönen, K., & Akbarov, A. (2015). Digital Natives in Higher Education Related to Language Learning. *Journal of Foreign Language Teaching and Applied Linguistics*. Available at www.j-fltal.org/storage/j-fltal-12.pdf

Gonye, J., Mareva, R., Dudu, W. T., & Sib, J. (2012). Academic writing challenges at universities in Zimbabwe: A case study of great Zimbabwe university. *International Journal of English and Literature*, *3*(3), 71–83.

González, J. C. (2008). TIC y la transformación de la práctica educativa en el contexto de las sociedades del conocimiento. *Revista de Universidad y Sociedad del Conocimiento, 5*(2). Retrieved from https://www.uoc.edu/rusc/5/2/dt/esp/gonzalez.pdf

González, A. B., Rodríguez, M.-J., Olmos, S., Borham, M., & García, F. (2013). Experimental evaluation of the impact of b-learning methodologies on engineering students in Spain. *Computers in Human Behavior*, *29*(2), 370–377. doi:10.1016/j.chb.2012.02.003

Goodhue, D. L. (2009). Understanding User Evaluations of Information Systems. *Management Science*, *41*(12), 1827–1844. doi:10.1287/mnsc.41.12.1827

Görgen, İ., Kömür, Ş., & Deniz, S. (2013). İngilizce öğretmen adaylarının güdüleme stratejilerini değerlendirmeleri. *Sosyal ve Beşeri Bilimler Araştırmaları Dergisi*, *23*, 147–160.

Gott, S. P., Lesgold, A., & Kane, R. S. (1996). Tutoring for Transfer of Technical Competence. In B. G. Wilson (Ed.), *Constructivist learning environments: Case studies in instructional design* (pp. 33–48). Englewood Cliffs, NJ: Educational Technology Publications.

Govindasamy, T. (2001). Successful implementation of e-learning: Pedagogical considerations. *The Internet and Higher Education*, *4*(3), 287–299. doi:10.1016/S1096-7516(01)00071-9

Grabinger, R. S., & Dunlap, J. C. (1996). Rich Environments for Active Learning in the Higher Education Classroom. In B. G. Wilson (Ed.), *Constructivist Learning Environments: Case Studies in Instructional Design* (pp. 65–81). Englewood Cliffs, NJ: Educational Technology Publications.

Graesser, A. C., Vanlehn, K., Rosé, C. P., Jordan, P. W., & Harter, D. (2001). Intelligent Tutoring Systems with Conversational Dialogue. In American Association for Artificial Intelligence (pp. 39–52). Academic Press.

Graham, C. R. (2006). Blended Learning Systems. Definition, Current Trends, and Future Directions. In C. R. Graham & C. J. Bonk (Eds.), *The Handbook of Blended Learning. Global Perspectives, Local Design* (pp. 3–21). San Francisco: Pfeiffer.

Graham, S., & Perin, D. (2007). A meta-analysis of writing instruction for adolescent students. *Journal of Educational Psychology*, *99*(3), 445–476. doi:10.1037/0022-0663.99.3.445

Grawemeyer, B., Holmes, W., Gutierrez-santos, S., & Wiedmann, M. (2016). Affecting Off-Task Behaviour : How Affect-aware Feedback Can Improve Student Learning. In Sixth International conference on learning analytics & knowledge (pp. 104–113). doi:10.1145/2883851.2883936

Green, K. C., & Gilbert, S. W. (1995). Great expectations: Content, communications, productivity, and the role of information technology in higher education. *Change*, *27*(2), 8–29. doi:10.1080/00091383.1995.9937733

Green, T. D., Brown, A., & Robinson, L. (2008). *Making the Most of the Web in your Classroom: A Teacher's Guide to Blogs, Podcasts, Wikis, Pages and Sites*. Thousand Oaks: Corwin.

Gregori-Signes, C. (2008). Integrating the old and the new: Digital storytelling in the EFL language classroom. *Greta*, *16*(1&2), 43–49.

Grgurovic, M., Chapelle, C., & Shelley, M. (2013). A meta-analysis of effectiveness studies on computer technology-supported language learning. *ReCALL Journal*, *25*(2), 165–198. doi:10.1017/S0958344013000013

Griffiths, C. (2013). *The strategy factor in successful language learning.* Bristol, UK: Multilingual Matters. doi:10.21832/9781847699428

Grivokostopoulou, F., & Hatzilygeroudis, I. (2013). Teaching AI Search Algorithms In A Web-Based Eeducational System. IADIS International Conference e-Learning.

Gross, J. M. (2018). *Document Analysis. In The SAGE Encyclopedia of Educational Research, Measurement, and Evaluation* (pp. 545–548). Thousand Oaks: SAGE Publications, Inc.

Grossman, B. (1996). *Intelligent Algebraic Tutoring Based on Student Misconceptions.* Massachusetts Institute of Technology.

Gruba, P., & Hinkelman, D. (2012). *Blending technologies in second language classrooms.* Basingstoke, UK: Palgrave McMillan. doi:10.1057/9780230356825

Guan, X. F., & Liu, Q. X. (2015). The introduction of a great help in college English composition teaching. In *Proceedings of the 2015 Joint International Social Science, Education, Language, Management and Business Conference* (pp. 133-136). Atlantis Press.

Guba, E. (1981). Criteria for assessing the trustworthiness of naturalistic inquiries. *Educational Resources Information Center Annual Review Paper, 29*, 75–91.

Guenther, S., Winkler, T., Ilgner, K., & Herczeg, M. (2008). Mobile Learning with Moles: A Case Study for Enriching Cognitive Learning by Collaborative Learning in Real World Contexts. In *Proceedings of World Conference on Educational Multimedia, Hypermedia and Telecommunications 2008* (pp. 374-380). Chesapeake, VA: AACE.

Guest, G., Bunce, A., & Johnson, L. (2006). How Many Interviews Are Enough? An Experiment with Data Saturation and Variability. *Field Methods, 18*(1), 59–82. doi:10.1177/1525822X05279903

Guest, G., MacQueen, K. M., & Namey, E. E. (2012). *Applied thematic analysis.* Los Angeles: Sage Publications. doi:10.4135/9781483384436

Güneş, M. (2015). *A Study of Teachers' Attitudes Towards Computer Technology and Their Use of Technology at the Preparatory School of Ufuk University* (Unpublished Thesis). Ufuk University, Ankara.

Hadžimehmedagić, M., & Akbarov, A. (2014). The importance of frequent usage of various motivational strategies in second language acquisition. *Linguistics, Culture and Identity in Foreign Language Education*, 1157.

Haines, K. (2016). Expanding the knowledge base of teachers' use of communication tools for language learning. *System, 62*, 102–112. doi:10.1016/j.system.2016.07.008

Hakan, K., Aydin, B., & Bulent, A. (2015). An investigation of undergraduates' language learning strategies. *Procedia: Social and Behavioral Sciences, 197*, 1348–1354. doi:10.1016/j.sbspro.2015.07.388

Hamdan, J. M., & Al-Hawamdeh, R. F. (2018). The Effects of 'Face' on Listening Comprehension: Evidence from Advanced Jordanian Speakers of English. *Journal of Psycholinguistic Research, 47*(5), 1121–1131. doi:10.100710936-018-9582-7 PMID:29637485

Hamed, T. (2016). Sampling methods in research methodology; how to choose a sampling technique for research. *International Journal of Academic Research in Management, 5*(2), 18–27.

Hammed, A., & Ola, M. U. (2012). Assessment of students' satisfaction with computer managed instruction in a gender-segregated. *The Journal of Educational Research, 5*(2), 94–103.

Hammed, T. U. (2015). A comparative study on computer-assisted instruction and its effect on secondary mathematics performance. *Dissertation Abstracts International*, *23*, 85–91.

Hampel, R. (2006). Rethinking task design for the digital age. *ReCALL*, *18*(1), 105–121. doi:10.1017/S0958344006000711

Hampel, R., & Hauck, M. (2006). Computer-mediated language learning: Making meaning in multimodal virtual learning space. *The JALT CALL Journal*, *2*(2), 3–18.

Hancock, D. R., & Algozzine, B. (2016). *Doing case study research: A practical guide for beginning researchers*. New York, NY: Teachers College Press.

Hao, K. (2019). This is how AI bias really happens—and why it's so hard to fix. *MIT Technology*. Review retrieved from https://www.technologyreview.com/s/612876/this-is-how-ai-bias-really-happensand-why-its-so-hard-to-fix/

Hao, S. (2020). Tolerance of diversity: Identity integration among People of all Ethnic groups. In *China's Solution to Its Ethno-national Issues* (p. 179). China Social Sciences Press, Springer; doi:10.1007/978-981-32-9519-3_6.

Haran, M. (2015). *A history of higher education*. Retrieved from http://institute-of-progressive-education-and-learning.org/a-history-of-education-technology/

Hardcastle, W. J., Laver, J., & Gibbon, F. E. (2013). *The Handbook of Phonetics Sciences*. Oxford: Blackwell Publishing.

Harding, L., Alderson, J. C., & Brunfaut, T. (2015). Diagnostic assessment of reading and listening in a second or foreign language: Elaborating on diagnostic principles. *Language Testing*, *32*(3), 317–336. doi:10.1177/0265532214564505

Harley, J. M., Bouchet, F., Hussain, S. M., Azevedo, R., & Calvo, R. A. (2015). A Multi-Componential Analysis of Emotions during Complex Learning with an Intelligent Multi-Agent System. *Computers in Human Behavior*, *48*, 615–625. doi:10.1016/j.chb.2015.02.013

Harman, B. A., & Sato, T. (2011). Cell phone use and grade point average among undergraduate university students. *College Student Journal*, *45*(3), 544–550.

Hatch, E., & Lazaraton, A. (1991). *The Research Manual: Design and Statistics for Applied Linguistics*. Rowley, MA: Newbury House.

Hathorn, P. P. (2005). Using digital storytelling as a literacy tool for the inner-city middle school youth. *The Charter Schools Resource Journal*, *1*(1), 32–38.

Hauck, M., & Youngs, B. (2008). Telecollaboration in multimodal environments: The impact on task design and learner interaction. *CALL*, *21*(2), 87–124. doi:10.1080/09588220801943510

Haynes, S. R., Spence, L., & Lenze, L. (2009). Scenario-based assessment of learning experiences. *Proceedings of the 39th ASEE/IEEE Frontiers in Education Conference*.

Healey, D. (1999). Theory and research: autonomy in language learning. In J. Egbert & E. Hanson-Smith (Eds.), *CALL Environments: Research, Practice and Critical Issues* (pp. 391–402). TESOL.

Heh, J. S., Li, S. C., Chang, A., Chang, M., & Liu, T. C. (2008). Diagnosis Mechanism and Feedback System to Accomplish the Full-Loop Learning Architecture. *Journal of Educational Technology & Society*, *11*, 29–44.

Heinrich, P. (2011). The iPad as a tool for education: A study of the introduction of iPads at Longfield AcademyNottingham: NAACE: The ICT Association.

Hémard, D., & Cushion, S. (2003). Design and evaluation of an online test: Assessment conceived as a complementary CALL tool. *Computer Assisted Language Learning*, *16*(2-3), 119–139. doi:10.1076/call.16.2.119.15879

Hemmati, F., & Ghaderi, E. (2014). The effect of four formats of multiple-choice questions on the listening comprehension of EFL learners. *Procedia: Social and Behavioral Sciences*, *98*, 637–644. doi:10.1016/j.sbspro.2014.03.462

Henderson, S., & Yeow, J. (2012). iPad in Education: A Case Study of iPad Adoption and Use in a Primary School. *45th Hawaii International Conference on System Science (HICSS)*, 78–87. 10.1109/HICSS.2012.390

Heo, M. (2009). Digital storytelling: An empirical study of the impact of digital storytelling on pre-service teachers' self-efficacy and dispositions towards educational technology. *Journal of Educational Multimedia and Hypermedia*, *18*(4), 405–428.

Hernández, R., Fernández, C., & Baptista, P. (2014). *Metodología de la investigación*. McGraw Hill.

Higher Education Opportunity Act (2008). *Higher Education Opportunity Act of 2008*. Pub. L. No. 110-315, § 204, 122 Stat. 70.

Hill, P. (2017). *Academic LMS market share: A view across four global regions*. Retrieved from https://eliterate.us/academic-lms-market-share-view-across-four-global-regions/

Hill, K. (2012). *Classroom-based assessment in the school foreign language classroom*. Frankfurt am Main: Peter Lang. doi:10.3726/978-3-653-01984-1

Hill, K., & McNamara, T. (2012). Developing a comprehensive, empirically based research framework for classroom-based assessment. *Language Testing*, *29*(3), 395–420. doi:10.1177/0265532211428317

Hismanoglu, M. (2001). Language learning strategies in foreign language learning and teaching. *The Internet and TESL Journal*, *8*. Retrieved December 3, 2019, from http://iteslj.org/Articles/Hismanoglu-Strategies.html

Hismanoglu, M. (2012a). The impact of a curricular innovation on prospective EFL teachers' attitudes towards ICT integration into language instruction. *International Journal of Instruction*, *5*(1), 183–202.

Hismanoglu, M. (2012b). Prospective EFL teachers' perceptions of ICT integration: A study of Distance Higher Education in Turkey. *Journal of Educational Technology & Society*, *15*(1), 185–196.

Ho, A. P., & Ng, L. (2016). Gender-based differences in language learning strategies among undergraduates in a Malaysian public university. *Issues in Language Studies*, *5*(2), 1–17. doi:10.33736/ils.1631.2016

Hoffmann, M. (2017). An exploratory study: Mobile device use for academics. *Research in Social Sciences and Technology*, *2*(1).

Hogle, P. S. (2019). Emerging Technology (S. Jacobs, Ed.). Santa Rosa, CA: The eLearning Guild. Retrieved from www.elearningGuild.com

Holec, H. (1981). Autonomy and Foreign Language Learning. Oxford, UK: Pergamon.

Holec, H. (1981). *Autonomy and Foreign Language Learning*. Oxford: Pergamon Press.

Honebein, P. C. (1996). Seven Goals for the Design of Constructivist Learning Environment. In B. G. Wilson (Ed.), *Constructivist learning environments: Case studies in instructional design* (pp. 11–24). Englewood Cliffs, NJ: Educational Technology Publications.

Honebein, P. C. (1996). Seven Goals for the Design of Constuctivist Learning Environment. In B. G. Wilson (Ed.), *Constructivist learning environments: Case studies in instructional design* (pp. 11–24). Englewood Cliffs, NJ: Educational Technology Publications.

Hooshyar, D., Ahmad, R. B., Yousefi, M., Yusop, F. D., & Horng, S. (2015). A flowchart-based intelligent tutoring system for improving problem-solving skills of novice programmers. *Journal of Computer Assisted Learning*, *31*(4), 1–17. doi:10.1111/jcal.12099

Horton, W., & Horton, K. (2003). *E-learning Tools and Technologies: A consumer's guide for trainers, teachers, educators, and instructional designers*. Chichester: Wiley.

Hsieh, S., & Cheng, Y.-T. (2014). Algorithm and intelligent tutoring system design for programmable controller programming. *International Journal of Advanced Manufacturing Technology*, *71*(5-8), 1099–1100. doi:10.1007/s00170-013-5539-z

Huang, S., & Renandya, W. A. (2018). Exploring the integration of automated feedback among lower-proficiency EFL learners. *Innovation in Language Learning and Teaching*, 1–12. doi:10.1080/17501229.2018.1471083

Hung, Y.-J., Samuelson, B. L., & Chen, S. (2016). The relationships between peer- and self-assessment and teacher assessment of young EFL learners' oral presentations. In M. Nikolov (Ed.), *Assessing young learners of English: Global and local perspectives* (pp. 317–338). Cham, Switzerland: Springer International Publishing. doi:10.1007/978-3-319-22422-0_13

Hymes, D. (1972). On Communicative Competence. In J. Pride & J. Holmes (Eds.), *Sociolinguistics* (pp. 269–293). Harmondsworth, UK: Penguin.

Ibrahim, F. M., Aziz, A. A., Zubairi, Y. Z., & Zaharim, A. (2012). Using The Rasch Model To Assess Examination Beyond Students Scores. *IEEE Global Engineering Education Conference.*

Ibrahim, R., & Jaafar, A. (2011). User Acceptance of Educational Games: A revised Unified Theory of Acceptance and Use of Technology (UTAUT). *World Academy of Science, Engineering and Technology*, *53*, 551–557.

Imhanlahimi, E. O., & Imhanlahimi, R. E. (2008). An Evaluation of the Effectiveness of Computer Assisted Learning Strategy and Expository Method of Teaching Biology: A Case Study of Lumen Christi International High School, Uromi, Nigeria. *Journal of Social Science*, *16*(3), 215–220.

Ince, A. (2015). *English Language Teachers' Perspectives towards Blended Learning in English Language Teaching* (Master's thesis). Çağ Üniversitesi Sosyal Bilimler Enstitüsü.

İnceelli, A. (2005). Dijital hikâye anlatımının bileşenleri. *The Turkish Online Journal of Educational Technology*, *4*(3), 132–142.

İncikabı, L., & Kıldan, A. O. (2013). An analysis of early childhood teacher candidates' digital stories for mathematics teaching. *International Journal of Academic Research*, *5*(2), 77–81. doi:10.7813/2075-4124.2013/5-2/B.10

Iruela, A. (2007). Principios didácticos para enseñanza de la pronunciación en lenguas extranjeras. *MarcoELE Revista de Didáctica, 4.* Retrieved from https://marcoele.com/principios-didacticos-para-la-ensenanza-de-la-pronunciacion-en-lenguas-extranjeras

Islim, O. F., & Cirak, N. S. (2017). Technology and college students: What faculty members think about the use of technology in higher education. *Malaysian Online Journal of Educational Technology*, *5*(2), 51–67.

Isotani, S., Mclaren, B. M., & Altman, M. (2010). *Towards Intelligent Tutoring with Erroneous Examples : A Taxonomy of Decimal Misconceptions. In 10th International Conference on Intelligent Tutoring Systems* (Vol. 6094, pp. 346–348). Berlin: Springer; doi:10.1007/978-3-642-13437-1_66.

Jadhav, A. S., & Sonar, R. M. (2011). Framework for evaluation and selection of the software packages: A hybrid knowledge based system approach. *Journal of Systems and Software*, *84*(8), 1394–1407. doi:10.1016/j.jss.2011.03.034

Jairak, K., Praneetpolgrang, P., & Mekhabunchakij, K. (2009). An Acceptance of Mobile Learning for Higher Education Students in Thailand. *Proceedings of the 6th International Conference on E Learning from Knowledge-Based Society.*

Jalil, J., & Sabir, S. (2019). Mobile Phone Usage and Distraction in Learning Sessions. *Pakistan Armed Forces Medical Journal, 69*(1), 54–59.

Jamieson, J. (2011). Assessment of classroom language learning. In C. Chapelle (Ed.), *Handbook of research in second language teaching and learning*. New York, NY: Routledge.

Jawaid, M., & Aly, S. M. (2014). Learning environment in undergraduate institutes in Pakistan: Determining factors and suggestions. *Journal of Postgraduate Medical Institute (Peshawar-Pakistan), 28*(3).

Jayachandran, A. (2009). *Technology integration practices of foreign language pre-service teachers: A case study* (Unpublished doctoral dissertation). The University of Iowa.

Jeffrey, L. M., Milne, J., Suddaby, G., & Higgins, A. (2014). Blended learning: How teachers balance the blend of online and classroom components. *Journal of Information Technology Education, 13*, 121–140. doi:10.28945/1968

Jeon, S. S. (2010). *Adaptive E-Learning using ECpAA Rules*. Bayesian Networks and Group Profile And Performance Data. Univeristy of Florida.

Jeremi, Z., Jovanovi, J., & Gaševi, D. (2009). Evaluating an Intelligent Tutoring System for Design Patterns : The DEPTHS Experience. *Journal of Educational Technology & Society, 12*, 111–130.

Jia, J., Chen, Y., Ding, Z., & Ruan, M. (2012). Effects of a vocabulary acquisition and assessment system on students' performance in a blended learning class for English subject. *Computers & Education, 58*(1), 63–76. doi:10.1016/j.compedu.2011.08.002

JISC. (2010). *Effective Assessment in a Digital Age*. Retrieved from www.jisc.ac.uk/digiassess

John, N., & Harrison, W. T. (2018). The effects of drill-and-practice computer instruction on learning basic mathematics. *Journal of Computing in Childhood Education, 6*, 349–356.

Johnson, D. W., & Johnson, R. T. (1996). Cooperation and the use of technology. In D. Jonassen (Ed.), *Handbook of research for educational communications and technology* (pp. 1017–1044). London: MacMillan.

Jones, D., & Matthews, D. (2002). *The transformation of instruction by information technology: Implications for state higher education policy*. Retrieved from https://wcet.wiche.edu/wcet/docs/whitepapers/Transformation_of_Instruction_by_IT_White_Paper.pdf

Jones, R. (2015). *Technology integration and higher education*. Retrieved from https://www.linkedin.com/pulse/technology-integration-higher-education-ronnie-jones/

Jugo, I., Kovačić, B., & Tijan, E. (2015). Cluster analysis of student activity in a web-based intelligent tutoring system. *Scientifc Journal of Maritime Research, 29*, 75–83.

Junco, R. (2012). *College students prefer to use Facebook in their courses*. Retrieved March 12, 2014, from http://blog.reyjunco.com/college-students-prefer-to-use-facebook-in-their-courses

Junco, R. (2012). Too much face and not enough books: The relationship between multiple indices of Facebook use and academic performance. *Computers in Human Behavior, 28*(1), 187–198. doi:10.1016/j.chb.2011.08.026

Jung, I. (2005). Cost-effectiveness of online teacher training. *Open Learning, 20*(2), 131–146. doi:10.1080/02680510500094140

Kaalberg, K. (2014). *Enhancing Teaching and Learning Through iPad Integration In*. Las Vegas: Department of Teaching and Learning, College of Education, The Graduate College, University of Nevada.

Kacalak, W., Majewski, M., & Zurada, J. M. (2010). Intelligent E-Learning Systems for Evaluation of User ' s Knowledge and Skills with Efficient Information Processing. In *International Conference on Artificial Intelligence and Soft Computing* (pp. 508–515). Springer.

Kajder, S., & Swenson, J. A. (2004). Digital images in the language arts classroom in the curriculum: Language arts. *Learning and Leading with Technology, 31*(8), 18–21.

Kalinga, E. A. (2008). *Development of an Interactive eTlearning Management System (eTLMS) for Tanzanian Secondary Schools*. Retrieved October 22, 2012, from https://www.bth.se/fou/forskinfo.nsf/alfs/078658eaeb62ee0ec12574570033056b/$file/Kalinga_lic.pdf

Karakaya, K. (2010). *An investigation of English language teachers' attitudes toward computer technology and their use of technology in language teaching*. Academic Press.

Karaoglan Yilmaz, F., & Durak, H. (2018). Examining pre-service teachers' opinions about digital story design. *Education and Information Technologies, 23*(3), 1277–1295. doi:10.100710639-017-9666-2

Karkouti, I. M. (2016). *University faculty members' perceptions of the factors that facilitate technology integration into their instruction: An exploratory case study in Qatar* (Unpublished doctoral dissertation). University of Hartford, West Hartford, CT.

Kasim, N. N. M., & Khalid, F. (2016). Choosing the Right Learning Management System (LMS) for the Higher Education Institution Context: A Systematic Review. *iJET, 11*(6), 55-61. Retrieved March 25, 2019, from http://www.i-jet.org

Kaur, M. (2013). Blended learning - its challenges and future. *Procedia: Social and Behavioral Sciences, 93*, 612–617. doi:10.1016/j.sbspro.2013.09.248

Kazi, H., Haddawy, P., & Suebnukarn, S. (2012). Employing UMLS for generating hints in a tutoring system for medical problem-based learning. *Journal of Biomedical Informatics, 45*(3), 557–565. doi:10.1016/j.jbi.2012.02.010 PubMed

Kearney, M. (2009). Towards A Learning Design for Student-Generated Digital Storytelling. In *Future of Learning Design Conference*. New South Wales, Australia: University of Wollongong. Retrieved from http://ro.uow.edu.au/cgi/viewcontent.cgi

Kearney, M., & Schuck, S. (2006). Spotlight on authentic learning: Student developed digital video projects. *Australasian Journal of Educational Technology, 22*(2), 189–208. doi:10.14742/ajet.1298

Keles, A., Ocak, R., Keles, A., & Gulcu, A. (2009). ZOSMAT : Web-based intelligent tutoring system for teaching – learning process. *Expert Systems with Applications, 36*(2), 1229–1239. doi:10.1016/j.eswa.2007.11.064

Keller, J. M. (1987). Development and Use of the ARCS Model of Instructional Design. *Journal of Instrcutional Development, 10*(3), 2–10. doi:10.1007/BF02905780

Kerlinger, F. N. (1985). *Investigación del comportamiento. Técnicas y metodología*. Nueva Editorial Interamericana.

Kerr, S., Muller, D., McKinon, W., & Mc Inerney, P. (2016). An online formative assessment tool to prepare students for summative assessment in physiology. *African Journal of Health Professions Education, 8*(1), 72–76. doi:10.7196/AJHPE.2016.v8i1.581

Kesan, C., & Crow, D. T. (2018). The effect of computer-assisted instruction on the achievement and attitudes towards mathematics of students in mathematics education. *International Journal of Global Education, 1*(2), 50–57.

Kessler, G. (2009). Student-initiated attention to form in wiki-based collaborative writing. *Language Learning & Technology, 13*(1), 79–95.

Khachatryan, G. A., Romashov, A. V., Khachatryan, A. R., Gaudino, S. J., Khachatryan, J. M., Guarian, K. R., & Yufa, N. V. (2014). Reasoning Mind Genie 2 : An Intelligent Tutoring System as a Vehicle for International Transfer of Instructional Methods in Mathematics. *International Journal of Artificial Intelligence in Education, 24*(3), 333–382. doi:10.1007/s40593-014-0019-7

Khamkhien, A. (2010). Factors Affecting Language Learning Strategy Reported Usage by Thai and Vietnamese EFL Learners. *Electronic Journal of Foreign Language Teaching, 7*(1), 66–85.

Khan, I. A. (2011). The teacher of English: Pedagogic relevance in Saudi Arabia. *English Language Teaching, 4*(2), 112–120. doi:10.5539/elt.v4n2p112

Khan, M. J., & Mustafa, K. (2019). Adaptive hypermedia instructional system (AHIS): A model. *Education and Information Technologies, 24*(6), 3329–3392. doi:10.1007/s10639-019-09927-x

Khatimin, N., Aziz, A. A., Zaharim, A., Sahari, J., & Rahmat, A. O. K. (2013). Setting the Standard for Project Design course using Rasch Measurement Model. In *IEEE Global Engineering Education Conference* (pp. 1062–1065). Berlin, Germany: IEEE; doi:10.1109/EduCon.2013.6530239.

Kiddle, T., & Kormos, J. (2011). The effect of mode of response on a semi-direct test of oral proficiency. *Language Assessment Quarterly, 8*(4), 342–360. doi:10.1080/15434303.2011.613503

Kim, J., & Craig, D. A. (2012). Validation of a video conferenced speaking test. *Computer Assisted Language Learning, 25*(3), 257–275. doi:10.1080/09588221.2011.649482

Kim, J., Guo, P. J., Cai, C. J., Li, S. W., Gajos, K. Z., & Miller, R. C. (2014, October). Data-driven interaction techniques for improving navigation of educational videos. In *Proceedings of the 27th annual ACM symposium on User interface software and technology* (pp. 563-572). 10.1145/2642918.2647389

Kirschner, P. A, & Karpinski, A. C. A. (2010). Facebook® and academic performance. *Computers in Human Behavior, 26*(6), 1237-1245. doi:10.1016/j.chb.2010.03.024

Kleftodimos, A., & Evangelidis, G. (2016). Using open source technologies and open internet resources for building an interactive video based learning environment that supports learning analytics. *Smart Learning Environments, 3*(9), 1–23. doi:10.118640561-016-0032-4

Klobas, J., & McGill, T. (2010). The role of involvement in learning management system success. *Journal of Computing in Higher Education, 22*(2), 114–134. doi:10.100712528-010-9032-5

Knuth, R. A., & Cunnigham, D. J. (1993). Tools for constrcutivism. In T. Duffy, J. Lowyck, & D. Jonassen (Eds.), *Designing environments for constructivist learning* (pp. 163–187). Berlín: Springer-Verlag. doi:10.1007/978-3-642-78069-1_9

Kocaman-Karoğlu, A. (2015). Öğretim sürecinde hikâye anlatmanın teknolojiyle değişen doğası: Dijital hikâye anlatımı. *Eğitim Teknolojisi Kuram ve Uygulama, 5*(2), 89–106.

Koh, J., Chai, C., Benjamin, W., & Hong, H. (2015). Technological Pedagogical Content Knowledge (TPACK) and Design Thinking: A Framework to Support ICT Lesson Design for 21st Century Learning. *The Asia-Pacific Education Researcher, 24*(3), 535–543. doi:10.1007/s40299-015-0237-2

Kohonen, V. (1992). *Experiential Language Learning: Second Language Learning as Cooperative Learner Education.* Cambridge: CUP.

Kolb, D. A. (1984). *Experiential Learning: experience as the source of learning and development.* Prentice Hall.

Kolekar, S. V. M., Pai, R., & Pai, M. M. M. (2019). Rule based adaptive user interface for adaptive E-learning system. *Education and Information Technologies, 24*(1), 613–641. doi:10.1007/s10639-018-9788-1

Koole, M., & Ally, M. (2006). Framework for the Rational Analysis of Mobile Education (FRAME) Model: Revising the ABCs of Educational Practices. *International Conference on Networking, International Conference on Systems and International Conference on Mobile Communications and Learning Technologies (ICNICONSMCL'06)*, 216. Available in: https://auspace.athabascau.ca/bitstream/2149/612/1/01628461.pdf

Kordaki, M. (2014). On the design of educational digital stories: The Ed-W model. *Procedia: Social and Behavioral Sciences, 116*, 1631–1635. doi:10.1016/j.sbspro.2014.01.447

Koruyan, K. (2016). *The influence of technology-enhanced task design on the development of language learner autonomy and motivation in an Anatolian high school; A case study* (Unpublished Doctoral dissertation). Open university, Milton Keynes, UK.

Koschmann, T. (2002). Dewey's Contribution to the Foundations of CSCL Research. Proceedings of CSCL 2002, 17–22. doi:10.3115/1658616.1658618

Koschmann, T., Stahl, G., & Zemel, A. (2004). The Video Analyst's Manifesto. In *Proceedings of the 6th International Conference on Learning Sciences* (pp. 278–285). International Society of the Learning Sciences.

Koscianski, A., & Farago, D. (2014). A Design Model for Educational Multimedia Software. Creative Education, 05(23), 5. doi:10.4236/ce.2014.523224

Krashen, S. (2004). *The power of reading: insights from the research.* Portsmouth, NH: Libraries Unlimited, Heineann.

Krathwohl, D. R. (2002). A Revision of Bloom's Taxonomy: An Overview. *Theory into Practice, 41*(1), 212–218. doi:10.1207/s15430421tip4104_2

Krathwohl, D. R., Bloom, B. S., & Masia, B. B. (1956). Taxnomy of Educational Objectives: The Classification of Eucational Goals. In *Handbook II*. Affective Domain. David McKay Company, Incorporated.

Kucirkova, N., Messer, D., Sheehy, K., & Panadero, C. (2014). Children's Engagement with Educational iPad Apps: Insights from a Spanish Classroom. *Computers & Education, 71*, 175–184. doi:10.1016/j.compedu.2013.10.003

Kulhavy, R. W. (1977). Feedback in Written Instruction. *American Educational Reserach Association, 47*(2), 211–232.

Kulik, J. A., & Fletcher, J. D. (2015). Effectiveness of Intelligent Tutoring Systems: A Meta-Analytic Review. *Review of Educational Research, 37*, 1–37. doi:10.3102/0034654315581420

Küngerü, A. (2016). Bir ifade aracı olarak dijital öykü anlatımı. *Abant Kültürel Araştırmalar Dergisi, 1*(2), 190–202.

Kurek, M., & Hauck, M. (2014). Closing the "digital divide" – a framework for multiliteracy training. In G.J. Pettes, & L. Williams (Eds.), Digital Literacies in Foreign and Second Language Education: Research, Perspectives, and Best Practice. CALICO Monograph Series 12. San Marcos, TX: CALICO.

Kurek, M., & Hauck, M. (2014). Closing the Digital Divide: A Framework for Multiliteracy Training. In J. Guikema & L. Williams (Eds.), *Digital Literacies in Foreign and Second Language Education* (pp. 119–140). San Marcos, TX: Calico.

Kurosu, M., & Kashimura, K. (1995). Apparent Usability vs. Inherent Usability. In CHI 95 Mosaic Of Creativity (pp. 1–2). doi:10.1145/223355.223680

Kurudayıoğlu, M., & Bal, M. (2014). Ana dili eğitiminde dijital hikâye anlatımlarının kullanımı. *Sakarya Üniversitesi Eğitim Fakültesi Dergisi,* (28), 74-95.

Lai, J. (2011). The challenge of assessing learner autonomy analytically. In C. J. Everhard, J. Mynar, & R. Smith (Eds.), Autonomy in language learning: opening a can of worms (pp. 43-49). Canterbury, UK: IATEFL.

Lai, J. (2001). Towards an analytic approach to assessing learner autonomy. *AILA Review, 15,* 34–44.

Lambert, J. (2002). *Digital storytelling: Capturing lives, creating community.* Berkeley, CA: Digital Diner Press.

Lamb, T. (2010). Assessment of autonomy or assessment for autonomy? Evaluating learner autonomy for formative purposes. In A. Paran & L. Sercu (Eds.), *Testing the Untestable in Language Education* (pp. 77–97). Bristol, UK: Multilingual Matters. doi:10.21832/9781847692672-008

Lang, J. (2017). *The Distracted Class.* Retrieved November 10, 2017, From: http://www.chronicle.com/article/The-Distracted-Classroom/239446

Lanzilotti, R., & Roselli, T. (2007). An Experimental Evaluation of Logiocando, an Intelligent Tutoring Hypermedia System. *International Journal of Artificial Intelligence in Education, 17*(1), 41–56.

Larsen-Freeman, D. (2003). *Techniques and Principles in Language Teaching.* Oxford: Oxford University Press.

Larsen-Freeman, D., & Long, M. (1994). *Introducción al estudio de la adquisición de segundas lenguas.* Madrid: Gredos.

Lau, M. A. I. (2009). *TBL in English Language Learning in Macau: Effects on Chinese Tertiary Learners' Beliefs and Motivations* (Unpublished PhD thesis). The University of Nottingham.

Laufer, B. (1994). The lexical profile of second language writing: Does it change over time? *RELC Journal, 25*(2), 21–33. doi:10.1177/003368829402500202

Laurillard, D., & Pachler, N. (2007). Pedagogical forms of mobile learning: framing research questions. In N. Pachler (Ed.), *Mobile learning: towards a research agenda* (pp. 33–54). London: WLE Centre, IOE.

Le, Q. X. (2013). *Fostering learner autonomy in language learning in tertiary education: an intervention study of university students in Hochiminh City, Vietnam* (Doctoral dissertation). University of Nottingham.

Leakey, J., & Ranchoux, A. (2006). BLINGUA. A blended language learning approach for CALL. *Computer Assisted Language Learning, 19*(4/5), 357–372. doi:10.1080/09588220601043016

Learning, V. (2007). *MY Access! Efficacy Report.* Newtown, PA: Author. Retrieved from http://www.vantagelearning.com/school/research/myaccess.html

Lebow, D. (1993). Constructivist Values for Instructional Systems Design: Five Principles toward a New Mindset. *Educational Technology Research and Development, 41*(3), 4–16. doi:10.1007/BF02297354

Lee, & Markey, A. (2014). A study of learners' perceptions of online intercultural exchange through Web 2.0 technologies. ReCALL, 26(3), 281–297. doi:10.1017/S0958344014000111

Lee, C. K. (2010). An overview of language learning strategies. *ARECLS, 7,* 132–152.

Lee, I. (2017). *Classroom writing assessment and feedback in L2 school contexts.* Singapore: Springer Singapore. doi:10.1007/978-981-10-3924-9

Lee, J. W. (2010). Online Support Service Quality, Online Learning Acceptance, and Student Satisfaction. *The Internet and Higher Education, 13*(4), 277–283. doi:10.1016/j.iheduc.2010.08.002

Lee, J., Lin, L., & Robertson, T. (2012). The impact of media multitasking on learning. *Learning, Media and Technology, 37*(1), 94–104. doi:10.1080/17439884.2010.537664

Lee, L. (2010). Exploring wiki-mediated collaborative writing: A case-study in an elementary Spanish course. *CALICO Journal, 27*(2), 260–276. doi:10.11139/cj.27.2.260-276

Lessard-Clouston, M. (1996). ESL vocabulary learning in a TOEFL preparation class: A case study. *Canadian Modern Language Review, 53*(1), 97–119. doi:10.3138/cmlr.53.1.97

LessonUp. (2019). Available online: https://www.lessonup.com/en/

Levett-Jones, T., Bowen, L., & Morris, A. (2015). Enhancing nursing students' understanding of threshold concepts through the use of digital stories and a virtual community called 'Wiimali'. *Nurse Education in Practice, 15*(2), 91–96. doi:10.1016/j.nepr.2014.11.014 PMID:25487056

Levis, J. M. (2005). Changing Contexts and Shifting Paradigms in Pronunciation Teaching. *TESOL Quarterly, 39*(3), 369–377. doi:10.2307/3588485

Levy, M. (2009). Technologies in use for second language learning. *Modern Language Journal, 93*(S1), 769–782. doi:10.1111/j.1540-4781.2009.00972.x

Levy, M., & Stockwell, G. (2006). *CALL Dimensions: Options and Issues in Computer-assisted Language Learning.* Lawrence Erlbaum Associates.

Levy, M., & Stockwell, G. (2006). *CALL Dimensions: Options and Issues in Computer-Assisted Language Learning.* Mahwah, NJ: Routledge.

Li, Z. X., Lu, Z. H., & Li, X. W. (2015). AWE-based corrective feedback on developing EFL learners' writing skill. In *Critical CALL – Proceedings of the 2015 EUROCALL Conference* (pp. 375-380). Padova, Italy: Research-publishing.net.

Liao, H. C. (2015). Using automated writing evaluation to reduce grammar errors in writing. *ELT Journal, 70*(3), 308–319. doi:10.1093/elt/ccv058

Li, C.-H. (2019). Using a Listening Vocabulary Levels Test to Explore the Effect of Vocabulary Knowledge on GEPT Listening Comprehension Performance. *Language Assessment Quarterly, 16*(3), 328–344. doi:10.1080/15434303.2019.1648474

Lieske, C. (2007). Teaching Effective Second Language Listening. 島根大学外国語教育センタージャーナル, *2*, 39-51.

Li, J., Link, S., & Hegelheimer, V. (2015). Rethinking the role of automated writing evaluation feedback in ESL writing instruction. *Journal of Second Language Writing, 27*, 1–18. doi:10.1016/j.jslw.2014.10.004

Lilian, C., & Musa, H. K. (2017). The attitudes on learning effects in computer managed instruction for Mathematics. *Journal of Technology and Computing, 12*(3), 21-28.

Li, M., & Zhu, W. (2017). Good or bad collaborative wiki writing: Exploring links between group interactions and writing products. *Journal of Second Language Writing, 35*, 38–53. doi:10.1016/j.jslw.2017.01.003

Lim, C., Han, H., Jung, D., Ozturk, Y. E., Hong, J., Kim, K., & Kwon, H. (2017). Exploring an e-learning platform prototype for supporting learning design. *Journal of Educational Technology, 33*(4), 799–837. doi:10.17232/KSET.33.4.799

Lin, H. Y., Chen, C. Y., & Chen, W. C. (2008). Scaffolding m-Learning approach of automotive practice courses in senior vocational high school. In *Frontiers in Education Conference, 2008. FIE 2008. 38th Annual* (pp. F1H-12). IEEE.

Lincoln, Y. S., & Guba, E. (1985). *Naturalistic Inquiry.* Beverley Hills, CA: Sage. doi:10.1016/0147-1767(85)90062-8

Lin, H.-Y., Hsu, P.-Y., & Sheen, G.-J. (2007). A fuzzy-based decision-making procedure for data warehouse system selection. *Expert Systems with Applications*, *32*(3), 939–953. doi:10.1016/j.eswa.2006.01.031

Lipponen, L., Rahikainen, M., Lallimo, J., & Hakkarainen, K. (2003). Patterns of participation and discourse in elementary students' computer-supported collaborative learning. *Learning and Instruction*, *13*(5), 487–509. doi:10.1016/S0959-4752(02)00042-7

Litman, D., Strik, H., & Lim, S. G. (2018). Speech Technologies and the Assessment of Second Language Speaking: Approaches, Challenges, and Opportunities. *Language Assessment Quarterly*, *15*(3), 294–309. doi:10.1080/15434303.2018.1472265

Little, D. (1999). Developing learner autonomy in the foreign language classroom: A social-interactive view of learning and three fundamental pedagogical principles. *Revista Canaria de Estudios Ingleses*, (38), 77-88.

Little, D. (2000). We're all in it together: exploring the interdependence of teacher and learner autonomy. In *The 7th Nordic Conference and Workshops on Autonomous Language Learning*. University of Helsinki.

Little, D. (2001). We're all in it together: exploring the interdependence of teacher and learner autonomy. In *The 7th Nordic Conference and Workshops on Autonomous Language Learning*. University of Helsinki.

Little, D. (1991). *Learner Autonomy 1: Definitions, Issues and Problems*. Dublin: Authentik.

Little, D. (1991). *Learner Autonomy 1: Definitions, Issues, Problems*. Dublin: Authentik.

Little, D. (1996). Freedom to learn and compulsion to interact: Promoting learner autonomy through the use of information systems and information technologies. In R. Pemberton, E. S. L. Li, W. W. F. Or, & H. Pierson (Eds.), *Taking control: Autonomy in language learning* (pp. 203–218). Hong Kong: Hong Kong University Press.

Little, D. (2007). Language learner autonomy: Some fundamental consideration revisited. *Innovation in Language Learning and Teaching*, *1*(1), 14–29. doi:10.2167/illt040.0

Littlejohn, A., & Pegler, C. (2007). *Preparing for Blended e-Learning*. London: Routledge. doi:10.4324/9780203961322

Littlewood, W. (1996). Autonomy: An anatomy and a framework. *System*, *24*(4), 427–435. doi:10.1016/S0346-251X(96)00039-5

Liu, Y. C., Huang, Y., & Lin, C. (2012). Organizational factors' effects on the success of e-learning systems and organizational benefits: An empirical study in Taiwan. *The International Review of Research in Open and Distributed Learning*. Retrieved April 2, 2015, from http://www.irrodl.org/index.php/irrodl/article/view/1203/2302

Liu, S. C., & Hung, P. Y. (2016). Teaching Pronunciation with Computer Assisted Pronunciation Instruction in a Technological University. *Universal Journal of Educational Research*, *4*(9), 1939–1943. doi:10.13189/ujer.2016.040902

Liu, S., & Kunnan, A. J. (2016). Investigating the application of automated writing evaluation to Chinese undergraduate English majors: A case study of "WriteToLearn". *CALICO Journal*, *33*(1), 71–91.

Liu, Y., Li, H., & Carlsson, C. (2010). Factors Driving the Adoption of M-learning: An empirical study. *Computers & Education*, *55*(3), 1211–1219. doi:10.1016/j.compedu.2010.05.018

Liyanage, I., & Bartlett, B. J. (2012). Gender and language learning strategies: Looking beyond the categories. *Language Learning Journal*, *40*(2), 237–253. doi:10.1080/09571736.2011.574818

Li, Z., Link, S., Ma, H., Yang, H., & Hegelheimer, V. (2014). The role of automated writing evaluation holistic scores in the ESL classroom. *System*, *44*, 66–78. doi:10.1016/j.system.2014.02.007

Llisterri, J. (2007). La enseñanza de la pronunciación asistida por ordenador. In *XXIV congreso internacional de AESLA. Aprendizaje de lenguas, uso del lenguaje y modelación cognitiva: Perspectivas aplicadas entre disciplinas* (91-120). España, Madrid: UNED.

Lofstrom, E., & Nevgi, A. (2007). From strategic planning to meaningful learning: Diverse perspectives on the development of web-based teaching and learning in higher education. *British Journal of Educational Technology*, *38*(2), 312–324. doi:10.1111/j.1467-8535.2006.00625.x

López, C., & Matesanz, M. (2009). *Las plataformas de aprendizaje. Del mito a la realidad.* Madrid: Editorial Biblioteca Nueva.

Lu, Z. H., & Li, Z. X. (2016). Exploring EFL learners' lexical application in AWE-based writing. In S. Papadima-Sophocleous, L. Bradley, & S. Thouësny (Eds.), CALL communities and culture – short papers from EUROCALL 2016 (pp. 295-301). Dublin, Ireland: Research-publishing.net.

Maldonado, M. (2016). Communication strategies used by different level L2 English learners in oral interaction. *Revista signos, 49*(90), 71-93. doi: 09342016000100004 doi:10.4067/S0718

Mandl, H., & Kopp, B. (2006). *Blended Learning*. Forschungsfragen und Perspektiven.

Man-Man, P. (2006). Developing Students' listening and speaking Skills Through ELT Podcasts. *Education Journal*, *34*(2), 115–134.

Marciniak, J. (2014). Building intelligent tutoring systems immersed in repositories of e-learning content. *Procedia Computer Science*, *35*, 541–550. doi:10.1016/j.procs.2014.08.135

Martin, F. (2008). Blackboard as the learning management system of a computer literacy course. *Journal of Online Learning and Teaching*, *4*(2), 138–145. http://libres.uncg.edu/ir/uncw/f/martinf2008-1.pdf

Martirosyan, N. M., Kennon, J. L., Saxon, D. P., Edmonson, S. L., & Skidmore, S. T. (2017). Instructional technology practices in developmental education in Texas. *Journal of College Reading and Learning*, *47*(1), 3–25. doi:10.1080/10790195.2016.1218806

Masrom, M., Zainon, O., & Rahiman, R. (2008). Critical success in e-learning: An examination of technological and institutional support factors. *International Journal of Cyber Society and Education*, *1*(2), 131–142. http://eprints.utm.my/6952/

Mbah, E. E., Mbah, B. M., Iloene, M. I., & Iloene, G. (2014). Podcasts for Learning English Pronunciation in Igboland: Students' Experiences and Expectations. *The EUROCALL Review*, *22*(2), 57–68. doi:10.4995/eurocall.2014.3635

McAfee, P. (2006). Enterprise 2.0: The dawn of emergent collaboration. *MIT Sloan Management Review*, *47*(1), 21–28. doi:10.1109/EMR.2006.261380

Mcdonald, J., Knott, A., Stein, S., & Zeng, R. (2013). An empirically-based, tutorial dialogue system: design, implementation and evaluation in a first year health sciences course. 30th ascilite Conference.

McDonough, J., Shaw, C., & Masuhara, H. (2013). *Materials and Methods in ELT.* Sussex, UK: John Wiley & Sons.

McFarlane, A. (2001). Perspectives on the relationships between ICT and assessment. *Journal of Computer Assisted Learning*, *17*(3), 227–235. doi:10.1046/j.0266-4909.2001.00177.x

McFarlane, A. (2002). *Educating the inheritors of the information age. Inaugural Lecture, 18 November 2002.* Bristol: University of Bristol.

Mcgee, P., & Green, M. (2008). Lifelong learning and systems: A postFordist analysis. *Journal of Online Learning and Teaching, 4*(2), 146–157.

McGill, T. J., & Klobas, J. (2009). A task–technology fit view of learning management system impact. *Computers & Education, 52*(2), 496–508. doi:10.1016/j.compedu.2008.10.002

McGill, T., Klobas, J. E., & Renz, S. (2008). The Relationship between LMS Use and Teacher Performance The Role of Task-Technology Fit. *19th Australasian Conference on Information Systems*, 648–657.

McMullen, M. G. (2009). Using language learning strategies to improve the writing skills of Saudi EFL students: Will it really work? *System: An International Journal of Educational Technology and Applied Linguistics, 37*, 418-433.

Meadows, D. (2003). Digital storytelling: Research-based practice in new media. *Visual Communication, 2*(2), 189–193. doi:10.1177/1470357203002002004

Mee-chin, W., Abrizah, A., & Lip, Y. P. (2012). Computer-managed instruction (CMI)-based online forums. *Journal of Educational Computing Research, 47*(2), 209–233. doi:10.2190/EC.47.2.e

Mehdiyev, E., Gonca, U. S. T. A., & Uğurlu, C. T. (2016). İngilizce dil öğreniminde motivasyon. *Elektronik Sosyal Bilimler Dergisi, 15*(57), 361–371.

Mehta, G., & Mokhasi, V. (2014). Item analysis of multiple choice questions-an assessment of the assessment tool. *International Journal of Health Sciences and Research, 4*(7), 197–202.

Mellow, J. D., Reeder, K., & Forster, E. (1996). Using time-series research designs to investigate the effects of instruction on SLA. *Studies in Second Language Acquisition, 18*(3), 325–350. doi:10.1017/S0272263100015059

Mercado, L. (2017). *Technology for the Language Classroom: Creating a 21st Century Learning Experience*. London: Macmillan International Higher Education. doi:10.1057/978-1-137-49785-7

Mercer-Mapstone, L. D., & Matthews, K. E. (2017). Student perceptions of communication skills in undergraduate science at an Australian research-intensive university. *Assessment & Evaluation in Higher Education, 42*(1), 98–114. doi:10.1080/02602938.2015.1084492

Meri, S. (2012). Autonomous computer-assisted language learning: Turkish primary school students' perceptions of Dyned software. *International Conference „ICT for Language Learning*, 1–4.

Merrill, M. D. (1983). Component Diaply Theory. In Instructional Design Theories and Models: An overview of their current status (pp. 282–333). Academic Press.

Mertens, D. M. (2005). *Research and Evaluation in Education and Psychology: Integrating Diversity with Quantitative, Qualitative, and Mixed Methods* (2nd ed.). Thousand Oaks, CA: Sage.

Metcalfe, J., & Noom-Ura, S. (2013). Communication strategy use of high and low proficiency learners of English at a Thai University. *LEARN Journal, 6*(1), 66–87.

Miles, M. B., & Huberman, A. (1994). *Qualitative Data Analysis: An Expanded Sourcebook*. Newbury Park, CA: SAGE.

Miles, M., & Huberman, A. (1994). *Qualitative data analysis: An expanded sourcebook*. Beverly Hills: Sage.

Millán, E., Loboda, T., & Pérez-de-la-Cruz, J. L. (2010). Bayesian networks for student model engineering. *Computers & Education, 55*(4), 1663–1683. doi:10.1016/j.compedu.2010.07.010

Mills, S. C., & Tincher, R. C. (2005). Be the technology: A developmental model for evaluating technology integration. *Journal of Research on Technology in Education, 35*(3), 382–401. doi:10.1080/15391523.2003.10782392

Mingyong, Z. (2015). Investigation into the use of mobile technology in English teaching and learning in institutes of higher vocational education in Hubei province in China. In *Futuristic Trends on Computational Analysis and Knowledge Management (ABLAZE), 2015 International Conference on* (pp. 505-509). IEEE. 10.1109/ABLAZE.2015.7155037

Ministry of Higher Education (MOHE). (2015). Malaysia Education Blueprint 2015-2025 (Higher Education) (Vol. 2025). Ministry of Education Malaysia. doi:10.5923/j.ijis.20120206.05

Mitul, M. (2018). *Artificial Intelligence in Testing: Tools and Advantages.* Retrieved from https://marutitech.com/artificial-intelligence-in-testing/

Mlitwa, N. B. W., & Van Belle, J. P. W. (2011). Mediators for Lecturer Perspectives on Learning Management Systems at Universities in The Western Cape, South Africa. In *Pacific Asia Conference on Information Systems, PACIS 2011: Quality Research in Pacific Asia, Brisbane, Queensland, Australia*, 7-11.

Mohammed, A. (2011). EFL effective factors: Anxiety and motivation and their effect on Saudi college student's achievement. *Proceedings of the 4th International Conference of Education, Research and Innovations.*

Mohammed, P., & Mohan, P. (2015). Dynamic Cultural Contextualisation of Educational Content in Intelligent Learning Environments using ICON. *International Journal of Artificial Intelligence in Education, 25*(2), 249–270. doi:10.1007/s40593-014-0033-9

MoLeNet. (2007). *What is the mobile learning?* Retrieved March 23, 2017, from: http://www.molenet.org.uk/about.html

Moodle. (2020a). Retrieved from https://moodle.org/plugins/

Moodle. (2020b). Retrieved from https://moodle.com/community/

Moore, M. G. (1993). Three types of interaction. In K. Harry, M. Hohn, & D. Keegan (Eds.), *Distance education: New perspectives* (pp. 12–24). London: Routledge.

Morgan, G. (2003). *Faculty use of course management systems.* Retrieved November 10, 2012, from https://www.educause.edu/ir/library/pdf/EKF/ekf0302.pdf

Morris, C. D., Bransford, J. D., & Franks, J. J. (1979). Levels of Processing versus Transfer Appropriate Processing. *Journal of Verbal Learning and Verbal Behavior, 16*(5), 519–533. doi:10.1016/S0022-5371(77)80016-9

Morrison, B. (2005). Evaluating learning gain in a self-access language learning centre. *Language Teaching Research, 9*(3), 267–293. doi:10.1191/1362168805lr167oa

Morshead, R. W. (1965). Taxonomy of Educational Objectives HandBook II : Affective Domain. In Studies in Phiolosophy and Education (pp. 164–170). Academic Press.

Moshagen, M., Musch, J., & Göritz, A. S. (2009). A blessing, not a curse : Experimental evidence for beneficial effects of visual aesthetics on performance. *Ergonomics, 52*(10), 1311–1311. doi:10.1080/00140130903061717 PubMed

Mosquera, L. H. (2017). Impact of implementing a virtual learning environment (VLE) in the EFL classroom. *Íkala, revista de lenguaje y cultura, 22*(3), 479-498.

Motteram, G. (2016). Membership, belonging, and identity in the twenty-first century. *ELT Journal, 70*(2), 150–159. doi:10.1093/elt/ccw001

Motteram, G. (Ed.). (2013). *Innovations in learning technologies for English language teaching.* London: The British Council.

Mtebe, J.S. (2015). Learning Management System success: Increasing Learning Management System usage in higher education in sub-Saharan Africa. *International Journal of Education and Development using Information and Communication Technology, 11*(2), 51-64.

Muho, A., & Kurani, A. (2014). The role of interaction in second language acquisition. *European Scientific Journal, 16*, 44–54. Retrieved from https://eujournal.org/index.php/esj/article/view/4696/4488

Mukandutiye, D., Sevilla, J., & Makhanu, E. (2014). Adoption of e-assessment in Strathmore University. In *Proceedings of IST-Africa Conference* Mauritius. IEEE.

Mullamaa, K. (2010). ICT in language learning – benefits and methodological implications. *International Education Studies, 3*(1), 38–44. doi:10.5539/ies.v3n1p38

Mullen, C. (2014). *iPad iPedagogy: A study of teacher perceptions on the impact of the iPad on teaching and assessment practices at a third level college in the United Arab Emirates* (MEd dissertation). The British University in Dubai.

Murase, F. (2010). *Developing a new instrument for measuring learner autonomy* (Unpublished doctoral dissertation). Macquarie University, Sydney, Australia.

Murase, F. (2015). Measuring language learner autonomy: problems and possibilities. In C. J. Everhard & L. Murphy (Eds.), *Assessment and Autonomy in Language Learning* (pp. 35–63). Basingstoke, UK: Palgrave Macmillan. doi:10.1057/9781137414380_3

Murphy, L., Hauck, M., Nicolson, M., & Adams, H. (2005). Reflection and self-evaluation. In S. Hurd, & L. Murphy (Eds.), Success with Languages. Abingdon: Routledge in association with The Open University.

Murray, D. (2005). Technologies for second language literacy. *Annual Review of Applied Linguistics, 25*, 188–201. doi:10.1017/S0267190505000103

Murray, G. (1999). Autonomy and language learning in a simulated environment. *System, 27*(3), 295–308. doi:10.1016/S0346-251X(99)00026-3

Mutlu, A., & Eroz-Tuga, B. (2013). The role of computer-assisted language learning (CALL) in promoting learner autonomy. *Eğitim Arastırmaları-Eurasian Journal of Educational Research, 51*, 107–122.

Myers, M., & Avison, D. (2002). *Qualitative research in information systems: a reader*. London: Sage Publications. Retrieved December 6, 2012, from http://en.scientificcommons.org/8816846

Mynard, J. (2004). Investigating evidence of learner autonomy in a virtual EFL classroom: a grounded theory approach. In J. Hull, J. Harris, & P. Darasawang (Eds.), Research In ELT: proceedings of the international conference (pp. 117-127). School of Liberal Arts and the Continuing Education Center, King Mongkut's University of Technology.

Mynard, J. (2006). Measuring learner autonomy: Can it be done? *Independence. Newsletter of the IATEFL Learner Autonomy Special Interest Group, 37*, 3–6.

Nafa, F., Othman, S., & Khan, J. (2016). Automatic Concepts Classification based on Bloom's Taxonomy using Text Analysis and the Naïve Bayes Classifier Method. CSEDU 2016 - Proceedings of the 8th International Conference on Computer Supported Education, 1, 391–396. 10.5220/0005813303910396

Nafa, F., & Khan, J. (2015). Conceptualize the Domain Knowledge Space in the Light of Cognitive Skills. CSEDU 2015 - 7th International Conference on Computer Supported Education. *Proceedings, 1*, 285–295. doi:10.5220/0005441602850295

Nakatsuhara, F., Inoue, C., Berry, V., & Galaczi, E. (2017). Exploring the Use of Video-Conferencing Technology in the Assessment of Spoken Language: A Mixed-Methods Study. *Language Assessment Quarterly, 14*(1), 1–18. doi:10.1080/15434303.2016.1263637

Nanayakkara, C. (2007). A model of user acceptance of learning management systems: a study within tertiary institutions in New Zealand. *The International Journal of Learning*. Retrieved November 7, 2012, from https://www.caudit.edu.au/educauseaustralasia07/authors_papers/Nanayakkara-361.pdf

Navarre, A. (2019). *Technology-Enhanced Teaching and Learning of Chinese as a Foreign Language*. Routledge.

Neal, L., & Miller, D. (2005). ACM Digital Library Communications of the ACM Human Factors. *eLearn Magazine Education and Technology in Perspective*. https://elearnmag.acm.org/index.cfm

Nedungadi, P., & Raman, R. (2012). A new approach to personalization: Integrating e-learning and m-learning. *Educational Technology Research and Development, 60*(4), 659–678. doi:10.100711423-012-9250-9

Neuhauser, P. C. (1993). *Corporate legends and lore: The power of storytelling as a management tool*. New York: McGraw-Hill.

Nicol, D. (2007). *Principles of good assessment and feedback: Theory and practice*. Paper presented at the REAP International Online Conference on Assessment Design for Learner Responsibility.

Nicol, D. (2007). E-assessment by design: Using multiple-choice tests to good effect. *Journal of Further and Higher Education, 31*(1), 53–64. doi:10.1080/03098770601167922

Nishioka, H. (2016). Analysing language development in a collaborative digital storytelling project: Sociocultural perspectives. *System, 62*, 39–52. doi:10.1016/j.system.2016.07.001

Nkambou, R., & Bourdeau, J. (2010). Building Intelligent Tutoring Systems : An Overview. In Advances in Intelligent Tutoring Systems (pp. 361–375). Academic Press.

Nomass, B. B. (2013). The impact of using technology in teaching English as a second language. *English Language and Literature Studies, 3*(1), 111–116.

Nunan, D. (1997). Listening in language learning. The Language Teacher: The Japan Association of Language Teaching, 21(9), 47-51.

Nunan, D. (2004). *Task-based Language Teaching*. Cambridge: CUP. doi:10.1017/CBO9780511667336

Nurhaeni, & Purnawarman, P. (2018). The use of smartphone and learning strategies. *Indonesian EFL Journal, 4*(1), 43–48. . doi:10.25134/ieflj.v4i1.797

O'Malley, J. M., & Chamot, A. (1990). *Learning strategies in second language acquisition*. Cambridge: Cambridge University Press. doi:10.1017/CBO9781139524490

Ockey, G. J., Gu, L., & Keehner, M. (2017). Web-based virtual environments for facilitating assessment of L2 oral communication ability. *Language Assessment Quarterly, 14*(4), 346–359. doi:10.1080/15434303.2017.1400036

OECD. (2010). *Inspired by Technology, Driven by Pedagogy: A systemic Approach to Technology-Based School Innovations*. Paris, France: OECD.

Okojie, M. C., Olinzock, A. A., & Okojie-Boulder, T. C. (2006). The pedagogy of technology integration. *The Journal of Technology Studies, 32*(2), 66–71. doi:10.21061/jots.v32i2.a.1

Okwuduba, E. N., Offiah, F. C., & Madichie, C. J. (2018). Effect of computer simulations on secondary school students' academic achievement in chemistry in Anambra State. *Asian Journal of Education and Training*, *4*(4), 284–289. doi:10.20448/journal.522.2018.44.284.289

Oliver, R. (2000). When Teaching Meets Learning: Design, Principles and Strategies for Web-based Learning Environments that Support Knowledge Construction. In R. Sims, M. O'Reilly & S. Sawkins (Eds.), *Learning to Choose: Choosing to Learn. Proceedings of the 17th Annual ASCILITE Conference* (pp. 17-28). Lismore, Australia: Southern Cross University Press.

Oliver, K. (2001). Recommendations for Student Tools in Online Course Management Systems. *Journal of Computing in Higher Education*, *13*(1), 47–70. doi:10.1007/BF02940944

Oliver, K. (2010). Integrating Web 2.0 across the curriculum. *TechTrends*, *54*(2), 50–60. doi:10.1007/s11528-010-0382-7

Oliver, K., & Moore, J. (2008). Faculty Recommendations for Web Management Systems. *Journal of Computing in Higher Education*, *19*(2), 3–24. doi:10.1007/BF03033424

Oloo, L. M. (2010). Digital learning management systems in Africa: myths and realities. *OpenLearning: The Journal of Open and Distance Learning*, *25*(1), 5–23. Retrieved May 6, 2012, from http://www.informaworld.com/openurl?genre=article&doi=10.1080/02680510903482033&magic=crossref||D404A21C5BB053405B1A640AFFD44AE3

Oscarson, M. (1984). *Self-assessment of foreign language skills: a survey of research and development work Council of Europe*. Strasbourg: Council for Cultural Cooperation.

Ouyang, J. R., & Stanley, N. (2014). Theories and research in educational technology and distance learning instruction through Blackboard. *Universal Journal of Educational Research*, *2*(2), 161–172. doi:10.13189/ujer.2014.020208

Oxford, R. L. (1999). Relationships between second language learning strategies and language proficiency in the context of learner autonomy and self-regulation. *Revista Canaria de Estudios Ingleses*, *38*, 109-126. Retrieved from: https://goo.gl/9AxkZo

Oxford, R. L. (1990). *Language learning strategies: What every teacher should know*. Boston: Heinle Publishers.

Oxford, R. L. (2011). Strategies for learning a second or foreign language. *Language Teaching*, *44*(2), 167–180. doi:10.1017/S0261444810000492

Oxford, R. L. (2011). *Teaching and Researching Language Learning Strategies* (2nd ed.). Harlow: Pearson Education.

Oxford, R. L., & Burry-Stock, J. A. (1995). Assessing the use of language learning strategies worldwide with the ESL/EFL version of the strategy inventory for language learning (SILL). *System*, *23*(I), 1–23. doi:10.1016/0346-251X(94)00047-A

Oxford, R., & Shearin, J. (1994). Language learning motivation: Expanding the theoretical framework. *Modern Language Journal*, *78*(1), 12–28. doi:10.1111/j.1540-4781.1994.tb02011.x

Özçalışan, H. (2013). *Yükseköğrenim öğrencilerinin ingilizceyi öğrenme motivasyonları*. Yüksek Lisans Tezi. Kocatepe Üniversitesi, Afyon.

Ozcinar, H., & Ozturk, H. T. (2013). Methods for Analyzing Computer-Mediated Communication in Educational Sciences. In N. Sappleton (Ed.), *Advancing Research Methods with New Media Technologies* (pp. 228–249). London: IGI Global. doi:10.4018/978-1-4666-3918-8.ch013

Özdemir, E. (2013). *Improving Pre-service English Language Teachers' ICT Skills and Developing Positive Attitudes Towards the Use of Technology in Language Teaching Through an Online Course* (Unpublished Thesis). Cukurova University.

Ozek, M., Akpolat, Z. H., & Orphan, A. (2013). A Web-Based Intelligent Tutoring System for a Basic Control Course. *Computer Applications in Engineering Education*, *21*(3), 561–571. doi:10.1002/cae.20501

Ozkan, S., & Koseler, R. (2009). Multi-dimensional students' evaluation of e-learning systems in the higher education context: An empirical investigation. *Computers & Education*, *53*(4), 1285–1296. doi:10.1016/j.compedu.2009.06.011

Ozkan, S., Koseler, R., & Baykal, N. (2009). Evaluating learning management systems. *Transforming Government: People. Process and Policy*, *3*(2), 111–130. doi:10.1108/17506160910960522

Padma, G. A., & Adi, Z. (2000). Computer managed instructions: Evaluation of alternate methods of technology integration in higher education. *Journal of Educational Technology & Society*, *3*(1), 84–87.

Page, E. B. (2003). Project essay grade: PEG. In M. D. Shermis & J. C. Burstein (Eds.), *Automated essay scoring: a cross-disciplinary perspective* (pp. 43–54). Lawrence Erlbaum.

Paker, T., & Höl, D. (2012). Attitudes and perceptions of the students and instructors towards testing speaking communicatively. *Pamukkale Universitesi Egitim Fakultesi Dergisi*, *32*(2), 13–24. doi:10.9779/PUJE544

Park, S. Y., Nam, M., & Cha, S. (2011). University Students'' Behavioral Intention to Use Mobile Learning: Evaluating the technology acceptance model. *British Journal of Educational Technology*, *43*(4), 592–605. doi:10.1111/j.1467-8535.2011.01229.x

Pastor, S. (2005). La enseñanza de segundas lenguas. In A. López & B. Gallardo (Eds.), *Conocimiento y lenguaje* (pp. 361–399). Valencia: PUV.

Paul, S. P. (2014). Student's academic performance and computer managed instruction. *Journal of Education*, *6*(2), 34–43.

Payne, C. R. (2009). *Information Technology and Constructivism in Higher Education Progressive Learning Frameworks*. Hershey, PA: IGI Global Snippet. doi:10.4018/978-1-60566-654-9

Pear Deck. (2019). Available online: https://www.peardeck.com

PebblePad. (2019). Available online: https://www.pebblepad.co.uk/

Pecheanu, E., Stefanescu, D., Dumitriu, L., & Segal, C. (2011). Methods to evaluate open source learning platforms. In *Proceedings of Global Engineering Education Conference (EDUCON)*, 2011 *IEEE* (pp. 1152-1161). IEEE. 10.1109/EDUCON.2011.5773292

Pedersen, E. (1995). Storytelling and the art of teaching. *Forum*, *33*(1), 2–5.

Pedro, L. F. M. G., & de Oliveira Barbosa, C. M. M. (2018). A critical review of mobile learning integration in formal educational contexts. *International Journal of Educational Technology in Higher Education*, *15*(1), 10. doi:10.118641239-018-0091-4

Peek, R. (2015). Exploring learner autonomy: Language learning locus of control in multilinguals. *International Journal of Multilingualism*, *13*(2), 230–248. doi:10.1080/14790718.2015.1090991

Pellegrino, J., & Quellmalz, E. (2010). Perspectives on the Integration of Technology and Assessment. *Journal of Research on Technology in Education*, *43*(2), 119–134. doi:10.1080/15391523.2010.10782565

Pérez, M. T., Arratia, O., Martín, M. A., & Galisteo, D. (2009). *Innovación en docencia universitaria con Moodle. Casos prácticos*. Alicante: Editorial Club Universitario.

Peter, J. B., & Bijik, A. H. (2018). Effect of Technology Distraction on Learning among Students in Higher Institutions in Central Nigeria. *Technology*, *14*, 16.

Picciano, A. G. (2009). Blending with purpose: The multimodal model. *Journal of Asynchronous Learning Networks*, *13*(1), 7–18.

Pillsbury, G. (2019). *2018-19 LMS Evaluation - Phase II, Part 1: Canvas.* Retrieved from https://www.csustan.edu/sites/default/files/groups/Office%20of%20Information%20Technology/documents/2018_canvas_evaluation_summary.pdf

Pineteh, E. A. (2013). The academic writing challenges of undergraduate students: A South African case study. *International Journal of Higher Education*, *3*(1), 12. doi:10.5430/ijhe.v3n1p12

Ping, H. A., & Luan, N. L. (2017). Effects of learners' language proficiency on their language learning strategies. *Malaysian Journal of Languages and Linguistics*, *6*(1), 10–25. doi:10.24200/mjll.vol6iss1pp10-25

Pinto-Llorente, A. M., Sánchez-Gómez, M. C., & García-Peñalvo, F. J. (2016). Assessing the Effectiveness of Interactive and Collaborative Resources to Improve Reading and Writing in English. *International Journal of Human Capital and Information Technology Professionals*, *7*(1), 66–85. doi:10.4018/IJHCITP.2016010105

Pinto-Llorente, A. M., Sánchez-Gómez, M. C., & García-Peñalvo, F. J. (2017). A Mixed Methods Research of Pre-service Teachers' Perceptions about the Benefits of Wiki-Based Tasks and Discussion Boards. In *Computer Supported Qualitative Research, Advances in Intelligent Systems and Computing* (pp. 260–276). Springer International Publishing.

Pinto-Llorente, A. M., Sánchez-Gómez, M. C., & García-Peñalvo, F. J. (2018a). A Research on Students' Perceptions on a B-Learning English Environment to Improve Written Skills. In V. Ahuja & S. Rathore (Eds.), *Multidisciplinary Perspectives on Human Capital and Information Technology Professionals* (pp. 179–201). Hershey, PA: IGI Global. doi:10.4018/978-1-5225-5297-0.ch010

Pinto-Llorente, A. M., Sánchez-Gómez, M. C., & García-Peñalvo, F. J. (2018b). Students Skills in a Blended Learning Environment: A Qualitative Research. In A. Borchers (Ed.), *Technology Management in Organizational and Societal Contexts* (pp. 249–280). Hershey, PA: IGI Global. doi:10.4018/978-1-5225-5279-6.ch011

Piontek, M., & Morrone, A. (2013). *Evaluation of the Pilot of the Canvas Learning Management System Implemented in Academic Year 2012-2013.* Retrieved from https://assets.uits.iu.edu/pdf/Faculty%20and%20Student%20Evaluation%20of%20Instructure%20Canvas.pdf

Playposit. (2020). Retrieved from www.playposit.com

Plummer, D. B., Dale, R., & Cox, R. (2012). Using Edit Distance to Analyse Errors in a Natural Language to Logic Translation Corpus. Retrieved from https://sro.sussex.ac.uk

Pourhosein Gilakjani, A. (2018). Teaching Pronunciation of English with Computer Technology: A Qualitative Study. *International Journal of Research in English Education*, *3*(2), 94–114. doi:10.29252/ijree.3.2.94

Prensky, M. (2001). Digital natives, digital immigrants. *On the Horizon*, *9*(5), 1–6. doi:10.1108/10748120110424816

Prensky, M. (2005). Engage me or enrage me: What today's learners demand. *EDUCAUSE Review*, *40*(5), 60–65.

Price, D. M., Strodtman, L., Brough, E., Lonn, S., & Luo, A. (2015). Digital storytelling: An innovative technological approach to nursing education. *Nurse Educator*, *40*(2), 66–70. doi:10.1097/NNE.0000000000000094 PMID:25290965

QSRInternational. (n.d.). *NVivo 10 research software for analysis and insight.* Retrieved October 5, 2012, from http://www.qsrinternational.com/products_nvivo.aspx

Quellmalz, E. S., Timms, M. J., & Buckley, B. (2010). The promise of simulation-based science assessment: The calipers project. *International Journal of Learning Technology*, *5*(3), 243–263. doi:10.1504/IJLT.2010.037306

Quizlet. (2019). Available online: https://quizlet.com

Rabovsky, T. M. (2012). Accountability in Higher Education: Exploring impacts on state budgets and institutional spending patters. Oxford University Press. doi:10.1093/jopart/mur069

Radwan, N. M., Senousy, M. B., & Riad, A. E. D. M. (2014). Current Trends and Challenges of Developing and Evaluating Learning Management Systems. *International Journal of e-Education, e-Business, e-. Management Learning*, *4*(5), 361–375.

Rahimi, M., & Yadollahi, S. (2017). Effects of offline vs. online digital storytelling on the development of EFL learners' literacy skills. *Cogent Education*, *4*(1), 1–13. doi:10.1080/2331186X.2017.1285531

Rahman, F., Jumani, N. B., & Basit, A. (2010). Motivating and demotivating factors among learners. *International Journal of Academic Research*, *2*(1), 206–212.

Ramesh, V. M., & Ramanathan, C. (2013). A rubric to Evaluate Learning Management Systems. In Proceedings of Teaching, Assessment and Learning for Engineering (TALE), 2013 IEEE (pp. 73-77). IEEE. doi:10.1109/TALE.2013.6654402

Ramirez, B. U. (2011). The sensory modality used for learning affects grades. *Advances in Physiology Education*, *35*(3), 270–274. doi:10.1152/advan.00010.2011 PMID:21908836

Ramírez-Noriega, A., Juárez-Ramírez, R., & Martínez-Ramírez, Y. (2017). Evaluation module based on Bayesian networks to Intelligent Tutoring Systems. *International Journal of Information Management*, *37*(1), 1488–1498. doi:10.1016/j.ijinfomgt.2016.05.007

Ranalli, J., Link, S., & Chukharev-Hudilainen, E. (2017). Automated writing evaluation for formative assessment of second language writing: Investigating the accuracy and usefulness of feedback as part of argument-based validation. *Educational Psychology*, *37*(1), 8–25. doi:10.1080/01443410.2015.1136407

Rarh, V., & Goel, A. (2011). A Methodology for E-quiz Content Production for E-learning. In *Proceedings of Second International Conference on Emerging Applications of Information Technology*. IEEE. 10.1109/EAIT.2011.72

Ravindram. (2001). Towards learner autonomy: evolution in practice: The certificate in independent language learning. In B. Sinclair, T. Lamb, & I. McGrath (Eds.), *Learner Autonomy, Teacher Autonomy: Future Directions* (pp. 60-72). London: Longman.

Razmia, M., Pouralib, S., & Nozad, S. (2014). Digital storytelling in EFL classroom (oral presentation of the story): A pathway to improve oral production. *Social and Behavioral Sciences*, *98*, 1541–1544. doi:10.1016/j.sbspro.2014.03.576

Reinders, H., & Cotterall, S. (2001). Language learners learning independently: How autonomous are they? *Toegepaste Taalwetenschap in Artikelen*, *65*(1), 85–97. doi:10.1075/ttwia.65.09rei

Reinders, H., & Lázaro, N. (2007). The assessment of self-access language learning: Practical challenges. *Language Learning Journal*, *36*(1), 55–64. doi:10.1080/09571730801988439

Reinders, H., & White, C. (2016). 20 years of autonomy and technology: How far have we come and where to next? *Language Learning & Technology*, *20*(2), 143–154.

Resta, P., & Laferriere, T. (2007). Technology in Support of Collaborative Learning. *Educational Psychology Review*, *19*(1), 65–83. doi:10.1007/s10648-007-9042-7

Rice, W. (2011). *Moodle 2.0 E-Learning Course Development*. Birmingham: Packt publishing.

Richard, J. C., & Schmidt, R. (2013). *Longman Dictionary of Language, Teaching and Applied Linguistics*. New York: Routledge; doi:10.4324/9781315833835

Richards, J. C., & Rodgers, T. S. (2001). *Approaches and Methods in Language Teaching*. Cambridge: Cambridge University Press; doi:10.1017/CBO9780511667305

Richards, J., & Platt, C. (1994). *Reflective teaching in second language classrooms*. Cambridge: Cambridge University Press. doi:10.1017/CBO9780511667169

Richtel, M. (2010). Digital devices deprive brain of needed downtime. *New York Times, 24*(8), 1-4.

Ricky, Y. K. N., & Rechell, Y. S. L. (2015, December). Using mobile and flexible technologies to enable, engage and enhance learning in Vocational Education and Training (VET). In *Teaching, Assessment, and Learning for Engineering (TALE), 2015 IEEE International Conference on* (pp. 96-101). IEEE.

Rivers, W. P. (2001). Autonomy at all costs: An ethnography of metacognitive self-assessment and self-management among experienced language learners. *Modern Language Journal, 85*(2), 279–290. doi:10.1111/0026-7902.00109

Robin, B. (2006, March). The Educational Uses of Digital Storytelling. In *Society for Information Technology & Teacher Education International Conference* (pp. 709-716). Association for the Advancement of Computing in Education (AACE).

Robin, B. R. (2008). Digital storytelling: A powerful technology tool for the 21st century classroom. *Theory into Practice, 47*(3), 220–228. doi:10.1080/00405840802153916

Rodríguez, A. I., Riaza, B. G., & Gómez, M. C. S. (2017). Collaborative learning and mobile devices: An educational experience in Primary Education. *Computers in Human Behavior, 72*, 664–677. doi:10.1016/j.chb.2016.07.019

Rogers, D. L. (2000). A paradigm shift: Technology integration for higher education in the new millennium. *Educational Technology Review, 1*(13), 19–33.

Rogers, E. M., & Shoemaker, F. F. (1971). *Communication of innovations: A cross-cultural approach* (2nd ed.). New York: Free Press.

Rogers, Y., Connelly, K., Hazlewood, W., & Tedesco, L. (2010). Enhancing learning: A study of how mobile devices can facilitate sense making. *Personal and Ubiquitous Computing, 14*(2), 111–124. doi:10.100700779-009-0250-7

Romiszowski, A. J. (1988). *The Selection and Use of Instructional Media*. Kogan Page Ltd.

Roscoe, R. D., Crossley, S. A., Snow, E. L., Varner, L. K., & McNamara, D. S. (2014). Writing quality, knowledge, and comprehension correlates of human and automated essay scoring. In *The Twenty-Seventh International Flairs Conference* (pp. 393-398). AAAI Press.

Roscoe, R. D., Wilson, J., Johnson, A. C., & Mayra, C. R. (2017). Presentation, expectations, and experience: Sources of student perceptions of automated writing evaluation. *Computers in Human Behavior, 70*, 207–221. doi:10.1016/j.chb.2016.12.076

Roulston, K. (2001). Data analysis and 'theorizing as ideology. *Qualitative Research, 1*(3), 279–302. doi:10.1177/146879410100100302

Rozema, R. (2011). *Heart of darkness. WebQuest: Using technology to social studies.* Retrieved on 30th December, 2014 from http://www.edrs.com/WebQuest/hod/

Rubin, J. (1987). Learner strategies: theoretical assumptions, research history and typology. *Learner strategies in language learning*, 15-30.

Ruiz, C. (2008). El Blended-learning: Evaluación de una experiencia de aprendizaje en el nivel de postgrado. *Investigación y Posgrado, 23*(1), 11–36.

Russell, C., Gregory, D., Ploeg, J., DiCenso, A., & Guyatt, G. (2005). Qualitative research. In A. DiCenso, G. Guyatt, & D. Ciliska (Eds.), *Evidence-based nursing: A guide to clinical practice* (pp. 120–135). St. Louis, MO: Elsevier Mosby.

Russell, M., & Haney, W. (2000). Bridging the gap between testing and technology in schools. *Education Policy Analysis Archives, 8*(19), 19. doi:10.14507/epaa.v8n19.2000

Saadawi, G. M., Tseytlin, E., Jukic, D., Castline, M., Gormley, R., & Crowley, R. S. (2008). A Natural Language Intelligent Tutoring System for Training Pathologists - Implementation and Evaluation. *Advances in Health Sciences Education : Theory and Practice, 13*(5), 709–722. doi:10.1007/s10459-007-9081-3 PubMed

Sachan, A., Agarwal, A., Rai, A., Sharma, S., Verma, J., & Mishra, M. (2006). *Software Requirement Specification (SRS) Learning Course Management System* (Version 1). Academic Press.

Salahshour, F., Sharifi, M., & Salahshour, N. (2013). The relationship between language learning strategy use, language proficiency level and learner gender. *Procedia - Social and Behavioral Sciences, 70*(1957), 634-643. doi:10.1016/j.sbspro.2013.01.103

Saldana, J. (2012). The coding manual for qualitative researchers (No. 14). Sage.

Salehi, H., & Salehi, Z. (2012). Integration of ICT in language teaching: Challenges and barriers. *In Proceedings of the 3rd International Conference on e-Education, e-Business, e- Management Learning, 27*, 215–219.

Sallam, N., & Alzouebi, K. (2014). Teacher Perceptions of the Use of Moodle to Enhance the Quality of Teaching and Learning in a K-12 Private School in the United Arab Emirates. *J. Tea. Tea. Edu., 2*(2), 93–101. doi:10.12785/jtte/020202

Samuels, P. (2007). Mathematics Support and New Technologies. *MSOR Connections, 7*(1), 10–13. doi:10.11120/msor.2007.07010010

Samur, Y., Garipağaoğlu, B. C., & Karadeniz, S. (2015). Student perceptions on tablet computer use. In *First International Congress on 'LE: Digital Life Environments'*. Istanbul University.

Sánchez, A. (1997). *Los métodos en la enseñanza de idiomas: evolución histórica y análisis didáctico*. Madrid: SGEL.

Santiago, D., King, T., & Clarke, P. (2018). *AI-Driven Test Generation: Machines Learning from Human Testers.* Retrieved from https://www.pnsqc.org

Santos, I. (1999). *Lingüística Aplicada a la enseñanza-aprendizaje del español como lengua extranjera*. Madrid: Arco Libros.

Saraç, S. (2013). Learner autonomy in Turkish territory context. *Independence, 56*, 21–2.

Sarıca, H. Ç., & Usluel, Y. K. (2016). Eğitsel bağlamda dijital hikâye anlatımı: Bir rubrik geliştirme çalışması. *Eğitim Teknolojisi Kuram ve Uygulama, 6*(2), 298–309.

Sarıca, H. Ç., & Usluel, Y. K. (2016). The effect of digital storytelling on visual memory and writing skills. *Computers & Education, 94*, 298–309. doi:10.1016/j.compedu.2015.11.016

Savignon, S. J. (1972). *Communicative Competence: An experiment in foreign language teaching*. Philadelphia, PA: Center for Curriculum Development.

Sawaki, Y. (2012). Technology in language testing. In G. Fulcher & F. Davidson (Eds.), *The Routledge handbook of language testing* (pp. 426–437). Abingdon, UK: Routledge.

Scalter, N. (2008, June 24). Web 2.0, Personal Learning Environments, and the Future of Learning Management Systems. *Educause Center for Applied Research Bulletin, 2008*(13), 2–13.

Scardamalia, M., & Bereiter, C. (2003). Knowledge building: theory, pedagogy, and technology. In J. W. Guthrie (Ed.), *Encyclopedia of Education* (2nd ed., pp. 1370–1373). New York: MacMillan Reference.

Schoology. (2019). Available online: https://www.schoology.com/

Schrire, S. (2006). Knowledge building in asynchronous discussion groups: Going beyond quantitative analysis. *Computers & Education, 46*(1), 49–70. doi:10.1016/j.compedu.2005.04.006

Schwienhorst, K. (2008). *Learner Autonomy and CALL Environments*. London: Routledge.

Seeman, T., & Tavares, C. (2000). Involving learners in their own learning: How to get started. In D. Little, L. Dam, & J. Timmer (Eds.), *Focus on learning rather than teaching: Why and how? Papers from the IATEFL conference on learner independence, Krakow, 14-16 May 1998* (pp. 59-70). Dublin: Trinity College.

Selçuk, M. (2015). *Demotivation in EFL classes*. Available at https://www.academia.edu/864982/Demotivation_in_EFL_Classes

Selim, H. M. (2007). Critical success factors for e-learning acceptance: Confirmatory factor models. *Computers & Education, 49*(2), 396–413. doi:10.1016/j.compedu.2005.09.004

Selinger, M. (2001). *Information and communication technology in schools*. Available at http:\\www.imfundo.org/papers/ict_in_s.doc/

Selingo, J. J. (2013). *College (un)bound: The future of higher education and what it means for students*. Las Vegas, NV: Amazon Publishing.

Serah, N. (2014). Challenges Facing Effective Information and Communications Technology (Ict) Implementation In Selected Public Secondary Schools In Nakuru North District Nakuru County. Kenyatta University, The School Of Business.

Setzer, J. C., Wise, S. L., van den Heuvel, J. R., & Ling, G. (2013). An Investigation of examinee test-taking effort on a large-scale assessment. *Applied Measurement in Education, 26*(1), 34–49. doi:10.1080/08957347.2013.739453

Shah, D. (2018). *By the numbers: MOOCs in 2018*. Retrieved from https://www.classcentral.com/report/mooc-stats-2018/

Shannon, J. (2016). M-learning: Effectiveness, Unknowns and Opportunities. *International Journal of Scientific Development and Research, 1*(9), 292–300.

Shih, R. C. (2011). Can Web 2.0 technology assist college students in learning English writing? Integrating Facebook and peer assessment with blended learning. *Australasian Journal of Educational Technology, 27*(5), 829–845. doi:10.14742/ajet.934

Sigala, M. (2007). Integrating web 2.0 in e-learning environ- ments: A socio-technical approach. *International Journal of Knowledge and Learning, 3*(6), 628–648. doi:10.1504/IJKL.2007.016837

Silseth, K. (2013). Surviving the impossible: Studying students' constructions of digital stories on World War II. *Learning, Culture and Social Interaction, 2*(3), 155–170. doi:10.1016/j.lcsi.2013.04.004

Silva, R. L. S., & Neiva, F. W. (2016). Systematic Literature Review in Computer Science - A Practical Guide. doi:10.13140/RG.2.2.35453.87524

Simpson, E., & Stansberry, S. (2008). Video Games and Teacher Development: Bridging the Gap in the Classroom. In C. T. Miller (Ed.), *Games: Purpose and Potential Education*. New York: Springer.

Sinclair, B. (2000) *Learner Autonomy and its Development in the Teaching of English to Speakers of Other Language (TESOL)* (Unpublished doctoral dissertation). University of Nottingham.

Sinclair, B. (1999). More than an Act of Faith? Evaluating Learner Autonomy. In C. Kennedy (Ed.), *Innovation and Best Practice* (pp. 96–107). Harlow: Longman.

Sinclair, B. (2009). The Teacher as Learner: Developing Autonomy in an Interactive Learning Environment. In R. Pemberton, S. Toogood, & A. Barfield (Eds.), *Maintaining Control: Autonomy and Language Learning* (pp. 175–198). Hong Kong: Hong Kong University Press. doi:10.5790/hongkong/9789622099234.003.0010

Singhal, M. (1997). The Internet and foreign language education: Benefits and challenges. *The Internet TESL Journal, 3*(6), 107.

Singh, U. G., & Gokool, R. (2018). Students' perceptions of the Moodle Quiz E-assessment tool in an isiZulu language course. *Journal for Language Teaching= Ijenali Yekufundzisa Lulwimi= Tydskrif vir Taalonderrig, 52*(1), 128–150. doi:10.4314/jlt.v52i1.7

Sinha, S., Rogat, T., Adams-Wiggins, K., & Hmelo-Silver, C. (2015). Collaborative group engagement in a computer-supported inquiry learning environment. *International Journal of Computer-Supported Collaborative Learning, 10*(3), 273–307. doi:10.1007/s11412-015-9218-y

Skehan, P. (1989). *Individual Differences in Second Language Learning*. London: Arnold.

Skehan, P. (1996). A Framework for the implementation of task-based instruction. *Applied Linguistics, 17*(1), 38–62. doi:10.1093/applin/17.1.38

Skehan, P. (2003). Focus on form, tasks, and technology. *Computer Assisted Language Learning, 16*(5), 391–411. doi:10.1076/call.16.5.391.29489

Smeda, N., Dakich, E., & Sharda, N. (2010, July). Developing a framework for advancing e-learning through digital storytelling. In *IADIS International Conference E-Learning* (pp. 169-176). Academic Press.

Smeda, N., Dakich, E., & Sharda, N. (2014). The Effectiveness of digital storytelling in the classrooms: A comprehensive study. *Smart Learning Environments, 1*(1), 6. doi:10.118640561-014-0006-3

Smith, A., Min, W., Mott, B. W., & Lester, J. C. (2015). Diagrammatic Student Models: Modeling Student Drawing Performance with Deep Learning. International Conference on User Modelling, Adaptation and Personalization, 2016–2227. doi:10.1007/978-3-319-20267-9_18

Smith, P., & Ragan, T. (1999). *Instructional design* (2nd ed.). Toronto: John Wiley &Sons.

Smith, R. (2008). Learner autonomy. *ELT Journal, 62*(4), 395–397. doi:10.1093/elt/ccn038

Snowball, J. (2014). Using interactive content and online activities to accommodate diversity in a large first year class. *Higher Education, 67*(6), 823–838. doi:10.100710734-013-9708-7

Soh, L., Khandaker, N., & Jiang, H. (2008). I-MINDS : A Multiagent System for Intelligent Computer- Supported Collaborative Learning and Classroom Management. Computer Science and Engineering Journal. Retrieved from https://digitalcommons.unl.edu/csearticles

Sökmen, İ. (2006). *İngilizce öğretmenlerinin strateji öğretimi ile ilgili inançları*. Eskişehir: Yüksek Lisans Tezi. Anadolu Üniversitesi.

Song, L., Singleton, E. S., Hill, J. R., & Koh, M. H. (2004). Improving online learning: Student perceptions of useful and challenging characteristics. *The Internet and Higher Education, 7*(1), 59–70. Retrieved October292012. doi:10.1016/j.iheduc.2003.11.003

Song, Y. (2008). SMS enhanced vocabulary learning for mobile audiences. *International Journal of Mobile Learning and Organisation, 2*(1), 81–98. doi:10.1504/IJMLO.2008.018719

Sotiriou, C., & Primalis, D. (2013). Literature strikes back! Teaching literature with technology. In T. Pattison (Ed.), IATEFL Liverpool Conference Selection (pp. 130–131). Academic Press.

South Africa Institute of Distance Education. (2013). *The use of Moodle to support teaching and learning at the university of Dar es salaam*. Tanzania: Author.

South Africa. (2001). Higher Education Act 101. Pretoria: Academic Press.

South African Government. (2004). *Government Gazette* (Vol. 470). Pretoria: Government Printer.

Spector, J. M., Merrill, M. D., van Merrienboer, J., & Driscoll, M. P. (2008). *HandBook Of Research On Educational Communications And Technology*. New York, NY: Taylor & Francis.

Spiral. (2019). Available online: https://spiral.ac/

Ssekakubo, G., Suleman, H., & Marsden, G. (2011). Issues of adoption: Have e-Learning Management Systems fulfilled their potential in developing countries? In *Proceedings of the South African Institute of Computer Scientists and Information Technologists Conference on Knowledge, Innovation and Leadership in a Diverse, Multidisciplinary Environment*. Cape Town, South Africa.: ACM.

Stahl, G., Koschmann, T., & Suthers, D. (2006). Computer-supported collaborative learning: An historical perspective. Cambridge Handbook of the Learning Sciences, 2006, 409–426. doi:10.1145/1124772.1124855

Stephanie, L. (2009). *Overview of the Federal Higher Education Opportunity Act*. Boston, MA: Institute for Community Inclusion.

Stern, H. H. (1975). What can we learn from the good language learner? *Canadian Modern Language Review, 31*(4), 304–319. doi:10.3138/cmlr.31.4.304

Stewart, B. (2000). IPTO - Information Processing Techniques Office. Retrieved August 10, 2019, from https://www.livinginternet.com/i/ii_ipto.htm

Stockwell, G. (2007). Vocabulary on the Move: Investigating an intelligent mobile phone-based vocabulary tutor. *Computer Assisted Language Learning, 20*(4), 365–383. doi:10.1080/09588220701745817

Stockwell, G. (2013). Technology and motivation in English-language teaching and learning. In *International perspectives on motivation* (pp. 156–175). London: Palgrave Macmillan. doi:10.1057/9781137000873_9

Storch, N. (2002). Patterns of interaction in ESL pair work. *Language Learning, 52*(1), 119–158. doi:10.1111/1467-9922.00179

Strauss, A., & Corbin, J. (1994). Grounded Theory Methodology. An Overview. In N. K. Denzin & Y. S. Lincoln (Eds.), *Handbook of Qualitative Research* (pp. 273–285). Thousand Oaks: SAGE.

Sung, Y., Chang, K., & Yang, J. (2015). How Effective are Mobile Devices for Language Learning? A Meta-Analysis. *Educational Research Review, 16*, 68–84. doi:10.1016/j.edurev.2015.09.001

Surry, D. W., Ensminger, D. C., & Haab, M. (2005). A model for integrating instructional technology into higher education. *British Journal of Educational Technology, 36*(2), 327–329. doi:10.1111/j.1467-8535.2005.00461.x

Suthers, D. (2006). Technology affordances for intersubjective meaning-making. *International Conference for Computers in Education*, 1(2), 1–24.

Suwardy, T., Pan, G., & Seow, P. S. (2013). Using digital storytelling to engage student learning. *Accounting Education, 22*(2), 109–124. doi:10.1080/09639284.2012.748505

Swan, K. (2009). Introduction to the Special Issue on Blended Learning. *Journal of the Research Center for Educational Technology, 5*(1), 1–3. http://www.rcetj.org/index.php/rcetj/article/view/20/25

Szabo, M., & Kanuka, H. (1998). Effects of Violating Screen Design Principles of Balance, Unity, and Focus on Recall Learning, Study Time, and Completion Rate. *Journal of Educational Multimedia and Hypermedia, 8*(1), 23–42.

Taele, P., & Hammond, T. (2015). BopoNoto : An Intelligent Sketch Education Application for Learning Zhuyin Phonetic Script. DMS, 101–107.

Talero, A., & Elizabeth, S. (2012). El podcast en la enseñanza de la lectoescritura. *Revista Virtual Universidad Católica del Norte, 37*, 9–26.

Tallei, J. I., & Coura, J. (2011). El uso del podcasts en la enseñanza secundaria. *Revista de humanidades, tecnología e cultura, 1*(1), 234-242.

Tal, T., Krajcik, S., & Blumenfeld, C. (2006). Urban schools' teachers enacting project- based science. *Journal of Research in Science Teaching, 43*(7), 722–745. doi:10.1002/tea.20102

Tamil, A. M. (2015). *Calculating Difficulty, Discrimination and Reliability Index/Standard Error of Measurement.* Retrieved from https://ppukmdotorg.wordpress.com/2015/04/02/calculating-omr-indexes/comment-page-1/

Tandberg, D. A. (2010). Politics, interest groups and state funding of public higher education. *Research in Higher Education, 51*(5), 416–450. doi:10.100711162-010-9164-5

Tang, K. S., & Tan, S. C. (2017). Intertextuality and Multimodal Meanings in High School Physics: Written and Spoken Language in Computer-supported Collaborative Student Discourse. Classroom Discourse, 8(1), 19–35. doi:10.1080/19463014.2016.1263576

Tarade, R. S., & Singh, N. (2014). Significance of Web 2.0 Technology and its Application in Academic Libraries. *International Journal of Computer Trends and Technology, 10*(5). doi:10.14445/22312803/IJCTT-V10P143

Tarhini, A., Hone, K., Liu, X., & Tarhini, T. (2017). Examining the moderating effect of individual level cultural values on users' acceptance of Elearning in developing countries: a structural equation modeling of an extended technology acceptance model. *Interactive Learning Environments.*

Taşdemir, A., & Tay, B. (2007). Fen bilgisi öğretiminde öğrencilerin öğrenme stratejilerini kullanmalarının akademik başarıya etkileri. *Uludağ Üniversitesi Eğitim Fakültesi Dergisi, 20*(1), 173–187.

Tassinari, M. G. (2012). Evaluating learner autonomy: A dynamic model with descriptors. *Studies in Self-Access Learning Journal, 3*(1), 24–40.

Tassinari, M. G. (2015). Assessing learner autonomy: a dynamic model. In C. J. Everhard & L. Murphy (Eds.), *Assessment and Autonomy in Language Learning* (pp. 64–88). Basingstoke, UK: Palgrave Macmillan. doi:10.1057/9781137414380_4

Tassinari, M. G. (2016). Assessment for learning; assessment for autonomy. In C. Gitsaki & C. Coombe (Eds.), *Current Issues in Language Evaluation, Assessment and Testing, Research and Practice* (pp. 118–136). Cambridge: Cambridge Scholars Publishing.

Tatlı, Z., & Aksoy, D. A. (2015). Yabancı dil konuşma eğitiminde dijital öykü kullanımı. *Marmara Üniversitesi Atatürk Eğitim Fakültesi Eğitim Bilimleri Dergisi, 45*, 137–152.

Tella, S. (2003). M-learning — Cybertextual travelling or a herald of post-modern, education. In H. Iahti & P. Seppälä (Eds.), *Mobile learning* (pp. 7–21). Helsinki, Finland: IT Press.

Tendero, A. (2006). Facing yourselves: The effects of digital storytelling on teacher education. *Contemporary Issues in Technology & Teacher Education*, *6*(2), 174–194.

Teo, A. (2012). Promoting EFL students' inferential reading skills through computerized dynamic assessment. *Language Learning & Technology*, *16*(3), 10–20.

The Glossary of Education Reform. (2013). *Learning Environment*. Retrieved From: https://www.edglossary.org/learning-environment/

The Peak Performance Center. (2019). *Bloom's Affective Domain*. Author.

The Star. (2019, February 19). Malaysia-China bilateral trade up 13% in 2018. The Star.

Thomas, D. R. (2006). A general inductive approach for analyzing qualitative evaluation data. *The American Journal of Evaluation*, *27*(2), 237–246. doi:10.1177/1098214005283748

Thomas, M., & Thomas, H. (2012). Using new social media and Web 2.0 technologies in business school teaching and learning. *Journal of Management Development*, *31*(4), 358–367. doi:10.1108/02621711211219013

Thomas, S. (2017). Journalogue: Voicing student challenges in writing through a classroom blog. *Journal of Educational Technology & Society*, *20*(1), 112–122.

Thomsen, H. (2000). Learners' favoured activities in the autonomous classroom. In D. Little, L. Dam, & J. Timmer (Eds.), *Focus On Learning Rather Than Teaching: Why and How?* (pp. 71–86). Dublin: CLCS.

Thorne, K. (2003). *Blended Learning: How to integrate online and traditional learning*. London: Kogan.

Tomlinson, C. (1999). *The Differentiated Classroom: Responding to the Needs of All Learners*. Alexandria, VA: Association for Supervision and Curriculum Development.

Toshalis, E., & Nakkula, M. J. (2012). Motivation, engagement, and student voice. *Education Digest*, *78*(1), 29.

Traxler, J. (2010). Distance education and mobile learning: Catching up, taking stock. *Distance Education*, *31*(2), 129–138. doi:10.1080/01587919.2010.503362

Trice, A. W., & Treacy, M. E. (1988). Utilization as a dependent variable in MIS research. *ACM SIGMIS Database*. Retrieved October 23, 2012, from https://dl.acm.org/citation.cfm?id=65771

Tugan, S. E. (2015). *The relationship among foreign language classroom anxiety, motivation and achievement of Turkish EFL students*. İstanbul: Yayımlanmamış Yüksek Lisans Tezi. Fatih Üniversitesi.

Turan, T., & Şeker, B. S. (2018). The effect of digital stories on fifth-grade students' motivation. *Journal of Education and Future*, *13*, 65–78.

Turgut, G., & Kışla, T. (2015). The use of computer-aided story in education: Literature review. *Turkish Online Journal of Qualitative Inquiry*, *6*(2), 97–121. doi:10.17569/tojqi.57305

Tuzi, F. (2004). The impact of e-feedback on the revisions of L2 writers in an academic writing course. *Computers and Composition*, *21*(2), 217–235. doi:10.1016/j.compcom.2004.02.003

Twu, H. (2010). A predictive study of Wiki interaction: Can attitude toward Wiki predict Wiki interaction in High-Context Cultures groups? *Journal of Educational Technology Development and Exchange*, *3*(1), 57–68. doi:10.18785/jetde.0301.05

U.S. Department of Education. (2017). *Reimagining the role of technology in education: 2017 national education technology plan update*. Retrieved from https://tech.ed.gov/files/2017/01/NETP17.pdf

UKZN. (2014). *Language Policy and Plan*. Retrieved from http://ukzn.ac.za

UKZN. (2015). *Phasing in Moodle from 2016 to 2018*. Retrieved from https://www.ukzn.ac.za/wp-content/miscFiles/docs/general-docs/phasing-in-of-moodle-2016---2018.pdf

Ülgen, G. (1995). *Eğitim psikolojisi: Birey ve öğrenme*. Ankara: Bilim Yayınları.

Ushioda, E. (2000). Tandem language learning via e-mail: From motivation to autonomy. *ReCALL*, *2*(2), 121–128. doi:10.1017/S0958344000000124

Ushioda, E. (2011). Why Autonomy? Insights from Motivation Theory and Research. *Innovation in Language Learning and Teaching*, *5*(2), 221–232. doi:10.1080/17501229.2011.577536

Uslupehlivan, E., & Erden, M. K. (2016). *Usage of digital storytelling method in higher education. International Conference on Quality in Higher Education, Sakarya, Turkey.*

Usó, L. (2008). La enseñanza de la pronunciación en LE: Algunas consideraciones. *Phonica*, *4*, 104–130.

Valiathan, P. (2002). *Designing a Blended Learning Solution*. Retrieved from http://www.docstoc.com/docs/2261631/Designing-a-Blended-Learning-Solution-What-is-Blended-Learning#

Vallance, M., & Martin, S. (2008). The Impact of Synchronous inter-networked teacher training in Information and Communication Technology Integration. *Computers & Education*, *51*(1), 34–53. doi:10.1016/j.compedu.2007.04.001

Vandergrift, L., & Baker, S. (2015). Learner variables in second language listening comprehension: An exploratory path analysis. *Language Learning*, *65*(2), 390–416. doi:10.1111/lang.12105

Vandergrift, L., & Goh, C. C. (2012). *Teaching and learning second language listening: Metacognition in action*. New York: Routledge. doi:10.4324/9780203843376

Vanlehn, K., Lynch, C., Schulze, K., Shapiro, J. A., Shelby, R., Taylor, L., ... Wintersgill, M. (2005). The Andes Physics Tutoring System : Lessons Learned. *International Journal of Artificial Intelligence in Education*, *15*(3), 1–47.

Vannatta, R. A., & Beyerbach, B. (2000). Facilitating a constructivist vision of technology integration among education faculty and preservice teachers. *Journal of Research on Computing in Education*, *33*(2), 132–148. doi:10.1080/08886504.2000.10782305

Vaughan, N. (2007). Perspectives on blended learning in higher education. *International Journal on E-Learning*, *6*(1), 81–94.

Venkatesh, V., Morris, M. G., Davis, G. B., & Davis, F. D. (2004). User Acceptance of Information Technology: Toward a unified view. *MIS Quarterly, 27*(3), 425–478. Retrieved November 1, 2012, from http://onlinelibrary.wiley.com/doi/10.1002/cbdv.200490137/abstract

Venkatesh, V., Morris, M. G., Davis, G. B., & Davis, F. D. (2003). User Acceptance of Information Technology: Toward a unified view. *Management Information Systems Quarterly*, *27*(3), 425–478. doi:10.2307/30036540

Vincent, T. (2016). *Know Students Better: A Visual Guide to Formative Assessment Tools.* Retrieved from https://learninginhand.com/blog/know

Vipond, S., & Clarey, J. (2018). Academic Learning Management Systems. *Research from the Elearning Guild and Adobe Systems.* www.eLearningGuild.com

Viriya, C., & Sapsirin, S. (2014). Gender differences in language learning style and language learning strategies. *Indonesian Journal of Applied Linguistics*, *3*(2), 77–88. doi:10.17509/ijal.v3i2.270

Vizia. (2020). Retrieved from www.vizia.co

Vuc, G., Baloi, F., & Litcanu, M. (2015). Adapting Methods of Student Evaluation and Grading in Electrical Power Engineering. *Procedia: Social and Behavioral Sciences*, *191*, 147–151. doi:10.1016/j.sbspro.2015.04.366

Vygotsky, L. S. (1978). *Mind in Society*. Cambridge: Harvard University Press.

Walker, A., & White, G. (2013). *Technology Enhanced Language Learning. Connecting Theory and Practice*. Oxford, UK: Oxford University Press.

Walker, D. J., Topping, K., & Rodrigues, S. (2008). Student reflections on formative e-assessment: Expectations and perceptions. *Learning, Media and Technology*, *33*(3), 221–234. doi:10.1080/17439880802324178

Walker, E., Rummel, N., & Koedinger, K. R. (2014). Adaptive Intelligent Support to Improve Peer Tutoring in Algebra. *International Journal of Artificial Intelligence in Education*, *24*(1), 33–61. doi:10.1007/s40593-013-0001-9

Walliman, N. (2005). *Your research project: a step-by-step guide for the first-time researcher*. Los Angeles: Sage.

Walsh, L., & Kahn, P. (2010). *Collaborative Working in Higher Education. The Social Academy*. New York: Routledge.

Walters, F. S. (2010). Cultivating assessment literacy: Standards evaluation through language-test specification reverse engineering. *Language Assessment Quarterly*, *7*(4), 317–342. doi:10.1080/15434303.2010.516042

Wan, L., Zhao, C., Liu, Q., & Sun, J. (2005). Work in progress-an evaluation model for learning content management systems: from a perspective of knowledge management. In *Frontiers in Education, FIE' 05. Proceedings 35th Annual Conference*. IEEE. Retrieved November 1, 2012, from. https://ieeexplore.ieee.org/xpls/abs_all.jsp?arnumber=1612111

Wang, Y.S., Wu, M. & Wang, H. (2009). Investigating the Determinants and Age and Gender Differences in the Acceptance of Mobile Learning. *British Journal of Educational Technology, 40*(1), 92-118.

Wang, F., & Reeves, T. C. (2003). Why do teachers need to use technology in their classrooms? Issues, problems, and solutions. *Computers in the Schools*, *20*(4), 49–65. doi:10.1300/J025v20n04_05

Wang, J., & Brown, M. S. (2007). Automated essay scoring versus human scoring: A comparative study. *The Journal of Technology, Learning, and Assessment*, *6*(2), 4–28. Retrieved from https://eric.ed.gov/?id=EJ838612

Wang, L. (2005). The advantages of using technology in second language education. *The Journal*, *32*(10), 38–42.

Wang, L. (2005). The advantages of using technology in second language education: Technology integration in foreign language teaching demonstrates the shift from a behavioral to a constructivist learning approach. *T.H.E. Journal*, *32*(10), 39–42.

Wang, S., & Zhan, H. (2010). Enhancing teaching and learning with digital storytelling. *International Journal of Information and Communication Technology Education*, *6*(2), 76–87. doi:10.4018/jicte.2010040107

Wang, Y. C. (2015). Promoting collaborative writing through wikis: A new approach for advancing innovative and active learning in an ESP context. *Computer Assisted Language Learning*, *28*(6), 499–512. doi:10.1080/09588221.2014.881386

Wang, Y. J., Shang, H. F., & Briody, P. (2013). Exploring the impact of using automated writing evaluation in English as a foreign language university students' writing. *Computer Assisted Language Learning*, *26*(3), 234–257. doi:10.1080/09588221.2012.655300

Ward, L., & Parr, J. M. (2010). Revisiting and reframing use: Implications for the integration of ICT. *Computers & Education, 54*(1), 113–122. doi:10.1016/j.compedu.2009.07.011

Warschauer, M., & Ware, P. (2006). Automated writing evaluation: Defining the classroom research agenda. *Language Teaching Research, 10*(2), 157–180. doi:10.1191/1362168806lr190oa

Watanabe-Crockett, L. (2019). 10 Innovative Formative Assessment Examples for Teachers to Know. Retrieved January 30, 2020, from https://www.wabisabilearning.com/blog/formative-assessment-examples

WCET. (n.d.). EduTools. *CMS: Product Comparison System.* Retrieved October 8, 2015, from https://wcet.wiche.edu/sites/default/files/docs/resources/OldEdutoolsCMSFeaturesandCriteriaRev041513.docx

Webpa. (2019). Available online: https://webpa.lboro.ac.uk/login.php

Weeden, P., Winter, J., & Broadfoot, P. (2002). *Assessment: What's in it for schools?* London, UK: Routledge Falmer.

Weller, M. (2002). Assessment issues on a web-based course. *Assessment & Evaluation in Higher Education, 27*(2), 109–116. doi:10.1080/02602930220128698

Wenden, A., & Rubin, J. (1987). *Learner strategies in language learning.* Englewood Cliffs, NJ: Prentice Hall.

Weragama, D., & Reye, J. (2014). Analysing Student Programs in the PHP Intelligent Tutoring System. *International Journal of Artificial Intelligence in Education, 24*(2), 162–188. doi:10.1007/s40593-014-0014-z

Weslake, A., & Christian, B. J. (2015). Brain Breaks: Help or Hindrance? *TEACH COLLECTION of Christian Education, 1*(1), 4.

Wilkins, D. A. (1972). *Linguistics in language teaching.* London: Edward Arnold.

Williams, M., & Burden, R. (1997). *Psychology for Language Teachers: A Social Constructivist Approach.* Cambridge: CUP.

Williams, M., & Robert, L. (1997). *Psychology for language teachers: A social constructivist approach.* Cambridge: Cambridge University Press.

Willis, J. (2009). *Constructivist Instructional Design (C-ID). Foundations, Models, and Examples.* Charlotte, NC: Information Age Publishing.

Wilson, J. A. (1997). *A program to develop the listening and speaking skills of children in a first grade classroom* (Master Thesis). University of Virginia.

Wilson, I. (2005). Using Praat and Moodle for teaching segmental and supra segmental pronunciation. *TESOL Quarterly, 3*, 33–43.

Wong, L.-H. (2015). A Brief History of Mobile Seamless Learning. In L.-H. Wong, M. Milrad, & M. Specht (Eds.), *Seamless Learning in the Age of Mobile Connectivity* (pp. 3–40). Springer. doi:10.1007/978-981-287-113-8_1

Wyatt-Smith, C., & Cumming, J. (Eds.). (2009). *Educational assessment in the 21st Century.* Dordrecht: Springer. doi:10.1007/978-1-4020-9964-9

Yang, Y. T. C., & Wu, W. C. I. (2012). Digital storytelling for enhancing student academic achievement, critical thinking and learning motivation: A year-long experimental study. *Computers & Education, 59*(2), 339–352. doi:10.1016/j.compedu.2011.12.012

Yanju, S., & Yanmei, S. (2016). Communication strategies used by Middle Eastern postgraduate students at service encounters in University of Malaya. *European Journal of Language and Literature Studies*, *5*(1), 40–45. doi:10.26417/ejls.v5i1.p40-45

Yaprak, Z. (2014). Computer-assisted collaborative language learning: With special reference to TBLL. *Turkish Studies*, *9*(6), 1117–1137. doi:10.7827/TurkishStudies.6783

Yarandi, M. (2013). Semantic Rule-based Approach for Supporting Personalised Adaptive E-Learning. Univeristy of East London.

Yasan, N. (2018). *The investigation of undergraduate students' mobile phone use in the academic environment: The Case of Middle East Technical University* (Unpublished doctoral dissertation). Middle East Technical University, Ankara.

Yeh, E., & Swinehart, N. (2017). A Learner-Centered Approach to Technology Integration: Online Geographical Tools in the ESL Classroom. In J. Keengwe & G. Onchwari (Eds.), Handbook of Research on Learner-Centered Pedagogy in Teacher Education and Professional Development (pp. 1-22). Hershey, PA: Information Science Reference, IGI Global.

Yerri, J., & Henry, D. (2016). A comparison of student knowledge between computer managed instruction and traditional method in a physical health education. *Journal of Educational Psychology*, *6*(2), 108–117.

Yi'an, W. (1998). What do tests of listening comprehension test?-A retrospection study of EFL test-takers performing a multiple-choice task. *Language Testing*, *15*(1), 21–44.

Yildirim, G., Elban, M., & Yildirim, S. (2018). Analysis of use of virtual reality technologies in history education: A case study. *Asian J. Educ. Train.*, *4*(2), 62–69. doi:10.20448/journal.522.2018.42.62.69

Yildirim, Z. Y., Ozden, M., & Aksu, M. (2011). Comparison of public schools and private schools WebQuest-based learning of social studies. *The Journal of Educational Research*, *4*(4), 125–132.

Yilmaz, R., Karaoglan Yilmaz, F. G., & Kilic Cakmak, E. (2017). The impact of transactive memory system and interaction platform in collaborative knowledge construction on social presence and self-regulation. *Interactive Learning Environments*, *25*(8), 949–969. doi:10.1080/10494820.2016.1224905

Yilmaz, R., & Keser, H. (2016). The impact of interactive environment and metacognitive support on academic achievement and transactional distance in online learning. *Journal of Educational Computing Research*. doi:10.1177/0735633116656453

Yılmaz, Y., Üstündağ, M. T., & Güneş, E. (2017). Öğretim materyali olarak dijital hikâye geliştirme aşamalarının ve araçlarının incelenmesi. *Abant İzzet Baysal Üniversitesi Eğitim Fakültesi Dergisi*, *17*(3), 1621–1640. doi:10.17240/aibuefd.2017.17.31178-338851

Yin, R. K. (2009). *Case study research: Design and methods*. Thousand Oaks, CA: Sage.

Yoohang, H. T. (2014). Students' perceptions toward the use of the digital library in weekly computer managed instruction assignments portion of a hybrid programme. *Journal of Educational Technology*, *42*, 712–725.

Young, S. C. (2003). Integrating ICT into second language education in a vocational high school. *Journal of Computer Assisted Learning*, *19*(4), 447–461. doi:10.1046/j.0266-4909.2003.00049.x

Yu, G., He, L., & Isaacs, T. (2017). *The Cognitive Processes of taking IELTS Academic Writing Task 1: An Eye-tracking Study*. IELTS Research Reports Online Series, British Council, IDP: IELTS Australia and Cambridge English Language Assessment. Available online: www.ielts.org/ /media/researchreports/ielts_online_rr_2017-2.ashx

Yu, G., & Zhang, J. (2017). Computer-Based English Language Testing in China: Present and Future. *Language Assessment Quarterly, 14*(2), 177–188. doi:10.1080/15434303.2017.1303704

Yuksel, G., & Kavanoz, S. (2011). In search of prospective EFL certificate teachers' attitudes towards technology. *Procedia Computer Science, 3*, 666–671. doi:10.1016/j.procs.2010.12.111

Yule, G. (2014). *The Study of Language*. Cambridge: Cambridge University Press.

Zain, J. M., Tey, M., & Goh, Y. (2007). Does Aesthetics of Web Page Interface Matters to Mandarin Learning? *Journal of Computer Science and Netwrok Security, 7*(8), 43–51.

Zare, P. (2010). An investigation into language learning strategy use and gender among Iranian undergraduate language learners. *World Applied Sciences Journal, 11*(10), 1238–1247.

Zhang, Z. (2016). Student engagement with computer-generated feedback: A case study. *ELT Journal, 71*(3), 317–328. doi:10.1093/elt/ccw089

Zhang, Z. V., & Hyland, K. (2017). Student engagement with teacher and automated feedback on L2 writing. *Assessing Writing, 36*, 90–102. doi:10.1016/j.asw.2018.02.004

Zhou, Y., & Wei, M. (2018). Strategies in technology-enhanced language learning. *Studies in Second Language Learning and Teaching, 8*(2), 471–495. doi:10.14746sllt.2018.8.2.13

Zimmerman, T. D. (2012). Exploring learner to content interaction as a success factor in online courses. *The International Review of Research in Open and Distributed Learning, 13*(4), 152–165. doi:10.19173/irrodl.v13i4.1302

ZoomUs. (2019). Available online: https://zoom.us/hc/en-us

About the Contributors

Serpil Meri Yilan received her MA and PhD degrees in Applied Linguistics for Language Teaching from University of Southampton in 2011 and 2017, respectively, and BA in English Language Teaching from Ataturk University in 2009. She has served as a language advisor and coach; editor, reviewer, and proofreader of academic papers; translator; and private tutor. She is currently working as an assistant professor at School of Foreign Languages, AICU, Turkey. She writes and presents about the topics of computer-assisted language learning, foreign and second language learning and teaching, virtual reality, e-learning, scaffolding, digital storytelling, humanization of ELT, learner autonomy, and motivation.

Kasim Koruyan is currently working as a trainer at Saudi Aramco and doing a further independent self-study at King Saud University. He has an MA in ELT from Reading University and a Doctorate in Education from the Open University, UK. He is also a member of IATEFL (International Association for Teachers of English as a Foreign Language). He has been mentoring and editing MA and PhD theses since 2014 and teaching IELTS and other exam courses.

* * *

Ahmed Mokhtar Abdelaziz is a head of an English Language Unit at one of Saudi Aramco's Industrial Training Centers in Saudi Arabia. He has a PhD in Educational Research and Technology Enhanced Learning from Lancaster University, UK. He has over 19 years of experience in educational administration and teaching English as a second language.

Muhammad Bashir Abdullahi is a trained Mathematician and Computer Scientist. He received his Doctor of Philosophy (PhD) degree in Computer Science and Technology from Central South University, Changsha, Hunan, P. R. China in 2012. His research interests include: Information and Network Security, Machine Learning, Data Science and Computer Science Education. His research results are published in refereed journals and conference proceedings. He is a chartered Information Technology practitioner and a member of the Computer Professionals Registration Council of Nigeria (CPN) and also a full member of Nigeria Computer Society (NCS). He is currently the Vice Chairman of Nigeria Computer Society, Niger State Chapter.

Salako E. Adekunle received a degree (B.Eng) in Electrical and Computer Engineering, Master of Technology (M.Tech) in Computer Science. He is a PhD student in Computer Science at the Federal University of Technology, Akure, Nigeria. He is a member of the Nigeria Computer Society and Teachers Registration Council of Nigeria (TRCN). His research interests include Biometric Security, Educational Technology and Control Technology. He has published papers in reputable local and international journals and his published textbooks included Introduction to Computer Logic, Learning Pascal Made Easy, A Handbook on Symbolic Logic and BASIC Programming Language.

Solomon A. Adepoju holds B. Tech (Mathematics/Computer Science) and M.Sc. (Computer Science) from the Federal University of Technology, Minna and University of Ibadan respectively. Presently, he is in Department of Computer Science, Federal University of Technology, Minna. He has co-authored papers which have appeared in some national and international journals He is a member Computer Professional Registration Council of Nigeria (CPN), International Association of Computer Science and Information Technology (IACST), SIGCHI, and International Society on Multi Criteria Decision Making (MCDM) among others. His areas of interest include Human Computer Interaction (website usability/accessibility), ICT4D and MCDM.

Abdu M. Talib Al-kadi obtained his PhD (Applied Linguistics) from ISLT, Carthage University, Tunisia. He has contributed to undergraduate courses in linguistics, English as a Foreign Language (EFL), and English for Specific Purposes (ESP) in Yemen. He has authored, co-authored, and reviewed some articles published in peer-reviewed journals within the realm of ELT, Applied Linguistics, Netlinguistics, ESP, and CALL. He serves now as a member of the International Editorial Board of the Journal of Education and Science (EĞİTİM VE BİLİM) as well as Language Teaching and Educational Research (LATER) - both based in Turkey.

Mansoor S. Almalki is an Associate Professor of Applied Linguistics, Dean of Supportive Studies, and Director of English Language Centre at Taif University in Saudi Arabia. He obtained his PhD from the University of Melbourne (Language Assessment) in 2014, MA in TESOL, Cambridge Teacher Trainer certificate, and CELTA Cambridge ESOL Examinations, and taught English for several years in Saudi Arabia as well as in Australia. His main research interests include language assessment, blended approaches in language education, and qualitative research methods in applied linguistics.

Sahar Alzahrani is the Vice director of the ELC at Umm AlQura University. She is Assistant Professor of Applied Linguistics. She has given conference papers and has been publishing in learner autonomy, innovations in teaching, blended learning, MOOCs, and online instructional design. Awards: best poster at LASIG Antwerp Conference; Faculty of Humanities 3MT competition at The University of Southampton; and CALICO Outstanding Graduate Student Award. Interests: learner autonomy, innovations in teaching, blended learning.

Ali Abbas Falah Alzubi earned his PhD in Applied Linguistics from Universiti Sains Malaysia, Malaysia. Currently, he is an Assistant Professor in the Department of English at the Faculty of Languages, Najran University, Saudi Arabia. He has been teaching English for over ten years. He does research in Teaching English as a Foreign Language, Language Acquisition, Mobile-Assisted Language Learning and Discourse Analysis.

Cansu Ayvali is a master student in the Department of Teaching Turkish to Foreigners at Bartin University in Turkey. She is interested in life long learning, educational technology, second language teaching.

Wagdi Rashad Ali Bin-Hady is currently an Assistant Professor of Applied Linguistics at Hadhramout University, Faculty of Education Socotra and the Head of the English Department, Yemen. He received his PhD degree in English in 2016 from Dr. Babasaheb Ambedkar Marathwada University, India. His research interests include communicative competence, novice teachers, cooperative learning, ICT-based informal learning, language learning strategies, task- based and process-genre approaches. He is also interested in quantitative, qualitative and mixed methods research design. He is also a reviewer in some respected international journals. https://orcid.org/0000-0002-4116-113X.

Zeynep Çetin Köroğlu received her MA and PhD degrees in English Language Teaching from Gazi University and has worked as an Assistant Professor Doctor at the Foreign Language Teaching Department, Bayburt University. She especially interested in Teacher Education, ICT, Intercultural Communication and Second Language Acquisition.

Suleiman Garba obtained his Master degree in Computer Science from Federal University of Technology, Minna, Niger State, Nigeria. Currently working FCT College of Education, Zuba, Abuja, Computer Science Department.

Roshni Gokool is a lecturer in the Discipline of African Languages at the University of KwaZulu Natal, South Africa. She lectures isiZulu as a second/additional language to undergraduate students and the module 'teaching isiZulu as an additional language' to postgraduate students'. Her research interests include computer-assisted language teaching (CALL), task-based language learning and teaching (TBLT) and language for specific purposes. She specialized in designing doctor-patient communication tasks in an isiZulu TBLT CALL syllabus design for health sciences students in her PhD study. She has collaborated with academics in the health sciences and IT Divisions on joint research projects.

Paul Gruba is an Associate Professor of Applied Linguistics, School of Languages and Linguistics, University of Melbourne. After an initial research interests in second language listening, Paul has pursued research in areas related to technology and language teaching, assessment and program evaluation. He is currently part of the team on the Petascale Campus Initiative, with a specific focus on the use of data analytics and technologies throughout humanities and social sciences.

Ismail Gürler is working, at present, in the Department of Translation and Interpretation at the Agri Ibrahim Cecen University, the author got his bachelor, MA and PhD degree in English Language Teaching. His major study areas are evaluation, curriculum, needs analysis and self-confidence.

Ibrahim M. Karkouti is an independent thinker, a young scholar, and a life-long learner who recently defended his doctoral dissertation at the University of Hartford, CT - USA. Ten years of professional experience in Lebanon, Qatar, and the United States have taught Ibrahim that learning has no boundaries and that education matters the most when it is used to remedy the deleterious effects of segregation, racism, sectarianism, and other forms of discriminatory practices that prevent historically excluded populations from attaining their basic rights to education, healthcare, and prosperity. Dr. Karkouti's research focuses on (a) diversity issues in higher education, (b) the elements that aid in the facilitation of the use of technology in the classroom, and (c) the types of social support K-12 teachers need to embrace and implement reform.

Mohd Javed Khan is conducting research in Instruction Design (e-learning) from Department of Computer Science, Jamia Millia Islamia, New Delhi, India. Formerly, he worked as an Instructional Design professional in both higher education and corporate settings. His research interest centres on learning environment, effective instruction designing and emerging technology. His work has been published in Journal of Multimedia Tools and Applications, International Journal of Education and Information Technology, Asian Journal of Education and e-learning (AJEEL) and IEEE, International Conference, Bangalore Section, and India. He was born on 5 May 1984 in Bhopal, Madhya Pradesh (M.P.), India. He graduated in Computer Application from Barkatullah University, Bhopal (M.P.) and completed his Master of Computer Application from Rajeev Gandhi Technical University, Bhopal (M.P.). Because of his interest in the domain of Computer Application he conducted research in the field of Computer Science by undertaking Master of Philosophy from Aisect University, Bhopal, (M.P.). After completing his M.Phill (C.S.) he moved to Delhi to further extend his research interests. He then got registered in PhD Computer Science under the supervision of Prof. Khurram Mustafa in Department of Computer Science of Jamia Millia Islamia, New Delhi, India.

Busra Koseoglu is a master student in the Department of Teaching Turkish to Foreigners at Bartin University in Turkey. She is interested in lifelong learning, educational technology, second language teaching.

Emily Lau Kui-Ling is a Senior Lecturer at the Department of English Language, Faculty of Languages and Linguistics, University of Malaya. Her core research domains include Discourse Studies and Multimodality with a particular attention to the representations of pathologized female appearance. Currently, her teaching of language in literary texts has fanned the flame of her interest in Literature and Stylistics. Alongside her academic engagements, she hopes to contribute to the preservation of mother tongues, focusing on the 'Foochow' dialect. She welcomes research collaboration with scholars, policy makers, NGOs, Institutions and graduate/postgraduate hopefuls who would be keen to work on the aforementioned areas.

Chia-An Lin graduated from the Department of English at National Taipei University of Technology in 2019.

Yen-Liang Lin is currently an Associate Professor in the Department of English, also serving as the Director of Media and Language Teaching Center, at National Taipei University of Technology. He received his Ph.D. in Applied Linguistics in 2013 from the University of Nottingham, UK. He has taught EFL at secondary and university levels for more than 10 years. His research interests include corpus linguistics, discourse analysis, intercultural communication and language teaching methodology.

Hassan Saleh Mahdi is an assistant professor of applied linguistics in the Department of English, University of Bisha, Saudi Arabia. His research interests are computer-assisted language learning (CALL),

Mobile-assisted language learning (MALL), second language vocabulary acquisition. He has published a number of articles related to these topics.

Shamila Naidoo is a Lecturer in the Discipline of African Languages at the University of KwaZulu-Natal in South Africa, where she teaches at under- and postgraduate level. Her research interests are in second language (L2) instruction, Experimental Phonetics and Theoretical Phonology and has published articles in scientific journals. Shamila is also engaged in research on technology supported learning for the L2 classroom. She also pursues an interest in Forensic Linguistics.

Tugba Ozturk did her PhD at the Centre for Studies in Advanced Learning Technology, Educational Research Department, UK. She has been working on educational technology for about 15 years.

Yunus Öztürk completed his B.S. degree on Computer Education and Educational Technology major in Bogazici University, Turkey and M.A. degree in Seoul National University, South Korea, majoring on Educational Technology. Currently, he is working in Ubion Co. Ltd., one of the well-known e-learning companies in South Korea, for 3 years. He is interested in online learning, learning design, interaction design, LMS and emerging technologies in education.

Indira Padayachee is a Senior Lecturer in Information Systems & Technology at the University of KwaZulu-Natal, where she has taught a number of subjects including Systems Analysis and Design, Database Design and Management, Software Engineering and Human Computer Interaction. Prior to that she was employed at the Durban University of Technology at the rank of Associate Director in the Department of Computer Studies. Indira has a PhD in Information Systems obtained from the University of South Africa. She has published articles in Alternation, the South African Computer Journal, and the Journal of Contemporary Management, as well as book chapters in IGI Global. In addition she has co-authored/presented research articles in various peer-reviewed conferences, namely Southern African Computer Lecturers' Association (SACLA) conference, Annual Conference on World Wide Web Applications, International Conference on e-Learning, International Conference on Society and Information Technologies, Business Management Conference (BMC), Conference of the South African Institute of Computer Scientists and Information Technologists (SAICSIT) and the European Conference on Social Media. She is a member of the International Federation for Information Processing (IFIP). Her research interests include eLearning, smart education, software engineering, information security, human-computer interaction and information technology adoption.

Ana María Pinto-Llorente holds PhD in Educational Technology, Bachelor in English as a second language (University of Salamanca) and Bachelor in Education (Pontifical University of Salamanca). She is a member of the research group GRIAL (Research Group Interaction and eLearning). She works as a professor in the Faculty of Education at the University of Salamanca in the Department of Education, Organization and Research Methods at the University of Salamanca. Her areas of work are related to new technologies, didactics and first and second languages. She has participated in several European and national projects as well as in different innovative experiences. She is a reviewer for several international journals and a member of the programme committee of several international conferences. She has been the Coordinator of the Postgraduate Programme in Bilingual Education and the Director of the Special Course in Bilingual Education in Infant, Primary and Secondary education. Her research interests focus on Second Language, eLearning and Computers & Education. She has an extensive experience of teaching Linguistics, Phonetics, English as a second language, and Technology in face-to-face and Blended Learning Modality.

Pei-Shan Tsai is an assistant professor at the Graduate Institute of Technological and Vocational Education, and Center for Teacher Education, National Taipei University of Technology, Taiwan. Her research interests have mainly focused on the design of Internet-based learning environments, online argumentation and conceptions of learning and teaching.

Vinothini Vasodavan is a PhD candidate in Department of Curriculum and Instructional Technology in Univeristy Malaya (UM). She was working with LeapEd Services Sdn Bhd project of facilitating education transformation in Malaysian schools through the Yayasan AMIR Trust Schools Programme through a Public-Private Partnership with the Ministry of Education Malaysia. Her research interest is in the field of collaborative learning and Technological Pedagogical Content Knowledge (TPACK) has driven her to design learning task for innovative teaching and learning. She won Gold medal award for project on Space Matters: The Impact of Mobile Augmented Reality (AR) From Student's Perspective for Learning Improvement and Teaching Enhancement (LITEC) Conference in 2019. She is also Silver award recipient for project on Collaborative Assessment Survey: A measure of group Teamwork and Browser recipient for Redesigning Assessment and Holistic Learning (RAHoLE) Conference in 2017.

Fatma Gizem Karaoglan Yilmaz is an associate professor in the Department of Computer Education & Instructional Technology (CEIT) at Bartin University in Turkey. She is the head of this department. She received her B.S. degree from Ankara University, Faculty of Educational Sciences, Department of CEIT in 2008. In 2010, she received her M.A. degree in CEIT from Çukurova University. In 2014, she received her Ph.D. degree in CEIT from Ankara University. She is interested in distance education, interactive learning environments, online learning and multimedia learning. The author has published articles in various journals such as Computers & Education, Computers in Human Behavior, Interactive Learning Environments, Journal of Educational Computing Research, Internet Research, etc.

Azlin Zaiti Zainal is Senior Lecturer at the Department of English Language, Faculty of Languages and Linguistics, University of Malaya. Her research interests include second language teacher education, second language writing, task-based language teaching, technology in language education and oral communication.

Ozlem Zengin has been teaching English for 9 years and now working at Sabancı University School of Languages. She holds CELTA and DELTA from Cambridge University. Besides being Pearson-certified master trainer, she has MSc degree on Curriculum and Instruction in Middle East Technical University and holds PhD on Curriculum and Instruction and Educational Technology in Middle East Technical University. She has been giving talks in national and international conferences on 21st century skills, teacher education, and mobile technologies in instruction.

Index

www.ingramcontent.com/pod-product-compliance
Lightning Source LLC
LaVergne TN
LVHW062108300926
849161LV00010B/2397
9781799830627